SCHAUM'S OUTLINE OF

THEORY AND PROBLEMS

OF

PROGRAMMING
WITH
C

.

BYRON S. GOTTFRIED, Ph.D.

Professor of Industrial Engineering
Engineering Management and Operations Research
University of Pittsburgh

SCHAUM'S OUTLINE SERIES

McGRAW-HILL, INC.

New York   St. Louis   San Francisco   Auckland   Bogotá   Caracas
Hamburg   Lisbon   London   Madrid   Mexico   Milan   Montreal
New Delhi   Paris   San Juan   São Paulo   Singapore
Sydney   Tokyo   Toronto

Byron S. Gottfried is a professor of Industrial Engineering at the University of Pittsburgh, where he teaches computer simulation, operations research, engineering economics, numerical methods and computer programming. He received his PhD from Case-Western Reserve University in 1962, and has been a member of the Pitt faculty since 1970. Dr. Gottfried is the author of several textbooks, including *Programming with C, Programming with Pascal,* and *Introduction to Engineering Calculations* in the Schaum's Outline Series.

DEC is a registered trademark of Digital Equipment Corporation.
IBM is a registered trademark of International Business Machines Corporation.
IBM PC-AT is a trademark of International Business Machines Corporation.
Microsoft is a registered trademark of Microsoft Corporation.
Quick C is a trademark of Microsoft Corporation.
Turbo C is a registered trademark of Borland International, Inc.
VAX is a trademark of Digital Equipment Corporation.
VMS is a trademark of Digital Equipment Corporation.

Schaum's Outline of Theory and Problems of
PROGRAMMING WITH C

4 5 6 7 8 0 20 SHP SHP9 9 8 7 6 5 4 3 2

ISBN 0-07-023854-5

Sponsoring Editor, John Aliano
Production Supervisor, Friederich W. Schulte
Project Supervision, The Total Book

Cover design by Amy E. Becker.

Library of Congress Cataloging-in-Publication Data

Gottfried, Byron S., (Date)
    Schaum's outline of theory and problems of programming with C.

    (Schaum outline series)
    Includes index.
    1. C (Computer program language).   I. Title.
II. Title: Outline of theory and problems of programming C.   III. Series.
QA76.73.C15G67 1989   005.13'3   88-13790
ISBN 0-07-023854-5

In memory of Sidney Gottfried:
father, teacher, and friend

Preface

In recent years, there has been a major trend toward the use of C among serious programmers. Among the many reasons for C's popularity are the following:

- C is a flexible, high-level, structured programming language.
- C includes certain low-level features that are normally available only in assembly or machine language.
- Programs written in C compile into small object programs that execute efficiently.
- C is widely available. Commercial C compilers are available for most personal computers, minicomputers, and mainframes.
- C is largely machine-independent. Programs written in C are easily ported from one computer to another.

This book provides instruction in computer programming with C. It includes complete and understandable explanations of the commonly used features of C. Most of the features recommended by the currently proposed ANSI standard, including function prototypes, are discussed. In addition, the book presents a contemporary approach to programming, stressing the importance of clarity, legibility, modularity, and efficiency in program design. Thus, the reader is exposed to the principles of good programming practice as well as the specific rules of C. Complete C programs are presented throughout the text, beginning with the first chapter. The use of an interactive programming style is emphasized throughout the text.

The book can be used by a wide reader audience, ranging from beginning programmers to practicing professionals. It is particularly well suited for beginning college-level students as a textbook for an introductory programming course, as a supplementary text, or as an effective independent-study guide.

Many examples are included as an integral part of the text. These include numerous programming examples of varying complexity, as well as illustrative drill-type problems. Many of the programming examples are solved using other programming languages in the companion Schaum's Outlines, thus providing the reader with a basis of comparison among several popular languages.

Sets of review questions and drill problems are provided at the end of each chapter. The review questions enable readers to test their recall of the material presented within each chapter. They also provide an effective chapter summary. The drill problems reinforce the principles presented within each chapter. The reader should solve as many of these problems as possible. Answers to most of the drill problems are provided at the end of the book.

In addition, problems that require the writing of complete C programs are presented at the end of each chapter, beginning with Chapter 5. The reader is encouraged to write and execute as many of these programs as possible. This will greatly enhance the reader's self-confidence and stimulate interest in the subject. (Computer programming is a demanding skill, much like creative writing or playing a musical instrument; such skills cannot be acquired simply by reading a textbook!)

Most of these programming problems require no special mathematical or technical background. Hence, they can be solved by a broad range of readers. When using this book in a programming course, the instructor may wish to supplement these problems with additional programming exercises that reflect particular disciplinary interests.

All of the programming examples and many of the end-of-chapter programming problems have been solved on an IBM PC-AT personal computer, using several different versions of the Microsoft C compiler. Many of the programs were also run using Microsoft's Quick C and Borland International's Turbo C, as those compilers became available. In addition, a number of programs were run on a Digital Equipment VAX 8600, using the versions of C provided by DEC for their VMS operating system.

The principal features of C are summarized in Appendixes A–H at the end of the book. This material should be used frequently for ready reference and quick recall. It is particularly helpful when writing or debugging new programs.

In closing, I would like to thank my students, particularly Jim Duray, for their comments and suggestions when working with early versions of the manuscript. Their suggestions have been very helpful in rewriting and refining the material. Also, I wish to express my appreciation to Professor Keith Harrow at Brooklyn College for his substantive, detailed reviews and his many excellent suggestions throughout the development of the manuscript.

BYRON S. GOTTFRIED

Table of Contents

Complete Programming Examples

The programming examples are listed in the approximate order in which they appear within the text. The examples vary from very simple to moderately complex. Multiple versions are presented for many of the programs, particularly the simpler programs.

1. Area of a Circle—Examples 1.6–1.13
2. Lowercase to Uppercase Character Conversion—Examples 3.31, 7.1
3. Lowercase to Uppercase Text Conversion—Examples 4.4, 6.6, 6.9, 6.13, 9.2
4. Reading and Writing a Line of Text—Examples 4.19, 4.31
5. Averaging Student Exam Scores—Example 4.32
6. Compound Interest Calculations—Examples 5.2, 5.3, 5.4, 8.13
7. Real Roots of a Quadratic Equation—Example 5.5
8. Evaluating a Polynomial (Logical Debugging)—Example 5.6
9. Generating Consecutive Integer Quantities—Examples 6.5, 6.8, 6.11, 6.12
10. Averaging a List of Numbers—Examples 6.7, 6.10, 6.14, 6.31
11. Repeated Averaging of a List of Numbers—Example 6.15
12. Converting Several Lines of Text to Uppercase—Examples 6.16, 6.34
13. Encoding a String of Characters—Example 6.19
14. Repeated Compound Interest Calculations with Error Trapping—Example 6.20
15. Solution of an Algebraic Equation—Example 6.21
16. Calculating Depreciation—Examples 6.26, 7.14, 7.15, 7.20
17. Searching for Palindromes—Example 6.32
18. Largest of Three Integer Quantities—Example 7.9
19. Calculating Factorials—Examples 7.10, 7.11, 7.21, 8.2
20. Simulation of a Game of Chance (Shooting Craps)—Examples 7.12, 7.16, 8.9
21. Printing Backwards—Example 7.22
22. The Towers of Hanoi—Example 7.23
23. Average Length of Several Lines of Text—Examples 8.3, 8.5
24. Search for a Maximum—Examples 8.4, 8.11
25. Generating Fibonacci Numbers—Examples 8.7, 8.12, 13.2
26. Deviations About an Average—Examples 9.8, 9.9
27. Reordering a List of Numbers—Examples 9.13, 10.15
28. A Piglatin Generator—Example 9.14
29. Adding Two Tables of Numbers—Examples 9.19, 10.22, 10.24
30. Reordering a List of Strings—Examples 9.20, 10.26
31. Analyzing a Line of Text—Example 10.8
32. Displaying the Day of the Year—Example 10.28
33. Future Value of Monthly Deposits (Compound Interest Calculations)—Examples 10.31, 14.13
34. Updating Customer Records—Examples 11.14, 11.28
35. Locating Customer Records—Example 11.26
36. Processing a Linked List—Example 11.32
37. Raising a Number to a Power—Examples 11.37, 14.5
38. Creating a Data File (Lowercase to Uppercase Text Conversion)—Example 12.3
39. Reading a Data File—Examples 12.4, 14.9
40. Creating a File Containing Customer Records—Example 12.5
41. Updating a File Containing Customer Records—Example 12.6
42. Creating an Unformatted Data File Containing Customer Records—Example 12.7
43. Updating an Unformatted Data File Containing Customer Records—Example 12.8
44. Displaying Bit Patterns—Example 13.16
45. Data Compression (Storing Names and Birthdates)—Example 13.23

Chapter 1

Introductory Concepts

This book offers instruction in computer programming using a popular, structured programming language called C. We will learn how programs can be written in C. In addition, we will see how problems that are initially described in very general terms can be analyzed, outlined and finally transformed into well-organized C programs. These concepts are demonstrated in detail by the many sample problems that are included in the text.

1.1 INTRODUCTION TO COMPUTERS

Today's computers come in a variety of shapes, sizes and costs. Huge, general-purpose computers are used by many businesses, universities, hospitals, and government agencies to carry out sophisticated scientific and business calculations. These large computers are generally referred to as *mainframes*. They are very expensive (some cost millions of dollars), and they require a carefully controlled environment (temperature, humidity, etc.). As a rule, they are not physically accessible to the people that use them.

Mainframes have been available since the early 1950's, though relatively few people knew how to use them in the earlier years. Those who did use them were generally scientists, engineers and financial analysts. Thus, it is not surprising that computers were viewed both with awe and with suspicion by the general public.

During the 1960's it became increasingly common for students at colleges and universities to learn how to program mainframe computers. This resulted in the emergence of many young professionals who understood both the capabilities and the limitations of computers. As a result, some of the mystery associated with the use of computers began to disappear.

The late 1960's and early 1970's witnessed the development of smaller, less expensive *minicomputers*. These machines offered the performance of earlier mainframes at a fraction of the cost. Many schools and businesses that could not afford mainframes therefore acquired minicomputers as they became increasingly available.

By the late 1970's, advances in integrated-circuit technology resulted in the development of still smaller and less expensive computers called *microcomputers*. Microcomputers are built with integrated circuits (i.e., "chips"); hence, they are small and inexpensive. In fact, some microcomputers are no larger, and no more expensive, than conventional office typewriters.

Microcomputers are often referred to as *personal computers*, because they are used by only one person at a time. This permits a high level of interaction between the user and the computer. Many applications (e.g., word processors, "paint" programs, spreadsheets and database management programs) are specifically designed to take advantage of this environment, thus providing the skilled user with a wide variety of creative tools to write, draw or carry out numerical computations. Figure 1.1 shows a student interacting with a personal computer.

Despite their small size and low cost, modern personal computers rival many minicomputers in computing power. Moreover, their performance continues to improve dramatically as their cost continues to drop. Personal computers are now used for many commercial, educational, scientific and technical applications that were formerly carried out on larger, more expensive computers. Hence, personal computers are now commonly available in most schools and businesses, and it appears likely that they will soon become common household items.

Many large organizations utilize personal computers as *terminals* or *workstations* that are connected to larger computers, or to other personal computers. Connections over telephone lines have become particularly common. Thus, personal computers can be used either as stand-alone devices or as a part of larger computer networks. When viewed in this context, we see that personal computers tend to *complement*, rather than *replace*, the use of larger computers.

1

Fig. 1.1

1.2 COMPUTER CHARACTERISTICS

All digital computers, regardless of their size, are basically electronic devices that can transmit, store and manipulate *information* (i.e., *data*). Several different types of data can be processed by a computer. These include *numerical data*, *character data* (names, addresses, etc.), *graphic data* (charts, drawings, photographs, etc.) and *sound* (music, speech patterns, etc.). The two most common types, from the standpoint of a beginning programmer, are numerical data and character data. Scientific and technical applications are concerned primarily with numerical data, whereas business applications usually involve processing both numerical and character data. This book is concerned exclusively with applications which involve either numerical or character data.

To process a particular set of data, the computer must be given an appropriate set of instructions, called a *program*. These instructions are entered into the computer and then stored in a portion of the computer's *memory*.

A stored program can be *executed* at any time. This causes the following things to happen.

1. A set of information, called the *input data*, will be entered into the computer (from a keyboard, floppy disk, etc.) and stored in a portion of the computer's memory.

2. The input data will then be processed to produce certain desired results, known as the *output data*.

3. The output data, and perhaps some of the input data, will be printed onto a sheet of paper or displayed on a monitor (i.e., a video-type display device).

This three-step procedure can be repeated many times if desired, thus causing a large quantity of data to be processed in rapid sequence. It should be understood, however, that each of these steps, particularly steps 2 and 3, can be lengthy and complicated.

Example 1.1 A computer has been programmed to calculate the area of a circle using the formula $a = \pi r^2$, given a numerical value for the radius r as input data. The following steps are required:

1. Read the numerical value for the radius of the circle.
2. Calculate the value of the area, using the above formula. This value will be stored, along with the input data, in the computer's memory.
3. Print (display) the values of the radius and the corresponding area.
4. Stop.

Each of these steps will require one or more instructions in a computer program.

The foregoing discussion illustrates two important characteristics of a digital computer: *memory* and *capability to be programmed*. A third important characteristic is its *speed and reliability*. We will say more about memory, speed and reliability in the next few paragraphs. Programmability will be discussed at length throughout the remainder of this book.

Memory

Every piece of information stored within the computer's memory is encoded as some unique combination of zeros and ones. These zeros and ones are called *bits* (*binary digits*). Each bit is represented by an electronic device that is, in some sense, either "off" (zero) or "on" (one).

Small computers have memories that are organized into 8-bit multiples called *bytes*, as illustrated in Fig. 1.2. Notice that the individual bits are numbered, beginning with 0 (for the rightmost bit) and extending to 7 (the leftmost bit). Normally, a single character (e.g., a letter, a single digit or a punctuation symbol) will occupy 1 byte of memory. An instruction may occupy 1, 2 or 3 bytes. A single numerical quantity may occupy anywhere from 1 to 8 bytes, depending on its *precision* (i.e., the number of significant figures) and its *type* (integer, floating-point, etc.).

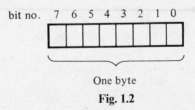

One byte

Fig. 1.2

The size of a computer's memory is usually expressed as some multiple of $2^{10} = 1024$ bytes. This is referred to as *1K* (1 kilobyte). Small computers have memories whose sizes typically range from 64K to several megabytes, where 1 megabyte (*1M*) is equivalent to $2^{10} \times 2^{10} = 1024K$ bytes.

Example 1.2 The memory of a small personal computer has a capacity of 256K bytes. Thus, as many as $256 \times 1024 = 262{,}144$ characters and/or instructions can be stored in the computer's memory. If the entire memory is used to represent character data (which is actually quite unlikely), then over 3200 names and addresses can be stored within the computer at any one time, assuming 80 characters for each name and address.

If the memory is used to represent numerical data rather than names and addresses, then over 65,000 individual numbers can be stored at any one time, assuming each numerical quantity requires 4 bytes of memory.

Large computers have memories that are organized into *words* rather than bytes. Each word will consist of a relatively large number of bits—typically 32 or 36. The bitwise organization of a 32-bit word is illustrated in Fig. 1.3. Notice that the bits are numbered, beginning with 0 (for the rightmost bit) and extending to 31 (the leftmost bit).

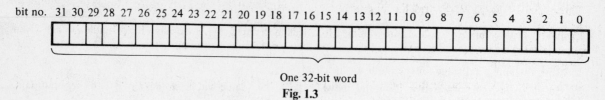

One 32-bit word

Fig. 1.3

Figure 1.4 shows the same 32-bit word organized into four consecutive bytes. The bytes are numbered in the same manner as individual bits, ranging from 0 (for the rightmost byte) to 3 (the leftmost byte).

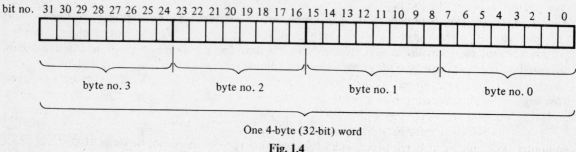

One 4-byte (32-bit) word

Fig. 1.4

The use of a 32- or a 36-bit word permits one numerical quantity, or a small *group* of characters (typically 4 or 5), to be represented within a single word of memory. Large computers commonly have several million words (i.e., several megawords) of memory.

Example 1.3 The memory of a large computer has a capacity of 2M (2048K) words, which is equivalent to $2048 \times 1024 = 2,097,152$ words. If the entire memory is used to represent numerical data (which is unlikely), then more than 2 million numbers can be stored within the computer at any one time, assuming each numerical quantity requires one word of memory.

If the memory is used to represent characters rather than numerical data, then about 8 million characters can be stored at any one time, based upon four characters per word. This is more than enough memory to store the contents of an entire book.

Most computers also employ *auxiliary storage devices* (e.g., magnetic tapes, disks, optical memory devices) in addition to their primary memories. These devices typically range from 10M or 20M bytes for a small computer, to several hundred megawords for a large computer. Moreover, they allow information to be permanently recorded, since they can often be physically disconnected from the computer and stored when not in use. However, the access time (i.e., the time required to store or retrieve information) is considerably greater for these auxiliary devices than for the computer's primary memory.

Speed and Reliability

Because of its extremely high speed, a computer can carry out calculations in just a few minutes that would require months—perhaps even years—if carried out by hand. Simple tasks, such as adding two numbers, can be carried out in a fraction of a *microsecond* ($1 \mu = 10^{-6}$ sec.). On a more practical level, the end-of-semester grades for all students in a large university can typically be processed in just a few minutes of computer time.

This very high speed is accompanied by an equally high level of reliability. Thus, a computer practically never makes a mistake of its own accord. Highly publicized "computer errors," such as a person receiving a telephone bill of over a million dollars, are the result of programming errors or data entry errors rather than errors caused by the computer itself.

1.3 MODES OF OPERATION

There are two different ways that a large digital computer facility can be utilized by many different users. These are the *batch mode* and the *interactive mode*. Each has its own advantages for certain types of problems.

Batch Processing

In the early days of computing, all jobs were processed via *batch processing*. This mode of operation is still in use in some schools and businesses, though it is much less common than it once was.

In batch processing a number of jobs are read into the computer, stored internally, and then processed sequentially. (A *job* refers to a computer program and its associated sets of input data that are to be processed.) Classical batch processing requires that the program and the data be recorded on punched cards. This information is read into the computer by means of a mechanical card reader and then processed. After the job is processed, the output, along with a listing of the computer program, is printed on multiple sheets of paper by a high-speed printer. This form of batch processing is now largely obsolete.

Modern batch processing is generally tied into a timesharing system (see p. 7). In this system the program and the data are typed into the computer via a *timesharing terminal* or a personal computer. The information is then stored within the computer's memory and processed in its proper sequence. This form of batch processing is preferable to classical batch processing, since it eliminates the need for punched cards and allows the input information (program and data) to be edited while it is being entered.

Large quantities of information (both programs and data) can be transmitted into and out of the computer very quickly in batch processing. Furthermore, the user need not be present while the job is being processed. Therefore, this mode of operation is well suited to jobs that require large amounts of computer time or are physically lengthy. On the other hand, the total time required for a job to be processed in this manner may vary from several minutes to several hours, even though the job may have required only a second or two of actual computer time. (Each job must wait its turn before it can be read, processed and printed out.) Thus, batch processing can be undesirable when it is necessary to process many small, simple jobs and return the results as quickly as possible.

Interactive Computing

Interactive computing is carried out with either a timesharing terminal (sometimes called a *console*), as illustrated in Fig. 1.5, or a personal computer, such as that shown in Fig. 1.1. In either case the user provides the computer with input information through a keyboard, which resembles an ordinary typewriter. The corresponding output information is then either printed onto large sheets of paper or displayed on a video-type *monitor*. Printed output may be more desirable for some types of applications, since it provides a "hard copy" of the interactive session, though the use of a monitor is usually more convenient.

The significant feature of interactive computing is that the user and the computer are able to interact with each other during the computational session. Thus, the user may periodically be asked to provide certain information that will determine what subsequent actions are to be taken by the computer, and vice versa.

Example 1.4 A student wishes to use a personal computer to calculate the radius of a circle whose area has a value of 100. A program is available which will calculate the area of a circle, given the radius. (Note that this is just the opposite of what the student wishes to do.) This program isn't exactly what is needed, but it does allow the student to proceed by trial and error. The procedure will be to guess a value for the radius and then calculate a corresponding area. This trial-and-error procedure continues until the student has found a value for the radius that yields an area sufficiently close to 100.

Once the program execution begins, the message

```
Radius = ?
```

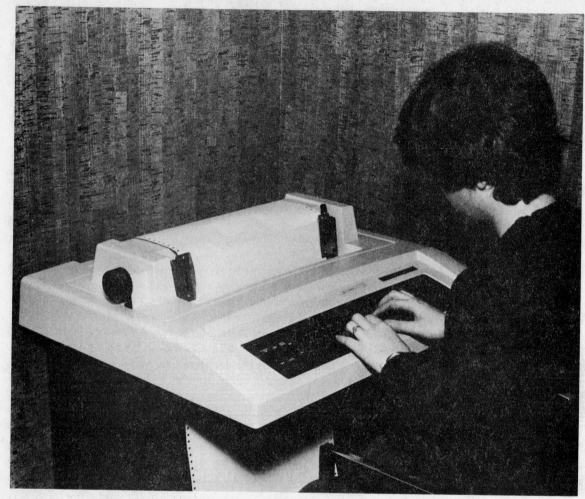

Fig. 1.5

is displayed. The student then enters a value for the radius. Let us assume that the student enters a value of 5 for the radius. The computer will respond by displaying

```
Area = 78.5398
```

```
Do you wish to repeat the calculation?
```

The student then types either yes or no. If the student types yes, then the message

```
Radius = ?
```

again appears, and the entire procedure is repeated. If the student types no, then the message

```
Goodbye
```

is displayed and the computation is terminated.

   Shown below is a hard copy of the information displayed during a typical interactive session, using the program described above. The information typed by the student has been underlined. In this session, an approximate value of $r = 5.6$ was determined after only three calculations.

```
Radius = ? 5
Area = 78.5398

Do you wish to repeat the calculation? yes

Radius = ? 6
Area = 113.097

Do you wish to repeat the calculation? yes

Radius = ? 5.6
Area = 98.5204

Do you wish to repeat the calculation? no

Goodbye
```

Notice the manner in which the student and the computer appear to be conversing with one another. Also, note that the student waits until he or she sees the calculated value of the area before deciding whether or not to carry out another calculation. If another calculation is initiated, the new value for the radius that the student supplies will depend on the previously calculated results.

Programs designed for interactive-type applications are sometimes said to be *conversational*. Computerized games are excellent examples of such interactive applications. This includes fast-action, graphical arcade games, even though the user's responses are reflexive rather than verbal.

Timesharing

Timesharing is a form of interactive computing in which many different users are able to use a single computer simultaneously. Each user will communicate with the computer through a terminal, such as that shown in Fig. 1.5. The terminals may be wired directly to the computer, or they may be connected to the computer over telephone lines, a microwave circuit or even an earth satellite. Thus, a timesharing terminal can be located far away—perhaps several hundred miles away—from its host computer.

Personal computers, such as that shown in Fig. 1.1, are often used in place of timesharing terminals. Systems in which personal computers are connected to large mainframes over telephone lines are particularly common. Such systems make use of *modems* (*modulator/demodulator* devices) to convert the digitized computer signals into analog telephone signals, and vice versa. Through such an arrangement, a person working at home, on his or her own personal computer, can easily access a remote computer at school or at the office.

Since a computer operates much faster than a human sitting at a terminal, one large computer can support many terminals at essentially the same time. Therefore, each user will be unaware of the presence of any other users, and will seem to have the remote computer at his or her own disposal.

Timesharing is best suited for processing relatively simple jobs that do not require extensive data transmission or large amounts of computer time. Many of the computer applications that arise in schools and commercial offices have these characteristics. Such applications can be processed quickly, easily, and at minimum expense using timesharing.

Example 1.5 A major university has a computer timesharing capability consisting of 200 timesharing terminals and 80 separate telephone connections. The timesharing terminals, which are located at various places around the campus, are wired directly to a large, central computer. Each terminal is able to transmit information to or from the main computer at a maximum speed of 960 characters per second.

The telephone connections allow students who are not on campus to connect their personal computers to the main computer. Each personal computer can transmit data to or from the main computer at a maximum speed of 240 characters per second. Thus, all 280 terminals and personal computers can interact with the main computer at the same time. However, each student will be unaware that others are also using the computer.

1.4 TYPES OF PROGRAMMING LANGUAGES

Many different languages can be used to program a computer. The most basic of these is *machine language*—a collection of very detailed, cryptic instructions that control the computer's internal circuitry. This is the natural dialect of the computer. Very few computer programs are actually written in machine language, however, for two significant reasons: first, because machine language is very cumbersome to work with, and second, because most computers have their own unique instruction sets. Thus, a machine-language program written for one type of computer cannot be run on another type of computer without significant alterations.

Usually, a computer program will be written in some *high-level language*, whose instruction set is more compatible with human languages and human thought processes. Most of these are *general-purpose* languages such as C, Pascal, PL/I, BASIC, FORTRAN and COBOL. There are also various *special-purpose* languages whose instruction sets are specifically designed for some particular type of application. Some common examples are GPSS and CSMP, which are special-purpose *simulation* languages, and LISP, a *list-processing* language which is widely used for artificial intelligence applications.

As a rule, a single instruction in a high-level language will be equivalent to several instructions in machine language. Moreover, the same general programming rules apply to all computers, so that a program written in a high-level language can generally be run on many different computers with little or no alteration. Therefore, the use of a high-level language offers three significant advantages over the use of machine language; namely, *simplicity*, *uniformity* and *portability* (machine independence).

A program written in a high-level language must, however, be translated into machine language before it can be executed. This is known as *compilation* or *interpretation*, depending on how it is carried out. (Compilers translate the entire program into machine language before executing any of the instructions. Interpreters, on the other hand, proceed through a program by translating and then executing single instructions, or small groups of instructions.) In either case, the translation is carried out automatically within the computer. In fact, inexperienced programmers may not even be aware that this process is taking place, since they typically see only their original high-level program, the input data, and the resulting output data.

A compiler or interpreter is itself a computer program that accepts a high-level program (e.g., a C program) as input data, and generates a corresponding machine-language program as output. The original high-level program is called the *source* program, and the resulting machine-language program is called the *object* program. Every high-level language must have its own compiler or interpreter for a particular computer. Most implementations of C operate as compilers, though interpreters are becoming increasingly common.

It is generally more convenient to develop a new program using an interpreter rather than a compiler. Once an error-free program has been developed, however, a compiled version will normally execute much faster than an interpreted version. The reasons for this are beyond the scope of our present discussion.

1.5 INTRODUCTION TO C

C is a general-purpose, structured programming language. Its instructions consist of terms that resemble algebraic expressions, augmented by certain English *keywords* such as if, else, for, do and while. In this respect C resembles other high-level structured programming languages such as Pascal and FORTRAN-77. C also contains certain additional features, however, that allow it to be used at a lower level, thus bridging the gap between machine language and the more conventional high-level languages. This flexibility allows C to be used for systems programming (e.g., for writing operating systems) as well as for applications programming (e.g., for writing a program to solve a complicated system of mathematical equations, or for writing a program to bill customers).

C is characterized by the ability to write very concise source programs, due in part to the large number of operators included within the language. It has a relatively small instruction set, though actual implementations include extensive *library functions* which enhance the basic instructions. Furthermore, the language encourages users to write additional library functions of their own. Thus, the features and capabilities of the language can easily be extended by the user.

C compilers are commonly available for computers of all sizes, and C interpreters are becoming increasingly common. The compilers are usually compact, and they generate object programs that are small and highly efficient when compared with programs compiled from other high-level languages. The interpreters are less efficient, though they are easier to use when developing a new program. Many programmers begin with an interpreter, and then switch to a compiler once the program has been debugged (once all of the programming errors have been removed).

Another important characteristic of C is that its programs are highly portable, even more so than with other high-level languages. The reason for this is that C relegates most computer-dependent features to its library functions. Thus, every version of C is accompanied by its own set of library functions, which are written for the particular characteristics of the host computer. These library functions are relatively standardized, however, and each individual library function is generally accessed in the same manner from one version of C to another. Therefore, most C programs can be processed on many different computers with little or no alteration.

History of C

C was originally developed in the 1970's by Dennis Ritchie at Bell Telephone Laboratories, Inc. (now AT&T Bell Laboratories). It is an outgrowth of two earlier languages, called BCPL and B, which were also developed at Bell Laboratories. C was largely confined to use within Bell Laboratories until 1978, when Brian Kernighan and Ritchie published a definitive description of the language.* The Kernighan and Ritchie description is commonly referred to as "K&R C."

Following the publication of the K&R description, computer professionals, impressed with C's many desirable features, began to promote the use of the language. By the mid 1980's, the popularity of C had become widespread. Numerous C compilers and interpreters had been written for computers of all sizes and many commercial application programs had been developed. Moreover, many commercial software products that were originally written in other languages were rewritten in C in order to take advantage of its efficiency and its portability.

Most commercial implementations of C differ somewhat from Kernighan and Ritchie's original definition. This has created some minor incompatibilities among different implementations of the language, thus diminishing the portability that the language attempts to provide. Consequently, the American National Standards Institute (ANSI)** has begun work on a standardized definition of the C language (ANSI committee X3J11). At the time of this writing, the ANSI project is nearing completion, though it is still in progress. Most commercial C compilers and interpreters are expected to adopt the ANSI standard once it has been completed (many now follow the partially completed recommendations). They may also provide additional features of their own.

This book describes the features of C that are generally supported by commercial C compilers and interpreters. Most of the features recommended by the currently proposed ANSI standard are included. The reader who has mastered this material should have no difficulty in customizing a C program to a particular version of the language.

Structure of a C Program

Every C program consists of one or more *functions*, one of which *must* be called `main`. The program will always begin by executing the `main` function. Additional function definitions may precede or follow `main` (more about this later, in Chaps. 7 and 8).

Each function must contain:

1. A function *heading*, which consists of the function name, followed by an optional list of *arguments* enclosed in parentheses.

2. A list of argument *declarations*, if arguments are included in the heading.

3. A *compound statement*, which comprises the remainder of the function.

---

* Brian W. Kernighan and Dennis M. Ritchie, *The C Programming Language*, Prentice-Hall, 1978.

** American National Standards Institute, 1430 Broadway, New York, NY 10018. (See also Brian W. Kernighan and Dennis M. Ritchie, *The C Programming Language*, 2d ed., Prentice-Hall, 1988.)

The arguments are symbols that represent information being passed between the function and other parts of the program. (Arguments are also referred to as *parameters*.)

Each compound statement is enclosed within a pair of braces, i.e., { and }. The braces may contain combinations of elementary statements (called *expression statements*) and other compound statements. Thus, compound statements may be nested, one within another. Each expression statement must end with a semicolon (;).

Comments (remarks) may appear anywhere within a program, as long as they are placed within the delimiters /* and */ (e.g., /* this is a comment */). Such comments are helpful in identifying the program's principal features or in explaining the underlying logic of various program features.

These program components will be discussed in much greater detail later in this book. For now, you should be concerned only with an overview of the basic features that characterize most C programs.

Example 1.6 Area of a Circle Here is an elementary C program that reads in the radius of a circle, calculates the area and then writes the calculated result.

```
#include <stdio.h>                        /* LIBRARY FILE ACCESS */

/* program to calculate area of a circle */  /* TITLE (COMMENT) */

main()                                    /* FUNCTION HEADING */

{
    float radius, area;                   /* VARIABLE DECLARATIONS */

    printf("Radius = ? ");                /* OUTPUT STATEMENT (PROMPT) */
    scanf("%f", &radius);                 /* INPUT STATEMENT */
    area = 3.14159 * radius * radius;     /* ASSIGNMENT STATEMENT */
    printf("Area = %f", area);            /* OUTPUT STATEMENT */
}
```

The comments at the end of each line have been added in order to emphasize the overall program organization. Normally a C program will not look like this. Rather, it might appear as shown below.

```
#include <stdio.h>

/* program to calculate the area of a circle */

main()

{
    float radius, area;

    printf("Radius = ? ");
    scanf("%f", &radius);
    area = 3.14159 * radius * radius;
    printf("Area = %f", area);
}
```

The following features should be pointed out in this last program.

1. The program is typed in lowercase. Either upper- or lowercase can be used, though it is customary to type ordinary instructions in lowercase. Most comments are also typed in lowercase, though comments are sometimes typed in uppercase for emphasis, or to distinguish certain comments from the instructions. (Uppercase and lowercase characters are not equivalent in C. Later in this book we will see some special situations where certain symbols are characteristically typed in uppercase.)

2. The first line contains a reference to a special file (called `stdio.h`) which contains information that must be `included` in the program when it is compiled. The inclusion of this required information will be handled automatically by the compiler.

3. The second line is a comment that identifies the purpose of the program.

4. The third line is a heading for the function `main`. The empty parentheses following the name of the function indicate that this function does not include any arguments.

5. The remaining five lines of the program are indented and enclosed within a pair of braces. These five lines comprise the compound statement within `main`.

6. The first indented line is a *variable declaration*. It establishes the symbolic names `radius` and `area` as *floating-point variables* (more about this in Chap. 2).

7. The remaining four indented lines are expression statements. The second indented line (`printf`) generates a request for information (namely, a value for the radius). This value is entered into the computer via the third indented line (`scanf`).

8. The fourth indented line is a particular type of expression statement called an *assignment statement*. This statement causes the area to be calculated from the given value of the radius. Within this statement the asterisks (∗) represent multiplication signs.

9. The last indented line (`printf`) causes the calculated value for the area to be displayed. The numerical value will be preceded by a brief label.

10. Notice that each expression statement within the compound statement ends with a semicolon. This is required of all expression statements.

11. Finally, notice the liberal use of spacing and indentation, creating *whitespace* within the program. The blank lines separate different parts of the program into logically identifiable components, and the indentation indicates subordinate relationships among the various instructions. These features are not grammatically essential, but their presence is strongly encouraged as a matter of good programming practice.

Execution of the program results in an interactive dialog such as that shown below. The user's response is underlined, for clarity.

```
Radius = ? 3
Area = 28.274309
```

1.6 SOME SIMPLE C PROGRAMS

In this section we present several C programs that illustrate some commonly used features of the language. All of the programs are extensions of Example 1.6; that is, each program calculates the area of a circle, or the areas of several circles. Each program illustrates a somewhat different approach to this problem.

The reader should not attempt to understand the syntactic details of these examples, though experienced programmers will recognize features similar to those found in other programming languages. Beginners should focus their attention only on the overall program logic. The details will be provided later in this book.

Example 1.7   Area of a Circle   Here is a variation of the program given in Example 1.6 for calculating the area of a circle.

```
#include <stdio.h>

#define PI 3.14159

/* program to calculate the area of a circle */
```

```
main()

{
    float radius, area;            /* variable declaration */
    float process(float radius);   /* function declaration */

    printf("Radius = ? ");
    scanf("%f", &radius);
    area = process(radius);
    printf("Area = %f", area);
}

float process(float r)      /* function definition */

{
    float a;                /* local variable declaration */

    a = PI * r * r;
    return(a);
}
```

This version utilizes a separate programmer-defined function, called process, to carry out the actual calculations (i.e., to process the data). Within this function, r is an argument (also called a *parameter*) that represents the value of the radius supplied to process from main, and a is the calculated result that is returned to main.

A reference to the function appears in main, within the statement

```
area = process(radius);
```

The main function also includes a *function declaration*, which indicates that process accepts a floating-point argument and returns a floating-point value. The use of functions will be discussed in detail in Chap. 7.

This program also contains a *symbolic constant*, PI, that represents the numerical value 3.14159. This is a form of shorthand that exists for the programmer's convenience. When the program is actually compiled, the symbolic constant will automatically be replaced by its equivalent numerical value.

When this program is executed, it behaves in the same manner as the program shown in Example 1.6.

Example 1.8   Area of a Circle with Error Checking   Now consider a variation of the program given in Example 1.7.

```
#include <stdio.h>

#define PI 3.14159

/* program to calculate the area of a circle, with error checking */

main()

{
    float radius, area;            /* variable declaration */
    float process(float radius);   /* function declaration */

    printf("Radius = ? ");
    scanf("%f", &radius);

    if (radius < 0)
        area = 0;
    else
        area = process(radius);

        printf("Area = %f", area);
}
```

```
float process(float r)          /* function definition */

{

    float a;                    /* local variable declaration */

    a = PI * r * r;
    return(a);
}
```

This program again calculates the area of a circle. It includes the function `process`, and the symbolic constant PI, as discussed in the previous example. Now, however, we have added a simple error-correction routine, which tests to see if the value of the radius is less than zero. (Mathematically, a negative value for the radius does not make any sense.) The test is carried out within `main`, using an `if-else` statement (see Sec. 6.6). Thus, if `radius` has a negative value, a value of zero is assigned to `area`; otherwise, the value for `area` is calculated within `process`, as before.

Example 1.9   Areas of Several Circles   The following program expands the previous sample programs by calculating the areas of several circles.

```
#include <stdio.h>

#define PI 3.14159

/* program to calculate the areas of circles, using a for loop */

main()

{
    float radius, area;             /* variable declaration */
    int count, n;                   /* variable declaration */
    float process(float radius);    /* function declaration */

    printf("How many circles? ");
    scanf("%d", &n);

    for (count = 1; count <= n; ++count)    {
        printf("\nCircle no. %d:    Radius = ? ", count);
        scanf("%f", &radius);

        if (radius < 0)
            area = 0;
        else
            area = process(radius);

        printf("Area = %f\n", area);
    }
}

float process(float r)          /* function definition */

{

    float a;                    /* local variable declaration */

    a = PI * r * r;
    return(a);
}
```

In this case the total number of circles, represented by the integer variable n, must be entered into the computer before any calculation is carried out. The `for` statement is then used to calculate the areas repeatedly, for all n circles (see Sec. 6.4).

Note the use of the variable count, which is used as a counter within the for loop (i.e., within the repeated portion of the program). The value of count will increase by 1 during each pass through the loop. Also, notice the expression ++count which appears in the for statement. This is a shorthand notation for increasing the value of the counter by 1; i.e., it is equivalent to count = count + 1 (see Sec. 3.2).

When the program is executed, it generates an interactive dialog, such as that shown below. The user's responses are again underlined.

```
How many circles? 3

Circle no. 1:    Radius = ? 3
Area = 28.274309

Circle no. 2:    Radius = ? 4
Area = 50.265442

Circle no. 3:    Radius = ? 5
Area = 78.539749
```

Example 1.10 Areas of an Unspecified Number of Circles The previous program can be improved by processing an unspecified number of circles, where the calculations continue until a value of zero is entered for the radius. This avoids the need to count, and then specify, the number of circles in advance. This feature is especially helpful when there are many sets of data to be processed.

Here is the complete program.

```c
#include <stdio.h>

#define PI 3.14159

/* program to calculate the areas of circles, using a for loop;
   number of circles is unspecified */

main()

{
    float radius, area;              /* variable declaration */
    int count;                       /* variable declaration */
    float process(float radius);     /* function declaration */

    printf("To STOP, enter 0 for the radius\n");
    printf("\nRadius = ? ");
    scanf("%f", &radius);

    for (count = 1; radius != 0; ++count)    {

        if (radius < 0)
            area = 0;
        else
            area = process(radius);

        printf("Area = %f\n", area);

        printf("\nRadius = ? ");
        scanf("%f", &radius);
    }
}
```

```
float process(float r)          /* function definition */

{
    float a;                    /* local variable declaration */

    a = PI * r * r;
    return(a);
}
```

Notice that this program will display a message at the beginning of the program execution, telling the user how to end the computation.

The dialog resulting from a typical execution of this program is shown below. Once again, the user's responses are underlined.

```
To STOP, enter 0 for the radius

Radius = ? 3
Area = 28.274309

Radius = ? 4
Area = 50.265442

Radius = ? 5
Area = 78.539749

Radius = ? 0
```

Example 1.11   Areas of an Unspecified Number of Circles   Here is a variation of the program shown in the previous example.

```
#include <stdio.h>

#define PI 3.14159

/* program to calculate the areas of circles, using a while loop;
   number of circles is unspecified */

main()

{
    float radius, area;            /* variable declaration */
    float process(float radius);   /* function declaration */

    printf("To STOP, enter 0 for the radius\n");
    printf("\nRadius = ? ");
    scanf("%f", &radius);

    while (radius != 0)  {

        if (radius <0)
            area = 0;
        else
            area = process(radius);

        printf("Area = %f\n", area);

        printf("\nRadius = ? ");
        scanf("%f", &radius);
    }
}
```

```
float process(float r)        /* function definition */

{

    float a;                  /* local variable declaration */

    a = PI * r * r;
    return(a);
}
```

This program includes the same features as the program shown in the previous example. Now, however, we use a `while` statement rather than a `for` statement to carry out the repeated program execution (see Sec. 6.2). The `while` statement will continue to execute as long as the value assigned to `radius` is not zero.

In more general terms, the `while` statement will continue to execute as long as the expression contained within the parentheses is considered to be *true*. Therefore, the first line of the `while` statement can be written more briefly, as

```
while (radius)    {
```

rather than

```
while (radius != 0)    {
```

because any nonzero value for `radius` will be interpreted as a *true* condition.

Some problems are better suited to the use of the `for` statement, while others are better suited to the use of `while`. The `while` statement is somewhat simpler in this particular application. There is also a third type of looping statement, called `do – while`, which is similar to the `while` statement shown above. (More about this in Chap. 6.)

When this program is executed, it generates an interactive dialog identical to that shown in Example 1.10.

Example 1.12   Calculating and Storing the Areas of Several Circles   Some problems require that a series of calculated results be stored within the computer, perhaps for recall in a later calculation. The corresponding input data may also be stored internally, along with the calculated results. This can be accomplished through the use of *arrays*.

The following program utilizes two arrays, called `radius` and `area`, to store the radius and the area for as many as 100 different circles. Each array can be thought of as a list of numbers. The individual numbers within each list are referred to as *array elements*. The array elements are numbered, beginning with 0. Thus, the radius of the first circle will be stored within the array element `radius[0]`, the radius of the second circle will be stored within `radius[1]`, and so on. Similarly, the corresponding areas will be stored in `area[0]`, `area[1]`, etc.

Here is the complete program.

```
#include <stdio.h>

#define PI 3.14159

/* program to calculate the areas of circles, using a while loop;
   results are stored in an array;
   number of circles is unspecified */

main()

{
    int n, i = 0;                        /* variable declaration */
    float radius[100], area[100];        /* array declaration    */
    float process(float radius);         /* function declaration */

    printf("To STOP, enter 0 for the radius\n\n");
    printf("Radius = ? ");
    scanf("%f", &radius[i]);
```

```
    while (radius[i])   {

        if (radius[i] < 0)
            area[i] = 0;
        else
            area[i] = process(radius[i]);

        printf("Radius = ? ");
        scanf("%f", &radius[++i]);
    }

    n = --i;          /* tag the highest value of i*/

    /* display the array elements */
    printf("\nSummary of Results\n\n");
    for (i = 0; i <= n; ++i)
        printf("Radius = %f   Area = %f\n", radius[i], area[i]);
}


float process(float r)        /* function definition */

{
    float a;                  /* local variable declaration */

    a = PI * r * r;
    return(a);
}
```

An unspecified number of radii will be entered into the comsputer, as before. As each value for the radius is entered (i.e., as the ith value is entered), it is stored within radius[i]. Its corresponding area is then calculated and stored within area[i]. This process will continue until all the radii have been entered, i.e., until a value of zero is entered for a radius. The entire set of stored values (i.e., the array elements whose values are nonzero) will then be displayed.

Notice the expression ++i, which appears twice within the program. Each of these expressions causes the value of i to increase by 1; i.e., they are equivalent to i = i + 1. Similarly, the statement

```
n = --i;
```

causes the current value of i to be decreased by 1 and the new value to be assigned to n. In other words, the statement is equivalent to

```
n = i - 1;
```

Expressions such as ++i and --i are discussed in detail in Sec. 3.2.

When the program is executed it results in an interactive dialog, such as that shown below. The user's responses are once again underlined.

```
To STOP, enter 0 for the radius

Radius = ? 3
Radius = ? 4
Radius = ? 5
Radius = ? 0

Summary of Results

Radius = 3.000000    Area = 28.274309
Radius = 4.000000    Area = 50.265442
Radius = 5.000000    Area = 78.539749
```

This simple program does not make any use of the values that have been stored within the arrays. Its only purpose is to demonstrate the mechanics of utilizing arrays. In a more complex example, we might want to determine an average value for the areas, and then compare each individual area with the average. To do this we would have to recall the individual areas (the individual array elements area[0], area[1], ..., etc.).

The use of arrays is discussed briefly in Chap. 2, and extensively in Chap. 9.

Example 1.13 Calculating and Storing the Areas of Several Circles Here is a more sophisticated approach to the problem described in the previous example.

```c
#include <stdio.h>

#define PI 3.14159

/* program to calculate the areas of circles, using a while loop;
   results are stored in an array of structures;
   number of circles is unspecified;
   string is entered to identify each data set */

main()

{
    int n, i = 0;                    /* variable declaration */

    struct  {
        char text[20];
        float radius;
        float area;
    } circle[10];                    /* structure variable declaration */

    float process(float radius);     /* function declaration */

    printf("To STOP, enter END for the identifier\n");
    printf("\nIdentifier: ");
    scanf("%s", circle[i].text);
    while (circle[i].text[0] != 'E'  ||  circle[i].text[1] != 'N')
                                     ||  circle[i].text[2] != 'D')   {
        printf("Radius: ");
        scanf("%f", &circle[i].radius);

        if (circle[i].radius < 0)
            circle[i].area = 0;
        else
            circle[i].area = process(circle[i].radius);

        ++i;
        printf("\nIdentifier: ");               /* next set of data */
        scanf("%s", circle[i].text);
    }

    n = --i;        /* tag the highest value of i */

    /* display the array elements */
    printf("\n\nSummary of Results\n\n");
    for (i = 0; i <= n; ++i)
        printf("%s   Radius = %f   Area = %f\n", circle[i].text,
                                                 circle[i].radius,
                                                 circle[i].area);
}
```

```
float process(float r)        /* function definition */

{
    float a;                  /* local variable declaration */

    a = PI * r * r;
    return(a);
}
```

In this program we enter a one-word *descriptor*, followed by a value of the radius, for each circle. The characters that comprise the descriptor are stored in an array called `text`. Collectively, these characters are referred to as a *string constant* (see Sec. 2.4). In this program, the maximum size of each string constant is 20 characters.

The descriptor, the radius and the corresponding area of each circle are defined as the components of a *structure* (see Chap. 11). We then define `circle` as an array of structures. That is, each element of `circle` will be a structure containing a descriptor, a radius and an area. For example, `circle[0].text` refers to the descriptor for the first circle, `circle[0].radius` refers to the radius of the first circle, and `circle[0].area` refers to the area of the first circle. (Remember that the numbering system for array elements begins with 0, not 1.)

When the program is executed, a descriptor is entered for each circle, followed by a value of the radius. This information is stored within `circle[i].text` and `circle[i].radius`. The corresponding area is then calculated and stored in `circle[i].area`. This procedure continues until the descriptor END is entered. All the information stored within the array elements (i.e., the descriptor, the radius and the area for each circle) will then be displayed, and the execution will stop.

Execution of this program results in an interactive dialog, such as that shown below. Note that the user's responses are once again underlined.

```
To STOP, enter END for the identifier

Identifier: RED
Radius: 3

Identifier: WHITE
Radius: 4

Identifier: BLUE
Radius: 5

Identifier: END


Summary of Results

RED    Radius = 3.000000   Area = 28.274309
WHITE    Radius = 4.000000    Area = 50.265442
BLUE    Radius = 5.000000    Area = 78.539749
```

1.7 DESIRABLE PROGRAM CHARACTERISTICS

Before concluding this chapter let us briefly examine some important characteristics of well-written computer programs. These characteristics apply to programs that are written in *any* programming language, not just C. They can provide us with a useful set of guidelines later in this book when we start writing our own C programs.

1. *Integrity.* This refers to the accuracy of the calculations. It should be clear that all other program enhancements will be meaningless if the calculations are not carried out correctly. Thus, the integrity of the calculations is an absolute necessity in any computer program.

2. *Clarity.* This refers to the overall readability of the program, with particular emphasis on its underlying logic. If a program is clearly written, it should be possible for another programmer to follow the program logic without undue effort. It should also be possible for the original author to follow his or her own program after being away from the program for an extended period of time. One of the

objectives in the design of C is the development of clear, readable programs through an orderly and disciplined approach to programming.

3. *Simplicity.* The clarity and accuracy of a program are usually enhanced by keeping things as simple as possible, consistent with the overall program objectives. In fact, it may be desirable to sacrifice a certain amount of computational efficiency in order to maintain a relatively simple, straightforward program structure.

4. *Efficiency.* This is concerned with execution speed and efficient memory utilization. These are generally important goals, though they should not be obtained at the expense of clarity or simplicity. Many complex programs require a tradeoff between these characteristics. In such situations, experience and common sense are key factors.

5. *Modularity.* Many programs can be broken down into a series of identifiable subtasks. It is good programming practice to implement each of these subtasks as a separate program module. In C, such modules are written as functions. The use of a modular programming design enhances the accuracy and clarity of a program, and it facilitates future program alterations.

6. *Generality.* Usually we will want a program to be as general as possible, within reasonable limits. For example, we may design a program to read in the values of certain key parameters rather than placing fixed values into the program. As a rule, a considerable amount of generality can be obtained with very little additional programming effort.

Review Questions

1.1 What is meant by a mainframe computer? Where can mainframes be found? For what are they generally used?

1.2 What is a minicomputer? How do minicomputers differ from mainframes?

1.3 What is a personal computer? How do personal computers differ from mainframes and minicomputers?

1.4 Name four different types of data.

1.5 What is meant by a computer program? What, in general, happens when a computer program is executed?

1.6 What is computer memory? What kinds of information are stored in a computer's memory?

1.7 What is a bit? What is a byte? What is the difference between a byte and a word of memory?

1.8 What terms are used to describe the size of a computer's memory? What are some typical memory sizes?

1.9 Name some typical auxiliary storage devices. How does this type of device differ from the computer's main memory?

1.10 What time unit is used to express the speed with which elementary tasks are carried out by a computer?

1.11 What is the difference between the batch mode and the interactive mode? What are their relative advantages and disadvantages?

1.12 What is meant by timesharing? For what types of applications is timesharing best suited?

1.13 What is machine language? How does machine language differ from high-level languages?

1.14 Name some commonly used high-level languages. What are the advantages of using high-level languages?

1.15 What is meant by compilation? What is meant by interpretation? How do these two processes differ?

1.16 What is a source program? An object program? Why are these concepts important?

1.17 What are the general characteristics of C?

1.18 Where was C originally developed and by whom?

1.19 To what extent do individual versions of C differ from one another? Has the language been standardized?

1.20 What are the major components of a C program? What significance is attached to the name `main`?

1.21 Describe the composition of a function in C.

1.22 What are arguments? Where do arguments appear within a C program? What other term is sometimes used for an argument?

1.23 What is a compound statement? How is a compound statement written?

1.24 What is an expression statement? Can an expression statement be included in a compound statement? Can a compound statement be included in an expression statement?

1.25　How can comments (remarks) be included within a C program? Where can comments be placed?

1.26　Are C programs required to be typed in lowercase? Can uppercase be used for anything in a C program? Explain.

1.27　What is an assignment statement? What is the relationship between an assignment statement and an expression statement?

1.28　What item of punctuation is used at the end of most C statements? Do all statements end this way?

1.29　Why are some of the statements within a C program indented? Why are blank spaces included within a typical C program?

1.30　Summarize the meaning of each of the following program characteristics: integrity, clarity, simplicity, efficiency, modularity and generality. Why is each of these characteristics important?

Problems

1.31　Determine, as best you can, the purpose of each of the following C programs. Identify all variables within each program. Identify all input and output statements, all assignment statements, and any other special features that you recognize.

(*a*)　main()

```
{
    printf("Welcome to the Wonderful World of Computing!\n");
}
```

(*b*)　#define MESSAGE "Welcome to the Wonderful World of Computing!\n"

```
main()

{
    printf(MESSAGE);
}
```

(*c*)　main()

```
{
    float base, height, area;

    printf("Base: ");
    scanf("%f", &base);
    printf("Height: ");
    scanf("%f", &height);
    area = (base * height) / 2.;
    printf("Area: %f", area);
}
```

(*d*)　main()

```
{
    float gross, tax, net;

    printf("Gross salary: ");
    scanf("%f", &gross);
    tax = 0.14 * gross;
    net = gross - tax;
    printf("Taxes withheld: %.2f\n", tax);
    printf("Net salary: %.2f", net);
}
```

(*e*) main()

```
    {
        int a, b, min;
        int smaller(int a, int b);

        printf("Please enter the first number: ");
        scanf("%d", &a);
        printf("Please enter the second number: ");
        scanf("%d", &b);

        min = smaller(a, b);

        printf("\nThe smaller number is: %d", min);
    }


    smaller(int a, int b)

    {
        if (a <= b)
            return(a);
        else
            return(b);
    }
```

(*f*) main()

```
    {
        int count, n, a, b, min;
        int smaller(int a, int b);

        printf("How many pairs of numbers? ");
        scanf("%d", &n);

        for (count = 1; count <= n; ++count)   {
            printf("\nPlease enter the first number: ");
            scanf("%d", &a);
            printf("Please enter the second number: ");
            scanf("%d", &b);

            min = smaller(a, b);

            printf("\nThe smaller number is: %d\n", min);
        }
    }


    smaller(int a, int b)

    {
        if (a <= b)
            return(a);
        else
            return(b);
    }
```

(g) main()

```
{
        int a, b, min;
        int smaller(int a, int b);

        printf("To STOP, enter 0 for each number\n");

        printf("\nPlease enter the first number: ");
        scanf("%d", &a);
        printf("Please enter the second number: ");
        scanf("%d", &b);

        while (a != 0 || b != 0)   {

            min = smaller(a, b);
            printf("\nThe smaller number is: %d\n", min);

            printf("\nPlease enter the first number: ");
            scanf("%d", &a);
            printf("Please enter the second number: ");
            scanf("%d", &b);

        }
}


smaller(int a, int b)

{
        if (a <= b)
            return(a);
        else
            return(b);
}
```

(h) main()

```
{
        int n, i = 0;
        int a[100], b[100], min[100];
        int smaller(int, int);

        printf("To STOP, enter 0 for each number\n");

        printf("\nPlease enter the first number: ");
        scanf("%d", &a[i]);
        printf("Please enter the second number: ");
        scanf("%d", &b[i]);

        while (a[i] || b[i])   {

            min[i] = smaller(a[i], b[i]);

            printf("\nPlease enter the first number: ");
            scanf("%d", &a[++i]);
            printf("Please enter the second number: ");
            scanf("%d", &b[i]);

        }
```

```
        n = --i;

        printf("\nSummary of Results\n\n");
        for (i = 0; i <= n; ++i)
            printf("a = %d    b = %d    min = %d\n", a[i], b[i], min[i]);
}


smaller(int a, int b)

{
        if (a <= b)
            return(a);
        else
            return(b);
}
```

## Chapter 2

C Fundamentals

This chapter is concerned with the basic elements used to construct simple C statements. These elements include the C character set, identifiers and keywords, data types, constants, variables and arrays, declarations, expressions and statements. We will see how these basic elements can be combined to form more comprehensive program components.

Some of this material is rather detailed and therefore somewhat difficult to absorb, particularly by an inexperienced programmer. Remember, however, that the purpose of this material is to introduce certain basic concepts and to provide some necessary definitions for the topics that follow in the next few chapters. Therefore, when reading this material for the first time, you need only acquire a general familiarity with the individual topics. A more comprehensive understanding will come later, from repeated references to this material in subsequent chapters.

2.1 THE C CHARACTER SET

C uses the uppercase letters A to Z, the lowercase letters a to z, the digits 0 to 9, and certain special characters as building blocks to form basic program elements (e.g., constants, variables, operators, expressions). The special characters are listed below.

```
    !      *      +      \      "      <
    #      (      =      |      {      >
    %      )      ~      ;      }      /
    ^      -      [      :      ,      ?
    &      _      ]      '      .      (blank)
```

Most versions of the language also allow certain other characters, such as @ and $, to be included within strings and comments.

C uses certain combinations of these characters, such as \b, \n and \t, to represent special conditions such as backspace, newline and horizontal tab, respectively. These character combinations are known as *escape sequences*. We will discuss escape sequences in Sec. 2.4. For now we simply mention that each escape sequence represents a single character, even though it is written as two or more characters.

2.2 IDENTIFIERS AND KEYWORDS

Identifiers are names given to various program elements, such as variables, functions and arrays. Identifiers consist of letters and digits, in any order, except that *the first character must be a letter*. Both upper- and lowercase letters are permitted, though common usage favors the use of lowercase letters for most types of identifiers. Upper- and lowercase letters are not interchangeable (i.e., an uppercase letter is *not* equivalent to the corresponding lowercase letter).

The underscore character (_) can also be included, and is considered to be a letter. An underscore is often used in the middle of an identifier. An identifier may also begin with an underscore, though this is rarely done in practice.

Example 2.1 The following names are valid identifiers.

```
    x       y12     sum_1       _temperature
    names   area    tax_rate    TABLE
```

25

The following names are *not* valid identifiers for the reasons stated.

`4th`	the first character must be a letter
`"x"`	illegal characters (")
`order-no`	illegal character (-)
`error flag`	illegal character (blank space)

An identifier can be arbitrarily long. Some implementations of C recognize only the first eight characters, though most implementations recognize more (typically, 31 characters). The ANSI standard recognizes 31 characters. Additional characters are carried along for the programmer's convenience.

Example 2.2 The identifiers `file_manager` and `file_management` are both grammatically valid. Some compilers may be unable to distinguish between them, however, because the first eight letters are the same for each identifier. Therefore, only one of these identifiers should be used with such compilers.

As a rule, an identifier should contain enough characters so that its meaning is readily apparent. On the other hand, an excessive number of characters should be avoided.

Example 2.3 A C program is being written to calculate the future value of an investment. The identifiers `value` or `future_value` are appropriate symbolic names. However, `v` or `fv` would probably be too brief, since the intended representation of these identifiers is not clear. On the other hand, a very long identifier such as `future_value_of_an_investment` would be unsatisfactory because it is too long and cumbersome.

There are certain reserved words, called *keywords*, that have standard, predefined meanings in C. These keywords can be used only for their intended purpose; they cannot be used as programmer-defined identifiers.

The standard keywords are:

`auto`	`extern`	`sizeof`
`break`	`float`	`static`
`case`	`for`	`struct`
`char`	`goto`	`switch`
`const`	`if`	`typedef`
`continue`	`int`	`union`
`default`	`long`	`unsigned`
`do`	`register`	`void`
`double`	`return`	`volatile`
`else`	`short`	`while`
`enum`	`signed`	

Some compilers may also include some or all of the following keywords:

`ada`	`far`	`near`
`asm`	`fortran`	`pascal`
`entry`	`huge`	

Some C compilers may recognize other keywords. The user is encouraged to consult a reference manual to obtain a complete list of keywords for his or her particular compiler.

Note that the keywords are all lowercase. Since uppercase and lowercase characters are not equivalent, it is possible to use an uppercase keyword as an identifier. Normally, however, this is not done; it is considered a poor programming practice.

2.3 DATA TYPES

C supports several different types of data, each of which may be represented differently within the computer's memory. The basic data types are listed below. Typical memory requirements are also given. (The memory requirements for each numerical data type will determine the permissible range of values for that data type. Note that the memory requirements for each data type may vary from one C compiler to another.)

Data Type	Description	Typical Memory Requirements
int	integer quantity	2 bytes or 1 word (varies from one compiler to another)
char	single character	1 byte
float	floating-point number (i.e., a number containing a decimal point and/or an exponent)	1 word (4 bytes)
double	double-precision floating-point number (i.e., more significant figures, and an exponent which may be larger in magnitude)	2 words (8 bytes)

C compilers that are written for personal computers or small minicomputers (i.e, computers whose natural word size is less than 32 bits) generally represent a word as 4 bytes (32 bits).

Some basic data types can be augmented by using the data type *qualifiers* short, long, signed and unsigned. For example, integer quantities can be defined as short int, long int or unsigned int (these data types are usually written simply as short, long or unsigned, and are understood to be integers). The interpretation of a qualified integer data type will vary from one C compiler to another, though there are some common-sense relationships. Thus, a short int may require less memory than an ordinary int or it may require the same amount of memory as an ordinary int, but it will never exceed an ordinary int in word length. Similarly, a long int may require the same amount of memory as an ordinary int or it may require more memory, but it will never be less than an ordinary int.

If short int and int both have the same memory requirements (e.g., 2 bytes), then long int will generally have double the requirements (e.g., 4 bytes). Or, if int and long int both have the same memory requirements (e.g., 4 bytes), then short int will generally have half the memory requirements (e.g., 2 bytes). Remember that the specifics will vary from one C compiler to another.

An unsigned int has the same memory requirements as an ordinary int. However, in the case of an ordinary int (or a short int or a long int), the leftmost bit is reserved for the sign. With an unsigned int, all the bits are used to represent the numerical value. Thus, an unsigned int can be approximately twice as large as an ordinary int (though, of course, negative values are not permitted). For example, if an ordinary int can vary from $-32,768$ to $+32,767$ (which is typical for a 2-byte int), then an unsigned int will be allowed to vary from 0 to 65,535. The unsigned qualifier can also be applied to other qualified ints, for example, unsigned short int or unsigned long int.

The char type is used to represent individual characters. Hence, the char type will generally require only 1 byte of memory. Each char type has an equivalent integer interpretation, however, so a char is a really a special kind of short integer (see Sec. 2.4). With most compilers, a char data type will permit a range of values extending from 0 to 255. References may also be made to unsigned char data (with typical values ranging from 0 to 255), or signed char data (with values ranging from -128 to $+127$).

Some compilers permit the qualifier long to be applied to float or to double, for example, long float or long double. However, the meaning of these data types will vary from one C compiler to another. Thus, long float may be equivalent to double. Moreover, long double may be equivalent to double, or it may refer to a separate, "extra-large," double-precision data type requiring more than 2 words of memory.

Two additional data types, void and enum will be introduced later in this book (void is discussed in Secs. 7.2 and 7.4; enum is discussed in Sec. 14.1).

Every identifier that represents a number or a character within a C program must be associated with one of the basic data types before the identifier appears in an executable statement. This is accomplished via a *type declaration*, as described in Sec. 2.6.

2.4 CONSTANTS

C has four basic types of constants. They are *integer constants*, *floating-point constants*, *character constants* and *string constants* (there are also *enumeration constants*, which are discussed in Sec. 14.1). Moreover, there are several different kinds of integer and floating-point constants, as discussed below.

Integer and floating-point constants represent numbers. They are often referred to collectively as *numeric-type* constants. The following rules apply to all numeric-type constants.

1. Commas and blank spaces cannot be included within the constant.

2. The constant can be preceded by a minus (−) sign if desired. (Actually, the minus sign is an *operator* that changes the sign of a positive constant, though it can be thought of as a part of the constant itself.)

3. The value of a constant cannot exceed specified minimum and maximum bounds. For each type of constant, these bounds will vary from one C compiler to another.

Let us consider each type of constant individually.

Integer Constants

An *integer constant* is an integer-valued number. Thus it consists of a sequence of digits. Integer constants can be written in three different number systems: decimal (base 10), octal (base 8) and hexadecimal (base 16). Beginning programmers rarely, however, use anything other than decimal integer constants.

A *decimal* integer constant can consist of any combination of digits taken from the set 0 through 9. If the constant contains two or more digits, the first digit must be something other than 0.

Example 2.4 Several valid decimal integer constants are shown below.

$$0 \qquad 1 \qquad 743 \qquad 5280 \qquad 32767 \qquad 9999$$

The following decimal integer constants are written incorrectly for the reasons stated.

12,245	illegal character (,)
36.0	illegal character (.)
10 20 30	illegal character (blank space)
123-45-6789	illegal character (−)
0900	the first digit cannot be a zero

An *octal* integer constant can consist of any combination of digits taken from the set 0 through 7. However, the first digit must be 0, in order to identify the constant as an octal number.

Example 2.5 Several valid octal integer constants are shown below.

$$0 \qquad 01 \qquad 0743 \qquad 077777$$

The following octal integer constants are written incorrectly for the reasons stated.

743	does not begin with 0
05280	illegal digit (8)
0777.777	illegal character (.)

A *hexadecimal* integer constant must begin with either Øx or ØX. It can then be followed by any combination of digits taken from the sets Ø through 9 and a through f (either upper- or lowercase). Note that the letters a through f (or A through F) represent the (decimal) quantities 1Ø though 15, respectively.

Example 2.6   Several valid hexadecimal integer constants are shown below.

$$Øx \qquad ØX1 \qquad ØX7FFF \qquad Øxabcd$$

The following hexadecimal integer constants are written incorrectly for the reasons stated.

ØX12.34	illegal character (.)
ØBE38	does not begin with Øx or ØX
Øx.4bff	illegal character (.)
ØXDEFG	illegal character (G)

The magnitude of an integer constant can range from zero to some maximum value that varies from one computer to another (and from one compiler to another on the same computer). A typical maximum value for most personal computers and many minicomputers is 32767 decimal (equivalent to 77777 octal or 7fff hexadecimal), which is $2^{15} - 1$. Mainframe computers generally permit larger values, such as 2,147,483,647 (which is $2^{31} - 1$).* Readers should determine the appropriate value for the version of C used with their particular computer.

Unsigned and Long Integer Constants

Unsigned integer constants may exceed the magnitude of ordinary integer constants by approximately a factor of 2, though they may not be negative.* An unsigned integer constant can be identified by appending the letter U (either upper- or lowercase) to the end of the constant.

Long integer constants may exceed the magnitude of ordinary integer constants, but require more memory within the computer. With some computers (and/or some compilers), a long integer constant will automatically be generated simply by specifying a quantity that exceeds the normal maximum value. It is *always* possible, however, to create a long integer constant by appending the letter L (either upper- or lowercase) to the end of the constant.

An unsigned long integer may be specified by appending the letters UL to the end of the constant. The letters may be written in either upper- or lowercase. However, the U must precede the L.

Example 2.7   Several unsigned and long integer constants are shown below.

Constant	Number System
5ØØØØU	decimal (unsigned)
123456789L	decimal (long)
123456789UL	decimal (unsigned long)
Ø123456L	octal (long)
Ø777777U	octal (unsigned)
ØX5ØØØØU	hexadecimal (unsigned)
ØXFFFFFUL	hexadecimal (unsigned long)

---

* Suppose a particular computer uses a *w*-bit word. Then an ordinary integer quantity may fall within the range -2^{w-1} to $+2^{w-1} - 1$, whereas an unsigned integer quantity may vary from 0 to $2^w - 1$. A short integer may substitute $w/2$ for w, and a long integer may substitute $2w$ for w. These rules may vary from one computer to another.

The maximum permissible values of unsigned and long integer constants will vary from one computer (and one compiler) to another. With some computers, the maximum permisssible value of a long integer constant may be the same as that for an ordinary integer constant; other computers may allow a long integer constant to be much larger than an ordinary integer constant. Readers are again advised to determine the appropriate values for their particular version of C.

Floating-Point Constants

A *floating-point constant* is a base-10 number that contains either a decimal point or an exponent (or both).

Example 2.8 Several valid floating-point constants are shown below.

0.	1.	0.2	827.602
50000.	0.000743	12.3	315.0066
2E-8	0.006e-3	1.6667E+8	.12121212e12

The following are *not* valid floating-point constants for the reasons stated.

1	either a decimal point or an exponent must be present
1,000.0	illegal character (,)
2E+10.2	the exponent must be an integer quantity (it cannot contain a decimal point)
3E 10	illegal character (blank space) in the exponent

If an exponent is present, its effect is to shift the location of the decimal point to the right if the exponent is positive, or to the left if the exponent is negative. If a decimal point is not included within the number, it is assumed to be positioned to the right of the last digit.

The interpretation of a floating-point constant with an exponent is essentially the same as for scientific notation, except that the base 10 is replaced by the letter E (or e). Thus, the number 1.2×10^{-3} would be written as 1.2E-3 or 1.2e-3. This is equivalent to 0.12e-2 or 12e-4, etc.

Example 2.9 The quantity 3×10^5 can be represented in C by any of the following floating-point constants:

300000.	3e5	3e+5	3E5	3.0e+5
.3e6	0.3E6	30E4	30.E+4	300e3

Similarly, the quantity 5.026×10^{-17} can be represented by any of the following floating-point constants.

5.026E-17	.5026e-16	50.26e-18	.0005026E-13

Floating-point constants have a much greater range than integer constants. Typically, the magnitude of a floating-point constant might range from a minimum value of approximately 3.4E-38 to a maximum of 3.4E+38. Some versions of the language permit floating-point constants that cover a wider range, such as 1.7E-308 to 1.7E+308. Also, the value 0.0 (which is less than either 3.4E-38 or 1.7E-308) is a valid floating-point constant. Readers should determine the appropriate values for the version of C used on their particular computer.

Floating-point constants are normally represented as double-precision quantities in C. Hence, each floating-point constant will typically occupy 2 words (8 bytes) of memory. Some versions of C permit the specification of a "single-precision," floating-point constant, by appending the letter F (in either upper- or lowercase) to the end of the constant (e.g., 3E5F). Similarly, some versions of C permit the specification of a "long" floating-point constant by appending the letter L (upper- or lowercase) to the end of the constant (e.g., 0.123456789E-33L).

The precision of floating-point constants (i.e., the number of significant figures) will vary from one version of C to another. Virtually all versions of the language permit at least six significant figures, and some versions permit as many as 18 significant figures. Readers should determine the appropriate number of significant figures for their particular version of C.

Numerical Accuracy

It should be understood that integer constants are exact quantities, whereas floating-point constants are approximations. The reasons for this are beyond the current scope of discussion. However, the reader should understand that the floating-point constant 1.0 might be represented within the computer's memory as 0.99999999..., even though it might appear as 1.0 when it is displayed (because of automatic rounding). Therefore, floating-point values cannot be used for certain purposes, such as counting or indexing, where exact values are required. We will discuss these restrictions as they arise in later chapters of this book.

Character Constants

A *character constant* is a single character, enclosed in apostrophes (single quotation marks).

Example 2.10   Several character constants are shown below.

$$\text{'A'} \qquad \text{'x'} \qquad \text{'3'} \qquad \text{'\$'} \qquad \text{' '}$$

Notice that the last constant consists of a blank space enclosed in apostrophes.

Character constants have integer values that are determined by the computer's particular character set. Thus, the value of a character constant may vary from one computer to another. The constants themselves, however, are independent of the character set. This feature eliminates the dependence of a C program on any particular character set.

Most computers, and virtually all personal computers, make use of the American Standard Code for Information Interchange (ASCII) character set, in which each individual character is numerically encoded with its own unique 7-bit combination. (Hence, a total of $2^7 = 128$ different characters.) Table 2-1 contains the ASCII character set, showing the decimal equivalent of the 7 bits that represent each character. Notice that the characters are ordered as well as encoded. In particular, the digits are ordered consecutively in their proper numerical sequence (0 to 9), and the letters are arranged consecutively in their proper alphabetical order, with uppercase characters preceding lowercase characters. This allows character-type data items to be compared with one another, based upon their relative order within the character set.

Example 2.11   Several character constants and their corresponding values, as defined by the ASCII character set, are shown below.

Constant	Value
'A'	65
'x'	120
'3'	51
'$'	36
' '	32

These values will be the same for all computers that use the ASCII character set. The values will be different, however, for computers that use an alternate character set.

IBM mainframe computers, for example, utilize the Extended Binary Coded Decimal Information Code (EBCDIC) character set, in which each individual character is numerically encoded with its own unique 8-bit combination. The EBCDIC character set is distinctly different from the ASCII character set.

Table 2-1 The ASCII Character Set

ASCII Value	Character	ASCII Value	Character	ASCII Value	Character	ASCII Value	Character
000	NUL	032	blank	064	@	096	`
001	SOH	033	!	065	A	097	a
002	STX	034	"	066	B	098	b
003	ETX	035	#	067	C	099	c
004	EOT	036	$	068	D	100	d
005	ENQ	037	%	069	E	101	e
006	ACK	038	&	070	F	102	f
007	BEL	039	'	071	G	103	g
008	BS	040	(	072	H	104	h
009	HT	041	)	073	I	105	i
010	LF	042	*	074	J	106	j
011	VT	043	+	075	K	107	k
012	FF	044	,	076	L	108	l
013	CR	045	-	077	M	109	m
014	SO	046	.	078	N	110	n
015	SI	047	/	079	O	111	o
016	DLE	048	0	080	P	112	p
017	DC1	049	1	081	Q	113	q
018	DC2	050	2	082	R	114	r
019	DC3	051	3	083	S	115	s
020	DC4	052	4	084	T	116	t
021	NAK	053	5	085	U	117	u
022	SYN	054	6	086	V	118	v
023	ETB	055	7	087	W	119	w
024	CAN	056	8	088	X	120	x
025	EM	057	9	089	Y	121	y
026	SUB	058	:	090	Z	122	z
027	ESC	059	;	091	[	123	{
028	FS	060	<	092	\	124	¦
029	GS	061	=	093	]	125	}
030	RS	062	>	094	↑	126	~
031	US	063	?	095	—	127	DEL

Note: The first 32 characters and the last character are control characters; they cannot be printed.

Escape Sequences

Certain nonprinting characters, as well as the double quote ("), the apostrophe ('), the question mark (?) and the backslash (\), can be expressed in terms of *escape sequences*. An escape sequence always begins with a backward slash and is followed by one or more special characters. For example, a line feed (LF), which is referred to as a *newline* in C, can be represented as \n. Such escape sequences always represent single characters, even though they are written in terms of two or more characters.

The commonly used escape sequences are listed below.

Character	Escape Sequence	ASCII Value
bell (alert)	\a	007
backspace	\b	008
horizontal tab	\t	009
vertical tab	\v	011
newline (line feed)	\n	010
form feed	\f	012
carriage return	\r	013
quotation mark (")	\"	034
apostrophe (')	\'	039
question mark (?)	\?	063
backslash (\)	\\	092
null	\0	000

Example 2.12   Shown below are several character constants, expressed in terms of escape sequences.

'\n'   '\t'   '\b'   '\''   '\\'   '\"'

Note that the last three escape sequences represent an apostrophe, a backslash and a quotation mark, respectively.

Of particular interest is the escape sequence \0. This represents the *null character* (ASCII 000), which is used to indicate the end of a *string* (see below). Note that the null character constant '\0' is *not* equivalent to the character constant '0'.

An escape sequence can also be expressed in terms of one, two or three octal digits which represent single-character bit patterns. The general form of such an escape sequence is \ooo, where each o represents an octal digit (0 through 7). Some versions of C also allow an escape sequence to be expressed in terms of one or more hexadecimal digits, preceded by the letter x. The general form of a hexadecimal escape sequence is \xhh, where each h represents a hexadecimal digit (0 through 9 and a through f). The letters can be either upper- or lowercase. Using an octal or hexadecimal escape sequence is usually less desirable than writing the character constant directly, however, since the bit patterns may be dependent upon some particular character set.

Example 2.13   The letter A is represented by the decimal value 065 in the ASCII character set. This value is equivalent to the octal value 101. (The equivalent binary bit pattern is 001 000 001.) Hence, the character constant 'A' can be expressed as the octal escape sequence '\101'.

In some versions of C, the letter A can also be expressed as a hexadecimal escape sequence. The hexadecimal equivalent of the decimal value 65 is 41. (The equivalent binary bit pattern is 0100 0001.) Hence, the character constant 'A' can be expressed as '\x41' or as '\X41'.

The preferred way to represent this character constant is simply 'A'. In this form, the character constant does not depend on its equivalent ASCII representation.

Escape sequences can only be written for certain special characters, such as those listed above, or in terms of octal or hexadecimal digits. If a backslash is followed by any other character, the result may be unpredictable. Usually, however, it will simply be ignored.

String Constants

A *string constant* consists of any number of consecutive characters (including none) enclosed in (double) quotation marks.

Example 2.14 Several string constants are shown below.

```
    "green"       "Washington, D.C. 20005"    "270-32-3456"
    "$19.95"      "THE CORRECT ANSWER IS:"     "2*(I+3)/J"
    "        "    "Line 1\nLine 2\nLine 3"     ""
```

Note that the string constant "Line 1\nLine 2\nLine 3" extends over three lines, because of the newline characters embedded within the string. Thus, this string would be displayed as

```
Line 1
Line 2
Line 3
```

Also, notice that the string "" is a *null* (empty) string.

Sometimes a backslash or a quotation mark must be included as a part of a string constant. These characters *must* be represented in terms of their escape sequences. Similarly, certain nonprinting characters (e.g., tab, newline) can be included in a string constant if they are represented in terms of their corresponding escape sequences. Most compilers permit the remaining printable escape characters (i.e., the apostrophe and the question mark) to appear within a string constant as either an ordinary character or an escape sequence.

Example 2.15 The following string constant includes three special characters represented by their corresponding escape sequences.

```
"\tTo continue, press the \"RETURN\" key\n"
```

The special characters are \t (horizontal tab), \" (double quotation marks, which appears twice), and \n (newline).

The compiler automatically places a null character ($\backslash 0$) at the end of every string constant, as the last character within the string (before the closing double quotation mark). This character is not visible when the string is displayed. However, we can easily examine the individual characters within a string and test to see whether or not each character is a null character (we will see how this is done in Chap. 6). Thus, the end of every string can be readily identified. This is very helpful if the string is scanned character-by-character, as is required in many applications. Also, in many situations this end-of-string designation eliminates the need to specify a maximum string length.

Example 2.16 The string constant shown in Example 2.15 actually contains 38 characters. This includes five blank spaces, four special characters (horizontal tab, two quotation marks and newline) represented by escape sequences, and the null character ($\backslash 0$) at the end of the string.

Remember that a character constant (e.g., 'A') and the corresponding single-character string constant ("A") are not equivalent. Also remember that a character constant has an equivalent integer value, whereas a single-character string constant does not have an equivalent integer value and, in fact, consists of *two* characters—the specified character followed by the null character ($\backslash 0$).

Example 2.17 The character constant 'w' has an integer value of 119 in the ASCII character set. It does not have a null character at the end. In contrast, the string constant "w" actually consists of two characters—the lowercase letter w and the null character $\backslash 0$. This constant does not have a corresponding integer value.

2.5 VARIABLES AND ARRAYS

A *variable* is an identifier that is used to represent some specified type of information within a designated portion of the program. In its simplest form, a variable represents a single data item, that is, a numerical quantity or a character constant. The data item must be assigned to the variable at some point in the program. The data item can then be accessed later in the program simply by referring to the variable name.

A given variable can be assigned different data items at various places within the program. Thus, the information represented by the variable can change during the execution of the program. However, the data type associated with the variable cannot change.

Example 2.18   A C program contains the following lines:

```
int a, b, c;
char d;
    :
a = 3;
b = 5;
c = a + b;
d = 'a';
    :
a = 4;
b = 2;
c = a - b;
d = 'W';
```

The first two lines are *type declarations*, which state that a, b and c are integer variables, and that d is a char-type variable. Thus a, b and c will each represent an integer-valued quantity, and d will represent a single character. These type declarations will apply throughout the program (more about this in Sec. 2.6).

The next four lines cause the following things to happen: the integer quantity 3 is assigned to a, 5 is assigned to b, and the quantity represented by the sum a + b (i.e., 8) is assigned to c. The character 'a' is then assigned to d.

In the third line within this group, notice that the values of the variables a and b are accessed simply by writing the variables on the righthand side of the equal sign.

The last four lines redefine the values assigned to the variables as follows: the integer quantity 4 is assigned to a, replacing the earlier value, 3; then 2 is assigned to b, replacing the earlier value, 5; then the difference between a and b (i.e., 2) is assigned to c, replacing the earlier value, 8. Finally, the character 'W' is assigned to d, replacing the earlier character, 'a'.

The *array* is another kind of variable that is used extensively in C. An array is an identifier that refers to a *collection* of data items which all have the same name. The data items must all be of the same type (for example, all integers, all characters). The individual data items are represented by their corresponding *array elements* (i.e., the first data item is represented by the first array element, and so on). The individual array elements are distinguished from one another by the value that is assigned to a *subscript*.

Example 2.19   Suppose that x is a 10-element array. The first element is referred to as $x[0]$, the second as $x[1]$, and so on. The last element will be $x[9]$.

The subscript associated with each element is shown in square brackets. Thus, the value of the subscript for the first element is 0, the value of the subscript for the second element is 1, and so on. For an n-element array, the subscripts always range from 0 to n-1.

There are several different ways to categorize arrays (e.g., integer arrays, character arrays, one-dimensional arrays, multidimensional arrays). For now, we will confine our attention to only one type of array: the one-dimensional *character* array, often called a char-type array. This type of array is generally used to represent a string. Each array element will represent one character within the string. Thus, the entire array can be thought of as an ordered list of characters.

Since the array is one dimensional, there will be a single *subscript* (sometimes called an *index*) whose value refers to individual array elements. If the array contains n elements, the subscript will be an integer quantity whose values range from 0 to n-1. Note that an n-character string will require an (n+1) element array, because of the null character ($\backslash 0$) automatically placed at the end of the string.

Example 2.20   Suppose that the string "California" is to be stored in a one-dimensional character array called letter. Since "California" contains 10 characters, letter will be an 11-element array. Thus, letter[∅] will represent the letter C, letter[1] will represent a, and so on, as summarized below. Note that the last (i.e., the 11th) array element, letter[1∅], represents the null character which signifies the end of the string.

Element Number	Subscript Value	Array Element	Corresponding Data Item (String Character)
1	∅	letter[∅]	C
2	1	letter[1]	a
3	2	letter[2]	l
4	3	letter[3]	i
5	4	letter[4]	f
6	5	letter[5]	o
7	6	letter[6]	r
8	7	letter[7]	n
9	8	letter[8]	i
10	9	letter[9]	a
11	1∅	letter[1∅]	\∅

From this list we can determine, for example, that the fifth array element, letter[4], represents the letter f, and so on.

The array elements and their contents are shown schematically in Fig. 2.1.

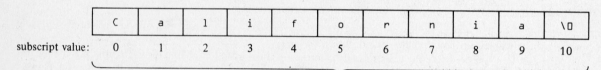

subscript value: 0   1   2   3   4   5   6   7   8   9   10

An 11-element character array

Fig. 2.1

We will discuss arrays in much greater detail in Chaps. 9 and 10.

2.6   DECLARATIONS

A *declaration* associates a group of variables with a specific data type. All variables must be declared before they can appear in executable statements.

A declaration consists of a data type, followed by one or more variable names, ending with a semicolon. (Recall that the permissible data types are discussed in Sec. 2.3.) Each array variable must be followed by a pair of square brackets, containing a positive integer which specifies the size (i.e., the number of elements) of the array.

Example 2.21   A C program contains the following type declarations:

```
int a, b, c;

float root1, root2;

char flag, text[8∅];
```

Thus, a, b and c are declared to be integer variables, root1 and root2 are floating-point variables, flag is a char-type variable and text is an 80-element, char-type array. Note the square brackets enclosing the size specification for text.

These declarations could also have been written as follows:

```
int a;

int b;

int c;

float root1;

float root2;

char flag;

char text[80];
```

This form may be useful if each variable is to be accompanied by a comment explaining its purpose. In small programs, however, items of the same type are usually combined in a single declaration.

Integer-type variables can be declared to be *short integer* for smaller integer quantities, or *long integer* for larger integer quantities. (Recall that some C compilers allocate less storage space to short integers, and additional storage space to long integers.) Such variables are declared by writing short int and long int, or simply short and long, respectively.

Example 2.22   A C program contains the following type declarations:

```
short int a, b, c;

long int r, s, t;

int p, q;
```

Some compilers will allocate less storage space to the short integer variables a, b and c than to the integer variables p and q. Typical values are 2 bytes for each short integer variable, and 4 bytes (1 word) for each ordinary integer variable. The maximum permissible values of a, b and c will be smaller than the maximum permissible values of p and q when using a compiler of this type.

Similarly, some compilers will allocate additional storage space to the long integer variables r, s and t than to the integer variables p and q. Typical values are 2 words (8 bytes) for each long integer variable, and 1 word (4 bytes) for each ordinary integer variable. The maximum permissible values of r, s and t will be larger than the maximum permissible values of p and q when using one of these compilers.

The above declarations could have been written as

```
short a, b, c;

long r, s, t;

int p, q;
```

Thus, short and short int are equivalent, as are long and long int.

An integer variable can also be declared to be *unsigned*, by writing unsigned int, or simply unsigned, as the type indicator. Unsigned integer quantities can be larger than ordinary integer quantities (approximately twice as large), but they cannot be negative.

Example 2.23   A C program contains the following type declarations:

```
int a, b;

unsigned x, y;
```

The unsigned variables x and y can represent values that are approximately twice as large as the values represented by a and b. However, x and y cannot represent negative quantities. For example, if the computer uses 2 bytes for each integer quantity, then a and b may take on values that range from -32768 to $+32767$, whereas the values of x and y may vary from 0 to $+65535$.

Floating-point variables can be declared to be *double precision* by using the type indicator double or long float rather than float. In most versions of C, the exponent within a double-precision quantity is larger in magnitude than the exponent within an ordinary floating-point quantity. Hence, the quantity represented by a double-precision variable can fall within a greater range. Moreover, a double-precision quantity will usually be expressed in terms of more significant figures.

Example 2.24   A C program contains the following type declarations:

```
float c1, c2, c3;

double root1, root2;
```

With a particular C compiler, the double-precision variables root1 and root2 represent values that can vary (in magnitude) from approximately 1.7×10^{-308} to $1.7 \times 10^{+308}$. However, the floating-point variables c1, c2 and c3 are restricted (in magnitude) to the range 3.4×10^{-38} to 3.4×10^{38}. Furthermore, the values represented by root1 and root2 will each be expressed in terms of 18 significant figures, whereas the values represented by c1, c2 and c3 will each be expressed in terms of only six significant figures.

The last declaration could have been written

```
long float root1, root2;
```

though the original form (i.e., double root1, root2;) is more common.

Initial values can be assigned to variables within a type declaration. To do so, the declaration must consist of a data type, followed by a variable name, an equal sign ($=$) and a constant of the appropriate type. A semicolon must appear at the end, as usual.

Example 2.25   A C program contains the following type declarations:

```
int c = 12;

char star = '*';

float sum = 0.;

double factor = 0.21023e-6;
```

Thus, c is an integer variable whose initial value is 12, star is a char-type variable initially assigned the character '*', sum is a floating-point variable whose initial value is 0., and factor is a double-precision variable whose initial value is 0.21023×10^{-6}.

A char-type array can also be initialized within a declaration. To do so, the array is usually written without an explicit size specification (the square brackets are empty). The array name is then followed by an equal sign, the string (enclosed in quotes) and a semicolon. This is a convenient way to assign a string to a char-type array.

Example 2.26   A C program contains the following type declaration:

```
char text[] = "California";
```

This declaration will cause text to be an 11-element character array. The first 10 elements will represent the 10 characters within the word California, and the 11th element will represent the null character (\0) which is automatically added at the end of the string.

The declaration could also have been written

```
char text[11] = "California";
```

where the size of the array is explicitly specified. In such situations it is important, however, that the size be specified correctly. If the size is too small, for example,

```
char text[10] = "California";
```

the characters at the end of the string (in this case, the null character) will be lost. If the size is too large, for example,

```
char text[20] = "California";
```

the extra array elements may be assigned zeros, or they may be filled with meaningless characters.

Array declarations that include the assignment of initial values can only appear in certain places within a C program (see Chap. 9).

In Chap. 8 we shall see that variables can be categorized by *storage class* as well as by data type. The storage class specifies the portion of the program within which the variables are recognized. Moreover, the storage class associated with an array determines whether or not the array can be initialized. This is explained in Chap. 9.

2.7   EXPRESSIONS

An *expression* represents a single data item, such as a number or a character. The expression may consist of a single entity, such as a constant, a variable, an array element or a reference to a function. It may also consist of some combination of such entities interconnected by one or more *operators*. The use of expressions involving operators is particularly common in C, as in most other programming languages.

Expressions can also represent logical conditions that are either true or false. However, in C the conditions *true* and *false* are represented by the integer values 1 and 0, respectively. Hence, logical-type expressions really represent numerical quantities.

Example 2.27   Several simple expressions are shown below.

```
a + b

x = y

c = a + b

x <= y

x == y

++i
```

The first expression involves use of the *addition operator* (+). This expression represents the sum of the values assigned to the variables a and b.

The second expression involves the *assignment operator* (=). In this case, the expression causes the value represented by y to be assigned to x. We have already encountered the use of this operator in several earlier examples (see Examples 1.6 through 1.13, 2.25 and 2.26). C includes several additional assignment operators, as discussed in Sec. 3.4.

The third expression combines the features of the first two expressions. In this case, the value of the expression a + b is assigned to the variable c.

The fourth expression will have the value 1 (true) if the value of x is less than or equal to the value of y. Otherwise, the expression will have the value $\emptyset$ (false). In this expression, <= is a *relational operator* that compares the values of the variables x and y (see Sec. 3.3).

The fifth expression is a test for equality (compare with the second expression, which is an assignment expression). Thus, the expression will have the value 1 (true) if the value of x is equal to the value of y. Otherwise, the expression will have the value $\emptyset$ (false).

The last expression causes the value of the variable i to be increased by 1 (i.e., *incremented*). Thus, the expression is equivalent to

```
i = i + 1
```

The operator ++, which indicates incrementing, is called a *unary* operator because it has only one *operand* (in this case, the variable i). C includes several other operators of this type, as discussed in Sec. 3.2.

The C language includes many different kinds of operators and expressions. Most are described in detail in Chap. 3. Others will be discussed elsewhere in this book, as the need arises.

2.8 STATEMENTS

A *statement* causes the computer to carry out some action. There are three different classes of statements in C. They are *expression statements*, *compound statements* and *control statements*.

An expression statement consists of an expression followed by a semicolon. The execution of an expression statement causes the expression to be evaluated.

Example 2.28   Several expression statements are shown below.

```
a = 3;

c = a + b;

++i;

printf("Area = %f", area);

;
```

The first two expression statements are assignment-type statements. Each causes the value of the expression on the right of the equal sign to be assigned to the variable on the left. The third expression statement is an incrementing-type statement, which causes the value of i to increase by 1.

The fourth expression statement causes the printf function to be evaluated. This is a standard C library function that writes information out of the computer (more about this in Sec. 3.6). In this case, the message Area = will be displayed, followed by the current value of the variable area. Thus, if area represents the value 100., the statement will generate the message

```
Area = 100.000000
```

The last expression statement does nothing, since it consists of only a semicolon. It is simply a mechanism for providing an empty expression statement in places where this type of statement is required. Consequently, it is called a null statement.

A compound statement consists of several individual statements enclosed within a pair of braces ({ and }). The individual statements may themselves be expression statements, compound statements or control statements. Thus, the compound statement provides capability for embedding statements within other statements. Unlike an expression statement, a compound statement does *not* end with a semicolon.

Example 2.29   A typical compound statement is shown below.

```
{
   pi = 3.141593;
   circumference = 2. * pi * radius;
   area = pi * radius * radius;
}
```

This particular compound statement consists of three assignment-type expression statements, though it is considered a single entity within the program in which it appears. Note that the compound statement does not end with a semicolon after the brace.

Control statements are used to create special program features, such as logical tests, loops and branches. Many control statements require that other statements be embedded within them, as illustrated in the following example.

Example 2.30   The following control statement creates a conditional loop in which several actions are executed repeatedly, until some particular condition is satisfied.

```
while (count <= n)   {
      printf("x = ");
      scanf("%f", &x);
      sum += x;
      ++count;
}
```

This statement contains a compound statement, which in turn contains four expression statements. The compound statement will continue to be executed as long as the value of count does not exceed the value of n. Note that count increases in value during each pass through the loop.

Chapter 6 presents a detailed discussion of control statements.

2.9   SYMBOLIC CONSTANTS

A *symbolic constant* is a name that substitutes for a sequence of characters. The characters may represent a numeric constant, a character constant or a string constant. Thus, a symbolic constant allows a name to appear in place of a numeric constant, a character constant or a string. When a program is compiled, each occurrence of a symbolic constant is replaced by its corresponding character sequence.

Symbolic constants are usually defined at the beginning of a program. The symbolic constants may then appear later in the program in place of the numeric constants, character constants, and so on, that the symbolic constants represent.

A symbolic constant is defined by writing

```
#define  name  text
```

where *name* represents a symbolic name, typically written in uppercase letters, and *text* represents the sequence of characters associated with the symbolic name. Note that *text* does not end with a semicolon, since a symbolic constant definition is not a true C statement. Moreover, if *text* were to end with a semicolon, this semicolon would be treated as though it were a part of the numeric constant, character constant or string constant that is substituted for the symbolic name.

Example 2.31   A C program contains the following symbolic constant definitions:

```
#define  TAXRATE  0.23

#define  PI  3.141593

#define  TRUE   1
#define  FALSE  0
#define  FRIEND  "Susan"
```

Notice that the symbolic names are written in uppercase, to distinguish them from ordinary C identifiers. Also, note that the definitions do not end with semicolons.

Now suppose that the program contains the statement

```
area = PI * radius * radius;
```

During the compilation process, each occurrence of a symbolic constant will be replaced by its corresponding text. Thus, the above statement will become

```
area = 3.141593 * radius * radius;
```

Now suppose that a semicolon had been (incorrectly) included in the definition for PI, that is

```
#define  PI  3.141593;
```

The assignment statement for area would then become

```
area = 3.141593; * radius * radius;
```

Note the semicolon preceding the first asterisk. This is clearly incorrect, and it will cause an error in the compilation.

The substitution of text for a symbolic constant will be carried out anywhere beyond the #define statement, *except* within a string. Thus, any text enclosed by (double) quotation marks will be unaffected by this substitution process.

Example 2.32   A C program contains the following statements:

```
#define  CONSTANT  6.023E23
int c;
 . . . . .
printf("CONSTANT = %f", c);
```

The printf statement will be unaffected by the symbolic constant definition, since the term "CONSTANT = %f" is a string constant. If, however, the printf statement were written as

```
printf("CONSTANT = %f", CONSTANT);
```

then the printf statement would become

```
printf("CONSTANT = %f", 6.023E23);
```

during the compilation process.

Symbolic constants are not required when writing C programs. Their use is recommended, however, since they contribute to the development of clear, orderly programs. For example, symbolic constants are more readily identified than the information that they represent, and the symbolic names usually suggest the significance of their associated data items. Furthermore, it is much easier to change the value of a single symbolic constant than to change every occurrence of some numerical constant that may appear in several places within the program.

The `#define` feature, which is used to define symbolic constants, is one of several features included in the C *preprocessor* (i.e., a program that provides the first step in the translation of a C program into machine language). A detailed discussion of the C preprocessor is presented in Sec. 14.6.

Review Questions

2.1 Which characters comprise the C character set?

2.2 Summarize the rules for naming identifiers. Are uppercase letters equivalent to lowercase letters? Can digits be included in an identifier name? Can any special characters be included?

2.3 How many characters can be included in an identifier name? Are all of these characters equally significant?

2.4 What are the keywords in C? What restrictions apply to their use?

2.5 Name and describe the four basic data types in C.

2.6 Name and describe the four data type qualifiers. To which data types can each qualifier be applied?

2.7 Name and describe the four basic types of constants in C.

2.8 Summarize the rules that apply to all numeric-type constants.

2.9 What special rules apply to integer constants?

2.10 When writing integer constants, how are decimal constants, octal constants and hexadecimal constants distinguished from one another?

2.11 Typically, what is the largest permissible magnitude of an integer constant? State your answer in decimal, octal and hexadecimal.

2.12 What are unsigned integer constants? What are long integer constants? How do these constants differ from ordinary integer constants? How can they be written and identified?

2.13 Describe two different ways that floating-point constants can be written. What special rules apply in each case?

2.14 What is the purpose of the (optional) exponent in a floating-point constant?

2.15 Typically, what is the largest permissible magnitude of a floating-point constant? Compare with an integer constant.

2.16 How can "single-precision" and "long" floating-point constants be written and identified?

2.17 Typically, how many significant figures are permitted in a floating-point constant?

2.18 Describe the differences in accuracy between integer and floating-point constants. Under what circumstances should each type of constant be used?

2.19 What is a character constant? How do character constants differ from numeric-type constants? Do character constants represent numerical values?

2.20 What is the ASCII character set? How common is its use?

2.21 What is an escape sequence? What is its purpose?

2.22 Summarize the standard escape sequences in C. Describe other, nonstandard escape sequences that are commonly available.

2.23 What is a string constant? How do string constants differ from character constants? Do string constants represent numerical values?

2.24 Can escape sequences be included in a string constant? Explain.

2.25 What is a variable? How can variables be characterized?

2.26 What is an array variable? How does an array variable differ from an ordinary variable?

2.27 What restriction must be satisfied by all of the data items represented by an array?

2.28 How can individual array elements be distinguished from one another?

2.29 What is a subscript? What range of values is permitted for the subscript of a one-dimensional, n-element array?

2.30   What is the purpose of a type declaration? What are the components of a type declaration?

2.31   Must all variables appearing within a C program be declared?

2.32   How are initial values assigned to variables within a type declaration? How are strings assigned to one-dimensional, character-type arrays?

2.33   What is an expression? What kind of information is represented by an expression?

2.34   What is an operator? Describe several different types of operators that are included within the C language.

2.35   Name the three different classes of statements in C. Describe the composition of each.

2.36   Can statements be embedded within other statements? Explain.

2.37   What is a symbolic constant? How is a symbolic constant defined? How is the definition written? Where must a symbolic constant definition be placed within a C program?

2.38   During the compilation process, what happens to symbolic constants that appear within a C program?

Problems

2.39   Determine which of the following are valid identifiers. If invalid, explain why.

    (a) `record1`   (d) `return`   (g) `name and address`   (j) `123-45-6789`
    (b) `1record`   (e) `$tax`   (h) `name_and_address`
    (c) `file_3`   (f) `name`   (i) `name-and-address`

2.40   Assume that your version of C can recognize only the first 8 characters of an identifier name, though identifier names may be arbitrarily long. Which of the following pairs of identifier names are considered to be identical and which are distinct?

    (a) `name, names`   (c) `identifier_1, identifier_2`   (e) `answer, ANSWER`
    (b) `address, Address`   (d) `list1, list2`   (f) `char1, char_1`

2.41   Determine which of the following numerical values are valid constants. If a constant is valid, specify whether it is integer or real. Also, specify the base for each valid integer constant.

    (a) `0.5`   (d) `9.3e-12`   (g) `0.8E+0.8`   (j) `018CDF`
    (b) `27,822`   (e) `12345678`   (h) `0.8E 8`   (k) `0XBCFDAL`
    (c) `9.3e12`   (f) `12345678L`   (i) `0515`   (l) `0x87e3ha`

2.42   Determine which of the following are valid character constants.

    (a) `'a'`   (c) `'\n'`   (e) `'\\'`   (g) `'T'`   (i) `'xyz'`
    (b) `'$'`   (d) `'/n'`   (f) `'\a'`   (h) `'\0'`   (j) `'\052'`

2.43   Determine which of the following are valid string constants.

    (a) `'8:15 P.M.'`
    (b) `"Red, White and Blue"`
    (c) `"Name:`
    (d) `"Chapter 3 (Cont\'d)"`
    (e) `"1.3e-12"`
    (f) `"NEW YORK, NY 10020"`
    (g) `"The professor said, "Please don't sleep in class"`

2.44   Write appropriate declarations for each group of variables and arrays.

    (a) Integer variables: `p, q`   (d) Character variables: `current, last`
        Floating-point variables: `x, y, z`   Unsigned integer variable: `count`
        Character variables: `a, b, c`   Floating-point variable: `error`
    (b) Floating-point variables: `root1, root2`   (e) Character variables: `first, last`
        Long integer variable: `counter`   80-element character array: `message`
        Short integer variable: `flag`
    (c) Integer variable: `index`
        Unsigned integer variable: `cust_no`
        Double-precision variables: `gross, tax, net`

2.45   Write appropriate declarations and assign the given initial values for each group of variables and arrays.

    (a) Floating-point variables: $a = -8.2$, $b = 0.005$
        Integer variables: $x = 129$, $y = 87$, $z = -22$
        Character variables: `c1 = 'w'`, `c2 = '&'`

(b) Double-precision variables: $d1 = 2.88 \times 10^{-8}$, $d2 = -8.4 \times 10^5$
     Integer variables: $u = 711$ (octal), $v = ffff$ (hexadecimal)
(c) Long integer variable: $big = 123456789$
     Double-precision variable: $c = 0.3333333333$
     Character variable: $eol = $ *newline character*
(d) One-dimensional character array: $message = $ "ERROR"

2.46 Explain the purpose of each of the following expressions.

(a) `a - b`   (c) `d = a * (b + c)`   (e) `(a % 5) == 0`   (g) `--a`
(b) `a * (b + c)`   (d) `a >= b`   (f) `a < (b / c)`

2.47 Identify whether each of the following statements is an expression statement, a compound statement or a control statement.

(a) `a * (b + c);`

(d)
```
{
    ++x;
    if (x > 0)
        y = 2.0;
    else
        y = 3.0;
    printf("%f", y);
}
```

(b)
```
while (a < 100)  {
    d = a * (b + c);
    ++a;
}
```

(e)
```
{
    ++x;
    if (x > 0)  {
        y = 2.0;
        z = 6.0;
    }
    else  {
        y = 3.0;
        z = 9.0;
    }
}
```

(c)
```
if (x > 0)
    y = 2.0;
else
    y = 3.0;
```

2.48 Write an appropriate definition for each of the following symbolic constants, as it would appear within a C program.

	Constant	Text
(a)	FACTOR	-18
(b)	ERROR	0.0001
(c)	BEGIN	{
	END	}
(d)	NAME	"Sharon"
(e)	EOLN	'\n'
(f)	COST	"$19.95"

Chapter 3

Operators and Expressions

We have already seen that individual constants, variables, array elements and function references can be joined by various operators to form expressions. We have also mentioned that C includes a large number of operators which fall into several different categories. In this chapter we examine certain of these categories in detail. Specifically, we will see how arithmetic operators, unary operators, relational and logical operators, assignment operators and the conditional operator are used to form expressions.

The data items that operators act upon are called *operands*. Some operators require two operands, while others act upon only one operand. Most operators allow the individual operands to be expressions. A few operators permit only single variables as operands (more about this in Sec. 3.2).

3.1 ARITHMETIC OPERATORS

There are five arithmetic operators in C. They are

Operator	Purpose
+	addition
–	subtraction
*	multiplication
/	division
%	remainder after integer division

The operator % is sometimes referred to as the *modulus operator*.

There is no exponentiation operator in C. However, there is a *library function* (pow) to carry out exponentiation (see Sec. 3.6).

The operands acted upon by arithmetic operators must represent numeric values. Thus, the operands can be integer quantities, floating-point quantities or characters (remember that character constants represent integer values, as determined by the computer's character set). The remainder operator (%) requires that both operands be integers and the second operand be nonzero. Similarly, the division operator (/) requires that the second operand be nonzero, though the operands need not be integers.

Division of one integer quantity by another is referred to as *integer division*. This operation always results in a truncated quotient (i.e., the decimal portion of the quotient will be dropped). On the other hand, if a division operation is carried out with two floating-point numbers, or with one floating-point number and one integer, the result will be a floating-point quotient.

Example 3.1 Suppose that a and b are integer variables whose values are 10 and 3, respectively. Several arithmetic expressions involving these variables are shown below, together with their resulting values.

Expression	Value
a + b	13
a - b	7
a * b	30
a / b	3
a % b	1

46

Notice the truncated quotient resulting from the division operation, since both operands represent integer quantites. Also, notice the integer remainder resulting from the use of the modulus operator in the last expression.

Now suppose that v1 and v2 are floating-point variables whose values are 12.5 and 2.0, respectively. Several arithmetic expressions involving these variables are shown below, together with their resulting values.

Expression	Value
v1 + v2	14.5
v1 - v2	10.5
v1 * v2	25.0
v1 / v2	6.25

Finally, suppose that c1 and c2 are character-type variables that represent the characters P and T, respectively. Several arithmetic expressions that make use of these variables are shown below, together with their resulting values (based upon the ASCII character set).

Expression	Value
c1	80
c1 + c2	164
c1 + c2 + 5	169
c1 + c2 + '5'	217

Note that P is encoded as (decimal) 80, T is encoded as 84, and 5 is encoded as 53 in the ASCII character set, as shown in Table 2-1.

If one or both operands represent negative values, then the addition, subtraction, multiplication and division operations will result in values whose signs are determined by the usual rules of algebra. Integer division will result in truncation toward zero, i.e., the resultant will always be smaller in magnitude than the true quotient.

The interpretation of the remainder operation is unclear when one of the operands is negative. Most versions of C assign the sign of the first operand to the remainder. Thus, the condition

```
a = ((a / b) * b) + (a % b)
```

will always be satisfied, regardless of the signs of the values represented by a and b.

Beginning programmers should be careful in using the remainder operation when one of the operands is negative. In general, it is best to avoid such situations.

Example 3.2 Suppose that a and b are integer variables whose values are 11 and -3, respectively. Several arithmetic expressions involving these variables are shown below, together with their resulting values.

Expression	Value
a + b	8
a - b	14
a * b	-33
a / b	-3
a % b	2

If a had been assigned a value of -11 and b had been assigned 3, then the value of a / b would still be -3 but the value of a % b would be -2. Similarly, if a and b had both been assigned negative values (-11 and -3, respectively), then the value of a / b would be 3 and the value of a % b would be -2.

Note that the condition

```
a = ((a / b) * b) + (a % b)
```

will be satisfied in each of the above cases. Most versions of C will determine the sign of the remainder in this manner, though this feature is unspecified in the formal definition of the language.

Example 3.3   Here is an illustration of the results obtained with floating-point operands having different signs. Let r1 and r2 be floating-point variables whose assigned values are -0.66 and 4.50. Several arithmetic expressions involving these variables are shown below, together with their resulting values.

Expression	Value
r1 + r2	3.84
r1 - r2	-5.16
r1 * r2	-2.97
r1 / r2	-0.146667

Operands that differ in type may undergo type conversion before the expression takes on its final value. In general, the final result will be expressed in the highest precision possible, consistent with the data types of the operands. The following rules apply when neither operand is unsigned.

1. If both operands are floating-point types whose precisions differ (e.g., a float and a double), the lower-precision operand will be converted to the precision of the other operand, and the result will be expressed in this higher precision. Thus, an operation between a float and a double will result in a double; a float and a long double will result in a long double; and a double and a long double will result in a long double. (*Note*: in some versions of C, all operands of type float are automatically converted to double.)

2. If one operand is a floating-point type (e.g., float, double or long double) and the other is a char or an int (including short int or long int), the char/int will be converted to the floating-point type of the other operand and the result will be expressed as such. Hence, an operation between an int and a double will result in a double.

3. If neither operand is a floating-point type but one is a long int, the other will be converted to long int and the result will be long int. Thus, an operation between a long int and an int will result in a long int.

4. If neither operand is a floating-point type or a long int, then both operands will be converted to int (if necessary) and the result will be int. Thus, an operation between a short int and an int will result in an int.

A detailed summary of these rules is given in Appendix D. Conversions involving unsigned operands are also presented in Appendix D.

Example 3.4   Suppose that i is an integer variable whose value is 7, f is a floating-point variable whose value is 5.5, and c is a character-type variable that represents the character w. Several expressions which include the use of these variables are shown below. Each expression involves operands of two different types. Assume the ASCII character set is being used.

Expression	Value	Type
i + f	12.5	double-precision
i + c	126	integer
i + c - '0'	78	integer
(i + c) - (2 * f / 5)	123.8	double-precision

Note that w is encoded as (decimal) 119 and Ø is encoded as 48 in the ASCII character set, as shown in Table 2-1.

The value of an expression can be converted to a different data type if desired. To do so, the expression must be preceded by the name of the desired data type, enclosed in parentheses; i.e.,

```
(data type) expression
```

This type of construction is known as a *cast*. (It is also called a *type cast*.)

Example 3.5   Suppose that i is an integer variable whose value is 7, and f is a floating-point variable whose value is 8.5. The expression

```
(i + f) % 4
```

is invalid, because the first operand (i + f) is floating-point rather than integer. However, the expression

```
((int) (i + f)) % 4
```

forces the first operand to be an integer and is therefore valid, resulting in the integer remainder 3.
Note that the explicit type specification applies only to the first operand, not the entire expression.

The data type associated with the expression itself is not changed by a cast. Rather, it is the *value* of the expression that undergoes type conversion wherever the cast appears. This is particularly relevant when the expression consists of only a single variable.

Example 3.6   Suppose that f is a floating-point variable whose value is 5.5. The expression

```
((int) f) % 2
```

contains two integer operands and is therefore valid, resulting in the integer remainder 1. Note, however, that f remains a floating-point variable whose value is 5.5, even though the value of f was converted to an integer (5) when carrying out the remainder operation.

The operators within C are grouped hierarchically according to their *precedence* (i.e., order of evaluation). Operations with a higher precedence are carried out before operations having a lower precedence. The natural order of evaluation can be altered, however, through the use of parentheses, as illustrated in Example 3.5.
Among the arithmetic operators, *, / and % fall into one precedence group, and + and - fall into another. The first group has a higher precedence than the second. Thus, multiplication, division and remainder operations will be carried out before addition and subtraction.
Another important consideration is the *order* in which consecutive operations within the same precedence group are carried out. This is known as *associativity*. Within each of the precedence groups described above, the associativity is left-to-right. In other words, consecutive addition and subtraction operations are carried out from left-to-right, as are consecutive multiplication, division and remainder operations.

Example 3.7   The arithmetic expression

```
a - b / c * d
```

is equivalent to the algebraic formula $a - [(b/c) \times d]$. Thus, if the floating-point variables a, b, c and d have been assigned the values 1., 2., 3. and 4., respectively, the expression would represent the value $-1.666666\cdots$, since

$$1. - [(2./3.) \times 4.] = 1. - [0.666666\cdots \times 4.] = 1. - 2.666666\cdots = -1.666666\cdots$$

Notice that the division is carried out first, since this operation has a higher precedence than subtraction. The resulting quotient is then multiplied by 4., because of left-to-right associativity. The product is then subtracted from 1., resulting in the final value of $-1.666666\cdots$.

The natural precedence of operations can be altered through the use of parentheses, thus allowing the arithmetic operations within an expression to be carried out in any desired order. In fact, parentheses can be *nested*, one pair within another. In such cases the innermost operations are carried out first, then the next innermost operations, and so on.

Example 3.8   The arithmetic expression

```
(a - b) / (c * d)
```

is equivalent to the algebraic formula $(a - b)/(c \times d)$. Thus, if the floating-point variables a, b, c and d have been assigned the values 1., 2., 3. and 4., respectively, the expression would represent the value $-0.08333333\cdots$, since

$$(1. - 2.)/(3. \times 4.) = -1./12. = -0.08333333\cdots$$

Compare this result with that obtained in Example 3.7.

Sometimes it is a good idea to use parentheses to clarify an expression, even though the parentheses may not be required. On the other hand, the use of overly complex expressions, such as that shown in the next example, should be avoided if at all possible. Such expressions are difficult to read, and they are often written incorrectly because of unbalanced parentheses.

Example 3.9   Consider the arithmetic expression

```
2 * ((i % 5) * (4 + (j - 3) /(k + 2)))
```

where i, j and k are integer variables. If these variables are assigned the values 8, 15 and 4, respectively, then the given expression would be evaluated as

$$2 \times ((8\% 5) \times (4 + (15 - 3)/(4 + 2))) = 2 \times (3 \times (4 + (12/6))) = 2 \times (3 \times (4 + 2)) = 2 \times (3 \times 6) = 2 \times 18 = 36$$

Suppose the value of this expression will be assigned to the integer variable w, that is,

```
w = 2 * ((i % 5) * (4 + (j - 3) / (k + 2)));
```

It is generally better to break this long arithmetic expression up into several shorter expressions, such as

```
u = i % 5;

v = 4 + (j - 3) / (k + 2);

w = 2 * (u * v);
```

where u and v are integer variables. These equivalent expressions are much more likely to be written correctly than the original lengthy expression.

Assignment expressions will be discussed in greater detail in Sec. 3.4.

3.2   UNARY OPERATORS

C includes a class of operators that act upon a single operand to produce a new value. Such operators are known as *unary operators*. Unary operators usually precede their single operands, though some unary operators are written after their operands.

Perhaps the most common unary operation is *unary minus*, where a minus sign precedes a numerical constant, a variable or an expression. (Some programming languages allow a minus sign to be included as a part of a numeric constant. In C, however, all numeric constants are positive. Thus, a negative number is actually an expression, consisting of the unary minus operator, followed by a positive numeric constant.)

Note that the unary minus operation is distinctly different from the arithmetic operator which denotes subtraction (-). The subtraction operator requires two separate operands.

Example 3.10 Here are several examples illustrating the use of the unary minus operation.

```
-743        -ØX7FFF         -Ø.2         -5E-8
-root1                  -(x + y)              -3 * (x + y)
```

In each case the minus sign is followed by a numerical operand which may be an integer constant, a floating-point constant, a numeric variable or an arithmetic expression.

Two other commonly used unary operators are the *increment operator*, ++, and the *decrement operator*, --. The increment operator causes its operand to be increased by one, whereas the decrement operator causes its operand to be decreased by one. The operand used with each of these operators must be a single variable.

Example 3.11 Suppose that i is an integer variable that has been assigned a value of 5. The expression ++i, which is equivalent to writing i = i + 1, causes the value of i to be increased to 6. Similarly, the expression --i, which is equivalent to i = i - 1, causes the (original) value of i to be decreased to 4.

The increment and decrement operators can each be utilized in two different ways, depending on whether the operator is written before or after the operand. If the operator precedes the operand (e.g., ++i), then the operand will be altered in value *before* it is utilized for its intended purpose within the program. If, however, the operator *follows* the operand (e.g., i++), then the value of the operand will be altered *after* it is utilized.

Example 3.12 A C program includes an integer variable i whose initial value is 1. Suppose the program includes the following three printf statements. (See Example 1.6 for a brief explanation of the printf statement.)

```
printf("i = %d\n", i);
printf("i = %d\n", ++i);
printf("i = %d\n", i);
```

These printf statements will generate the following three lines of output. (Each printf statement will generate one line.)

```
i = 1
i = 2
i = 2
```

The first statement causes the original value of i to be displayed. The second statement increments i and then displays its value. The final value of i is displayed by the last statement.

Now suppose that the program includes the following three printf statements, rather than the three statements given above.

```
printf("i = %d\n", i);
printf("i = %d\n", i++);
printf("i = %d\n", i);
```

Note that the first and third statements are identical to those shown above. In the second statement, however, the unary operator follows the integer variable rather than precedes it.

These statements will generate the following three lines of output:

```
i = 1
i = 1
i = 2
```

The first statement causes the original value of i to be displayed, as before. The second statement causes the current value of i (1) to be displayed and then incremented (to 2). The final value of i (2) is displayed by the last statement.

We will say much more about the use of the printf statement in Chap. 4. For now, simply note the distinction between the expression ++i in the first group of statements and the expression i++ in the second group.

Another unary operator worth mentioning at this time is the sizeof operator. This operator returns the size of its operand, in bytes. The sizeof operator always precedes its operand. The operand may be an expression, or it may be a cast.

Elementary programs rarely make use of this operator. However, the operator allows a determination of the number of bytes allocated to various types of data items. This information can be very useful when transferring a program to a different computer or to a new version of C. It is also used for dynamic memory allocation, as explained in Sec. 10.4.

Example 3.13   Suppose that i is an integer variable, x is a floating-point variable, d is a double-precision variable, and c is a character-type variable. The statements

```
printf("integer: %d\n", sizeof i);
printf("float: %d\n", sizeof x);
printf("double: %d\n", sizeof d);
printf("character: %d\n", sizeof c);
```

might generate the following output:

```
integer: 2
float: 4
double: 8
character: 1
```

Thus, we see that this version of C allocates 2 bytes to each integer quantity, 4 bytes to each floating-point quantity, 8 bytes to each double-precision quantity, and 1 byte to each character. These values may vary from one version of C to another, as explained in Sec. 2.3.

Another way to generate the same information is to use a cast rather than a variable within each printf statement. Thus, the printf statements could have been written as

```
printf("integer: %d\n", sizeof (integer));
printf("float: %d\n", sizeof (float));
printf("double: %d\n", sizeof (double));
printf("character: %d\n", sizeof (char));
```

These printf statements will generate the same output as that shown above. Note that each cast is enclosed in parentheses, as described in Sec. 3.1.

Finally, consider the array declaration

```
char text[] = "California";
```

The statement

```
printf("Number of characters = %d", sizeof text);
```

will generate the following output.

```
Number of characters = 11
```

Thus, we see that the array text contains 11 characters, as explained in Example 2.26.

A *cast* is also considered to be a unary operator (see Example 3.5 and the preceding discussion). In general terms, a reference to the cast operator is written as (*type*). Thus, the unary operators we have encountered so far in this book are -, ++, --, sizeof and (*type*).

Unary operators have a higher precedence than arithmetic operators. Hence, if a unary minus operator acts upon an arithmetic expression that contains one or more arithmetic operators, the unary minus operation will be carried out first (unless, of course, the arithmetic expression is enclosed in parentheses). Also, the associativity of the unary operators is right-to-left, though consecutive unary operators rarely appear in elementary programs.

Example 3.14   Suppose that x and y are integer variables whose values are 10 and 20, respectively. The value of the expression -x + y will be $-10 + 20 = 10$. Note that the unary minus operation is carried out before the addition.

Now suppose that parentheses are introduced, so that the expression becomes -(10 + 20). The value of this expression is $-(10 + 20) = -30$. Note that the addition now precedes the unary minus operation.

C includes several other unary operators. They will be discussed in later sections of this book, as the need arises.

3.3   RELATIONAL AND LOGICAL OPERATORS

There are four *relational operators* in C. They are

Operator	Meaning
<	less than
<=	less than or equal to
>	greater than
>=	greater than or equal to

These operators all fall within the same precedence group, which is lower than the unary and arithmetic operators. The associativity of these operators is left-to-right.

Closely associated with the relational operators are the following two *equality operators*:

Operator	Meaning
==	equal to
!=	not equal to

The equality operators fall into a separate precedence group, beneath the relational operators. These operators also have a left-to-right associativity.

These six operators are used to form logical expressions representing conditions that are either true or false. The resulting expressions will be of type integer, since *true* is represented by the integer value 1 and *false* is represented by the value 0.

Example 3.15   Suppose that i, j and k are integer variables whose values are 1, 2 and 3, respectively. Several logical expressions involving these variables are shown below.

Expression	Interpretation	Value
i < j	true	1
(i + j) >= k	true	1
(j + k) > (i + 5)	false	0
k != 3	false	0
j == 2	true	1

When carrying out relational and equality operations, operands that differ in type will be converted in accordance with the rules discussed in Sec. 3.1.

Example 3.16 Suppose that i is an integer variable whose value is 7, f is a floating-point variable whose value is 5.5, and c is a character variable that represents the character `'w'`. Several logical expressions that make use of these variables are shown below. Each expression involves two different type operands. (Assume that the ASCII character set applies.)

Expression	Interpretation	Value
f > 5	true	1
(i + f) <= 10	false	0
c == 119	true	1
c != 'p'	true	1
c >= 10 * (i + f)	false	0

In addition to the relational and equality operators, C contains two *logical operators* (also called *logical connectives*). They are

Operator	Meaning
&&	and
||	or

These operators are referred to as *logical and* and *logical or*, respectively.

The logical operators act upon operands that are themselves logical expressions. The net effect is to combine the individual logical expressions into more complex conditions that are either true or false. The result of a *logical and* operation will be true only if both operands are true, whereas the result of a *logical or* operation will be true if either operand is true or if both operands are true. In other words, the result of a *logical or* operation will be false only if both operands are false.

In this context, *any* nonzero value, not just 1, is interpreted as true.

Example 3.17 Suppose that i is an integer variable whose value is 7, f is a floating-point variable whose value is 5.5, and c is a character variable that represents the character `'w'`. Several complex logical expressions that make use of these variables are shown below.

Expression	Interpretation	Value
(i >= 6) && (c == 'w')	true	1
(i >= 6) || (c == 119)	true	1
(f < 11) && (i > 100)	false	0
(c != 'p') || ((i + f) <= 10)	true	1

The first expression is true because both operands are true. In the second expression, both operands are again true; hence the overall expression is true. The third expression is false because the second operand is false. And finally, the fourth expression is true because the first operand is true.

Each of the logical operators falls into its own precedence group. *Logical and* has a higher precedence than *logical or*. Both precedence groups are lower than the group containing the equality operators. The associativity is left-to-right. The precedence groups are summarized on p. 55.

C also includes the unary operator ! that negates the value of a logical expression, i.e., it causes an expression that is originally true to become false, and vice versa. This operator is referred to as the *logical negation* (or *logical not*) operator.

Example 3.18 Suppose that i is an integer variable whose value is 7 and f is a floating-point variable whose value is 5.5. Several logical expressions that make use of these variables and the logical negation operator are shown below.

Expression	Interpretation	Value
f > 5	true	1
!(f > 5)	false	∅
i <= 3	false	∅
!(i <= 3)	true	1
i > (f + 1)	true	1
!(i > (f + 1))	false	∅

We will see other examples illustrating the use of the logical negation operator in later chapters of this book.

The hierarchy of operator precedences covering all of the operators discussed so far has become extensive. These operator precedences are summarized below, from highest to lowest.

Operator Category	Operators	Associativity
unary operators	- ++ -- ! sizeof (type)	R → L
arithmetic multiply, divide and remainder	* / %	L → R
arithmetic add and subtract	+ -	L → R
relational operators	< <= > >=	L → R
equality operators	== !=	L → R
logical *and*	&&	L → R
logical *or*	¦¦	L → R

A more complete list is given in Table 3-1 on p. 60.

Example 3.19 Consider once again the variables i, f and c, as described in Examples 3.16 and 3.17, i.e., i = 7, f = 5.5 and c = 'w'. Some logical expressions that make use of these variables are shown below.

Expression	Interpretation	Value
i + f <= 1∅	false	∅
i >= 6 && c == 'w'	true	1
c != 'p' ¦¦ i + f <= 1∅	true	1

Each of these expressions has been presented before (the first in Example 3.16, and the other two in Example 3.17), though pairs of parentheses were included in the previous examples. The parentheses are not necessary because of the natural operator precedences. Thus, the arithmetic operations will automatically be carried out before the relational or equality operations, and the relational and equality operations will automatically be carried out before the logical connectives.

Consider the last expression in particular. The first operation to be carried out will be addition (i.e., i + f); then the relational comparison (i.e., i + f <= 1∅); then the equality comparison (i.e., c != 'p'); and finally, the *logical or* condition.

Complex logical expressions that consist of individual logical expressions joined by the logical operators && and ¦¦ are evaluated left-to-right, but only until the overall true/false value has been established. Thus, a complex logical expression will not be evaluated in its entirety if its value can be established from its constituent operands.

Example 3.20 Consider the complex logical expression shown below.

```
error > .0001 && count < 100
```

If `error > .0001` is false, then the second operand (i.e., `count < 100`) will not be evaluated, because the entire expression will be considered to be false.

On the other hand, suppose the expression had been written

```
error > .0001 ¦¦ count < 100
```

If `error > .0001` is true, then the entire expression will be true. Hence, the second operand will not be evaluated. If `error > .0001` is false, however, then the second expression (i.e., `count < 100`) must be evaluated to determine if the entire expression is true or false.

3.4 ASSIGNMENT OPERATORS

There are several different assignment operators in C. All of them are used to form *assignment expressions*, which assign the value of an expression to an identifier.

The most commonly used assignment operator is =. Assignment expressions that make use of this operator are written in the form

identifier = expression

where *identifier* generally represents a variable and *expression* represents a constant, a variable or a more complex expression.

Example 3.21 Here are some typical assignment expressions that make use of the = operator.

```
a = 3

x = y

delta = 0.001

sum = a + b

area = length * width
```

The first assignment expression causes the integer value 3 to be assigned to the variable a, and the second assignment causes the value of y to be assigned to x. In the third assignment, the floating-point value 0.001 is assigned to `delta`. The last two assignments each result in the value of an arithmetic expression being assigned to a variable (i.e., the value of a + b is assigned to sum, and the value of `length * width` is assigned to `area`).

Remember that the *assignment operator* = and the *equality operator* == are *distinctly different*. The assignment operator is used to assign a value to an identifier, whereas the equality operator is used to determine if two expressions have the same value. These operators cannot be used in place of one another. Beginning programmers often incorrectly use the assignment operator when they want to test for equality. This results in a logical error that is usually difficult to detect.

Assignment expressions are often referred to as *assignment statements*, since they are usually written as complete statements. However, assignment expressions can also be written as expressions that are included within other statements (more about this in later chapters).

If the two operands in an assignment expression are of different data types, then the value of the expression on the right (i.e., the righthand operand) will automatically be converted to the type of the identifier on the left. The entire assignment expression will then be of this same data type.

Under some circumstances, this automatic type conversion can result in an alteration of the data being assigned. For example:

- A floating-point value may be truncated if assigned to an integer identifier.
- A double-precision value may be rounded if assigned to a floating-point (single-precision) identifier.
- An integer quantity may be altered if assigned to a shorter integer identifier or to a character identifier (some high-order bits may be lost).

Moreover, the value of a character constant assigned to a numeric-type identifier will depend on the particular character set in use. This may result in inconsistencies from one version of C to another.

The careless use of type conversions is a frequent source of errors among beginning programmers.

Example 3.22   In the following assignment expressions, suppose that `i` is an integer-type variable.

Expression	Value
i = 3.3	3
i = 3.9	3
i = -3.9	-3

Now suppose that `i` and `j` are both integer-type variables, and that `j` has been assigned a value of 5. Several assignment expressions that make use of these two variables are shown below.

Expression	Value	
i = j	5	
i = j / 2	2	
i = 2 * j / 2	5	(left-to-right associativity)
i = 2 * (j / 2)	4	(truncated division, followed by multiplication)

Finally, assume that `i` is an integer-type variable, and that the ASCII character set applies.

Expression	Value
i = 'x'	120
i = '∅'	48
i = ('x' - '∅') / 3	24
i = ('y' - '∅') / 3	24

Multiple assignments of the form

identifier 1 = identifier 2 = · · · = expression

are permissible in C. In such situations, the assignments are carried out from right to left. Thus, the multiple assignment

identifier 1 = identifier 2 = expression

is equivalent to

identifier 1 = (identifier 2 = expression)

and so on, with right-to-left nesting for additional multiple assignments.

Example 3.23   Suppose that i and j are integer variables. The multiple assignment expression

i = j = 5

will cause the integer value 5 to be assigned to both i and j. (To be more precise, 5 is first assigned to j, and the value of j is then assigned to i.)

Similarly, the multiple assignment expression

i = j = 5.9

will cause the integer value 5 to be assigned to both i and j. Remember that truncation occurs when the floating-point value 5.9 is assigned to the integer variable j.

C contains the following five additional assignment operators: +=, -=, *=, /= and %=. To see how they are used, consider the first operator, +=. The assignment expression

expression 1 += *expression 2*

is equivalent to

expression 1 = *expression 1* + *expression 2*

Similarly, the assignment expression

expression 1 -= *expression 2*

is equivalent to

expression 1 = *expression 1* - *expression 2*

and so on for all five operators.

Usually, *expression 1* is an identifier, such as a variable or an array element.

Example 3.24   Suppose that i and j are integer variables whose values are 5 and 7, and f and g are floating-point variables whose values are 5.5 and −3.25. Several assignment expressions that make use of these variables are shown below. Each expression utilizes the *original* values of i, j, f and g.

Expression	*Equivalent Expression*	*Final Value*
i += 5	i = i + 5	10
f -= g	f = f - g	8.75
j *= (i - 3)	j = j * (i - 3)	14
f /= 3	f = f / 3	1.833333
i %= (j - 2)	i = i % (j - 2)	0

Assignment operators have a lower precedence than any of the other operators that have been discussed so far. Therefore unary operations, arithmetic operations, relational operations, equality operations and logical operations are all carried out before assignment operations. Moreover, the assignment operations have a right-to-left associativity.

The hierarchy of operator precedences presented in the last section can now be modified as follows to include assignment operators.

Operator Category	Operators	Associativity
unary operators	- ++ -- ! sizeof (type)	R → L
arithmetic multiply, divide and remainder	* / %	L → R
arithmetic add and subtract	+ -	L → R
relational operators	< <= > >=	L → R
equality operators	== !=	L → R
logical *and*	&&	L → R
logical *or*	¦¦	L → R
assignment operators	= += -= *= /= %=	R → L

See Table 3-1 on p. 60 for a more complete list.

Example 3.25 Suppose that x, y and z are integer variables which have been assigned the values 2, 3 and 4, respectively. The expression

```
x *= -2 * (y + z) / 3
```

is equivalent to the expression

```
x = x * (-2 * (y + z) / 3)
```

Either expression will cause the value −8 to be assigned to x.

Consider the order in which the operations are carried out in the first expression. The arithmetic operations precede the assignment operation. Therefore, the expression (y + z) will be evaluated first, resulting in 7. Then the value of this expression will be multiplied by −2, yielding −14. This product will then be divided by 3 and truncated, resulting in −4. Finally, this truncated quotient is multiplied by the original value of x (i.e., 2) to yield the final result of −8.

Note that all of the explicit arithmetic operations are carried out before the final multiplication and assignment are made.

C contains other assignment operators in addition to those discussed above. We will discuss them in Chap. 13.

3.5 THE CONDITIONAL OPERATOR

Simple conditional operations can be carried out with the *conditional operator* (? :). An expression that makes use of the conditional operator is called a *conditional expression*. Such an expression can be written in place of the more traditional if-else statement, which is discussed in Chap. 6.

A conditional expression is written in the form

expression 1 ? *expression 2* : *expression 3*

When evaluating a conditional expression, *expression 1* is evaluated first. If *expression 1* is true (i.e., if its value is nonzero), then *expression 2* is evaluated and this becomes the value of the conditional expression. However, if *expression 1* is false (i.e., if its value is zero), then *expression 3* is evaluated and this becomes the value of the conditional expression. Note that only one of the embedded expressions (either *expression 2* or *expression 3*) is evaluated when determining the value of a conditional expression.

Example 3.26 In the conditional expression shown below, assume that i is an integer variable.

```
(i < 0) ? 0 : 100
```

The expression (i < 0) is evaluated first. If it is true (i.e., if the value of i is less than 0), the entire conditional expression takes on the value 0. Otherwise (if the value of i is not less than 0), the entire conditional expression takes on the value 100.

In the following conditional expression, assume that f and g are floating-point variables.

```
(f < g) ? f : g
```

This conditional expression takes on the value of f if f is less than g; otherwise, the conditional expression takes on the value of g. In other words, the conditional expression returns the value of the smaller of the two variables.

If the operands (i.e., *expression 2* and *expression 3*) differ in type, then the resulting data type of the conditional expression will be determined by the rules given in Sec. 3.1.

Example 3.27 Now suppose that i is an integer variable, and f and g are floating-point variables. The conditional expression

```
(f < g) ? i : g
```

involves both integer and floating-point operands. Thus, the resulting expression will be floating-point, even if the value of i is selected as the value of the expression (because of rule 2 in Sec. 3.1).

Conditional expressions frequently appear on the righthand side of a simple assignment statement. The resulting value of the conditional expression is assigned to the identifier on the left.

Example 3.28 Here is an assignment statement that contains a conditional expression on the righthand side.

```
flag = (i < 0) ? 0 : 100;
```

If the value of i is negative, then 0 will be assigned to flag. If i is not negative, however, then 100 will be assigned to flag.

Here is another assignment statement that contains a conditional expression on the righthand side.

```
min = (f < g) ? f : g;
```

This statement causes the value of the smaller of f and g to be assigned to min.

The conditional operator has its own precedence, just above the assignment operators. The associativity is right-to-left.

Table 3-1 summarizes the precedences for all of the operators discussed in this chapter.

Table 3-1 Operator Precedence Groups

Operator Category	*Operators*	*Associativity*
unary operators	− ++ −− ! sizeof (*type*)	R → L
arithmetic multiply, divide and remainder	* / %	L → R
arithmetic add and subtract	+ −	L → R
relational operators	< <= > >=	L → R
equality operators	== !=	L → R
logical *and*	&&	L → R
logical *or*	||	L → R
conditional operator	? :	R → L
assignment operators	= += −= *= /= %=	R → L

A complete list of all C operators, which is more extensive than that given in Table 3-1, is shown in Appendix C.

Example 3.29   In the following assignment statement, a, b and c are assumed to be integer variables. The statement includes operators from six different precedence groups.

```
c += (a > 0 && a <= 10) ? ++a : a/b;
```

The statement begins by evaluating the complex expression

```
(a > 0 && a <= 10)
```

If this expression is true, the expression ++a is evaluated. Otherwise, the expression a/b is evaluated. Finally, the assignment operation (+=) is carried out, causing the value of c to be increased by the value of the conditional expression.

If, for example, a, b and c have the values 1, 2 and 3, respectively, then the value of the conditional expression will be 2 (because the expression ++a will be evaluated), and the value of c will increase to 5 (c = 3 + 2). On the other hand, if a, b and c have the values 50, 10 and 20, respectively, then the value of the conditional expression will be 5 (because the expression a/b will be evaluated), and the value of c will increase to 25 (c = 20 + 5).

3.6   LIBRARY FUNCTIONS

The C language is accompanied by a number of *library functions* that carry out various commonly used operations or calculations. These library functions are not a part of the language per se, though all implementations of the language include them. Some functions return a data item to their access point; others indicate whether a condition is true or false by returning a 1 or a 0, respectively; still others carry out specific operations on data items but do not return anything. Features which tend to be computer-dependent are generally written as library functions.

For example, there are library functions that carry out standard input/output operations (read and write characters, read and write numbers, open and close files, test for *end-of-file*, etc.), functions that perform operations on characters (convert from lower-to uppercase, test to see if a character is uppercase, etc.), functions that perform operations on strings (copy a string, compare strings, concatenate strings, etc.), and functions that carry out various mathematical calculations (evaluate trigonometric, logarithmic and exponential functions, compute absolute values, square roots, etc.). Other kinds of library functions are also available.

Functionally similar library functions are usually grouped together as (compiled) object programs in separate library files. These library files are supplied as a part of each C compiler. All C compilers contain similar groups of library functions, though they lack precise standardization. Thus, there may be some variation in the library functions that are available in different versions of the language.

A typical set of library functions will include a large number of functions that are common to most C compilers, such as those shown in Table 3-2. Within this table, the column labeled "type" refers to the data type of the quantity returned by the function. The *void* entry shown for function srand indicates that nothing is returned by this function.

A more extensive list, which includes all of the library functions appearing in the programming examples presented in this book, is shown in Appendix H. For a complete list, the reader is referred to the programmer's reference manual that accompanies his or her particular version of C.

A library function is accessed simply by writing the function name, followed by a list of *arguments* that represent information being passed to the function. The arguments must be enclosed in parentheses and separated by commas. The arguments can be constants, variable names, or more complex expressions. The parentheses must be present, even if there are no arguments.

A function that returns a data item can appear anywhere within an expression in place of a constant or an identifier (i.e., in place of a variable or an array element). A function that carries out operations

Table 3-2   Some Commonly Used Library Functions

Function	Type	Purpose
abs(i)	int	return the absolute value of i.
ceil(d)	double	round up to the next integer value (the smallest integer that is greater than or equal to d)
cos(d)	double	return the cosine of d
cosh(d)	double	return the hyperbolic cosine of d
exp(d)	double	raise e to the power d ($e = 2.7182818 \ldots$ is the base of the natural (Naperian) system of logarithms)
fabs(d)	double	return the absolute value of d
floor(d)	double	round down to the next integer value (the largest integer that does not exceed d)
fmod(d1,d2)	double	return the remainder (i.e., the noninteger part of the quotient) of d1/d2, with same sign as d1
getchar()	int	enter a character from the standard input device.
log(d)	double	return the natural logarithm of d
pow(d1,d2)	double	return d1 raised to the d2 power
printf(...)	int	send data items to the standard output device (arguments are complicated— see Chap. 4)
putchar(c)	int	send a character to the standard output device
rand()	int	return a random positive integer
sin(d)	double	return the sine of d
sqrt(d)	double	return the square root of d
srand(u)	void	initialize the random number generator
scanf(...)	int	enter data items from the standard input device (arguments are complicated—see Chap. 4)
tan(d)	double	return the tangent of d
toascii(c)	int	convert value of argument to ASCII
tolower(c)	int	convert letter to lowercase
toupper(c)	int	convert letter to uppercase

Note: *Type* refers to the data type of the quantity returned by the function.

   c denotes a character-type argument

   i denotes an integer argument

   d denotes a double-precision argument

   u denotes an unsigned integer argument

on data items but does not return anything can be accessed simply by writing the function name, since this type of function reference constitutes an expression statement.

Example 3.30   Shown below is a portion of a C program that solves for the roots of the quadratic equation

$$ax^2 + bx + c = 0$$

using the well-known quadratic formula

$$x = [-b \pm (b^2 - 4ac)^{1/2}]/2a$$

This program uses the sqrt library function to evaluate the quantity $(b^2 - 4ac)^{1/2}$.

```
main()   /* solution of a quadratic equation */

{
    double a, b, c, root, x1, x2;

    /* read values for a, b and c */

    root = sqrt(b * b - 4 * a * c);
    x1 = (-b + root) / (2 * a);
    x2 = (-b - root) / (2 * a);

    /* write values for a, b, c, x1 and x2 */

}
```

In order to use a library function it may be necessary to include certain specific information within the main portion of the program. For example, forward function declarations and symbolic constant definitions are usually required when using library functions (see Secs. 7.3, 8.5 and 8.6). This information is generally stored in special files supplied with the compiler. Thus, the required information can be obtained simply by accessing these special files. This is accomplished with the preprocessor statement #include, that is

#include ⟨*filename*⟩

where *filename* represents the name of a special file.

The names of these special files are specified by each individual implementation of C, though there are certain commonly used file names such as stdio.h, stdlib.h and math.h. The suffix "h" designates a "header" file, which indicates that it is to be included at the beginning of the program. (Header files are discussed in Sec. 8.6.)

Note the similarity between the preprocessor statement #include and the preprocessor statement #define, which was discussed in Sec. 2.9.

Example 3.31   Lowercase to Uppercase Character Conversion   Here is a complete C program that reads in a lower-case character, converts it to uppercase and then writes out the uppercase equivalent.

```
#include ⟨stdio.h⟩

main()

/* read a lower-case character and print its upper-case equivalent */

{
    int lower, upper;

    lower = getchar();
    upper = toupper(lower);
    putchar(upper);
}
```

This program contains three library functions: getchar, toupper and putchar. The first two functions each return a single character (getchar returns a character that is entered from the keyboard, and toupper returns the uppercase equivalent of its argument). The last function (putchar) causes the value of the argument to be displayed. Notice that the last two functions each have one argument but the first function does not have any arguments, as indicated by the empty parentheses.

Also, notice the preprocessor statement #include ⟨stdio.h⟩, which appears at the start of the program. This statement causes the contents of the file stdio.h to be inserted into the program at the start of the compilation process. The information contained in this file is essential for the proper functioning of the library functions getchar and putchar.

Review Questions

3.1   What is an expression? What are its components?

3.2   What is an operator? Describe several different types of operators included in C.

3.3   What is an operand? What is the relationship between operators and operands?

3.4   Describe the five arithmetic operators in C. Summarize the rules associated with their use.

3.5   Summarize the rules that apply to expressions whose operands are of different types.

3.6   How can the value of an expression be converted to a different data type? What is this called?

3.7   What is meant by operator precedence? What are the relative precedences of the arithmetic operators?

3.8   What is meant by associativity? What is the associativity of the arithmetic operators?

3.9   When should parentheses be included within an expression? When should the use of parentheses be avoided?

3.10 In what order are the operations carried out within an expression that contains nested parentheses?

3.11 What are unary operators? How many operands are associated with a unary operator?

3.12 Describe the six unary operators discussed in this chapter. What is the purpose of each?

3.13 Describe two different ways to utilize the increment and decrement operators. What is the difference between them?

3.14 What is the relative precedence of the unary operators compared with the arithmetic operators? What is their associativity?

3.15 How can the number of bytes allocated to each data type be determined for a particular C compiler?

3.16 Describe the four relational operators included in C. With what type of operands can they be used? What type of expression is obtained?

3.17 Describe the two equality operators included in C. How do they differ from the relational operators?

3.18 Describe the two logical operators included in C. What is the purpose of each? With what type of operands can they be used? What type of expression is obtained?

3.19 What are the relative precedences of the relational, equality and logical operators with respect to one another and with respect to the arithmetic and unary operators? What are their associativities?

3.20 Describe the *logical not* (logical negation) operator. What is its purpose? Within which precedence group is it included? How many operands does it require? What is its associativity?

3.21 Describe the six assignment operators discussed in this chapter. What is the purpose of each?

3.22 How is the type of an assignment expression determined when the two operands are of different data types? In what sense is this situation sometimes a source of programming errors?

3.23 How can multiple assignments be written in C? In what order will the assignments be carried out?

3.24 What is the precedence of assignment operators relative to other operators? What is their associativity?

3.25 Describe the use of the conditional operator to form conditional expressions. How is a conditional expression evaluated?

3.26 How is the type of a conditional expression determined when its operands differ in type?

3.27 How can the conditional operator be combined with the assignment operator to form an "if-else" type statement?

3.28 What is the precedence of the conditional operator relative to the other operators described in this chapter? What is its associativity?

3.29 Describe, in general terms, the kinds of operations and calculations carried out by the C library functions.

3.30 Are the library functions actually a part of the C language? Explain.

3.31 How are the library functions usually packaged within a C compiler?

3.32 How are library functions accessed? How is information passed to a library function from the access point?

3.33 What are arguments? How are arguments written? How is a call to a library function written if there are no arguments?

3.34 How is specific information that may be required by the library functions stored? How is this information entered into a C program?

3.35 In what general category do the #define and #include statements fall?

Problems

3.36 Suppose a, b and c are integer variables that have been assigned the values a = 8, b = 3 and c = −5. Determine the value of each of the following arithmetic expressions.

(a) a + b + c	(d) a % b	(g) a * b / c	(j) a * (c % b)
(b) 2 * b + 3 * (a - c)	(e) a / c	(h) a * (b / c)	
(c) a / b	(f) a % c	(i) (a * c) % b	

3.37 Suppose x, y and z are floating-point variables that have been assigned the values x = 8.8, y = 3.5 and z = −5.2. Determine the value of each of the following arithmetic expressions.

(a) x + y + z	(c) x / y	(e) x / (y + z)	(g) 2 * x / 3 * y
(b) 2 * y + 3 * (x - z)	(d) x % y	(f) (x / y) + z	(h) 2 * x / (3 * y)

3.38 Suppose c1, c2 and c3 are character-type variables that have been assigned the characters E, 5 and ?, respectively. Determine the numerical value of the following expressions, based upon the ASCII character set (see Table 2-1).

(a) c1	(d) c2 - '2'	(g) '2' + '2'	(j) '3' * c2
(b) c1 - c2 + c3	(e) c3 + '#'	(h) (c1 / c2) * c3	
(c) c2 - 2	(f) c1 % c3	(i) 3 * c2	

3.39 A C program contains the following declarations:

```
int i, j;
long ix;
short s;
float x;
double dx;
char c;
```

Determine the data type of each of the following expressions:

(a) i + c	(d) ((int) dx) + ix	(g) ix + j
(b) x + c	(e) i + x	(h) s + c
(c) dx + x	(f) s + j	(i) ix + c

3.40 A C program contains the following declarations and initial assignments:

```
int i = 8, j = 5;
float x = 0.005, y = -0.01;
char c = 'c', d = 'd';
```

Determine the value of each of the following expressions. Use the values initially assigned to the variables for each expression.

(a) (3 * i - 2 * j) % (2 * d - c)
(b) 2 * ((i / 5) + (4 * (j - 3)) % (i + j - 2))
(c) (i - 3 * j) % (c + 2 * d) / (x - y)
(d) -(i + j)
(e) ++i
(f) i++
(g) --j
(h) ++x
(i) y--
(j) i <= j
(k) c > d
(l) x >= 0
(m) x < y
(n) j != 6
(o) c == 99
(p) 5 * (i + j) > 'c'
(q) (2 * x + y) == 0
(r) 2 * x + (y == 0)

(s)   2 * x + y == 0
(t)   !(i <= j)
(u)   !(c == 99)
(v)   !(x > 0)
(w)   (i > 0) && (j < 5)
(x)   (i > 0) ¦¦ (j < 5)
(y)   (x > y) && (i > 0) ¦¦ (j < 5)
(z)   (x > y) && (i > 0) && (j < 5)

3.41   A C program contains the following declarations and initial assignments:

```
int i = 8, j = 5, k;
float x = 0.005, y = -0.01, z;
char a, b, c = 'c', d = 'd';
```

Determine the value of each of the following assignment expressions. Use the values originally assigned to the variables for each expression.

(a)	k = (i + j)	(i)	z = k = x	(p)	i += (j - 2)
(b)	z = (x + y)	(j)	k = z = x	(q)	k = (j == 5) ? i : j
(c)	i = j	(k)	i += 2	(r)	k = (j > 5) ? i : j
(d)	k = (x + y)	(l)	y -= x	(s)	z = (x >= 0) ? x : 0
(e)	k = c	(m)	x *= 2	(t)	z = (y >= 0) ? y : 0
(f)	z = i / j	(n)	i /= j	(u)	a = (c < d) ? c : d
(g)	a = b = d	(o)	i %= j	(v)	i -= (j > 0) ? j : 0
(h)	i = j = 1.1				

3.42   Each of the following expressions involves the use of a library function. Identify the purpose of each expression. (See Appendix H for an extensive list of library functions.)

(a)	abs(i - 2 * j)	(i)	isupper(j)	(p)	toascii(10 * j)
(b)	fabs(x + y)	(j)	exp(x)	(q)	fmod(x, y)
(c)	isprint(c)	(k)	log(x)	(r)	tolower(65)
(d)	isdigit(c)	(l)	sqrt(x * x + y * y)	(s)	pow(x - y, 3.0)
(e)	toupper(d)	(m)	isalnum(10 * j)	(t)	sin(x - y)
(f)	ceil(x)	(n)	isalpha(10 * j)	(u)	strlen("hello\0")
(g)	floor(x + y)	(o)	isascii(10 * j)	(v)	strpos("hello\0", 'e')
(h)	islower(c)				

3.43   A C program contains the following declarations and initial assignments:

```
int i = 8, j = 5;
double x = 0.005, y = -0.01;
char c = 'c', d = 'd';
```

Determine the value of each of the follow expressions, which involve the use of library functions. (See Appendix H for an extensive list of library functions.)

(a)	abs(i - 2 * j)	(j)	islower(c)	(s)	toascii(10 * j)
(b)	fabs(x + y)	(k)	isupper(j)	(t)	fmod(x, y)
(c)	isprint(c)	(l)	exp(x)	(u)	tolower(65)
(d)	isdigit(c)	(m)	log(x)	(v)	pow(x - y, 3.0)
(e)	toupper(d)	(n)	log(exp(x))	(w)	sin(x - y)
(f)	ceil(x)	(o)	sqrt(x * x + y * y)	(x)	strlen("hello\0")
(g)	ceil(x + y)	(p)	isalnum(10 * j)	(y)	strpos("hello\0", 'e')
(h)	floor(x)	(q)	isalpha(10 * j)	(z)	sqrt(sin(x) + cos(y))
(i)	floor(x + y)	(r)	isascii(10 * j)		

3.44   Determine which of the library functions shown in Appendix H are available for your particular version of C. Are some of the functions available under a different name? What header files are required?

## Chapter 4

Data Input and Output

We have already seen that the C language is accompanied by a collection of library functions that includes a number of input/output (I/O) functions. In this chapter we will make use of six of these functions: `getchar`, `putchar`, `scanf`, `printf`, `gets` and `puts`. These six functions permit the transfer of information between the computer and the standard input/output devices (e.g., a keyboard and a TV monitor). The first two functions, `getchar` and `putchar`, allow single characters to be transferred into and out of the computer; `scanf` and `printf` are more complicated, but they permit the transfer of single characters, numerical values and strings; `gets` and `puts` facilitate the input and output of strings. Once we have learned how to use these functions, we will be able to write a number of complete, though simple, C programs.

4.1 PRELIMINARIES

An input/output function can be accessed from anywhere within a program simply by writing the function name, followed by a list of arguments enclosed in parentheses. The arguments represent data items that are sent to the function. Some input/output functions do not require arguments, though the empty parentheses must still appear.

The names of those functions that return data items may appear within expressions, as though each function reference were an ordinary variable (e.g., `c = getchar();`), or they may be referenced as separate statements (e.g., `scanf(...);`). Some functions do not return any data items. Such functions are referenced as though they were separate statements (e.g., `putchar(...);`).

Most versions of C include a collection of header files that provide necessary information (e.g., symbolic constants) in support of the various library functions. Each file contains information in support of a group of related library functions. These files are entered into the program via an `#include` statement at the beginning of the program. As a rule, the header file required by the standard input/output library functions is called `stdio.h` (see Sec. 8.6 for more information about the contents of these header files).

Example 4.1. Here is an outline of a typical C program that makes use of several input/output routines from the standard C library.

```
#include <stdio.h>

main()

/* sample setup illustrating the use
   of input/output library functions */
```

```
{
      char c,d;                       /* declarations */
      float x,y;
      int i,j,k;

      c = getchar();                  /* character input */

      scanf("%f", &x);                /* floating-point input */

      scanf("%d %d", &i, &j);         /* integer input */

      ...                             /* action statements */

      putchar(d);                     /* character output */

      printf("%3d %7.4f", k, y);      /* numerical output */
}
```

The program begins with the preprocessor statement #include ⟨stdio.h⟩. This statement causes the contents of the header file stdio.h to be included within the program. The header file supplies required information for the library functions scanf and printf. (The syntax of the #include statement may vary from one version of C to another; some versions of the language use quotes instead of angle brackets, for example, #include "stdio.h".)

Following the preprocessor statement are the program heading main() and some variable declarations. Several input/output statements are shown in the skeletal outline that follows the declarations. In particular, the assignment statement c = getchar(); causes a single character to be entered from the keyboard and assigned to the character variable c. The first reference to scanf causes a floating-point value to be entered from the keyboard and assigned to the floating-point variable x, whereas the second reference to scanf causes two decimal integer quantities to be entered from the keyboard and assigned to the integer variables i and j, respectively.

The output statements behave similarly. Thus, the reference to putchar causes the value of the character variable d to be displayed. Similarly, the reference to printf causes the values of the integer variable k and the floating-point variable y to be displayed.

The details of each input/output statement will be discussed in subsequent sections of this chapter. For now, you should consider only a general overview of the input/output statements appearing in this typical C program.

4.2 SINGLE CHARACTER INPUT—THE getchar FUNCTION

Single characters can be entered into the computer using the C library function getchar. We have already encountered the use of this function in Chaps. 1 and 2, and in Example 4.1. Let us now examine it more thoroughly.

The getchar function is a part of the standard C language I/O library. It returns a single character from a standard input device (typically a keyboard). The function does not require any arguments, though a pair of empty parentheses must follow the word getchar.

In general terms, a reference to the getchar function is written as

character variable = getchar();

where *character variable* refers to some previously declared character variable.

Example 4.2 A C program contains the following statements.

```
char c;

...

c = getchar();
```

The first statement declares that c is a character-type variable. The second statement causes a single character to be entered from the standard input device (usually a keyboard) and then assigned to c.

If an *end-of-file* condition is encountered when reading a character with the getchar function, the value of the symbolic constant EOF will automatically be returned. (This value will be assigned within the stdio.h file. Typically, EOF will be assigned the value -1, though this may vary from one compiler to another.) The detection of EOF in this manner offers a convenient way to detect an end-of-file, whenever and wherever it may occur. Appropriate corrective action can then be taken. Both the detection of the EOF condition and the corrective action can be carried out using the if - else statement described in Chap. 6.

The getchar function can also be used to read multicharacter strings, by reading one character at a time within a multipass loop. We will see one illustration of this in Example 4.4. Additional examples will be presented in later chapters of this book.

4.3　SINGLE CHARACTER OUTPUT—THE putchar FUNCTION

Single characters can be displayed (i.e., written out of the computer) using the C library function putchar. This function is complementary to the character input function getchar, which we discussed in the last section. We have already seen illustrations of the use of these two functions in Chaps. 1 and 2, and in Example 4.1. We now examine the use of putchar in more detail.

The putchar function, like getchar, is a part of the standard C language I/O library. It transmits a single character to a standard output device (typically a TV monitor or a timesharing terminal). The character being transmitted will normally be represented as a character-type variable. It must be expressed as an argument to the function, enclosed in parentheses, following the word putchar.

In general, a reference to the putchar function is written as

```
putchar(character variable)
```

where *character variable* refers to some previously declared character variable.

Example 4.3　A C program contains the following statements.

```
char c;

. . .

putchar(c);
```

The first statement declares that c is a character-type variable. The second statement causes the current value of c to be transmitted to the standard output device (e.g., a TV monitor) where it will be displayed. (Compare with Example 4.2, which illustrates the use of the getchar function.)

The putchar function can be used to output a string constant by storing the string within a one-dimensional, character-type array, as explained in Chap. 2. Each character can then be written separately within a loop. The most convenient way to do this is to utilize a *for* statement, as illustrated in the following example. (The *for* statement is discussed in detail in Chap. 6.)

Example 4.4　Lowercase to Uppercase Text Conversion　Here is a complete program that reads in a line of lowercase text, stores it within a one-dimensional, character-type array, and then writes it out in uppercase.

```
#include <stdio.h>

main()

/* read in a line of lower-case text and write it out in upper-case */

{
    char letter[80];
    int count, tag;

    /* read in the line */

    for (count = 0; (letter[count] = getchar()) != '\n'; ++count)
        ;

    /* tag the character count */

    tag = count;

    /* write out the line in upper-case */

    for (count = 0; count < tag; ++count)
        putchar(toupper(letter[count]));
}
```

Notice the declaration

```
char letter[80];
```

This declares letter to be an 80-element, character-type array whose elements will represent the individual characters within the line of text.

Now consider the statement

```
for (count = 0; (letter[count] = getchar()) != '\n'; ++count)
    ;
```

This statement creates a loop which causes the individual characters to be read into the computer and assigned to the array elements. The loop begins with a value of count equal to zero. A character is then read into the computer from the standard input device and assigned to letter[0] (the first element in letter). The value of count is then incremented, and the process is repeated for the next array element. This looping action continues as long as a *newline* character (i.e., '\n') is not encountered. The *newline* character will signify the end of the line, and will therefore terminate the process.

Once all of the characters have been entered, the value of count corresponding to the last character is assigned to tag. Another for loop is then initiated, in which the uppercase equivalents of the original characters are displayed on the standard output device. Characters that were originally uppercase, digits, punctuation characters, and so on, will be displayed in their original form. Thus, if the message

```
Now is the time for all good men to come to the aid of their country!
```

is entered as input, the corresponding output will be

```
NOW IS THE TIME FOR ALL GOOD MEN TO COME TO THE AID OF THEIR COUNTRY!
```

Note that tag will be assigned the value 69 after all the characters have been entered, since the 69th character will be the newline character following the exclamation point.

Chapter 6 contains more detailed information on the use of the for statement to control a character array. For now, you should only attempt to gain a general understanding of what is happening.

4.4   ENTERING INPUT DATA—THE scanf FUNCTION

Input data can be entered into the computer from a standard input device by means of the C library function scanf. This function can be used to enter any combination of numerical values, single characters and strings. The function returns the number of data items that have been entered successfully.

In general terms, the scanf function is written as

scanf(*control string*, arg1, arg2, ..., argn)

where *control string* refers to a string containing certain required formatting information, and arg1, arg2, ..., argn are arguments that represent the individual input data items. (Actually, the arguments represent *pointers* that indicate the *addresses* of the data items within the computer's memory. More about this later, in Chap. 10.)

The control string comprises individual groups of characters, with one character group for each input data item. Each character group must begin with a percent sign (%). In its simplest form, a single character group will consist of the percent sign, followed by a *conversion character* which indicates the type of the corresponding data item.

Within the control string, multiple character groups can be contiguous, or they can be separated by whitespace characters (i.e., blank spaces, tabs or newline characters). If whitespace characters are used to separate multiple character groups in the control string, then all consecutive whitespace characters in the input data will be read but ignored. The use of blank spaces as character-group separators is very common.

The more frequently used conversion characters are listed in Table 4-1.

Table 4-1   Commonly Used Conversion Characters for Data Input

Conversion Character	Meaning
c	data item is a single character
d	data item is a decimal integer
e	data item is a floating-point value
f	data item is a floating-point value
g	data item is a floating-point value
h	data item is a short integer
i	data item is a decimal, hexadecimal or octal integer
o	data item is an octal integer
s	data item is a string followed by a whitespace character (the null character \0 will automatically be added at the end)
u	data item is an unsigned decimal integer
x	data item is a hexadecimal integer
[...]	data item is a string which may include whitespace characters (see explanation below)

The arguments are written as variables or arrays, whose types match the corresponding character groups in the control string. *Each variable name must be preceded by an ampersand* (&). (The arguments are actually pointers which indicate where the data items are stored in the computer's memory, as explained in Chap. 10.) However, array names should *not* begin with an ampersand.

Example 4.5   Here is a typical application of a scanf function.

```
#include ⟨stdio.h⟩

main()

{
    char item[2Ø];
    int partno;
    float cost;

    ...

    scanf("%s %d %f", item, &partno, &cost);

    ...

}
```

Within the scanf function, the control string is "%s %d %f". It contains three character groups. The first character group, %s, indicates that the first argument (item) represents a string. The second character group, %d, indicates that the second argument (&partno) represents a decimal integer value, and the third character group, %f, indicates that the third argument (&cost) represents a floating-point value.

Notice that the numerical variables partno and cost are preceded by ampersands within the scanf function. An ampersand does not precede item, however, since item is an array name.

Notice, also, that the scanf function could have been written

```
scanf("%s %d %f", item, &partno, &cost);
```

with no whitespace characters in the control string. This is also valid, though the input data could be interpreted differently when using c-type conversions (more about this later in this section).

The actual data items are numeric values, single characters or strings, or some combination thereof. They are entered from a standard input device (typically a keyboard). The data items must correspond to the arguments in the scanf function in number, in type and in order. Numeric data items are written in the same form as numeric constants (see Sec. 2.4), though octal values need not be preceded by a Ø, and hexadecimal values need not be preceded by Øx or ØX. Floating-point values may include either a decimal point or an exponent (or both).

If two or more data items are entered, they must be separated by whitespace characters. (An exception to this rule occurs with c-type conversions, as described in Sec. 4.5.) Note that the data items may continue onto two or more lines, since the newline character is considered to be a whitespace character.

Example 4.6 Consider once again the skeletal outline of a C program shown in Example 4.5, that is,

```
#include ⟨stdio.h⟩

main()

{
    char item[2Ø];
    int partno;
    float cost;

    ...

    scanf("%s %d %f", item, &partno, &cost);

    ...

}
```

The following data items could be entered from the standard input device when the program is executed:

```
fastener 12345 Ø.Ø5
```

Thus, the characters that make up the string `fastener` would be assigned to the first eight elements of the array `item`; the integer value `12345` would be assigned to `partno`, and the floating-point value `0.05` would be assigned to `cost`.

Notice that the individual data items are entered on one line, separated by blank spaces. The data items could also be entered on separate lines, however, since newline characters are also whitespace characters. Therefore, the data items could be written as

```
fastener
12345
0.05
```

or as

```
fastener
12345    0.05
```

or

```
fastener    12345
0.05
```

and so on.

Note that the `s`-type conversion character applies to a string terminated by a whitespace character. Therefore, a string that *includes* whitespace characters cannot be entered in this manner. There are ways, however, to work with strings that include whitespace characters. One way is to use the `getchar` function within a loop, as illustrated in Example 4.4. It is also possible to use the `scanf` function to enter such strings. To do so, the `s`-type conversion character within the control string is replaced by a sequence of characters enclosed in square brackets, designated as `[ . . . ]`. Whitespace characters may be included within the brackets, thus accommodating strings that contain such characters.

When the program is executed, successive characters will continue to be read from the standard input device as long as each input character matches one of the characters enclosed within the brackets. The order of the characters within the square brackets need not correspond to the order of the characters being entered. Input characters may be repeated. The string will terminate, however, once an input character is encountered that does not match any of the characters within the brackets. A null character (`/0`) will then automatically be added to the end of the string.

Example 4.7 This example illustrates the use of the `scanf` function to enter a string consisting of uppercase letters and blank spaces. The string will be of undetermined length, but it will be limited to 79 characters (actually, 80 characters including the null character that is added at the end).

```
#include <stdio.h>

main()

{
    char line[80];

    ...

    scanf("%[ ABCDEFGHIJKLMNOPQRSTUVWXYZ]", line);

    ...
}
```

If the string

```
NEW YORK CITY
```

is entered from the standard input device when the program is executed, the entire string will be assigned to the array `line` since the string is composed entirely of uppercase letters and blank spaces. If the string were written as

```
New York City
```

however, then only the single letter N would be assigned to `line`, since the first lowercase letter (in this case, e) would be interpreted as the first character beyond the string. It would, of course, be possible to include both uppercase and lowercase characters within the brackets, but this becomes cumbersome.

A variation of this feature, which is often more useful, is to precede the characters within the square brackets by a *circumflex* (^). This causes the subsequent characters within the brackets to be interpreted in the opposite manner. Thus, when the program is executed, successive characters will continue to be read from the standard input device as long as each input character *does not* match one of the characters enclosed within the brackets.

If the characters within the brackets are simply the circumflex followed by a newline character, then the string entered from the standard input device can contain any ASCII characters except the newline character (line feed). Thus, the user may enter whatever he or she wishes and then press the RETURN (or ENTER) key. The RETURN (ENTER) key will issue the newline character, thus signifying the end of the string.

Example 4.8 Suppose that a C program contains the following statements.

```
#include <stdio.h>

main()

{
   char line [80];

   ...

   scanf("%[^\n]", line);

   ...

}
```

When the `scanf` function is executed, a string of undetermined length (but not more than 79 characters) will be entered from the standard input device and assigned to `line`. There will be no restrictions on the characters that compose the string, except that they all fit on one line. For example, the string

```
The PITTSBURGH STEELERS is one of America's favorite football teams!
```

could be entered from the keyboard and assigned to `line`.

4.5 MORE ABOUT THE scanf FUNCTION

This section contains some additional details about the `scanf` function. Beginning C programmers may wish to skip over this material for the time being.

The consecutive nonwhitespace characters that compose a data item collectively define a *field*. It is possible to limit the number of such characters by specifying a maximum *field width* for that data item. To do so, an unsigned integer indicating the field width is placed within the control string, between the percent sign (%) and the conversion character.

The data item may be composed of fewer characters than the specified field width. However, the number of characters in the actual data item cannot exceed the specified field width. Any characters that extend beyond the specified field width will not be read. Such leftover characters may be incorrectly interpreted as the components of the next data item.

Example 4.9 The skeletal structure of a C program is shown below.

```
#include <stdio.h>

main()

{
    int a, b, c;

    . . .

    scanf("%3d %3d %3d", &a, &b, &c);

    . . .

}
```

When the program is executed, three integer quantities will be entered from the standard input device (the keyboard). Suppose the input data items are entered as

1 2 3

Then the following assignments will result:

a = 1,   b = 2,   c = 3

If the data had been entered as

123 456 789

Then the assignments would be

a = 123,   b = 456,   c = 789

Now suppose that the data had been entered as

123456789

Then the assignments would be

a = 123,   b = 456,   c = 789

as before, since the first three digits would be assigned to a, the next three digits to b, and the last three digits to c.
Finally, suppose that the data had been entered as

1234 5678 9

The resulting assignments would now be

a = 123,   b = 4,   c = 567

The remaining two digits (8 and 9) would be ignored, unless they were read by a subsequent scanf statement.

Example 4.10 Consider a C program that contains the following statements.

```
#include (stdio.h)

main()

{
    int i;
    float x;
    char c;

    . . .

    scanf("%3d %5f %c", &i, &x, &c);

    . . .
}
```

If the data items are entered as

```
1Ø 256.875 T
```

when the program is executed, then 10 will be assigned to i, 256.8 will be assigned to x and the character 7 will be assigned to c. The remaining two input characters (5 and T) will be ignored.

Most versions of C allow certain conversion characters within the control string to be preceded by a single-letter *prefix*, which indicates the length of the corresponding argument. For example, an l (lowercase L) is used to indicate either a signed or unsigned long integer argument, or a double-precision argument. Similarly, an h is used to indicate a signed or unsigned short integer. Also, some versions of C permit the use of an uppercase L to indicate a long double.

Example 4.11 Suppose the following statements are included in a C program:

```
#include (stdio.h)

main()

{
    short ix,iy;
    long lx,ly;
    double dx,dy;

    . . .

    scanf("%hd %ld %lf", &ix, &lx, &dx);

    . . .

    scanf("%3ho %7lx %15le", &iy, &ly, &dy);

    . . .
}
```

The control string in the first scanf function indicates that the first data item will be assigned to a short decimal integer variable, the second will be assigned to a long decimal integer variable, and the third will be assigned to a double-precision variable. The control string in the second scanf function indicates that the first data item will have a maximum field width of three characters and it will be assigned to a short octal integer variable; the second data item will have a maximum field width of seven characters and it will be assigned to a long hexadecimal integer variable, and the third data item will have a maximum field width of 15 characters and it will be assigned to a double-precision variable.

Some versions of C permit the use of uppercase conversion characters to indicate long integers (signed or unsigned). This feature may be available in addition to the prefix "l", or it may replace the use of the prefix.

Example 4.12   Consider once again the skeletal outline of the C program given in Example 4.11. With some versions of C, it may be possible to write the scanf functions somewhat differently, as follows:

```
#include <stdio.h>

main()

{
    short ix,iy;
    long lx,ly;
    double dx,dy;

    . . .

    scanf("%hd %D %f", &ix, &lx, &dx);

    . . .

    scanf("%3ho %7X %15e", &iy, &ly, &dy);

    . . .
}
```

Notice the use of uppercase conversion characters (in the scanf functions) to indicate long integers. The interpretation of the scanf functions will be the same as in the previous example.

In most versions of C it is possible to skip over a data item without assigning it to the designated variable or array. To do so, the % sign within the appropriate control group is followed by an asterisk (*). This feature is referred to as *assignment suppression*.

Example 4.13   Here is a variation of the scanf features shown in Example 4.6.

```
#include <stdio.h>

main()

{
    char item[20];
    int partno;
    float cost;

    . . .

    scanf("%s %*d %f", item, &partno, &cost);

    . . .
}
```

Notice the asterisk in the second character group.

If the corresponding data items are

```
fastener 12345 0.05
```

then fastener will be assigned to item and 0.05 will be assigned to cost. However, 12345 will not be assigned to partno because of the asterisk, which is interpreted as an assignment-suppression character.

The integer quantity 12345 will be read into the computer along with the other data items, even though it is not assigned to its corresponding variable.

If the control string contains multiple character groups without interspersed whitespace characters, then some care must be taken with c-type conversion. In such cases a whitespace character within the input data will be interpreted as a data item. To skip over such whitespace characters and read the next nonwhitespace character, the conversion group %1s should be used.

Example 4.14 Consider the following skeletal outline of a C program:

```
#include <stdio.h>

main()

{
    char c1, c2, c3;

    . . .

    scanf("%c%c%c", &c1, &c2, &c3);

    . . .
}
```

If the input data consisted of

```
a b c
```

(with blank spaces between the letters), then the following assignments would result:

```
c1 = a,        c2 = <blank space>,        c3 = b
```

If the scanf function were written as

```
scanf("%c%1s%1s", &c1, &c2, &c3);
```

however, then the same input data would result in the following assignments:

```
c1 = a,        c2 = b,        c3 = c
```

as intended.

Note that there are some other ways around this problem. We could have written the scanf function as

```
scanf("%c %c %c", &c1, &c2, &c3);
```

with blank spaces within the control string, or we could have used the original scanf function but written the input data as consecutive characters without blanks, i.e., abc.

Unrecognized characters within the control string are expected to be matched by the same characters in the input data. Such input characters will be read into the computer, but not assigned to an identifier. Execution of the scanf function will terminate if a match is not found.

Example 4.15 Consider the following skeletal outline of a C program:

```
#include <stdio.h>

main()

{
    int i;
    float x;

    . . .

    scanf("%d a %f", &i, &x);

    . . .

}
```

If the input data consist of

```
1 a 2.0
```

then the decimal integer 1 will be read in and assigned to i, the character a will be read in but subsequently ignored, and the floating-point value 2.0 will be read in and assigned to x.

On the other hand, if the input were entered simply as

```
1 2.0
```

then the scanf function would stop executing once the expected character (a) is not found. Therefore, i would be assigned the value 1 but x would automatically represent the value 0.

Finally, the reader should realize that there is some variation in the features supported by the scanf function from one version of C to another. The features described above are quite common and are available in virtually all versions of the language. However, there may be slight differences in their implementation. Moreover, additional features may be available in some versions of the language.

4.6 WRITING OUTPUT DATA—THE printf FUNCTION

Output data can be written from the computer onto a standard output device using the library function printf. This function can be used to output any combination of numerical values, single characters and strings. It is similar to the input function scanf, except that its purpose is to display data rather than to enter data into the computer. That is, the printf function moves data from the computer's memory to the standard output device, whereas the scanf function enters data from the standard input device and stores it in the computer's memory.

In general terms, the printf function is written as

```
printf(control string, arg1, arg2, . . ., argn)
```

where *control string* refers to a string that contains formatting information, and *arg1*, *arg2*, . . ., *argn* are arguments that represent the individual output data items. The arguments can be written as constants, single variable or array names, or more complex expressions. Function references may also be included. In contrast to the scanf function discussed in the last section, the arguments in a printf function do *not* represent memory addresses and therefore they are *not* preceded by ampersands.

The control string is composed of individual groups of characters, with one character group for each output data item. Each character group must begin with a percent sign (%). In its simplest form, an individual character group will consist of the percent sign followed by a *conversion character* indicating the type of the corresponding data item.

Multiple character groups can be contiguous, or they can be separated by other characters, including whitespace characters. These "other" characters are simply transferred directly to the output device where they are displayed. The use of blank spaces as character-group separators is particularly common.

Several of the more frequently used conversion characters are listed in Table 4-2.

Table 4-2   Commonly Used Conversion Characters for Data Output

Conversion Character	Meaning
c	data item is displayed as a single character
d	data item is displayed as a signed decimal integer
e	data item is displayed as a floating-point value with an exponent
f	data item is displayed as a floating-point value without an exponent
g	data item is displayed as a floating-point value using either e-type or f-type conversion, depending on value; trailing zeros, trailing decimal point will not be displayed
i	data item is displayed as a signed decimal integer
o	data item is displayed as an octal integer, without a leading zero
s	data item is displayed as a string
u	data item is displayed as an unsigned decimal integer
x	data item is displayed as a hexadecimal integer, without the leading 0x

Note that some of these characters are interpreted differently than with the scanf function (see Table 4-1).

Example 4.16   Here is a simple program that makes use of the printf function.

```
#include <stdio.h>
#include <math.h>

main()   /* print several floating-point numbers */

{
    float i = 2.0, j = 3.0;
    printf("%f %f %f %f", i, j, i + j, sqrt(i + j));
}
```

Notice that the first two arguments within the printf function are single variables, the third argument is an arithmetic expression, and the last argument is a function reference which has a numeric expression as an argument.
    Executing the program produces the following output:

```
2.000000 3.000000 5.000000 2.236068
```

Example 4.17   The following skeletal outline of a C program indicates how several different types of data can be displayed using the printf function.

```
#include <stdio.h>

main()

{
    char item[20];
    int partno;
    float cost;

    . . .

    printf("%s %d %f", item, partno, cost);

    . . .

}
```

Within the `printf` function, the control string is `"%s %d %f"`. It contains three character groups. The first character group, `%s`, indicates that the first argument (`item`) represents a string. The second character group, `%d`, indicates that the second argument (`partno`) represents a decimal integer value, and the third character group, `%f`, indicates that the third argument (`cost`) represents a floating-point value.

Notice that the arguments are not preceded by ampersands. This differs from the `scanf` function, which requires ampersands for all arguments other than array names (see Example 4.5).

Now suppose that `name`, `partno` and `cost` have been assigned the values `fastener`, 12345 and 0.05, respectively, within the program. When the `printf` statement is executed, the following output will be generated.

```
fastener 12345 0.050000
```

The single space between data items is generated by the blank spaces that appear within the control string in the `printf` statement.

Suppose the `printf` statement had been written as

```
printf("%s%d%f", item, partno, cost);
```

This `printf` statement is syntactically valid, though it has the disadvantage of causing the output items to run together, that is,

```
fastener123450.050000
```

The f-type conversion and the e-type conversion are both used to output floating-point values. However, the latter causes an exponent to be included in the output, whereas the former does not.

Example 4.18   The following program generates the same floating-point output in two different forms.

```
#include <stdio.h>

main()  /* display floating-point output 2 different ways */

{
    double x = 5000.0, y = 0.0025;

    printf("%f %f %f %f\n\n", x, y, x*y, x/y);
    printf("%e %e %e %e", x, y, x*y, x/y);
}
```

Both `printf` statements have the same arguments. However, the first `printf` statement makes use of f-type conversion, whereas the second `printf` statement uses e-type conversion. Also, notice the repeated newline character in the first `printf` statement. This causes the output to be double spaced, as shown below.

When the program is executed, the following output is generated.

```
5000.000000 0.002500 12.500000 2000000.000000

5.000000e+003 2.500000e-003 1.250000e+001 2.000000e+006
```

The first line of output shows the quantities represented by x, y, x*y and x/y in standard floating-point format, without exponents. The second line of output shows these same quantities in a form resembling scientific notation, with exponents.

Notice that six decimal places are shown for each value. The number of decimal places can be altered, however, by specifying the *precision* as a part of each character group within the control string (more about this in Sec. 4.7).

The `printf` function interprets s-type conversion differently than the `scanf` function. In the `printf` function, s-type conversion is used to output a string terminated by the null character (/∅). Whitespace characters may be included within the string.

Example 4.19 Reading and Writing a Line of Text Here is a short C program that will read in a line of text and then write it back out, just as it was entered. The program illustrates the syntactic differences in reading and writing a string that contains a variety of characters, including whitespace characters.

```
#include <stdio.h>

main()           /* read and write a line of text */

{
    char line[8∅];

    scanf("%[^\n]", line);
    printf("%s", line);
}
```

Notice the difference in the control strings within the `scanf` function and the `printf` function.

Now suppose that the following string is entered from the standard input device when the program is executed.

```
The PITTSBURGH STEELERS is one of America's favorite football teams!
```

This string contains lowercase characters, uppercase characters, punctuation characters and whitespace characters. The entire string can be entered with the single `scanf` function, as long as it is terminated by a newline character (by pressing the RETURN key). The `printf` function will then cause the entire string to be displayed on the standard output device, just as it had been entered. Thus, the message

```
The PITTSBURGH STEELERS is one of America's favorite football teams!
```

will be generated by the computer.

A *minimum* field width can be specified by preceding the conversion character by an unsigned integer. If the number of characters in the corresponding data item is less than the specified field width, then the data item will be preceded by enough leading blanks to fill the specified field. If the number of characters in the data item exceeds the specified field width, however, then additional space will be allocated to the data item, so that the entire data item will be displayed. This is just the opposite of the field width indicator in the `scanf` function, which specifies a *maximum* field width.

Example 4.20 The following C program illustrates the use of the minimum field width feature.

```
#include <stdio.h>

main()         /* minimum field width specifications */

{
    int i = 12345;
    float x = 345.678;

    printf("%3d %5d %8d\n\n", i, i, i);
    printf("%3f %10f %13f\n\n", x, x, x);
    printf("%3e %13e %16e", x, x, x);
}
```

Notice the double newline characters in the first two `printf` statements. They will cause the lines of output to be double spaced, as shown below.

When the program is executed, the following output is generated.

```
12345 12345    12345

345.678000 345.678000    345.678000

3.456780e+002 3.456780e+002    3.456780e+002
```

The first line of output displays a decimal integer using three different minimum field widths (three characters, five characters and eight characters). The entire integer value is displayed within each field, even if the field width is too small (as with the first field in this example).

The second output value is preceded by one blank space. This is generated by the blank space separating the first two character groups within the control string.

The third output value is preceded by four blank spaces. One blank space comes from the blank space separating the last two character groups within the control field. The other three blank spaces fill the minimum field width, which exceeds the number of characters in the output value (the minimum field width is 8, but there are only five characters in the output value).

A similar situation is seen in the next two lines, where the floating-point value is displayed using f-type conversion (line 2) and e-type conversion (line 3).

Example 4.21   Here is a variation of the program presented in Example 4.20, which makes use of g-type conversion.

```
#include <stdio.h>

main()        /* minimum field width specifications */

{
   int i = 12345;
   float x = 345.678;

   printf("%3d %5d %8d\n\n", i, i, i);
   printf("%3g %10g %13g\n\n", x, x, x);
   printf("%3g %13g %16g", x, x, x);
}
```

Execution of this program causes the following output to be displayed.

```
12345 12345    12345

345.678    345.678    345.678

345.678    345.678    345.678
```

The floating-point values are displayed with an f-type conversion, since this results in a shorter display. The minimum field widths conform to the specifications within the control string.

4.7   MORE ABOUT THE printf FUNCTION

This section contains additional details about the printf function. Beginning C programmers may wish to skip over this material for the time being.

We have already learned how to specify a minimum field width in a printf function. It is also possible to specify the maximum number of decimal places for a floating-point value, or the maximum number of characters for a string. This specification is known as *precision*. The precision is an unsigned integer that is always preceded by a decimal point. If a minimum field width is specified in addition to the precision (as is usually the case), then the precision specification follows the field width specification. Both of these integer specifications precede the conversion character.

A floating-point number will be *rounded* if it must be shortened to conform to a precision specification.

Example 4.22 Here is a program that illustrates the use of the precision feature with floating-point numbers.

```
#include <stdio.h>

main()   /* displaying a floating-point number with
                         several different precisions */

{
    float x = 123.456;

    printf("%7f %7.3f %7.1f\n\n", x, x, x);
    printf("%12e %12.5e %12.3e", x, x, x);
}
```

When the program is executed, the following output is generated:

```
123.456000 123.456    123.5

1.234560e+002 1.23456e+002    1.235e+002
```

The first line is produced by f-type conversion. Notice the rounding that occurs in the third number because of the precision specification (one decimal place). Also, notice the leading blanks that are added to fill the specified minimum field width (seven characters).

The second line, produced by e-type conversion, has similar characteristics. Again, we see that the third number is rounded to conform to the specified precision (three decimal places). Also, note the leading blanks added to fill the specified minimum field width (12 characters).

A minimum field width specification need not necessarily accompany the precision specification. It is possible to specify the precision without the minimum field width, though the precision must still be preceded by a decimal point.

Example 4.23 Now let us rewrite the program shown in the last example without any minimum field width specifications, but with precision specifications.

```
#include <stdio.h>

main()   /* displaying a floating-point number with
                         several different precisions */

{
    float x = 123.456;

    printf("%f %.3f %.1f\n\n", x, x, x);
    printf("%e %.5e %.3e", x, x, x);
}
```

Execution of this program produces the following output.

```
123.456000 123.456 123.5

1.234560e+002 1.23456e+002 1.235e+002
```

Notice that the third number in each line does not have multiple leading blanks, since there is no minimum field width that must be satisfied. In all other respects, however, this output is the same as the output generated in the last example.

Minimum field width and precision specifications can be applied to character data as well as numerical data. When applied to a string, the minimum field width is interpreted in the same manner as with a numerical quantity, i.e., leading blanks will be added if the string is shorter than the specified field width, and additional space will be allocated if the string is longer than the specified field width. Hence, the field width specification will not prevent the entire string from being displayed.

However, the precision specification will determine the maximum number of characters that can be displayed. If the precision specification is less than the total number of characters in the string, the excess rightmost characters will not be displayed. This will occur even if the minimum field width is larger than the entire string, resulting in the addition of leading blanks to the truncated string.

Example 4.24 The following program outline illustrates the use of field width and precision specifications in conjunction with string output.

```
#include ⟨stdio.h⟩

main()

{
    char line[12];

    ...

    printf("%1Øs %15s %15.5s %.5s", line, line, line, line);

}
```

Now suppose that the string hexadecimal is assigned to the character array line. When the program is executed, the following output will be generated.

```
hexadecimal     hexadecimal             hexad hexad
```

The first string is shown in its entirety, even though this string consists of 11 characters, but the fieldwidth specification is only 10 characters. Thus, the first string overrides the minimum field width specification. The second string is padded with four leading blanks to fill out the 15-character minimum; hence, the second string is *right-justified* within its field. The third string consists of only five nonblank characters because of the five-character precision specification; however, 10 leading blanks are added to fill out the minimum field width specification, which is 15 characters. The last string also consists of five nonblank characters. Leading blanks are not added, however, because there is no minimum field width specification.

Most versions of C permit the use of prefixes within the control string to indicate the length of the corresponding argument. The allowable prefixes are the same as the prefixes used with the scanf function. Thus, an l (lowercase L) indicates a signed or unsigned integer argument, or a double-precision argument; an h indicates a signed or unsigned short integer. Some versions of C permit an L (uppercase) to indicate a long double.

Example 4.25 Suppose the following statements are included in a C program:

```
#include ⟨stdio.h⟩

main()

{
    short a, b;
    long c, d;

    ...

    printf("%5hd %6hx %8lo %lu", a, b, c, d);

    ...

}
```

The control string indicates that the first data item will be a short decimal integer, the second will be a short hexadecimal integer, the third will be a long octal integer, and the fourth will be a long unsigned (decimal) integer. Note that the first three fields have minimum field width specifications, but the fourth does not.

Some versions of C allow the conversion characters X, E and G to be written in uppercase. These uppercase conversion characters cause any letters within the output data to be displayed in uppercase. (Note that this use of uppercase conversion characters is distinctly different than their use with the scanf function.)

Example 4.26   The following program illustrates the use of uppercase conversion characters in the printf function.

```
#include <stdio.h>

main()       /* use of upper-case conversion characters */

{
    int a = 0x80ec;
    float b = 0.3e-12;

    printf("%4x %10.2e\n\n", a, b);
    printf("%4X %10.2E", a, b);
}
```

Notice that the first printf statement contains lowercase conversion characters, whereas the second printf statement contains uppercase conversion characters.

When the program is executed, the following output is generated.

```
80ec   3.00e-013

80EC   3.00E-013
```

The first quantity on each line is a hexadecimal number. Note that the letters ec (which are a part of the hexadecimal number) are shown in lowercase on the first line, and in uppercase on the second line.

Table 4-3   Commonly Used Flags

Flag	Meaning
–	data item is left-justified within the field (blank spaces required to fill the minimum field width will be added *after* the data item rather than *before* the data item)
+	a sign (either + or –) will precede each signed numerical data item; without this flag, only negative data items are preceded by a sign
0	causes leading zeros to appear instead of leading blanks; applies only to data items that are right-justified within a field whose minimum size is larger than the data item.
	(*Note:* Some compilers consider the zero flag to be a part of the field width specification rather than an actual flag. This assures that the 0 is processed last, if multiple flags are present.)
' ' (blank space)	a blank space will precede each positive signed numerical data item; this flag is overridden by the + flag if both are present.
# (with o- and x-type conversion)	causes octal and hexadecimal data items to be preceded by 0 and 0x, respectively
# (with e-, f- and g-type conversion)	causes a decimal point to be present in all floating-point numbers, even if the data item is a whole number; also prevents the truncation of trailing zeros in g-type conversion.

The second quantity on each line is a decimal floating-point number which includes an exponent. Notice that the letter e, which indicates the exponent, is shown in lowercase on the first line and uppercase on the second.

The reader is again reminded that not all compilers support the use of uppercase conversion characters.

In addition to the field width, the precision and the conversion character, each character group within the control string can include a *flag*, which affects the appearance of the output. The flag must be placed immediately after the percent sign (%). Some compilers allow two or more flags to appear consecutively, within the same character group. The more commonly used flags are listed in Table 4-3

Example 4.27 Here is a simple C program that illustrates the use of flags with integer and floating-point quantities.

```
#include <stdio.h>

main()      /* use of flags with integer and floating-point numbers */

{
   int i = 123;
   float x = 12.0, y = -3.3;

   printf(":%6d %7.0f %10.1e:\n\n", i, x, y);
   printf(":%-6d %-7.0f %-10.1e:\n\n", i, x, y);
   printf(":%+6d %+7.0f %+10.1e:\n\n" , i, x, y);
   printf(":%-+6d %-+7.0f %-+10.1e:\n\n", i, x, y);
   printf(":%7.0f %#7.0f %7g %#7g:", x, x, y, y);
}
```

When the program is executed, the following output is produced. (The colons indicate the beginning of the first field and the end of the last field in each line.)

```
:   123      12   -3.3e+000:

:123    12       -3.3e+000 :

:  +123     +12  -3.3e+000:

:+123    +12     -3.3e+000 :

:     12   12.    -3.3 -3.30000:
```

The first line illustrates how integer and floating-point numbers appear without any flags. Each number is right-justified within its respective field. The second line shows the same numbers, using the same conversions, with a – flag included within each character group. Note that the numbers are now left-justified within their respective fields. The third line shows the effect of using a + flag. The numbers are now right-justified, as in the first line, but each number (whether positive or negative) is preceded by an appropriate sign.

In the fourth line we see the effect of combining a – flag with a + flag. The numbers are now left-justified and preceded by an appropriate sign. Finally, the last line shows two floating-point numbers, each displayed first without and then with the # flag. Note that the effect of the flag is to include a decimal point in the number 12. (which is printed with f-type conversion) and to include the trailing zeros in the number -3.30000 (printed with g-type conversion).

Example 4.28 Now consider the following program, which displays decimal, octal and hexadecimal numbers.

```
#include <stdio.h>

main()     /* use of flags with unsigned decimal,
                        octal and hexadecimal numbers */

{
    int i = 1234, j = 01777, k = 0xa08c;

    printf(":%8u %8o %8x:\n\n", i, j, k);
    printf(":%-8u %-8o %-8x:\n\n", i, j, k);
    printf(":%#8u %#8o %#8X:\n\n", i, j, k);
    printf(":%08u %08o %08X:\n\n", i, j, k);
}
```

Execution of this program results in the following output. (The colons indicate the beginning of the first field and the end of the last field in each line.)

```
:    1234     1777      a08c:

:1234     1777      a08c     :

:    1234    01777    0XA08C:

:00001234 00001777 0000A08C:
```

The first line illustrates the display of unsigned integer, octal and hexadecimal output without any flags. Notice that the numbers are right-justified within their respective fields. The second line shows the same data, using the same conversions, with a – flag included within each character group. Now the numbers are left-justified within their respective fields.

In the third line we see the output that is obtained when the # flag is used. This flag causes the octal number 1777 to be preceded by a 0 (appearing as 01777) and the hexadecimal number to be preceded by 0X (i.e., 0XA08C). Notice that the unsigned decimal integer 1234 is unaffected by this flag. Also, notice that the hexadecimal number now contains uppercase characters, since the conversion character was written in uppercase (X).

The last line illustrates the use of the 0 flag. This flag causes the fields to be filled with leading 0s rather than leading blanks. Once again we see uppercase hexadecimal characters, in response to the uppercase conversion character (X).

Example 4.29   The following program outline illustrates the use of flags with string output.

```
#include <stdio.h>

main()

{
    char line[12];
    :
    printf(":%15s %15.5s %.5s:\n\n" line, line, line);
    printf(":%-15s %-15.5s %-.5s:" line, line, line);
}
```

Now suppose that the string lower-case is assigned to the character array line. The following output will be generated when the program is executed.

```
:     lower-case          lower lower:

:lower-case      lower          lower:
```

The first line illustrates how strings are displayed when flags are not present, as explained in Example 4.24. The second line shows the same strings, left-justified, in response to the – flag in each character group.

Unrecognized characters within the control string will be displayed just as they appear. This feature allows us to include labels and messages with the output data items, if we wish.

Example 4.30 The following program illustrates how printed output can be labeled.

```
#include <stdio.h>

main()     /* labeling of floating-point numbers */

{
    float a = 2.2, b = -6.2, x1 = .005, x2 = -12.88;

    printf("$%4.2f   %7.1f%%\n\n", a, b);
    printf("x1=%7.3f   x2=%7.3f", x1, x2);
}
```

This program causes the value of a (2.2) to be preceded by a dollar sign ($), and the value of b (-6.2) to be followed by a percent sign (%). Note the two consecutive percent signs in the first printf statement. The first percent sign indicates the start of a character group, whereas the second percent sign is interpreted as a label.

The second printf statement causes the value of x1 to be preceded by the label x1=, and the value of x2 to be preceded by the label x2=. Three blank spaces will separate these two labeled data items.

The actual output is shown below.

```
$2.20       -6.2%

x1=  0.005   x2=-12.880
```

The reader should be aware that there is some variation in the features supported by the printf function in different versions of C. The features described in this section are very common, though there may be differences in the way these features are implemented. Additional features are also available in many versions of the language.

4.8 THE gets AND puts FUNCTIONS

C contains a number of other library functions that permit some form of data transfer into or out of the computer. We will encounter several such functions in Chap. 12, where we discuss data files. Before leaving this chapter, however, we mention the gets and puts functions, which facilitate the transfer of strings between the computer and the standard input/output devices.

Each of these functions accepts a single argument. The argument must be a data item that represents a string (e.g., a character array). The string may include whitespace characters. In the case of gets, the string will be entered from the keyboard, and will terminate with a newline character (i.e., the string will end when the user presses the RETURN key).

The gets and puts functions offer simple alternatives to the use of scanf and printf for reading and displaying strings, as illustrated in the following example.

Example 4.31 Reading and Writing a Line of Text Here is another version of the simple program presented in Example 4.19, that reads a line of text into the computer and then writes it back out in its original form.

```
#include <stdio.h>

main()         /* read and write a line of text */

{
    char line[80];

    gets(line);
    puts(line);
}
```

This program utilizes `gets` and `puts`, rather than `scanf` and `printf`, to transfer the line of text into and out of the computer. Note that the syntax is simpler in the present program (compare carefully with the program shown in Example 4.19). On the other hand, the `scanf` and `printf` functions in the earlier program can be expanded to include additional data items, whereas the present program cannot.

When this program is executed, it will behave in exactly the same manner as the program shown in Example 4.19.

4.9 INTERACTIVE (CONVERSATIONAL) PROGRAMMING

Many modern computer programs are designed to create an interactive dialog between the computer and the person using the program (the "user"). These dialogs usually involve some form of question-answer interaction, where the computer asks the questions and the user provides the answers, or vice versa. The computer and the user thus appear to be carrying on some limited form of conversation.

In C, such dialogs can be created by alternate use of the `scanf` and `printf` functions. The actual programming is straightforward, though sometimes confusing to beginners, since the `printf` function is used both when entering data (to create the computer's questions) and when displaying results. On the other hand, `scanf` is used only for actual data entry.

The basic ideas are illustrated in the following example.

Example 4.32 Averaging Student Exam Scores This example presents a simple, interactive C program that reads in a student's name and three exam scores, and then calculates an average score. The data will be entered interactively, with the computer asking the user for information and the user supplying the information in a free format, as requested. Each input data item will be entered on a separate line. Once all the data have been entered, the computer will compute the desired average and write out all the data (both the input data and the calculated average).

The actual program is shown below.

```
#include <stdio.h>

main()      /* sample interactive program */

{
   char name[20];
   float score1, score2, score3, avg;

   printf("Please enter your name: ");              /* enter name */
   scanf("%[^\n]", name);

   printf("Please enter the first score:  ");       /* enter 1st score */
   scanf("%f", &score1);

   printf("Please enter the second score: ");       /* enter 2nd score */
   scanf("%f", &score2);

   printf("Please enter the third score:  ");       /* enter 3rd score */
   scanf("%f", &score3);

   avg = (score1+score2+score3)/3;                  /* calculate avg */

   printf("\n\nName: %-s\n\n", name);               /* write output */
   printf("Score 1: %-5.1f\n", score1);
   printf("Score 2: %-5.1f\n", score2);
   printf("Score 3: %-5.1f\n\n", score3);
   printf("Average: %-5.1f\n\n", avg);

}
```

Notice that two statements are associated with each input data item. The first is a `printf` statement, which generates a request for the item. The second statement, a `scanf` function, causes the data item to be entered from the standard input device (i.e., the keyboard).

After the student's name and all three exam scores have been entered, an average exam score is calculated. The input data and the calculated average are then displayed as a result of the group of printf statements at the end of the program.

A typical interactive session is shown below. To illustrate the nature of the dialog, the user's responses have been underlined.

```
Please enter your name: Robert Smith
Please enter the first score: 88
Please enter the second score: 62.5
Please enter the third score: 90


Name: Robert Smith

Score 1: 88.0
Score 2: 62.5
Score 3: 90.0

Average: 80.2
```

Additional interactive programs will be seen in many of the programming examples presented in succeeding chapters of this book.

Review Questions

4.1   What are the commonly used input/output functions in C? How are they accessed?

4.2   What is the standard input/output header file called in most versions of C? How is the file included within a program?

4.3   What is the purpose of the getchar function? How is it used within a C program?

4.4   What happens when an end-of-file condition is encountered when reading characters with the getchar function? How is the end-of-file condition recognized?

4.5   How can the getchar function be used to read multicharacter strings?

4.6   What is the purpose of the putchar function? How is it used within a C program? Compare with the getchar function.

4.7   How can the putchar function be used to write multicharacter strings?

4.8   What is a character-type array? What does each element of a character-type array represent? How are character-type arrays used to represent multicharacter strings?

4.9   What is the purpose of the scanf function? How is it used within a C program? Compare with the getchar function.

4.10   What is the purpose of the control string in a scanf function? What type of information does it convey? Of what is the control string composed?

4.11   How is each character group within the control string identified? What are the constituent characters within a character group?

4.12   If a control string within a scanf function contains multiple character groups, how are the character groups separated? Are whitespace characters required?

4.13   If whitespace characters are present within a control string, how are they interpreted?

4.14   Summarize the meaning of the more commonly used conversion characters within the control string of a scanf function.

4.15   What special symbol must be included with the arguments, other than the control string, in a scanf function? In what way are array names treated differently than other arguments?

4.16   When entering data via the scanf function, what relationships must there be between the data items and the corresponding arguments? How are multiple data items separated from one another?

4.17   When entering data via the scanf function, must octal data be preceded by 0? Must hexadecimal data be preceded by 0x (or 0X)? How must floating-point data be written?

4.18   When entering a string via the scanf function using an s-type conversion factor, how is the string terminated?

4.19   When entering a string via the scanf function, how can a single string which includes whitespace characters be entered?

4.20   Summarize a convenient method for entering a string of undetermined length, which may contain whitespace characters and all printable characters, and which is terminated by pressing the RETURN key. Answer this question relative to the type of conversion required within the control string of a scanf function.

4.21   What is meant by a field?

4.22   How can the maximum field width for a data item be specified within a scanf function?

4.23   What happens if an input data item contains more characters than the maximum allowable field width? What if the data item contains fewer characters?

4.24   How can short integer, long integer and double-precision arguments be indicated within the control string of a scanf function?

4.25   How can long double arguments be indicated within the control string of a scanf function? Is this feature available in most versions of C?

4.26   How can the assignment of an input data item to its corresponding argument be suppressed?

4.27   If the control string within a scanf function contains multiple character groups without interspersed whitespace characters, what difficulty can arise when using c-type conversion? How can this difficulty be avoided?

4.28   How are unrecognized characters within the control string of a scanf function interpreted?

4.29   What is the purpose of the printf function? How is it used within a C program? Compare with the putchar function.

4.30   In what ways does the control string within a printf function differ from the control string within a scanf function?

4.31   If the control string within a printf function contains multiple character groups, how are the character groups separated? How are the separators interpreted?

4.32   Summarize the meaning of the more commonly used conversion characters within the control string of a printf function. Compare with the conversion characters that are used in a scanf function.

4.33   In a printf function, must the arguments (other than the control string) be preceded by ampersands? Compare with the scanf function and explain any differences.

4.34   What is the difference between f-type conversion, e-type conversion and g-type conversion when outputting floating-point data with a printf function?

4.35   Compare the use of s-type conversion in the printf and the scanf functions. How does s-type conversion differ when processing strings containing whitespace characters?

4.36   How can the minimum field width for a data item be specified within the printf function?

4.37   What happens if an output data item contains more characters than the minimum field width? What if the data item contains fewer characters? Contrast with the field width specifications in the scanf function.

4.38   What is meant by the precision of an output data item? To what types of data does this apply?

4.39   How can the precision be specified within a printf function?

4.40   What happens to a floating-point number if it must be shortened to conform to a precision specification? What happens to a string?

4.41   Must a precision specification be accompanied by a minimum field width specification in a printf function?

4.42   How can short integer, long integer and double-precision arguments be indicated within the control string of a printf function? How can long double arguments be indicated?

4.43   How are uppercase conversion characters interpreted compared to the corresponding lowercase conversion characters in a printf function? To what types of conversion does this feature apply? Do all versions of C recognize this distinction?

4.44   Summarize the purpose of the flags commonly used within the printf function.

4.45   Can two or more flags appear consecutively within the same character group?

4.46   How are unrecognized characters within the control string of a printf function interpreted?

4.47   How can labeled data items be generated by the printf function?

4.48   Summarize the use of the gets and puts functions to transfer strings between the computer and the standard input/output devices. Compare the use of these functions with the string transfer features in the scanf and printf functions.

4.49   Explain, in general terms, how an interactive dialog can be generated by repeated use of pairs of scanf and printf functions.

Problems

4.50   A C program contains the following statements:

```
#include <stdio.h>

char a, b, c;
```

    (a) Write appropriate getchar statements that will allow values for a, b, and c to be entered into the computer.

    (b) Write appropriate putchar statements that will allow the current values of a, b and c to be written out of the computer.

4.51   Solve Problem 4.50 using a single scanf function and a single printf function rather than the getchar and putchar statements. Compare your answer with the solution to Problem 4.50.

4.52   A C program contains the following statements:

```
#include <stdio.h>

char text[80];
```

    (a) Write a for statement that will permit a 60-character message to be entered into the computer and stored in the character array text. Include a reference to the getchar function in the for loop, as in Example 4.4.

    (b) Write a for statement that will permit the first 60 characters of the character array text to be written out. Include a reference to the putchar function in the for loop, as in Example 4.4.

4.53   Modify the solution to Problem 4.52 (a) so that a character array whose length is unspecified can be read into the computer. Assume that the message does not exceed 79 characters, and that it is terminated by a *newline* character (\n). (See Example 4.4.)

4.54   Solve Problem 4.53 using a scanf statement in place of a for statement (see Example 4.8). What additional information is provided by the method described in Problem 4.53?

4.55   A C program contains the following statements:

```
#include <stdio.h>

int i, j, k;
```

Write an appropriate scanf function to enter numerical values for i, j and k, assuming

    (a) The values for i, j and k will be decimal integers.

    (b) The value for i will be a decimal integer, j an octal integer and k a hexadecimal integer.

    (c) The values for i and j will be hexadecimal integers and k will be an octal integer.

4.56   A C program contains the following statements:

```
#include <stdio.h>

int i, j, k;
```

Write an appropriate scanf function to enter numerical values for i, j and k into the computer, assuming

    (a) The values for i, j and k will be decimal integers not exceeding six characters each.

(b) The value for i will be a decimal integer, j an octal integer and k a hexadecimal integer, with each quantity not exceeding eight characters.

(c) The values for i and j will be hexadecimal integers and k will be an octal integer. Each quantity will be seven or fewer characters.

4.57 Interpret the meaning of the control string in each of the following scanf functions:

(a) `scanf("%12ld %5hd %15lf %15le", &a, &b, &c, &d);`

(b) `scanf("%10lx %6ho %5hu %14lu", &a, &b, &c, &d);`

(c) `scanf("%12D %hd %15f %15e", &a, &b, &c, &d);`

(d) `scanf("%8d %*d %12lf %12lf", &a, &b, &c, &d);`

4.58 A C program contains the following statements:

```
#include <stdio.h>

int i, j;
long ix;
short s;
unsigned u;
float x;
double dx;
char c;
```

For each of the following groups of variables, write a scanf function that will allow a corresponding set of data items to be read into the computer and assigned to the variables. Assume that all integers will be read in as decimal quantities.

(a) i, j, x and dx   (c) i, u and c

(b) i, ix, j, x and u   (d) c, x, dx and s

4.59 A C program contains the following statements:

```
#include <stdio.h>

int i, j;
long ix;
short s;
unsigned u;
float x;
double dx;
char c;
```

Write an appropriate scanf function to accommodate each of the following situations, assuming that all integers will be read in as decimal quantities.

(a) Enter values for i, j, x and dx, assuming that each integer quantity does not exceed four characters, the floating-point quantity does not exceed eight characters, and the double-precision quantity does not exceed 15 characters.

(b) Enter values for i, ix, j, x and u, assuming that each integer quantity does not exceed five characters, the long integer does not exceed 12 characters, and the floating-point quantity does not exceed 10 characters.

(c) Enter values for i, u and c, assuming that each integer quantity does not exceed six characters.

(d) Enter values for c, x, dx and s, assuming that the floating-point quantity does not exceed nine characters, the double-precision quantity does not exceed 16 characters and the short integer does not exceed six characters.

4.60 A C program contains the following statements:

```
#include <stdio.h>

char text[80];
```

Write a scanf function that will allow a string to be read into the computer and assigned to the character array text. Assume that the string does not contain any whitespace characters.

4.61　Solve Problem 4.60 assuming that the string contains only lowercase letters, blank spaces and newline characters.

4.62　Solve Problem 4.60 assuming that the string contains only uppercase letters, digits, dollar signs and blank spaces.

4.63　Solve Problem 4.60 assuming that the string contains anything other than an asterisk (i.e., assume that an asterisk will be used to indicate the end of the string).

4.64　A C program contains the following statements:

```
#include <stdio.h>

char a, b, c;
```

Suppose that $ is to be entered into the computer and assigned to a, * assigned to b and @ assigned to c. Show how the input data must be entered for each of the following scanf functions:

(a) scanf("%c%c%c", &a, &b, &c);
(b) scanf("%c %c %c ", &a, &b, &c);　　(d) scanf("%s %s %s", &a, &b, &c);
(c) scanf("%s%s%s", &a, &b, &c);　　　　(e) scanf("%1s%1s%1s", &a, &b, &c);

4.65　A C program contains the following statements:

```
#include <stdio.h>

int a, b;
float x, y;
```

Suppose that 12 is to be entered into the computer and assigned to a, -8 assigned to b, 0.011 assigned to x and -2.2×10^6 assigned to y. Show how the input data might most conveniently be entered for each of the following scanf functions:

(a) scanf("%d %d %f %f", &a, &b, &x, &y);
(b) scanf("%d %d %e %e", &a, &b, &x, &y);
(c) scanf("%2d %2d %5f %6e", &a, &b, &x, &y);
(d) scanf("%3d %3d %8f %8e", &a, &b, &x, &y);

4.66　A C program contains the following statements:

```
#include <stdio.h>

int i, j, k;
```

Write a printf function for each of the following groups of variables or expressions. Assume all variables represent decimal integers.

(a) i, j and k　　　(b) (i + j), (i - k)　　　(c) sqrt(i + j), abs(i - k)

4.67　A C program contains the following statements:

```
#include <stdio.h>

int i, j, k;
```

Write a printf function for each of the following groups of variables or expressions. Assume all variables represent decimal integers.

(a) i, j and k, with a minimum field width of three characters per quantity.
(b) (i + j), (i - k), with a minimum field width of five characters per quantity.
(c) sqrt(i + j), abs(i - k), with a minimum field width of nine characters for the first quantity and seven characters for the second quantity.

4.68   A C program contains the following statements:

```
#include <stdio.h>

float x, y, z;
```

Write a `printf` function for each of the following groups of variables or expressions:

(*a*) x, y and z   (*b*) (x + y), (x - z)   (*c*) sqrt(x + y), fabs(x - z)

4.69   A C program contains the following statements:

```
#include <stdio.h>

float x, y, z;
```

Write a `printf` function for each of the following groups of variables or expressions, using f-type conversion for each floating-point quantity.

(*a*) x, y and z, with a minimum field width of six characters per quantity.
(*b*) (x + y), (x - z), with a minimum field width of eight characters per quantity.
(*c*) sqrt(x + y), fabs(x - z), with a minimum field width of 12 characters for the first quantity and nine characters for the second.

4.70   Repeat the previous problem using e-type conversion.

4.71   A C program contains the following statements:

```
#include <stdio.h>

float x, y, z;
```

Write a `printf` function for each of the following groups of variables or expressions, using f-type conversion for each floating-point quantity.

(*a*) x, y and z, with a minimum field width of eight characters per quantity, with no more than four decimal places.
(*b*) (x + y), (x - z), with a minimum field width of nine characters per quantity, with no more than three decimal places.
(*c*) sqrt(x + y), fabs(x - z), with a minimum field width of 12 characters for the first quantity and 10 characters for the second. Display a maximum of four decimal places for each quantity.

4.72   A C program contains the following statements:

```
#include <stdio.h>

float x, y, z;
```

Write a `printf` function for each of the following groups of variables or expressions, using e-type conversion for each floating-point quantity.

(*a*) x, y and z, with a minimum field width of 12 characters per quantity, with no more than four decimal places.
(*b*) (x + y), (x - z), with a minimum field width of 14 characters per quantity, with no more than five decimal places.
(*c*) sqrt(x + y), fabs(x - z), with a minimum field width of 12 characters for the first quantity and 15 characters for the second. Display a maximum of seven decimal places for each quantity.

4.73   A C program contains the following statements:

```
#include <stdio.h>

int a = 0177, b = 055, c = 0xa8, d = 0x1ff;
```

Write a `printf` function for each of the following groups of variables or expressions:

(a) a, b, c and d   (b) (a + b), (c - d)

4.74 A C program contains the following statements:

```
#include <stdio.h>

int i, j;
long ix;
unsigned u;
float x;
double dx;
char c;
```

For each of the following groups of variables, write a `printf` function that will allow the values of the variables to be written out of the computer. Assume that all integers will be displayed as decimal quantities.

(a) i, j, x and dx   (c) i, u and c
(b) i, ix, j, x and u   (d) c, x, dx and ix

4.75 A C program contains the following statements:

```
#include <stdio.h>

int i, j;
long ix;
unsigned u;
float x;
double dx;
char c;
```

Write an appropriate `printf` function for each of the following situations, assuming that all integers will be displayed as decimal quantities.

(a) Write out the values of i, j, x and dx, assuming that each integer quantity will have a minimum field width of four characters and each floating-point quantity is displayed in exponential notation with a total of at least 14 characters and no more than eight decimal places.

(b) Repeat part (a), displaying each quantity on a separate line.

(c) Write out the values of i, ix, j, x and u, assuming that each integer quantity will have a minimum field width of five characters, the long integer will have a minimum field width of 12 characters, and the floating-point quantity will be at least 10 characters with a maximum of five decimal places. Do not include an exponent.

(d) Repeat part (c), displaying the first three quantities on one line, followed by a blank line and then the remaining two quantities on the next line.

(e) Write out the values of i, u and c, with a minimum field width of six characters for each integer quantity. Place three blank spaces between each output quantity.

(f) Write out the values for j, u and x. Display the integer quantities with a minimum field width of five characters. Display the floating-point quantity using f-type conversion, with a minimum field width of 11 characters and a maximum of four decimal places.

(g) Repeat part (f), with each data item left-justified within its respective field.

(h) Repeat part (f), with a sign (either + or −) preceding each signed data item.

(i) Repeat part (f), with leading zeros filling out the field for each of the integer quantities.

(j) Repeat part (f), with a provision for a decimal point in the value of x regardless of its value.

4.76 Assume that i, j and k are integer variables, and that i represents an octal quantity, j represents a decimal quantity and k represents a hexadecimal quantity. Write an appropriate `printf` function for each of the following situations.

(a) Write out the value for i, j and k, with a minimum field width of eight characters for each value.

(b) Repeat part (a) with each data item left-justified within its respective field.

(c) Repeat part (a) with each data item preceded by zeros (0x, in the case of the hexadecimal quantity).

4.77 A C program contains the following variable declarations:

```
int i = 12345, j = -13579, k = -24680;
long ix = 123456789;
short sx = -2222;
unsigned ux = 5555;
```

Show the output resulting from each of the following `printf` statements

(a) `printf("%d %d %d %ld %d %u", i, j, k, ix, sx, ux);`
(b) `printf("%3d %3d %3d\n\n%3ld %3d %3u", i, j, k, ix, sx, ux);`
(c) `printf("%8d %8d %8d\n\n%15ld %8d %8u", i, j, k, ix, sx, ux);`
(d) `printf("%-8d %-8d\n%-8d %-15ld\n%-8d %-8u", i, j, k, ix, sx, ux);`
(e) `printf("%+8d %+8d\n%+8d %+15ld\n%+8d %8u", i, j, k, ix, sx, ux);`
(f) `printf("%08d %08d\n%08d %015ld\n%08d %08u", i, j, k, ix, sx, ux);`

4.78 A C program contains the following variable declarations:

```
int i = 12345, j = 0xabcd9, k = 077777;
```

Show the output resulting from each of the following `printf` statements:

(a) `printf("%d %x %o", i, j, k);`
(b) `printf("%3d %3x %3o", i, j, k);`
(c) `printf("%8d %8x %8o", i, j, k);`
(d) `printf("%-8d %-8x %-8o", i, j, k);`
(e) `printf("%+8d %+8x %+8o", i, j, k);`
(f) `printf("%08d %#8x %#8o", i, j, k);`

4.79 A C program contains the following variable declarations:

```
float a = 2.5, b = 0.0005, c = 3000.;
```

Show the output resulting from each of the following `printf` statements:

(a) `printf("%f %f %f", a, b, c);`
(b) `printf("%3f %3f %3f", a, b, c);`
(c) `printf("%8f %8f %8f", a, b, c);`
(d) `printf("%8.4f %8.4f %8.4f", a, b, c);`
(e) `printf("%8.3f %8.3f %8.3f", a, b, c);`
(f) `printf("%e %e %e", a, b, c);`
(g) `printf("%3e %3e %3e", a, b, c);`
(h) `printf("%12e %12e %12e", a, b, c);`
(i) `printf("%12.4e %12.4e %12.4e", a, b, c);`
(j) `printf("%8.2e %8.2e %8.2e", a, b, c);`
(k) `printf("%-8f %-8f %-8f", a, b, c);`
(l) `printf("%+8f %+8f %+8f", a, b, c);`
(m) `printf("%08f %08f %08f", a, b, c);`
(n) `printf("%#8f %#8f %#8f", a, b, c);`
(o) `printf("%g %g %g", a, b, c);`
(p) `printf("%#g %#g %#g", a, b, c);`

4.80 A C program contains the following variable declarations:

```
char c1 = 'A', c2 = 'B', c3 = 'C';
```

Show the output resulting from each of the following `printf` statements:

(a) `printf("%c %c %c", c1, c2, c3);`
(b) `printf("%c%c%c", c1, c2, c3);`
(c) `printf("%3c %3c %3c", c1, c2, c3);`
(d) `printf("%3c%3c%3c", c1, c2, c3);`
(e) `printf("c1=%c c2=%c c3=%c", c1, c2, c3);`

4.81   A C program contains the following statements:

```
#include <stdio.h>

char text[80];
```

Write a `printf` function that will allow the contents of `text` to be displayed in the following ways:

(a) Entirely on one line.

(b) Only the first eight characters.

(c) The first eight characters, preceded by five blanks.

(d) The first eight characters, followed by five blanks.

4.82   A C program contains the following array declaration:

```
char text[80];
```

Suppose that the following string has been assigned to `text`:

```
Programming with C can be a challenging creative activity.
```

Show the output resulting from the following `printf` statements:

(a) `printf("%s", text);`

(b) `printf("%18s", text);`

(c) `printf("%.18s", text);`

(d) `printf("%18.7s", text);`

(e) `printf("%-18.7s", text);`

4.83   Write the necessary `scanf` or `printf` statements for each of the following situations:

(a) Generate the message

```
Please enter your name:
```

Then enter the name on the same line. Assign the name to a character-type array called `name`.

(b) Suppose that `x1` and `x2` are floating-point variables whose values are 8.0 and −2.5, respectively. Display the values of `x1` and `x2`, with appropriate labels, i.e., generate the message

```
x1 = 8.0    x2 = -2.5
```

(c) Suppose that `a` and `b` are integer variables. Prompt the user for input values of these two variables, then display their sum. Label the output accordingly.

4.84   Determine which conversion characters are available with your particular version of C. Also, determine which flags are available for data output.

Chapter 5

Preparing and Running
a Complete C Program

By now we have learned enough about C to write complete, though simple, C programs. Let us therefore pause briefly from our coverage of new features, and devote some attention to planning, writing and executing such programs. Moreover, we will consider some of the more creative aspects of programming, such as logical program development and good programming style, as well as the mechanics of complete program development.

5.1 PLANNING A C PROGRAM

It is essential that the overall program strategy be completely mapped out before any of the detailed programming actually begins. This way the programmer can concentrate on the general program logic, without becoming bogged down in the syntactic details of the individual instructions. In fact, this entire process might be repeated several times, with more programming detail added at each stage. Once the overall program strategy has been clearly established, then the syntactic details of the language can be considered. Such an approach is often referred to as "top-down" programming.

Top-down program organization is normally carried out by developing an informal outline, consisting of phrases or sentences that are part English and part C. In the initial stages of program development, the amount of C is minimal, consisting only of various elements that define major program components, such as function headings, function references, braces defining compound statements, and portions of control statements describing major program structures. Additional detail is then provided by descriptive English material inserted between these elements, often in the form of program comments. The resulting outline is usually referred to as *pseudocode*.

Example 5.1 Compound Interest A common problem in personal finance is that of determining how much money will accumulate in a bank account after n years if a known amount, P, is deposited initially and the account collects interest at a rate of r percent per year, compounded annually. The answer to this question can be determined by the well-known formula

$$F = P(1 + i)^n$$

where F represents the future accumulation of money (including the original sum, P, which is known as the *principal*) and i is the decimal representation of the interest rate, i.e., $i = r/100$ (for example, an interest rate of $r = 5\%$ would correspond to $i = 0.05$).

Consider the organization of a C program that will solve this problem. The program will be based upon the following general outline:

1. Declare the required program variables.
2. Read in values for the principal (P), the interest rate (r) and the number of years (n).
3. Calculate the decimal representation of the interest rate (i), using the formula

    ```
    i = r/100
    ```

4. Determine the future accumulation (F) using the formula

    ```
    F = P(1 + i)ⁿ
    ```

100

5. Write out the calculated value for F.

Here is the outline in the form of pseudocode.

```
/* compound interest calculations */

main()

{
    /* declare the program variables */

    /* read in values for P, r and n */

    /* calculate a value for i */

    /* calculate a value for F */

    /* write out the calculated value for F */
}
```

Each of these steps appears very simple when viewed from the top. However, some of the steps require more detail before they can actually be programmed. For example, the data input step will be carried out interactively. This will require some dialog generated by pairs of scanf and printf statements, as explained in Chap. 4. Moreover, C does not have an exponentiation operator; hence, some additional detail will be required to evaluate the formula $F = P(1 + i)^n$.

Here is a more detailed version of the above outline.

```
/* compound interest calculations */

main()

{
    /* declare p, r, n, i and f to be floating-point variables */

    /* write a prompt for p and then read in its value */
    /* write a prompt for r and then read in its value */
    /* write a prompt for n and then read in its value */

    /* calculate i = r/100 */

    /* calculate f = p(1 + i)ⁿ as follows:

         f = p * pow((1+i),n)

    where pow is a library function for exponentiation */

    /* write the value for f, with an accompanying label */
}
```

This outline may involve more detail than is actually necessary for a program this simple, though it does illustrate the top-down approach to program development.

We will consider the detailed development and implementation of this program in Examples 5.2, 5.4 and 5.5.

Another method sometimes used when planning a C program is the "bottom-up" approach. This method may be useful for programs that make use of self-contained program modules (e.g., user-defined functions). The bottom-up approach involves the detailed development of these program modules early in the overall planning process. The overall program development is then based upon the known characteristics of these available program modules.

In practice we often use both approaches: top-down for the overall program planning, bottom-up in developing individual modules before the main part of the program, and top-down with respect to the development of each individual module.

5.2 WRITING A C PROGRAM

Once an overall program strategy has been formulated and a program outline has been written, attention can be given to the detailed development of a working C program. At this point the emphasis becomes one of translating each step of the program outline (or each portion of the pseudocode) into one or more equivalent C instructions. This should be a straightforward activity provided the overall program strategy has been thought through carefully and in enough detail.

You should understand, however, that there is more to writing a complete C program than simply arranging the individual declarations and statements in the right order and then punctuating them correctly. Attention should also be given to the inclusion of certain additional features that will improve the program's readability and its resulting output. These features include the logical sequencing of the statements, the use of indentation, the use of comments and the generation of clearly labeled output.

The selection of program statements and their logical sequencing within the program is, to a large extent, determined by the underlying logic of the program. Often, however, there will be several different choices available for obtaining the same result. This is particularly true of more complex programs that involve the use of conditional or repeated program segments. In such cases, the manner in which the program is organized can have a major effect on the logical clarity of the program and the efficiency of execution. Therefore it is important that the statements be selected and sequenced in the most effective manner. We will say more about this in Chap. 6 where we discuss the various types of conditional and repetitive features available in C.

The use of indentation is closely related to the sequencing of groups of statements within a program. Whereas sequencing affects the order in which a group of operations is carried out, indentation illustrates the subordinate nature of individual statements within a group. The advantages of indentation are fairly obvious, even in the simple programs presented earlier in this book. This will become even more apparent later, as we encounter C programs whose structures are more complex.

Comments should always be included within a C program. If written properly, these comments can provide a useful overview of the general program logic. They can also delineate major segments of a program, identify certain key items within the program and provide other useful information about the program. Generally, the comments need not be extensive; a few well-placed comments can shed a great deal of light on an otherwise obscure program. Such comments can be of great use to a programmer as well as to anyone else trying to read and understand a program, since programmers sometimes forget the details of their own programs over a period of time. This is especially true of long, complicated programs.

Another important characteristic of a well-written program is its ability to generate clear, legible output. Two factors contribute to this legibility. The first is labeling the output data, as we have discussed in Chap. 4. The second is the appearance of some of the input data along with the output, so that each instance of program execution (if there are more than one) can be clearly identified. The manner in which this is accomplished depends upon the environment in which the C program will be executed. In an interactive environment the input data will usually be displayed on the terminal at the time of data entry, during program execution. Hence, the input data may not need to be written out again.

When executing an interactive program, the user may not know how to enter the required input data. For example, the user may not know what data items are required, when the data items should be entered, or the order in which they should be entered. Thus a well-written interactive program should generate prompts at appropriate times during the program execution in order to provide this information.

Example 5.2 Compound Interest Let us now consider an interactive program corresponding to the outline presented in Example 5.1.

```
#include <stdio.h>
#include <math.h>

/* simple compound interest problem */
main()

{
    float p,r,n,i,f;

    /* read input data (include prompts) */

    printf("Please enter a value for the principal (P): ");
    scanf("%f", &p);
    printf("Please enter a value for the interest rate (r): ");
    scanf("%f", &r);
    printf("Please enter a value for the number of years (n): ");
    scanf("%f", &n);

    /* calculate i, then f */

    i = r/100;
    f = p * pow((1 + i),n);

    /* write output */

    printf("\nThe final value (F) is: %.2f\n", f);
}
```

The program shown in this example is logically very straightforward. Thus, we did not have to concern ourselves with alternate ways to sequence the statements. There are, however, some other desirable features that might have been included. For example, we might want to execute the program repetitively, for several different sets of input data. Or, we might have added error traps, preventing the user from entering negative values for any of the input parameters. In Chap. 6 we will see how features such as these can be added.

5.3   ENTERING THE PROGRAM INTO THE COMPUTER

Once the program has been written it must be entered into the computer before it can be compiled and executed. This is usually accomplished by one of two possible methods, the most common being the use of an *editor*.

Most computer systems include an editor that is used to create and alter *text files* (programs, or textual documents such as memos, data files, etc.). Some editors are *line-oriented*, while others are *character-oriented*.

The commands within a line-oriented editor permit various editing operations, such as insert, delete, copy, to be carried out on specified lines within the text file. The use of a line editor is convenient for making small changes to known lines of text. On the other hand, its use for more extensive editing requires that a listing of the text file be available, showing the individual line numbers. Since the line numbers may change as the file is edited (because of insertions and deletions), the use of a line-oriented editor may be cumbersome when extensive editing is required.

Character-oriented editors are generally used with interactive, TV-type terminals. They are also referred to as *full-screen* editors, because they permit the entire screen to be filled with multiple lines of the file being edited. Their use is very convenient for all types of editing, no matter how extensive.

To edit a file with a full-screen editor, the portion of the file that requires editing is located and viewed on the screen. A flashing *cursor* is then moved to the location where the editing is to take place, and the required changes are entered directly. This procedure can be repeated as often as necessary, until all the required changes have been made.

There are many text editors available for virtually all types of computers. Some editors include both full-screen features and line-oriented commands, thus combining the capabilities of both types of editors. Any editor can be used to enter a C program and its accompanying data files, though some C compilers are associated with operating systems that include their own editors. For example, the UNIX® operating system includes an editor and a file-management system, in addition to a compiler and a library of various support routines. The editor includes a number of sophisticated features that make it particularly well suited for C program development. For example, the editor can be used in conjunction with the compiler by displaying a portion of an unsuccessfully compiled program and indicating exactly where the compilation error occurred.

Regardless of the particular editor being used, the procedure for creating a new program is to enter the program into a text file line-by-line. The text file is then assigned a file name and stored either in the computer's memory or on an auxiliary storage device. Usually a suffix, such as c, is attached to the file name, thus identifying the file as a C program. Such suffixes are called *extensions*. (For example, the program developed in Example 5.2 might be called `interest.c`.) The program will remain in this form until it is ready to be processed by the C compiler.

Many large systems support both batch processing and timesharing, with some form of on-line editing. This allows the user to choose whichever mode of operation is most convenient for the particular task at hand. For example, a new program and its accompanying data might be entered via an editor, but the calculated results, in the form of an output file, might be routed to a line printer operating in the batch mode.

The reader should determine what type of program-entry procedure is available at his or her particular installation. If an editor is available, the reader should obtain a user's manual or other set of instructions that describes exactly how the editor can be used.

5.4 COMPILING AND EXECUTING THE PROGRAM

Once a complete program has been correctly entered into the computer, it can be compiled and executed. The compilation is usually accomplished automatically in response to a single command, such as `compile name`, where *name* refers to the name of the file containing the program. It may also be necessary to *link* the compiled object program with one or more library routines in order to execute the program. This is also accomplished automatically in most cases, simply by issuing a single command, such as `link name`. In the UNIX operating system, the compile and link steps can both be carried out using the single instruction `cc name.c`, resulting in an object program called `a.out`.

The successful compilation and linking of a C program will result in an executable (machine language) object program that can then be executed in response to an appropriate system command, such as `execute`. The details of the execution will differ, however, from one operating system to another. In UNIX, the execution can be initiated simply by typing the name of the object program, i.e., `a.out`.

A typical microcomputer application is illustrated below.

Example 5.3 Compound Interest Suppose we wish to determine how much money will accumulate after 20 years if we deposit $1000 in a savings account that pays interest at the rate of 6 percent per year, compounded annually. Let us use the C program presented in the last example to answer this question. The program will be entered, compiled, linked and executed (and edited, if necessary) on a personal computer.

We first type the program into the computer using a text editor, being careful to correct any typing errors. Once the program has been entered it must be given a recognizable file name, such as `interest.c`, so that it can be saved for later compilation and execution. At this point it is a good idea to list the program on a printer and check it for accuracy. Typing errors, syntactic errors, and so on can easily be corrected by reentering the editor and making the required changes.

Once the program has been entered correctly, it can be compiled. This is accomplished by entering the single command

```
compile interest
```

With this particular compiler, the extension `.c` is not required. The computer will respond by compiling the program, resulting in a nonexecutable object program called `interest.obj`.

Many of the C compilers available for microcomputers are *multiple-pass* compilers, requiring a separate command to initiate each pass. Usually, however, it is possible to create a single "macro" command, such as `compile`, that will automatically carry out all passes in the proper sequence.

If the compilation is carried out successfully, the next step is to link the program with the program library routines. This is accomplished with the command

```
link interest
```

Once again, the extension `.obj` is not required. The result of the linking process will be the creation of an executable object program, called (typically) `interest.exe`.

If the compilation had not been successful, it would not have been possible to proceed with the link step. The programmer must then find the source of error, reenter the editor, and correct the original source program so that it can again be compiled (more about this in Sec. 5.5).

To execute the final object program, we simply type the program name, e.g.,

```
interest
```

Note once more that the extension `.exe` is not required. The instructions contained in the original C program will then be carried out, even though it is the object program rather than the original source program that is being executed. Thus, the following interactive dialog will be generated. (The user's responses are underlined for clarity.)

```
Please enter a value for the principal (P): 1000.
Please enter a value for the interest rate (r): 6.
Please enter a value for the number of years (n): 20.

The final value (F) is: 3207.14
```

The last line of output provides the answer to our original question: $1000 will increase to $3207.14 over a 20-year period at an interest rate of 6 percent per year, compounded annually.

The procedures shown in the above example are representative of those commonly used with compiled programs, though there will be some variation from one version of C to another. For example, some C compilers include a single command, such as `run`, that will cause a C source program to be compiled, linked and executed in succession. In such cases each step will be initiated only if the previous steps have been completed successfully.

C *interpreters* translate a source program into object code on a line-by-line basis and then execute the newly generated object code directly. Thus, the generation and execution of object code occur simultaneously, and there is no link step. In such an environment, a C program will begin execution immediately in response to a single command, such as `run`. The reader should determine whether his or her particular C system is a compiler or an interpreter and should then determine the exact procedures required to execute a program.

Finally, the reader is again reminded that the successful compilation, linking and execution of a C program often requires several attempts, because of the presence of errors that are almost always present in a new program. This is true of programs written by experienced programmers as well as by beginners. Thus, the entire procedure may seem tedious, particularly to the beginning programmer. It should be understood, however, that the frequency of such errors will decrease as the programmer gains a modest amount of experience. Beginners are therefore cautioned against becoming unduly discouraged with their first few programs, as things really do get better.

5.5   ERROR DIAGNOSTICS

Programming errors often remain undetected until an attempt is made to compile or execute the program. Once the `compile` or the `run` command has been issued, however, the presence of certain errors will become readily apparent, since these errors will prevent the program from being compiled or executed successfully. Some particularly common errors of this type are improperly declared variables, a reference to an undeclared variable, or incorrect punctuation. Such errors are referred to as *syntactic* (or *grammatical*) errors.

Most C compilers will generate diagnostic messages when syntactic errors have been detected during the compilation process. The compiler may come to an abrupt halt when this happens (though some compilers proceed to scan the entire source program, even though syntactic errors have been detected).

These diagnostic messages are not always straightforward in their meaning, but they are nevertheless helpful in identifying the nature and location of errors.

Example 5.4 Here is another version of the compound interest program shown in Example 5.2. This version contains several syntactic errors.

```
#include <stdio.h>
include <math.h>

/* simple compound interest problem */

main

{
   float p,r,n,i;

   /* read input data (include prompts) */

   printf("Please enter a value for the principal (P): ");
   scanf("%f", &p);
   printf("Please enter a value for the interest rate (r): );
   scanf("%f", &r);
   printf("Please enter a value for the number of years (n): ");
   scanf("%f", n)

   /* calculate i, then f */

   i = r/100
   f = p * pow(1 + i),n);

   /* write output *

   printf("\nThe final value (F) is: %.2f\n", f);
```

The errors are as follows:

1. The second `include` statement does not begin with a `#`-sign; `main` does not include a pair of parentheses.
2. The variable `f` is not declared to be a floating-point variable.
3. The control string in the second `printf` statement does not have a closing quotation mark.
4. The last `scanf` statement does not have an ampersand (&) preceding the last argument.
5. The last `scanf` statement and the assignment statement for `i` do not end with semicolons.
6. The assignment statement for `f` contains unbalanced parentheses.
7. The last comment lacks a final slash (/).
8. The program does not end with a closing brace (}).

When a compilation was attempted, the following nine messages were obtained. (These results were obtained on an IBM Personal Computer using the Microsoft C compiler, version 4.0.)

```
interest.C(2) : error 54: expected '(' to follow 'include'
interest.C(2) : error 59: syntax error : 'rel op'
interest.C(13) : error 61: syntax error : identifier 'printf'
interest.C(14) : error 61: syntax error : identifier 'scanf'
interest.C(15) : error 61: syntax error : identifier 'printf'
interest.C(16) : error 1: newline in constant
interest.C(17) : error 61: syntax error : identifier 'printf'
interest.C(18) : error 61: syntax error : identifier 'scanf'
interest.C(27) : fatal error 4: unexpected EOF
```

Notice that the error messages are very cryptic. In particular, each error message consists of the file name, followed by the line number (in parentheses) where an error has been detected. This information is followed by a numbered reference to an error type, which is then followed by a very brief message. The numbered error types refer to explanations that appear in the accompanying user's reference manual, though in most cases these explanations consist of little more than the brief messages shown above.

The specific error messages and warnings will vary from one version of C to another. These are merely representative. Some compilers may generate messages that are longer or more informative than those shown in this example. However, the brief, cryptic messages shown above are typical of the error messages generated by most compilers. Brief explanations are usually provided in the user's reference manual, though they may be too vague to be useful. The proper interpretation of these error messages may require considerable resourcefulness on the part of the programmer.

Another common type of error is the *execution* error. Execution errors occur during program execution after a successful compilation. For example, some common execution errors are the generation of an excessively large numerical quantity (exceeding the largest permissible number that can be stored in the computer), division by zero, or an attempt to compute the logarithm or the square root of a negative number. Diagnostic messages will often be generated in this type of situation, making it easy to identify and correct the errors. These diagnostics are sometimes called *execution* diagnostics, to distinguish them from the *compilation* diagnostics described earlier.

Example 5.5   Real Roots of a Quadratic Equation   Suppose we want to calculate the real roots of the quadratic equation

$$ax^2 + bx + c = 0$$

using the quadratic formula

$$x = \frac{-b \pm \sqrt{b^2 - 4ac}}{2a}$$

Here is a C program that will carry out these calculations.

```c
#include <stdio.h>
#include <math.h>

/* real roots of a quadratic equation */

main()

{
   float a, b, c, d, x1, x2;

   /* read input data */

   printf("a = ");
   scanf("%f", &a);
   printf("b = ");
   scanf("%f", &b);
   printf("c = ");
   scanf("%f", &c);

   /* carry out the calculations */

   d = sqrt(b*b - 4*a*c);
   x1 = (-b+d) / (2*a);
   x2 = (-b-d) / (2*a);

   /* write output */

   printf("x1 = %e    x2 = %e", x1, x2);
}
```

This program is completely free of syntactic errors, but it is unable to accommodate negative values for the quantity $b^2 - 4ac$. Furthermore, numerical difficulties may be encountered if the variable a has a very small or a very large numerical value, or if $a = 0$. A separate error message will be generated for each of these errors.

Suppose, for example, that the program is run with the following input values:

```
a=1.0        b=2.0        c=3.0
```

The program compiles without any difficulty. When the object program is executed, however, the following error message is generated, after the input values have been entered into the computer.

```
sqrt: DOMAIN error
```

Everything then comes to a halt, since the program execution cannot continue beyond this point.

Similarly, suppose that the program is run with the input values

```
a=1E-30        b=1E+10        c=1E+36
```

The system now generates the error message

```
error 2100: Floating point error: Overflow
```

when an attempt is made to execute the program.

Interpreters operate differently than compilers. Recall that a compiler translates an entire program into object code (i.e., machine language) before any execution can be attempted, whereas an interpreter translates the source program into object code line-by-line and then executes the object code as it is generated. Thus, an interpreter can detect both compilation-type errors and execution-type errors line-by-line, at approximately the same time. When an error is detected during the interpretation process, the interpreter will stop and issue an error message, indicating which line was being processed when the error was detected. Thus, interpreters are usually more convenient than compilers when debugging a new program.

On the other hand, interpreters are generally much slower than compilers when executing a program. Interpreters are therefore less suitable for running debugged programs. Many professional programmers exploit the advantages of both types of systems by using an interpreter to debug a program and then switching to a compiler once the program has been debugged.

5.6 LOGICAL DEBUGGING

We have just seen that syntactic errors and execution errors usually result in the generation of error messages when compiling or executing a program. Errors of this type are usually quite easy to find and correct, even if the error messages are unclear. Much more insidious, however, are *logical* errors. Here the program correctly conveys the programmer's instructions, free of syntactic errors, but the programmer has supplied the computer with instructions that are logically incorrect. Logical errors can be very difficult to detect, since the output resulting from a logically incorrect program may appear to be error free. Moreover, logical errors are often hard to find even when they are known to exist (as, for example, when the computed output is obviously incorrect). Thus, a good bit of probing may be required in order to find and correct errors of this type. Such probing is known as *logical debugging*.

Detecting Errors

The first step in attacking logical errors is to find out if they are present. This can sometimes be accomplished by testing a new program with data that will yield a known answer. If the correct results are not obtained, then the program obviously contains errors. Even if the correct results are obtained, however, you cannot be absolutely certain that the program is error free, since some errors cause incorrect results only under certain circumstances (as, for example, with certain values of the input data or with certain program options). Therefore, a new program should receive thorough testing before it is considered to be debugged. This is especially true of complicated programs or programs that will be used extensively by others.

As a rule, a calculation will have to be carried out by hand (with the aid of a calculator) in order to obtain a known answer. For some problems, however, the amount of work involved in carrying out a hand calculation is prohibitive, since a calculation that requires a few minutes of computer time may require *several weeks* to solve by hand. Therefore, a sample calculation cannot always be developed to test a new program. The logical debugging of such programs can be particularly difficult, though an observant programmer can often detect the presence of logical errors by studying the computed results carefully to see if they are reasonable.

Correcting Errors

Once it has been established that a program contains a logical error, some resourcefulness and ingenuity may be required to find the error. Error detection should always begin with a thorough review of each logical group of statements within the program. Knowing that an error exists somewhere, the programmer can often spot the error by such careful study. If the error cannot be found, it sometimes helps to set the program aside for a while. This is especially true if the programmer is experiencing some fatigue or frustration; it is not unusual for a tired, tense programmer to miss an obvious error the first time around.

If an error cannot be located simply by inspection, the program should be modified to print out certain intermediate results and then be rerun. This technique is referred to as *tracing*. The source of error will often become evident once these intermediate calculations have been carefully examined. In particular, the programmer can usually identify the particular area within the program where things begin to go wrong. The greater the amount of intermediate output, the more likely the chances of pin-pointing the source of error.

Sometimes an error simply cannot be located, despite the most elaborate debugging techniques. On such occasions beginning programmers are often inclined to suspect a problem that is beyond their control, such as a hardware error or an error in the compiler. In almost all cases, however, the problem turns out to be some subtle error in the program logic. Thus, the beginning programmer should resist the temptation to simply blame the computer and not look further for that elusive programming error. Although hardware errors do occur *on rare occasions*, they usually produce very bizarre results, such as the computer "dying" or the terminal spewing out random, unintelligible characters. Also, compiler errors occasionally crop up with a new compiler but are usually corrected after a compiler has been in use for a short period of time.

Finally, the reader should recognize the fact that some logical errors are inescapable in computer programming, though a conscientious programmer will make every attempt to minimize their occurrence. The beginning programmer should therefore anticipate the need for some logical debugging when writing realistic, meaningful C programs.

Example 5.6 Evaluating a Polynomial A student has written a C program to evaluate the formula

$$y = \left(\frac{x-1}{x}\right) + \frac{1}{2}\left(\frac{x-1}{x}\right)^2 + \frac{1}{3}\left(\frac{x-1}{x}\right)^3 + \frac{1}{4}\left(\frac{x-1}{x}\right)^4 + \frac{1}{5}\left(\frac{x-1}{x}\right)^5$$

To simplify the programming the student has defined a new variable, u, as

$$u = \left(\frac{x-1}{x}\right)$$

so that the formula becomes

$$y = u + \frac{u^2}{2} + \frac{u^3}{3} + \frac{u^4}{4} + \frac{u^5}{5}$$

Here is the student's complete C program.

```
#include <stdio.h>
#include <math.h>

/* program to evaluate an algebraic formula */

main()

{
    float u,x,y;

    /* read input data */

    printf("x = ");
    scanf("%f", &x);

    /* carry out the calculations */

    u = x-1 / x;
    y = u + pow((u/2),2.) + pow((u/3),3.) + pow((u/4),4.) + pow((u/5),5.);

    /* write output */

    printf("x = %f      y = %f", x, y);
}
```

The student knows that y should have a value of about 0.69 when $x = 2$, but the output generated by the program appears as follows:

```
x = 2.000000      y = 2.209705
```

The student concludes, therefore, that the program contains logical errors which must be found and corrected.

After inspecting the program carefully the student realized that the first assignment statement was incorrect. This statement should have been written as

```
u = (x-1) / x;
```

The student then corrected the program and reran it, again using a value of $x = 2$. The output,

```
x = 2.000000      y = 0.567384
```

indicates that a logical error is still present.

After some additional study the student discovered that the second assignment statement was also incorrect. This statement should appear as

```
y = u + pow(u,2.)/2 + pow(u,3.)/3 + pow(u,4.)/4 + pow(u,5.)/5;
```

The program was then modified and rerun, resulting in the correct answer (finally!), as indicated below.

```
x = 2.000000      y = 0.688542
```

Some C compilers include a *debugger*, which is a special program that facilitates the detection of errors in other C programs. In particular, a debugger allows the execution of a source program to be suspended at designated places, called *break points*, revealing the values assigned to the program variables and array elements at the time the execution stops. Some debuggers also allow a program to execute continuously until some specified error condition has occurred. By examining the values assigned to the variables at the break points, it is easier to determine when and where an error originates.

Review Questions

5.1   What is meant by "top-down" programming? What are its advantages? How is it carried out?

5.2   What is pseudocode?

5.3   What is meant by "bottom-up" programming? How does it differ from top-down programming?

5.4   How much flexibility does the programmer have in the logical sequencing of the statements within a C program? Explain.

5.5   Why are some statements indented within a C program? Is this indentation absolutely necessary?

5.6   What are the reasons for placing comments within a C program? How extensive should these comments be?

5.7   Name two factors that contribute to the generation of clear, legible output data.

5.8   What useful information is provided by prompts?

5.9   What is a text file?

5.10 What is the difference between a line-oriented editor and a character-oriented editor?

5.11 How is a program entered into the computer in most typical C programming environments?

5.12 What is a program name extension?

5.13 What is the difference between compilation and execution of a C program?

5.14 What is meant by linking? How does linking differ from compiling?

5.15 What is a syntactic error? What is an execution error? How do syntactic errors and execution errors differ from one another?

5.16 Name some common syntactic errors. Name some common execution errors.

5.17 What is a logical error? How do logical errors differ from syntactic and execution errors?

5.18 What are diagnostic messages?

5.19 What is the difference between compilation diagnostics and execution diagnostics? Name some situations in which each type of diagnostic message would be generated.

5.20 How does the operation of an interpreter differ from that of a compiler? What are the advantages and disadvantages of each?

5.21 What is meant by logical debugging? Name some common debugging procedures.

5.22 What is meant by tracing? In what way is tracing useful?

5.23 What is a debugger? What special features are made available by a debugger?

Problems

The following questions are concerned with information gathering rather than actual problem solving.

5.24 If timesharing is used at your particular school or office, obtain answers to the following questions.

   (*a*) Are video display terminals available? Are hard-copy terminals available?

   (*b*) How can a terminal be turned on or off?

   (*c*) How can a single character be deleted from a typed line before it has been sent to the computer? How can an entire line be deleted?

   (*d*) How can a typed line be transmitted to the computer?

   (*e*) Can a hard copy of your timesharing session be obtained? If so, how?

   (*f*) Is a telephone dialup required to establish a connection with the computer? If so, what is the dialup procedure?

   (*g*) Exactly how do you log on and log off your computer?

   (*h*) Can your timesharing terminal be operated in a local mode (i.e., as a stand-alone device, independent of the mainframe computer)? If so, how is this done?

   (*i*) What editor or editors are available on your system? How are normal editing functions (e.g., insert, delete) carried out?

   (*j*) How can C be accessed on your system? What procedures are required to compile, link and execute a C program?

   (*k*) How much does it cost to use your particular computer?

5.25 If batch processing is used at your particular school or office, obtain answers to the following questions.

    (a)   How is the C system accessed? What procedures are required to compile, link and execute a C program?

    (b)   How can a program or a data file be stored in your system? How can a program or data file be accessed? How can it be deleted?

    (c)   Where is the line printer located? What does the printed output look like?

    (d)   What does it cost to use your particular computer?

5.26 If personal computers are used at your particular school or office, obtain answers to the following questions.

    (a)   Exactly what equipment is available (printers, auxiliary memory devices, etc.)?

    (b)   What operating system is available?

    (c)   How can programs be saved, displayed, and transferred from one memory device to another?

    (d)   How can a single character be deleted from a typed line before it has been sent to the computer? How can an entire line be deleted?

    (e)   How can a typed line be transmitted to the computer?

    (f)   How is the editor accessed? How are normal editing functions (i.e., insert, delete) carried out?

    (g)   How is C accessed on your computer? What procedures are required to compile, link and execute a C program?

    (h)   What is the cost of one complete personal computer system?

Programming Problems

5.27 Example 1.6 presents a C program for calculating the area of a circle, given its radius. Enter this program into your computer and make any necessary modifications, such as `#include <stdio.h>`. Be sure to correct any typing errors. List the program after it has been stored within the computer. When you are sure that it is correct, compile the program and then execute the object program using several different values for the radius. Verify that the computed answers are correct by comparing them with hand calculations.

5.28 Enter, compile and execute the C programs given in Examples 1.7 through 1.13. Verify that they run correctly with your particular version of C. (If any of the programs do not run, try to determine why.)

5.29 Repeat Problem 5.28 for a few of the programs given in Problem 1.31.

5.30 Example 5.2 presents a C program for determining the future value of a savings account if the interest is allowed to accumulate and compound annually. Enter this program into the computer and save it; then run the program using several different sets of input data. Verify that the calculated results are correct by comparing them with calculations carried out by hand, with the aid of a calculator.

5.31 Write a complete C program for each of the following problem situations. Enter each program into the computer, being sure to correct any typing errors. Save and then list the program. When you are sure that it has been entered correctly, compile and then execute the program. Repeat as often as necessary in order to obtain an error-free program. Use interactive programming wherever appropriate.

    (a)   Print HELLO! at the beginning of a line.

    (b)   Have the computer print

```
HI, WHAT'S YOUR NAME?
```

    on one line. The user then enters his or her name immediately after the question mark. The computer then skips two lines and prints

```
WELCOME (name)

LET'S BE FRIENDS!
```

    on two consecutive lines. Use a character-type array to represent the user's name. Assume the name contains fewer than 20 characters.

    (c)   Convert a temperature reading in degrees Fahrenheit to degrees Celsius, using the formula

$$C = (5/9) \times (F - 32)$$

    Test the program with the following values: 68, 150, 212, 0, -22, -200 (degrees Fahrenheit).

(d)   Determine how much money (in dollars) is in a piggy bank that contains several half dollars, quarters, dimes, nickels and pennies. Use the following values to test your program: 11 half dollars, 7 quarters, 3 dimes, 12 nickels and 17 pennies. (Answer: $8.32).

(e)   Calculate the volume and area of a sphere using the formulas

$$V = 4\pi r^3/3$$
$$A = 4\pi r^2$$

Test the program using the following values for the radius: 1, 6, 12.2, 0.2.

(f)   Calculate the mass of air in an automobile tire, using the formula

$$PV = 0.37m\,(T + 460)$$

where P = pressure, pounds per square inch (psi)

   V = volume, cubic feet

   m = mass of air, pounds

   T = temperature, degrees Fahrenheit

The tire contains two cubic feet of air. Assume that the pressure is 32 psi at room temperature.

(g)   Read a five-letter word into the computer, then encode the word letter-by-letter by subtracting 30 from the numerical value that is used to represent each letter. Thus, if the ASCII character set is being used, the letter a (which is represented by the value 97) would become a C (represented by the value 67), and so on.

  Write out the encoded version of the word. Test the program with the following words: white, roses, Japan, zebra.

(h)   Read into the computer a five-letter word that has been encoded using the scheme described above. Decode the word by reversing the above procedure, then write out the decoded word.

(i)   Read an entire line of text into the computer, encoding it as it is read in, using the method described in part (g). Display the entire line of text in encoded form. Then decode the text and write it out (displaying the text as it originally appeared), using the method described in part (h).

(j)   Read into the computer a line of text containing both uppercase and lowercase letters. Write out the text with the uppercase and lowercase letters reversed, but all other characters intact. (Hint: Use the conditional operator ?: and the library functions islower, tolower and toupper.

Chapter 6

Control Statements

In most of the C programs we have encountered so far, the instructions were executed in the same order in which they appeared in the program. Each instruction was executed once and once only. Programs of this type are unrealistically simple, since they do not include any logical control structures. In particular, such programs do not include tests to determine if certain conditions are true or false, they do not require the repeated execution of groups of statements, and they do not involve the execution of individual groups of statements on a selective basis. Most programs that are of practical interest make extensive use of features such as these.

For example, many programs require that a group of instructions be executed repeatedly, until some logical condition has been satisfied. This is known as *looping*. Sometimes the required number of repetitions will not be known in advance; the computation simply continues until the logical condition becomes true. Situations also arise, however, in which a group of consecutive instructions is repeated some specified number of times. This is another form of looping.

Many programs require that a logical test be carried out at some particular point within the program. An action will then be carried out whose exact nature depends upon the outcome of the logical test. This is known as *conditional execution*. And finally, there is a special kind of conditional execution in which one group of statements is selected from several available groups. This is sometimes referred to as *selection*.

All of these operations can be carried out using the various control statements included in C. We will see how this is accomplished in this chapter. The use of these statements will open the door to programming problems that are much broader and more interesting than those considered earlier.

6.1 PRELIMINARIES

Before considering the detailed control statements available in C, let us review some concepts presented in Chaps. 2 and 3 that must be used in conjunction with these statements. Understanding these concepts is essential in order to proceed further.

First, we will need to form logical expressions that are either true or false. To do so, we can use the four relational operators, <, <=, >, >=, and the two equality operators, == and != (see Sec. 3.3).

Example 6.1 Several logical expressions are shown below.

```
count <= 100

sqrt(a+b+c) > 0.005

answer == 0

balance >= cutoff

ch1 < 'T'

letter != 'x'
```

The first four expressions involve numerical operands. Their meaning should be readily apparent.

In the fifth expression, ch1 is assumed to be a char-type variable. This expression will be true if the character represented by ch1 comes before T in the character set. That is, if the numerical value used to encode the character is less than the numerical value used to encode the letter T.

The last expression makes use of the char-type variable letter. This expression will be true if the character represented by letter is something other than x.

In addition to the relational and equality operators, C contains two logical connectives (also called logical operators), && (AND) and ¦¦ (OR), and the unary negation operator ! (see Sec. 3.3). The logical connectives are used to combine logical expressions, thus forming more complex expressions. The negation operator is used to reverse the meaning of a logical expression (e.g., from true to false).

Example 6.2 Here are some logical expressions that illustrate the use of the logical connectives and the negation operator.

```
(count <= 100) && (ch1 != '*')

(balance < 1000.0) ¦¦ (status == 'R')

(answer < 0) ¦¦ ((answer > 5.0) && (answer <= 10.0))

!((pay >= 1000.0) && (status == 's'))
```

Note that ch1 and status are assumed to be char-type variables in these examples. The remaining variables are assumed to be numeric (either integer or floating-point).

Since the relational and equality operators have a higher precedence than the logical operators, some of the parentheses are not needed in the above expressions (see Table 3-1 in Sec. 3.5). Thus, we could have written these expressions as

```
count <= 100 && ch1 != '*'

balance < 1000.0 ¦¦ status == 'R'

answer < 0 ¦¦ answer > 5.0 && answer <= 10.0

!(pay >= 1000.0 && status == 's')
```

It is a good idea, however, to include pairs of parentheses if there is any doubt about the operator precedences. This is particularly true of relatively complicated expressions, such as the expression above which involves the variable answer.

The conditional operator ?: also makes use of an expression that is either true or false (see Sec. 3.5). An appropriate value is selected, depending on the outcome of this logical expression. This operator is equivalent to a simple *if-then-else* structure, as found in most high-level programming languages, including C.

Example 6.3 Suppose that status is a char-type variable and balance is a floating-point variable. We wish to assign the character C (current) to status if balance has a value of zero, and O (overdue) if balance has a value greater than zero. This can be accomplished by writing

```
status = (balance == 0) ? 'C' : 'O'
```

Finally, recall that there are three different kinds of statements in C: expression statements, compound statements and control statements (see Sec. 2.8). An expression statement consists of an expression, followed by a semicolon (see Sec. 2.7). A compound statement consists of a sequence of two or more consecutive statements enclosed in braces ({ and }); the statements within the braces may be expression statements, other (embedded) compound statements or control statements. Every function (and hence every program) must contain at least one compound statement. Moreover, most control statements contain expression statements or compound statements (or both). Control statements that contain embedded compound statements are very common.

Example 6.4 Here is an elementary compound statement which we have seen before, in Example 3.31.

```
{
    int lower, upper;

    lower = getchar();
    upper = toupper(lower);
    putchar(upper);
}
```

Here is a more complicated compound statement:

```
{
    float sum = 0, sumsq = 0, sumsqrt = 0, x;

    scanf("%f", &x);
    while (x != 0) {
        sum += x;
        sumsq += x*x;
        sumsqrt += sqrt(x);
        scanf("%f", &x);
    }
}
```

This last example contains one compound statement embedded within another.

The control statements presented within this chapter make extensive use of logical expressions and compound statements. Assignment operators, such as the one used in the above example (i.e., +=), will also be utilized.

6.2   THE while STATEMENT

The while statement is used to carry out looping operations. The general form of the statement is

```
while (expression) statement
```

The included *statement* will be executed repeatedly, as long as the value of *expression* is not zero. This *statement* can be simple or compound, though it is typically a compound statement. It must include some feature which eventually alters the value of *expression*, thus providing a stopping condition for the loop.

In practice, the included *expression* is usually a logical expression that is either true or false. (Remember that *true* corresponds to a nonzero value, and *false* corresponds to 0.) Thus, the *statement* will continue to execute as long as the logical expression is true.

Example 6.5   Consecutive Integer Quantities Suppose we want to display the consecutive digits 0, 1, 2, . . . , 9, with one digit on each line. This can be accomplished with the following program.

```
#include <stdio.h>

main()    /* display the integers 0 through 9 */

{
    int digit = 0;

    while (digit <= 9)  {
         printf("%d\n", digit);
         ++digit;
    }
}
```

Initially, digit is assigned a value of 0. The while loop then displays the current value of digit, increases its value by 1 and then repeats the cycle, until the value of digit exceeds 9. The net effect is that the body of the loop will be repeated 10 times, resulting in 10 consecutive lines of output. Each line will contain a successive integer value, beginning with 0 and ending with 9. Thus, when the program is run, the following output will be generated.

```
0
1
2
3
4
5
6
7
8
9
```

This program can be written more concisely as

```
#include <stdio.h>

main()    /* display the integers 0 through 9 */

{
    int digit = 0;

    while (digit <= 9)
         printf("%d\n", digit++);
}
```

When executed, this program will generate the same output as the first program.

Example 6.6   Lowercase to Uppercase Text Conversion   Here is another example of a C program that makes use of the while statement. In this example we will read a line of lowercase text character-by-character and store the characters in a char-type array called letter. The characters will then be converted to uppercase, using the library function toupper, and written out.

Two separate while statements will be used. One will read in the text. The other will perform the conversion and write out the converted text. The complete program is shown below.

```
#include <stdio.h>

#define EOL  '\n'

/* convert a line of lower-case text to upper-case */
main()

{
    char letter[80];
    int tag, count = 0;

    /* read in the lower-case text */
    while ((letter[count] = getchar()) != EOL) ++count;
    tag = count;

    /* write out the upper-case text */
    count = 0;
    while (count < tag)  {
          putchar(toupper(letter[count]));
          ++count;
    }
}
```

Notice that count is initially assigned a value of zero.

The first while loop, i.e.,

```
while ((letter[count] = getchar()) != EOL)  ++count;
```

is written very concisely. This single-statement loop is equivalent to the following:

```
letter[count] = getchar();
while (letter[count] != EOL)  {
    count = count + 1;
    letter[count] = getchar();
}
```

This latter form will be more familiar to those readers experienced with other high-level programming languages, such as Pascal or BASIC. Either form is correct, though the original concise form is more representative of typical C programming style.

When the program is executed, any line of text entered into the computer will be displayed in uppercase. Suppose, for example, that the following line of text had been entered:

```
Fourscore and seven years ago our fathers brought forth ...
```

The computer would respond by printing

```
FOURSCORE AND SEVEN YEARS AGO OUR FATHERS BROUGHT FORTH ...
```

Example 6.7   Averaging a List of Numbers   Let us now use a while statement to calculate the average of a list of n numbers. Our strategy will be based on the use of a partial sum that is initially set equal to zero, then updated as each new number is read into the computer. Thus, the problem very naturally lends itself to the use of a loop.

The calculations will be carried out in the following manner.

1. Assign a value of 1 to the integer variable count. This variable will be used as a loop counter.

2. Assign a value of 0 to the floating-point variable sum.

3. Read in a value for the integer variable n.

4. Carry out the following steps repeatedly, as long as count does not exceed n.
   (*a*) Read in one of the numbers in the list. Each number will be represented by the floating-point variable x.
   (*b*) Add the value of x to the current value of sum.
   (*c*) Increase the value of count by 1.
5. Divide the value of sum by n to obtain the desired average.
6. Write out the calculated value for the average.

Here is the actual C program. Notice that the input operations are all accompanied by prompts asking the user for the required information.

```c
#include <stdio.h>

/* calculate the average of n numbers */

main()

{

    int n, count = 1;
    float x, average, sum = 0;

    /* initialize and read in a value for n */
    printf("How many numbers? ");
    scanf("%d", &n);

    /* read in the numbers */
    while (count <= n)  {
        printf("x = ");
        scanf("%f", &x);
        sum += x;
        ++count;
    }

    /* calculate the average and write out the answer */
    average = sum/n;
    printf("\nThe average is %f\n", average);
}
```

Notice that the while loop contains a compound statement which, among other things, causes the value of count to increase. Eventually, this will cause the logical expression

```c
count <= n
```

to become false, thus terminating the loop. Also, note that the loop will not be executed at all if n is assigned a value less than 1 (which would make no sense).

Now suppose that the program will be used to process the following six values: 1, 2, 3, 4, 5, 6. Execution of the program will produce the following interactive dialog. (Note that the user's responses have been underlined.)

```
How many numbers? 6
x = 1
x = 2
x = 3
x = 4
x = 5
x = 6

The average is 3.500000
```

6.3   THE do-while STATEMENT

When a loop is constructed using the `while` statement described in Sec. 6.2, the test for continuation of the loop is carried out at the beginning of each pass. Sometimes, however, it is desirable to have a loop with the test for continuation at the *end* of each pass. This can be accomplished by means of the `do - while` statement.

The general form of the `do - while` statement is

```
do statement while (expression);
```

The included *statement* will be executed repeatedly, as long as the value of *expression* is not zero. Notice that *statement* will always be executed at least once, since the test for repetition does not occur until the end of the first pass through the loop. The *statement* can be either simple or compound, though most applications will require it to be a compound statement. It must include some feature which eventually alters the value of *expression* so that the looping action can terminate.

In practice, *expression* is usually a logical expression which is either true (with a nonzero value) or false (with a value of 0). The included *statement* will be repeated (i.e., another pass will be made through the loop) if the logical expression is true.

For most applications it is more natural to test for continuation of a loop at the beginning rather than at the end of the loop. For this reason, the `do - while` statement is used less frequently than the `while` statement described in Sec. 6.2. For illustrative purposes, however, the programming examples shown in Sec. 6.2 are repeated below using the `do - while` statement for the conditional loops.

Example 6.8   Consecutive Integer Quantities   In Example 6.5 we saw two complete C programs that use the `while` statement to display the consecutive digits $0, 1, 2, \ldots, 9$. Here is another program to do the same thing, using the `do - while` statement in place of the `while` statement.

```c
#include <stdio.h>

main()     /* display the integers 0 through 9 */

{
    int digit = 0;

    do
        printf("%d\n", digit++);
    while (digit <= 9);
}
```

As in the earlier example, `digit` is initially assigned a value of 0. The `do - while` loop displays the current value of `digit`, increases its value by 1, and then tests to see if the current value of `digit` exceeds 9. If so, the loop terminates; otherwise, the loop continues, using the new value of `digit`. Note that the test is carried out at the *end* of each pass through the loop. The net effect is that the loop will be repeated 10 times, resulting in 10 successive lines of output. Each line will appear exactly as shown in Example 6.5.

Comparing this program with the second program presented in Example 6.5, we see about the same level of complexity in both programs. Neither of the conditional looping structures (i.e., `while` or `do - while`) appears more desirable than the other.

Example 6.9   Lowercase to Uppercase Text Conversion   Now let us rewrite the program shown in Example 6.6, which converts lowercase text to uppercase, so that the two `while` loops are replaced by `do - while` loops. As in the earlier program, our overall strategy will be to read in a line of lowercase text character-by-character, store the characters in a char-type array called `letter`, and then write them out in uppercase using the library function `toupper`. We will make use of a `do - while` statement to read in the text character-by-character, and another `do - while` statement to convert the characters to uppercase and then write them out.

Here is the complete C program.

```
#include <stdio.h>

#define EOL   '\n'

* convert a line of lower-case text to upper-case */

main() /

{
    char letter[80];
    int tag, count = -1;

    /* read in the text */
    do ++count; while ((letter[count] = getchar()) != EOL);
    tag = count;

    /* write out the text */
    count = 0;
    do {
        putchar(toupper(letter[count]));
        ++count;
    }  while (count < tag);
}
```

The first loop, i.e.,

```
do ++count; while ((letter[count] = getchar()) != EOL);
```

is simple and concise, but the second loop,

```
do {
    putchar(toupper(letter[count]));
    ++count;
}  while (count < tag);
```

is somewhat more complex. Both loops resemble the corresponding while loops presented in Example 6.6. Note, however, that the first loop in the current program begins with a value of −1 assigned to count, whereas the initial value of count was 0 in Example 6.6.

When the program is executed, it behaves in exactly the same way as the program shown in Example 6.6.

Before leaving this example, we mention that the last loop could have been written more concisely as

```
do
    putchar(toupper(letter[count++]));
while (count < tag);
```

This may appear a bit strange to the beginner, though it is characteristic of the programming style commonly used by most experienced C programmers.

Example 6.10   Averaging a List of Numbers   The program shown in Example 6.7 can easily be rewritten to illustrate the use of the do - while statement. The logic will be the same, except that the test to determine if all n numbers have been entered into the computer will not be made until the end of the loop rather than the beginning. Thus, the program will always make at least one pass through the loop, even if n is assigned a value of 0 (which would make no sense).

Here is the modified version of the program.

```
#include <stdio.h>

/* calculate the average of n numbers */

main()

{
    int n, count = 1;
    float x, average, sum = 0;

    /* initialize and read in a value for n */
    printf("How many numbers? ");
    scanf("%d", &n);

    /* read in the numbers */
    do {
        printf("x = ");
        scanf("%f", &x);
        sum += x;
        ++count;
    } while (count <= n);

    /* calculate the average and write out the answer */
    average = sum/n;
    printf("\nThe average is %f\n", average);
}
```

When the program is executed it will behave in exactly the same manner as the earlier version shown in Example 6.7.

6.4   THE for STATEMENT

The for statement is the third and perhaps the most commonly used looping statement in C. This statement includes an expression that specifies an initial value for an index, another expression that determines whether or not the loop is continued and a third expression that allows the index to be modified at the end of each pass.

The general form of the for statement is

for (*expression 1*; *expression 2*; *expression 3*) *statement*

where *expression 1* is used to initialize some parameter (called an index) that controls the looping action, *expression 2* represents a condition that must be satisfied for the loop to continue execution, and *expression 3* is used to alter the value of the parameter initially assigned by *expression 1*. Typically, *expression 1* is an assignment expression, *expression 2* is a logical expression and *expression 3* is a unary expression or an assignment expression.

When the for statement is executed, *expression 2* is evaluated and tested before each pass through the loop, and *expression 3* is evaluated at the end of each pass. Thus, the for statement is equivalent to

```
expression 1;
while (expression 2) {
    statement
    expression 3;
}
```

The looping action will continue as long as the value of *expression 2* is not zero; that is, as long as the logical condition represented by *expression 2* is true.

Example 6.11 Consecutive Integer Quantities We have already seen several different versions of a C program that will display the consecutive digits 0, 1, 2, ... , 9, with one digit on each line (see Examples 6.5 and 6.8). Here is another program to do the same thing. Now, however, we will make use of the `for` statement rather than the `while` statement or the `do - while` statement, as in the earlier examples.

```
#include <stdio.h>

main()   /* display the numbers 0 through 9 */

{
    int digit;

    for (digit = 0; digit <= 9; ++digit)
        printf("%d\n", digit);
}
```

Notice that the first line of the `for` statement contains three expressions, enclosed in parentheses. The first expression assigns an initial value of 0 to the integer variable `digit`, the second expression states that the looping action will continue as long as the current value of `digit` does not exceed 9 and the third expression increases the value of `digit` by 1 after each pass through the loop. Also, note that the value of `digit` is tested at the beginning of each pass through the loop. And finally, notice that the `printf` function, referenced within the `for` statement, produces the desired output, as shown in Example 6.5.

From a syntactic standpoint all three expressions need not be present in the `for` statement, though the semicolons must be shown. However, the consequences of an omission should be clearly understood. The first and third expressions may be omitted if other means are provided for initializing the index and/or altering the index. If the second expression is omitted, however, it will be assumed to have a permanent value of 1 (true); thus, the loop will continue indefinitely unless it is terminated by some other means, such as a `break` or a `return` statement (see Secs. 6.8 and 7.2). As a practical matter, most applications of the `for` statement include all three expressions.

Example 6.12 Consecutive Integer Quantities Here is still another example of a C program that generates the consecutive integers 0, 1, 2, ... , 9 with one digit on each line. We now use a `for` statement in which two of the three expressions are omitted.

```
#include <stdio.h>

main()   /* display the numbers 0 through 9 */

{
    int digit = 0;

    for (; digit <= 9; )
        printf("%d\n", digit++);
}
```

This version of the program is more obscure than that shown in Example 6.11, and hence less desirable.

Note the similarity between this program and the second program in Example 6.5, which makes use of the `while` statement.

Example 6.13   Lowercase to Uppercase Text Conversion   Here once again is a C program that converts lowercase text to uppercase. We have already seen other programs that do this, in Examples 6.6 and 6.9. Now, however, we make use of the `for` statement rather than the `while` statement or the `do - while` statement.

As before, our overall strategy will be to read in a line of lowercase text character-by-character, store the characters in a char-type array called `letter`, and then write them out in uppercase using the library function `toupper`. Two separate loops will be required; one to read and store the lowercase characters, the other to display the characters in uppercase.

Here is the complete C program.

```
#include <stdio.h>

#define EOL '\n'

/* convert a line of lower-case text to upper-case */

main()

{
    char letter[80];
    int tag, count;

    /* read in the text */
    for (count = 0; (letter[count] = getchar()) != EOL; ++count)
        ;
    tag = count;

    /* write out the text */
    for (count = 0; count < tag; ++count)
        putchar(toupper(letter[count]));
}
```

Comparing this program with the corresponding programs given in Examples 6.6 and 6.9, we see that the loops are more concise in this example. Thus, the `for` statement appears more desirable than the `while` or `do - while` statement for forming loops of this type, where the number of passes is known in advance.

Example 6.14   Averaging a List of Numbers   Now let us modify the program given in Example 6.7, which calculates the average of a list of n numbers, so that the looping action is accomplished by means of a `for` statement. The logic will be essentially the same, though some of the steps will be carried out in a slightly different order. In particular:

1. Assign a value of 0 to the floating-point variable `sum`.
2. Read in a value for the integer variable n.
3. Assign a value of 1 to the integer variable `count`, where `count` is an index that counts the number of passes through the loop.
4. Carry out the following steps repeatedly, as long as the value of `count` does not exceed n.
   (*a*)   Read in one of the numbers in the list. Each number will be represented by the floating-point variable x.
   (*b*)   Add the value of x to the current value of `sum`.
   (*c*)   Increase the value of `count` by 1.
5. Divide the value of `sum` by n to obtain the desired average.
6. Write out the calculated value for the average.

Here is the complete C program. Notice that steps 3 and 4 are combined in the `for` statement, and that steps 3 and 4(*c*) are both carried out in the first line (first and third expressions, respectively). Also, notice that the input operations are all accompanied by prompts that ask the user for the desired information.

```
#include <stdio.h>

/* calculate the average of n numbers */

main()

{
    int n, count;
    float x, average, sum = 0;

    /* initialize and read in a value for n */
    printf("How many numbers? ");
    scanf("%d", &n);

    /* read in the numbers */
    for (count = 1; count <= n; ++count)  {
         printf("x = ");
         scanf("%f", &x);
         sum += x;
    }

    /* calculate the average and write out the answer */
    average = sum/n;
    printf("\nThe average is %f\n", average);
}
```

Comparing this program to the corresponding programs shown in Examples 6.7 and 6.10, we again see a more concise loop specification when the for statement is used rather than while or do - while. Now, however, the for statement is somewhat more complex than in the preceding programming examples. In particular, notice that the *statement* part of the loop is now a compound statement. Moreover, we must explicitly assign an initial value to sum before encountering the for statement.

When the program is executed it will generate exactly the same output as the earlier versions presented in Examples 6.7 and 6.10.

6.5 NESTED LOOPS

Loops can be *nested* (i.e., embedded) one within another. The inner and outer loops need not be generated by the same type of control structure. It is essential, however, that one loop be completely embedded within the other—there can be no overlap. Also, each loop must be controlled by a different index.

Example 6.15 Repeated Averaging of a List of Numbers Suppose we want to calculate the average of several consecutive lists of numbers, using nested loops. If we know in advance how many lists are to be averaged, then we can use a for statement to control the number of times that the inner (averaging) loop is executed. The actual averaging can be accomplished using any of the three methods presented earlier in Examples 6.7, 6.10 and 6.14 (using a while, a do - while, or a for statement).

Let us arbitrarily use the for statement to carry out the averaging, as in Example 6.14. Thus, we will proceed in the following manner.

1. Read in a value of loops, an integer quantity that indicates the number of lists that will be averaged.

2. Repeatedly read in a list of numbers and determine its average. That is, calculate the average of a list of numbers for each successive value of loopcount ranging from 1 to loops. Follow the steps given in Example 6.14 to calculate each average.

Here is the actual C program.

```
#include <stdio.h>

/* calculate averages for several different lists of numbers */

main()

{
    int n, count, loops, loopcount;
    float x, average, sum;

    /* read in the number of lists */
    printf("How many lists? ");
    scanf("%d", &loops);

    /* outer loop (process each list of numbers) */
    for (loopcount = 1; loopcount <= loops; ++loopcount)  {

        /* initialize and read in a value for n */
        sum = 0;
        printf("\nList number %d\nHow many numbers? ", loopcount);
        scanf("%d", &n);

        /* read in the numbers */
        for (count = 1; count <= n; ++count)  {
            printf("x = ");
            scanf("%f", &x);
            sum += x;
        }   /* end inner loop */

        /* calculate the average and write out the answer */
        average = sum/n;
        printf("\nThe average is %f\n", average);

    }   /* end outer loop */
}
```

This program contains several interesting features. First, notice that it contains two for statements, one embedded within the other. Each for statement includes a compound statement, composed of several individual statements enclosed in braces. Also, a different index is used in each for statement (the indices are loopcount and count, respectively).

Note that sum must now be initialized within the outer loop, rather than within the declaration. This allows sum to be reset to zero each time a new set of data is encountered (i.e., at the beginning of each pass through the outer loop).

The data input operations are all accompanied by prompts, indicating to the user what data are required. Thus, we see pairs of printf and scanf functions at several places throughout the program. Two of the printf functions contain multiple newline characters to control the line spacing of the output. This causes the output associated with each set of data (each pass through the outer loop) to be easily identified.

Finally, notice that the program is organized into separate identifiable segments, with each segment preceded by a blank space and a comment.

When the program is executed using three simple sets of data, the following dialog is generated. As usual, the user's responses to the input prompts have been underlined.

```
How many lists? 3

List number 1
How many numbers? 4
x = 1.5
x = 2.5
x = 6.2
x = 3.0

The average is 3.300000

List number 2
How many numbers? 3
x = 4
x = -2
x = 7

The average is 3.000000

List number 3
How many numbers? 5
x = 5.4
x = 8.0
x = 2.2
x = 1.7
x = -3.9

The average is 2.680000
```

Example 6.16 Converting Several Lines of Text to Uppercase This example illustrates the use of two different types of loops, with one nested within the other. Let us extend the lowercase to uppercase conversion programs presented in Examples 6.6, 6.9 and 6.13 so that multiple lines of lowercase text can be converted to uppercase, with the conversion taking place one line at a time. In other words, we will read in a line of lowercase text, display it in uppercase, then process another line, and so on. The procedure will continue until a line is detected in which the first character is an asterisk.

We will use nested loops to carry out the computation. The outer loop will be used to process multiple lines of text. Two separate inner loops will be embedded within the outer loop. The first will read in a line of text, and the second will display the converted uppercase text. Note that these inner loops are not nested. Let us arbitrarily utilize a while statement for the outer loop and a for statement for each of the inner loops.

In general terms, the computation will proceed as follows:

1. Assign an initial value of 1 to the outer loop index (linecount).

2. Carry out the following steps repeatedly, for each successive line of text, as long as the first character in the line is not an asterisk.
   (a) Read in a line of text and assign the individual characters to the elements of the char-type array letter. A line will be defined as a succession of characters terminated by an end-of-line (newline) designation.
   (b) Assign the character count (including the end-of-line character) to tag.
   (c) Write out the line in uppercase, using the library function toupper to carry out the conversion. Then write out two newline characters so that the next line of input will be separated from the current output by a blank line, and increment the line counter (linecount).

3. Once an asterisk has been detected as the first character of a new line, write out "Good bye." and terminate the computation.

Here is the complete C program.

```
#include ⟨stdio.h⟩

#define EOL '\n'

/* convert several lines of text to upper-case

   continue conversion until the first character
   in a line is an asterisk (*)                          */

main()

{
    char letter[80];
    int tag, count, linecount = 1;

    while((letter[0] = getchar()) != '*')    {

        /* read in a line of text */
        for (count = 1; (letter[count] = getchar()) != EOL; ++count)
            ;
        tag = count;

        /* write out the line of text */
        for (count = 0; count < tag; ++count)
            putchar(toupper(letter[count]));
        printf("\n\n");
        ++linecount;
    }    /* end outer loop */

    printf("Good bye.");
}
```

A typical interactive session, illustrating the execution of the program, is shown below. Note that the input text supplied by the user is underlined, as usual.

```
Now is the time for all good men to come to the aid ...
NOW IS THE TIME FOR ALL GOOD MEN TO COME TO THE AID ...

Fourscore and seven years ago our fathers brought forth ...
FOURSCORE AND SEVEN YEARS AGO OUR FATHERS BROUGHT FORTH ...

*
Good bye.
```

It should be understood that the decision to use a `while` statement for the outer loop and `for` statements for the inner loops is arbitrary. Other loop structures could also have been selected.

6.6   THE if-else STATEMENT

The `if - else` statement is used to carry out a logical test and then take one of two possible actions, depending on the outcome of the test (i.e., whether the outcome is true or false).

The `else` portion of the `if - else` statement is optional. Thus, in its simplest general form, the statement can be written

```
if (expression) statement
```

The *expression* must be placed in parentheses, as shown. In this form, the *statement* will be executed only if the *expression* has a nonzero value (i.e., if *expression* is true). If the *expression* has a value of zero (i.e., if *expression* is false), then the *statement* will be ignored.

The *statement* can be either simple or compound. In practice, it is often a compound statement which may include other control statements.

Example 6.17 Several representative if statements are shown below.

```
if (x < 0) printf("%f", x);

if (flag != 0)  {
    printf("account number: %d", accountno);
    credit = 0;
}


if (flag)
    for (digit = 0; digit <= 9; ++digit)
       printf("%d\n", digit);


if ((balance < 1000.) || (status == 'R'))
    printf("%f", balance);
```

The first statement causes the value of the floating-point variable x to be printed (displayed) if its value is negative. The second statement contains a compound statement that is executed if flag has a nonzero value. Notice that the second and third statements make use of the same logical expression, though the expression is written more concisely in the third statement. Also, notice that the third if statement contains another control statement (i.e., for). And finally, notice the last statement, which makes use of a more complex logical expression.

The general form of an if statement which includes the else clause is

```
if (expression) statement 1 else statement 2
```

If the *expression* has a nonzero value (i.e., if *expression* is true), then *statement 1* will be executed. Otherwise (i.e., if *expression* is false), *statement 2* will be executed.

Example 6.18 Here are several examples illustrating the full if - else statement.

```
if (status == 'S') tax = 0.20 * pay;
else tax = 0.14 * pay;


if (flag) {
    printf("account number: %d", accountno);
    credit = 0;
}
else
    credit = 1000.0;

if (circle) {
    scanf("%f", &radius);
    area = 3.14159 * radius * radius;
    printf("Area of circle = %f", area);
}
else {
    scanf("%f %f", &length, &width);
    area = length * width;
    printf("Area of rectangle = %f", area);
}
```

In the first example the value of tax is determined in one of two possible ways, depending on the character that has been assigned to the variable status. Notice the semicolon at the end of each statement, particularly the first statement (tax = 0.2 * pay;).

This statement can be written with more indentation, as

```
if (status == 'S')
    tax = 0.20 * pay;
else
    tax = 0.14 * pay;
```

A more concise way to accomplish the same thing is to write

```
tax = (status == 'S') ? (0.20 * pay) : (0.14 * pay);
```

though this approach is much more cryptic.

The second example looks for certain "flagged" accounts. If an account is flagged (i.e., if flag has a nonzero value), then the account number is displayed and the credit limit is set at zero; otherwise, the credit limit is set at 1000.0.

The third example shows how an area can be calculated for either of two different geometric figures. If circle is assigned a nonzero value, then the radius of a circle is read into the computer and the area is calculated and then displayed. If the value of circle is zero, however, then the length and width of a rectangle are read into the computer and the area is calculated and then displayed. In each case, the type of geometric figure is included in the label that accompanies the value of the area.

It is possible to nest if - else statements within one another, just as we did with loops. There are several different forms that nested if - else statements can take. The most general form of two-layer nesting is

```
if e1 if e2 s1
        else s2
else   if e3 s3
        else s4
```

where e1, e2 and e3 represent expressions, and s1, s2, s3 and s4 represent statements. In this situation, one complete if - else statement will be executed if e1 is nonzero (true), and another complete if - else statement will be executed if e1 is zero (false). It is, of course, possible that s1, s2, s3 and s4 will contain other if - else statements. We would then have multilayer nesting.

Some other forms of two-layer nesting are

```
if e1 s1
else if e2 s2
```

```
if e1 s1
else if e2 s2
        else s3
```

```
if e1 if e2 s1
        else s2
else s3
```

```
if e1 if e2 s1
        else s2
```

In the first three cases the association between the else clauses and their corresponding expressions is straightforward. In the last case, however, it is not clear which expression (e1 or e2) is associated with the else clause. The answer is e2. The rule is that the else clause is always associated with the closest preceding unmatched (i.e., else-less) if. This is suggested by the indentation, though the indentation itself is not the deciding factor. Thus, the last example is equivalent to

```
if e1  {
   if e2 s1 else s2
}
```

If we wanted to associate the else clause with *e1* rather than *e2*, we could do so by writing

```
if e1  {
   if e2 s1
}
else s2
```

This type of nesting must be carried out carefully in order to avoid possible ambiguities.

When an expression is encountered whose value is nonzero (true) within a group of nested if - else statements, the corresponding statement will be executed and the remainder of the nested if - else statements will be bypassed. Thus, control will be transferred out of the entire nest once a true condition is encountered.

Example 6.19 Encoding a String of Characters Let us write a simple C program that will read in a sequence of ASCII characters and write out a sequence of encoded characters in its place. If a character is a letter or a digit, we will replace it with the next character in the character set, except that Z will be replaced by A, z by a, and 9 by 0. Thus, 1 becomes 2, C becomes D, p becomes q, and so on. Any character other than a letter or a digit will be replaced by a period (.).

The computation will begin by reading in the characters. The scanf function will be used for this purpose. All the characters, up to, but not including, the newline (\n) character used to terminate the input, will be entered and stored in an 80-element, character-type array called line.

The characters will then be encoded and displayed individually within a for loop. The loop will process each of the characters in line, until the escape character \0, which designates the end of the character sequence, is encountered. (Recall that the escape sequence \0 is automatically added at the end of each string.) Several nested if - else statements will be included within the loop to carry out the appropriate encoding. Each encoded character will then be displayed using the putchar function.

The complete C program is shown below.

```
#include <stdio.h>

/* read in a string, then replace each character
                  with an equivalent encoded character */

main()

{
    char line[80];
    int count;

    /* read in the entire string */

    printf("Enter a line of text below:\n");
    scanf("%[^\n]", line);

    /* encode each individual character and write it out */

    for (count = 0; line[count] != '\0'; ++count)  {
          if (((line[count] >= '0') && (line[count] < '9')) ||
              ((line[count] >= 'A') && (line[count] < 'Z')) ||
              ((line[count] >= 'a') && (line[count] < 'z')))
                    putchar(line[count] + 1);
          else if (line[count] == '9') putchar('0');
              else if (line[count] == 'Z') putchar('A');
                  else if (line[count] == 'z') putchar('a');
                      else putchar('.');
    }

}
```

Execution of this program generates the following representative dialog. The input provided by the user is again underlined.

```
Enter a line of text below:
The White House, 1600 Pennsylvania Avenue, Washington, DC
Uif.Xijuf.Ipvtf..2711.Qfootzmwbojb.Bwfovf..Xbtijohupo..ED
```

Example 6.20   Repeated Compound Interest Calculations with Error Trapping   In Example 5.2 we saw a complete C program to carry out simple compound interest calculations, as outlined in Example 5.1. However, this program does not allow for repetitive execution (i.e., for several successive calculations, using different input data for each calculation), nor does it attempt to detect errors in the input data. Let us now add these features to the earlier program.

In particular, let us embed the earlier calculations within a `while` statement, which will continue to execute as long as the value entered for the principal (P) is positive. Thus, a zero value for P will be interpreted as a stopping condition. We will include a message explaining the stopping condition when prompting for the value of P.

In addition, let us test the value of each input quantity to determine if it is negative, since a negative value would not make any sense and should be interpreted as an error. Each test will be carried out with a separate `if` statement. If an error (i.e., a negative value) is detected, a message will be written asking the user to reenter the data.

Here is the entire C program.

```c
#include <stdio.h>
#include <math.h>

/* simple compound interest problem */

main()

{
   float p,r,n,i,f;

   /* read initial value for the principal */

   printf("Please enter a value for the principal (P) ");
   printf("\n(To end program, enter 0 for the principal): ");
   scanf("%f", &p);
   if (p < 0)   {
      printf("\nERROR - Please try again: ");
      scanf("%f", &p);
   }

   while (p > 0)  {     /* main loop */

      /* read remaining input data */

      printf("\nPlease enter a value for the interest rate (r): ");
      scanf("%f", &r);
      if (r < 0)   {
         printf("\nERROR - Please try again: ");
         scanf("%f", &r);
      }
      printf("\nPlease enter a value for the number of years (n): ");
      scanf("%f", &n);
      if (n < 0)   {
         printf("\nERROR - Please try again: ");
         scanf("%f", &n);
      }
```

```
    /* calculate i, then f */

    i = r/100;
    f = p * pow((1 + i),n);

    /* write output */

    printf("\nThe final value (F) is: %.2f\n", f);

    /* read principal for next pass */

    printf("\n\nPlease enter a value for the principal (P) ");
    printf("\n(To end program, enter 0 for the principal): ");
    scanf("%f", &p);
    if (p < 0)    {
        printf("\nERROR - Please try again: ");
        scanf("%f", &p);
    }
  }
}
```

A typical interactive session is shown below. Note that the user's responses are underlined.

```
Please enter a value for the principal (P)
(To end program, enter 0 for the principal): 1000

Please enter a value for the interest rate (r): 6

Please enter a value for the number of years (n): 20

The final value (F) is: 3207.14


Please enter a value for the principal (P)
(To end program, enter 0 for the principal): 5000

Please enter a value for the interest rate (r): -7.5

ERROR - Please try again: 7.5

Please enter a value for the number of years (n): 12

The final value (F) is: 11908.90


Please enter a value for the principal (P)
(To end program, enter 0 for the principal): 0
```

Notice that two sets of input data are provided. The first set of data is entered correctly, resulting in a calculated future value of 3207.14 (as in Example 5.3). In the second data set, a negative value is initially supplied for the interest rate (r). This is detected as an error, resulting in an error message and a request for another value. Once the corrected value is supplied, the remaining program execution proceeds as expected.

After the second data set has been processed, the user enters a value of 0 for the principal, in response to the prompt. This causes the execution of the program to terminate.

It should be understood that the error trapping used in this program applies only to negative floating-point quantities entered as input data. Another type of error occurs if a letter or punctuation mark is entered for one of the required input quantities. This will produce a type mismatch in the scanf function, resulting in an input error. Individual compilers deal with this type of error differently, thus preventing a simple, general error trap.

Example 6.21   Solution of an Algebraic Equation   For the more mathematically inclined reader, this example illustrates how computers can be used to solve algebraic equations, including those that cannot be solved by more direct methods. Consider, for example, the equation

$$x^5 + 3x^2 - 10 = 0$$

This equation cannot be arranged to yield an exact solution for x. However, we can determine the solution by a repeated trial-and-error procedure (called an *iterative* procedure) that successively refines an initially crude guess.

We begin by rearranging the equation into the form

$$x = (10 - 3x^2)^{1/5}$$

Our procedure will then be to guess a value for x, substitute this value into the righthand side of the rearranged equation, and thus calculate a new value for x. If this new value is equal (or very nearly equal) to the old value, then we will have obtained a solution to the equation. Otherwise, this new value will be substituted into the righthand side and still another value obtained for x, and so on. This procedure will continue until either the successive values of x have become sufficiently close (i.e., until the computation has *converged*), or until a specified number of iterations has been exceeded. This last condition prevents the computation from continuing indefinitely in the event that the computed results do not converge.

To see how the method works, suppose we choose an initial value of $x = 1.0$. Substituting this value into the righthand side of the equation, we obtain

$$x = \lceil 10 - 3(1.0)^2 \rceil^{0.2} = 1.47577$$

We then substitute this new value of x into the equation, resulting in

$$x = [10 - 3(1.47577)^2]^{0.2} = 1.28225$$

Continuing this procedure, we obtain

$$x = [10 - 3(1.28225)^2]^{0.2} = 1.38344$$
$$x = [10 - 3(1.38344)^2]^{0.2} = 1.33613$$

and so on. Notice that the successive values of x appear to be converging to some final answer.

The success of the method depends on the value chosen for the initial guess. If this value is too large in magnitude, then the quantity in brackets will be negative, and a negative value cannot be raised to a fractional power. Therefore, we should test for a negative value of $10 - 3x^2$ whenever we substitute a new value of x into the righthand side.

In order to write a program outline, let us define the following symbols.

count	= an iteration counter (count will increase by 1 at each successive iteration)
guess	= the value of x substituted into the righthand side of the equation
root	= the newly calculated value of x
test	= the quantity $(10 - 3x^2)$
error	= the absolute difference between root and guess
flag	= an integer variable that signifies whether or not to continue the iteration

We will continue the computation until one of the following conditions is satisfied.

1.   The value of error becomes less than 0.00001, in which case we have obtained a satisfactory solution.

2.   Fifty iterations have been completed (i.e., count = 50).

3.   The variable test takes on a negative value, in which case the computation cannot be continued.

Let us monitor the progress of the computation by writing out each successive value of root.

We can now write the following program outline:

1.   For convenience, define the symbolic constants TRUE and FALSE.

2. Declare all variables, and initialize the integer variables `flag` and `count` (assign TRUE to `flag` and 0 to `count`).

3. Read in a value for the initial `guess`.

4. Carry out the following looping procedure, while `flag` remains TRUE.

   (*a*) Increase the value of `count` by 1.

   (*b*) Assign FALSE to `flag` if the new value of `count` equals 50. This will signify the last pass through the loop.

   (*c*) Examine the value of `test`. If its value is positive, proceed as follows:

      (*i*) Calculate a new value for `root`; then write out the current value for `count`, followed by the current value for `root`.

      (*ii*) Evaluate `error`, which is the absolute value of the differences between `root` and `guess`. If this value is greater than 0.00001, assign the current value of `root` to `guess` and proceed with another iteration. Otherwise write out the current values of `root` and `count`, and set `flag` to FALSE. The current value of `root` will be considered to be the desired solution.

   (*d*) If the current value of `test` is not positive, then the computation cannot proceed. Hence, write an appropriate error message (e.g., "numbers out of range") and set `flag` to FALSE.

5. Upon completion of step 4, write an appropriate error message (e.g., "Convergence not obtained") if `count` has a value of 50 and the value of `error` is greater than 0.00001.

Now let use express the program outline in the form of pseudocode in order to simplify the transition from a general outline to a working C program.

```
#include files

#define symbolic constants

main()

{
    /* variable declarations and initialization */

    /* read input parameters */

    while (flag)  {

        /* increment count */

        /* flag becomes FALSE if count = 50 */

        /* evaluate test */

        if (test > 0)  {

            /* evaluate root */

            /* display count and loop */

            /* evaluate error */

            if (error > 0.00001) guess = root;
            else  {

                /* flag becomes FALSE */

                /* display the final answer (root and count)*/
            }
        }
```

```
            else  {

                /* flag becomes FALSE */

                /* numbers out of range — write error message */
            }
    }      /* end while */

    if ((count == 50) && (error > 0.00001))

        /* convergence not obtained — write error message */
}
```

Here is the complete C program.

```
#include <stdio.h>
#include <math.h>

#define TRUE 1
#define FALSE 0

/* determine the roots of an algebraic equation using an iterative procedure */

main()

{

    int flag = TRUE, count = 0;
    float guess, root, test, error;

    /* read input parameters */

    printf("Initial guess: ");
    scanf("%f", &guess);
    while (flag)  {                              /* begin the main loop */
        ++count;
        if (count == 50) flag = FALSE;
        test = 10. - 3. * guess * guess;
        if (test > 0)  {                         /* another iteration */
            root = exp(0.2 * log(test));
            printf("\nIteration number: %2d", count);
            printf("    x= %7.5f", root);
            error = fabs(root - guess);
            if (error > 0.00001) guess = root;   /* repeat the calculation */
            else {                               /* write the final answer */
                flag = FALSE;
                printf("\n\nRoot= %7.5f", root);
                printf("    No. of iterations= %2d", count);
            }
        }
        else {                                   /* error message */
            flag = FALSE;
            printf("\nNumbers out of range — try another initial guess");
        }
    }
    if ((count == 50) && (error > 0.00001))      /* another error message */
        printf("\n\nConvergence not obtained after 50 iterations");
}
```

Notice that the program contains a while statement and several if - else statements. A for statement could easily have been used instead of the while statement. Also, notice the nested if - else statements near the middle of the program.

The statement

```
root = exp(0.2 * log(test));
```

is used to raise the value of test to the 0.2 power, since C does not include an exponentiation operator. Thus, we perform the required exponentiation by obtaining the natural log of test, multiplying by 0.2, and then raising e to a power equal to the resulting product. The functions exp and log, which are used to carry out the exponentiation, are provided in the system library. The corresponding header file math.h is accessed at the beginning of the program. (We could also have used the pow function, as in Example 6.20.)

The output that is generated for an initial guess of $x = 1$ is shown below, with the user's response underlined. Notice that the computation has converged to the solution $x = 1.35195$ after 16 iterations. The printed output shows the successive values of x becoming closer and closer, leading to the final solution.

```
Initial guess: 1

Iteration number:    1      x= 1.47577
Iteration number:    2      x= 1.28225
Iteration number:    3      x= 1.38344
Iteration number:    4      x= 1.33613
Iteration number:    5      x= 1.35951
Iteration number:    6      x= 1.34826
Iteration number:    7      x= 1.35375
Iteration number:    8      x= 1.35109
Iteration number:    9      x= 1.35238
Iteration number:   10      x= 1.35175
Iteration number:   11      x= 1.35206
Iteration number:   12      x= 1.35191
Iteration number:   13      x= 1.35198
Iteration number:   14      x= 1.35196
Iteration number:   15      x= 1.35196
Iteration number:   16      x= 1.35195

Root= 1.35195    No. of iterations= 16
```

Now suppose that a value of $x = 10$ has been selected as an initial guess. This value generates a negative number for test in the first iteration. Therefore the output would appear as follows.

```
Initial guess: 10
Numbers out of range — try another initial guess
```

It is interesting to see what happens when the initial guess is once again chosen as $x = 1$, but the maximum number of iterations is changed from 50 to 10. Try this and observe the result.

It should be mentioned that there are many other iterative methods for solving algebraic equations. Most converge faster than the method described above (i.e., they require fewer iterations to obtain a solution), though the mathematics is more involved.

In some situations it may be desirable to nest multiple if - else statements in order to create a situation in which one of several different courses of action will be selected. For example, the general form of four nested if - else statements could be written as

```
if e1 s1
else if e2 s2
    else if e3 s3
        else if e4 s4
            else s5
```

The final else clause will apply if none of the expressions is true. It can be used to provide a default condition or an error message.

Example 6.22   Here is an illustration of three nested if - else statements.

```
if ((time >= Ø.) && (time < 12.)) printf ("Good Morning");
else if ((time >= 12.) && (time < 18.)) printf("Good Afternoon");
    else if ((time >= 18.) && (time < 24.)) printf("Good Evening");
        else printf("Time is out of range");
```

This example causes a different message to be displayed at different times of the day. Specifically, the message Good Morning will be displayed if time has a value between 0 and 12; Good Afternoon will be displayed if time has a value between 12 and 18; and Good Evening will be displayed if time has a value between 18 and 24. An error message ("Time is out of range") will be displayed if the value of time is less than zero, or greater than or equal to 24.

6.7   THE switch STATEMENT

The switch statement causes a particular group of statements to be chosen from several available groups. The selection is based upon the current value of an expression that is included within the switch statement.
   The general form of the switch statement is

```
switch (expression) statement
```

where *expression* results in an integer value. Note that *expression* may also be of type char, since individual characters have equivalent integer values.
   The embedded *statement* is generally a compound statement that specifies alternate courses of action. Each alternative is expressed as a group of one or more individual statements within the overall embedded *statement*.
   For each alternative, the first statement within the group must be preceded by one or more *case labels* (also called *case prefixes*). The case labels identify the different groups of statements (i.e., the different alternatives) and distinguish them from one another. The case labels must therefore be unique within a given switch statement.
   In general terms, each group of statements is written as

```
case expression :
    statement 1
    statement 2
        :
    statement n
```

or, in the case of multiple case labels,

```
case expression 1 :
case expression 2 :
    :
case expression m :
    statement 1
    statement 2
        :
    statement n
```

where *expression 1*, *expression 2*, ..., *expression m* represent constant, integer-valued expressions. Usually, each of these expressions will be written as either an integer constant or a character constant. Each individual *statement* following the case labels may be either simple or complex.

When the `switch` statement is executed, the *expression* is evaluated and control is transferred directly to the group of statements whose case-label value matches the value of the *expression*. If none of the case-label values matches the value of the *expression*, then none of the groups within the `switch` statement will be selected. In this case control is transferred directly to the statement that follows the `switch` statement.

Example 6.23   A simple `switch` statement is illustrated below. In this example, `choice` is assumed to be a char-type variable.

```
switch (choice = getchar())  {

case 'r':
case 'R':
     printf("RED");
     break;

case 'w':
case 'W':
     prinf("WHITE");
     break;

case 'b':
case 'B':
     printf("BLUE");
}
```

Thus, RED will be displayed if `choice` represents either r or R, WHITE will be displayed if `choice` represents either w or W, and BLUE will be displayed if `choice` represents either b or B. Nothing will be displayed if any other character has been assigned to `choice`.

Notice that each group of statements has two case labels, to account for either upper- or lowercase. Also, note that each of the first two groups ends with the `break` statement (see Sec. 6.8). The `break` statement causes control to be transferred out of the `switch` statement, thus preventing more than one group of statements from being executed.

One of the labeled groups of statements within the `switch` statement may be labeled `default`. This group will be selected if none of the case labels matches the value of the `expression`. (This is a convenient way to generate error messages or error correction routines.) The `default` group may appear anywhere within the `switch` statement—it need not necessarily be placed at the end. If none of the case labels matches the value of the `expression` and the `default` group is not present (as in the above example), then the `switch` statement will take no action.

Example 6.24   Here is a variation of the `switch` statement presented in Example 6.23.

```
switch (choice = toupper(getchar()))  {

case 'R':
     printf("RED");
     break;

case 'W':
     printf("WHITE");
     break;

case 'B':
     printf("BLUE");
     break;

default:
     printf("ERROR");
}
```

The switch statement now contains a default group (consisting of only one statement) which generates an error message if none of the case labels matches the original *expression*.

Each of the first three groups of statements now has only one case label. Multiple case labels are not necessary in this example, since the library function toupper causes all incoming characters to be converted to uppercase. Hence, choice will always be assigned an uppercase character.

Example 6.25 Here is another typical switch statement. In this example flag is assumed to be an integer variable, and x and y are assumed to be floating-point variables.

```
switch (flag)  {

case -1:
     y = fabs(x);
     break;

case 0:
     y = sqrt(x);
     break;

case 1:
     y = x;
     break;

case 2:
case 3:
     y = 2 * (x - 1);
     break;

default:
     y = 0;
}
```

In this example y will be assigned some value related to the value of x if flag equals −1, 0, 1, 2 or 3. The exact relationship between y and x will depend upon the particular value of flag. If flag represents some other value, however, then y will be assigned a value of 0.

Notice that the case labels are numeric in this example. Also, note that the fourth group of statements has two case labels, whereas each of the other groups has only one case label. And finally, notice that a default group (consisting of only one statement) is included within this switch statement.

In a practical sense, the switch statement may be thought of as an alternative to the use of nested if - else statements, though it can only replace those if - else statements that test for equality. In such situations, using the switch statement is generally much more convenient.

Example 6.26 Calculating Depreciation Let us consider how to calculate the yearly depreciation for some depreciable item, such as a building or a machine. There are three commonly used methods for calculating depreciation, known as the *straight-line* method, the *double-declining-balance* method, and the *sum-of-the-years'-digits* method. We wish to write a C program that will allow us to select any one of these methods for each set of calculations.

The computation will begin by reading in the original (undepreciated) value of the item, the life of the item (i.e., the number of years over which it will be depreciated) and an integer that indicates which method will be used. The yearly depreciation and the remaining (undepreciated) value of the item will then be calculated and written out for each year.

The *straight-line* method is the easiest to use. In this method the original value of the item is divided by its life (total number of years). The resulting quotient will be the amount by which the item depreciates each year. For example, if an $8000 item is to be depreciated over 10 years, then the annual depreciation would be $8000/10 = $800. Therefore, the value of the item would decrease by $800 each year. Notice that the annual depreciation is the same each year when using straight-line depreciation.

When using the *double-declining-balance* method, the value of the item will decrease by a constant *percentage* each year. Hence the *actual amount* of the depreciation, in dollars, will vary from one year to the next. To obtain the depreciation factor, we divide 2 by the life of the item. This factor is multiplied by the value of the item at the beginning of each year (*not the original* value of the item) to obtain the annual depreciation.

Suppose, for example, that we wish to depreciate an $8000 item over 10 years, using the double-declining-balance method. The depreciation factor will be 2/10 = 0.20. Hence, the depreciation for the first year will be 0.20 × $8000 = $1600. The second year's depreciation will be 0.20 × ($8000 − $1600) = 0.20 × $6400 = $1280; the third year's depreciation will be 0.20 × $5120 = $1024, and so on.

In the *sum-of-the-years'-digits* method, the value of the item will decrease by a percentage that is different each year. The depreciation factor will be a fraction whose denominator is the sum of the digits from 1 to n, where n represents the life of the item. If, for example, we consider a 10-year lifetime, the denominator will be $1 + 2 + 3 + \cdots + 10 = 55$. For the first year the numerator will be n, for the second year it will be $(n - 1)$, for the third year $(n - 2)$, and so on. The yearly depreciation is obtained by multiplying the depreciation factor by the *original* value of the item.

To see how the sum-of-the-years'-digits method works, we again depreciate an $8000 item over 10 years. The depreciation for the first year will be (10/55) × $8000 = $1454.55; for the second year it will be (9/55) × $8000 = $1309.09, and so on.

Now let us define the following symbols, so that we can write the actual program.

`val`	= the current value of the item
`tag`	= the original value of the item (i.e., the original value of `val`)
`deprec`	= the annual depreciation
`n`	= the number of years over which the item will be depreciated
`year`	= a counter ranging from 1 to n
`choice`	= an integer indicating which method to use

Our C program will follow the outline presented below.

1. Declare all variables, and initialize the integer variable `choice` to 0 (actually, we can assign any value other than 4 to `choice`).
2. Repeat all the following steps as long as the value of `choice` is not equal to 4. Use a `while` loop for this purpose.
    (*a*) Read a value for `choice` which indicates the type of calculation to be carried out. This value can only be 1, 2, 3 or 4. (Any other value will be an error.)
    (*b*) If `choice` is assigned a value of 1, 2 or 3, read values for `val` and `n`.
    (*c*) Depending on the value assigned to `choice`, branch to the appropriate part of the program and carry out the indicated calculations. In particular,
       (*i*)   If `choice` is assigned a value of 1, 2 or 3, calculate the yearly depreciation and the new value of the item year-by-year, using the appropriate method indicated by the value of `choice`. Print out the results as they are calculated, year-by-year.
       (*ii*) If `choice` is assigned a value of 4, write out a "goodbye" message and end the computation by terminating the `while` loop.
       (*iii*) If `choice` is assigned any value other than 1, 2, 3 or 4, write out an error message and begin another pass through the `while` loop.

Now let's express this outline in pseudocode.

```
#include files

main()

{

    /* variable declarations and initialization */

    while (choice != 4)  {

        /* generate menu and read choice */

        if  (choice >= 1 && choice <= 3)

            /* read val and n */

        switch (choice)  {

        case  1:     /* straight-line method */

            /* write out title */

            /* calculate depreciation */

            /* for each year:
                calculate a new value
                write out year, depreciation, value */

        case  2:     /* double-declining-balance method */

            /* write out title */

            /* for each year:
                calculate depreciation
                calculate a new value
                write out year, depreciation, value */

        case  3:     /* sum-of-the-years'-digits method */

            /* write out title */

            /* tag original value */

            /* for each year:
                calculate depreciation
                calculate a new value
                write out year, depreciation, value */

        case  4:     /* end of computation */

            /* write "goodbye" message */

            /* write out title */

        default:     /* generate error message */

            /* write error message */
        }
    }
}
```

Most of the pseudocode is straightforward, though a few comments are in order. First, we see that a `while` statement is used to repeat the entire set of calculations. Within this overall loop, the `switch` statement is used to select a particular depreciation method. Each depreciation method uses a `for` statement to carry out the required calculations.

At this point it is not difficult to write a complete C program, as shown below.

```c
#include <stdio.h>

/* calculate depreciation using one of three different methods */

main()

{
    int n, year, choice = 0;
    float val, tag, deprec;

    while (choice != 4)  {
        /* read input data */

        printf("\nMethod: (1-SL  2-DDB  3-SYD  4-End) ");
        scanf("%d", &choice);
        if (choice >= 1 && choice <= 3)  {
            printf("Original value: ");
            scanf("%f", &val);
            printf("Number of years: ");
            scanf("%d", &n);
        }

        switch (choice)  {

        case 1:     /* straight-line method */

            printf("\nStraight-Line Method\n\n");
            deprec = val/n;
            for (year = 1; year <= n; ++year)  {
                val -= deprec;
                printf("End of Year %2d", year);
                printf("  Depreciation: %7.2f", deprec);
                printf("  Current Value: %8.2f\n", val);
            }
            break;

        case 2:     /* double-declining-balance method */

            printf("\nDouble-Declining-Balance Method\n\n");
            for (year = 1; year <= n; ++year)  {
                deprec = 2*val/n;
                val -= deprec;
                printf("End of Year %2d", year);
                printf("  Depreciation: %7.2f", deprec);
                printf("  Current Value: %8.2f\n", val);
            }
            break;

        case 3:     /* sum-of-the-years'-digits method */

            printf("\nSum-of-the-Years\'-Digits Method\n\n");
            tag = val;
```

```
                    for (year = 1; year <= n; ++year)  {
                        deprec = (n-year+1)*tag / (n*(n+1)/2);
                        val -= deprec;
                        printf("End of Year %2d", year);
                        printf("  Depreciation: %7.2f", deprec);
                        printf("  Current Value: %8.2f\n", val);
                    }
                    break;

            case 4:    /* end of computation */

                    printf("\nGoodbye, have a nice day!\n");
                    break;

            default:    /* generate error message */

                    printf("\nIncorrect data entry - please try again\n");
            }
        }
}
```

The calculation of the depreciation for the sum-of-the-years'-digits method may be somewhat obscure. In particular, the term (n-year+1) in the numerator requires some explanation. This quantity is used to count *backward* (from n down to 1) as year progresses *forward* (from 1 to n). These declining values are required by the sum-of-the-years'-digits method. We could, of course, have set up a backward-counting loop instead, that is,

```
for (year = n; year >= 1; --year)
```

but then we would have required a corresponding forward-counting loop to write out the results of the calculations on a yearly basis. Also, the term (n*(n+1)/2) which appears in the denominator is a formula for the sum of the first n digits, i.e., $1 + 2 + \cdots + n$.

The program is designed to be run interactively, with prompts for the required input data. Notice that the program generates a "menu" with four choices, to calculate the depreciation using one of the three methods or to end the computation. The computer will continue to accept new sets of input data, and carry out the appropriate calculations for each data set, until a value of 4 is selected from the menu. The program automatically generates an error message and returns to the menu if some value other than 1, 2, 3 or 4 is entered in response to the menu request.

Some representative output is shown below. In each case, an $8000 item is depreciated over a 10-year period, using one of the three methods. The error message generated by an incorrect data entry is also illustrated. Finally, the computation is terminated in response to the last menu selection.

```
Method: (1-SL  2-DDB  3-SYD  4-End) 1
Original value: 8000
Number of years: 10

Straight-Line Method

End of Year  1  Depreciation:  800.00  Current Value:  7200.00
End of Year  2  Depreciation:  800.00  Current Value:  6400.00
End of Year  3  Depreciation:  800.00  Current Value:  5600.00
End of Year  4  Depreciation:  800.00  Current Value:  4800.00
End of Year  5  Depreciation:  800.00  Current Value:  4000.00
End of Year  6  Depreciation:  800.00  Current Value:  3200.00
End of Year  7  Depreciation:  800.00  Current Value:  2400.00
End of Year  8  Depreciation:  800.00  Current Value:  1600.00
End of Year  9  Depreciation:  800.00  Current Value:   800.00
End of Year 10  Depreciation:  800.00  Current Value:     0.00

Method: (1-SL  2-DDB  3-SYD  4-End) 2
Original value: 8000
Number of years: 10
```

```
Double-Declining-Balance Method

End of Year  1  Depreciation:  1600.00  Current Value:  6400.00
End of Year  2  Depreciation:  1280.00  Current Value:  5120.00
End of Year  3  Depreciation:  1024.00  Current Value:  4096.00
End of Year  4  Depreciation:   819.20  Current Value:  3276.80
End of Year  5  Depreciation:   655.36  Current Value:  2621.44
End of Year  6  Depreciation:   524.29  Current Value:  2097.15
End of Year  7  Depreciation:   419.43  Current Value:  1677.72
End of Year  8  Depreciation:   335.54  Current Value:  1342.18
End of Year  9  Depreciation:   268.44  Current Value:  1073.74
End of Year 10  Depreciation:   214.75  Current Value:   858.99

Method: (1-SL  2-DDB  3-SYD  4-End) 3
Original value: 8000
Number of years: 10

Sum-of-the-Years'-Digits Method

End of Year  1  Depreciation:  1454.55  Current Value:  6545.45
End of Year  2  Depreciation:  1309.09  Current Value:  5236.36
End of Year  3  Depreciation:  1163.64  Current Value:  4072.73
End of Year  4  Depreciation:  1018.18  Current Value:  3054.55
End of Year  5  Depreciation:   872.73  Current Value:  2181.82
End of Year  6  Depreciation:   727.27  Current Value:  1454.55
End of Year  7  Depreciation:   581.82  Current Value:   872.73
End of Year  8  Depreciation:   436.36  Current Value:   436.36
End of Year  9  Depreciation:   290.91  Current Value:   145.45
End of Year 10  Depreciation:   145.45  Current Value:     0.00

Method: (1-SL  2-DDB  3-SYD  4-End) 5

Incorrect data entry — please try again

Method: (1-SL  2-DDB  3-SYD  4-End) 4

Goodbye, have a nice day!
```

Notice that the double-declining-balance method and the sum-of-the-years'-digits method result in a large annual depreciation during the early years but a very small annual depreciation in the last few years of the item's lifetime. Also, we see that the item has a value of zero at the end of its lifetime when using the straight-line method and the sum-of-the-years'-digits method, but a small value remains undepreciated when using the double-declining-balance method.

6.8 THE break STATEMENT

The break statement is used to terminate loops or to exit from a switch. It can be used within a while, a do - while, a for or a switch statement.

The break statement is written simply as

```
break;
```

without any embedded expressions or statements.

We have already seen several examples of the use of the break statement within a switch statement, in Sec. 6.7. The break statement causes a transfer of control out of the entire switch statement, to the first statement following the switch statement.

Example 6.27   Consider once again the switch statement originally presented in Example 6.24.

```
switch (choice = toupper(getchar()))  {

case 'R':
     printf("RED");
     break;

case 'W':
     printf("WHITE");
     break;

case 'B':
     printf("BLUE");
     break;

default:
     printf("ERROR");
     break;
}
```

Notice that each group of statements ends with a `break` statement in order to transfer control out of the `switch` statement. The `break` statement is required within each of the first three groups in order to prevent the succeeding groups of statements from executing. The last group does not require a `break` statement, since control will automatically be transferred out of the `switch` statement after the last group has been executed. This last `break` statement is included, however, as a matter of good programming practice, so that it will be present if another group of statements is added later.

If a `break` statement is included in a `while`, `do` - `while` or `for` loop, then control will immediately be transferred out of the loop when the `break` statement is encountered. This provides a convenient way to terminate the loop if an error or other irregular condition is detected.

Example 6.28 Here are some illustrations of loops that contain `break` statements. In each situation, the loop will continue to execute as long as the current value for the floating-point variable x does not exceed 100. However, the computation will break out of the loop if a negative value for x is detected.

First, consider a `while` loop.

```
scanf("%f", &x);
while (x <= 100)  {
     if (x < 0)      {
        printf("ERROR - NEGATIVE VALUE FOR X");
        break;
     }

     /* process the nonnegative value of x */
       :
     scanf("%f", &x);
}
```

Now consider a `do` - `while` loop which does the same thing.

```
do  {
    scanf("%f", &x);
    if (x < 0)  {
       printf("ERROR - NEGATIVE VALUE FOR X");
       break;
    }

    /* process the nonnegative value of x */
      :
} while (x <= 100);
```

Finally, here is a `for` loop that is similar.

```
for (count = 1; x <= 100; ++count)  {
    scanf("%f", &x);
    if (x < 0)  {
        printf("ERROR — NEGATIVE VALUE FOR X");
        break;
    }

    /* process the nonnegative value of x */
    :
}
```

In the event of several nested `while`, `do - while`, `for` or `switch` statements, a `break` statement will cause a transfer of control out of the immediate enclosing statement, but not out of the outer surrounding statements. We have seen one illustration of this in Example 6.26, where a `switch` statement is embedded within a `while` statement. Another illustration is shown below.

Example 6.29 Consider the following outline of a `while` loop embedded within a `for` loop.

```
for (count = 0; count <= n; ++count)  {
    :
    while ((c = getchar()) != '\n')  {
        if (c = '*')  break;
        :
    }
}
```

If the character variable `c` is assigned an asterisk (*), then the `while` loop will be terminated. However, the `for` loop will continue to execute. Thus, if the value of `count` is less than n when the breakout occurs, the computer will increment `count` and make another pass through the `for` loop.

6.9 THE continue STATEMENT

The `continue` statement is used to *bypass* the remainder of the current pass through a loop. The loop does *not* terminate when a `continue` statement is encountered. Rather, the remaining loop statements are skipped and the computation proceeds directly to the next pass through the loop. (Note this important distinction between `continue` and `break`.)

The `continue` statement can be included within a `while`, a `do - while` or a `for` statement. It is written simply as

```
continue;
```

without any embedded statements or expressions.

Example 6.30 Here are some illustrations of loops that contain `continue` statements.

First, consider a `do - while` loop.

```
do  {
    scanf("%f", &x);
    if (x < 0)  {
        printf("ERROR — NEGATIVE VALUE FOR X");
        continue;
    };

    /* process the nonnegative value of x */
    :
} while (x <= 100);
```

Here is a similar `for` loop

```
for (count = 1; x <= 100; ++count)   {
    scanf("%f", &x);
    if (x < 0)   {
        printf("ERROR - NEGATIVE VALUE FOR X");
        continue;
    }

    /* process the nonnegative value of x */
    :
}
```

In each case, the processing of the current value of x will be bypassed if the value of x is negative. Execution of the loop will then continue with the next pass.

It is interesting to compare these control statements with those shown in Example 6.28, which make use of the `break` statement instead of the `continue` statement. (Why is a modification of the `while` loop shown in Example 6.28 not included in this example?)

Example 6.31   Averaging a List of Nonnegative Numbers   In Example 6.14 we saw a complete C program that uses a `for` loop to calculate the average of a list of n numbers. Let us now modify this program so that it processes only nonnegative numbers.

The earlier program requires two minor changes to accommodate this modification. First, the `for` loop must include an `if` statement to determine whether or not each new value of x is nonnegative. A `continue` statement will be included in the `if` statement to bypass the processing of negative values of x. Secondly, we require a special counter (navg) to determine how many nonnegative numbers have been processed. This counter will appear in the denominator when the average is calculated (i.e., the average will be determined as `average = sum/navg`).

Here is the actual C program. It is interesting to compare it with the program shown in Example 6.14.

```
#include <stdio.h>

/* calculate the average of the nonnegative numbers
                              in a list of n numbers */

main()

{
    int n, count, navg = 0;
    float x, average, sum = 0;

    /* initialize and read in a value for n */
    printf("How many numbers? ");
    scanf("%d", &n);

    /* read in the numbers */
    for (count = 1; count <= n; ++count)  {
        printf("x = ");
        scanf("%f", &x);
        if (x < 0) continue;
        sum += x;
        ++navg;
    }

    /* calculate the average and write out the answer */
    average = sum/navg;
    printf("\nThe average is %f\n", average);
}
```

When the program is executed with nonnegative values for x, it behaves exactly like the earlier version presented in Example 6.14. When some of the x's are assigned negative values, however, the negative values are ignored in calculating the average.

A sample interactive session is shown below. As usual, the user's responses are underlined.

```
How many numbers? 6
x = 1
x = -1
x = 2
x = -2
x = 3
x = -3

The average is 2.000000
```

This is the correct average of the positive numbers. Note that the average would be zero if all of the numbers had been averaged.

6.10 THE COMMA OPERATOR

We now introduce the comma operator (,) which is used primarily in conjunction with the `for` statement. This operator permits two different expressions to appear in situations where only one expression would ordinarily be used. For example, it is possible to write

```
for (expression 1a, expression 1b; expression 2; expression 3) statement
```

where *expression 1a* and *expression 1b* are the two expressions, separated by the comma operator, where only one expression (*expression 1*) would normally appear. These two expressions would typically initialize two separate indices that would be used simultaneously within the `for` loop.

Similarly, a `for` statement might make use of the comma operator in the following manner:

```
for (expression 1; expression 2; expression 3a, expression 3b) statement
```

Here *expression 3a* and *expression 3b*, separated by the comma operator, appear in place of the usual single expression. In this application the two separate expressions would typically be used to alter (e.g., increment or decrement) the two different indices used simultaneously within the loop. For example, one index might count forward while the other counts backward.

Example 6.32 Searching for Palindromes A *palindrome* is a word, phrase or sentence that reads the same way either forward or backward. For example, words such as *noon, peep,* and *madam* are palindromes. If we disregard punctuation and blank spaces, then the sentence *Rise to vote, sir*! is also a palindrome.

Let us write a C program that will enter a line of text containing a word, a phrase or a sentence and determine whether or not the text is a palindrome. To do so, we will compare the first character with the last, the second character with the next to last, and so on, until we have reached the middle of the text. The comparisons will include punctuation and blank spaces.

In order to outline a computational strategy, let us define the following variables:

letter   = a character-type array containing as many as 80 elements. These elements will be the characters in the line of text.

tag   = an integer variable indicating the number of characters assigned to letter, excluding the escape character \0 at the end.

count   = an integer variable used as an index when moving forward through letter.

countback   = an integer variable used as an index when moving backward through letter.

flag   = an integer variable that will be used to indicate a true/false condition. True will indicate that a palindrome has been found.

loop   = an integer variable whose value will always equal 1, thus appearing always to be true. The intent here is to continue execution of a main loop until a particular stopping condition causes a breakout.

We can now outline our overall strategy as follows.

1. Define the symbolic constants EOL (end-of-line), TRUE and FALSE.

2. Declare all variables and initialize loop (i.e., assign TRUE to loop).

3. Enter the main loop.
   (a) Assign TRUE to flag, in anticipation of finding a palindrome.
   (b) Read in the line of text character-by-character, and store in letter.
   (c) Test to see if the uppercase equivalents of the first three characters are E, N and D, respectively. If so, break out of the main loop and exit the program.
   (d) Assign the final value of count, less 1, to tag. This value will indicate the number of characters in the line of text, not including the final escape character \∅.
   (e) Compare each character in the first half of letter with the corresponding character in the second half. If a mismatch is found, assign FALSE to flag and break out of the (inner) comparison loop.
   (f) If flag is TRUE, write a message indicating that a palindrome has been found. Otherwise, write a message indicating that a palindrome has not been found.

4. Repeat step 3 (i.e., make another pass through the outer loop), thus processing another line of text.

Here is the corresponding pseudocode.

```
#include files

#define symbolic constants

main()

{
    /* declare all variables and initialize as required */
    while (loop)  {

        flag = TRUE;   /* anticipating a palindrome */

        /* read in a line of text and store in letter */

        /* break out of while loop if first three characters
            of letter spell END (test upper-case equivalents) */

        /* assign number of characters in text to tag */

        for ((count = ∅, countback = tag); count <= (tag - 1)/2;
            (++count, --countback))   {

            if (letter[count] != letter[countback])  {
                flag = FALSE;

                /* not a palindrome — break out of for loop */
            }
        }

        /* write out message indicating whether or not letter
            contains a palindrome */

    }
}
```

The program utilizes the comma operator within a `for` loop to compare each character in the first half of `letter` with the corresponding character in the second half. Thus, as `count` increases from Ø to `(tag - 1) / 2`, `countback` decreases from `tag` to `(tag / 2) + 1`. Note that integer division (resulting in a truncated quotient) is involved in establishing these limiting values.

Also, observe that there will be two distinct comma operators within the `for` statement. Each comma operator and its associated operands are enclosed in parentheses. This is not necessary, but it does emphasize that each operand pair comprises one argument within the `for` statement.

The complete C program is shown below.

```c
#include <stdio.h>

#define EOL  '\n'
#define TRUE 1
#define FALSE Ø

/* search for a palindrome */

main()

{
    char letter[80];
    int tag, count, countback, flag, loop = TRUE;

    /* main loop */

    while (loop)   {
        flag = TRUE;

        /* read the text */

        printf("Please enter a word, phrase or sentence below:\n");
        for (count = Ø; (letter[count] = getchar()) != EOL; ++count)
            ;
        if ((toupper(letter[Ø]) == 'E') && (toupper(letter[1]) == 'N') &&
            (toupper(letter[2]) == 'D')) break;
        tag = count - 1;

        /* carry out the search */

        for ((count = Ø, countback = tag); count <= tag/2;
            (++count, --countback))   {

                if (letter[count] != letter[countback])   {
                    flag = FALSE;
                    break;
                }
        }

        /* print out message */

        for (count = Ø; count <= tag; ++count)
            putchar(letter[count]);
        if (flag) printf(" IS a palindrome\n\n");
        else printf(" is NOT a palindrome\n\n");
    }
}
```

A typical interactive session is shown below, indicating the type of output generated when the program is executed. As usual, the user's responses are underlined.

```
Please enter a word, phrase or sentence below:
TOOT

TOOT IS a palindrome

Please enter a word, phrase or sentence below:
FALSE

FALSE is NOT a palindrome

Please enter a word, phrase or sentence below:
PULLUP

PULLUP IS a palindrome

Please enter a word, phrase or sentence below:
ABLE WAS I ERE I SAW ELBA

ABLE WAS I ERE I SAW ELBA IS a palindrome

Please enter a word, phrase or sentence below:
END
```

Remember that the comma operator accepts two distinct expressions as operands. These expressions will be evaluated from left to right. In situations that require the evaluation of the overall expression (i.e., the expression formed by the two operands and the comma operator), the type and value of the overall expression will be determined by the type and value of the right operand.

Within the collection of C operators, the comma operator has the lowest precedence. Thus, the comma operator falls within its own unique precedence group, beneath the precedence group containing the various assignment operators (see Appendix C). Its associativity is left-to-right.

6.11   THE goto STATEMENT

The goto statement is used to alter the normal sequence of program execution by transferring control to some other part of the program. In its general form, the goto statement is written as

goto *label*;

where *label* is an identifier used to label the target statement to which control will be transferred.

Control may be transferred to any other statement within the program. (To be more precise, control may be transferred anywhere within the current *function*. We will discuss functions in the next chapter.) The target statement must be labeled, and the label must be followed by a colon. Thus, the target statement will appear as

label: *statement*

Each labeled statement within the program (more precisely, within the current function) must have a unique label, i.e., no two statements can have the same label.

Example 6.33   The following skeletal outline illustrates how the goto statement can be used to transfer control out of a loop if an unexpected condition arises.

```
/* main loop */
scanf("%f", &x);
while (x <= 100)   {
        .
        .
        if (x < 0) goto errorcheck;
        .
        .
        scanf("%f", &x);
}
        .                                                    .
        .                                                    .

/* error detection routine */

errorcheck: {
                printf("ERROR — NEGATIVE VALUE FOR X");
                .
                .
        }
```

Notice that control is transferred out of the `while` loop, to the compound statement whose label is `errorcheck`, if a negative value is detected for the input variable x.

The same thing could have been accomplished using the `break` statement, as illustrated in Example 6.28. The use of the `break` statement is actually the preferred approach. The use of the `goto` statement is presented here only to illustrate the syntax.

All of the popular, general-purpose programming languages contain a `goto` statement, though modern programming practice discourages its use. In some of the older languages, such as FORTRAN and BASIC, the `goto` statement is used extensively. The most common applications are:

1. Branching around statements or groups of statements under certain conditions.

2. Jumping to the end of a loop under certain conditions, thus bypassing the remainder of the loop during the current pass.

3. Jumping completely out of a loop under certain conditions, thus terminating the execution of a loop.

The structured features in C enable all of these operations to be carried out without resorting to the `goto` statement. For example, branching around statements can be accomplished with the `if - else` statement; jumping to the end of a loop can be carried out with the `continue` statement; and jumping out of a loop is easily accomplished using the `break` statement. The use of these structured features is preferrable to the use of the `goto` statement because the use of `goto` tends to encourage (or at least, not discourage) logic that skips all over the program; the structured features in C require that the entire program be written in an orderly, sequential manner. For this reason, *use of the `goto` statement should generally be avoided in a C program.*

Occasional situations do arise, however, in which the `goto` statement can be useful. Consider, for example, a situation in which it is necessary to jump out of a doubly nested loop if a certain condition is detected. This can be accomplished with two `if - break` statements, one within each loop, though this is awkward. A better solution in this particular situation might make use of the `goto` statement to transfer out of both loops at once. The procedure is illustrated in the following example.

Example 6.34 Converting Several Lines of Text to Uppercase   Example 6.16 presents a program to convert several successive lines of text to uppercase, processing one line of text at a time, until the first character in a new line is an asterisk (*). Let us now modify this program to detect a break condition, as indicated by two successive dollar signs ($$) anywhere within a line of text. If the break condition is encountered, the program will print the line of text containing the dollar signs, followed by an appropriate message. Execution of the program will then terminate.

The logic will be the same as that given in Example 6.16, except that an additional loop will now be added to test for two consecutive dollar signs. Thus the program will proceed as follows.

1. Assign an initial value of 1 to the outer loop index (`linecount`).

2. Carry out the following steps repeatedly, for successive lines of text, as long as the first character in the line is not an asterisk.

(a) Read in a line of text and assign the individual characters to the elements of the char-type array `letter`. A line will be defined as a succession of characters terminated by an end-of-line (i.e, a newline) designation.

(b) Assign the character count, including the end-of-line character, to `tag`.

(c) Write out the line in uppercase, using the library function `toupper` to carry out the conversion. Then write out two newline characters (so that the next line of input will be separated from the current output by a blank line) and increment the line counter (`linecount`).

(d) Test all successive characters in the line for two successive dollar signs. If two successive dollar signs are detected, then write out a message indicating that a break condition has been found and jump to the terminating condition at the end of the program (see below).

3. Once an asterisk has been detected as the first character of a new line, write out "Good bye." and terminate the computation.

Here is the complete C program.

```
#include <stdio.h>

#define EOL '\n'

/* convert several lines of text to upper-case

   Continue conversion until the first character in a line is
   an asterisk (*).  Break out of the program, however, if two
   successive dollar signs ($$) are detected within a line.    */

main()

{
    char letter[80];
    int tag, count, linecount = 1;

    while((letter[0] = getchar()) != '*')   {

        /* read in a line of text */
        for (count = 1; (letter[count] = getchar()) != EOL; ++count)
            ;
        tag = count;

        /* write out the line of text */
        for (count = 0; count < tag; ++count)
            putchar(toupper(letter[count]));
        printf("\n\n");
        ++linecount;

        /* test for a break condition */
        for (count=1; count < tag; ++count)
            if (letter[count-1] == '$' && letter[count] == '$')   {
                printf("BREAK CONDITION DETECTED - TERMINATE EXECUTION\n\n");
                goto end;
            }
    }
    end: printf("Good bye.");
}
```

It is interesting to compare this program with the corresponding program presented earlier, in Example 6.16. The present program contains an additional `for` loop embedded at the end of the `while` loop. This `for` loop examines consecutive pairs of characters for a break condition ($$) after the entire line has already been written out in uppercase. If a break condition is encountered, then control is transferred to the final `printf` statement

("Good bye.") which is now labeled end. Note that this transfer of control causes a breakout from the if statement, the current for loop, and the outer while loop.

You should run this program, using both the regular terminating condition (an asterisk at the start of a new line) and the breakout condition. Compare the results obtained with the output shown in Example 6.16.

Review Questions

6.1 What is meant by looping? Describe two different forms of looping.

6.2 What is conditional execution?

6.3 What is selection?

6.4 Summarize the rules associated with the use of the four relational operators, the two equality operators, the two logical connectives and the unary negation operator. What types of operands are used with each type of operator?

6.5 How are char-type constants and char-type variables interpreted when used as operands with a relational operator?

6.6 How do expression statements differ from compound statements? Summarize the rules associated with each.

6.7 What is the purpose of the while statement? When is the logical expression evaluated? What is the minimum number of times that a while loop can be executed?

6.8 How is the execution of a while loop terminated?

6.9 Summarize the syntactic rules associated with the while statement.

6.10 What is the purpose of the do - while statement? How does it differ from the while statement?

6.11 What is the minimum number of times a do - while loop can be executed? Compare with a while loop and explain the reasons for the differences.

6.12 Summarize the syntactic rules associated with the do - while statement. Compare with the while statement.

6.13 What is the purpose of the for statement? How does it differ from the while statement and the do - while statement?

6.14 How many times will a for loop be executed? Compare with the while loop and the do - while loop.

6.15 What is the purpose of the index in a for statement?

6.16 Can any of the three initial expressions in the for statement be omitted? If so, what are the consequences of each omission?

6.17 Summarize the syntactic rules associated with the for statement.

6.18 What rules apply to nested loops? Can one type of loop be embedded within another?

6.19 What is the purpose of the if - else statement? In what way is this statement different from the while, the do - while and the for statements?

6.20 Describe the two different forms of the if - else statement. How do they differ?

6.21 Compare the use of the if - else statement with the use of the ?: operator. In particular, in what way can the ?: operator be used in place of an if - else statement?

6.22 Summarize the syntactic rules associated with the if - else statement.

6.23 How are nested if - then statements interpreted? In particular, how is the following interpreted?

```
if e1 if e2 s1
     else s2
```

Which logical expression is associated with the else clause?

6.24 What happens when an expression is encountered whose value is nonzero within a group of nested if - else statements?

6.25 Describe how the exp and the log functions can be used to carry out exponentiation operations.

6.26 What is the purpose of the switch statement? How does this statement differ from the other statements described in this chapter?

6.27 What are case labels (case prefixes)? What type of expression must be used to represent a case label?

6.28 Summarize the syntactic rules associated with the use of the `switch` statement. Can multiple case labels be associated with a single group of statements?

6.29 What happens when the value of the expression in the `switch` statement matches the value of one of the case labels? What happens when the value of this expression does not match any of the case labels?

6.30 Can a default alternative be defined within a `switch` statement? If so, how would the default alternative be labeled?

6.31 Compare the use of the `switch` statement with the use of nested `if - else` statements. Which is more convenient?

6.32 What is the purpose of the `break` statement? Within which control statements can the `break` statement be included?

6.33 Suppose a `break` statement is included within the innermost of several nested control statements. What happens when the `break` statement is executed?

6.34 What is the purpose of the `continue` statement? Within which control statements can the `continue` statement be included? Compare with the `break` statement.

6.35 What is the purpose of the comma operator? Within which control statement does the comma operator usually appear?

6.36 In situations that require the evaluation of an expression containing the comma operator, which operand will determine the type and the value of the entire expression (i.e., the expression to the left of the comma operator or the expression to the right)?

6.37 What is the precedence of the comma operator compared with other C operators?

6.38 What is the purpose of the `goto` statement? How is the associated target statement identified?

6.39 Are there any restrictions that apply to where control can be transferred within a given C program?

6.40 Summarize the syntactic rules associated with the `goto` statement.

6.41 Compare the syntax associated with statement labels with that of case labels (case prefixes).

6.42 Why is the use of the `goto` statement generally discouraged? Under what conditions might the `goto` statement be helpful? What types of usage should be avoided, and why? Discuss thoroughly.

Problems

6.43 Explain what happens when the following statement is executed.

```
if (abs(x) < xmin) x = (x > 0) ? xmin : -xmin;
```

Is this a compound statement? Is a compound statement embedded within this statement?

6.44 Identify all compound statements that appear within the following program segment.

```
{
    sum = 0;
    do  {
            scanf("%d", &i);
            if (i < 0)    {
                i = -i;
                ++flag;
            }
            sum += i;
    } while (i != 0);
}
```

6.45 Write a loop that will calculate the sum of every third integer, beginning with $i = 2$ (i.e., calculate the sum $2 + 5 + 8 + 11 + \cdots$) for all values of i that are less than 100. Write the loop three different ways.

(a)　using a `while` statement
(b)　using a `do - while` statement
(c)　using a `for` statement

6.46　Repeat Problem 6.45 calculating the sum of every n^{th} integer, beginning with `nstart` (i.e., `i = nstart`, `nstart + n, nstart + 2 * n, nstart + 3 * n,` and so on). Continue the looping process for all values of `i` that do not exceed `nstop`.

6.47　Write a loop that will examine each character in a character-type array called `text`, and write out the ASCII equivalent (i.e., the numerical value) of each character. Assume that the number of characters in the array is specified in advance by the integer variable n. Write the loop three different ways.

(a)　using a `while` statement
(b)　using a `do - while` statement
(c)　using a `for` statement

6.48　Repeat Problem 6.47 assuming that the number of characters in the array is not specified in advance. Continue the looping action until an asterisk (*) is encountered. Write the loop three different ways, as before.

6.49　Generalize Problem 6.45 by generating a *series* of loops, each loop generating the sum of every j^{th} integer, where j ranges from 2 to 13. Begin each loop with a value of `i = 2`, and increase i by j until i takes on the largest possible value that is less than 100. (In other words, the first loop will calculate the sum $2 + 4 + 6 + \cdots + 98$; the second loop will calculate the sum $2 + 5 + 8 + \cdots + 98$; the third loop will calculate the sum $2 + 6 + 10 + \cdots + 98$; and so on. The last loop will calculate the sum $2 + 15 + 28 + \cdots + 93$.) Print the value of each complete sum.

Use a nested loop structure to solve this problem, with one loop embedded within another. Calculate each sum with the inner loop, and let the outer loop control the value of j used by each pass through the inner loop. Use a `for` statement to structure the outer loop, and use each of the three different loop statements (`while`, `do - while` and `for`) for the inner loop. Develop a separate solution for each type of inner loop.

6.50　Write a loop that will generate every third integer, beginning with `i = 2` and continuing for all integers that are less than 100. Calculate the sum of those integers that are evenly divisible by 5. Use two different methods to carry out the test.

(a)　use the conditional operator (`?:`)
(b)　use an `if - else` statement

6.51　Generalize Problem 6.50 by generating every n^{th} integer, beginning with `nstart` (i.e., `i = nstart`, `nstart + n, nstart + 2 * n, nstart + 3 * n,` and so on). Continue the looping process for all values of `i` that do not exceed `nstop`. Calculate the sum of those integers evenly divisible by k, where k represents some positive integer.

6.52　Write a loop that will examine each character in a character-type array called `text` and determine how many of the characters are letters, how many are digits, how many are whitespace characters, and how many are other kinds of characters (e.g., punctuation characters). Assume that `text` contains 80 characters.

6.53　Write a loop that will examine each character in a character-type array called `text` and determine how many of the characters are vowels and how many are consonants. (*Hint*: First determine whether or not a character is a letter; if so, determine the type of letter.) Assume that `text` contains 80 characters.

6.54　Write a `switch` statement that will examine the value of an integer variable called `flag` and print one of the following messages, depending on the value assigned to `flag`.

(a)　HOT, if `flag` has a value of 1
(b)　LUKE WARM, if `flag` has a value of 2
(c)　COLD, if `flag` has a value of 3
(d)　OUT OF RANGE, if `flag` has any other value

6.55　Write a `switch` statement that will examine the value of a char-type variable called `color` and print one of the following messages, depending on the character assigned to `color`.

(a)　RED, if either r or R is assigned to `color`
(b)　GREEN, if either g or G is assigned to `color`
(c)　BLUE, if either b or B is assigned to `color`
(d)　BLACK, if `color` is assigned any other character

6.56　Write an appropriate control structure that will examine the value of a floating-point variable called `temp` and print one of the following messages, depending on the value assigned to `temp`.

(a)   ICE, if the value of temp is less than 0
(b)   WATER, if the value of temp lies between 0 and 100
(c)   STEAM, if the value of temp exceeds 100
Can a switch statement be used in this instance?

6.57   Write a for loop that will read the characters in a character-type array called text and write the characters backwards into another character-type array called backtext. Assume that text contains 80 characters. Use the comma operator within the for loop.

6.58   Describe the output that will be generated by each of the following C programs.

(a)
```
#include <stdio.h>

main()

{
    int i = 0, x = 0;

    while (i < 20)  {
        if (i % 5 == 0)  {
            x += i;
            printf("%d ", x);
        }
        ++i;
    }
    printf("\nx = %d", x);
}
```

(b)
```
#include <stdio.h>

main()

{
    int i = 0, X = 0;

    do {
        if (i % 5 == 0)  {
            x++;
            printf("%d ", x);
        }
        ++i;
    } while (i < 20);
    printf("\nx = %d", x);
}
```

(c)
```
#include <stdio.h>

main()

{
    int i = 0, x = 0;

    for (i = 1; i < 10; i *= 2)  {
        x++;
        printf("%d ", x);
    }
    printf("\nx = %d", x);
}
```

(d)
```
#include <stdio.h>

main()

{
    int i = 0, x = 0;

    for (i = 1; i < 10; ++i)  {
        if (i % 2 == 1)
            x += i;
        else
            x--;
        printf("%d ", x);
    }
    printf("\nx = %d", x);
}
```

(e) #include ⟨stdio.h⟩

```
main()

{
    int i = 0, x = 0;

    for (i = 1; i < 10; ++i)    {
        if (i % 2 == 1)
            x += i;
        else
            x--;
        printf("%d ", x);
        continue;
    }
    printf("\nx = %d", x);
}
```

(f) #include ⟨stdio.h⟩

```
main()

{
    int i = 0, x = 0;

    for (i = 1; i < 10; ++i)    {
        if (i % 2 == 1)
            x += i;
        else
            x--;
        printf("%d ", x);
        break;
    }
    printf("\nx = %d", x);
}
```

(g) #include ⟨stdio.h⟩

```
main()

{
    int i, j, x = 0;

    for (i = 0; i < 5; ++i)
        for (j = 0; j < i; ++j)    {
            x += (i + j - 1);
            printf("%d ", x);
        }
    printf("\nx = %d", x);
}
```

(h) #include ⟨stdio.h⟩

```
main()

{
    int i, j, x = 0;

    for (i = 0; i < 5; ++i)
        for (j = 0; j < i; ++j)   {
            x += (i + j - 1);
            printf("%d ", x);
            break;
        }
    printf("\nx = %d", x);
}
```

(i) #include ⟨stdio.h⟩

```
main()

{
    int i, j, x = 0;

    for (i = 0; i < 5; ++i)   {
        for (j = 0; j < i; ++j)
            x += (i + j - 1);
            printf("%d ", x);
            break;
    }
    printf("\nx = %d", x);
}
```

(j) #include ⟨stdio.h⟩

```
main()

{
    int i, j, k, x = 0;

    for (i = 0; i < 5; ++i)
        for (j = 0; j < i; ++j)   {
            k = (i + j - 1);
            if (k % 2 == 0)
                x += k;
            else
                if (k % 3 == 0)
                    x += k - 2;
            printf("%d ", x);
        }
    printf("\nx = %d", x);
}
```

```
(k)   #include <stdio.h>

      main()

      {
          int i, j, k, x = 0;

          for (i = 0; i < 5; ++i)
             for (j = 0; j < i; ++j)   {

                 switch (i + j - 1)   {

                 case -1:
                 case  0:
                        x += 1;
                        break;

                 case  1:
                 case  2:
                 case  3:
                        x += 2;
                        break;

                 default:
                        x += 3;
                 }
                 printf("%d ", x);
             }
          printf("\nx = %d", x);
      }

(l)   #include <stdio.h>

      main()

      {
          int i, j, k, x = 0;

          for (i = 0; i < 5; ++i)
             for (j = 0; j < i; ++j)   {

                 switch (i + j - 1)   {

                 case -1:
                 case  0:
                        x += 1;
                        break;

                 case  1:
                 case  2:
                 case  3:
                        x += 2;

                 default:
                        x += 3;
                 }
                 printf("%d ", x);
             }
          printf("\nx = %d", x);
      }
```

Programming Problems

6.59   Modify the programs given in Examples 6.6, 6.9 and 6.13 so that each program does the following:

    (*a*)   Read in a line of uppercase text, store it in an appropriate array, and then write it out in lowercase.

    (*b*)   Read in a line of mixed text, store it in an appropriate array, and then write it out with all lowercase and uppercase letters reversed, all digits replaced by 0's, and all other characters (nonletters and nondigits) replaced by asterisks (*).

6.60   Compile and execute the programs given in Examples 6.7, 6.10 and 6.14, using the following 10 numbers:

27.5	87.0
13.4	39.9
53.8	47.7
29.2	8.1
74.5	63.2

6.61   Compile and execute the program given in Example 6.31 using the following 10 numbers:

27.5	87.0
−13.4	39.9
53.8	−47.7
−29.2	−8.1
74.5	63.2

    Compare the calculated result with the results obtained for the last problem.

6.62   Modify the program given in Example 6.7 so that the size of the list of numbers being averaged is not specified in advance. Continue looping (i.e., reading in a new value for x and adding it to sum) until a value of zero is entered. Thus, x = 0 will signal a stopping condition.

6.63   Repeat Problem 6.62 for the program given in Example 6.14.

6.64   Rewrite the depreciation program given in Example 6.26 to use the `if - else` statement instead of the `switch` statement. Test the program using the data given in Example 6.26. Which version do you prefer? Why?

6.65   The equation

$$x^5 + 3x^2 - 10 = 0$$

which was presented in Example 6.21, can be rearranged into the form

$$x = [(10 - x^5)/3]^{1/2}$$

Rewrite the program presented in Example 6.21 to make use of the above form of the equation. Run the program and compare the calculated results with those presented in Example 6.21. Why are the results different? (Do computers always generate correct answers?)

6.66   Modify the program given in Example 6.21, which solves for the roots of an algebraic equation, so that the `while` statement is replaced by a `do - while` statement. Which structure is best suited for this particular problem?

6.67   Modify the program given in Example 6.21, which solves for the roots of an algebraic equation, so that the `while` statement is replaced by a `for` statement. Compare the use of the `for`, `while` and `do - while` statements. Which version do you prefer, and why?

6.68   Add an error-trapping routine similar to that given in Example 6.20 to the depreciation program in Example 6.26. The routine should generate an error message followed by a request to reenter the data whenever a nonpositive input value is detected.

6.69   Write a complete C program for each of the problems presented below. Use the most natural type of control statement for each problem. Begin with a detailed outline; then rewrite the outline in pseudocode if the translation into a working C program is not entirely clear. Be sure to use good programming style (comments, indentation, etc.).

(a) Calculate the *weighted average* of a list of n numbers, using the formula

$$x_{avg} = f_1 x_1 + f_2 x_2 + \cdots + f_n x_n$$

where the f's are fractional *weighting factors*, i.e.,

$$0 <= f_i < 1, \text{ and } f_1 + f_2 + \cdots + f_n = 1.$$

Test your program with the following data:

$i = 1$	$f = 0.06$	$x = 27.5$
2	0.08	13.4
3	0.08	53.8
4	0.10	29.2
5	0.10	74.5
6	0.10	87.0
7	0.12	39.9
8	0.12	47.7
9	0.12	8.1
10	0.12	63.2

(b) Calculate the cumulative product of a list of n numbers. Test your program with the following set of data ($n = 6$): 6.2, 12.3, 5.0, 18.8, 7.1, 12.8.

(c) Calculate the geometric average of a list of numbers, using the formula

$$x_{avg} = [x_1 x_2 x_3 \cdots x_n]^{1/n}$$

Test your program using the values of x given in part (b) above. Compare the results obtained with the arithmetic average of the same data. Which average is larger?

(d) Determine the roots of the quadratic equation

$$ax^2 + bx + c = 0$$

using the well-known quadratic formula

$$x = \frac{-b \pm \sqrt{b^2 - 4ac}}{2a}$$

(see Example 5.5). Allow for the possibility that one of the constants has a value of zero, and that the quantity $b^2 - 4ac$ is less than or equal to zero. Test the program using the following sets of data:

$a = 2$	$b = 6$	$c = 1$
3	3	0
1	3	1
0	12	−3
3	6	3
2	−4	3

(e) The *Fibonacci numbers* are members of an interesting sequence in which each number is equal to the sum of the previous two numbers. In other words,

$$F_i = F_{i-1} + F_{i-2}$$

where F_i refers to the ith Fibonacci number. The first two Fibonacci numbers are, by definition, equal to 1; i.e., $F_1 = F_2 = 1$. Hence,

$$F_3 = F_2 + F_1 = 1 + 1 = 2$$
$$F_4 = F_3 + F_2 = 2 + 1 = 3$$
$$F_5 = F_4 + F_3 = 3 + 2 = 5$$

and so on.

Write a program that will determine the first n Fibonacci numbers. Test the program with $n = 7$, $n = 10$, $n = 17$ and $n = 23$.

(f) A *prime number* is a positive integer quantity that is evenly divisible (without a remainder) only by 1 or by itself. For example, 7 is a prime number, but 6 is not.

Calculate and tabulate the first n prime numbers. (*Hint*: a number, n, will be a prime if the remainders of $n/2$, $n/3$, $n/4$, ..., $n/\sqrt{n}$ are all nonzero.) Test your program by calculating the first 100 prime numbers.

(g) Write an interactive program that will read in a positive integer value and determine the following:

(i) if the integer is a prime number
(ii) if the integer is a Fibonacci number

Write the program in such a manner that it will execute repeatedly, until a zero value is detected for the input quantity. Test the program with several integer values of your choice.

(h) Calculate the sum of the first n odd integers (i.e., $1 + 3 + 5 + \cdots + 2*n - 1$). Test the program by calculating the sum of the first 100 odd integers (note that the last integer will be 199).

(i) The sine of x can be calculated approximately by summing the first n terms of the infinite series

$$\sin x = x - x^3/3! + x^5/5! - x^7/7! + \cdots$$

where x is expressed in radians (*Note*: π radians = 180°). Write a C program that will read in a value for x and then calculate its sine. Write the program two different ways:

(1) Sum the first n terms, where n is a positive integer that is read into the computer along with the numerical value for x.
(2) Continue adding successive terms in the series until the value of the next term becomes smaller (in magnitude) than 10^{-5}.

Test the program for $x = 1$, $x = 2$ and $x = -3$. In each case write out the number of terms used to obtain the final answer.

(j) Suppose that P dollars are borrowed from a bank, with the understanding that A dollars will be repaid each month until the entire loan has been repaid. Part of the monthly payment will be interest, calculated as i percent of the current unpaid balance. The remainder of the monthly payment will be applied toward reducing the unpaid balance.

Write a C program that will determine the following information:

(i) The amount of interest paid each month.
(ii) The amount of money applied toward the unpaid balance each month.
(iii) The cumulative amount of interest that has been paid at the end of each month.
(iv) The amount of the loan that is still unpaid at the end of each month.
(v) The number of monthly payments required to repay the entire loan.
(vi) The amount of the last payment (since it will probably be less than A).

Test your program using the following data: P = \$40,000; A = \$2000; i = 1% per month.

(k) A class of students earned the following grades for the 6 examinations taken in a C programming course.

Name	*Exam Scores (percent)*					
Adams	45	80	80	95	55	75
Brown	60	50	70	ˉ75	55	80
Davis	40	30	10	45	60	55
Fisher	0	5	5	0	10	5
Hamilton	90	85	100	95	90	90
Jones	95	90	80	95	85	80
Ludwig	35	50	55	65	45	70
Osborne	75	60	75	60	70	80
Prince	85	75	60	85	90	100
Richards	50	60	50	35	65	70
Smith	70	60	75	70	55	75
Thomas	10	25	35	20	30	10
Wolfe	25	40	65	75	85	95
Zorba	65	80	70	100	60	95

Write an interactive C program that will accept each student's name and exam grades as input, determine an average grade for each student, and then write out the student's name, the individual exam grades and the calculated average.

(*l*) Modify the program written for part (*k*) above to allow for unequal weighting of the individual exam grades. In particular, assume that each of the first four exams contributes 15 percent to the final score, and each of the last two exams contributes 20 percent.

(*m*) Extend the program written for part (*l*) above so that an overall class average is determined in addition to the individual student averages.

(*n*) Write a C program that will allow the computer to be used as an ordinary desk calculator. Consider only the common arithmetic operations (addition, subtraction, multiplication and division). Include a memory that can store one number.

(*o*) Generate the following "pyramid" of digits, using nested loops.

$$1$$
$$232$$
$$34543$$
$$4567654$$
$$567898765$$
$$67890109876$$
$$7890123210987$$
$$890123454321098$$
$$90123456765432109$$
$$0123456789876543210$$

Do *not* simply write out 10 multidigit strings. Instead, develop a formula to *generate* the appropriate output for each line.

(*p*) Generate a plot of the function

$$y = e^{-0.1t} \sin 0.5t$$

on a printer, using an asterisk (*) for each of the points that makes up the plot. Have the plot run vertically down the page, with one point (one asterisk) per line. (*Hint*: Each printed line should consist of one asterisk, preceded by an appropriate number of blank spaces. Determine the position of the asterisk by rounding the value of *y* to the nearest integer, scaled to the maximum number of characters per line.)

(*q*) Write an interactive C program that will convert a positive integer quantity to a roman numeral (e.g., 12 will be converted to XII, 14 will be converted to XIV, and so on). Design the program so that it will execute repeatedly, until a value of zero is read in from the keyboard.

(*r*) Write an interactive C program that will convert a date, entered in the form `mm-dd-yy` (example: 4-12-69) into an integer that indicates the number of days beyond January 1, 1960. To do so, make use of the following relationships:

  (*i*)   The day of the current year can be determined approximately as

```
day = (int) (30.42 * (mm - 1)) + dd
```

  (*ii*)   If `mm == 2` (February), increase the value of `day` by 1
  (*iii*) If `mm > 2` and `mm < 8` (March, April, May, June or July), decrease the value of `day` by 1
  (*iv*)   If `yy % 4 == 0` and `mm > 2` (leap year), increase the value of `day` by 1
  (*v*)   Increase the value of `day` by 1461 for each full four-year cycle beyond 1-1-60.
  (*vi*)   Increase `day` by 365 for each additional full year beyond the completion of the last full four-year cycle, then add 1 (for the most recent leap year).

Test the program with today's date, or any other date of your choice.

Chapter 7

Functions

We have already seen that C supports the use of library functions, which are used to carry out a number of commonly used operations or calculations (see Sec. 3.6). However, C also allows programmers to define their own functions for carrying out various individual tasks. This chapter concentrates on the creation and utilization of such programmer-defined functions.

The use of programmer-defined functions allows a large program to be broken down into a number of smaller, self-contained components, each of which has some unique, identifiable purpose. Thus, a C program can be *modularized* through the intelligent use of such functions. (C does not support other forms of modular program development, such as the procedures in Pascal or the subroutines in Fortran.)

There are several advantages to this modular approach to program development. For example, many programs require a particular group of instructions to be accessed repeatedly from several different places within the program. The repeated instructions can be placed within a single function, which can then be accessed whenever it is needed. Moreover, a different set of data can be transferred to the function each time it is accessed. Thus, the use of a function avoids the need for redundant (repeated) programming of the same instructions.

Equally important is the logical clarity resulting from the decomposition of a program into several concise functions, where each function represents some well-defined part of the overall problem. Such programs are easier to write and easier to debug, and their logical structure is more apparent than that of programs which lack this type of structure. This is especially true of lengthy, complicated programs. Most C programs are therefore modularized in this manner, even though they may not involve repeated execution of the same tasks. In fact, the decomposition of a program into individual program modules is generally considered to be an important part of good programming practice.

The use of functions also enables a programmer to build a customized library of frequently used routines or of routines containing system-dependent features. Each routine can be programmed as a separate function and stored within a special library file. If a program requires a particular routine, the corresponding library function can be accessed and attached to the program during the compilation process. Hence, many different programs can utilize a single function. This avoids repetitive programming between programs. It also promotes portability, since programs can be written that are independent of system-dependent features.

In this chapter we will see how functions are defined and how they are accessed from various places within a C program. We will then consider the manner in which information is passed to a function. Our discussion will include the use of function prototypes, as recommended by the proposed American National Standards Institute (ANSI) standard. And finally, we will discuss an interesting and important programming technique known as *recursion*, in which a function can access itself repeatedly.

7.1 A BRIEF OVERVIEW

A *function* is a self-contained program segment that carries out some specific, well-defined task. Every C program consists of one or more functions (see Sec. 1.5). One of these functions must be called main. Program execution will always begin by carrying out the instructions in main. Additional functions will be subordinate to main, and perhaps to one another.

If a program contains multiple functions, their definitions may appear in any order, though they must be independent of one another. That is, one function definition cannot be embedded within another.

A function will carry out its intended action whenever it is accessed (i.e., whenever the function is "called") from some other portion of the program. The same function can be accessed from several dif-

166

ferent places within a program. Once the function has carried out its intended action, control will be returned to the point from which the function was accessed.

Generally, a function will process information passed to it from the calling portion of the program, and return a single value. Information will be passed to the function via special identifiers called *arguments* (also called *parameters*) and returned via the return statement. Some functions, however, accept information but do not return anything (for example, the library function printf), whereas other functions (the library function scanf, for example) return multiple values.

Example 7.1   Lowercase to Uppercase Character Conversion   In Example 3.31 we saw a simple C program that read in a single lowercase character, converted it to uppercase using the library function toupper and then wrote out the uppercase equivalent. We will now consider a similar program, though we will define and utilize our own function for carrying out the lowercase to uppercase conversion.

Our purpose in doing this is to illustrate the principal features involved in the use of functions. Hence, concentrate on the overall logic and do not worry about the details of each individual statement.

Here is the complete program.

```c
#include <stdio.h>

/* convert a lower-case character to upper-case
                            using a programmer-defined function */

main()

{
    char lower, upper;
    char lower_to_upper(char lower);    /* function declaration */

    printf("Please enter a lower-case character: ");
    scanf("%c", &lower);
    upper = lower_to_upper(lower);
    printf("\nThe upper-case equivalent is %c\n\n", upper);
}


char lower_to_upper(char c1)              /* function definition */

{
    char c2;

    c2 = (c1 >= 'a' && c1 <= 'z') ? ('A' + c1 - 'a') : c1;
    return(c2);
}
```

This program consists of two functions — the required main function, and the programmer-defined function lower_to_upper, which converts lowercase characters to uppercase. Notice that main reads in a character (which may or may not be a lowercase letter) and assigns it to the char-type variable lower. Then main calls lower_to_upper, transferring the lowercase character (lower) to lower_to_upper and receiving the equivalent uppercase character (upper). The uppercase character is then written out, and the program ends.

Now consider the function lower_to_upper. This function converts only lowercase letters; all other characters are returned intact. The lowercase letter is transferred via the argument c1, and the uppercase equivalent, c2, is returned to the calling portion of the program via the return statement. Notice that the variables lower and upper in main correspond to the variables c1 and c2 within lower_to_upper, respectively.

We will consider the rules associated with function definitions and function accesses in the remainder of this chapter.

7.2 DEFINING A FUNCTION

As originally conceived, a function definition has three principal components: the first line, the argument declarations and the body of the function.

The first line of a function definition contains the type specification of the value returned by the function, followed by the function name, and (optionally) a set of arguments, separated by commas and enclosed in parentheses. The type specification can be omitted if the function returns an integer or a character (recall that a character is represented as an integer quantity). An empty pair of parentheses must follow the function name if the function definition does not include any arguments.

In general terms, the first line can be written as

```
data-type name(formal argument 1, formal argument 2, ...,
                                            formal argument n)
```

where *data-type* represents the data type of the value which is returned, and *name* represents the function name. (See Sec. 8.5 for a more inclusive form.)

The formal arguments allow information to be transferred from the calling portion of the program to the function. They are also known as *parameters* or *formal parameters*. (The corresponding arguments in the *function reference* are called *actual arguments*, since they define the information actually being transferred. Some writers refer to actual arguments simply as *arguments*, or as *actual parameters*.) The identifiers used as formal arguments are "local" in the sense that they are not recognized outside of the function. Hence, the names of the formal arguments may be the same as the names of other identifiers that appear outside the function definition.

The argument declarations follow the first line. All formal arguments must be declared at this point in the function (unless function prototypes are used, as described in Sec. 7.6). Each formal argument must have the same data type as its corresponding actual argument. That is, each formal argument must be of the same data type as the data item it receives from the calling portion of the program.

The remainder of the function definition is a compound statement that defines the action to be taken by the function. This compound statement is sometimes referred to as the *body* of the function. It must follow the formal argument declarations. Like any other compound statement, this statement can contain expression statements, other compound statements, control statements, and so on. As a result, it can also access other functions. In fact, it can even access itself (this process is known as *recursion* and is discussed in Sec. 7.7).

Example 7.2   Consider once again the function `lower_to_upper`, which was originally presented in Example 7.1.

```
lower_to_upper(c1)    /* programmer-defined conversion function */

char c1;

{
    char c2;

    c2 = (c1 >= 'a' && c1 <= 'z') ? ('A' + c1 - 'a') : c1;
    return(c2);
}
```

The first line contains the title, `lower_to_upper`, followed by the formal argument `c1`, which is enclosed in parentheses. Note that `c1` represents the lowercase character that is transferred to the function from the calling portion of the program. A comment identifying the purpose of the function is also present, though this is not a part of the actual function.

Note that this function returns a character constant, which is actually an integer value. Therefore, a type specification is not required in the first line. It would be permissible, however, to write the first line as

```
char lower_to_upper(c1)    /* programmer-defined conversion function */
```

The formal argument c1 is declared to be a char-type variable on the second line. This is followed by the body of the function, which begins on the third line. Notice that the body contains the declaration of the local char-type variable c2. (Observe the distinction between the formal argument c1, and the local variable c2. Also, note that these two identifiers are declared in different places within the function.) Following the declaration of c2 is a statement that tests whether c1 represents a lowercase letter and then carries out the conversion. The original character is returned intact if it is not a lowercase letter. Finally, the return statement (see below) causes the converted character to be returned to the calling portion of the program.

Information is returned from the function to the calling portion of the program via the return statement. The return statement also causes control to be returned to the point from which the function was accessed.

In general terms. the return statement is written as

```
return expression;
```

The value of the *expression* is returned to the calling portion of the program, as in Example 7.2 above. The *expression* is optional, however; a return statement can be written without it. If the *expression* is omitted, the return statement simply causes control to revert back to the calling portion of the program, without any information transfer.

Only one expression can be included in the return statement. Thus, a function can return only one value to the calling portion of the program via return.

A function definition can include multiple return statements, each containing a different expression. Functions that include multiple branches often require multiple returns.

Example 7.3   Here is a variation of the function lower_to_upper, which appeared in Examples 7.1 and 7.2.

```
lower_to_upper(c1)    /* programmer-defined conversion function */

char c1;

{
    if (c1 >= 'a' && c1 <= 'z')
        return('A' + c1 - 'a');
    else
        return(c1);

}
```

This function utilizes the if - else statement rather than the conditional operator. It is somewhat less compact than the original version, though the logic may be clearer. On the other hand, the current function does not require the local variable c2.

Notice that the function contains two different return statements. The first returns an expression which represents a single uppercase character (actually, an integer); the second returns the original character, unchanged.

The return statement can be absent altogether from a function definition, though this is generally regarded as poor programming practice. If a function reaches the end of the block without encountering a return statement, control simply reverts back to the calling portion of the program without returning any information. Using an empty return statement (without the accompanying expression) is recommended in such situations, to clarify the logic and to accommodate future modifications to the function.

Example 7.4   The following function accepts two integer quantities and determines the larger value, which is then written out. The function does not return any information to the calling program.

```
maximum(x, y)

/* determine the larger of two integer quantities */

int x, y;

{
    int z;

    z = (x >= y) ? x : y;
    printf("\n\nMaximum value = %d", z);
    return;
}
```

Notice that an empty return statement is included as a matter of good programming practice. The function would still work properly, however, if the return statement were not present.

Now let us momentarily return to the function type specification, which appears in the first line of the function definition. We have already stated that this type specification can be omitted if the function returns an integer quantity or a character. If the function returns a different type of quantity, such as a long integer, floating-point or double-precision quantity, however, the first line of the function definition must include a corresponding type specification. An example is shown below.

Example 7.5 The *factorial* of a positive integer quantity, n, is defined as $n! = 1 \times 2 \times 3 \times \cdots \times n$. Thus, $2! = 1 \times 2 = 2$, $3! = 1 \times 2 \times 3 = 6$, $4! = 1 \times 2 \times 3 \times 4 = 24$, and so on.

The function shown below calculates the factorial of a given positive integer n. The factorial is returned as a long integer quantity, since factorials grow in magnitude very rapidly as n increases. (For example, $8! = 40,320$. This value, expressed as an ordinary integer, may be too large for some computers.)

```
long int factorial(n)

/* calculate the factorial of n */

int n;

{
    int i;
    long int prod = 1;

    if (n > 1)
        for (i = 2; i <= n; ++i)
            prod *= i;
    return(prod);
}
```

Notice the long int type specification included in the first line of the function definition. Also, the local variable prod is declared to be a long integer within the function. Note that prod is assigned an initial value of 1. Its value is then recalculated within a for loop. The final value of prod, which is returned by the function, represents the desired value of *n* factorial.

Now suppose the data type specified in the first line is inconsistent with the expression that appears in the return statement. Under such conditions the compiler will attempt to convert the quantity represented by the expression to the data type specified in the first line. This could result in a compilation error, or it might involve a partial loss of data (for instance, due to truncation). In any event, you should avoid inconsistencies of this type.

Example 7.6   The following function definition is identical to that in Example 7.5 except that the first line does not contain a type specification.

```
factorial(n)

/* calculate the factorial of n */

int n;

{
    int i;
    long int prod = 1;

    if (n > 1)
       for (i = 2; i <= n; ++i)
            prod *= i;
    return(prod);
}
```

The function expects to return an ordinary integer quantity, since there is no explicit type declaration in the first line of the function definition. However, the quantity being returned (prod) is declared to be a long integer within the function. This inconsistency can result in an error. (Some compilers will generate a diagnostic error and then stop without completing the compilation.) The problem can be avoided, however, by adding a long int type declaration to the first line of the function definition, as in Example 7.5.

Most newer C compilers permit the keyword void to appear as a type specifier when defining a function that does not return anything. It is good programming practice to use this feature if it is available.

Example 7.7   Consider once again the function presented in Example 7.4, which accepts two integer quantities and writes out the larger of the two. Recall that this function does not return anything to the calling portion of the program. Therefore, many compilers will permit the function to be written as

```
void maximum(x, y)

/* determine the larger of two integer quantities */

int x, y;

{
    int z;

    z = (x >= y) ? x : y;
    printf("\n\nMaximum value = %d", z);
    return;
}
```

This function is identical to that shown in Example 7.4 except that the keyword void has been added to the first line, indicating that the function does not return anything.

7.3 ACCESSING A FUNCTION

A function can be accessed (i.e., *called*) by specifying its name, followed by a list of arguments enclosed in parentheses and separated by commas. If the function call does not require any arguments, an empty pair of parentheses must follow the function's name. The function call may appear by itself (that is, it may comprise a simple expression), or it may be one of the operands within a more complex expression.

The arguments appearing in the function call are referred to as *actual arguments*, in contrast to the formal arguments that appear in the first line of the function definition. (They are also known simply as *arguments*, or as *actual parameters*.) In a normal function call, there will be one actual argument for each formal argument. The actual arguments may be expressed as constants, single variables, or more complex expressions. However, each actual argument must be of the same data type as its corresponding formal argument.

Example 7.8 Consider once again the program originally shown in Example 7.1, which reads in a single lower-case character, converts it to uppercase using a programmer-defined function, and then writes out the uppercase equivalent.

```
#include <stdio.h>

/* convert a lower-case character to upper-case
                          using a programmer-defined function */

main()

{
    char lower, upper;

    printf("Please enter a lower-case character: ");
    scanf("%c", &lower);
    upper = lower_to_upper(lower);
    printf("\nThe upper-case equivalent is %c\n\n", upper);
}

lower_to_upper(c1)     /* this is the programmer-defined conversion function */

char c1;

{
    char c2;

    c2 = (c1 >= 'a' && c1 <= 'z') ? ('A' + c1 - 'a') : c1;
    return(c2);
}
```

This program contains only one call to the programmer-defined function lower_to_upper. The call is a part of the assignment expression upper = lower_to_upper(lower).

The function call contains one actual argument, the char-type variable lower. Note that the corresponding formal argument, c1, within the function definition is also a char-type variable.

Activating the function via the function call causes the value of lower to be transferred to the function. This value is represented by c1 within the function. The value of the uppercase equivalent, c2, is then generated and returned to the calling portion of the program, where it is assigned to the char-type variable upper.

Note that the last two statements in main can be combined to read

```
printf("\nThe upper-case equivalent is %c\n\n", lower_to_upper(lower));
```

The call to lower_to_upper is now an actual argument for the library function printf. Also, note that the variable upper is no longer necessary.

There may be several different calls to the same function from various places within a program. The actual arguments may differ from one function call to another. Within each function call, however, the actual arguments must correspond to the formal arguments in the function definition; i.e., the number of actual arguments must be the same as the number of formal arguments and each actual argument must be of the same data type as its corresponding formal argument.

Example 7.9 Largest of Three Integer Quantities The following program determines the largest of three integer quantities. This program makes use of a function that determines the larger of two integer quantities. The function is similar to that defined in Example 7.4, except that the current function returns the larger value to the calling program rather than displaying it.

The overall strategy is to determine the larger of the first two quantities, and then compare this value with the third quantity. The largest quantity is then written by the main part of the program.

```c
#include <stdio.h>

/* determine the largest of three integer quantities */

main()

{
    int a, b, c, d;

    /* read the integer quantities */

    printf("\na = ");
    scanf("%d", &a);
    printf("\nb = ");
    scanf("%d", &b);
    printf("\nc = ");
    scanf("%d", &c);

    /* calculate and display the maximum value */

    d = maximum(a, b);
    printf("\n\nmaximum = %d", maximum(c, d));
}


maximum(x, y)   /* determine the larger of two integer quantities */

int x, y;

{
    int z;

    z = (x >= y) ? x : y;
    return(z);
}
```

The function `maximum` is accessed from two different places in `main`. In the first call to `maximum` the actual arguments are the variables `a` and `b`, whereas the arguments are `c` and `d` in the second call (`d` is a temporary variable representing the maximum value of `a` and `b`).

Note that the two statements which access `maximum`, i.e.,

```c
d = maximum(a, b);
printf("\n\nmaximum = %d", maximum(c, d));
```

can be replaced by the single statement

```c
printf("\n\nmaximum = %d", maximum(c, maximum(a, b)));
```

In this statement we see that one of the calls to `maximum` is an argument for the other call. Thus, the calls are embedded, one within the other, and the intermediary variable, `d`, is not required. Such embedded function calls are permissible, though their logic may be less clear to the beginning programmer.

If a function returns a noninteger quantity and the portion of the program containing the function call precedes the function definition, then there must be a *function declaration* in the calling portion of the program. This is sometimes referred to as a *forward declaration*. The function declaration effectively informs the compiler that a function will be accessed before it is defined. (Note the important distinction between a function declaration and a function definition.) Many programmers include forward declarations in their programs, whether they are needed or not, simply as a matter of good programming practice.

In its simplest form, a function declaration can be written as

```
data-type  name();
```

where *data-type* refers to the data type of the quantity returned by the function, and *name* refers to the function name.

Example 7.10 Calculating Factorials   Here is a complete program to calculate the factorial of a positive integer quantity. The program utilizes the function factorial, defined in Example 7.5.

```
#include <stdio.h>

/* calculate the factorial of an integer quantity */

main()

{
    int n;
    long int factorial();       /* function declaration */

    /* read in the integer quantity */

    printf("\nn = ");
    scanf("%d", &n);

    /* calculate and display the factorial */

    printf("\nn! = %ld", factorial(n));
}


long int factorial(n)

/* calculate the factorial of n */

int n;

{
    int i;
    long int prod = 1;

    if (n > 1)
        for (i = 2; i <= n; ++i)
            prod *= i;
    return(prod);
}
```

The function makes use of an integer argument (n) and two local variables—an ordinary integer (i) and a long integer (prod). Since the function returns a long integer, the type declaration long int appears in the first line of the function definition. Also, notice that the calling portion of the program (main) contains the forward declaration

```
long int factorial();
```

This declaration indicates that the function factorial, which returns a long integer quantity, will be defined later in the program. The declaration is required because the function returns a quantity that is not an ordinary integer, and the function call precedes the function definition.

If the function definition precedes all function calls, then it is not necessary to include a function declaration within the calling portion of the program. This is true regardless of the type of data returned by the function. It is, however, good programming practice to include such declarations, whether or not they are actually required.

Example 7.11   Calculating Factorials   The following program calculates the factorial of a positive integer quantity, just like the program presented in Example 7.10. In this program, however, the function definition precedes the first (and only) function call. Therefore, main need not include a function declaration, even though the function (factorial) returns a long integer quantity. The function definition is nevertheless included, as a matter of good programming practice.

```
#include <stdio.h>

/* calculate the factorial of an integer quantity */

long int factorial(n)

/* calculate the factorial of n */

int n;

{
    int i;
    long int prod = 1;

    if (n > 1)
        for (i = 2; i <= n; ++i)
            prod *= i;
    return(prod);
}


main()

{
    int n;
    long int factorial();        /* function declaration */

    /* read in the integer quantity */

    printf("\nn = ");
    scanf("%d", &n);

    /* calculate and display the factorial */

    printf("\nn! = %ld", factorial(n));
}
```

Function calls can span several levels within a program; function A can call function B, which can call function C, and so on. Also, function A can call function C directly, and so on.

Example 7.12 Simulation of a Game of Chance (Shooting Craps) Here is an interesting programming problem that includes multiple function calls at several different levels. Both library functions and programmer-defined functions are required.

Craps is a popular dice game in which you throw a pair of dice one or more times until you either win or lose. The game can be simulated on a computer by substituting the generation of random numbers for the actual throwing of the dice.

There are two ways to win in craps. You can throw the dice once and obtain a score of either 7 or 11; or you can obtain a 4, 5, 6, 8, 9 or 10 on the first throw and then repeat the same score on a subsequent throw before obtaining a 7. Conversely, there are two ways to lose. You can throw the dice once and obtain a 2, 3 or 12; or you can obtain a 4, 5, 6, 8, 9 or 10 on the first throw and then obtain a 7 on a subsequent throw before repeating your original score.

We will develop the game interactively, so that one throw of the dice will be simulated each time you press the RETURN key on the keyboard. A message will then appear indicating the outcome of each throw. At the end of each game, you will be asked whether or not you want to continue to play.

Our program will require a random number generator that produces uniformly distributed integers between 1 and 6. (By *uniformly distributed* we mean that any integer between 1 and 6 is just as likely to appear as any other integer.) Most versions of C include a random number generator in their library routines. These random number generators typically return a floating-point number uniformly distributed between 0 and 1, or an integer quantity uniformly distributed between 0 and some very large integer value.

We will employ a library function called rand, which returns a uniformly distributed integer between 0 and $2^{15} - 1$ (i.e., between 0 and 32,767). We then convert each random integer quantity to a floating-point number, x, which varies from 0 to 0.99999 $\cdots$. To do so, we write

```
x = rand() / 32768.0
```

Note that the denominator is written as a floating-point constant. This forces the quotient, and hence x, to be floating-point.

The quantity

```
(int) (6 * x)
```

will be a truncated integer whose value will be uniformly distributed between 0 and 5. Thus, we obtain the desired result simply by adding 1, that is,

```
n = 1 + (int) (6 * x)
```

This value will represent the random outcome of rolling one die. If we repeat this process a second time and add the results, we obtain the result of rolling two dice.

The following function utilizes the above strategy to simulate one throw of a pair of dice.

```
throw()   /* simulate one throw of a pair of dice */

{

    float x1, x2;  /* random floating-point numbers between 0 and 1 */
    int n1, n2;    /* random integers between 1 and 6 */

    x1 = rand() / 32768.0;
    x2 = rand() / 32768.0;

    n1 = 1 + (int) (6 * x1);   /* simulate first die */
    n2 = 1 + (int) (6 * x2);   /* simulate second die */

    return(n1 + n2);           /* score is sum of two dice */

}
```

The function returns the result of each throw (an integer quantity whose value varies between 2 and 12). Note that this final result will *not* be uniformly distributed, even though the individual values of n1 and n2 are.

Now let us define another function, called play, that can simulate one complete game of craps. Thus, the dice will be thrown as many times as necessary to establish either a win or a loss. This function will access throw. The complete rules of craps will also be built into this function.

In pseudocode, we can write the function play as

```
play()   /* simulate one complete game */

{
    int score1, score2;

    /* instruct the user to throw the dice */

    /* initialize the random number generator */

    score1 = throw();

    switch (score1)  {

    case 7:
    case 11:

        /* write a message indicating a win on the first throw */

    case 2:
    case 3:
    case 12:

        /* write a message indicating a loss on the first throw */

    case 4:
    case 5:
    case 6:
    case 8:
    case 9:
    case 10:

        do  {
                /* instruct the user to throw the dice again */

                score2 = throw();

        }     while (score2 != score1 && score2 != 7);


        if (score2 == score1)

            /* write a message indicating a win */

        else

            /* write a message indicating a loss */
    }

    return;
}
```

Finally, the main routine will control the execution of the game. This routine will consist of a while loop containing some interactive input/output and a call to play. Thus, we can write the pseudocode for main as

```
main()

{

    /* declarations */

    /* initialize the random number generator */

    /* generate a welcoming message */

    while ( /* player wants to continue */ )   {

        play();

        /* ask if player wants to continue */
    }

    /* generate a sign-off message */
}
```

The library function srand will be used to initialize the random number generator. This function requires a positive integer, called a *seed*, which establishes the sequence of random numbers generated by rand. A different sequence will be generated for each seed. For convenience, we can include a value for the seed as a symbolic constant within the program. (If the program is executed repeatedly with the same seed, the same sequence of random numbers will be generated each time. This is helpful when debugging the program.)

Here is the complete C program.

```
/* simulation of a craps game */

#include <stdio.h>
#include <stdlib.h>

#define  SEED   12345

main()

{
    char answer = 'Y';

    printf("Welcome to the Game of CRAPS\n\n");
    printf("To throw the dice, press RETURN\n\n");

    srand(SEED);   /* initialize the random number generator */

    /* main loop */

    while (toupper(answer) != 'N')   {
        play();
        printf("\nDo you want to play again? (Y/N) ");
        scanf("%1s", &answer);
        printf("\n");
    }
    printf("Bye, have a nice day");
}
```

```
play()   /* simulate one complete game */

{
    int score1, score2;
    char dummy;

    printf("\nPlease throw the dice ...");
    scanf("%c", &dummy);
    printf("\n");
    score1 = throw();
    printf("\n%2d", score1);

    switch (score1)  {

    case 7:   /* win on first throw */
    case 11:

        printf(" - Congratulations! You WIN on the first throw\n");
        break;

    case 2:   /* lose on first throw */
    case 3:
    case 12:

        printf(" - Sorry, you LOSE on the first throw\n");
        break;

    case 4:   /* additional throws are required */
    case 5:
    case 6:
    case 8:
    case 9:
    case 10:

        do  {
                printf(" - Throw the dice again ...");
                scanf("%c", &dummy);
                score2 = throw();
                printf("\n%2d", score2);
        }  while (score2 != score1 && score2 != 7);

        if (score2 == score1)
           printf(" - You WIN by matching your first score\n");
        else
           printf(" - You LOSE by failing to match your first score\n");
        break;
    }

    return;
}
```

```
throw()   /* simulate one throw of a pair of dice */

{
    float x1, x2;   /* random floating-point numbers between 0 and 1 */
    int n1, n2;     /* random integers between 1 and 6 */

    x1 = rand() / 32768.0;
    x2 = rand() / 32768.0;

    n1 = 1 + (int) (6 * x1);   /* simulate first die */
    n2 = 1 + (int) (6 * x2);   /* simulate second die */

    return(n1 + n2);            /* score is sum of two dice */
}
```

Notice that main calls srand and play. One argument is in the call to srand (the value of the seed), but no arguments are passed to play. Also, note that play calls throw from two different places, and throw calls rand from two different places. No arguments are passed from play to throw or from throw to rand. However, rand returns a random integer to throw, and throw returns the value of an integer expression (the outcome of one throw of the dice) to play. Notice that play does not return any information to main.

Within play, there are two references to the scanf function, each of which enters a value for the variable dummy. It should be understood that dummy is not actually used within the program. The scanf functions are present simply to generate a time delay, until the user presses the RETURN key.

This program must be run in an interactive environment, such as on a personal computer or within a time-sharing system. A typical set of output is shown below. The user's responses are underlined for clarity.

```
Welcome to the Game of CRAPS

To throw the dice, press RETURN (return)


Please throw the dice ...

 6 — Throw the dice again ...

10 — Throw the dice again ...

 7 — You LOSE by failing to match your first score

Do you want to play again? (Y/N) y


Please throw the dice ...

 7 — Congratulations!  You WIN on the first throw

Do you want to play again? (Y/N) y


Please throw the dice ...

11 — Congratulations!  You WIN on the first throw

Do you want to play again? (Y/N) y
```

```
Please throw the dice ...

  8 — Throw the dice again ...

  5 — Throw the dice again ...

  7 — You LOSE by failing to match your first score

Do you want to play again? (Y/N) y


Please throw the dice ...

  6 — Throw the dice again ...

  4 — Throw the dice again ...

  6 — You WIN by matching your first score

Do you want to play again? (Y/N) y


Please throw the dice ...

  3 — Sorry, you LOSE on the first throw

Do you want to play again? (Y/N) n

Bye, have a nice day
```

7.4 PASSING ARGUMENTS TO A FUNCTION

When a single value is passed to a function via an actual argument, the value of the actual argument is *copied* into the function. Therefore, the value of the corresponding formal argument can be altered within the function, but the value of the actual argument within the calling routine will not change. This procedure for passing the value of an argument to a function is known as *passing by value*.

Example 7.13   Here is a simple C program containing a function that alters the value of its argument.

```c
#include <stdio.h>

main()
{
    int a = 2;

    printf("\na = %d  (from main, before calling the function)", a);
    modify(a);
    printf("\n\na = %d  (from main, after calling the function)", a);
}

modify(a)
int a;
{
    a *= 3;
    printf("\n\na = %d  (from the function, after being modified)", a);
    return;
}
```

The original value of a (i.e., a = 2) is displayed when main begins execution. This value is then passed to the function modify, where it is multiplied by three and the new value displayed. Note that it is the altered value of the formal argument that is displayed within the function. Finally, the value of a within main (i.e., the actual argument) is again displayed, after control is transferred back to main from modify.

When the program is executed, the following output is generated:

```
a = 2   (from main, before calling the function)

a = 6   (from the function, after being modified)

a = 2   (from main, after calling the function)
```

These results show that a is not altered within main, even though the corresponding value of a is changed within modify.

Passing an argument by value has advantages and disadvantages. On the plus side, it allows a single-valued actual argument to be written as an expression rather than being restricted to a single variable. Moreover, if the actual argument is expressed as a single variable, it protects the value of this variable from alterations within the function. On the other hand, it prevents information from being transferred back to the calling portion of the program via arguments. Thus, passing by value is restricted to a one-way transfer of information.

Example 7.14 Calculating Depreciation   Let us consider a variation of the depreciation program presented in Example 6.26. The overall objective is to calculate depreciation as a function of time using any one of three different commonly used methods, as before. Now, however, we will rewrite the program so that a separate function is used for each method. This approach offers us a cleaner way to organize the program into its logical components. In addition, we will move a block of repeated output instructions into a separate function, thus eliminating some redundant programming from the program's original version.

We will also expand the generality of the program somewhat by permitting different sets of depreciation calculations to be carried out on the same input data. Thus, at the end of each set of calculations the user will be asked if another set of calculations is desired. If the answer is yes, then the user will be asked whether or not to enter new data.

Here is the new version of the program.

```
#include <stdio.h>

/* calculate depreciation using one of three different methods */

main()

{
    int n, choice = 0;
    float val;
    char answer1 = 'Y', answer2 = 'Y';

    while (toupper(answer1) != 'N')  {

        /* read input data */

        if (toupper(answer2) != 'N')  {
            printf("\nOriginal value: ");
            scanf("%f", &val);
            printf("Number of years: ");
            scanf("%d", &n);
        }
        printf("\nMethod: (1-SL  2-DDB  3-SYD) ");
        scanf("%d", &choice);
```

```
        switch (choice)  {

        case 1:      /* straight-line method */

            printf("\nStraight-Line Method\n\n");
            sl(val, n);
            break;

        case 2:      /* double-declining-balance method */

            printf("\nDouble-Declining-Balance Method\n\n");
            ddb(val, n);
            break;

        case 3:      /* sum-of-the-years'-digits method */

            printf("\nSum-of-the-Years\'-Digits Method\n\n");
            syd(val, n);
        }

        printf("\n\nAnother calculation? (Y/N) ");
        scanf("%1s", &answer1);
        if (toupper(answer1) != 'N')   {
            printf("Enter a new set of data? (Y/N) ");
            scanf("%1s", &answer2);
        }
    }
    printf("\nGoodbye, have a nice day!\n");
}


sl(val, n)

/* calculate depreciation using the straight-line method */

float val;
int n;

{
    float deprec;
    int year;

    deprec = val/n;
    for (year = 1; year <= n; ++year)  {
        val -= deprec;
        writeoutput(year, deprec, val);
    }
    return;
}


ddb(val, n)

/* calculate depreciation using the double-declining-balance method */

float val;
int n;
```

```
{

    float deprec;
    int year;

    for (year = 1;  year <= n;  ++year)  {
        deprec = 2*val/n;
        val -= deprec;
        writeoutput(year, deprec, val);
    }
    return;
}

syd(val, n)

/* calculate depreciation using the sum-of-the-years'-digits method */

float val;
int n;

{

    float tag, deprec;
    int year;

    tag = val;
    for (year = 1;  year <= n;  ++year)  {
        deprec = (n-year+1)*tag / (n*(n+1)/2);
        val -= deprec;
        writeoutput(year, deprec, val);
    }
    return;
}

writeoutput(year, depreciation, value)

/* write output data */

int year;
float depreciation, value;

{

    printf("End of Year %2d", year);
    printf("  Depreciation: %7.2f", depreciation);
    printf("  Current Value: %8.2f\n", value);
    return;
}
```

Notice that the switch statement is still employed, as in Example 6.26, though there are now only three choices rather than four. (The fourth choice, which ended the computation in the previous version, is now handled through interactive dialog at the end of each set of calculations.) A separate function is now provided for each type of calculation. In particular, the straight-line calculations are carried out within function sl, the double-declining-balance calculations within ddb and the sum-of-the-years'-digits calculations within syd. Each of these functions includes the formal arguments val and n, which represent the original value of the item and its lifetime, respectively. Note that the value of val is altered within each function, although the original value assigned to val remains unaltered within main. It is this feature that allows repeated sets of calculations with the same input data.

The last function, writeoutput, causes the results of each set of calculations to be written out year-by-year. This function is accessed from sl, ddb and syd. In each call to writeoutput, the *altered* value of val is transferred as an actual argument, along with the current year (year) and the current year's depreciation (deprec). Note that these quantities are called value, year and depreciation, respectively, within writeoutput.

A sample interactive session that makes use of this program is shown below.

```
Original value: 8000
Number of years: 10

Method: (1-SL  2-DDB  3-SYD) 1

Straight-Line Method

End of Year  1  Depreciation:  800.00  Current Value:  7200.00
End of Year  2  Depreciation:  800.00  Current Value:  6400.00
End of Year  3  Depreciation:  800.00  Current Value:  5600.00
End of Year  4  Depreciation:  800.00  Current Value:  4800.00
End of Year  5  Depreciation:  800.00  Current Value:  4000.00
End of Year  6  Depreciation:  800.00  Current Value:  3200.00
End of Year  7  Depreciation:  800.00  Current Value:  2400.00
End of Year  8  Depreciation:  800.00  Current Value:  1600.00
End of Year  9  Depreciation:  800.00  Current Value:   800.00
End of Year 10  Depreciation:  800.00  Current Value:     0.00


Another calculation? (Y/N) y
Enter a new set of data? (Y/N) n

Method: (1-SL  2-DDB  3-SYD) 2

Double-Declining-Balance Method

End of Year  1  Depreciation: 1600.00  Current Value:  6400.00
End of Year  2  Depreciation: 1280.00  Current Value:  5120.00
End of Year  3  Depreciation: 1024.00  Current Value:  4096.00
End of Year  4  Depreciation:  819.20  Current Value:  3276.80
End of Year  5  Depreciation:  655.36  Current Value:  2621.44
End of Year  6  Depreciation:  524.29  Current Value:  2097.15
End of Year  7  Depreciation:  419.43  Current Value:  1677.72
End of Year  8  Depreciation:  335.54  Current Value:  1342.18
End of Year  9  Depreciation:  268.44  Current Value:  1073.74
End of Year 10  Depreciation:  214.75  Current Value:   858.99


Another calculation? (Y/N) y
Enter a new set of data? (Y/N) n

Method: (1-SL  2-DDB  3-SYD) 3

Sum-of-the-Years'-Digits Method

End of Year  1  Depreciation: 1454.55  Current Value:  6545.45
End of Year  2  Depreciation: 1309.09  Current Value:  5236.36
End of Year  3  Depreciation: 1163.64  Current Value:  4072.73
End of Year  4  Depreciation: 1018.18  Current Value:  3054.55
End of Year  5  Depreciation:  872.73  Current Value:  2181.82
End of Year  6  Depreciation:  727.27  Current Value:  1454.55
End of Year  7  Depreciation:  581.82  Current Value:   872.73
End of Year  8  Depreciation:  436.36  Current Value:   436.36
End of Year  9  Depreciation:  290.91  Current Value:   145.45
End of Year 10  Depreciation:  145.45  Current Value:     0.00
```

```
Another calculation? (Y/N) y
Enter a new set of data? (Y/N) y

Original value: 5000
Number of years: 4

Method: (1-SL  2-DDB  3-SYD) 1

Straight-Line Method

End of Year  1  Depreciation: 1250.00  Current Value:  3750.00
End of Year  2  Depreciation: 1250.00  Current Value:  2500.00
End of Year  3  Depreciation: 1250.00  Current Value:  1250.00
End of Year  4  Depreciation: 1250.00  Current Value:     0.00


Another calculation? (Y/N) y
Enter a new set of data? (Y/N) n

Method: (1-SL  2-DDB  3-SYD) 2

Double-Declining-Balance Method

End of Year  1  Depreciation: 2500.00  Current Value:  2500.00
End of Year  2  Depreciation: 1250.00  Current Value:  1250.00
End of Year  3  Depreciation:  625.00  Current Value:   625.00
End of Year  4  Depreciation:  312.50  Current Value:   312.50


Another calculation? (Y/N) n

Goodbye, have a nice day!
```

Notice that two different sets of input data are processed. Depreciation is calculated for the first set using all three methods, and for the second set using only the first two methods. Thus, it is not necessary to re-enter the input data simply to recalculate the depreciation using a different method.

Arrays are passed differently than single-valued entities. If an array name is specified as an actual argument, the individual array elements are not copied to the function. Instead, the *location* of the array (i.e., the location of the first element) is passed to the function. If an element of the array is accessed within the function, the access will refer to the location of that array element relative to the location of the first element. Thus, any alteration to an array element within the function will carry over to the calling routine. We will discuss this in greater detail in Chap. 9, when we formally consider arrays.

Other kinds of data structures can also be passed as arguments to a function. We will discuss the transfer of such arguments in later chapters, as the additional data structures are introduced.

7.5 SPECIFYING ARGUMENT DATA TYPES

In Sec. 7.3 we saw that the calling portion of a program must contain a function declaration (i.e., a *forward declaration*) if a function returns a noninteger value and the function call precedes the function definition. Moreover, we saw that a function declaration *may* be included in the calling portion of a program even if its presence is not absolutely necessary. We now mention an additional reason for including a function declaration within the calling portion of a program; namely, it is possible to include the data types of the *arguments* within the function declaration. The compiler will then convert the value of each actual argument to the declared data type (if necessary) and then compare each (converted) actual data type with its corresponding formal argument. A compilation error will result if the data types do not agree. Thus, the use of function declarations will allow the programmer to be informed of data-type inconsistencies detected during the compilation process.

When the argument data types are specified in a function declaration, the general form of the function declaration can be written as

```
data-type name(argument type 1, argument type 2, ..., argument type n);
```

where `data-type` represents the data type of the quantity returned by the function, *name* represents the function name, and `argument type 1, argument type 2, ..., argument type n` refer to the data types of the first argument, the second argument, and so on. Remember that the argument data types are optional, even in situations that require a function declaration.

Note that this is an expansion of the general form of a function declaration presented in Sec. 7.3. More inclusive forms of function declarations are discussed in Secs. 7.6 and 8.3.

Example 7.15 Depreciation Revisited Consider once again the problem of calculating depreciation several different ways, as discussed in Example 6.26. We saw a modularized depreciation program, utilizing a separate function for each type of depreciation calculation, in Example 7.14. That program, however, did not include function declarations. We now present a modified version of that program, which includes function declarations with argument-type specifications. The addition of the type specifications permits type checking between the actual and the formal arguments when the program is compiled.

The modified form of the program, which includes the function declarations, is given below.

```c
#include <stdio.h>

/* calculate depreciation using one of three different methods */

main()

{
    int n, choice = 0;
    float val;
    char answer1 = 'Y', answer2 = 'Y';

    void sl(float, int);          /* function declaration */
    void ddb(float, int);         /* function declaration */
    void syd(float, int);         /* function declaration */

    while (toupper(answer1) != 'N')   {

        /* read input data*/

        if (toupper(answer2) != 'N')   {
            printf("\nOriginal value: ");
            scanf("%f", &val);
            printf("Number of years: ");
            scanf("%d", &n);
        }
        printf("\nMethod: (1-SL  2-DDB  3-SYD) ");
        scanf("%d", &choice);
```

```
        switch (choice)  {

        case 1:      /* straight-line method */

            printf("\nStraight-Line Method\n\n");
            sl(val, n);
            break;

        case 2:      /* double-declining-balance method */

            printf("\nDouble-Declining-Balance Method\n\n");
            ddb(val, n);
            break;

        case 3:      /* sum-of-the-years'-digits method */

            printf("\nSum-of-the-Years\'-Digits Method\n\n");
            syd(val, n);
        }

        printf("\n\nAnother calculation? (Y/N) ");
        scanf("%1s", &answer1);
        if (toupper(answer1) != 'N')   {
           printf("Enter a new set of data? (Y/N) ");
           scanf("%1s", &answer2);
        }
    }
    printf("\nGoodbye, have a nice day!\n");
}


void sl(val, n)

/* calculate depreciation using the straight-line method */

float val;
int n;

{
    float deprec;
    int year;
    void writeoutput(int, float, float);      /* function declaration */

    deprec = val/n;
    for (year = 1; year <= n; ++year)  {
        val -= deprec;
        writeoutput(year, deprec, val);
    }
    return;
}


void ddb(val, n)

/* calculate depreciation using the double-declining-balance method */

float val;
int n;
```

```
{
    float deprec;
    int year;
    void writeoutput(int, float, float);     /* function declaration */

    for (year = 1; year <= n; ++year)  {
        deprec = 2*val/n;
        val -= deprec;
        writeoutput(year, deprec, val);
    }
    return;
}


void syd(val, n)

/* calculate depreciation using the sum-of-the-years'-digits method */

float val;
int n;

{
    float tag, deprec;
    int year;
    void writeoutput(int, float, float);     /* function declaration */

    tag = val;
    for (year = 1; year <= n; ++year)  {
        deprec = (n-year+1)*tag / (n*(n+1)/2);
        val -= deprec;
        writeoutput(year, deprec, val);
    }
    return;
}


void writeoutput(year, depreciation, value)

/* write output data */

int year;
float depreciation, value;

{
    printf("End of Year %2d", year);
    printf("  Depreciation: %7.2f", depreciation);
    printf("  Current Value: %8.2f\n", value);
    return;
}
```

Note that main now contains type declarations for the functions sl, ddb and syd. These declarations specify that each function call will include two actual arguments, the first of which will be floating-point and the second, integer.

Within each of these functions (i.e., within sl, ddb and syd) we see a declaration for writeoutput (since each of these functions calls writeoutput). These declarations state that the calls to writeoutput will each include three actual arguments, the first of which will be integer and the remaining two, floating-point.

Finally, note that the function declarations and their corresponding definitions each include the data type `void` for the return value. This specifies that each function does not return anything, as discussed in Sec. 7.2.

Execution of this program results in exactly the same output as the program presented earlier in Example 7.14. (It is instructive to change the order of the argument type specifications in one or more of the function declarations and then observe what happens when an attempt is made to compile the program.)

We have already seen that most C compilers support the use of the keyword `void` in function definitions, as a return data type indicating that the function does not return anything (see Sec. 7.2.). Function declarations may also include `void` for the same purpose. In addition, `void` may appear in an argument list, in both function definitions and function declarations, to indicate that a function does not require arguments. In this latter case, `void` appears by itself in the area normally used for argument specifications. The following example illustrates this full use of `void`:

Example 7.16   Shooting Craps   Here is a variation of the program that simulates a game of craps, originally shown in Example 7.12.

```c
/* simulation of a craps game */

#include <stdio.h>
#include <stdlib.h>

#define  SEED  12345

main()

{
    void play(void);      /* function declaration */
    char answer = 'Y';

    printf("Welcome to the Game of CRAPS\n\n");
    printf("To throw the dice, press RETURN\n\n");

    srand(SEED);  /* initialize the random number generator */

    /* main loop */

    while (toupper(answer) != 'N')   {
        play();
        printf("\nDo you want to play again? (Y/N) ");
        scanf("%1s", &answer);
        printf("\n");
    }
    printf("Bye, have a nice day");
}


void play(void)    /* simulate one complete game */

{
    int throw(void);      /* function declaration */
    int score1, score2;
    char dummy;

    printf("\nPlease throw the dice ...");
    scanf("%c", &dummy);
    printf("\n");
    score1 = throw();
    printf("\n%2d", score1);
```

```
    switch (score1)  {

    case 7:    /* win on first throw */
    case 11:

        printf(" - Congratulations!  You WIN on the first throw\n");
        break;

    case 2:    /* lose on first throw */
    case 3:
    case 12:

        printf(" - Sorry, you LOSE on the first throw\n");
        break;

    case 4:    /* additional throws are required */
    case 5:
    case 6:
    case 8:
    case 9:
    case 10:

        do   {
                printf(" - Throw the dice again ...");
                scanf("%c", &dummy);
                score2 = throw();
                printf("\n%2d", score2);
        }  while (score2 != score1 && score2 != 7);

        if (score2 == score1)
           printf(" - You WIN by matching your first score\n");
        else
           printf(" - You LOSE by failing to match your first score\n");
        break;
    }

    return;
}


int throw(void)    /* simulate one throw of a pair of dice */

{

    float x1, x2;   /* random floating-point numbers between 0 and 1 */
    int n1, n2;     /* random integers between 1 and 6 */

    x1 = rand() / 32768.0;
    x2 = rand() / 32768.0;

    n1 = 1 + (int) (6 * x1);    /* simulate first die */
    n2 = 1 + (int) (6 * x2);    /* simulate second die */

    return(n1 + n2);            /* score is sum of two dice */
}
```

In this program, the function play, which is called from main, does not accept any arguments and does not return a value to main. Hence, void appears twice within the declaration for play (in main) and within the definition for play. The first appearance of void refers to the data type of the value returned by play, and the second appearance of void indicates the absence of arguments.

Similarly, the function throw, which is called from play, does not accept any arguments, though it does return an integer value to play. Therefore, the declaration for throw (in play) and the definition for throw include the data type int for the return type and void to indicate the absence of arguments.

7.6 FUNCTION PROTOTYPES

Many C compilers support a more comprehensive system for handling argument specifications in function declarations and function definitions. In particular, the proposed ANSI standard permits each of the argument data types within a function declaration to be followed by an argument name, that is,

```
data-type  name(type 1  arg 1,  type 2  arg 2, ...,  type n  arg n);
```

where arg 1, arg 2, ..., arg n refer to the first argument, the second argument, and so on.

Function declarations written in this form are called *function prototypes*. Their use is not mandatory in C. Function prototypes are desirable, however, because they further facilitate error checking between the calls to a function and the corresponding function definition.

Example 7.17 Several function declarations (function prototypes) are shown below. Two different forms of each declaration are presented, illustrating the older method for specifying argument types described in Sec. 7.5 and the newer method discussed in this section.

Older Method	*Newer Method*
int sample(int, int);	int sample(int a, int b);
float funct(int, float);	float funct(int i, float x);
void f(char, long, double);	void f(char c, long j, double z);
void demo(void);	void demo(void);

The names of the arguments within the function declaration need not be declared elsewhere in the program, since these are "dummy" argument names recognized only within the declaration. In practice, however, the argument names are often the same as the names of the actual arguments appearing in one of the function calls.

When the function is called, the names of the actual arguments need not be the same as the names shown in the declaration. However, the data types of the actual arguments must conform to the data types of the arguments within the declaration.

Example 7.18 The skeletal outline of a C program is shown below.

```
main()

{
    int a, b, c, d, i, j;            /* variable declarations */

    int funct(int a, int b);         /* function declaration
                                        (function prototype) */

    . . .

    i = funct(a, b);

    . . .

    j = funct(c, d);
}
```

The function prototype indicates that a and b are integer-type arguments. The function funct is called twice within main. In the first call, the actual arguments are the integer variables a and b. In the second call, the actual arguments are the integer variables c and d.

The ANSI standard also allows function *definitions* to be written more concisely, by combining formal argument declarations with the first line of the function definition. Thus, the first line in the function definition can be written as follows:

```
data-type  name(type 1  arg 1,   type 2  arg 2, ...,   type n  arg n)
```

Here *data-type* represents the type of the quantity returned by a function, *name* represents the function name, and *type 1*, *type 2*, . . . , *type n* represent the data types of the arguments *arg 1*, *arg 2*, . . . , *arg n*.

Example 7.19   Here is an expanded version of the program outline shown in Example 7.18.

```
main()

{
    int a, b, c, d, i, J;           /* variable declarations */

    int funct(int a, int b);        /* function declaration
                                       (function prototype) */

    ...

    i = funct(a, b);

    ...

    j = funct(c, d);

}



int funct(int a, int b)             /* function definition */

{

    /* body of function definition */

}
```

Notice that the first line of the function definition includes the formal argument declarations.

Example 7.20   More Depreciation   A variation of the program presented in Example 7.15 is shown below. This outline makes use of function prototypes. It also utilizes the concise form of the function definitions.

```c
#include <stdio.h>

/* calculate depreciation using one of three different methods */

main()

{
    int n, choice = 0;
    float val;
    char answer1 = 'Y', answer2 = 'Y';

    void sl(float val, int n);              /* function prototype */
    void ddb(float val, int n);             /* function prototype */
    void syd(float val, int n);             /* function prototype */

    while (toupper(answer1) != 'N')   {

        ...

    }
    printf("\nGoodbye, have a nice day!\n");
}


void sl(float val, int n)

{
    float deprec;
    int year;
    void writeoutput(int year, float deprec, float value); /* funct prototype */

    ...

    return;
}


void ddb(float val, int n)

{

    float deprec;
    int year;
    void writeoutput(int year, float deprec, float value); /* funct prototype */

    ...

    return;
}


void syd(float val, int n)

{
    float tag, deprec;
    int year;
    void writeoutput(int year, float deprec, float value); /* funct prototype */

    ...

    return;
}
```

```
void writeoutput(int year, float depreciation, float value)

{

    ...

    return;
}
```

7.7 RECURSION

Recursion is a process by which a function calls itself repeatedly, until some specified condition has been satisfied. The process is used for repetitive computations in which each action is stated in terms of a previous result. Many iterative (i.e., repetitive) problems can be written in this form.

In order to solve a problem recursively, two conditions must be satisfied. First, the problem must be written in a recursive form, and second, the problem statement must include a stopping condition. Suppose, for example, we wish to calculate the factorial of a positive integer quantity. We would normally express this problem as $n! = 1 \times 2 \times 3 \times \cdots \times n$, where n is the specified positive integer (see Example 7.5). However, we can also express this problem in another way, by writing $n! = n \times (n-1)!$ This is a recursive statement of the problem, in which the desired action (the calculation of $n!$) is expressed in terms of a previous result (the value of $(n-1)!$, which is assumed to be known). Also, we know that $1! = 1$ by definition. This last expression provides a stopping condition for the recursion.

Example 7.21 Calculating Factorials In Examples 7.10 and 7.11 we saw a program for calculating the factorial of a given input quantity, using a nonrecursive function to perform the actual calculations. Here is a program that carries out this same calculation using recursion. (Note that an argument type specification is now included in the function declaration in main.)

```
#include <stdio.h>

/* calculate the factorial of an integer quantity using recursion */

main()

{
    int n;
    long int factorial(int n);

    /* read in the integer quantity */

    printf("n = ");
    scanf("%d", &n);

    /* calculate and display the factorial */

    printf("n! = %ld\n",  factorial(n));
}


long int factorial(int n)     /* calculate the factorial */

{
    if (n <= 1)
        return(1);
    else
        return(n * factorial(n - 1));
}
```

The main portion of the program simply reads the integer quantity n and then calls the long-integer recursive function `factorial`. (Recall that we use long integers for this calculation because factorials are such large integer quantities, even for modest values of n.) The function `factorial` calls itself recursively, with an actual argument (n - 1) that decreases in magnitude for each successive call. The recursive calls terminate when the value of the actual argument becomes equal to 1.

Notice that the current form of `factorial` is simpler than the function presented in Examples 7.10 and 7.11. The close correspondence between this function and the original problem definition, in recursive terms, should be readily apparent. In particular, note that the `if - then` statement includes a termination condition that becomes active when the value of n becomes less than or equal to 1. (Note that the value of n will never be less than 1 unless an improper initial value is entered into the computer.)

When the program is executed, the function `factorial` will be accessed repeatedly, once in `main` and $(n-1)$ times within itself, though the person using the program will not be aware of this. Only the final answer will be displayed, for example,

```
n = 10
```

```
n! = 3628800
```

When a recursive program is executed, the recursive function calls are not executed immediately. Rather, they are placed on a *stack* until the condition that terminates the recursion is encountered.* The function calls are then executed in reverse order, as they are "popped" off the stack. Thus, when evaluating a factorial recursively, the function calls will proceed in the following order:

$$n! = n \times (n-1)!$$
$$(n-1)! = (n-1) \times (n-2)!$$
$$(n-2)! = (n-2) \times (n-3)!$$
$$\cdots$$
$$2! = 2 \times 1!$$

The actual values will then be returned in the following reverse order:

$$1! = 1$$
$$2! = 2 \times 1! = 2 \times 1 = 2$$
$$3! = 3 \times 2! = 3 \times 2 = 6$$
$$4! = 4 \times 3! = 4 \times 6 = 24$$
$$\cdots$$
$$n! = n \times (n-1)! = \cdots$$

This reversal in the order of execution is a characteristic of all functions executed recursively.

If a recursive function contains local variables, a *different* set of local variables will be created during each call. The names of the local variables will, of course, always be the same, as declared within the function. However, the variables will represent a different set of values each time the function is executed. Each set of values will be stored on the stack, so that they will be available as the recursive process "unwinds," i.e., as the various function calls are "popped" off the stack and executed.

Example 7.22   Printing Backwards   The following program reads in a line of text on a character-by-character basis and then writes out the characters in reverse order. The program utilizes recursion to carry out the reversal of the characters.

---

* A *stack* is a *last-in, first-out* data structure in which successive data items are "pushed down" upon preceding data items. The data items are later removed (i.e., they are "popped") from the stack in reverse order, as indicated by the last-in, first-out designation.

```
#include <stdio.h>

#define EOLN '\n'

/* read a line of text and write it out backwards, using recursion */

main()

{
    void reverse(void);

    printf("Please enter a line of text below\n");
    reverse();
}


void reverse(void)

/* read a line of characters and write it out backwards */

{
    char c;

    if ((c = getchar()) != EOLN) reverse();
    putchar(c);
    return;
}
```

The main portion of this program simply displays a prompt and then calls the function reverse, thus initiating the recursion. The recursive function reverse then proceeds to read single characters until an end-of-line designation (\n) is encountered. Each function call causes a new character (a new value for c) to be pushed onto the stack. Once the end-of-line is encountered, the successive characters are popped from the stack and displayed on a last-in, first-out basis. Thus, the characters are displayed in reverse order.

Suppose that the program is executed with the following line of input:

```
Now is the time for all good men to come to the aid of their country!
```

Then the corresponding output will be

```
!yrtnuoc rieht fo dia eht ot emoc ot nem doog lla rof emit eht si woN
```

Sometimes a complicated repetitive process can be programmed very concisely using recursion, though the logic may be tricky. The following example provides a well-known illustration.

Example 7.23   The Towers of Hanoi   The Towers of Hanoi is a well-known children's game, played with three poles and a number of different sized disks. Each disk has a hole in the center, allowing it to be stacked around any of the poles. Initially, the disks are stacked on the leftmost pole in the order of decreasing size, i.e., the largest on the bottom and the smallest on the top, as illustrated in Fig. 7.1.

The object of the game is to transfer the disks from the leftmost pole to the rightmost pole, without ever placing a larger disk on top of a smaller disk. Only one disk may be moved at a time, and each disk must always be placed around one of the poles.

The general strategy is to consider one of the poles to be the origin, and another to be the destination. The third pole will be used for intermediate storage, thus allowing the disks to be moved without placing a larger disk over a smaller one. Assume there are n disks, numbered from smallest to largest, as in Fig. 7.1. If the disks are initially stacked on the left pole, the problem of moving all n disks to the right pole can be stated in the following

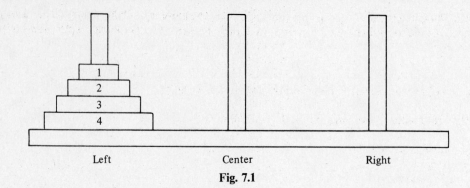

Fig. 7.1

recursive manner:

1. Move the top $n - 1$ disks from the left pole to the center pole.
2. Move the nth disk (the largest disk) to the right pole.
3. Move the $n - 1$ disks on the center pole to the right pole.

The problem can be solved in this manner for any value of n greater than 0 ($n = 0$ represents a stopping condition).

In order to program this game we first label the poles, so that the left pole is represented as L, the center pole as C and the right pole as R. We then construct a recursive function called transfer that will transfer n disks from one pole to another. Let us refer to the individual poles with the char-type variables from, to and temp for the origin, destination, and temporary storage, respectively. As a result, if we assign the character L to from, R to to and C to temp, we will, in effect, be specifying the movement of n disks from the leftmost pole to the rightmost pole, using the center pole for intermediate storage.

With this notation, the function will have the following skeletal structure:

```
void transfer(int n, char from, char to, char temp)

/* n    = number of disks
   from = origin
   to   = destination
   temp = temporary storage */

{
   if (n > 0)  {

      /* move n-1 disks from their origin to the temporary pole */

      /* move the nth disk from its origin to its destination */

      /* move the n-1 disks from the temporary pole to their destination */

   }
}
```

The transfer of the $n - 1$ disks can be accomplished by a recursive call to transfer. Thus, we can write

```
transfer(n-1, from, temp, to);
```

for the first transfer, and

```
transfer(n-1, temp, to, from);
```

for the second. (Note the order of the arguments in each call.) The movement of the nth disk from the origin to the destination simply requires writing out the current values of from and to. The complete function can be written as follows:

```
void transfer(int n, char from, char to, char temp)

/* transfer n disks from one pole to another */

/* n    = number of disks
   from = origin
   to   = destination
   temp = temporary storage */

{
    if (n > 0)    {
        /* move n-1 disks from origin to temporary */
        transfer(n-1, from, temp, to);

        /* move nth disk from origin to destination */
        printf("Move disk %d from %c to %c\n", n, from, to);

        /* move n-1 disks from temporary to destination */
        transfer(n-1, temp, to, from);
    }
    return;
}
```

It is now a simple matter to add the main portion of the program, which merely reads in a value for *n* and then initiates the computation by calling transfer. In this first function call, the actual parameters will be specified as character constants, that is,

```
transfer(n, 'L', 'R', 'C');
```

This function call specifies the transfer of all *n* disks from the leftmost pole (the origin) to the rightmost pole (the destination), using the center pole for intermediate storage.

Here is the complete program.

```
#include <stdio.h>

/* the TOWERS OF HANOI — solved using recursion */

main()

{
    void transfer(int, char, char, char);
    int n;

    printf("Welcome to the TOWERS OF HANOI\n\n");
    printf("How many disks? ");
    scanf("%d", &n);
    printf("\n");
    transfer(n, 'L', 'R', 'C');
}
```

```
void transfer(int n, char from, char to, char temp)

/* transfer n disks from one pole to another */

/* n    = number of disks
   from = origin
   to   = destination
   temp = temporary storage */

{
    if (n > 0)   {
        /* move n-1 disks from origin to temporary */
        transfer(n-1, from, temp, to);

        /* move nth disk from origin to destination */
        printf("Move disk %d from %c to %c\n", n, from, to);

        /* move n-1 disks from temporary to destination */
        transfer(n-1, temp, to, from);
    }
    return;
}
```

It should be understood that the function `transfer` receives a different set of values for its arguments each time the function is called. These sets of values will be pushed onto the stack so that each set is independent of the others. They are then popped from the stack at the proper time during the execution of the program. It is this ability to store and retrieve these independent sets of values that allows the recursion to work.

When the program is executed for the case where $n = 3$, the following output is obtained:

```
Welcome to the TOWERS OF HANOI

How many disks? 3

Move disk 1 from L to R
Move disk 2 from L to C
Move disk 1 from R to C
Move disk 3 from L to R
Move disk 1 from C to L
Move disk 2 from C to R
Move disk 1 from L to R
```

Study this example carefully. The logic is very tricky, despite the apparent simplicity of the program. Think through each move to verify that the solution is indeed correct.

We will see another programming example that utilizes recursion in Sec. 11.6, when we discuss linked lists (see Example 11.32).

The use of recursion is not necessarily the best way to approach a problem, even though the problem definition may be recursive in nature. A nonrecursive implementation may be more efficient in terms of memory utilization and execution speed. As a result, the use of recursion may involve a tradeoff between simplicity and performance. Each problem should therefore be judged on its own individual merits.

Review Questions

7.1   What is a function? Is the use of functions required when writing a C program?

7.2   State several advantages to the use of functions.

7.3   What is meant by a function call? From what parts of a program can a function be called?

7.4   What are arguments? What is their purpose? What other term is sometimes used for an argument?

7.5   What is the purpose of the `return` statement?

7.6   What are the three principal components of a function definition?

7.7   How is the first line of a function definition written? What is the purpose of each item, or group of items?

7.8   What are formal arguments? What are actual arguments? What is the relationship between formal arguments and actual arguments?

7.9   Describe some alternate terms used in place of *formal argument* and *actual argument*.

7.10   Can the names of the formal arguments within a function coincide with the names of other variables defined outside of the function? Explain.

7.11   Can the names of the formal arguments within a function coincide with the names of other variables defined within the function? Explain, and compare your answer with the answer to the last question.

7.12   How are formal arguments declared within a function?

7.13   Summarize the rules governing the use of the `return` statement. Can multiple expressions be included in a `return` statement? Can multiple `return` statements be included in a function?

7.14   What relationship must exist between the data type that appears in the first line of the function definition and the expression that is included in the `return` statement?

7.15   Summarize the rules that apply to a function call. What relationships must be maintained between the actual arguments and the corresponding formal arguments? Are the actual arguments subject to the same restrictions as the formal arguments?

7.16   Can a function be called from more than one place within a program?

7.17   Explain the difference between a function declaration and a function definition. When is a function declaration required?

7.18   Summarize the rules associated with function declarations. What is the purpose of each item or group of items?

7.19   Suppose function F1 calls function F2 within a C program. Does the order of the function definitions make any difference? Explain.

7.20   Describe the manner in which an actual argument passes information to a function. What name is associated with this process? What are the advantages and disadvantages to passing arguments in this manner?

7.21   How are argument data types specified in a function declaration? What value is there in including argument data types in a function declaration?

7.22   What is the purpose of the keyword `void` in a function declaration? What is the purpose of `void` in a function definition?

7.23   What is a function prototype? How do function prototypes differ from the more traditional function declarations described in Sec. 7.2?

7.24   What advantage is there in using function prototypes within a program?

7.25   When a function is accessed, must the names of the actual arguments agree with the names of the arguments in the corresponding function declaration?

7.26   When a function is accessed, must the data types of the actual arguments agree with the data types of the arguments in the corresponding function declaration? Compare your answer with that of Problem 7.25 above.

7.27   What is recursion? What advantage is there in its use?

7.28   What is a stack? In what order is information added to and removed from a stack?

7.29   Explain what happens when a program containing recursive function calls is executed (in terms of information being added to and removed from a stack).

7.30   When a program containing recursive function calls is executed, how are the local variables within the recursive function interpreted?

7.31   If a repetitive process is programmed recursively, will the resulting program necessarily be more efficient than a nonrecursive version?

Problems

7.32   Explain the meaning of each of the following function declarations:

(*a*) `int f(int a);`
(*b*) `double f(double a, int b);`
(*c*) `void f(long a, short b, unsigned c);`
(*d*) `char f(void);`
(*e*) `unsigned f(unsigned a, unsigned b);`

7.33 Each of the following is the first line of a function definition. Explain the meaning of each.

(*a*) `float f(float a, float b)`   (*c*) `void f(int a)`
(*b*) `long f(long a)`   (*d*) `char f(void)`

7.34 Several function definitions are outlined below. Rewrite each, combining the first line with the formal argument declarations.

(*a*) `float funct(a, b)`   (*b*) `char funct(c1, c2)`   (*c*) `long funct(x, y)`
    `float a, b;`   `char c1, c2;`   `int x;`
    `{`   `{`   `long y;`
    `   ...`   `   ...`   `{`
                                                                 `...`
    `}`   `}`   `}`

7.35 Write the first line of the function definition and the formal argument declarations for each of the situations described below.

(*a*) A function called `sample` generates and returns an integer quantity.
(*b*) A function called `root` accepts two integer arguments and returns a floating-point result.
(*c*) A function called `convert` accepts a character and returns another character.
(*d*) A function called `transfer` accepts a long integer and returns a character.
(*e*) A function called `inverse` accepts a character and returns a long integer.
(*f*) A function called `process` accepts an integer and two floating-point quantities (in that order) and returns a double-precision quantity.
(*g*) A function called `value` accepts two double-precision quantities and a short-integer quantity (in that order). The input quantities are processed to yield a double-precision value which is written out as a final result.

7.36 Add the required (or suggested) function declarations for each of the skeletal outlines shown below.

(*a*)
```
main()
{
    int a, b, c;

    ...

    c = funct1(a, b);

    ...
}


funct1(int x, int y)
{

    ...

}
```

(*b*)
```
main()
{
    double a, b, c;

    ...

    c = funct1(a, b);

    ...
}
```

```
        double funct1(double x, double y)
        {

            ...

        }

(c)  main()
     {
         int a;
         float b;
         long int c;

         ...

         c = funct1(a, b);

         ...

     }

     long int funct1(int x, float y)
     {

         ...

     }


(d)  main()
     {
         double a, b, c, d;

         ...

         c = funct1(a, b);

         ...

         d = funct2(a + b, a + c);
     }


     double funct1(double x, double y)
     {
         double z;

         ...

         z = funct2(x, y);

         ...

     }


     double funct2(double x, double y)
     {

         ...

     }
```

7.37   Describe the output generated by each of the following programs:

(a)   `#include <stdio.h>`

```
main()
{
    int a, count;
    int funct(int count);

    for (count = 1; count <= 5; ++count)    {
        a = funct1(count);
        printf("%d  ", a);
    }
}

int funct1(int x)
{
    int y;

    y = x * x;
    return(y);
}
```

(b)   Show how the preceding program can be written more concisely.

(c)   `#include <stdio.h>`

```
main()
{
    int n = 10;
    int funct1(int n);

    printf("%d", funct1(n));
}

int funct1(int n)
{
    if (n > 0) return(n + funct1(n - 1));
}
```

(d)   `#include <stdio.h>`

```
main()
{
    int n = 10;
    int funct1(int n);

    printf("%d", funct1(n));
}

int funct1(int n)
{
    if (n > 0) return(n + funct1(n - 2));
}
```

7.38   Express each of the following algebraic formulas in a recursive form:

(a) $y = (x_1 + x_2 + \cdots + x_n)$
(b) $y = 1 - x + x^2/2 - x^3/6 + x^4/24 + \cdots + (-1)^n x^n/n!$
(c) $p = (f_1 * f_2 * \cdots * f_t)$

Programming Problems

7.39   Write a function that will calculate and display the real roots of the quadratic equation

$$ax^2 + bx + c = 0$$

using the quadratic formula

$$x = \frac{-b \pm \sqrt{b^2 - 4ac}}{2a}$$

Assume that a, b and c are floating-point arguments whose values are given, and that x_1 and x_2 are floating-point variables. Also, assume that $b^2 > 4 * a * c$, so that the calculated roots will always be real.

7.40   Write a complete C program that will calculate the real roots of the quadratic equation

$$ax^2 + bx + c = 0$$

using the quadratic formula, as described in the previous problem. Read the coefficients a, b and c in the main portion of the program. Then access the function written for the preceding problem in order to obtain the desired solution. Finally, write out the values of the coefficients, followed by the calculated values of x_1 and x_2. Be sure that all of the output is clearly labeled.

   Test the program using the following data:

a	b	c
2	6	1
3	3	0
1	3	1

7.41   Modify the function written for Problem 7.39 so that *all* roots of the quadratic equation

$$ax^2 + bx + c = 0$$

will be calculated, given the values of a, b and c. Note that the roots will be repeated (i.e., there will only be one real root) if $b^2 = 4 * a * c$. Also, the roots will be complex if $b^2 < 4 * a * c$. In this case, the real part of each root will be determined as

$$-b/(2 * a)$$

and the imaginary parts will be calculated as

$$\pm(\sqrt{4ac - b^2})i$$

where i represents $\sqrt{-1}$.

7.42   Modify the C program written for Problem 7.40 so that *all* roots of the quadratic equation

$$ax^2 + bx + c = 0$$

will be calculated, using the function written for Problem 7.41. Be sure that all output is clearly labeled. Test the program using the following data:

a	b	c
2	6	1
3	3	0
1	3	1
0	12	-3
3	6	3
2	-4	3

7.43   Write a function that will allow a floating-point number to be raised to an integer power. In other words, we wish to evaluate the formula

$$y = x^n$$

where y and x are floating-point variables and n is an integer variable.

7.44   Write a complete C program that will read in numerical values for x and n, evaluate the formula

$$y = x^n$$

using the function written for Problem 7.43, and then write out the calculated result. Test the program using the following data:

x	n
2	3
2	12
2	-5
-3	3
-3	7
-3	-5
1.5	3
1.5	10
1.5	-5
0.2	3
0.2	5
0.2	-5

7.45   Expand the function written for Problem 7.43 so that positive values of x can be raised to *any* power, integer or floating-point. (*Hint:* Use the formula

$$y = x^n = e^{(n \ln x)}$$

Remember to include a test for inappropriate values of x.)

Include this function in the program written for Problem 7.44. Test the program using the data given in Problem 7.44 and the following additional data:

x	n
2	0.2
2	-0.8
-3	0.2
-3	-0.8
1.5	0.2
1.5	-0.8
0.2	0.2
0.2	-0.8
0.2	0.0

7.46   Modify the program for calculating the solution of an algebraic equation, given in Example 6.21, so that each iteration is carried out within a separate function. Compile and execute the program to be sure that it runs correctly.

7.47   Modify the program for averaging a list of numbers, given in Example 6.14, so that it makes use of a function to read in the numbers and return their sum. Test the program using the following 10 numbers:

27.5	87.0
13.4	39.9
53.8	47.7
29.2	8.1
74.5	63.2

7.48   Modify the program for carrying out compound interest calculations given in Example 5.2 so that the actual calculations are carried out in a programmer-defined function. Write the function so that the values of P, r and n are entered as arguments, and the calculated value of F is returned. Test the program using the following data:

P	r	n
1000	6	20
1000	6.25	20
333.33	8.75	20
333.33	8.75	22.5

7.49   For each of the following problems, write a complete C program that includes a recursive function.
   (a)   The *Legendre polynomials* can be calculated by means of the formulas $P_0 = 1$, $P_1 = x$,

$$P_n = [(2n - 1)/n] \times P_{n-1} - [(n - 1)/n]P_{n-2}$$

   where $n = 2, 3, 4, \ldots$ and x is any floating-point number between -1 and 1. (Note that the Legendre polynomials are floating-point quantities.)
         Generate the first n Legendre polynomials. Let the values of n and x be input parameters.
   (b)   Determine the cumulative sum of n floating-point numbers [see Problem 7.38(a)]. Read a new number into the computer during each call to the recursive function.
   (c)   Evaluate the first n terms in the series specified in Problem 7.38(b). Enter n as an input parameter.
   (d)   Determine the cumulative product of n floating-point numbers [see Problem 7.38(c)]. Read a new number into the computer during each call to the recursive function.

Additional programming problems involving the use of functions can be found at the end of Chap. 8.

Chapter 8

Program Structure

This chapter considers several topics associated with the structure of programs that utilize multiple functions. For example, in some situations it may be desirable to introduce certain "global" variables that are recognized throughout the entire program (or within major portions of the program, e.g., two or more functions). Such variables are defined differently than the usual "local" variables, which are recognized only within a single function. We will see how global variables are defined and utilized.

In addition, we will consider the issue of static vs. dynamic retention of information by a local variable. That is, a local variable normally does not retain its value once control has been transferred out of its defining function. In some circumstances, however, it may be desirable to have certain local variables retain their values, so that the function can be reentered later and the computation resumed.

And finally, it may be desirable to develop a large, multifunction program in terms of several independent files, with a small number of functions (perhaps only one) defined within each file. In such programs the individual functions can be defined and accessed locally within a single file, or globally within multiple files. This is similar to the definition and use of local vs. global variables in a multifunction, single-file program.

8.1 STORAGE CLASSES

We have already mentioned that there are two different ways to characterize variables: by *data type*, and by *storage class* (see Sec. 2.6). Data type refers to the type of information represented by a variable, for example, integer number, floating-point number, or character. Storage class refers to the permanence of a variable and its *scope* within the program, that is, the portion of the program over which the variable is recognized.

There are four different storage-class specifications in C: *automatic*, *external*, *static* and *register*. They are identified by the keywords `auto`, `extern`, `static` and `register`, respectively. We will discuss the *automatic*, *external* and *static* storage classes within this chapter. The *register* storage class will be discussed in Sec. 13.1.

The storage class associated with a variable can sometimes be established simply by the location of the variable declaration within the program. In other situations, however, the keyword which specifies a particular storage class must be placed at the beginning of the variable declaration.

Example 8.1 Shown below are several typical variable declarations that include the specification of a storage class.

```
auto int a, b, c;

extern float root1, root2;

static int count = 0;

extern char star;
```

The first declaration states that a, b and c are automatic integer variables, and the second declaration establishes root1 and root2 as external floating-point variables. The third declaration states that count is a static integer variable whose initial value is 0, and the last declaration establishes star as an external character-type variable.

208

The exact procedure for establishing a storage class for a variable depends upon the particular storage class, and the manner in which the program is organized (i.e., single file vs. multiple file). We will consider these rules in the next few sections of this chapter.

8.2 AUTOMATIC VARIABLES

Automatic variables are always declared within a function and are local to the function in which they are declared; that is, their scope is confined to that function. Automatic variables defined in different functions will therefore be independent of one another, even though they may have the same name.

Any variable declared within a function is interpreted as an automatic variable unless a different storage-class specification is included within the declaration. This includes formal argument declarations. All the variables in the programming examples encountered in the earlier chapters of this book have been automatic variables.

Since the location of the variable declarations within the program determine the automatic storage class, the keyword `auto` is not required at the beginning of each variable declaration. There is no harm in including an `auto` specification within a declaration if the programmer wishes, though this is normally not done.

Example 8.2 Calculating Factorials Consider once again the program for calculating factorials, originally shown in Example 7.10. Within `main`, n is an automatic variable. Within `factorial`, i and prod, as well as the formal argument n, are automatic variables.

The storage-class designation `auto` could have been included explicitly in the variable declarations if we had wished. Thus, the program could have been written as follows:

```c
#include <stdio.h>

/* calculate the factorial of an integer quantity */

main()

{
    auto int n;
    long int factorial(int n);

    /* read in the integer quantity */

    printf("\nn = ");
    scanf("%d", &n);

    /* calculate and display the factorial */

    printf("\nn! = %ld", factorial(n));
}


long int factorial(auto int n)    /* calculate the factorial */

{
    auto int i;
    auto long int prod = 1;

    if (n > 1)
        for (i = 2; i <= n; ++i)
            prod *= i;
    return(prod);
}
```

Either method is acceptable. As a rule, however, the auto designation is not included in variable or formal argument declarations, since this is the default storage class. Thus, the program shown in Example 7.10 is preferred.

Automatic variables can be assigned initial values by including appropriate expressions within the variable declarations, as in the above example, or by explicit assignment expressions elsewhere in the function. Such values will be reassigned each time the function is re-entered. If an automatic variable is not initialized in some manner, however, its initial value will be unpredictable, and probably unintelligible.

An automatic variable does not retain its value once control is transferred out of its defining function. Therefore, any value assigned to an automatic variable within a function will be lost once the function is exited. If the program logic requires that an automatic variable be assigned a particular value each time the function is executed, that value will have to be reset whenever the function is re-entered (i.e., whenever the function is accessed).

Example 8.3   Average Length of Several Lines of Text   Let us now write a C program that will read several lines of text and determine the average number of characters (including punctuation and blank spaces) in each line. We will structure the program in such a manner that it continues to read additional lines of text until an empty line (i.e., a line whose first character is \n) is encountered.

We will utilize a function (linecount) that reads a single line of text and counts the number of characters, excluding the newline character (\n) that signifies the end of the line. The calling routine (main) will maintain a cumulative sum, as well as a running total, of the number of lines that have been read. The function will be called repeatedly (thus reading a new line each time), until an empty line is encountered. The program will then divide the cumulative number of characters by the total number of lines to obtain an average.

Here is the entire program.

```c
#include <stdio.h>

/* read several lines of text and determine
   the average number of characters per line */

main()

{
    int n;                  /* number of chars in given line */
    int count = 0;          /* number of lines */
    int sum = 0;            /* total number of characters */
    float avg;              /* average number of chars per line */
    void linecount(void);   /* function declaration */

    printf("Enter the text below\n");

    /* read a line of text and update the cumulative counters */

    while ((n = linecount()) > 0)   {
         sum += n;
         ++count;
    }

    avg = (float) sum / count;
    printf("\nAverage number of characters per line: %5.2f", avg);
}
```

```
void linecount(void)

/* read a line of text and count the number of characters */

{
    char line[80];
    int count = 0;

    while ((line[count] = getchar()) != '\n')
         ++count;
    return (count);
}
```

We see that `main` contains four automatic variables: `n`, `count`, `sum` and `avg`, whereas `linecount` contains two: `line` and `count`. (Notice that `line` is an 80-element character array representing the contents of one line of text.) Three of these automatic variables are assigned initial values of zero.

Also, note that `count` has different meanings within each function. Within `linecount`, `count` represents the number of characters in a single line, whereas within `main`, `count` represents the total number of lines that have been read. Moreover, `count` is reset to zero within `linecount` whenever the function is accessed. This does not affect the value of `count` within `main`, since the variables are independent of one another. It would have been clearer if we had named these variables differently, for example, `count` and `lines`, or perhaps `chars` and `lines`. We have used the same name for both variables to illustrate the independence of automatic variables within different functions.

A sample interactive session, resulting from executing this program, is shown below. As usual, the user's responses are underlined.

```
Enter the text below
Now is the time for all good men
to come to the aid of their country.
```

```
Average number of characters per line: 34.00
```

The scope of an automatic variable can be smaller than an entire function if we wish. In fact, automatic variables can be declared within a single compound statement. With small, simple programs there is usually no advantage in doing this, but it is sometimes desirable in larger programs.

8.3   EXTERNAL VARIABLES

External variables, in contrast to automatic variables, are not confined to single functions. Their scope extends from the point of definition through the remainder of the program. Hence, they usually span two or more functions, and often an entire program.

Since external variables are recognized globally, they can be accessed from any function that falls within their scope. They retain their assigned values within this scope. Therefore, an external variable can be assigned a value within one function, and this value can be used (by accessing the external variable) within another function.

The use of external variables provides a convenient mechanism for transferring information back and forth between functions. In particular, we can transfer information into a function without using arguments. This is especially convenient when a function requires numerous input data items. Moreover, we now have a way to transfer multiple data items out of a function, since the `return` statement can return only one data item. (We will see another way to transfer information back and forth between functions in Chap. 10, where we discuss pointers.)

When working with external variables, we must distinguish between external variable *definitions* and external variable *declarations*. An external variable *definition* is written in the same manner as an ordinary variable declaration. It must appear outside of, and usually before, the functions that access the external variables. An external variable definition will automatically allocate the required storage space (within the computer's memory) for the external variables. The assignment of initial values can be included within an external variable definition if desired (more about this later).

The storage-class specifier `extern` is not required in an external variable definition, since the external variables will be identified by the location of their definition within the program. In fact, many C compilers forbid the appearance of the storage-class specifier `extern` within an external variable definition. We will follow this convention within this book.

If a function requires an external variable that has been defined earlier in the program, then the function may access the external variable freely, without any special declaration within the function. (Remember, however, that any alteration to the value of an external variable within a function will be recognized within the entire scope of the external variable.) On the other hand, if the function definition *precedes* the external variable definition, then the function must include a *declaration* for that external variable. The function definitions within a large program often include external variable declarations, whether they are needed or not, as a matter of good programming practice.

An external variable *declaration must* begin with the storage-class specifier `extern`. The name of the external variable and its data type must agree with the corresponding external variable definition that appears outside of the function. Storage space for external variables will *not* be allocated as a result of an external variable declaration. Moreover, an external variable declaration *cannot* include the assignment of initial values. These are important distinctions between an external variable definition and an external variable declaration.

Example 8.4   Search for a Maximum   Suppose we wish to find the particular value of x that causes the function

$$y = x \cos(x)$$

to be maximized within the interval bounded by $x = 0$ on the left and $x = \pi$ on the right. We will require that the maximizing value of x be known quite accurately. We will also require that the search scheme be relatively efficient in the sense that the function $y = x \cos(x)$ should be evaluated as few times as possible.

An obvious way to solve this problem would be to generate a large number of closely spaced trial functions (that is, evaluate the function at $x = 0$, $x = 0.0001$, $x = 0.0002, \ldots, x = 3.1415$, and $x = 3.1416$) and determine the largest of these by visual inspection. This would not be very efficient, however, and it would require human intervention to obtain the final result. Instead, let us use the following *elimination scheme*, which is a highly efficient computational procedure for all functions that have only one maximum (i.e., only one "peak") within the search interval.

The computation will be carried out as follows: We begin with two search points at the center of the search interval, located a very small distance from each other, as shown in Fig. 8.1.

The following notation is used:

`a`   = left end of the search interval

`xl`   = lefthand interior search point

`xr`   = righthand interior search point

`b`   = right end of the search interval

`sep`   = distance between `xl` and `xr`

If `a`, `b`, and `sep` are known, then the interior points can be calculated as

```
xl = a + .5 * (b - a - sep)
```

```
xr = a + .5 * (b - a + sep) = xl + sep
```

Let us evaluate the function `y = x cos(x)` at `xl` and at `xr`, and let us call these values `yl` and `yr`, respectively. Suppose `yl` turns out to be greater than `yr`. Then the maximum will lie somewhere between `a` and `xr`. Hence, we retain only that portion of the search interval which ranges from `x = a` to `x = xr`. We will now refer to the old point `xr` as `b`, since it is now the right end of the new search interval, and generate two *new* search points, `xl` and `xr`. These points will be located at the center of the new search interval, a distance `sep` apart, as shown in Fig. 8.2.

On the other hand, suppose now that in our *original* search interval the value of `yr` turned out to be greater than `yl`. This would indicate that our new search interval should lie between `xl` and `b`. Hence, we rename the point which was originally called `xl` to be `a` and we generate two *new* search points, `xl` and `xr`, at the center of the new search interval, as shown in Fig. 8.3.

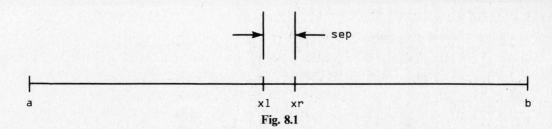

Fig. 8.1

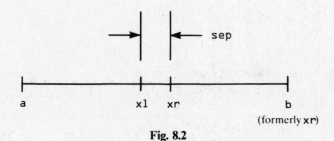

Fig. 8.2

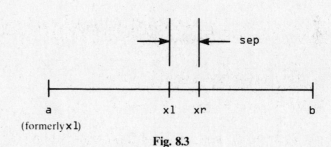

Fig. 8.3

We continue to generate a new pair of search points at the center of each new interval, compare the respective values of y, and eliminate a portion of the search interval until the new search interval becomes smaller than 3 * sep. Once this happens we can no longer distinguish the interior points from the boundaries. Hence, the search is ended.

Each time we make a comparison between yl and yr, we eliminate that portion of the search interval that contains the smaller value of y. If both interior values of y should happen to be identical (which can happen, though it is unusual), then the search procedure stops, and the maximum is assumed to occur at the center of the last two interior points.

Once the search has ended, either because the search interval has become sufficiently small or because the two interior points yield identical values of y, we can calculate the approximate location of the maximum as

```
xmax = 0.5 * (xl + xr)
```

The corresponding maximum value of the function can then be obtained as xmax cos (xmax).

Let us consider a program outline for the general case where a and b are input quantities but sep has a fixed value of 0.0001.

1. Assign a value of sep = 0.0001.

2. Read in the values of a and b.

3. Repeat the following until either yl becomes equal to yr (the desired maximum will be at the midpoint), or the most recent value of (b - a) becomes less than or equal to (3 * sep):
    (a) Generate the two interior points, xl and xr.
    (b) Calculate the corresponding values of yl and yr, and determine which is larger.
    (c) Reduce the search interval, by eliminating that portion that does not contain the larger value of y.

4.   Evaluate xmax and ymax.

5.   Write out the values of xmax and ymax, and stop.

To translate this outline into a program, we first create a programmer-defined function to evaluate the mathematical function $y = x \cos(x)$. Let us call this function curve. This function can easily be written as follows:

```
double curve(double x)

/*  evaluate the function y = x * cos(x)  */

{
    return (x * cos(x));
}
```

Note that cos(x) is a call to a C library function.

Now consider step 3 in the above program outline, which carries out the interval reduction. This step can also be programmed as a function, which we will call reduce. Notice, however, that the values represented by the variables a, b, xl, xr, yl and yr, which change through the course of the computation, must be transferred back and forth between this function and main. Therefore, let these variables be external variables whose scope includes both reduce and main.

Function reduce can be written as

```
void reduce(void)

/* interval reduction routine */

{
    double curve(double xl);

    xl = a + 0.5 * (b - a - CNST);
    xr = xl + CNST;
    yl = curve(xl);
    yr = curve(xr);

    if (yl > yr)   {      /* retain left interval */
       b = xr;
       return;
    }
    if (yl < yr)          /* retain right interval */
       a = xl;
    return;
}
```

Notice that the parameter we have referred to earlier as sep is now represented as the character constant CNST. Also, notice that this function does not include any formal arguments and that it does not return anything via the return statement. All the information transfers involve external variables.

It is now quite simple to write the main portion of the program, which calls the two functions defined above. Here is the entire program.

```
#include <stdio.h>
#include <math.h>

#define  CNST  0.0001

/* find the maximum of a function within a specified interval */

double a, b, xl, yl, xr, yr;        /* global variables */
```

```
main()

{
    double xmax, ymax;
    void reduce(void);
    double curve(double xl);

    /* read input data (interval end points) */

    printf("\na = ");
    scanf("%lf", &a);
    printf("b = ");
    scanf("%lf", &b);

    /* interval reduction loop */

    do
        reduce();
    while ((yl != yr) && ((b - a) > 3 * CNST));

    /* calculate xmax and ymax, and write out the results */

    xmax = 0.5 * (xl + xr);
    ymax = curve(xmax);
    printf("\nxmax = %8.6lf   ymax = %8.6lf", xmax, ymax);
}


void reduce(void)

/* interval reduction routine */

{
    double curve(double xl);

    xl = a + 0.5 * (b - a - CNST);
    xr = xl + CNST;
    yl = curve(xl);
    yr = curve(xr);

    if (yl > yr)   {      /* retain left interval */
        b = xr;
        return;
    }
    if (yl < yr)         /* retain right interval */
        a = xl;
    return;
}


double curve(double x)

/*  evaluate the function y = x * cos(x)  */

{
    return (x * cos(x));
}
```

The variables a, b, xl, yl, xr and yr are defined as external variables whose scope includes the entire program. Notice that these variables are declared before main begins.

Executing the program, with a = 0 and b = 3.141593, produces the following interactive session. The user's responses are underlined, as usual.

```
a = 0
b = 3.141593

xmax = 0.860394    ymax = 0.561096
```

Thus, we have obtained the location and the value of the maximum within the given original interval.

External variables can be assigned initial values as a part of the variable definitions, but the initial values must be expressed as *constants* rather than as expressions. These initial values will be assigned only once, at the beginning of the program. The external variables will then retain these initial values unless they are later altered during the execution of the program.

If an initial value is not included in the definition of an external variable, the variable will automatically be assigned a value of zero. Thus, external variables are never left dangling with undefined, garbled values. Nevertheless, it is good programming practice to assign an explicit initial value of zero when required by the program logic.

Example 8.5   Average Length of Several Lines of Text   Shown below is a modification of the program, previously presented in Example 8.3, for determining the average number of characters in several lines of text. The current version makes use of external variables to represent the total (cumulative) number of characters read and the total number of lines.

```
#include <stdio.h>

/* read several lines of text and determine
   the average number of characters per line */


int sum = 0;            /* total number of characters */
int lines = 0;          /* total number of lines */


main()

{
    int n;                 /* number of chars in given line */
    float avg;             /* average number of chars per line */
    void linecount(void);  /* function declaration */

    printf("Enter the text below\n");

    /* read a line of text and update the cumulative counters */

    while ((n = linecount()) > 0)   {
         sum += n;
         ++lines;
    }

    avg = (float) sum / lines;
    printf("\nAverage number of characters per line: %5.2f", avg);
}
```

```
void linecount(void)

/* read a line of text and count the number of characters */

{
    char line[80];
    int count = 0;

    while ((line[count] = getchar()) != '\n')
          ++count;
    return (count);
}
```

Notice that sum and lines are external variables representing the total (cumulative) number of characters read and the total number of lines, respectively. Both of these variables are assigned initial values of zero. These values are successively modified within main, as additional lines of text are read.

Also, recall that the earlier version of the program used two different automatic variables called count in different parts of the program. In the current version of the program, however, the variables that represent these same quantities have different names, since one of the variables (lines) is now an external variable.

It should be pointed out that sum and lines need not be assigned zero values explicitly, since external variables are always set equal to zero unless some other initial value is designated. We include the explicit zero initialization in order to clarify the program logic.

Arrays can also be declared either automatic or external, though automatic arrays cannot be initialized. We will see how initial values are assigned to array elements in Chap. 9.

Finally, it should be pointed out that there are inherent dangers in the use of external variables, since an alteration in the value of an external variable within a function will be carried over into other parts of the program. Sometimes this happens inadvertently, as a *side effect* of some other action. Thus, there is the possibility that the value of an external value will be changed unexpectedly, resulting in a subtle programming error. The programmer should decide carefully which storage class is most appropriate for each particular programming situation.

8.4 STATIC VARIABLES

In this section and the next, we make the distinction between a *single-file* program, in which the entire program is contained within a single source file, and a *multifile* program, where the functions that compose the program are contained in separate source files. The rules governing the static storage class are different in each situation.

In a single-file program, static variables are defined within individual functions and therefore have the same scope as automatic variables, i.e., they are local to the functions in which they are defined. Unlike automatic variables, however, static variables retain their values throughout the life of the program. As a result, if a function is exited and then re-entered later, the static variables defined within that function will retain their former values. This feature allows functions to retain information permanently throughout the execution of a program.

Static variables are defined within a function in the same manner as automatic variables, except that the variable declaration must begin with the static storage-class designation. Static variables can be utilized within the function in the same manner as other variables. They cannot, however, be accessed outside of their defining function.

It is not unusual to define automatic or static variables having the same names as external variables. In such situations the local variables will take precedence over the external variables, though the values of the external variables will be unaffected by any manipulation of the local variables. Thus, the external variables maintain their independence with locally defined automatic and static variables. The same is true of local variables within one function that have the same names as local variables within another function.

Example 8.6 Shown below is the skeletal structure of a C program that includes variables belonging to several different storage classes.

```
float a, b, c;

main()
{
    static float a;
    void dummy(void);
    ...
}


void dummy(void)
{
    static int a;
    int b;


    ...
}
```

Within this program a, b and c are external, floating-point variables. However, a is redefined as a static floating-point variable within main. Therefore, b and c are the only external variables that will be recognized within main. Note that the static local variable a will be independent of the external variable a.

Similarly, a and b are redefined as integer variables within dummy. Note that a is a static variable, but b is an automatic variable. Thus, a will retain its former value whenever dummy is reentered, whereas b will lose its value whenever control is transferred out of dummy. Furthermore, c is the only external variable that will be recognized within dummy.

Since a and b are local to dummy, they will be independent of the external variables a, b and c, and the static variable a defined within main. The fact that a and b are declared to be integer variables within dummy and floating-point variables elsewhere is therefore immaterial.

Initial values can be included in static variable declarations. The rules associated with the assignment of these values are essentially the same as the rules associated with the initialization of external variables, even though the static variables are defined locally within a function. In particular:

1. The initial values must be expressed as constants, not expressions.

2. The initial values are assigned to their respective variables at the beginning of program execution. The variables retain these values throughout the life of the program, unless different values are assigned during the course of the computation.

3. Zeros will be assigned to all static variables whose declarations do not include explicit initial values. Hence, static variables will always have assigned values.

Example 8.7 Generating Fibonacci Numbers The Fibonacci numbers form an interesting sequence in which each number is equal to the sum of the previous two numbers. In other words,

$$F_i = F_{i-1} + F_{i-2}$$

where F_i refers to the ith Fibonacci number. The first two Fibonacci numbers are defined to equal 1, that is,

$$F_1 = F_2 = 1$$

Hence,

$$F_3 = F_2 + F_1 = 1 + 1 = 2$$
$$F_4 = F_3 + F_2 = 2 + 1 = 3$$
$$F_5 = F_4 + F_3 = 3 + 2 = 5$$

and so on.

Let us write a C program that generates the first n Fibonacci numbers, where n is a value specified by the user. The main portion of the program will read in a value for n, and then enter a loop that generates and writes out each of the Fibonacci numbers. A function called fibonacci will be used to calculate each Fibonacci number from its two preceding values. Thus, this function will be called once during each pass through the main loop.

When fibonacci is entered, the computation of the current Fibonacci number, f, is very simple, provided the two previous values are known. These values can be retained from one function call to the next if we assign them to the static variables f1 and f2, which represent F_{i-1} and F_{i-2}, respectively. (We could, of course, have used external variables for this purpose, but it is better to use local variables, since F_{i-1} and F_{i-2} are required only within the function.) We then calculate the desired Fibonacci number as f = f1 + f2, and update the values of f2 and f1 using the formulas f2 = f1, and f1 = f.

Here is the complete C program.

```c
#include <stdio.h>

/* program to calculate successive Fibonacci numbers */

main()

{
    int count, n;
    long int fibonacci(int count);

    printf("How many Fibonacci numbers? ");
    scanf("%d", &n);
    printf("\n");

    for (count = 1; count <= n; ++count)
        printf("\ni = %2d   F = %ld", count, fibonacci(count));
}

long int fibonacci(int count)

/* calculate a Fibonacci number using the formulas

   F = 1 for i < 3, and F = F1 + F2 for i >= 3 */

{
    static long int f1 = 1, f2 = 1;
    long int f;

    f = (count < 3) ? 1 : f1 + f2;
    f2 = f1;
    f1 = f;
    return(f);
}
```

Notice that long integers are used to represent the Fibonacci numbers. Also, note that f1 and f2 are static variables that are each assigned an initial value of 1. These initial values are assigned only once, at the beginning of the program execution. The subsequent values are retained between successive function calls, as they are assigned. It should be understood that f1 and f2 are strictly local variables, even though they retain their values from one function call to another.

The output corresponding to a value of n = 30 is shown below. As usual, the user's response is underlined.

How many Fibonacci numbers? 30

```
i =  1     F = 1
i =  2     F = 1
i =  3     F = 2
i =  4     F = 3
i =  5     F = 5
i =  6     F = 8
i =  7     F = 13
i =  8     F = 21
i =  9     F = 34
i = 10     F = 55
i = 11     F = 89
i = 12     F = 144
i = 13     F = 233
i = 14     F = 377
i = 15     F = 610
i = 16     F = 987
i = 17     F = 1597
i = 18     F = 2584
i = 19     F = 4181
i = 20     F = 6765
i = 21     F = 10946
i = 22     F = 17711
i = 23     F = 28657
i = 24     F = 46368
i = 25     F = 75025
i = 26     F = 121393
i = 27     F = 196418
i = 28     F = 317811
i = 29     F = 514229
i = 30     F = 832040
```

It is possible to define and initialize static arrays as well as static single-valued variables. The use of arrays will be discussed in Chap. 9.

8.5   MULTIFILE PROGRAMS

A *file* is a collection of information stored as a separate entity within the computer or on an auxiliary storage device. A file can be a collection of data, a source program, a portion of a source program, an object program, and so on. In this chapter we will consider a file to be either an entire C program or a portion of a C program, i.e., one or more functions. (See Chap. 12 for a discussion of data files and their relationship to C programs.)

Until now, we have restricted our attention to C programs that are contained entirely within a single file. Many programs, however, are composed of multiple files. This is especially true of programs that make use of lengthy functions, where each function may occupy a separate file. Or, if there are many small related functions within a program, it may be desirable to place a few functions within each of several files. The individual files can then be compiled separately and linked to form one executable object program (see Sec. 5.4). This makes editing and debugging the program easier, since each file can be maintained at a manageable size.

Multifile programs allow the programmer greater flexibility in defining the scope of both functions and variables. The rules associated with the use of storage classes become more complicated, however, because they apply to functions as well as to variables, and there are more options available in the use of both external and static variables.

Functions

Let us begin by considering the rules associated with the use of functions. Within a multifile program, a function definition may be either *external* or *static*. An external function will be recognized throughout the entire program, whereas a static function will be recognized only within the file in which it is defined. In each case, the storage class is established by placing the appropriate storage-class designation (i.e., either `extern` or `static`) at the beginning of the function definition. The function is assumed to be *external* if a storage-class designation does not appear.

In general terms, the first line of a function *definition* can be written as

```
storage-class  data-type  name(formal argument 1,
                          formal argument 2,..., formal argument n)
```

Within this definition, `storage-class` refers to the storage-class associated with the function, `data-type` refers to the data-type of the value returned by the function, and *name* refers to the function name. (Note that this is a broader form of the definition originally given in Sec. 7.2). The first line of a function definition can also include the formal argument declarations, as explained in Sec. 7.6. Hence, the first line of a function definition may appear as

```
storage-class  data-type  name(type 1  arg 1,   type 2  arg 2,...,
                                                  type n  arg n);
```

where *type 1*, *type 2*, ..., *type n* refer to the formal argument types, and *arg 1*, *arg 2*, ..., *arg n* refer to the formal arguments themselves. Remember that the storage-class, the data-type, and the formal arguments need not all be present in every function definition.

When a function is defined in one file and accessed in another, the latter file must include a function *declaration*. This declaration identifies the function as an external function whose definition appears elsewhere. Such declarations are usually placed at the beginning of the file, ahead of any function definitions.

It is good programming practice to begin the declaration with the storage-class specifier `extern`. This storage-class specifier is not absolutely necessary, however, since the function will be assumed to be external if a storage-class specifier is not present.

In general terms, a function *declaration* can be written as

```
storage-class  data-type  name(argument type 1,   argument type 2,...,
                                                  argument type n);
```

(Note that this is an expanded form of the function declaration presented in Sec. 7.5.) A function declaration can also be written using full function prototyping (see Sec. 7.6) as

```
storage-class  data-type  name(type 1  arg 1,   type 2  arg 2,...,
                                                  type n  arg n);
```

The reader is again reminded that the storage-class, the data-type and the argument types need not all be present in every function declaration.

Example 8.8   Here is a simple program that generates the message "Hello, there!" from within a function. The program consists of two functions: `main` and `output`. Each function appears in a separate file.

First file:

```
#include <stdio.h>

/* simple, multifile program to write "Hello, there!" */

extern void output(void);   /* external function declaration */

main ()
{
    output();
}
```

Second file:

```
extern void output(void)   /* external function definition */
{
    printf("Hello, there!");
    return;
}
```

Notice that output is assigned the storage class extern, since it must be accessed from a file other than the one in which it is defined; it must therefore be an external function. Hence, the keyword extern is included in both the function declaration (in the first file) and the function definition (in the second file). Since extern is a default storage class, however, we could have omitted the keyword extern from both the function declaration and the function definition. As a result, the program could be written as follows:

First file:

```
#include <stdio.h>

/* simple, multifile program to write "Hello, there!" */

void output(void);   /* external function declaration */

main ()
{
    output();
}
```

Second file:

```
void output(void)   /* external function definition */
{
    printf("Hello, there!");
    return;
}
```

The details involved in compiling and linking the two files will differ from one C compiler to another. Typically, however, the appropriate commands might be written

```
compile file1

compile file2

link file1 + file2
```

where file1 and file2 are the names of the two files containing main and output, respectively.

The resulting object program will usually have the same name as the first of the files listed in the link command, i.e., file1.exe. Thus, the final program might be executed simply by writing

```
file1
```

Execution of the program will then generate the message

```
Hello, there!
```

as desired.

If a file contains a static function, it may be necessary to include static declarations for that function elsewhere in the file. In particular, a declaration will be required if the static function is accessed by another function whose definition appears ahead of the static function. Declarations of this type are generally placed within the calling functions as required. This is comparable to the use of forward declarations, described in Sec. 7.3.

Example 8.9   Simulation of a Game of Chance (Shooting Craps)   Here is another version of the craps game simulation, originally presented in Example 7.12. In this version the program consists of two separate files. The first file contains main, whereas the second file contains the functions play and throw.

First file:

```c
/* simulation of a craps game */

#include <stdio.h>
#include <stdlib.h>

#define  SEED   12345

extern void play(void);    /* external function declaration */

main()

{
    char answer = 'Y';

    printf("Welcome to the Game of CRAPS\n\n");
    printf("To throw the dice, press RETURN\n\n");

    srand(SEED);   /* initialize the random number generator */

    /* main loop */

    while (toupper(answer) != 'N')   {
        play();
        printf("\nDo you want to play again? (Y/N)");
        scanf("%1s", &answer);
        printf("\n");
    }
    printf("Bye, have a nice day");
}
```

Second file:

```
#include <stdio.h>
#include <stdlib.h>

extern void play(void)    /* external function definition */

/* simulate one complete game */

{
    static int throw(void);    /* static function declaration */
    int score1, score2;
    char dummy;

    printf("\nPlease throw the dice...");
    scanf("%c", &dummy);
    printf("\n");
    score1 = throw();
    printf("\n%2d", score1);

    switch (score1)  {

    case 7:    /* win on first throw */
    case 11:

        printf(" - Congratulations!  You WIN on the first throw\n");
        break;

    case 2:    /* lose on first throw */
    case 3:
    case 12:

        printf(" - Sorry, you LOSE on the first throw\n");
        break;

    case 4:    /* additional throws are required */
    case 5:
    case 6:
    case 8:
    case 9:
    case 10:

        do   {
                printf(" - Throw the dice again...");
                scanf("%c", &dummy);
                score2 = throw();
                printf("\n%2d", score2);
        }  while (score2 != score1 && score2 != 7);

        if (score2 == score1)
            printf(" - You WIN by matching your first score\n");
        else
            printf(" - You LOSE by failing to match your first score\n");
        break;
    }

    return;
}
```

```
static int throw(void)   /* static function definition */

/* simulate one throw of a pair of dice */

{
    float x1, x2;    /* random floating-point numbers between 0 and 1 */
    int n1, n2;      /* random integers between 1 and 6 */

    x1 = rand() / 32768.0;
    x2 = rand() / 32768.0;

    n1 = 1 + (int) (6 * x1);   /* simulate first die */
    n2 = 1 + (int) (6 * x2);   /* simulate second die */

    return(n1 + n2);           /* score is sum of two dice */
}
```

Notice that play is defined as an external function, so that it can be accessed from main (because main and play are defined in separate files). Therefore, play is declared to be an external function within the first file. On the other hand, throw is accessed only by play, which is defined in the same file as throw. Hence, throw need not be recognized in the first file. We can therefore define throw to be a static function, confining its scope to the second file. Observe that *throw* is declared to be a static function within play, as required.

Also, notice that each file has a separate set of #include statements for the library function header files stdio.h and stdlib.h. This ensures that the necessary declarations for the library functions are included in each file.

When the individual files are compiled and linked and the resulting object program is executed, the program generates a dialog identical to that shown in Example 7.12, as expected.

Variables

Within a multifile program, external variables can be defined in one file and accessed in another. The programmer must again exercise some care between the *definition* of an external variable and its *declarations*. An external variable *definition* can appear in only one file. Its location within the file must be external to any function definition. Usually, it will appear at the beginning of the file, ahead of the first function definition.

External variable definitions may include initial values. Any external variable that is not assigned an initial value will automatically be initialized to zero. The storage-class specifier extern is not required within the definition; in fact, many versions of C specifically forbid the appearance of this storage-class specifier in external variable *definitions*. Thus, external variable definitions are recognized by their location within the defining files. We will follow this convention in this book.

In order to access an external variable in another file, the variable must first be *declared* within that file. This declaration may appear anywhere within the file. Usually, however, it will be placed at the beginning of the file, ahead of the first function definition. The declaration *must* begin with the storage-class specifier extern. Initial values *cannot* be included in external variable declarations.

The value assigned to an external variable may be altered within any file in which the variable is recognized. Such changes will be recognized in all other files that fall within the scope of the variable. Thus, external variables provide a convenient means of transferring information between files.

Example 8.10   Shown below is a skeletal outline of a two-file C program that makes use of external variables.

First file:

```
int a = 1, b = 2, c = 3;    /* external variable DEFINITION */

extern void funct1(void);   /* external function DECLARATION */

main()                      /* function DEFINITION */
{
    ...
}
```

Second file:

```
extern int a, b, c;           /* external variable DECLARATION */

extern void funct1(void)    /* external function DEFINITION */
{
   ...
}
```

The variables a, b and c are defined as external variables within the first file, and assigned the initial values 1, 2 and 3, respectively. The first file also contains a *definition* of the function main, and a *declaration* for the external function funct1, defined elsewhere. Within the second file we see the *definition* of funct1, and a *declaration* for the external variables a, b and c.

Notice that the storage-class specifier extern appears in both the *definition* and the *declaration* of the external function funct1. This storage-class specifier is also present in the *declaration* for the external *variables* (in the second file), but it does *not* appear in the *definition* of the external variables (in the first file).

The scope of a, b and c is the entire program. Therefore, these variables can be accessed and their values altered in either file, i.e., in either main or funct1.

Example 8.11 Search for a Maximum   In Example 8.4 we presented a C program that determines the value of *x* which causes the function

$$y = x \cos(x)$$

to be maximized within a specified interval. We now present another version of this program, in which each of the three functions composing the program is placed in a separate file.

First file:

```
#include <stdio.h>

/* find the maximum of a function within a specified interval */

double a, b, xl, yl, xr, yr, cnst = 0.0001;     /* ext var def */

extern void reduce(void);                        /* ext funct decl */
extern double curve(double xl);                  /* ext funct decl */

main()                                           /* funct def */

{
    double xmax, ymax;

    /* read input data (interval end points) */

    printf("\na = ");
    scanf("%lf", &a);
    printf("b = ");
    scanf("%lf", &b);

    /* interval reduction loop */

    do
       reduce();
    while ((yl != yr) && ((b - a) > 3 * cnst));

    /* calculate xmax and ymax, and write out the results */

    xmax = 0.5 * (xl + xr);
    ymax = curve(xmax);
    printf("\nxmax = %8.6lf   ymax = %8.6lf", xmax, ymax);
}
```

Second file:

```
extern double a, b, xl, yl, xr, yr, cnst;     /* ext var decl */

extern double curve(double xl);               /* ext funct decl */

extern void reduce(void)                      /* ext funct def */

/* interval reduction routine */

{
    xl = a + 0.5 * (b - a - cnst);
    xr = xl + cnst;
    yl = curve(xl);
    yr = curve(xr);

    if (yl > yr)   {      /* retain left interval */
        b = xr;
        return;
    }
    if (yl < yr)          /* retain right interval */
        a = xl;
    return;
}
```

Third file:

```
#include <math.h>

extern double curve(double x)                 /* ext funct def */

/* evaluate the function y = x * cos(x)  */

{
    return (x * cos(x));
}
```

The external function `reduce`, which is defined in the second file, is declared in the first file. Therefore, its scope is the first two files. Similarly, the external function `curve`, which is defined in the third file, is declared in the first and second files. Hence, its scope is the entire program. Notice that the storage-class specifier `extern` appears in both the function definitions and the function declarations.

Now consider the external variables a, b, xl, yl, xr, yr and cnst, which are defined in the first file. Observe that cnst is assigned an initial value within the definition. These variables are utilized, and hence declared, in the second file, but not in the third file. Note that the variable declaration (in the second file) includes the storage-class specifier `extern`, but the variable definition (in the first file) does not include a storage-class specifier.

Finally, notice the `#include <math.h>` statement at the beginning of the third file. This statement causes the header file `math.h` to be included in the third source file, in support of the `cos` library function.

Executing this program results in output identical to that shown in Example 8.4.

Within a file, external variables can be defined to be static. To do so, the storage-class specifier `static` is placed at the beginning of the definition. The scope of a static external variable will be the remainder of the file in which it is defined. It will not be recognized elsewhere in the program (i.e., in other files). Thus, the use of static external variables within a file permits a group of variables to be "hidden" from the remainder of a program. Other external variables having the same names can be defined in the remaining files (though it may not be a good idea to do so). Such identically named variables will not conflict with one another syntactically, though they may cause some confusion in understanding the program logic.

Example 8.12   Generating Fibonacci Numbers   Let us return to the problem of calculating Fibonacci numbers, which we originally considered in Example 8.7. If we rewrite the program as a two-file program employing static external variables, we obtain the following complete program:

First file:

```
#include <stdio.h>

/* program to calculate successive Fibonacci numbers */

extern long int fibonacci(int count);    /* ext funct decl */

main()                                    /* funct def */

{
    int count, n;

    printf("How many Fibonacci numbers? ");
    scanf("%d", &n);
    printf("\n");

    for (count = 1; count <= n; ++count)
        printf("\ni = %2d   F = %ld", count, fibonacci(count));
}
```

Second file:

```
static long int f1 = 1, f2 = 1;          /* static ext var def */

long int fibonacci(int count)             /* ext funct def */

/* calculate a Fibonacci number using the formulas

   F = 1 for i < 3, and F = F1 + F2 for i >= 3 */

{
    long int f;

    f = (count < 3) ? 1 : f1 + f2;
    f2 = f1;
    f1 = f;
    return(f);
}
```

In this program the function `fibonacci` is defined in the second file and declared in the first file so that its scope is the entire program. On the other hand, the variables `f1` and `f2` are defined as static external variables in the second file. Their scope is therefore confined to the second file. Note that the variable definition in the second file includes the assignment of initial values.

Executing this program results in output identical to that shown in Example 8.7, as expected.

8.6   MORE ABOUT LIBRARY FUNCTIONS

Our discussion of multifile programs can provide additional insight into the use of library functions. Recall that library functions are routines that carry out various commonly used operations or calculations (see Sec. 3.6). They are contained within one or more library files that accompany each C compiler.

During the process of converting a C source program into an executable object program, the compiled source program is linked with the library files to produce the final executable program (see Sec.

5.4). Thus, the final program will be assembled from two or more separate files, even though the original source program may have been contained within a single file. The source program must therefore include declarations for the library functions, just as it would for programmer-defined functions that are defined in separate files.

One way to provide the necessary library-function declarations is for the programmer to write them explicitly, as in the multifile programs presented in the last section. This can become tedious, however, since a small program may make use of several library functions. We wish to simplify the use of library functions to the greatest extent possible. C offers us a clever way to do this, by placing the required library-function declarations in special source files, called *header files*.

Most C compilers include several header files, each of which contains declarations that are functionally related (see Appendix H). For example, `stdio.h` is a header file containing declarations for input/output routines; `math.h` contains declarations for certain mathematical functions, and so on. The header files also contain other information related to the use of the library functions, such as symbolic constant definitions.

The required header files must be merged with the source program during the compilation process. This is accomplished by placing one or more `#include` statements at the beginning of the source program (or at the beginning of the individual program files). We have been following this procedure in all of the programming examples presented in this book.

Example 8.13 Compound Interest Example 5.2 originally presented the following C program for carrying out simple compound interest calculations:

```
#include <stdio.h>
#include <math.h>

/* simple compound interest problem */

main()

{
    float p, r, n, i, f;

    /* read input data (include prompts) */

    printf("Please enter a value for the principal (P): ");
    scanf("%f", &p);
    printf("Please enter a value for the interest rate (r): ");
    scanf("%f", &r);
    printf("Please enter a value for the number of years (n): ");
    scanf("%f", &n);

    /* calculate i, then f */

    i = r / 100;
    f = p * pow((1 + i), n);

    /* write output */

    printf("\nThe final value (F) is: %.2f\n", f);
}
```

This program makes use of two header files, `stdio.h` and `math.h`. The first header file contains declarations for the `printf` and `scanf` functions, whereas the second file contains a declaration for the power function, `pow`.

We can rewrite the program if we wish, removing the #include statements and adding our own function declarations, as follows:

```
/* simple compound interest problem */

extern int printf();                    /* lib funct decl */
extern int scanf();                     /* lib funct decl */
extern double pow(double, double);      /* lib funct decl */

main()

{
    float p,r,n,i,f;

    /* read input data (include prompts) */

    printf("Please enter a value for the principal (P): ");
    scanf("%f", &p);
    printf("Please enter a value for the interest rate (r): ");
    scanf("%f", &r);
    printf("Please enter a value for the number of years (n): ");
    scanf("%f", &n);

    /* calculate i, then f */

    i = r / 100;
    f = p * pow((1 + i),n);

    /* write output */

    printf("\nThe final value (F) is: %.2f\n", f);
}
```

This version of the program is compiled in the same way as the earlier version and will generate the same output when executed. In practice the use of such programmer-supplied function declarations is not done, however, because it is more complicated and provides additional sources of error. Moreover, the error checking that occurs during the compilation process will be less complete, because the argument types are not specified for the printf and scanf functions. (Note that the number of arguments in printf and scanf can vary from one function call to another. The manner in which argument types are specified under these conditions is beyond the scope of our current discussion.)

Machine independence is a significant advantage in this approach to the use of library functions and header files. Thus machine-dependent features can be provided as library functions, as character constants or as *macros* (see Sec. 14.4) that are included within the header files. A typical C program will therefore run on many different computers without alteration, provided the appropriate library functions and header files are utilized. The portability resulting from this approach is a major contributor to the popularity of C.

Review Questions

8.1   What is meant by the storage class of a variable?

8.2   Name the four storage-class specifications included in C.

8.3   What is meant by the scope of a variable within a program?

8.4   What is the purpose of an automatic variable? What is its scope?

8.5   How is an automatic variable defined? How is it initialized? What happens if an automatic variable is not explicitly initialized within a function?

8.6   Does an automatic variable retain its value once control is transferred out of its defining function?

8.7   What is the purpose of an external variable? What is its scope?

8.8   Summarize the distinction between an external variable definition and an external variable declaration.

8.9   How is an external variable defined? How is it initialized? What happens if an external variable definition does not include the assignment of an initial value? Compare your answers with those for automatic variables.

8.10   Suppose that an external variable is defined outside of function A and accessed within the function. Does it matter whether the external variable is defined before or after the function? Explain.

8.11   In what way is the initialization of an external variable more restricted than the initialization of an automatic variable?

8.12   What is meant by side effects?

8.13   What inherent dangers are there in the use of external variables?

8.14   What is the purpose of a static variable in a single-file program? What is its scope?

8.15   How is a static variable defined in a single-file program? How is a static variable initialized? Compare with automatic variables.

8.16   Under what circumstances might it be desirable to have a program composed of several different files?

8.17   Compare the definition of functions within a multifile program with the definition of functions within a single-file program. What additional options are available in the multifile case?

8.18   In a multifile program, what is the default storage class for a function if a storage class is not explicitly specified in the function definition?

8.19   What is the purpose of a static function in a multifile program?

8.20   Compare the definition of external variables within a multifile program with the definition of external variables within a single-file program. What additional options are available in the multifile case?

8.21   Compare external variable definitions with external variable declarations in a multifile program. What is the purpose of each? Can an external variable declaration include the assignment of an initial value?

8.22   Under what circumstances can an external variable be defined to be static? What advantage might there be in doing this?

8.23   What is the scope of a static external variable?

8.24   What is the purpose of a header file? Is the use of a header file absolutely necessary?

Problems

8.25   Describe the output generated by each of the following programs:

(a)
```
#include <stdio.h>

main()
{
    int a, count;
    int funct1(int count);

    for (count = 1; count <= 5; ++count)   {
        a = funct1(count);
        printf("%d  ", a);
    }
}


funct1(int x)
{
    int y = 0;

    y += x;
    return(y);
}
```

(b) #include ⟨stdio.h⟩

```
    main()
    {
        int a, count;
        int funct1(int count);

        for (count = 1; count <= 5; ++count)    {
            a = funct1(count);
            printf("%d  ", a);
        }
    }


    funct1(int x)
    {
        static int y = Ø;

        y += x;
        return(y);
    }
```

(c) #include ⟨stdio.h⟩

```
    main()
    {
        int a = Ø, b = 1, count;
        int funct1(int a);
        int funct2(int a);

        for (count = 1; count <= 5; ++count)    {
            b += funct1(a) + funct2(a);
            printf("%d  ", b);
        }
    }


    funct1(int a)
    {
        int b;
        int funct2(int a);

        b = funct2(a);
        return(b);
    }


    funct2(int a)
    {
        static int b = 1;

        b += 1;
        return(b + a);
    }
```

8.26   Write the first line of the function definition for each of the situations described below.

(a)   The second file of a two-file program contains a function called `solver` which accepts two floating-point quantities and returns a floating-point argument. The function will be called by other functions that are defined in both files.

(b)   The second file of a two-file program contains a function called `solver` which accepts two floating-point quantities and returns a floating-point argument, as in the preceding problem. Recognition of this function is to remain local within the second file.

8.27   Add the required (or suggested) function declarations for each of the skeletal outlines shown below.

(a)   This is a two-file program.

First file:

```
main()
{
    double x, y, z;

    . . .

    z = funct1(x, y);

    . . .
}
```

Second file:

```
double funct1(double a, double b)
{
    . . .
}
```

(b)   This is a two-file program.

First file:

```
main()
{
    double x, y, z;

    . . .

    z = funct1(x, y);

    . . .
}
```

Second file:

```
double funct1(double a, double b)
{
    double c;

    c = funct2(a, b);

    . . .
}


static double funct2(double a, double b)
{

    . . .

}
```

8.28   Describe the output generated by each of the following programs:

(a)   ```
#include <stdio.h>

int a = 3;

main()
{
    int count;
    int funct1(int count);

    for (count = 1; count <= 5; ++count)   {
        a = funct1(count);
        printf("%d ", a);
    }
}

funct1(int x)
{
    a += x;
    return(a);
}
```

(b)   ```
#include <stdio.h>

int a = 100, b = 200;

main()
{
    int count, c, d;
    int funct1(int a, int b);

    for (count = 1; count <= 5; ++count)   {
        c = 20 * (count - 1);
        d = 4 * count * count;
        printf("%d  %d  ", funct1(a, c), funct1(b, d));
    }
}


funct1(int x, int y)
{
    return(x - y);
}
```

(c)   ```
#include <stdio.h>

int a = 100, b = 200;

main()
{
    int count, c;
    int funct1(int c);

    for (count = 1; count <= 5; ++count)   {
        c = 4 * count * count;
        printf("%d ", funct1(c));
    }
}
```
```

```
        funct1(int x)
        {
            int c;

            c = (x < 50) ? (a + x) : (b - x);
            return(c);
        }
```

(d) #include ⟨stdio.h⟩

```
        int a = 100, b = 200;

        main()
        {
            int count;
            int funct1(int count);

            for (count = 1; count <= 5; ++count)
                printf("%d  ", funct1(count));
        }


        funct1(int x)
        {
            int c, d;
            int funct2(int c);

            c = funct2(x);
            d = (c < 100) ? (a + c) : b;
            return(d);
        }


        funct2(int x)
        {
            static int prod = 1;

            prod *= x;
            return(prod);
        }
```

(e) #include ⟨stdio.h⟩

```
        main()
        {
            int a = 0, b = 1, count;
            int funct1(int a);

            for (count = 1; count <= 5; ++count)   {
                b += funct1(a + 1) + 1;
                printf("%d  ", b);
            }
        }
```

```
funct1(int a)
{
    int b;
    int funct2(int b);

    b = funct2(a + 1) + 1;
    return(b);
}


funct2(int a)
{
    return(a + 1);
}
```

(f)   #include ⟨stdio.h⟩

```
int a = Ø, b = 1;

main()
{
    int count;
    int funct1(int a);

    for (count = 1; count <= 5; ++count)    {
        b += funct1(a + 1) + 1;
        printf("%d  ", b);
    }
}


funct1(int a)
{
    int b;
    int funct2(int b);

    b = funct2(a + 1) + 1;
    return(b);
}

funct2(int a)
{
    return(a + 1);
}
```

(g)   #include ⟨stdio.h⟩

```
int a = Ø, b = 1;

main()
{
    int count;
    int funct1(int a);

    for (count = 1; count <= 5; ++count)    {
        b += funct1(a + 1) + 1;
        printf("%d  ", b);
    }
}
```

```
funct1(int a)
{
    int funct2(int b);

    b = funct2(a + 1) + 1;
    return(b);
}



funct2(int a)
{
    return(b + a);
}
```

(h)   #include <stdio.h>

```
int count = 0;

main()
{
    void funct1(void);

    printf("Please enter a line of text below\n");
    funct1();
    printf("%d", count);
}


void funct1(void)
{
    char c;

    if ((c = getchar()) != '\n')    {
        ++count;
        funct1();
    }
    return;
}
```

Programming Problems

8.29 The program given in Example 8.4 can easily be modified to *minimize* a function of *x*. This minimization procedure can provide us with a highly effective technique for calculating the roots of a nonlinear algebraic equation. For example, suppose we want to find the particular value of *x* that causes some function $f(x)$ to equal zero. A typical function of this nature might be

$$f(x) = x + \cos(x) - 1 - \sin(x)$$

If we let $y(x) = f(x)^2$, then the function $y(x)$ will always be positive, except for those values of *x* that are roots of the given function (i.e., for which $f(x)$, and hence $y(x)$, will equal zero). Therefore, any value of *x* that causes $y(x)$ to be minimized will also be a root of the equation $f(x) = 0$.

Modify the program shown in Example 8.4 to minimize a given function. Use the program to obtain the roots of the following equations:

(a) $x + \cos(x) = 1 + \sin(x)$, $\pi/2 < x < \pi$
(b) $x^5 + 3x^2 = 10$, $0 \le x \le 3$ (see Example 6.21)

8.30 Modify the program shown in Example 7.12 so that a sequence of craps games will be simulated automatically and noninteractively. Enter the total number of games as an input variable. Include within the program a counter that will determine the total number of wins. Use the program to simulate some large number of games (e.g., 1000). Estimate the probability of coming out ahead when playing multiple games of craps. This value, expressed as a decimal, is equal to the number of wins divided by the total number of games played. If the probability exceeds 0.500, it favors the player; otherwise it favors the house.

8.31   Rewrite each of the following programs so that it includes at least one programmer-defined function, in addition to the main function. Be careful with your choice of arguments and (if necessary) external variables.

(a)   Calculate the weighted average of a list of numbers [see Problem 6.69(a)].
(b)   Calculate the cumulative product of a list of numbers [see Problem 6.69(b)].
(c)   Calculate the geometric average of a list of numbers [see Problem 6.69(c)].
(d)   Calculate and tabulate a list of prime numbers [see Problem 6.69(f)].
(e)   Compute the sine of x, using the method described in Problem 6.69(i).
(f)   Compute the repayments on a loan [see Problem 6.69(j)].
(g)   Determine the average exam score for each student in a class, as described in Problem 6.69(k).

8.32   Write a complete C program to solve each of the problems described below. Utilize programmer-defined functions wherever appropriate. Compile and execute each program using the data given in the problem description.

(a)   Suppose you place a given sum of money, A, into a savings account at the beginning of each year for n years. If the account earns interest at the rate of i percent annually, then the amount of money that will have accumulated after n years, F, is given by

$$F = A[(1 + i/100) + (1 + i/100)^2 + (1 + i/100)^3 + \cdots + (1 + i/100)^n]$$

Write a conversational-style C program to determine the following:

(i)   How much money will accumulate after 30 years if $1000 is deposited at the beginning of each year and the interest rate is 6 percent per year, compounded annually?

(ii)   How much money must be deposited at the beginning of each year in order to accumulate $100,000 after 30 years, again assuming that the interest rate is 6 percent per year, with annual compounding?

In each case, first determine the unknown amount of money. Then create a table showing the total amount of money that will have accumulated at the end of each year. Use the function written for Problem 7.43 to carry out the exponentiation.

(b)   Modify the above program to accommodate quarterly rather than annual compounding of interest. Compare the calculated results obtained for both problems. *Hint:* The proper formula is

$$F = A[(1 + i/100m)^m + (1 + i/100m)^{2m} + (1 + i/100m)^{3m} + \cdots + (1 + i/100m)^{nm}]$$

where m represents the number of interest periods per year.

(c)   Home mortgage costs are determined in such a manner that the borrower pays the same amount of money to the lending institution each month throughout the life of the mortgage. The fraction of the total monthly payment that is required as an interest payment on the outstanding balance of the loan varies, however, from month to month. Early in the life of the mortgage most of the monthly payment is required to pay interest, and only a small fraction of the total monthly payment is applied toward reducing the amount of the loan. Gradually, the outstanding balance becomes smaller, which causes the monthly interest payment to decrease; the amount used to reduce the outstanding balance therefore increases. As a result, the balance of the loan is reduced at an accelerated rate.

Typically, prospective home buyers know how much money they must borrow and the time required for repayment. They then ask a lending institution how much their monthly payment will be at the prevailing interest rate. They should also be concerned with how much of each monthly payment is charged to interest, how much total interest they have paid since they first borrowed the money, and how much money they still owe the lending institution at the end of each month.

Write a C program that can be used by a lending institution to provide a potential customer with this information. Assume that the amount of the loan, the annual interest rate and the duration of the loan are specified. The amount of the monthly payment is calculated as

$$A = iP(1 + i)^n/[(1 + i)^n - 1]$$

where A = monthly payment, dollars

   P = total amount of the loan, dollars

   i = monthly interest rate, expressed as a decimal (e.g., 1/2 percent would be written 0.005)

   n = total number of monthly payments

The monthly interest payment can then be calculated from the formula

$$I = iB$$

where I = monthly interest payment, dollars

B = current outstanding balance, dollars

The current outstanding balance is simply equal to the original amount of the loan, less the sum of the previous payments toward principal. The monthly payment toward principal (i.e., the amount which is used to reduce the outstanding balance) is simply

$$T = A - I$$

where T = monthly payment toward principal.

Make use of the function written for Problem 7.43 to carry out the exponentiation.

Use the program to calculate the cost of a 25-year, $50,000 mortgage at an annual interest rate of 8 percent. Then repeat the calculations for an annual interest rate of 8.5 percent. How significant is the additional 0.5 percent in the interest rate over the entire life of the mortgage?

(d) The method used to calculate the cost of a home mortgage in the previous problem is known as a *constant payment* method, since each monthly payment is the same. Suppose, instead, that the monthly payments were computed by the method of simple interest. That is, suppose that the same amount is applied toward reducing the loan each month. Hence,

$$T = P/n$$

The monthly interest, however, will depend on the amount of the outstanding balance, that is,

$$I = iB$$

Thus, the total monthly payment, $A = T + I$, will decrease each month as the outstanding balance diminishes.

Write a C program to calculate the cost of a home mortgage using this method of repayment. Label the output clearly. Use the program to calculate the cost of a 25-year, $50,000 loan at 8 percent annual interest. Compare the results with those obtained in Problem 8.32(c) above.

(e) Suppose we are given a number of discrete points $(x_1, y_1), (x_2, y_2), \ldots, (x_n, y_n)$ read from a curve $y = f(x)$, where x is bounded by x_1 and x_n. We wish to approximate the area under the curve by breaking up the curve into a number of small rectangles and calculating the area of these rectangles. (This is known as the *trapezoidal rule*.) The appropriate formula is

$$A = (y_1 + y_2)(x_2 - x_1)/2 + (y_2 + y_3)(x_3 - x_2)/2 + \cdots + (y_{n-1} + y_n)(x_n - x_{n-1})/2$$

Notice that the average height of each rectangle is given by $(y_i + y_{i+1})/2$ and the width of each rectangle is equal to $(x_{i+1} - x_i)$; $i = 1, 2, \ldots, n - 1$.

Write a C program to implement this strategy, using a function to evaluate the mathematical formula $y = f(x)$. Use the program to calculate the area under the curve $y = x^3$ between the limits $x = 1$ and $x = 4$. Solve this problem first with 16 evenly spaced points, then with 61 points, and finally with 301 points. Note that the accuracy of the solution will improve as the number of points increases. (The exact answer to this problem is 63.75.)

(f) The preceding problem describes a method known as the *trapezoidal rule* for calculating the area under a curve $y(x)$, where a set of tabulated values $(x_1, y_1), (x_2, y_2), \ldots, (x_n, y_n)$ is used to describe the curve. If the tabulated values of x are equally spaced, then the equation given in the preceding problem can be simplified to read

$$A = (y_1 + 2y_2 + 2y_3 + 2y_4 + \cdots + 2y_{n-1} + y_n)h/2$$

where h is the distance between successive values of x.

Another technique that applies when there is an even number of equally spaced intervals (i.e., an odd number of data points) is *Simpson's rule*. The computational equation for implementing Simpson's rule is

$$A = (y_1 + 4y_2 + 2y_3 + 4y_4 + 2y_5 + \cdots + 4y_{n-1} + y_n)h/3$$

For a given value of h, this method will yield a more accurate result than the trapezoidal rule. (Note that the method requires about the same amount of computational complexity as the trapezoidal rule.)

Write a C program for calculating the area under a curve using either of the above techniques, assuming an odd number of equally spaced data points. Implement each method with a separate function, and utilize another independent function to evaluate $y(x)$.

Use the program to calculate the area under the curve

$$y = e^{-x^2}$$

where x ranges from 0 to 1. Calculate the area using each method, and compare the results with the correct answer of $A = 0.7468241$.

(g) Still another technique for calculating the area under a curve is to employ the *Monte Carlo* method, which makes use of randomly generated numbers. Suppose that the curve $y = f(x)$ is positive for any value of x between the specified lower and upper limits $x = a$ and $x = b$. Let the largest value of y within these limits be y^*. The Monte Carlo method proceeds as follows:

(*i*)   Begin with a counter set equal to zero.

(*ii*) Generate a random number, r_x, whose value lies between a and b.

(*iii*) Evaluate $y(r_x)$.

(*iv*) Generate a second random number, r_y, whose value lies between 0 and y^*.

(*v*)   Compare r_y with $y(r_x)$. If r_y is less than or equal to $y(r_x)$, then this point will fall on or under the given curve. Hence, the counter is incremented by 1.

(*vi*) Repeat steps (*ii*) through (*v*) a large number of times. Each time will be called a *cycle*.

(*vii*) When a specified number of cycles has been completed, the fraction of points which fell on or under the curve, F, is computed as the value of the counter divided by the total number of cycles. The area under the curve is then obtained as

$$A = Fy^*(b - a)$$

Write a C program to implement this strategy. Use this program to find the area under the curve $y = e^{-x^2}$ between the limits $a = 0$ and $b = 1$. Determine how many cycles are required to obtain an answer that is accurate to three significant figures. Compare the computer time required for this problem with the time required for the preceding problem. Which method is better?

(h) A normally distributed random variate x, with mean μ and standard deviation σ, can be generated from the formula

$$x = \mu + \sigma \frac{\sum\limits_{i=1}^{N} r_i - N/2}{\sqrt{N/12}}$$

where r_i is a uniformly distributed random number whose value lies between 0 and 1. A value of $N = 12$ is frequently selected when using this formula. The underlying basis for the formula is the *central limit theorem*, which states that a set of mean values of uniformly distributed random variates tends to be normally distributed for moderately large values of N.

Write a C program that will generate a specified number of normally distributed random variates with a given mean and a given standard deviation. Let the number of random variates, the mean and the standard deviation be input quantities to the program. Generate each random variate within a function that accepts the mean and standard deviation as arguments.

(i) Write a C program that will allow a person to play a game of tic-tac-toe against the computer. Write the program in such a manner that the computer can be either the first or the second player. If the computer is to be the first player, let the first move be generated randomly. Write out the complete status of the game after each move. Have the computer acknowledge a win by either player when it occurs.

(j) Write a complete C program that includes a recursive function to determine the value of the nth Fibonacci number, F_n, where $F_n = F_{n-1} + F_{n-2}$ and $F_1 = F_2 = 1$ (see Example 8.7). Let the value of n be an input quantity.

Chapter 9

Arrays

Many applications require the processing of multiple data items that have common characteristics (e.g., a set of numerical data, represented by $x_1, x_2, \ldots, x_n$). In such situations it is often convenient to place the data items into an *array*, where they will all share the same name (e.g., x). The individual data items can be characters, integers, floating-point numbers, and so on. They must all, however, be of the same type and the same storage class.

Each array element (i.e., each individual data item) is referred to by specifying the array name followed by one or more *subscripts*, with each subscript enclosed in square brackets. Each subscript must be expressed as a nonnegative integer. Thus, in the n-element array x, the array elements are x[0], x[1], x[2], ..., x[n-1], as illustrated in Fig. 9.1. The value of each subscript can be expressed as an integer constant, an integer variable or a more complex integer expression.

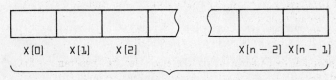

x is an n-element, one-dimensional array

Fig. 9.1

The number of subscripts determines the dimensionality of the array. For example, x[i] refers to an element in the one-dimensional array x. Similarly, y[i][j] refers to an element in the two-dimensional array y. (We can think of a two-dimensional array as a table, where y[i][j] is the jth element of the ith row.) Higher dimensional arrays can also be formed, by adding additional subscripts in the same manner (e.g., z[i][j][k]).

Recall that we have used one-dimensional character arrays earlier in this book, in conjunction with the processing of strings and lines of text. Thus, arrays are not entirely new, even though our previous references to them were somewhat casual. We will now consider arrays in greater detail. In particular, we will discuss the manner in which arrays are defined and processed, the passing of arrays to functions, and the use of multidimensional arrays. Both numerical and character-type arrays will be considered. Initially we will concentrate on one-dimensional arrays, though multidimensional arrays will be considered in Sec. 9.4.

9.1 DEFINING AN ARRAY

Arrays are defined in much the same manner as ordinary variables, except that each array name must be accompanied by a size specification (i.e., the number of elements). For a one-dimensional array, the size is specified by a positive integer expression enclosed in square brackets. The expression is usually written as a positive integer constant.

In general terms, a one-dimensional array definition may be expressed as

storage-class data-type array[*expression*];

where *storage-class* refers to the storage class of the array, *data-type* is the data type, *array* is the array name, and *expression* is a positive-valued integer expression that indicates the number of array elements. The *storage-class* is optional; default values are *automatic* for arrays defined within a function or a block, and *external* for arrays defined outside of a function.

Example 9.1   Several typical one-dimensional array definitions are shown below.

```
int x[100];
char text[80];
static char message[25];
static float n[12];
```

The first line states that x is a 100-element integer array, and the second defines text to be an 80-element character array. In the third line, message is defined as a static 25-element character array, whereas the fourth line establishes n as a static 12-element floating-point array.

It is sometimes convenient to define an array size in terms of a symbolic constant rather than a fixed integer quantity. This makes it easier to modify a program that utilizes an array, since all references to the maximum array size (e.g., within for loops as well as in array definitions) can be altered simply by changing the value of the symbolic constant.

Example 9.2   Lowercase to Uppercase Text Conversion   Here is a complete program that reads in a one-dimensional character array, converts all the elements to uppercase, and then writes out the converted array. (Similar programs are shown in Examples 4.4, 6.6, 6.9 and 6.13.)

```
#include <stdio.h>

#define  SIZE  80

main()

/* read in a line of lower-case text and write it out in upper-case */

{
    char letter[SIZE];
    int count;

    /* read in the line */

    for (count = 0; count < SIZE; ++count)
        letter[count] = getchar();

    /* write out the line in upper-case */

    for (count = 0; count < SIZE; ++count)
        putchar(toupper(letter[count]));
}
```

Notice that the symbolic constant SIZE is assigned a value of 80. This symbolic constant, rather than its value, appears in the array definition and in the two for statements. (Remember that the value of the symbolic constant will be substituted for the constant itself during the compilation process.) Therefore, in order to alter the program to accommodate a different size array, only the #define statement must be changed.

For example, to alter the above program so that it will process a 60-element array, the original #define statement is simply replaced by

```
#define  SIZE  60
```

This one change takes care of all of the necessary program alterations; there is no possibility that some required program modification will be overlooked.

Automatic arrays, unlike automatic variables, *cannot* be initialized. However, external and static array definitions can include the assignment of initial values if desired. The initial values must appear in the order in which they will be assigned to the individual array elements, enclosed in braces and separated by commas. The general form is

```
storage-class  data-type  array[expression] = {value 1, value 2, ...,    value n};
```

where *value 1* refers to the value of the first array element, *value 2* refers to the value of the second element, and so on. The appearance of the `expression`, which indicates the number of array elements, is optional when initial values are present.

Example 9.3 Shown below are several array definitions that include the assignment of initial values.

```
int digits[10] = {1, 2, 3, 4, 5, 6, 7, 8, 9, 10};

static float x[6] = {0, 0.25, 0, -0.50, 0, 0};

char color[3] = {'R', 'E', 'D'};
```

Note that x is a static array. The other two arrays (`digits` and `color`) are assumed to be external arrays by virtue of their placement within the program.

The results of these initial assignments, in terms of the individual array elements, are as follows:

digits[0] = 1	x[0] = 0	color[0] = 'R'
digits[1] = 2	x[1] = 0.25	color[1] = 'E'
digits[2] = 3	x[2] = 0	color[2] = 'D'
digits[3] = 4	x[3] = -0.50	
digits[4] = 5	x[4] = 0	
digits[5] = 6	x[5] = 0	
digits[6] = 7		
digits[7] = 8		
digits[8] = 9		
digits[9] = 10		

Remember that the subscripts in an n-element display range from 0 to n - 1.

All individual array elements that are not assigned explicit initial values will automatically be set to zero. This includes the remaining elements of an array in which certain elements have been assigned nonzero values.

Example 9.4 Consider the following array definitions:

```
int digits[10] = {3, 3, 3};

static float x[6] = {-0.3, 0, 0.25};
```

The results, on an element-by-element basis, are:

$$
\begin{array}{ll}
\texttt{digits[0] = 3} & \texttt{x[0] = -0.3} \\
\texttt{digits[1] = 3} & \texttt{x[1] = 0} \\
\texttt{digits[2] = 3} & \texttt{x[2] = 0.25} \\
\texttt{digits[3] = 0} & \texttt{x[3] = 0} \\
\texttt{digits[4] = 0} & \texttt{x[4] = 0} \\
\texttt{digits[5] = 0} & \texttt{x[5] = 0} \\
\texttt{digits[6] = 0} & \\
\texttt{digits[7] = 0} & \\
\texttt{digits[8] = 0} & \\
\texttt{digits[9] = 0} &
\end{array}
$$

In each case, all of the array elements are automatically set to zero except those that have been explicitly initialized within the array definitions. Note that the repeated values (i.e., 3, 3, 3) must be shown individually.

The array size need not be specified explicitly when initial values are included as a part of an array definition. With a numerical array, the array size will automatically be set equal to the number of initial values included within the definition.

Example 9.5 Consider the following array definitions, which are variations of the definitions shown in Examples 9.3 and 9.4.

```
int digits[] = {1, 2, 3, 4, 5, 6};

static float x[] = {0, 0.25, 0, -0.5};
```

Thus, `digits` will be a six-element integer array, and x will be a static, four-element floating-point array. The individual elements will be assigned the following values:

$$
\begin{array}{ll}
\texttt{digits[0] = 1} & \texttt{x[0] = 0} \\
\texttt{digits[1] = 2} & \texttt{x[1] = 0.25} \\
\texttt{digits[2] = 3} & \texttt{x[2] = 0} \\
\texttt{digits[3] = 4} & \texttt{x[3] = -0.5} \\
\texttt{digits[4] = 5} & \\
\texttt{digits[5] = 6} &
\end{array}
$$

Strings are handled somewhat differently, as discussed in Sec. 2.6. In particular, when a string constant is assigned to an external or a static character array as a part of the array definition, the array size specification is usually omitted. The proper array size will be assigned automatically. This will include a provision for the null character \0, which is automatically added at the end of every string (see Examples 2.20 and 2.26).

Example 9.6 Consider the following two character array definitions. Each includes the initial assignment of the string constant "RED".

```
char color[3] = "RED";

char color[] = "RED";
```

The results of these initial assignments are not the same because of the null character, \∅, which is automatically added at the end of the second string. Specifically, the first line defines a three-element character array whose individual elements are

```
color[∅] = 'R'

color[1] = 'E'

color[2] = 'D'
```

The second line, however, defines the following four-element character array:

```
color[∅] = 'R'

color[1] = 'E'

color[2] = 'D'

color[3] = '\∅'
```

Thus, the first form is incorrect, since the null character \∅ is not included in the array.
    The array definition could have been written as

```
char color[4] = "RED";
```

This definition is correct, since we are now defining a four-element array which includes an element for the null character. However, the earlier form, which omits the size specifier, is preferred.

If a program requires a one-dimensional array *declaration* (because the array is defined elsewhere in the program), the declaration is written in the same manner as the array definition with the following exceptions:

1. The square brackets may be empty, since the array size will have been specified as a part of the array definition. Array declarations are customarily written in this form.
2. Initial values cannot be included in the declaration.

These rules apply to formal argument declarations within functions as well as to external variable declarations. However, the rules for defining *multidimensional* formal arguments are more complex (see Sec. 9.4).

Example 9.7 Here is a skeletal outline of a two-file C program that makes use of external arrays.

First file:

```
int c[] = {1, 2, 3};            /* external array DEFINITION */

char message[] = "Hello!";      /* external array DEFINITION */

extern void funct1(void);       /* external function DECLARATION */

main()
{
   ...
}
```

Second file:

```
extern int c[];                    /* external array DECLARATION */

extern char message[];             /* external array DECLARATION */

extern void funct1(void)           /* external function DEFINITION */
{
   ...
}
```

This program outline includes two external arrays, c and message. The first array (c) is a three-element integer array that is defined and initialized in the first file. The second array (message) is a character array that is also defined and initialized in the first file. The arrays are then *declared* in the second file, because they are global arrays that must be recognized throughout the entire program.

Neither the array definitions in the first file nor the array declarations in the second file include explicit size specifications. Such size specifications are permissible in the first file, but are omitted because of the initialization. Moreover, array size specifications serve no useful purpose within the second file, since the array sizes have already been established.

9.2 PROCESSING AN ARRAY

Single operations involving entire arrays are not permitted in C. Thus, if a and b are similar arrays (i.e., same data type, same dimensionality and same size), assignment operations, comparison operations, and so on must be carried out on an element-by-element basis. This is usually accomplished within a loop, where each pass through the loop is used to process one array element. The number of passes through the loop will therefore equal the number of array elements to be processed.

We have already seen several examples in which the individual elements of a character array are processed in one way or another (see Examples 4.4, 4.19, 6.6, 6.9, 6.13, 6.16, 6.19, 6.32, 6.34, 8.3, 8.5 and 9.2). Numerical arrays are processed in much the same manner. In a numerical array, each array element represents a single numerical quantity, as illustrated in Example 9.8.

Example 9.8 Deviations About an Average Suppose we want to read in a list of *n* floating-point quantities and then calculate their average, as in Example 6.14. In addition to simply calculating the average, however, we will also compute the deviation of each of the numerical quantities about the average, using the formula

$$d = x_i - avg$$

where x_i represents each of the given quantities, $i = 1, 2, \ldots, n$, and *avg* represents the calculated average.

In order to solve this problem we must store each of the given quantities in a one-dimensional, floating-point array. This is an essential part of the program. The reason, which must be clearly understood, is as follows.

In all the earlier examples where we calculated the average of a list of numbers, each number was replaced by its successor in the given list (see Examples 6.7, 6.10, 6.14 and 6.31). Hence, each individual number was no longer available for subsequent calculations once the next number had been entered. Now, however, these individual quantities must be retained within the computer in order to calculate their corresponding deviations after the average has been determined. We therefore store them in a one-dimensional array, which we shall call list.

Let us define list to be a 100-element, floating-point array. We need not, however, make use of all 100 elements. Rather, we shall specify the actual number of elements by entering a positive integer quantity (not exceeding 100) for the integer variable n.

Here is the complete C program.

```
#include <stdio.h>

/* calculate the average of n numbers, then compute
   the deviation of each number about the average */
```

```
main()

{
    int n, count;
    float avg, d, sum = 0;
    float list[100];

    /* read in a value for n */
    printf("\nHow many numbers will be averaged? ");
    scanf("%d", &n);
    printf("\n");

    /* read in the numbers and calculate their sum */
    for (count = 0; count < n; ++count)  {
        printf("i = %d    x = ", count + 1);
        scanf("%f", &list[count]);
        sum += list[count];
    }

    /* calculate and write out the average */
    avg = sum / n;
    printf("\nThe average is %5.2f\n\n", avg);

    /* calculate and write out the deviations about the average */
    for (count = 0; count < n; ++count)   {
        d = list[count] - avg;
        printf("i = %d    x = %5.2f    d = %5.2f\n", count + 1, list[count], d);
    }
}
```

Note that the second scanf function (within the for loop) includes an ampersand (&) when referring to list[count], since it refers to a single array element rather than to an entire array (see Sec. 4.4).

Now suppose the program is executed using the following five numerical quantities: $x_1 = 3$, $x_2 = -2$, $x_3 = 12$, $x_4 = 4.4$, $x_5 = 3.5$. The interactive session, including the data entry and the calculated results, is shown below. The user's responses are underlined.

```
How many numbers will be averaged? 5

i = 1    x = 3
i = 2    x = -2
i = 3    x = 12
i = 4    x = 4.4
i = 5    x = 3.5

The average is 4.18

i = 1    x =   3.00    d = -1.18
i = 2    x =  -2.00    d = -6.18
i = 3    x =  12.00    d =  7.82
i = 4    x =   4.40    d =  0.22
i = 5    x =   3.50    d = -0.68
```

For some applications it may be desirable to assign initial values to the elements of an array. This requires that the array either be defined globally or locally (within the function) as a static array. The next example illustrates the use of a global array definition.

Example 9.9 Deviations About an Average Revisited Let us again calculate the average of a given set of numbers and then compute the deviation of each number about the average, as in Example 9.8. Now, however, let us assign the given numbers to the array within the array definition. To do so, let us move the definition of the array list outside of the main portion of the program. Thus, list will become an external array. Moreover, we will remove the explicit size specification from the definition, since the number of initial values will now determine the array size.

The initial values included in the following program are the same five values that were specified as input data for Example 9.8. To be consistent, we will also assign an initial value for n. This can be accomplished by defining n as either an automatic variable within main, or as an external variable. We have chosen the latter, so that all initial assignments that might otherwise be entered as input data are grouped together.

Here is the complete program.

```
#include <stdio.h>

/* calculate the average of n numbers, then compute
   the deviation of each number about the average */

int n = 5;
float list[] = {3, -2, 12, 4.4, 3.5};

main()

{
    int count;
    float avg, d, sum = 0;

    /* calculate and write out the average */
    for (count = 0; count < n; ++count)
        sum += list[count];
    avg = sum / n;
    printf("\nThe average is %5.2f\n\n", avg);

    /* calculate and write out the deviations about the average */
    for (count = 0; count < n; ++count)  {
        d = list[count] - avg;
        printf("i = %d   x = %5.2f   d = %5.2f\n", count + 1, list[count], d);
    }
}
```

Note that this version of the program does not require any input data.

Execution of this program will generate the following output:

```
The average is 4.18

i = 1    x =   3.00    d = -1.18
i = 2    x =  -2.00    d = -6.18
i = 3    x =  12.00    d =  7.82
i = 4    x =   4.40    d =  0.22
i = 5    x =   3.50    d = -0.68
```

9.3 PASSING ARRAYS TO A FUNCTION

An array name can be used as an argument to a function, thus permitting the entire array to be passed to the function. The manner in which the array is passed differs markedly, however, from that of an ordinary variable.

To pass an array to a function, the array name must appear by itself, without brackets or subscripts, as an actual argument within the function call. The corresponding formal argument is written in the same manner, though it must be declared as an array within the formal argument declarations. When declaring a one-dimensional array as a formal argument, the array name is written with a pair of empty square brackets. The size of the array is not specified within the formal argument declaration.

Example 9.10 The following program outline illustrates the passing of an array from the main portion of the program to a function.

```
main()
{
    int n;                  /* variable DECLARATION */
    float avg;              /* variable DECLARATION */
    float list[100];        /* array DEFINITION */
    float average();        /* function DECLARATION */


    ...


    avg = average(n, list);


    ...


}



float average(a, x)        /* function DEFINITION */
int a;                     /* formal argument DECLARATION */
float x[];                 /* formal argument (array) DECLARATION */
{

    ...

}
```

Within main we see a call to the function average. This function call contains two actual arguments—the integer variable n, and the one-dimensional, floating-point array list. Notice that list appears as an ordinary variable within the function call.

In the first line of the function definition, we see two formal arguments, called a and x. The formal argument declarations establish a as an integer variable and x as a one-dimensional, floating-point array. Thus, there is a correspondence between the actual argument n and the formal argument a. Similarly, there is a correspondence between the actual argument list and the formal argument x. Note that the size of x is not specified within the formal argument declaration.

Some care is required when writing function declarations that include argument type specifications. If any of the arguments are arrays, an empty pair of square brackets must follow the data type of each array argument, thus indicating that the argument is an array. In the case of function prototypes, an empty pair of square brackets must follow the name of each array argument.

Similarly, if the first line of a function definition includes the formal argument declarations, each array name appearing as a formal argument must be followed by an empty pair of square brackets.

Example 9.11 The program outline shown below is similar to that shown in Example 9.10. Now, however, argument type specifications are included within the function declaration. Moreover, the formal argument declarations are combined with the first line of the function definition.

```
main()
{
    int n;                           /* variable DECLARATION */
    float avg;                       /* variable DECLARATION */
    float list[100];                 /* array DEFINITION */
    float average(int, float[]);     /* function DECLARATION */


    ...


    avg = average(n, list);


    ...


}
```

```
float average(int a, float x[])       /* function DEFINITION */
{

    ...

}
```

Note that the function declaration appearing in main could have been written as a function prototype, that is,

```
float average(int n, float list[]);
```

We have already discussed the fact that arguments are passed to a function *by value* when the arguments are ordinary variables (see Sec. 7.4). When an array is passed to a function, however, the values of the array elements *are not* passed to the function. Rather, the array name is interpreted as the *address* of the first array element (i.e., the address of the memory location containing the first array element). This address is assigned to the corresponding formal argument when the function is called. The formal argument therefore becomes a *pointer* to the first array element (more about this in Chap. 10). Arguments passed in this manner are said to be passed *by reference* rather than by value.

When a reference is made to an array element within the function, the value of the element's subscript is added to the value of the pointer to indicate the address of the specified array element. Therefore, any array element can be accessed from within the function. Moreover, if an array element is altered within the function, the alteration will be recognized in the calling portion of the program (actually, throughout the entire scope of the array definition).

Example 9.12 Here is a simple C program that passes a three-element integer array to a function where the array elements are altered. The values of the array elements are written out at three different places in the program, thus illustrating the effects of the alterations.

```
#include <stdio.h>

main()

{

    int count, a[3];          /* array definition */
    void modify(int a[]);     /* function declaration */

    printf("\nFrom main, before calling the function:\n");
    for (count = 0; count <= 2; ++count)    {
        a[count] = count + 1;
        printf("a[%d] = %d\n", count, a[count]);
    }

    modify(a);

    printf("\nFrom main, after calling the function:\n");
    for (count = 0; count <= 2; ++count)
        printf("a[%d] = %d\n", count, a[count]);
}
```

```
void modify(int a[])       /* function definition */

{
    int count;

    printf("\nFrom the function, after modifying the values:\n");
    for (count = 0; count <= 2; ++count)    {
        a[count] = -9;
        printf("a[%d] = %d\n", count, a[count]);
    }
    return;
}
```

The array elements are assigned the values $a[0] = 1$, $a[1] = 2$ and $a[2] = 3$ within the first loop appearing in main. These values are displayed as soon as they are assigned. The array is then passed to the function modify, where each array element is assigned the value -9. These new values are then displayed from within the function. Finally, the values of the array elements are again displayed from main, after control has been transferred back to main from modify.

When the program is executed, the following output is generated:

```
From main, before calling the function:
a[0] = 1
a[1] = 2
a[2] = 3

From the function, after modifying the values:
a[0] = -9
a[1] = -9
a[2] = -9

From main, after calling the function:
a[0] = -9
a[1] = -9
a[2] = -9
```

These results show that the elements of a are altered within main as a result of the changes made within modify.

Example 7.13 presents a similar program in which the value of an ordinary variable is altered within a function, with output generated before and after the alteration. It is interesting to compare the results obtained in this example with those shown in Example 7.13.

The fact that an array can be altered globally within a function provides a convenient mechanism for moving multiple data items back and forth between the function and the calling portion of the program. Simply pass the array to the function and then alter its elements within the function. Or, if the original array must be preserved, copy the array (element-by-element) within the calling portion of the program, pass the copy to the function and perform the alterations. The programmer must exercise some caution in altering an array within a function, however, since it is very easy to unintentionally alter the array outside of the function.

Example 9.13 Reordering a List of Numbers Consider the well-known problem of rearranging a list of n integer quantities into a sequence of algebraically increasing values. Let us write a program that will carry out the rearrangement in such a manner that unnecessary storage will not be used. Therefore, the program will contain only one array—a one-dimensional, integer array called x—which will be reordered one element at a time.

The rearrangement will begin by scanning the entire array for the smallest number (in the algebraic sense). This number will then be interchanged with the first number in the array, thus placing the smallest number at the top of the list. Next the remaining $n-1$ numbers will be scanned for the smallest, which will be exchanged with the second number. The remaining $n-2$ numbers will then be scanned for the smallest, which will be interchanged with the third number, and so on, until the entire array has been rearranged. The complete rearrangement will require a total of $n-1$ passes through the array, though the length of each scan will become progressively smaller with each pass.

In order to find the smallest number within each pass, we sequentially compare each number in the array, $x[i]$, with the starting number, $x[item]$, where item is an integer variable that is used to identify a particular array element. If $x[i]$ is smaller than $x[item]$, then we interchange the two numbers; otherwise we leave the two numbers in their original positions. Once this procedure has been applied to the entire array, the first number in the array will be the smallest. We then repeat the entire procedure $n - 2$ times, for a total of $n - 1$ passes ($item = 0, 1, \ldots, n - 2$).

The only remaining question is how the two numbers are actually interchanged. To carry out the interchange, we first temporarily save the value of $x[item]$ for future reference. Then we assign the current value of $x[i]$ to $x[item]$. Finally, we assign the *original* value of $x[item]$, which has temporarily been saved, to $x[i]$. The interchange is now complete.

The strategy described above can be written in C as follows:

```c
/* reorder all array elements */
for (item = 0; item < n - 1; ++item)

    /* find the smallest of all remaining elements */
    for (i = item + 1; i < n; ++i)

        if (x[i] < x[item])   {

            /* interchange two elements */
            temp = x[item];
            x[item] = x[i];
            x[i] = temp;
        }
```

We are assuming that item and i are integer variables that are used as counters, and that temp is an integer variable that is used to temporarily store the value of $x[item]$.

It is now a simple matter to add the required variable and array definitions, and the input/output statements which will allow the original array elements to be entered and the rearranged array elements to be displayed. Here is a complete C program.

```c
#include <stdio.h>

#define  SIZE  100

/* reorder a one-dimensional, integer array from smallest to largest */

main()

{
    int i, n, x[SIZE];
    void reorder(int n, int x[]);

    /* read in a value for n */
    printf("\nHow many numbers will be entered? ");
    scanf("%d", &n);
    printf("\n");

    /* read in the list of numbers */
    for (i = 0; i < n; ++i)   {
        printf("i = %d    x = ", i + 1);
        scanf("%d", &x[i]);
    }

    /* reorder all array elements */
    reorder(n, x);

    /* display the reordered list of numbers */
    printf("\n\nReordered List of Numbers:\n\n");
    for (i = 0; i < n; ++i)
        printf("i = %d    x = %d\n", i + 1, x[i]);
}
```

```
void reorder(int n, int x[])    /* rearrange the list of numbers */

{
    int i, item, temp;

    for (item = 0; item < n - 1; ++item)

        /* find the smallest of all remaining elements */
        for (i = item + 1; i < n; ++i)

            if (x[i] < x[item])   {

                /* interchange two elements */
                temp = x[item];
                x[item] = x[i];
                x[i] = temp;
            }
    return;
}
```

In this program x is defined initially as a 100-element integer array. (Notice the use of the symbolic constant SIZE to define the size of x.) A value for n is first read into the computer, followed by numerical values for the first n elements of x (i.e., x[0], x[1], . . . , x[n-1]). Following the data input, n and x are passed to the function reorder, where the first n elements of x are rearranged into ascending order. The reordered elements of x are then written from main at the conclusion of the program.

The declaration for reorder that appears in main is written as a function prototype, as a matter of good programming practice. Notice the manner in which the function arguments are written. In particular, note that the second argument is identified as an integer array by the empty square brackets that follow the array name, i.e., int x[]. The square brackets are a required part of this argument specification.

Now suppose that the program is used to reorder the following six numbers: 595, 78, −1505, 891, −29, −7. The program will generate the following interactive dialog. (The user's responses are underlined, as usual.)

```
How many numbers will be entered? 6

i = 1     x = 595
i = 2     x = 78
i = 3     x = -1505
i = 4     x = 891
i = 5     x = -29
i = 6     x = -7


Reordered list of numbers:

i = 1     x = -1505
i = 2     x = -29
i = 3     x = -7
i = 4     x = 78
i = 5     x = 595
i = 6     x = 891
```

It should be mentioned that the return statement cannot be used to return an array. (Recall that the return statement can return only a *single-valued* expression to the calling portion of the program.) Therefore, if the elements of an array are to be passed back to the calling portion of the program, the array must either be defined as an external array whose scope includes both the function and the calling portion of the program, or it must be passed to the function as a formal argument.

Example 9.14 A Piglatin Generator   Piglatin is an encoded form of English that is often used by children as a game. A piglatin word is formed from an English word by transposing the first sound (usually the first letter) to the end of the word, and then adding the letter "a". Thus, the word "dog" becomes "ogda," "computer" becomes "omputerca," "piglatin" becomes "iglatinpa" (or "igpa atinla," if spelled as two separate words), and so on.

Let us write a C program that will accept a line of English text and then print out the corresponding text in piglatin. We will assume that each textual message can be typed on one 80-column line, with a single blank space between successive words. (Actually, we will require that the *piglatin* message not exceed 80 characters. Therefore, the original message must be somewhat less than 80 characters, since the corresponding piglatin message will be lengthened by the addition of the a's after each word.) For simplicity, we will transpose only the first letter (not the first sound) of each word. Also, we will ignore any special consideration that might be given to capital letters and to punctuation marks.

We will use two character arrays in this program. One array will contain the original line of English text, and the other will contain the translated piglatin.

The overall computational strategy will be straightforward, consisting of the following major steps:

1.   Initialize both arrays by assigning blank spaces to all of the elements.

2.   Read in an entire line of text (several words).

3.   Determine the number of words in the line (by counting the number of single blank spaces followed by a non-blank space).

4.   Rearrange the words into piglatin, word-by-word, as follows:
     (*a*)   locate the end of the word
     (*b*)   transpose the first letter to the end of the word and then add an "a"
     (*c*)   locate the beginning of the next word

5.   Write out the entire line of piglatin.

We will continue this procedure repetitively, until the computer reads a line of text whose first three letters are "end" (or "END").

In order to implement this strategy we will make use of two markers, called m1 and m2, respectively. The first marker (m1) will indicate the position of the beginning of a particular word within the original line of text. The second marker (m2) will indicate the end of the word. Note that the character in the column preceding column number m1 will be a blank space (except for the first word). Also, note that the character in the column beyond column number m2 will be a blank space.

This program lends itself to the use of a function for carrying out each of the major tasks. Before discussing the individual functions, however, we define the following program variables:

english   = a one-dimensional character array that represents the original line of text

piglatin   = a one-dimensional character array that represents the new line of text (i.e., the piglatin)

words   = an integer variable that indicates the number of words in the given line of text

n   = an integer variable that is used as a word counter (n = 1, 2, . . . , words)

count   = an integer variable that is used as a character counter within each line of text
                (count = 0, 1, 2, . . . , 79)

We will also make use of the integer variables m1 and m2 discussed earlier.

Now let us return to the overall program outline presented above. The first step, array initialization, can be carried out straightforwardly with the following function:

```
void initialize(char english[], char piglatin[])

/* initialize the character arrays with blank spaces */

{
    int count;

    for (count = Ø; count < 8Ø; ++count)
        english[count] = piglatin[count] = ' ';
    return;
}
```

Step 2 can also be carried out with a simple function. This function will contain a while loop that will continue to read characters from the keyboard until an end-of-line is detected. This sequence of characters will become the elements of the character array english. Here is the complete function.

```
void readinput(char english[])

/* read one line of English text */

{
    int count = 0;
    char c;

    while ((c = getchar()) != '\n')   {
        english[count] = c;
        ++count;
    }
    return;
}
```

Step 3 of the overall outline is equally straightforward. We simply scan the original line for occurrences of single blank characters followed by nonblank characters. The word counter (words) is then incremented each time a single blank character is encountered. Here is the word-count routine.

```
int countwords(char english[])

/* scan the English text and determine the number of words */

{
    int count, words = 1;

    for (count = 0; count < 79; ++count)
        if (english[count] == ' ' && english[count + 1] != ' ')
            ++words;
    return (words);
}
```

Now consider step 4 (rearranging the English text into piglatin), which is really the heart of the program. The logic for carrying this out is rather involved since it requires three separate, though related, operations. We must first identify the end of each word by finding the first blank space beyond m1. We then assign the characters that make up the word to the character array piglatin, with the first character at the end of the word. Finally, we must add the trailing letter "a" and then reset the initial marker, to identify the beginning of the next word.

The logic must be handled carefully, since the new line of text will be longer than the original line (because of the additional a's). Hence, the characters in the first piglatin word will occupy locations m1 to m2+1. The characters in the second word will occupy locations m1+1 to m2+2 (note that these are new values for m1 and m2), and so on. These rules can be generalized as follows:

First, for word number n, transfer all characters except the first from the original line to the new line. This can be accomplished by writing

```
for (count = m1; count < m2; ++count)
    piglatin[count + (n - 1)] = english[count + 1];
```

The last two characters (i.e., the first character in the original word plus the letter "a") can then be added in the following manner:

```
piglatin[m2 + (n - 1)] = english[m1];
piglatin[m2 + n] = 'a';
```

We then reset the value of m1

```
m1 = m2 + 2;
```

in preparation for the next word.

This entire group of calculations is repeated for each word in the original line.
Here is the function that accomplishes all of this.

```
void convert(int words, char english[], char piglatin[])

/* convert each word into piglatin */

{
    int n, count;
    int m1 = Ø;              /* marker -> beginning of word */
    int m2;                  /* marker -> end of word       */

    /* convert each word */
    for (n = 1; n <= words; ++n)   {

        /* locate the end of the current word */
        count = m1;
        while (english[count] != ' ')
            m2 = count++;

        /* transpose the first letter and add 'a' */
        for (count = m1; count < m2; ++count)
            piglatin[count + (n - 1)] = english[count + 1];
        piglatin[m2 + (n - 1)] = english[m1];
        piglatin[m2 + n] = 'a';

        /* reset the initial marker */
        m1 = m2 + 2;
    }
    return;
}
```

Step 5 (write out the piglatin) requires little more than a for loop. The complete function can be written as

```
void writeoutput(char piglatin[])

/* write out the line of text in piglatin */

{
    int count = Ø;

    for (count = Ø; count < 8Ø; ++count)
        putchar(piglatin[count]);
    printf("\n");
    return;
}
```

Now consider the main portion of the program. This is nothing more than a group of definitions and declarations, an initial message, a do - while loop that allows for repetitious program execution (until the word "end" is detected, in either upper- or lowercase, as the first word in the English text), and a closing message. The do - while loop can be made to continue indefinitely by using the test (words >= Ø) at the end of the loop. Since words is assigned an initial value of 1 and its value does not decrease, the test will always be true.

The complete program is shown below.

```c
#include <stdio.h>
#include <stdlib.h>

/* convert English to piglatin, one line at a time */

main()

{
    char english[80], piglatin[80];
    int words;
    void initialize(char english[], char piglatin[]);
    void readinput(char english[]);
    int countwords(char english[]);
    void convert(int words, char english[], char piglatin[]);
    void writeoutput(char piglatin[]);

    printf("Welcome to the piglatin generator\n\n");
    printf("Type \'END\' when finished\n\n");

    do {    /* process a new line of text */

            initialize(english, piglatin);
            readinput(english);

            /* test for stopping condition */
            if (toupper(english[0]) == 'E' &&
                toupper(english[1]) == 'N' &&
                toupper(english[2]) == 'D')    break;

            /* count the number of words in the line */
            words = countwords(english);

            /* convert english into piglatin */
            convert(words, english, piglatin);
            writeoutput(piglatin);
        }
    while (words >= 0);

    printf("\naveHa aa icena ayda (Have a nice day)\n");
}


void initialize(char english[], char piglatin[])

/* initialize the character arrays with blank spaces */

{
    int count;

    for (count = 0; count < 80; ++count)
        english[count] = piglatin[count] = ' ';
    return;
}
```

```
void readinput(char english[])

/* read one line of English text */

{
    int count = 0;
    char c;

    while ((c = getchar()) != '\n')   {
            english[count] = c;
            ++count;
    }
    return;
}



int countwords(char english[])

/* scan the English text and determine the number of words */

{
    int count, words = 1;

    for (count = 0; count < 79; ++count)
        if (english[count] == ' ' && english[count + 1] != ' ')
            ++words;
    return (words);
}



void convert(int words, char english[], char piglatin[])

/* convert each word into piglatin */

{
    int n, count;
    int m1 = 0;              /* marker -> beginning of word */
    int m2;                  /* marker -> end of word       */

    /* convert each word */
    for (n = 1; n <= words; ++n)   {

        /* locate the end of the current word */
        count = m1;
        while (english[count] != ' ')
            m2 = count++;

        /* transpose the first letter and add 'a' */
        for (count = m1; count < m2; ++count)
            piglatin[count + (n - 1)] = english[count + 1];
        piglatin[m2 + (n - 1)] = english[m1];
        piglatin[m2 + n] = 'a';

        /* reset the initial marker */
        m1 = m2 + 2;
    }
    return;
}
```

```
void writeoutput(char piglatin[])

/* write out the line of text in piglatin */

{
    int count = 0:

    for (count = 0; count < 80; ++count)
        putchar(piglatin[count]);
    printf("\n");
    return;
}
```

Notice that each function requires at least one array as an argument. In countwords and writeoutput, the array arguments simply provide input to the functions. In convert, however, one array argument provides input to the function and the other provides output to main. And in initialize and readinput, the arrays represent information that is returned to main.

The function declarations within main are written as full function prototypes. Note that each array argument is identified by an empty pair of square brackets following the array name.

Now consider what happens when the program is executed. Here is a typical interactive session, in which the user's entries are underlined.

```
Welcome to the piglatin generator

Type 'END' when finished

C is a popular structured programming language
Ca sia aa opularpa tructuredsa rogrammingpa anguagela

baseball is the great American pastime,
aseballba sia heta reatga mericanAa astime,pa

though there are many who prefer football
houghta hereta reaa anyma howa referpa ootballfa

please do not sneeze in the computer room
leasepa oda otna neezesa nia heta omputerca oomra

end

aveHa aa icena ayda   (Have a nice day)
```

The program does not include any special accommodations for punctuation marks, uppercase letters, or double-letter sounds (e.g., "th" or "sh"). These refinements are left as exercises for the reader.

9.4 MULTIDIMENSIONAL ARRAYS

Multidimensional arrays are defined in much the same manner as one-dimensional arrays, except that a separate pair of square brackets is required for each subscript. Thus, a two-dimensional array will require two pairs of square brackets, a three-dimensional array will require three pairs of square brackets, and so on.

In general terms, a multidimensional array definition can be written as

```
storage-class  data-type
                    array[expression 1][expression 2]...[expression n];
```

where *storage-class* refers to the storage class of the array, *data-type* is its data type, *array* is the array name, and *expression 1, expression 2, . . . , expression n* are positive-valued integer expressions that indicate the number of array elements associated with each subscript. Remember that the *storage-class* is optional; the default values are *automatic* for arrays that are defined inside of a function, and *external* for arrays defined outside of a function.

We have already seen that an n-element, one-dimensional array can be thought of as a *list* of values, as illustrated in Fig. 9.1. Similarly, an m × n, two-dimensional array can be thought of as a *table* of values having m rows and n columns, as illustrated in Fig. 9.2. Extending this idea, a three-dimensional array can be visualized as a *set* of tables (e.g., a book in which each page is a table), and so on.

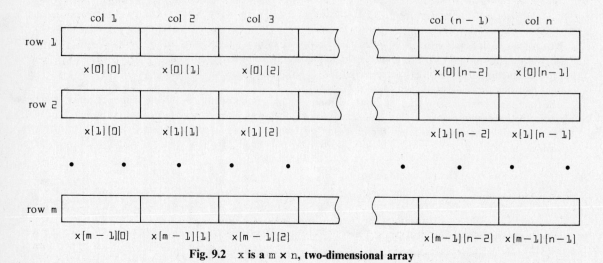

Fig. 9.2   x is a m × n, **two-dimensional array**

Example 9.15   Several typical multidimensional array definitions are shown below.

```
float table[50][50];
char page[24][80];
static double records[100][66][255];
static double records[L][M][N];
```

The first line defines `table` as a floating-point array having 50 rows and 50 columns (hence, 50 × 50 = 2500 elements), and the second line establishes `page` as a character array with 24 rows and 80 columns (24 × 80 = 1920 elements). The third array can be thought of as a set of 100 static, double-precision tables, each having 66 lines and 255 columns (hence, 100 × 66 × 255 = 1,683,000 elements).

The last definition is similar to the preceding definition except that the symbolic constants L, M and N define the array size. Thus, the values assigned to these symbolic constants will determine the actual size of the array.

If a multidimensional array definition includes the assignment of initial values, then care must be given to the order in which the initial values are assigned to the array elements. (Remember, only external and static arrays can be initialized.) The rule is that the last (rightmost) subscript increases most rapidly, and the first (leftmost) subscript increases least rapidly. Thus, the elements of a two-dimensional array will be assigned by rows, that is, the elements of the first row will be assigned, then the elements of the second row, and so on.

Example 9.16   Consider the following two-dimensional array definition:

```
int values[3][4] = {1, 2, 3, 4, 5, 6, 7, 8, 9, 10, 11, 12};
```

Note that `values` can be thought of as a table having three rows and four columns (four elements per row). Since the initial values are assigned by rows (i.e., last subscript increasing most rapidly), the results of this initial assignment are as follows:

```
values[0][0] = 1     values[0][1] = 2      values[0][2] = 3     values[0][3] = 4
values[1][0] = 5     values[1][1] = 6      values[1][2] = 7     values[1][3] = 8
values[2][0] = 9     values[2][1] = 10     values[2][2] = 11    values[2][3] = 12
```

(Remember that the first subscript ranges from 0 to 2, and the second subscript ranges from 0 to 3.)

The natural order in which the initial values are assigned can be altered by forming groups of initial values enclosed within braces (i.e., { . . . }). The values within each innermost pair of braces will be assigned to those array elements whose last subscript changes most rapidly. In a two-dimensional array, for example, the values within an inner pair of braces will be assigned to the elements of a row, since the second (column) subscript increases most rapidly. If there are too few values within a pair of braces, the remaining elements of that row will be assigned zeros. On the other hand, the number of values within each pair of braces cannot exceed the defined row size.

Example 9.17   Here is a variation of the two-dimensional array definition presented in the last example.

```
int values[3][4] = {
                    {1,  2,  3,  4},
                    {5,  6,  7,  8},
                    {9,  10,  11,  12}
                   };
```

This definition results in the same initial assignments as in the last example. Thus, the four values in the first inner pair of braces are assigned to the array elements in the first row, the values in the second inner pair of braces are assigned to the array elements in the second row, and so on. Note that an outer pair of braces is required, containing the inner pairs.

Now consider the following two-dimensional array definition:

```
int values[3][4] = {
                    {1,  2,  3},
                    {4,  5,  6},
                    {7,  8,  9}
                   };
```

This definition assigns values only to the first three elements in each row. Therefore, the array elements will have the following initial values:

```
values[0][0] = 1     values[0][1] = 2      values[0][2] = 3     values[0][3] = 0

values[1][0] = 4     values[1][1] = 5      values[1][2] = 6     values[1][3] = 0

values[2][0] = 7     values[2][1] = 8      values[2][2] = 9     values[2][3] = 0
```

Notice that the last element in each row is assigned a value of zero.

If the preceding array definition is written as

```
int values[3][4] = {1, 2, 3, 4, 5, 6, 7, 8, 9};
```

then three of the array elements will again be assigned zeros, though the order of the assignments will be different. In particular, the array elements will have the following initial values:

```
values[0][0] = 1     values[0][1] = 2      values[0][2] = 3     values[0][3] = 4

values[1][0] = 5     values[1][1] = 6      values[1][2] = 7     values[1][3] = 8

values[2][0] = 9     values[2][1] = 0      values[2][2] = 0     values[2][3] = 0
```

Now the initial values are assigned with the last subscript increasing most rapidly, on a row-by-row basis, until all of the initial values have been assigned. Without the inner pairs of braces, however, the initial values cannot be grouped for assignment to specific rows.

Finally, consider the array definition

```
int values[3][4] = {
                     {1,  2,  3,  4,  5},
                     {6,  7,  8,  9,  10},
                     {11, 12, 13, 14, 15}
                    };
```

This will result in a compilation error, since the number of values in each inner pair of braces (five values in each pair) exceeds the defined array size (four elements in each row).

The use of embedded groups of initial values can be generalized to higher dimensional arrays.

Example 9.18   Consider the following three-dimensional array definition:

```
int t[10][20][30] = {
                      {                             /* table 1 */
                       {1,  2,  3,  4},             /* row 1 */
                       {5,  6,  7,  8},             /* row 2 */
                       {9,  10, 11, 12}             /* row 3 */
                      },
                      {                             /* table 2 */
                       {21, 22, 23, 24},            /* row 1 */
                       {25, 26, 27, 28},            /* row 2 */
                       {29, 30, 31, 32}             /* row 3 */
                      }
                     };
```

Think of this array as a collection of 10 tables, each having 20 rows and 30 columns. The groups of initial values will result in the assignment of the following nonzero values in the first two tables.

$t[0][0][0] = 1$	$t[0][0][1] = 2$	$t[0][0][2] = 3$	$t[0][0][3] = 4$
$t[0][1][0] = 5$	$t[0][1][1] = 6$	$t[0][1][2] = 7$	$t[0][1][3] = 8$
$t[0][2][0] = 9$	$t[0][2][1] = 10$	$t[0][2][2] = 11$	$t[0][2][3] = 12$
$t[1][0][0] = 21$	$t[1][0][1] = 22$	$t[1][0][2] = 23$	$t[1][0][3] = 24$
$t[1][1][0] = 25$	$t[1][1][1] = 26$	$t[1][1][2] = 27$	$t[1][1][3] = 28$
$t[1][2][0] = 29$	$t[1][2][1] = 30$	$t[1][2][2] = 31$	$t[1][2][3] = 32$

All of the remaining array elements will be assigned zeros.

Multidimensional arrays are processed in the same manner as one-dimensional arrays, on an element-by-element basis. However, some care is required when passing multidimensional arrays to a function. In particular, the formal argument declarations within the function definition *must* include explicit size specifications in all of the subscript positions *except the first*. These size specifications must be consistent with the corresponding size specifications in the calling program. The first subscript position may be written as an empty pair of square brackets, as with a one-dimensional array. The corresponding function prototypes must be written in the same manner.

Example 9.19   Adding Two Tables of Numbers   Suppose we want to read two tables of integers into the computer, calculate the sums of the corresponding elements, that is,

```
c[i][j] = a[i][j] + b[i][j]
```

and then write out the new table containing these sums. We will assume that all of the tables contain the same number of rows and columns, not exceeding 20 rows and 30 columns.

Let us make use of the following variable and array definitions:

a, b, c   = two-dimensional arrays, each having the same number of rows and the same number of columns, not exceeding 20 rows and 30 columns

nrows   = an integer variable indicating the actual number of rows in each table

ncols   = an integer variable indicating the actual number of columns in each table

row   = an integer counter that indicates the row number

col   = an integer counter that indicates the column number

The program will be modularized by writing separate functions to read in an array, calculate the sum of the array elements, and write out an array. Let us call these functions readinput, computesums and writeoutput, respectively.

The logic within each function is quite straightforward. Here is a complete C program for carrying out the computation.

```c
#include <stdio.h>

#define MAXROWS  20
#define MAXCOLS  30

/* calculate the sum of the elements in two tables of integers */

main()

{
    int nrows, ncols;

    /* array definitions */
    int a[MAXROWS][MAXCOLS], b[MAXROWS][MAXCOLS], c[MAXROWS][MAXCOLS];

    /* function prototypes */
    void readinput(int a[][MAXCOLS], int nrows, int ncols);
    void computesums(int a[][MAXCOLS], int b[][MAXCOLS],
                     int c[][MAXCOLS], int nrows, int ncols);
    void writeoutput(int c[][MAXCOLS], int nrows, int ncols);

    printf("How many rows? ");
    scanf("%d", &nrows);
    printf("How many columns? ");
    scanf("%d", &ncols);

    printf("\n\nFirst table:\n");
    readinput(a, nrows, ncols);

    printf("\n\nSecond table:\n");
    readinput(b, nrows, ncols);

    computesums(a, b, c, nrows, ncols);

    printf("\n\nSums of the elements:\n\n");
    writeoutput(c, nrows, ncols);
}
```

```
void readinput(int a[][MAXCOLS], int m, int n)
/* read in a table of integers */

{
    int row, col;

    for (row = 0; row < m; ++row)   {
        printf("\nEnter data for row no. %2d\n", row + 1);
        for (col = 0; col < n; ++col)
            scanf("%d", &a[row][col]);
    }
    return;
}


void computesums(int a[][MAXCOLS], int b[][MAXCOLS],
                                   int c[][MAXCOLS], int m, int n)
/* add the elements of two integer tables */

{
    int row, col;

    for (row = 0; row < m; ++row)
        for (col = 0; col < n; ++col)
            c[row][col] = a[row][col] + b[row][col];
    return;
}


void writeoutput(int a[][MAXCOLS], int m, int n)
/* write out a table of integers */

{
    int row, col;

    for (row = 0; row < m; ++row)   {
        for (col = 0; col < n; ++col)
            printf("%4d", a[row][col]);
        printf("\n");
    }
    return;
}
```

The array definitions are expressed in terms of the symbolic constants MAXROWS and MAXCOLS, whose values are specified as 20 and 30, respectively, at the beginning of the program.

Notice the manner in which the formal argument declarations are written within each function definition. For example, the first line of function readinput is written as

```
void readinput(int a[][MAXCOLS], int m, int n)
```

The array name, a, is followed by two pairs of square brackets. The first pair is empty because the number of rows need not be specified explicitly. However, the second pair contains the symbolic constant MAXCOLS, which provides an explicit size specification for the number of columns. The array names appearing in the other function definitions (i.e., in functions computesums and writeoutput) are written in the same manner.

Also, notice the function declarations (i.e., the function prototypes) within main. These declarations are analogous to the first lines of the corresponding function definitions. In particular, each array name is followed by two pairs of brackets, the first of which is empty. The second pair of brackets contains the size specification for the number of columns, as required.

Now suppose that the program is used to sum the following two tables of numbers:

First Table				Second Table			
1	2	3	4	10	11	12	13
5	6	7	8	14	15	16	17
9	10	11	12	18	19	20	21

Execution of the program will generate the following dialog. (The user's responses are underlined, as usual.)

```
How many rows? 3
How many columns? 4


First table:

Enter data for row no.    1
1 2 3 4

Enter data for row no.    2
5 6 7 8

Enter data for row no.    3
9 10 11 12


Second table:

Enter data for row no.    1
10 11 12 13

Enter data for row no.    2
14 15 16 17

Enter data for row no.    3
18 19 20 21


Sums of the elements:

   11   13   15   17
   19   21   23   25
   27   29   31   33
```

Some C compilers are unable to pass sizeable multidimensional arrays to functions. In such situations it may be possible to redesign the program so that the multidimensional arrays are defined as external (global) arrays. Hence, the arrays need not be passed to functions as arguments. This strategy will not always work, however, because some programs use the same function to process different arrays (see, for example, the program shown in Example 9.19.) Problems of this type can usually be circumvented through the use of pointers, as will be discussed in Chap. 10.

9.5 ARRAYS AND STRINGS

We have already seen that a string can be represented as a one-dimensional character-type array. Each character within the string will be stored within one element of the array. Some problems require that the characters within a string be processed individually (e.g., the piglatin generator shown in Example 9.14). However, there are many other problems which require that strings be processed as complete entities. Such problems can be simplified considerably using special, string-oriented library functions.

For example, most C compilers include library functions that allow strings to be compared, copied or concatenated (i.e., combined, one behind another). Other library functions permit operations on individual characters within strings, for example, they allow individual characters to be found within strings, and so on. The following example illustrates the use of some of these library functions.

Example 9.20 Reordering a List of Strings Suppose we wish to enter a list of strings into the computer, rearrange them alphabetically, and then write out the rearranged list. The strategy for doing this is very similar to that shown in Example 9.13, where we rearranged a list of numbers into ascending order. Now, however, there is the additional complication of comparing entire strings, rather than single numerical values. We will therefore store the strings within a two-dimensional character array. Each string will be stored in a separate row within the array.

To simplify the computation, let us make use of the library functions strcmpi and strcpy. These functions are used to compare two strings and to copy one string to another, respectively. (Note that strcmpi is a variation of the more common function strcmp, which compares the strings but differentiates between upper- and lowercase characters. The function strcmpi, on the other hand, does not distinguish between upper- and lowercase.)

The strcmpi function accepts two strings as arguments and returns an integer value, depending upon the relative order of the two strings, as follows:

1. A negative value is returned if the first string alphabetically precedes the second string.

2. A value of zero is returned if the first string and the second string are identical (disregarding case).

3. A positive value is returned if the second string alphabetically precedes the first string.

Therefore, if strcmpi(*string1, string2*) returns a positive value, it would indicate that *string2* must be placed ahead of *string1* in order to alphabetize the two strings properly.

The strcpy function also accepts two strings as arguments. Its first argument is generally an identifier that represents a string. The second argument can be a string constant or an identifier representing a string. The function copies the value of *string2* to *string1*. Hence, it effectively causes one string to be assigned to another.

The complete program is very similar to the numerical reordering program presented in Example 9.13. Now, however, we will allow the program to accept an unspecified number of strings, until a string is entered whose first three characters are END (in either upper- or lowercase). The program will count the strings as they are entered, ignoring the last string, which contains END.

Here is the entire program.

```
#include <stdio.h>
#include <stdlib.h>

/* sort a list of strings into alphabetical order

   this program uses a two-dimensional character array */

main()

{
    int i, n = 0;
    char x[10][12];
    void reorder(int n, char x[][12]);        /* function prototype */

    printf("Enter each string on a separate line below\n\n");
    printf("Type \'END\' when finished\n\n");

    /* read in the list of strings */
    do  {
            printf("string %d: ", n + 1);
            scanf("%s", x[n]);
        }
    while (strcmpi(x[n++], "END"));

    /* reorder the list of strings */
    reorder(--n, x);

    /* display the reordered list of strings */
    printf("\n\nReordered List of Strings:\n");
    for (i = 0; i < n; ++i)
        printf("\nstring %d: %s", i + 1, x[i]);
}
```

```
void reorder(int n, char x[][12])    /* rearrange the list of strings */

{
   char temp[12];
   int i, item;

   for (item = 0; item < n - 1; ++item)

        /* find the lowest of all remaining strings */
        for (i = item + 1; i < n; ++i)

            if (strcmpi(x[item], x[i]) > 0) {
            /* interchange the two strings */
                strcpy(temp, x[item]);
                strcpy(x[item], x[i]);
                strcpy(x[i], temp);
        }
   return;
}
```

The strcmpi function appears in two different places within this program; in main, when testing for a stopping condition, and in rearrange, when testing for the need to interchange two strings. The actual string interchange is carried out using strcpy.

The dialog resulting from a typical execution of the program is shown below. The user's responses are underlined, as usual.

```
Enter each string on a separate line below

Type 'END' when finished

string 1: Pacific
string 2: Atlantic
string 3: Indian
string 4: Caribbean
string 5: Bering
string 6: Black
string 7: Red
string 8: North
string 9: Baltic
string 10: Caspian
string 11: end


Reordered List of Strings:

string 1: Altantic
string 2: Baltic
string 3: Bering
string 4: Black
string 5: Caribbean
string 6: Caspian
string 7: Indian
string 8: North
string 9: Pacific
string 10: Red
```

In the next chapter we will see a different way to represent lists of strings, which is more efficient in terms of its memory requirements (see Sec. 10.7).

Review Questions

9.1   In what way does an array differ from an ordinary variable?

9.2   What conditions must be satisfied by all of the elements of any given array?

9.3   How are individual array elements identified?

9.4   What are subscripts? How are they written? What restrictions apply to the values that can be assigned to subscripts?

9.5   Suggest a practical way to visualize one-dimensional arrays and two-dimensional arrays.

9.6   How does an array definition differ from that of an ordinary variable?

9.7   Summarize the rules for writing a one-dimensional array definition.

9.8   What advantage is there in defining an array size in terms of a symbolic constant rather than a fixed integer quantity?

9.9   Can initial values be specified within an external array definition? Can they be specified within a static array definition? Can they be specified within an automatic array definition?

9.10 How are initial values written in a one-dimensional array definition? Must the entire array be initialized?

9.11 What value is automatically assigned to those array elements not explicitly initialized?

9.12 Describe the manner in which an initial string constant is most commonly assigned to a one-dimensional character array. Can a similar procedure be used to assign values to a one-dimensional numerical array?

9.13 When a one-dimensional character array of unspecified length is assigned an initial value, what extra character is automatically added to the end of the string?

9.14 When are array declarations (in contrast to array definitions) required in a C program? How do such declarations differ from array definitions?

9.15 How are arrays usually processed in C? Can entire arrays be processed with single instructions, without repetition?

9.16 When passing an array to a function, how must the array argument be written? How is the corresponding formal argument written?

9.17 How is an array name interpreted when it is passed to a function?

9.18 Suppose a function declaration includes argument type specifications, and one of the arguments is an array. How must the array type specification be written?

9.19 When passing an argument to a function, what is the difference between passing by value and passing by reference? To what types of arguments does each apply?

9.20 If an array is passed to a function and several of its elements are altered within the function, are these changes recognized in the calling portion of the program? Explain.

9.21 Can an array be passed from a function to the calling portion of the program via a `return` statement?

9.22 How are multidimensional arrays defined? Compare with the manner in which one-dimensional arrays are defined.

9.23 State the rule that determines the order in which initial values are assigned to multidimensional array elements.

9.24 When assigning initial values to the elements of a multidimensional array, what advantage is there to forming groups of initial values, where each group is enclosed in its own set of braces?

9.25 When a multidimensional array is passed to a function, how are the formal argument declarations written? Compare with one-dimensional arrays.

9.26 How can a list of strings be stored within a two-dimensional array? How can the individual strings be processed? What library functions are available to simplify string processing?

Problems

9.27 Describe the array defined in each of the following statements:

(a) `char name[30];`   (e) `#define A 66`
(b) `float c[6];`   `#define B 132`
(c) `#define N 50`   `...`
      `...`   `char memo[A][B];`
     `int a[N];`   (f) `double accounts[50][20][80];`
(d) `int params[5][5];`

9.28 Describe the array defined in each of the following statements. Indicate what values are assigned to the individual array elements.

(a) `float c[8] = {2., 5., 3., -4., 12., 12., 0., 8.};`
(b) `float c[8] = {2., 5., 3., -4.};`
(c) `int z[12] = {0, 0, 8, 0, 0, 6};`
(d) `char flag[4] = {'T', 'R', 'U', 'E'};`
(e) `char flag[5] = {'T', 'R', 'U', 'E'};`
(f) `char flag[] = "TRUE";`
(g) `char flag[] = "FALSE";`
(h) `int p[2][4] = {1, 3, 5, 7};`
(i) `int p[2][4] = {1, 1, 3, 3, 5, 5, 7, 7};`
(j) `int p[2][4] = {`
                  `{1, 3, 5, 7},`
                  `{2, 4, 6, 8}`
              `};`
(k) `int p[2][4] = {`
                  `{1, 3},`
                  `{5, 7}`
              `};`
(l) `int c[2][3][4] = {`
                  `{`
                    `{1, 2, 3},`
                    `{4, 5},`
                    `{6, 7, 8, 9}`
                  `},`
                  `{`
                    `{10, 11},`
                    `{},`
                    `{12, 13, 14}`
                  `}`
              `};`
(m) `char colors[3][6] = {`
                  `{'R', 'E', 'D'},`
                  `{'G', 'R', 'E', 'E','N'},`
                  `{'B', 'L', 'U', 'E'}`
              `};`

9.29 Write an appropriate array definition for each of the following problem situations:

(a) Define a one-dimensional, 12-element integer array called c. Assign the values 1, 4, 7, 10,..., 34 to the array elements.

(b) Define a one-dimensional character array called `point`. Assign the string "NORTH" to the array elements. End the string with the null character.

(c) Define a one-dimensional, four-element character array called `letters`. Assign the characters 'N', 'S', 'E' and 'W' to the array elements.

(d) Define a one-dimensional, six-element floating-point array called `consts`. Assign the following values to the array elements:

$$0.005, \quad -0.032, \quad 1e-6, \quad 0.167, \quad -0.3e8, \quad 0.015$$

(e) Define a two-dimensional, 3 × 4 integer array called n. Assign the following values to the array elements:

$$
\begin{array}{cccc}
10 & 12 & 14 & 16 \\
20 & 22 & 24 & 26 \\
30 & 32 & 34 & 36
\end{array}
$$

(f) Define a two-dimensional, 3 × 4 integer array called n. Assign the following values to the array elements:

$$
\begin{array}{cccc}
10 & 12 & 14 & 0 \\
0 & 20 & 22 & 0 \\
0 & 30 & 32 & 0
\end{array}
$$

(g) Define a two-dimensional, 3 × 4 integer array called n. Assign the following values to the array elements:

$$
\begin{array}{cccc}
10 & 12 & 14 & 16 \\
20 & 22 & 0 & 0 \\
0 & 0 & 0 & 0
\end{array}
$$

9.30 In each of the following situations, write the definitions and declarations required to transfer the indicated variables and arrays from main to a function called sample (see Examples 9.10 and 9.11). In each case, assign the value returned by the function to the floating-point variable x.

(a) Transfer the floating-point variables a and b, and the one-dimensional, 20-element integer array jstar.

(b) Transfer the integer variable n, the character variable c and the one-dimensional, 50-element double-precision array values.

(c) Transfer the two-dimensional, 12 × 80 character array text.

(d) Transfer the one-dimensional, 40-element character array message, and the two-dimensional, 50 × 100 floating-point array accounts.

9.31 Describe the output generated by each of the following programs:

(a)
```c
#include <stdio.h>

main()
{
    int a, b = 0;
    static int c[10] = {1, 2, 3, 4, 5, 6, 7, 8, 9, 0};

    for (a = 0; a < 10; ++a)
        if ((c[a] % 2) == 0) b += c[a];
    printf("%d", b);
}
```

(b)
```c
#include <stdio.h>

main()
{
    int a, b = 0;
    static int c[10] = {1, 2, 3, 4, 5, 6, 7, 8, 9, 0};

    for (a = 0; a < 10; ++a)
        if ((a % 2) == 0) b += c[a];
    printf("%d", b);
}
```

(c) ```
     #include ⟨stdio.h⟩

     main()
     {
        int a, b = 0;
        int c[10] = {1, 2, 3, 4, 5, 6, 7, 8, 9, 0};

        for (a = 0; a < 10; ++a)
            b += c[a];
        printf("%d", b);
     }
     ```

(d)  ```
     #include ⟨stdio.h⟩

     int c[10] = {1, 2, 3, 4, 5, 6, 7, 8, 9, 0};

     main()
     {
        int a, b = 0;

        for (a = 0; a < 10; ++a)
            if ((c[a] % 2) == 1) b += c[a];
        printf("%d", b);
     }
     ```

(e) ```
     #include ⟨stdio.h⟩

     #define ROWS 3
     #define COLUMNS 4

     int z[ROWS][COLUMNS] = {1, 2, 3, 4, 5, 6, 7, 8, 9, 10, 11, 12};

     main()
     {
        int a, b, c = 999;

        for (a = 0; a < ROWS; ++a)
            for (b = 0; b < COLUMNS; ++b)
                if (z[a][b] < c) c = z[a][b];
        printf("%d", c);
     }
     ```

(f)  ```
     #include ⟨stdio.h⟩

     #define  ROWS  3
     #define  COLUMNS  4

     int z[ROWS][COLUMNS] = {1, 2, 3, 4, 5, 6, 7, 8, 9, 10, 11, 12};

     main()
     {
        int a, b, c;

        for (a = 0; a < ROWS; ++a)   {
            c = 999;
            for (b = 0; b < COLUMNS; ++b)
                if (z[a][b] < c) c = z[a][b];
            printf("%d  ", c);
        }
     }
     ```

(*g*) #include ⟨stdio.h⟩

```
#define   ROWS   3
#define   COLUMNS   4

main()
{
    static int z[ROWS][COLUMNS] = {1, 2, 3, 4, 5, 6, 7, 8, 9, 10, 11, 12};
    void sub1(int z[][COLUMNS]);

    sub1(z);
}

void sub1(int x[][4])
{
    int a, b, c;

    for (b = 0; b < COLUMNS; ++b)    {
        c = 0;
        for (a = 0; a < ROWS; ++a)
            if (x[a][b] > c) c = x[a][b];
        printf("%d  ", c);
    }
    return;
}
```

(*h*) #include ⟨stdio.h⟩

```
#define   ROWS   3
#define   COLUMNS   4

main()
{
    int a, b;
    static int z[ROWS][COLUMNS] = {1, 2, 3, 4, 5, 6, 7, 8, 9, 10, 11, 12};
    void sub1(int z[][COLUMNS]);

    sub1(z);
    for (a = 0; a < ROWS; ++a)    {
        for (b = 0; b < COLUMNS; ++b)
            printf("%d  ", z[a][b]);
        printf("\n");
    }
}

void sub1(int x[][COLUMNS])
{
    int a, b;

    for (a = 0; a < ROWS; ++a)
        for (b = 0; b < COLUMNS; ++b)
            if ((x[a][b] % 2) == 1) x[a][b]--;
    return;
}
```

```
(i)    #include <stdio.h>

       main()
       {
           int a;
           static char c[] = "Programming with C can be great fun!";

           for (a = 0; c[a] != '\0'; ++a)
               if ((a % 2) == 0)
                   printf("%c%c", c[a], c[a]);
       }
```

Programming Problems

9.32 Modify the program given in Example 9.8 (deviations about an average) to include two additional functions. Have the first function read in the numbers to be averaged, calculating their sum as they are read in. The second function should calculate the deviations about the average. All remaining program features (reading in a value for n, calculating a value for the average, displaying the calculated average and displaying the deviations about the average) should be carried out in the main portion of the program.

9.33 Modify the program given in Example 9.9 (deviations about an average revisited) to include two additional functions. Calculate and write out the average in the first function. Calculate and write out the deviations about the average in the second function.

9.34 Modify the program given in Example 9.13 (reordering a list of numbers) so that the numbers are rearranged into a sequence of decreasing values (i.e., from largest to smallest). Test the program using the data given in Example 9.13.

9.35 Modify the program given in Example 9.13 (reordering a list of numbers) so that any one of the following rearrangements can be carried out:

(a) smallest to largest, by magnitude
(b) smallest to largest, algebraic (by sign)
(c) largest to smallest, by magnitude
(d) largest to smallest, algebraic

Include a menu that will allow the user to select which rearrangement will be used each time the program is executed. Test the program using the following 10 values:

4.7	−8.0
−2.3	11.4
12.9	5.1
8.8	−0.2
6.0	−14.7

9.36 Modify the piglatin generator given in Example 9.14 so that it can accommodate punctuation marks, upper-case letters and double-letter sounds.

9.37 Modify the program given in Example 9.19 (adding two tables of numbers) so that it calculates the differences rather than the sums of the corresponding elements in two tables of integer numbers. Test the program using the data given in Example 9.19.

9.38 Modify the program given in Example 9.19 (adding two tables of numbers) so that it utilizes one 3-dimensional array rather than three 2-dimensional arrays. Let the first subscript refer to one of the three tables. The second subscript should refer to the row number, and the third subscript should refer to the column number.

9.39 Write a C program that will enter a line of text, store it in an array, and then write it out backwards. Allow the length of the line to be unspecified (terminated by a carriage return), but assume that it will not exceed 80 characters.

Test the program with any line of text of your own choosing. Compare with the program given in Example 7.22, which makes use of recursion rather than an array. Which approach is better, and why?

9.40 Write an interactive C program to process the exam scores for a group of students in a C programming course. Begin by specifying the number of exam scores for each student (assume this value is the same for all students in the class). Then enter each student's name and exam scores. Calculate an average score for each student, and an overall class average (an average of the individual student averages). Write out the overall class average, followed by the name, the individual exam scores and the average score for each student.

Store the student names in a two-dimensional character array, and store the exam scores in a two-dimensional floating-point array. Make the program as general as possible. Label the output clearly.

Test the program using the following set of student exam grades:

Name	Exam Scores (percent)					
Adams	45	80	80	95	55	75
Brown	60	50	70	75	55	80
Davis	40	30	10	45	60	55
Fisher	0	5	5	0	10	5
Hamilton	90	85	100	95	90	90
Jones	95	90	80	95	85	80
Ludwig	35	50	55	65	45	70
Osborne	75	60	75	60	70	80
Prince	85	75	60	85	90	100
Richards	50	60	50	35	65	70
Smith	70	60	75	70	55	75
Thomas	10	25	35	20	30	10
Wolfe	25	40	65	75	85	95
Zorba	65	80	70	100	60	95

Compare with the program written for Problem 6.69 (k).

9.41 Modify the program written for the above problem to allow for unequal weighting of the individual exam scores. In particular, assume that each of the first four exams contributes 15 percent to the final score, and each of the last two exams contributes 20 percent [see Problems 6.69(l) and 6.69(m)].

9.42 Extend the program written for the previous problem so that the deviation of each student's average about the overall class average will be determined. Write out the class average, followed by each student's name, individual exam scores, final score, and the deviation about the class average. Be sure the output is logically organized and clearly labeled.

9.43 Write a C program that will produce a table of values of the equation

$$y = 2e^{-0.1t} \sin 0.5t$$

where t varies between 0 and 60. Allow the size of the t-increment to be entered as an input parameter.

9.44 Write a complete C program that will generate a table of compound interest factors, F/P, where

$$F/P = (1 + i/100)^n$$

In this formula F represents the future value of a given sum of money, P represents its present value, i represents the annual interest rate, expressed as a percentage, and n represents the number of years.

Let each row in the table correspond to a different value of n, with n ranging from 1 to 30 (hence, 30 rows). Let each column represent a different interest rate. Include the following interest rates: 4, 4.5, 5, 5.5, 6, 6.5, 7, 7.5, 8, 8.5, 9, 9.5, 10, 11, 12 and 15 percent (hence, a total of 16 columns). Be sure to label the rows and columns appropriately.

9.45   Consider the following foreign currencies and their equivalents to one U.S. dollar:

British pound:	0.6 pounds per U.S. dollar
Canadian dollar:	1.3 dollars per U.S. dollar
Dutch guilder:	2.0 guilders per U.S. dollar
French franc:	6.0 francs per U.S. dollar
Italian lira:	1250 lira per U.S. dollar
Japanese yen:	140 yen per U.S. dollar
Mexican peso:	1600 pesos per U.S. dollar
Swiss franc:	1.4 francs per U.S. dollar
West German mark:	1.7 marks per U.S. dollar

Write an interactive, menu-driven program that will accept two different currencies and return the value of the second currency per one unit of the first currency. (For example, if the two currencies are Japanese yen and Mexican pesos, the program will return the number of Mexican pesos equivalent to one Japanese yen.) Use the data given above to carry out the conversions. Design the program so that it executes repetitiously, until an ending condition is selected from the menu.

9.46   Consider the following list of countries and their capitals:

Canada	Ottawa
England	London
France	Paris
India	New Delhi
Israel	Jerusalem
Italy	Rome
Japan	Tokyo
Mexico	Mexico City
People's Republic of China	Beijing
United States	Washington, D.C.
U.S.S.R	Moscow
West Germany	Bonn

Write an interactive C program that will accept the name of a country as input and write out the corresponding capital, and vice versa. Design the program so that it executes repetitively, until the word *End* is entered as input.

9.47   Write a complete C program for each of the problems presented below. Include the most appropriate types of arrays for each problem. Be sure to modularize each program, label the output clearly, and make use of natural data types and efficient control structures.

(a)   Suppose we are given a table of integers, A, having m rows and n columns, and a list of integers, X, having n elements. We wish to generate a new list of integers, Y, that is formed by carrying out the following operations:

```
Y[1] = A[1][1]*X[1] + A[1][2]*X[2] + · · · + A[1][N]*X[N]

Y[2] = A[2][1]*X[1] + A[2][2]*X[2] + · · · + A[2][N]*X[N]
   · · ·

Y[M] = A[M][1]*X[1] + A[M][2]*X[2] + · · · + A[M][N]*X[N]
```

Write out the input data (i.e., the values of the elements A and X), followed by the values of the elements of Y.

Use the program to process the following data:

$$A = \begin{bmatrix} 1 & 2 & 3 & 4 & 5 & 6 & 7 & 8 \\ 2 & 3 & 4 & 5 & 6 & 7 & 8 & 9 \\ 3 & 4 & 5 & 6 & 7 & 8 & 9 & 10 \\ 4 & 5 & 6 & 7 & 8 & 9 & 10 & 11 \\ 5 & 6 & 7 & 8 & 9 & 10 & 11 & 12 \\ 6 & 7 & 8 & 9 & 10 & 11 & 12 & 13 \end{bmatrix}$$

$$X = \begin{bmatrix} 1 \\ -8 \\ 3 \\ -6 \\ 5 \\ -4 \\ 7 \\ -2 \end{bmatrix}$$

(b) Suppose that A is a table of floating-point numbers having k rows and m columns, and B is a table of floating-point numbers having m rows and n columns. We wish to generate a new table, C, where each element of C is determined by

```
C[i][j] = A[i][1]*B[1][j] + A[i][2]*B[2][j] + · · · + A[i][m]*B[m][j]
```

where $i = 1, 2, \ldots, k$ and $j = 1, 2, \ldots, n$ (this is matrix multiplication).
Use the program to process the following set of data:

$$A = \begin{bmatrix} 2 & -1/3 & 0 & 2/3 & 4 \\ 1/2 & 3/2 & 4 & -2 & 1 \\ 0 & 3 & -9/7 & 6/7 & 4/3 \end{bmatrix}$$

$$B = \begin{bmatrix} 6/5 & 0 & -2 & 1/3 \\ 5 & 7/2 & 3/4 & -3/2 \\ 0 & -1 & 1 & 0 \\ 9/2 & 3/7 & -3 & 3 \\ 4 & -1/2 & 0 & 3/4 \end{bmatrix}$$

Write out the elements of A, B and C. Be sure that everything is clearly labeled.

(c) Consider a sequence of floating-point numbers, x_i, $i = 1, 2, \ldots, m$. The *mean* is defined as

$$\bar{x} = (x_1 + x_2 + \cdots + x_m)/m$$

the deviation about the mean is

$$d_i = (x_i - \bar{x}), \qquad i = 1, 2, \ldots, m$$

and the *standard deviation* is

$$s = \sqrt{(d_1^2 + d_2^2 + \cdots + d_m^2)/m}$$

Read in the first *m* elements of a one-dimensional floating-point array. Calculate the sum of these elements, the mean, the deviations, the standard deviation, the algebraic maximum and the algebraic minimum. Use the program to process the following set of data:

27.5	87.0
13.4	39.9
53.8	47.7
29.2	8.1
74.5	63.2

Repeat the computation for k different lists of numbers. Calculate the overall mean, the overall standard deviation, the overall (largest) maximum and the overall (algebraically smallest) minimum.

(d) Suppose we are given a set of tabulated values of y vs. x, that is,

$$y_0 \quad y_1 \quad y_2 \quad \cdots \quad y_n$$
$$x_0 \quad x_1 \quad x_2 \quad \cdots \quad x_n$$

and we wish to obtain a value of y at some x that lies between two of the tabulated values. This problem is commonly solved by *interpolation*, i.e., by passing a polynomial $y(x)$ through n points such that $y(x_0) = y_0$, $y(x_1) = y_1, \ldots, y(x_n) = y_n$ and then evaluating y at the desired value of x.

A common way to carry out the interpolation is to use the *Lagrange form* of the interpolation polynomial. To do this we write

$$y(x) = f_0(x)*y_0 + f_1(x)*y_1 + \cdots + f_n(x)*y_n$$

where $f_i(x)$ is a polynomial such that

$$f_i(x) = \left[\frac{(x - x_0)(x - x_1) \cdots (x - x_{i-1})(x - x_{i+1}) \cdots (x - x_n)}{(x_i - x_0)(x_i - x_1) \cdots (x_i - x_{i-1})(x_i - x_{i+1}) \cdots (x_i - x_n)} \right]$$

Notice that $f_i(x_i) = 1$ and $f_i(x_j) = 0$, where x_j is a tabulated value of x different from x_i. Therefore, we are assured that $y(x_i) = y_i$.

Write a C program to read in n pairs of data, where n does not exceed 10, and then obtain an interpolated value of y at one or more specified values of x. Use the program to obtain interpolated values of y at x = 13.7, x = 37.2, x = 112 and x = 147 from the data listed below. Determine how many tabulated pairs of data are required in each calculation in order to obtain a reasonably accurate interpolated value for y.

$y =$	$x =$
0.21073	0
0.37764	10
0.45482	20
0.49011	30
0.50563	40
0.49245	50
0.47220	60
0.43433	80
0.33824	120
0.19390	180

9.48 The following problems are concerned with games of chance (gambling games). Each problem requires the use of random numbers, as described in Example 7.12. Each program also requires the use of an array. The programs should be interactive and modularized.

(a) Write a C program that will simulate a game of blackjack between two players. Note that the computer will not be a participant in this game but will simply deal the cards to each player and then provide each player with one or more "hits" (additional cards) when requested.

The cards are dealt in order, first one card to each player, then a second card to each player. Additional hits may then be requested.

The object of the game is to obtain 21 points, or as many points as possible without exceeding 21 points, on each hand. A player is automatically disqualified if his or her hand exceeds 21 points. Picture cards count 10 points, and an ace can count either one point or 11 points. Thus a player can obtain 21 points (blackjack!) if he or she is dealt an ace and either a picture card or a 10. If the player has a low score with his (her) first two cards, he (she) may request one or more hits, as long as his (her) total score does not exceed 21.

Random numbers should be used to simulate the dealing of the cards. Be sure to include a provision that the same card is not dealt more than once.

(b) Roulette is played with a wheel containing 38 different squares along its circumference. Two of these squares, numbered 0 and 00, are green; 18 squares are red, and 18 are black. The red and black squares alternate in color, and are numbered 1 through 36 in random order.

A small marble is spun within the wheel, which eventually comes to rest within a groove beneath one of the squares. The game is played by betting on the outcome of each spin, in any one of the following ways:

(*i*)   By selecting a single red or black square, at 35-to-1 odds. Thus, if a player were to bet $1.00 and win, he or she would receive a total of $36.00: the original $1.00, plus an additional $35.00.

(*ii*) By selecting a color, either red or black, at 1-to-1 odds. Thus, if a player chose red on a $1.00 bet, he or she would receive $2.00 if the marble came to rest beneath any red square.

(*iii*) By selecting either the odd or the even numbers (excluding 0 and 00), at 1-to-1 odds.

(*iv*) By selecting either the low 18 or the high 18 numbers at 1-to-1 odds.

The player will automatically lose if the marble comes to rest beneath one of the green squares (0 or 00).

Write an interactive C program that will simulate a roulette game. Allow the players to select whatever type of bets they wish by choosing from a menu. Then print the outcome of each game followed by an appropriate message indicating whether each player has won or lost.

(*c*)   Write an interactive C program that will simulate a game of BINGO. Print each letter-number combination as it is drawn (generated). Be sure that no combination is drawn more than once. Remember that each of the letters B-I-N-G-O corresponds to a certain range of numbers, as indicated below.

B: 1—15

I: 16—30

N: 31—45

G: 46—60

O: 61—75

Each player will have a card with five columns, labeled B-I-N-G-O. Each column will contain five numbers, within the ranges indicated above. No two players will have the same card. The first player to have one entire row of numbers drawn (either vertically, horizontally or diagonally) wins.

Note: The center position of each card is sometimes covered before the game begins (a "free" call). Also, the game is sometimes played such that a player must have *all* of the numbers on his or her card drawn before he (she) can win.

9.49   Write an interactive C program that will encode or decode a line of text. To encode a line of text, proceed as follows:

1.   Convert each character, including blank spaces, to its ASCII equivalent.

2.   Generate a positive random integer. Add this integer to the ASCII equivalent of each character. The same random integer will be used for the entire line of text.

3.   Suppose that N1 represents the lowest permissible value in the ASCII code, and N2 represents the highest permissible value. If the number obtained in step 2 above (i.e., the original ASCII equivalent plus the random integer) exceeds N2, then subtract the largest possible multiple of N2 from this number, and add the remainder to N1. Hence, the encoded number will always fall between N1 and N2, and will always represent some ASCII character.

4.   Print the characters that correspond to the encoded ASCII values.

The procedure is reversed when decoding a line of text. Be certain, however, that the same random number is used in decoding as was used in encoding.

Chapter 10

Pointers

A *pointer* is a variable that represents the location (rather than the value) of a data item, such as a variable or an array element. Pointers are used frequently in C, as they have a number of useful applications. For example, pointers can be used to pass information back and forth between a function and its reference point. In particular, pointers provide a way to return multiple data items from a function via function arguments. Pointers also permit references to other functions to be specified as arguments to a given function. This has the effect of passing functions as arguments to the given function.

Pointers are also closely associated with arrays and therefore provide an alternate way to access individual array elements. Moreover, pointers provide a convenient way to represent multidimensional arrays, allowing a single multidimensional array to be replaced by a lower-dimensional array of pointers. This feature permits a collection of strings to be represented within a single array, even though the individual strings may differ in length.

10.1 FUNDAMENTALS

Within the computer's memory, every stored data item occupies one or more contiguous memory cells (i.e., adjacent words or bytes). The number of memory cells required to store a data item depends on the type of data item. For example, a single character will typically be stored in 1 byte (8 bits) of memory; an integer usually requires two contiguous bytes. A floating-point number may require four contiguous bytes, and a double-precision quantity may require eight contiguous bytes. (See Chap. 2 and Appendix D.)

Suppose v is a variable that represents some particular data item. The compiler will automatically assign memory cells for this data item. The data item can be accessed if we know the location (i.e., the *address*) of the first memory cell.* The address of v's memory location can be determined by the expression &v, where & is a unary operator, called the *address operator*, that evaluates the address of its operand.

Now let us assign the address of v to another variable, pv. Thus,

```
pv = &v
```

This new variable is called a *pointer* to v, since it "points" to the location where v is stored in memory. Remember, however, that pv represents v's *address*, not its value. Thus, pv is referred to as a *pointer variable*. The relationship between pv and v is illustrated in Fig. 10.1.

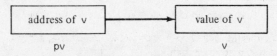

Fig. 10.1 **Relationship between** pv **and** v **(where** pv = &v **and** v = *pv**)**

The data item represented by v (i.e., the data item stored in v's memory cells) can be accessed by the expression *pv, where * is a unary operator, called the *indirection operator*, that operates only on a

---

* Adjacent memory cells within a computer are numbered consecutively, from the beginning to the end of the memory area. The number associated with each memory cell is known as the memory cell's *address*. Most computers use a hexadecimal numbering system to designate the addresses of consecutive memory cells, though some computers use an octal numbering system (see Appendix A).

279

pointer variable. Therefore, *pv and v both represent the same data item (i.e., the contents of the same memory cells). Furthermore, if we write pv = &v and u = *pv, then u and v will both represent the same value, i.e., the value of v will indirectly be assigned to u. (It is assumed that u and v are declared to have the same data type.)

Example 10.1   Shown below is a simple program that illustrates the relationship between two integer variables, their corresponding addresses and their associated pointers.

```
#include <stdio.h>

main()
{
    int u = 3;
    int v;
    int *pu;               /* pointer to an integer */
    int *pv;               /* pointer to an integer */

    pu = &u;               /* assign address of u to pu */
    v = *pu;               /* assign value of u to v */
    pv = &v;               /* assign address of v to pv */

    printf("\nu=%d   &u=%X   pu=%X   *pu=%d", u, &u, pu, *pu);
    printf("\n\nv=%d   &v=%X   pv=%X   *pv=%d", v, &v, pv, *pv);
}
```

Note that pu is a pointer to u, and pv is a pointer to v. Therefore pu represents the address of u, and pv represents the address of v. (Pointer declarations will be discussed in the next section.)

Executing this program results in the following output:

$$
\begin{array}{llll}
u=3 & \&u=F8E & pu=F8E & *pu=3 \\
v=3 & \&v=F8C & pv=F8C & *pv=3
\end{array}
$$

In the first line, we see that u represents the value 3, as specified in the declaration statement. The address of u is determined automatically by the compiler as F8E (hexadecimal). The pointer pu is assigned this value; hence, pu also represents the (hexadecimal) address F8E. Finally, the value to which pu points (i.e., the value stored in the memory cell whose address is F8E) is 3, as expected.

Similarly, the second line shows that v also represents the value 3. This is expected, since we have assigned the value *pu to v. The address of v, and hence the value of pv, is F8C. Notice that u and v have different addresses. And finally, we see that the value to which pv points is 3, as expected.

The relationships between pu and u, and pv and v, are shown in Fig. 10.2. Note that the memory locations of the pointer variables (i.e., address EC7 for pu and EC5 for pv) are not displayed by the program.

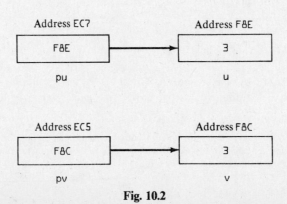

Fig. 10.2

The unary operators & and * are members of the same precedence group as the other unary operators, i.e., -, ++, --, !, sizeof and (*type*), which were presented in Chap. 3. The reader is reminded that this group of operators has a higher precedence than the groups containing the arithmetic operators and that the associativity of the unary operators is right-to-left (see Appendix C).

The address operator (&) must act upon operands associated with unique addresses, such as ordinary variables or single array elements. Thus, *the address operator cannot act upon arithmetic expressions*, such as 2 * (u + v).

The indirection operator (*) can only act upon operands that are pointers (e.g., pointer variables). However, if pv points to v (i.e., pv = &v), then an expression such as *pv can be used interchangeably with its corresponding variable v. Thus, an indirect reference (e.g., *pv) can appear in place of an ordinary variable (e.g., v) within a more complicated expression.

Example 10.2　Consider the simple C program shown below.

```c
#include <stdio.h>

main()
{

    int u1, u2;
    int v = 3;
    int *pv;                /* pv points to v */

    u1 = 2 * (v + 5);       /* ordinary expression */

    pv = &v;
    u2 = 2 * (*pv + 5);     /* equivalent expression */

    printf("\nu1=%d   u2=%d", u1, u2);
}
```

This program involves the use of two integer expressions. The first, 2 * (v + 5), is an ordinary arithmetic expression, whereas the second, 2 * (*pv + 5), involves the use of a pointer. The expressions are equivalent, since v and *pv each respresent the same integer value.

The following output is generated when the program is executed:

```
u1=16   u2=16
```

An indirect reference can also appear on the left side of an assignment statement. This provides another method for assigning a value to a variable or an array element.

Example 10.3　A simple C program is shown below.

```c
#include <stdio.h>

main()
{
    int v = 3;
    int *pv;

    pv = &v;                                /* pv points to v */
    printf("\n*pv=%d   v=%d", *pv, v);

    *pv = 0;                                /* reset v indirectly */
    printf("\n\n*pv=%d   v=%d", *pv, v);
}
```

The program begins by assigning an initial value of 3 to the integer variable v and then assigns the address of v to the pointer variable pv. Thus, pv becomes a pointer to v. The expression *pv therefore represents the value 3. The first printf statement is intended to illustrate this by displaying the current values of *pv and v.

Following the first printf statement, the value of *pv is reset to ∅. Therefore, v will be reassigned the value ∅. This is illustrated by the second printf statement, which causes the new values of *pv and v to be displayed. When the program is executed, the following output is generated.

$$*pv=3 \qquad v=3$$
$$*pv=\emptyset \qquad v=\emptyset$$

Thus, the value of v has been altered by assigning a new value to *pv.

Pointer variables can point to numeric or character variables, arrays, functions or other pointer variables. (They can also point to certain other data structures that will be discussed later in this book.) Thus, a pointer variable can be assigned the address of an ordinary variable (e.g., pv = &v). Also, a pointer variable can be assigned the value of another pointer variable (e.g., pv = px), provided both pointer variables point to data items of the same type. Moreover, a pointer variable can be assigned a null (zero) value, as explained in Sec. 10.2. On the other hand, ordinary variables *cannot* be assigned arbitrary addresses (i.e., an expression such as &x cannot appear on the lefthand side of an assignment statement).

Section 10.5 presents additional information concerning those operations that can be carried out on pointers.

10.2 POINTER DECLARATIONS

Pointer variables, like all other variables, must be declared before they may be used in a C program. The interpretation of a pointer declaration is somewhat different, however, than the interpretation of other variable declarations. When a pointer variable is declared, the variable name must be preceded by an asterisk (*). This identifies the fact that the variable is a pointer. The data type that appears in the declaration refers to the *object* of the pointer, i.e., the data item that is stored in the address represented by the pointer, rather than the pointer itself.

Thus, a pointer declaration may be written in general terms as

```
data-type *ptvar;
```

where *ptvar* is the name of the pointer variable, and *data-type* refers to the data type of the pointer's object. Remember that an asterisk must precede ptvar.

Example 10.4 A C program contains the following declarations:

```
float u, v;
float *pv;
```

The first line declares u and v to be floating-point variables. The second line declares pv to be a pointer variable whose object is a floating-point quantity, i.e., pv points to a floating-point quantity. Note that pv represents an address, not a floating-point quantity. (Some additional pointer declarations are shown in Examples 10.1 to 10.3.)

Within a variable declaration, a pointer variable can be initialized by assigning it the address of another variable. Remember that the variable whose address is assigned to the pointer variable must have been declared earlier in the program.

Example 10.5 A C program contains the following declarations:

```
float u, v;
float *pv = &v;
```

The variables u and v are declared to be floating-point variables and pv is declared as a pointer variable that points to a floating-point quantity, as in Example 10.4. In addition, the address of v is initially assigned to pv.

This terminology can be confusing. Remember that these declarations are equivalent to writing

```
float u, v;          /* floating-point variable declarations */
float *pv;           /* pointer variable declaration */
   ...
pv = &v;             /* assign v's address to pv */
```

Notice that an asterisk is not included in the assignment statement.

In general, it does not make sense to assign an integer value of a pointer variable. An exception, however, is an assignment of ∅, which is sometimes used to indicate some special condition. In such situations the recommended programming practice is to define a symbolic constant NULL which represents ∅, and to use NULL in the pointer assignment. This practice emphasizes the fact that the zero assignment represents a special situation.

Example 10.6   A C program contains the following symbolic constant definitions and array declarations:

```
#define  NULL  ∅

float u, v;
float *pv = NULL;
```

The variables u and v are declared to be floating-point variables and pv is declared as a pointer variable that points to a floating-point quantity. In addition, pv is initially assigned a value of ∅ to indicate some special condition dictated by the logic of the program (which is not shown in this example). The use of the symbolic constant NULL suggests that this initial assignment is something other than the assignment of an ordinary integer value.

We will see other kinds of pointer declarations later in this chapter.

10.3   PASSING POINTERS TO A FUNCTION

Pointers are often passed to a function as arguments. This allows data items within the calling portion of the program to be accessed by the function, altered within the function, and then returned to the calling portion of the program in altered form. We refer to this use of pointers as passing arguments by *reference* (or by *address* or by *location*), in contrast to passing arguments by *value* as we discussed in Chap. 7.

When an argument is passed by value, the data item is *copied* to the function. Thus, any alteration made to the data item within the function is not carried over into the calling routine (see Sec. 7.4). When an argument is passed by reference, however (i.e., when a pointer is passed to a function), the *address* of a data item is passed to the function. The contents of that address can be accessed freely, either within the function or within the calling routine. Moreover, any change that is made to the data item (i.e., to the contents of the address) will be recognized in both the function and the calling routine. Thus, the use of a pointer as a function argument permits the corresponding data item to be altered globally from within the function.

When pointers are used as arguments to a function, some care is required with the formal argument declarations within the function. Specifically, the formal arguments that are pointers must each be preceded by an asterisk. Also, if a function declaration is included in the calling portion of the program, the data type of each argument that corresponds to a pointer must be followed by an asterisk. Both of these points are illustrated in the following example.

Example 10.7   Here is a simple C program that illustrates the difference between ordinary arguments, which are passed by value, and pointer arguments, which are passed by reference.

```
#include <stdio.h>

main()

{
    int u = 1;
    int v = 3;
    void funct1(int u, int v);      /* function declaration */
    void funct2(int *pu, int *pv);  /* function declaration */

    printf("\nBefore calling funct1:  u=%d   v=%d", u, v);
    funct1(u, v);
    printf("\nAfter calling funct1:   u=%d   v=%d", u, v);

    printf("\n\nBefore calling funct2:  u=%d   v=%d", u, v);
    funct2(&u, &v);
    printf("\nAfter calling funct2:   u=%d   v=%d", u, v);
}


void funct1(int u, int v)

{
    u = 0;
    v = 0;
    printf("\nWithin funct1:          u=%d   v=%d", u, v);
    return;
}


void funct2(int *pu, int *pv)

{
    *pu = 0;
    *pv = 0;
    printf("\nWithin funct2:          *pu=%d *pv=%d", *pu, *pv);
    return;
}
```

This program contains two functions, called funct1 and funct2. The first function, funct1, receives two integer variables as arguments. These variables are originally assigned the values 1 and 3, respectively. The values are then changed, to 0, 0, within funct1. The new values are not recognized in main, however, because the arguments were passed by value, and any changes to the arguments are local to the function in which the changes occur.

Now consider the second function, funct2. This function receives two *pointers* to integer variables as its arguments. The arguments are identified as pointers by the indirection operators (i.e., the asterisks) that appear in the argument declaration. In addition, the argument declaration indicates that the pointers represent the addresses of *integer* quantities.

Within funct2, the contents of the pointer addresses are reassigned the values 0, 0. Since the addresses are recognized in both funct2 and main, the reassigned values will be recognized within main after the call to funct2. Therefore, the integer variables u and v will have their values changed from 1, 3 to 0, 0.

The six printf statements illustrate the values of u and v, and their associated values *pu and *pv, within main and within the two functions. Hence, the following output is generated when the program is executed:

```
Before calling funct1:   u=1    v=3
Within funct1:           u=0    v=0
After calling funct1:    u=1    v=3

Before calling funct2:   u=1    v=3
Within funct2:           *pu=0 *pv=0
After calling funct2:    u=0    v=0
```

Notice that the values of u and v are unaltered within main after the call to funct1, though the values of these variables are changed within main after the call to funct2. Thus, the output illustrates the local nature of the alterations within funct1, and the global nature of the alterations within funct2.

This example contains some additional features that should be pointed out. Notice, for example, the manner in which funct2 is declared within main, that is,

```
void funct2(int *pu, int *pv);
```

The items in parentheses identify the arguments as pointers to integer quantities. The pointer variables, pu and pv, have not been declared elsewhere in main. This is permitted in the function prototype, however, because pu and pv are dummy arguments rather than actual arguments.

Second, notice the declaration of the formal arguments within the first line of funct2, that is,

```
void funct2(int *pu, int *pv)
```

The formal arguments pu and pv are consistent with the dummy arguments in the function prototype. In this example the corresponding variable names are the same, though this is generally not required.

Finally, notice the manner in which u and v are accessed within funct2, that is,

```
*pu = 0;
*pv = 0;
```

Thus, u and v are accessed indirectly, by referencing the contents of the addresses represented by the pointers pu and pv. This is necessary because the variables u and v are not recognized as such within funct2.

We have already mentioned the fact that an array name is actually a pointer to the array, i.e., the array name represents the address of the first element in the array (see Sec. 9.3). Therefore, an array name is treated as a pointer when it is passed to a function. However, it is not necessary to precede the array name with an ampersand within the function call.

An array name that appears as a formal argument within a function definition can be declared either as a pointer or as an array of unspecified size, as shown in Sec. 9.3. The choice is a matter of personal preference, though it will often be determined by the manner in which the individual array elements are accessed within the function (more about this in the next section).

Example 10.8   Analyzing a Line of Text Suppose we wish to analyze a line of text by examining each of the characters and determining into which of several different categories it falls. In particular, suppose we count the number of vowels, consonants, digits, whitespace characters and "other" characters (punctuation, operators, brackets, etc.) This can easily be accomplished by reading in a line of text, storing it in a one-dimensional character array, and then analyzing the individual array elements. An appropriate counter will be incremented for each character. The value of each counter (number of vowels, number of consonants, etc.) can then be written out after all of the characters have been analyzed.

Let us write a complete C program that will carry out such an analysis. To do so, we first define the following symbols.

> line = an 80-element character array that will contain the line of text

> vowels = an integer counter that indicates the number of vowels

> consonants = an integer counter that indicates the number of consonants

> digits = an integer counter that indicates the number of digits

> whitespc = an integer counter that indicates the number of whitespace characters (blank spaces or tabs)

> other = an integer counter that indicates the number of characters that do not fall into any of the preceding categories

Notice that newline characters are not included in the "whitespace" category, because there can be no newline characters within a single line of text.

We will structure the program so that the line of text is read into the main portion of the program, and then passed to a function where it will be analyzed. The function will return the value of each counter after all the characters have been analyzed. The results of the analysis (i.e., the value of each counter) will then be displayed from the main portion of the program.

The actual analysis can be carried out by creating a loop to examine each of the characters. Within the loop we first convert each character that is a letter to uppercase. This avoids the need to distinguish between uppercase and lowercase letters. We can then categorize the character using a nest of if - else statements. Once the proper category has been identified, the corresponding counter is incremented. The entire process is repeated until the string termination character (\∅) has been found.

The complete C program is shown below.

```
#include <stdio.h>

/* count the number of vowels, consonants, digits, whitespace
   characters, and "other" characters in a line of text */

main()

{
    char line[8∅];              /* line of text */
    int vowels = ∅;             /* vowel counter */
    int consonants = ∅;         /* consonant counter */
    int digits = ∅;             /* digit counter */
    int whitespc = ∅;           /* whitespace counter */
    int other = ∅;              /* remaining character counter */

    /* function prototype */
    void scan_line(char line[], int *pv, int *pc, int *pd, int *pw, int *po);

    printf("Enter a line of text below:\n");
    scanf("%[^\n]", line);

    scan_line(line, &vowels, &consonants, &digits, &whitespc, &other);

    printf("\nNo. of vowels: %d", vowels);
    printf("\nNo. of consonants: %d", consonants);
    printf("\nNo. of digits: %d", digits);
    printf("\nNo. of whitespace characters: %d", whitespc);
    printf("\nNo. of other characters: %d", other);
}


void scan_line(char line[], int *pv, int *pc, int *pd, int *pw, int *po)

/* analyze the characters in a line of text */

{
    char c;                     /* uppercase character */
    int count = ∅;              /* character counter */

    while ((c = toupper(line[count])) != '\∅')     {

        if (c == 'A' || c == 'E' || c == 'I' || c == 'O' || c == 'U')
            ++ *pv;                                                 /* vowel */
        else if (c >= 'A' && c <= 'Z')
                ++ *pc;                                             /* consonant */
            else if (c >= '∅' && c <= '9')
                    ++ *pd;                                         /* digit */
                else if (c == ' ' || c == '\t')
                        ++ *pw;                                     /* whitespace */
                    else
                        ++ *po;                                     /* other */
        ++count;
    }
    return;
}
```

Notice the function prototype for scan_line that appears in main. In particular, notice the use of the void data type, and notice the manner in which the argument data types are specified. Note the distinction between the array argument and the remaining pointer arguments.

Also, observe the manner in which the actual arguments are written in the call to scan_line. An ampersand does not precede the array argument, line, since arrays are, by definition, pointers. An ampersand must precede each of the remaining arguments so that its address, rather than its value, is passed to the function.

Now consider the function scan_line. All of the formal arguments, including line, are pointers. However, line is declared as an array whose size is unspecified, whereas the remaining arguments are specifically declared as pointers. It is possible (and quite common) to declare line as a pointer rather than as an array. Thus, the first line of scan_line could have been written as

```
void scan_line(char *line, int *pv, int *pc, int *pd, int *pw, int *po)
```

rather than as shown in the program listing. To be consistent, the corresponding function prototype in main would then be written similarly.

Incrementing the various counters also requires some explanation. First, note that it is the *content* of each address (i.e., the *object* of each pointer) that is incremented. Second, note that each indirection expression (e.g., *pv) is *preceded* by the unary operator ++. Since the unary operators are evaluated from right-to-left, we are assured that the content of each address, rather the address itself, is increased in value.

Here is a typical dialog that might be encountered when the program is executed. (The line of text entered by the user is underlined.)

```
Enter a line of text below:
Personal computers with memories in excess of 1024 KB are now quite common.
```

The corresponding output is:

```
No. of vowels: 23
No. of consonants: 35
No. of digits: 4
No. of whitespace characters: 12
No. of other characters: 1
```

Thus, we see that this particular line of text contains 23 vowels, 35 consonants, four digits, 12 whitespace characters (blank spaces), and one other character (the period).

Recall that the scanf function requires those arguments that are ordinary variables to be preceded by ampersands (see Sec. 4.4). However, array names are exempted from this requirement. This may have seemed somewhat mysterious back in Chap. 4, but it should make sense now, considering what we know about array names and addresses. Thus, the scanf function requires that the *addresses* of the data items being entered into the computer's memory be specified. The ampersands provide a means for accessing the addresses of ordinary single-valued variables. Ampersands are not required with array names, since array names themselves represent addresses.

Example 10.9　The skeletal structure of a C program is shown below (repeated from Example 4.5).

```
#include <stdio.h>

main()

{
    char item[20];
    int partno;
    float cost;

    . . .

    scanf("%s %d %f", item, &partno, &cost);

    . . .

}
```

The scanf statement causes a character string, an integer quantity and a floating-point quantity to be entered into the computer and stored in the addresses associated with the item, partno and cost, respectively. Since item is the name of an array, it is understood to represent an address. Hence, item is not preceded by an ampersand within the scanf statement. On the other hand, partno and cost are conventional variables. Therefore, they must be written as &partno and &cost within the scanf statement. The ampersands are required in order to access the addresses of these variables rather than their values.

It is interesting to compare this program with the program shown in Example 9.8, where the scanf function is used to enter a single array element rather than an entire array. When a single array element is entered, the name of the array element appearing in the scanf function must be preceded by an ampersand, for example,

```
scanf("%f", &list[count]);
```

(This last statement is taken from Example 9.8.)

It is possible to pass a portion of an array, rather than an entire array, to a function. To do so, the address of the first array element to be passed must be specified as an argument. The remainder of the array, starting with the specified array element, will then be passed to the function.

Example 10.10   The skeletal structure of a C program is shown below.

```
#include <stdio.h>

main()

{
    float z[100];
    void process(float z[]);

    . . .

    /* enter values for elements of z */

    . . .

    process(&z[50]);

    . . .
}


void process(float f[])

{

    . . .

    /* process elements of f */

    . . .

    return;
}
```

Notice that z is declared within main to be a 100-element, floating-point array. After the elements of z are entered into the computer, the address of z[50] (i.e., &z[50]) is passed to the function process. Hence, the last 50 elements of z (i.e., the elements z[50] through z[99]) will be available to process.

In the next section we shall see that the address of z[50] can be written as z + 50 rather than as &z[50]. Therefore, the call to process can appear as process(z + 50) rather than process(&z[50]), as shown above. Either method may be used, depending on the programmer's preferences.

Within process, the corresponding array is referred to as f. This array is declared to be a floating-point array whose size is unspecified. As a result, the fact that the function receives only a portion of z is immaterial; if all the array elements are altered within process, only the last 50 elements will be affected within main.

Within process, it may be desirable to declare the formal argument f as a pointer to a floating-point quantity rather than as an array name. Thus, the outline of process may be written as

```
void process(float *f)

{

    ...

    /* process elements of f */

    ...

    return;
}
```

Notice the difference between the formal argument declarations in the two function outlines. Both declarations are valid.

A function can also return a pointer to the calling portion of the program. To do so, the function definition and any corresponding function declarations must indicate that the function will return a pointer. This is accomplished by preceding the function name with an asterisk. The asterisk must appear in both the function definition and the function declarations.

Example 10.11 Shown below is the skeletal structure of a C program that transfers a double-precision array to a function and returns a pointer to one of the array elements.

```
#include <stdio.h>

main()

{
    double z[100];            /* array declaration */
    double *pz;               /* pointer declaration */
    double *scan(double z[]); /* function declaration */

    ...

    /* enter values for elements of z */

    ...

    pz = scan(z);

    ...
}
```

```
double *scan(double f[])

{

    double *pf;          /* pointer declaration */

    ...

    /* process elements of f */

    pf = ...;

    return(pf);
}
```

Within main, we see that z is declared to be a 100-element, double-precision array, and pz is a pointer to a double-precision quantity. We also see a declaration for the function scan. Note that scan will accept a double-precision array as an argument, and it will return a pointer to (i.e., the address of) a double-precision quantity. The asterisk preceding the function name (*scan) indicates that the function will return a pointer.

Within the function definition, the first line indicates that scan accepts one formal parameter (f[ ]) and returns a pointer to a double-precision quantity. The formal parameter will be a one-dimensional, double-precision array. The outline suggests that the address of one of the array elements is assigned to the pointer pf during or after the processing of the array elements. This address is then returned to main, where it is assigned to the pointer variable pz.

10.4   POINTERS AND ONE-DIMENSIONAL ARRAYS

Recall that an array name is really a pointer to the first element in that array. Therefore, if x is a one-dimensional array, then the address of the first array element can be expressed as either &x[0] or simply as x. Moreover, the address of the second array element can be written as either &x[1] or as (x + 1), and so on. In general, the address of the $(i + 1)^{st}$ array element can be expressed as either &x[i] or as (x + i). Thus, we have two different ways to write the address of any array element: we can write the actual array element, preceded by an ampersand; or we can write an expression in which the subscript is added to the array name.

In the latter case, it should be understood that we are dealing with a very special and unusual type of expression. In the expression (x + i), for example, x represents an address, whereas i represents an integer quantity. Moreover, x is the name of an array whose elements may be characters, integers, floating-point quantities, and so on (though all of the array elements will be of the same data type). Thus, we are not simply adding numerical values. Rather, we are specifying an address that is a certain number of memory cells beyond the address of the first array element. Or, in simpler terms, we are specifying a location that is i array elements beyond the first. As a result, the expression (x + i) is a symbolic representation for an address specification rather than an arithmetic expression.

Recall that the number of memory cells associated with an array element will depend on the data type of the array as well as on the particular computer's architecture. With some computers, for example, an integer quantity occupies 2 bytes (two memory cells), a floating-point quantity requires 4 bytes, and a double-precision quantity requires 8 bytes. With other computers, an integer quantity might require 4 bytes, and floating-point and double-precision quantities might each require 8 bytes. And so on.

When writing the address of an array element in the form (x + i), however, the C programmer need not be concerned with the number of memory cells associated with each type of array element; the C compiler adjusts for this automatically. The programmer must specify only the address of the first array element (i.e., the name of the array) and the number of array elements beyond the first (i.e., a value for the subscript). The value of i is sometimes referred to as an *offset* when used in this manner.

Since &x[i] and (x + i) both represent the address of the ith element of x, it would seem reasonable that x[i] and *(x + i) both represent the contents of that address, i.e., the value of the ith element of x. This is indeed the case. The two terms are interchangeable. Hence, either term can be used in any particular application. The choice depends upon the programmer's individual preferences.

Example 10.12 Here is a simple program that illustrates the relationship between array elements and their addresses.

```
#include <stdio.h>

main()
{
    static int x[10] = {10, 11, 12, 13, 14, 15, 16, 17, 18, 19};
    int i;

    for (i = 0; i <= 9; ++i)
        printf("\ni= %d        x[i]= %d    *(x+i)= %d      &x[i]= %X    x+i= %X",
                                i, x[i], *(x+i), &x[i], x+i);

}
```

This program defines a one-dimensional, 10-element integer array x, whose elements are assigned the values 10, 11, ..., 19. The action portion of the program consists of a loop that displays the value and the corresponding address of each array element. Note that the value of each array element is specified in two different ways, as x[i] and as *(x+i), in order to illustrate their equivalence. Similarly, the address of each array element is specified in two different ways, as &x[i] and as (x+i), for the same reason. Therefore, the value and the address of each array element should appear twice.

Executing this program results in the following output:

```
i=0        x[i]= 10    *(x+i)= 10        &x[i]= 72    x+i= 72
i=1        x[i]= 11    *(x+i)= 11        &x[i]= 74    x+i= 74
i=2        x[i]= 12    *(x+i)= 12        &x[i]= 76    x+i= 76
i=3        x[i]= 13    *(x+i)= 13        &x[i]= 78    x+i= 78
i=4        x[i]= 14    *(x+i)= 14        &x[i]= 7A    x+i= 7A
i=5        x[i]= 15    *(x+i)= 15        &x[i]= 7C    x+i= 7C
i=6        x[i]= 16    *(x+i)= 16        &x[i]= 7E    x+i= 7E
i=7        x[i]= 17    *(x+i)= 17        &x[i]= 80    x+i= 80
i=8        x[i]= 18    *(x+i)= 18        &x[i]= 82    x+i= 82
i=9        x[i]= 19    *(x+i)= 19        &x[i]= 84    x+i= 84
```

The output clearly illustrates the distinction between x[i], which represents the value of the ith array element, and &x[i], which represents its address. Moreover, we see that the value of the ith array element can be represented by either x[i] or *(x+i), and the address of the ith element can be represented by either &x[i] or x+i. Thus, we see another comparison, between *(x+i), which also represents the value of the ith element, and x+i, which also represents its address.

In particular, notice that the first array element (corresponding to i = 0) has been assigned a value of 10 and a (hexadecimal) address of 72. The second array element has a value of 11 and an address of 74, etc. Thus, memory location 72 will contain the integer value 10, location 74 will contain 11, and so on.

It should be understood that the compiler automatically assigns these addresses.

When assigning a *value* to an array element such as x[i], the left side of the assignment statement may be written as either x[i] or as *(x + i). Thus, a value may be assigned directly to an array element, or it may be assigned to the memory area whose address is that of the array element. On the other hand, it is sometimes necessary to assign an *address* to an identifier. In such situations a pointer variable must appear on the left side of the assignment statement. It is not possible to assign an arbitrary address to an array name or to an array element. Thus, expressions such as x, (x + i) and &x[i] cannot appear on the left side of an assignment statement. Moreover, the address of an array cannot arbitrarily be altered, so that expressions such as ++x are not permitted.

Example 10.13   Consider the skeletal structure of the C program shown below.

```
#include <stdio.h>

main()
{
    int line[80];
    int *pl;

    . . .

    /* assign values */
    line[2] = line[1];
    line[2] = *(line + 1);
    *(line + 2) = line[1];
    *(line + 2) = *(line + 1);

    /* assign addresses */
    pl = &line[1];
    pl = line + 1;
}
```

Each of the first four assignment statements assigns the value of the second array element (i.e., line[1]) to the third array element (line[2]). Thus, the four statements are all equivalent. An experienced programmer would probably choose either the first or the fourth, however, so that the notation would be consistent.

Each of the last two assignment statements assigns the *address* of the second array element to the pointer pl. We might choose to do this in an actual program if it was necessary to "tag" the address of line[1] for some reason.

Note that the address of one array element cannot be assigned to some other array element. We *cannot* write a statement such as

```
&line[2] = &line[1];
```

On the other hand, we can assign the *value* of one array element to another through a pointer if we wish, for example,

```
pl = &line[1];
line[2] = *pl;
```

or

```
pl = line + 1;
*(line + 2) = *pl;
```

We have established that an array name is actually a pointer to the first element within the array. Therefore, it should be possible to define the array as a pointer variable rather than as a conventional array. Syntactically, the two definitions are equivalent. However, a conventional array definition results in a fixed block of memory being reserved at the beginning of program execution, whereas this does not occur if the array is represented in terms of a pointer variable. As a result the use of a pointer variable to represent an array requires some sort of initial memory assignment before the array elements are processed. Generally, such initial memory allocations are accomplished by using the malloc library function, though the exact method will vary from one application to another. Some typical applications are shown in a few of the programming examples in the remainder of this chapter.

Numerical array elements cannot be assigned initial values if the array is defined as a pointer variable. Therefore, a conventional array definition is required if initial values will be assigned to the elements of a numerical array. (Later in this section we shall see that *strings* can be assigned to *character-type* pointer variables as a part of the variable declarations.)

Example 10.14   Suppose that x is to be defined as a one-dimensional, 10-element array of integers. It is possible to define x as a pointer variable rather than as an array. Thus, we can write

```
int *x;
```

instead of

```
int x[10];
```

or instead of

```
#define SIZE 10

int x[SIZE];
```

However, x is not automatically assigned a memory block when it is defined as a pointer variable, though a block of memory large enough to store 10 integer quantities will be reserved in advance when x is defined as an array.
    To assign sufficient memory for x, we can make use of the library function `malloc`, as follows:

```
x = malloc(10 * sizeof(int));
```

This function reserves a block of memory whose size (in bytes) is equivalent to the size of an integer quantity. The function returns a pointer to a character. To be consistent with the definition of x, we really want a pointer to an integer. However, characters and integers are equivalent in C. Therefore, the statement is acceptable as shown above, though we could include a type cast to be on the safe side, that is,

```
x = (int *) malloc(10 * sizeof(int));
```

The allocation of memory in this manner, as it is required, is known as *dynamic memory allocation.*
    If the declaration is to include the assignment of initial values, then x *must* be defined as an array rather than as a pointer variable. For example,

```
int x[10] = {1, 2, 3, 4, 5, 6, 7, 8, 9, 10};
```

or

```
int x[] = {1, 2, 3, 4, 5, 6, 7, 8, 9, 10};
```

When programming in C, it is not unusual to use pointer expressions rather than references to individual array elements. The resulting programs may appear strange to the uninitiated, though they are straightforward once the programmer becomes comfortable accessing the values stored in specific addresses. Generally, a small amount of practice is all that is required.

Example 10.15   Reordering a List of Numbers   To illustrate the use of pointers, let us once again consider the problem of reordering a list of integers, as described in Example 9.13. Now, however, we will utilize pointer expressions to access individual values rather than refer explicitly to individual array elements. In all other respects, we present a program identical to that given in Example 9.13.
    Here is the complete C program.

```
#include <stdio.h>

/* reorder a one-dimensional, integer array from smallest to largest —
   version using pointer notation */

main()

{
    int i, n, *x;
    void reorder(int n, int *x);

    /* read in a value for n */
    printf("\nHow many numbers will be entered? ");
    scanf("%d", &n);
    printf("\n");

    /* allocate memory */
    x = (int *) malloc(n * sizeof(int));

    /* read in the list of numbers */
    for (i = 0; i < n; ++i)   {
        printf("i = %d   x = ", i + 1);
        scanf("%d", x + i);
    }

    /* reorder all array elements */
    reorder(n, x);

    /* display the reordered list of numbers */
    printf("\n\nReordered List of Numbers:\n\n");
    for (i = 0; i < n; ++i)
        printf("i = %d   x = %d\n", i + 1, *(x + i));
}

void reorder(int n, int *x)     /* rearrange the list of numbers */

{
   int i, item, temp;

   for (item = 0; item < n - 1; ++item)

        /* find the smallest of all remaining elements */
        for (i = item + 1; i < n; ++i)

            if (*(x + i) < *(x + item))   {

                /* interchange two elements */
                temp = *(x + item);
                *(x + item) = *(x + i);
                *(x + i) = temp;
            }
   return;
}
```

In this program the integer array is defined as a pointer to an integer. Memory is initially assigned to the pointer variable via the `malloc` library function. Elsewhere in the program, pointer notation is used to process the individual array elements. Within `main`, for example, the forward declaration of the function `reorder` now specifies that the second argument is a pointer to an integer quantity rather than an integer array. This pointer will identify the beginning of the integer array.

We also see that the scanf function now specifies the address of the ith element as x + i rather than &x[i]. Similarly, the printf function now represents the value of the ith element as *(x + i) rather than x[i]. The call to reorder, however, is the same in both programs, namely, reorder(n, x);.

Within the function reorder, we see that the second formal argument is now defined as a pointer variable rather than as an integer array. This is consistent with the function declaration in main. Even more pronounced, however, are the differences in the if statement. In particular, notice that each reference to an array element is now written as the content of an address. Thus, x[i] is now written as *(x + i), and x[item] is now written as *(x + item). This compound if statement can be viewed as a conditional interchange involving the contents of two different addresses, rather than as an interchange of two different elements within a conventional array.

Compare this program with that shown in Example 9.13 in order to appreciate the differences. Both programs will generate identical results with the same input data. The reader should, however, understand the syntactic differences between the two programs.

We have already discussed the fact that a numerical pointer variable cannot be initialized in the same manner as a numerical array, i.e., it cannot be assigned multiple numerical values as a part of the variable declaration. However, a character-type pointer variable can be assigned an entire string as a part of the variable declaration. Thus, a string can conveniently be represented by either a one-dimensional character array or by a character pointer.

Example 10.16 Shown below is a simple C program in which two strings are represented as one-dimensional character arrays.

```
#include <stdio.h>

char x[] = "This string is declared externally\n\n";

main()
{
    static char y[] = "This string is declared within main";

    printf("%s", x);
    printf("%s", y);
}
```

The first string is assigned to the external array x[]. The second string is assigned to the static array y[], which is defined within main. This second definition occurs within a function; therefore y[] must be defined as a static array so that it can be initialized.

Here is a different version of the same program. The strings are now assigned to pointer variables rather than to conventional one-dimensional arrays.

```
#include <stdio.h>

char *x = "This string is declared externally\n\n";

main()
{
    char *y = "This string is declared within main";

    printf("%s", x);
    printf("%s", y);
}
```

The external pointer variable x points to the beginning of the first string, whereas the pointer variable y, declared within main, points to the beginning of the second string. Note that y can now be initialized without being declared static.

Executing either program produces the following output:

```
This string is declared externally

This string is declared within main
```

Syntactically, of course, it is possible to declare a pointer variable static. However, there is no reason to do so in this example.

10.5 OPERATIONS ON POINTERS

In the previous section we saw that an integer value can be added to an array name in order to access an individual array element. The integer value is interpreted as an array subscript; it represents the location of the desired array element relative to the first element in the array. This works because all of the array elements are of the same data type, and therefore each array element occupies the same number of memory cells (i.e., the same number of bytes or words). The actual number of memory cells separating the two array elements will depend on the data type of the array, though this is taken care of automatically by the compiler and therefore need not concern the programmer directly.

This concept can be extended to pointer variables. In particular, an integer value can be added to or subtracted from a pointer variable, though the resulting expression must be interpreted very carefully. Suppose, for example, that px is a pointer variable representing the address of some variable x. We can write expressions such as ++px, --px, (px + 3), (px + i), and (px - i), where i is an integer variable. Each expression will represent an address located some distance from the original address represented by px. The exact distance will be the product of the integer quantity and the number of bytes or words associated with the data item to which px points. Suppose, for example, that px points to an integer quantity, and each integer quantity requires 2 bytes of memory. Then the expression (px + 3) will result in an address 6 bytes beyond the integer to which px points, as illustrated in Fig. 10.3. It should be understood, however, that this new address will *not* necessarily represent the address of another data item, particularly if the data items stored between the two addresses involve different data types.

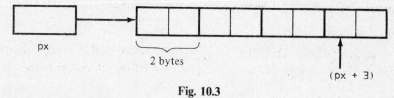

Fig. 10.3

Example 10.17   Consider the simple C program shown below.

```
#include <stdio.h>

main()

{
    int *px;          /* pointer to an integer */
    int i = 1;
    float f = 0.3;
    double d = 0.005;
    char c = '*';

    px = &i;
    printf("Values:      i=%i   f=%f    d=%f    c=%c\n\n", i, f, d, c);
    printf("Addresses:      &i=%X    &f=%X    &d=%X    &c=%X\n\n", &i, &f, &d, &c);
    printf("Pointer values:     px=%X    px + 1=%X    px + 2=%X    px + 3=%X",
                                 px, px + 1, px + 2, px + 3);
}
```

This program displays the values and addresses associated with four different types of variables: i, an integer variable; f, a floating-point variable; d, a double-precision variable; and c, a character variable. The program also makes use of a pointer variable, px, that represents the address of i. The values of px, px + 1, px + 2 and px + 3 are also displayed, so that they may be compared with the addresses of the different variables.

Execution of the program results in the following output:

```
Values:    i=1    f=0.300000   d=0.005000    c=*

Addresses:    &i=117E    &f=1180    &d=1186    &c=118E

Pointer values:    px=117E    px + 1=1180    px + 2=1182    px + 3=1184
```

The first line simply displays the values of the variables, and the second line displays their addresses, as assigned by the compiler. Notice that the number of bytes associated with each data item is different. Thus, the integer value represented by i requires 2 bytes (specifically, addresses 117E and 117F). The floating-point value represented by f appears to be assigned 6 bytes (addresses 1180 through 1185), though only 4 bytes (addresses 1180 through 1183) are actually used for this purpose. (Compilers allocate memory space according to their own rules.) Eight bytes, however, are required for the double-precision value represented by d (addresses 1186 through 118D). And finally, the character represented by c begins in address 118E. Although the output does not indicate the number of bytes between this character and the next data item, only 1 byte is required to store this single character.

Now consider the third line of output, which contains the addresses represented by the pointer expressions. Clearly, px represents the address of i (i.e., 117E). This comes as no surprise, since this address was explicitly assigned to px by the expression px = &i. However, px + 1 moves over only 2 bytes, to 1180, and px + 2 moves over another 2 bytes, to 1182, and so on. The reason is that px points to an integer quantity, and integer quantities each require 2 bytes with this particular C compiler. As a result, when integer constants are added to px, the constants are interpreted in terms of 2-byte multiples.

If px is defined as a pointer to a different type of object (e.g., a character or a floating-point quantity), then any integer constant added to or subtracted from the pointer will be interpreted differently. In particular, each integer value will represent an equivalent number of individual bytes if px points to a character, or a corresponding number of 4-byte multiples if px points to a floating-point quantity. Interested readers are encouraged to verify this on their own.

One pointer variable can be subtracted from another provided both variables point to elements of the same array. The resulting value indicates the number of words or bytes separating the corresponding array elements.

Example 10.18   In the program shown below, two different pointer variables point to the first and the last elements of an integer array.

```
#include <stdio.h>

main()
{
    int *px, *py;          /* integer pointers */
    static int a[6] = {1, 2, 3, 4, 5, 6};

    px = &a[0];
    py = &a[5];
    printf("px=%X   py=%X", px, py);
    printf("\n\npy - px=%X", py - px);
}
```

In particular, the pointer variable px points to a[0], and py points to a[5]. The difference, py - px, should be 5, since a[5] is the fifth element beyond a[0].

Executing the program results in the following output:

```
px=52    py=5C

py - px=5
```

The first line indicates that the address of a[0] is 52, and the address of a[5] is 5C. The difference between these two hexadecimal numbers is 10 (when converted to decimal). Thus, a[5] is stored at an address 10 bytes beyond the address of a[∅]. Since each integer quantity occupies 2 bytes, we would expect the difference between py and px to be 10/2 = 5. The second line of output confirms this value.

Pointer variables can be compared provided both variables point to objects of the same data type. Such comparisons can be useful when both pointer variables point to elements of the same array. The comparisons can test for either equality or inequality. Moreover, a pointer variable can be compared with zero (usually expressed as NULL when used in this manner, as explained in Sec. 10.2).

Example 10.19   Suppose px and py are pointer variables that point to elements of the same array. Several logical expressions involving these two variables are shown below. All of the expressions are syntactically correct.

```
(px < py)

(px >= py)

(px == py)

(px != py)

(px == NULL)
```

These expressions can be used in the same manner as any other logical expression. For example,

```
if (px < py)
    printf("px < py");
else
    printf("px >= py");
```

Moreover, expressions such as (px < py) indicate whether or not the element associated with px is ranked ahead of the element associated with py (i.e., whether or not the subscript associated with *px is less than the subscript associated with *py).

Finally, it should be understood that the operations discussed previously are the *only* operations that can be carried out on pointers. These permissible operations are summarized below.

1. A pointer variable can be assigned the address of an ordinary variable (e.g., pv = &v).
2. A pointer variable can be assigned the value of another pointer variable (e.g., pv = px) provided both pointers point to objects of the same data type.
3. A pointer variable can be assigned a null (zero) value (e.g., pv = NULL, where NULL is a symbolic constant that represents the value ∅).
4. An integer quantity can be added to or subtracted from a pointer variable (e.g., pv + 3, ++pv.)
5. One pointer variable can be subtracted from another provided both pointers point to elements of the same array.
6. Two pointer variables can be compared provided both pointers point to objects of the same data type.

Other arithmetic operations on pointers are not allowed. Thus, a pointer variable cannot be multiplied by a constant, two pointer variables cannot be added, and so on. The reader is also reminded that an ordinary variable cannot be assigned an arbitrary address (i.e., an expression such as &x cannot appear on the lefthand side of an assignment statement).

10.6   POINTERS AND MULTIDIMENSIONAL ARRAYS

Since a one-dimensional array can be represented in terms of a pointer (the array name) and an offset (the subscript), it is reasonable to expect that a multidimensional array can also be represented with an equivalent pointer notation. This is indeed the case. A two-dimensional array, for example, is actually a collection of one-dimensional arrays. Therefore, we can define a two-dimensional array as a pointer to a group of contiguous one-dimensional arrays. A two-dimensional array declaration can be written as

```
data-type  (*ptvar)[expression 2];
```

rather than

```
data-type  array[expression 1][expression 2];
```

This concept can be generalized to higher dimensional arrays, that is,

```
data-type (*ptvar)[expression 2][expression 3]...[expression n];
```

replaces

```
data-type  array[expression 1][expression 2]...[expression n];
```

In these declarations *data-type* refers to the data type of the array, *ptvar* is the name of the pointer variable, *array* is the corresponding array name, and *expression 1, expression 2, . . . , expression n* are positive-valued integer expressions that indicate the maximum number of array elements associated with each subscript.

Notice the parentheses that surround the array name and the preceding asterisk in the pointer version of each declaration. These parentheses *must be present*. Without them we would be defining an array of pointers rather than a pointer to a group of arrays, since these particular symbols (i.e., the square brackets and the asterisk) would normally be evaluated right-to-left. We will say more about this in the next section.

Example 10.20 Suppose that x is a two-dimensional integer array having 10 rows and 20 columns. We can declare x as

```
int (*x)[20];
```

rather than

```
int x[10][20];
```

In the first declaration, x is defined to be a pointer to a group of contiguous, one-dimensional, 20-element integer arrays. Thus, x points to the first 20-element array, which is actually the first row (row 0) of the original two-dimensional array. Similarly, (x + 1) points to the second 20-element array, which is the second row (row 1) of the original two-dimensional array, and so on, as illustrated in Fig. 10.4.

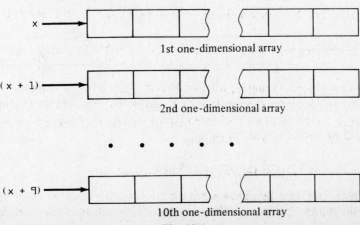

1st one-dimensional array

2nd one-dimensional array

10th one-dimensional array

Fig. 10.4

Now consider a three-dimensional floating-point array t. This array can be defined as

```
float (*t)[20][30];
```

rather than

```
float t[10][20][30];
```

In the first declaration, t is defined as a pointer to a group of contiguous, two-dimensional, 20 × 30 floating-point arrays. Hence, t points to the first 20 × 30 array, (t + 1) points to the second 20 × 30 array, and so on.

An individual array element within a multidimensional array can be accessed by repeatedly using the indirection operator. Usually, however, this procedure is more awkward than the conventional method for accessing an array element. The following example illustrates the use of the indirection operator.

Example 10.21 Suppose that x is a two-dimensional integer array having 10 rows and 20 columns, as declared in the previous example. The item in row 2, column 5 can be accessed by writing either

```
x[2][5]
```

or

```
*(*(x + 2) + 5)
```

The second form requires some explanation. First, note that (x + 2) is a pointer to row 2. Therefore, the object of this pointer, *(x + 2), refers to the entire row. Since row 2 is a one-dimensional array, *(x + 2) is actually a pointer to the first element in row 2. We now add 5 to this pointer. Hence, (*(x + 2) + 5) is a pointer to element 5 (the sixth element) in row 2. The object of this pointer, *(*(x + 2) + 5), therefore refers to the item in column 5 of row 2, which is x[2][5]. Figure 10.5 illustrates these relationships.

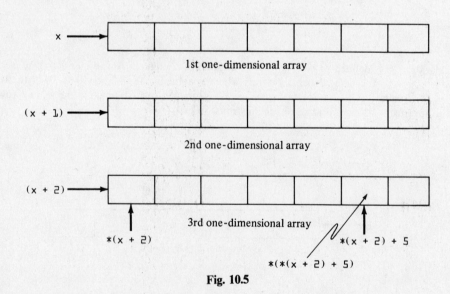

Fig. 10.5

Programs that make use of multidimensional arrays can be written in several different ways. In particular, there are different ways to define the arrays, and different ways to process the individual array elements. The choice of one method over another is often a matter of personal preference. In applications involving numerical arrays, it is often easier to define the arrays in the conventional manner, thus avoiding any possible subtleties associated with initial memory assignments. The following example, however, illustrates the use of pointer notation to process multidimensional numerical arrays.

Example 10.22   Adding Two Tables of Numbers   In Example 9.19 we developed a C program to calculate the sum of the corresponding elements of two tables of integers. That program required three separate, two-dimensional arrays, which were defined and processed in the conventional manner. Here is a variation of this program, in which each two-dimensional array is defined as a pointer to a set of one-dimensional integer arrays.

The complete program is shown below.

```c
#include <stdio.h>

#define MAXCOLS  30

/* calculate the sum of the elements in two tables of integers */

/* each 2-dimensional array is processed as a pointer
   to a set of 1-dimensional integer arrays */

main()

{
    int nrows, ncols;

    /* pointer definitions */
    int (*a)[MAXCOLS], (*b)[MAXCOLS], (*c)[MAXCOLS];

    /* function prototypes */
    void readinput(int (*a)[MAXCOLS], int nrows, int ncols);
    void computesums(int (*a)[MAXCOLS], int (*b)[MAXCOLS],
                     int (*c)[MAXCOLS], int nrows, int ncols);
    void writeoutput(int (*c)[MAXCOLS], int nrows, int ncols);

    printf("How many rows? ");
    scanf("%d", &nrows);
    printf("How many columns? ");
    scanf("%d", &ncols);

    /* allocate initial memory */
    *a = (int *) malloc(nrows * ncols * sizeof(int));
    *b = (int *) malloc(nrows * ncols * sizeof(int));
    *c = (int *) malloc(nrows * ncols * sizeof(int));

    printf("\n\nFirst table:\n");
    readinput(a, nrows, ncols);

    printf("\n\nSecond table:\n");
    readinput(b, nrows, ncols);

    computesums(a, b, c, nrows, ncols);

    printf("\n\nSums of the elements:\n\n");
    writeoutput(c, nrows, ncols);
}
```

```
void readinput(int (*a)[MAXCOLS], int m, int n)
/* read in a table of integers */

{
    int row, col;

    for (row = Ø; row < m; ++row)   {
        printf("\nEnter data for row no. %2d\n", row + 1);
        for (col = Ø; col < n; ++col)
            scanf("%d", (*(a + row) + col));
    }
    return;
}


void computesums(int (*a)[MAXCOLS], int (*b)[MAXCOLS],
                                    int (*c)[MAXCOLS], int m, int n)
/* add the elements of two integer tables */

{
    int row, col;

    for (row = Ø; row < m; ++row)
        for (col = Ø; col < n; ++col)
            *(*(c + row) + col) = *(*(a + row) + col) + *(*(b + row) + col);
    return;
}


void writeoutput(int (*a)[MAXCOLS], int m, int n)
/* write out a table of integers */

{
    int row, col;

    for (row = Ø; row < m; ++row)   {
        for (col = Ø; col < n; ++col)
            printf("%4d", *(*(a + row) + col));
        printf("\n");
    }
    return;
}
```

In this program a, b and c are defined as pointers to groups of contiguous, one-dimensional integer arrays of size MAXCOLS. The function declarations within main and the formal argument declarations within the subordinate functions also represent the arrays in this manner.

Since a, b and c are defined as pointers rather than as arrays, we must allocate initial memory for each array using the malloc function, as described in Sec. 10.4. These memory allocations appear in main, after the values for nrows and ncols have been entered. Consider the first memory allocation, that is,

```
*a = (int *) malloc(nrows * ncols * sizeof(int));
```

In this statement, *a points to the first element in the first array. (Similarly, *(a + 1) points to the first element in the second array, *(a + 2) points to the first element in the third array, and so on, as explained in Example 10.21.) Thus, a block of memory large enough to store nrows × ncols integer quantities begins at the first element of the first array. Similar memory allocations are written for the other two arrays.

The individual array elements are processed by using the indirection operator repeatedly. In readinput, for example, each array element is referenced as

```
scanf("%d", (*(a + row) + col));
```

Similarly, the addition of the array elements within computesums is written as

```
*(*(c + row) + col) = *(*(a + row) + col) + *(*(b + row) + col);
```

and the first `printf` statement within `writeoutput` is written as

```
printf("%4d", *(*(a + row) + col));
```

We could, of course, have used the more conventional array notation within the functions. Thus, in `readinput` we could have written

```
scanf("%d", &a[row][col]);
```

instead of

```
scanf("%d", (*(a + row) + col));
```

Similarly, in `computesums` we could have written

```
c[row][col]= a[row][col] + b[row][col];
```

instead of

```
*(*(c + row) + col) = *(*(a + row) + col) + *(*(b + row) + col);
```

and in `writeoutput` we could have written

```
printf("%4d", a[row][col]);
```

rather than

```
printf("%4d", *(*(a + row) + col));
```

This program will generate output identical to that shown in Example 9.19 when executed with the same input data.

10.7   ARRAYS OF POINTERS

A multidimensional array can be expressed in terms of an array of pointers rather than as a pointer to a group of contiguous arrays. In such situations the newly defined array will have one less dimension than the original multidimensional array. Each pointer will indicate the beginning of a separate $(n-1)$-dimensional array.

In general terms, a two-dimensional array can be defined as a one-dimensional array of pointers by writing

data-type   *array[*expression 1*];

rather than the conventional array definition

data-type   array[*expression 1*][*expression 2*];

Similarly, an n-dimensional array can be defined as an $(n-1)$-dimensional array of pointers by writing

data-type   *array[*expression 1*][*expression 2*]...[*expression n-1*];

rather than

data-type   array[*expression 1*][*expression 2*]...[*expression n*];

In these declarations *data-type* refers to the data type of the original n-dimensional array, *array* is the array name, and *expression 1, expression 2, ..., expression n* are positive-valued integer expressions that indicate the maximum number of elements associated with each subscript.

Notice that the array name and its preceding asterisk *are not enclosed in parentheses* in this type of declaration. (Compare carefully with the pointer declarations presented in the last section.) Thus, a right-to-left rule first associates the pairs of square brackets with array, defining the named object as an array. The preceding asterisk then establishes that the array will contain pointers.

Moreover, note that the *last* (the rightmost) expression is omitted when defining an array of pointers, whereas the *first* (the leftmost) expression is omitted when defining a pointer to a group of arrays. (Again, compare carefully with the declarations presented in the last section.) The reader should understand the distinction between this type of declaration and that presented in the last section.

When an *n*-dimensional array is expressed in this manner, an individual array element within the *n*-dimensional array can be accessed by a single use of the indirection operator. The following example illustrates how this is done.

Example 10.23 Suppose that x is a two-dimensional integer array having 10 rows and 20 columns, as in Example 10.20. We can define x as a one-dimensional array of pointers by writing

```
int *x[10];
```

Hence, x[0] points to the beginning of the first row, x[1] points to the beginning of the second row, and so on. Note that the number of elements within each row is not explicitly specified.

An individual array element, such as x[2][5], can be accessed by writing

```
*(x[2] + 5)
```

In this expression, x[2] is a pointer to the first element in row 2, so that (x[2] + 5) points to element 5 (actually, the sixth element) within row 2. The object of this pointer, *(x[2] + 5), therefore refers to x[2][5]. These relationships are illustrated in Fig. 10.6.

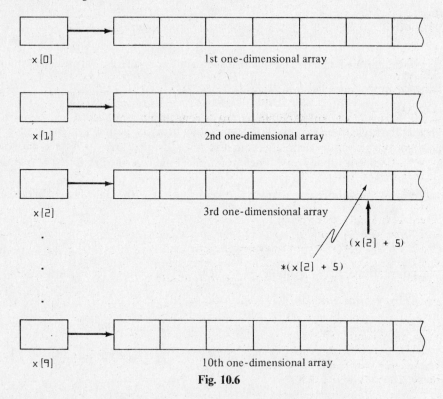

Fig. 10.6

Now consider a three-dimensional floating-point array t. Suppose the dimensionality of t is 10 × 20 × 30. This array can be expressed as a two-dimensional array of pointers by writing

```
float *t[10][20];
```

Therefore, we have 200 pointers (10 rows, 20 columns), each pointing to a one-dimensional array.

An individual array element, such as t[2][3][5], can be accessed by writing

```
*(t[2][3] + 5)
```

In this expression, t[2][3] is a pointer to the first element in the one-dimensional array represented by t[2][3]. Hence, (t[2][3] + 5) points to element 5 (the sixth element) within this array. The object of this pointer, *(t[2][3] + 5), therefore represents t[2][3][5]. This situation is, of course, directly analogous to the two-dimensional case described above.

Example 10.24   Adding Two Tables of Numbers   Here is yet another version of the programs presented in Examples 9.19 and 10.22, which calculate the sum of the corresponding elements of two tables of integers. Now each two-dimensional array is represented as an array of pointers to one-dimensional arrays. Each one-dimensional array will correspond to one row within the original two-dimensional array.

```
#include <stdio.h>

#define MAXROWS  20

/* calculate the sum of the elements in two tables of integers */

/* each 2-dimensional array is represented as an array of pointers
   each pointer indicates a row in the original 2-dimensional array */

main()

{
    int row, nrows, ncols;

    /* array definitions */
    int *a[MAXROWS], *b[MAXROWS], *c[MAXROWS];

    /* function prototypes */
    void readinput(int *a[MAXROWS], int nrows, int ncols);
    void computesums(int *a[MAXROWS], int *b[MAXROWS],
                     int *c[MAXROWS], int nrows, int ncols);
    void writeoutput(int *c[MAXROWS], int nrows, int ncols);

    printf("How many rows? ");
    scanf("%d", &nrows);
    printf("How many columns? ");
    scanf("%d", &ncols);

    /* allocate initial memory */
    for (row = 0; row <= nrows; row++)    {
        a[row] = (int *) malloc(ncols * sizeof(int));
        b[row] = (int *) malloc(ncols * sizeof(int));
        c[row] = (int *) malloc(ncols * sizeof(int));
    }

    printf("\n\nFirst table:\n");
    readinput(a, nrows, ncols);

    printf("\n\nSecond table:\n");
    readinput(b, nrows, ncols);

    computesums(a, b, c, nrows, ncols);

    printf("\n\nSums of the elements:\n\n");
    writeoutput(c, nrows, ncols);
}
```

```
void readinput(int *a[MAXROWS], int m, int n)
/* read in a table of integers */

{
    int row, col;

    for (row = 0; row < m; ++row)    {
        printf("\nEnter data for row no. %2d\n", row + 1);
        for (col = 0; col < n; ++col)
            scanf("%d", (a[row] + col));
    }
    return;
}


void computesums(int *a[MAXROWS], int *b[MAXROWS],
                                  int *c[MAXROWS], int m, int n)
/* add the elements of two integer tables */

{
    int row, col;

    for (row = 0; row < m; ++row)
        for (col = 0; col < n; ++col)
            *(c[row] + col) = *(a[row] + col) + *(b[row] + col);
    return;
}


void writeoutput(int *a[MAXROWS], int m, int n)
/* write out a table of integers */

{
    int row, col;

    for (row = 0; row < m; ++row)    {
        for (col = 0; col < n; ++col)
            printf("%4d", *(a[row] + col));
        printf("\n");
    }
    return;
}
```

Notice that a, b and c are now defined as one-dimensional arrays of pointers. Each array will contain MAXROWS elements (i.e., MAXROWS pointers). Each array element will point to a one-dimensional array of integers. The function prototypes within main and the formal argument declarations within the subordinate functions also represent the arrays in this manner.

Each one-dimensional array that is the object of a pointer (i.e., each row within each of the tables) must be allocated an initial block of memory. The malloc function accomplishes this. For example, each row within the first table is allocated an initial block of memory in the following manner:

```
a[row] = (int *) malloc(ncols * sizeof(int));
```

This statement associates a block of memory large enough to store ncols integer quantities with each pointer (i.e., with each element of a). Similar memory allocations are written for b and c. These malloc statements are placed within a for loop in order to allocate a block of memory for each of the nonzero rows within the three tables.

Notice the way the individual array elements are processed, using a combination of array and pointer notation. For example, in `readinput` each array element is now referenced as

```
scanf("%d", (a[row] + col));
```

Similarly, in `computesums` and `writeoutput` the individual array elements are referenced as

```
*(c[row] + col) = *(a[row] + col) + *(b[row] + col);
```

and

```
printf("%4d", *(a[row] + col));
```

respectively. These statements could have been written using conventional two-dimensional array notation if we had wanted.

This program, as well as the program presented in Example 10.22, will generate output identical to that shown in Example 9.19 when executed with the same input data. You may wish to verify this on your own. If this problem were being programmed from scratch, however, the conventional approach shown in Example 9.19, using two-dimensional arrays, would most likely be chosen.

Pointer arrays offer a particularly convenient method for storing strings. In this situation, each array element is a character-type pointer that indicates the beginning of a separate string. Thus, an *n*-element array can point to *n* different strings. Each individual string can be accessed by referring to its corresponding pointer.

Example 10.25 Suppose that the following strings are to be stored in a character-type array:

```
Pacific

Atlantic

Indian

Caribbean

Bering

Black

Red

North

Baltic

Caspian
```

These strings can be stored in a two-dimensional, character-type array, for example,

```
char names[10][12];
```

Note that `names` contains 10 rows, to accommodate the 10 strings. Each row must be large enough to store at least 10 characters, since `Caribbean` contains nine letters as well as the null character (\∅) at the end. To provide for larger strings, we are allowing each row to contain as many as 12 characters.

A better way to do this is to define a 10-element array of pointers, that is,

```
char *names[10];
```

Thus, names[Ø] will point to Pacific, names[1] will point to Atlantic, and so on. Note that it is not necessary to include a maximum string size within the array declaration. However, a specified amount of memory will have to be allocated for each string later in the program, for example,

```
names[i] = malloc(12 * sizeof(char));
```

Just as individual strings can be accessed by referring to the corresponding pointer (i.e., the corresponding array element), so can individual string elements be accessed through the use of the indirection operator. For example, *(*(names + 2) + 3) refers to the fourth character (character number 3) in the third string (row number 2) of the array names, as defined in the preceding example.

Rearranging the strings can be accomplished simply by reassigning the pointers (i.e., by reassigning the elements in an array of pointers). The strings themselves need not be moved.

Example 10.26   Reordering a List of Strings   Consider once again the problem of entering a list of strings into the computer and rearranging them into alphabetical order. We saw one approach to this problem in Example 9.20, where the list of strings was stored in a two-dimensional array. Let us now approach this problem using a one-dimensional array of pointers, where each pointer indicates the beginning of a string. The string interchanges can now be carried out simply by reassigning the pointers, as required.

The complete program is presented below.

```
#include <stdio.h>
#include <stdlib.h>

/* sort a list of strings into alphabetical order

   this program uses an array of pointers */

main()

{
    int i, n = Ø;
    char *x[1Ø];
    int reorder(int n, char *x[]);

    printf("Enter each string on a separate line below\n\n");
    printf("Type \'END\' when finished\n\n");

    /* read in the list of strings */
    do  {
         /* allocate memory */
         x[n] = malloc(12 * sizeof(char));

         printf("string %d: ", n + 1);
         scanf("%s", x[n]);
     }
    while (strcmpi(x[n++], "END"));

    /* reorder the list of strings */
    reorder(--n, x);

    /* display the reordered list of strings */
    printf("\n\nReordered List of Strings:\n");
    for (i = Ø; i < n; ++i)
        printf("\nstring %d: %s", i + 1, x[i]);
}
```

```
reorder(int n, char *x[])      /* rearrange the list of strings */

{
   char *temp;
   int i, item;

   for (item = 0; item < n - 1; ++item)

         /* find the lowest of all remaining strings */
         for (i = item + 1; i < n; ++i)

             if (strcmpi(x[item], x[i]) > 0)   {
                 /* interchange the two strings */
                 temp = x[item];
                 x[item] = x[i];
                 x[i] = temp;
             }
   return;
}
```

The logic is essentially the same as that shown in Example 9.20, though the array containing the strings is now defined as an array of pointers. Notice that the second formal argument in the function reorder is declared in the same manner. Also, notice the string interchange routine (i.e., the if statement) within reorder. It is now the pointers, not the actual strings, that are interchanged. Hence, the library function strcpy, which was used in Example 9.20, is not required. The program will therefore run somewhat faster than the earlier version.

Execution of this program will generate the same dialog as that shown in Example 9.20.

If the elements of an array are string pointers, a set of initial values can be specified as a part of the array declaration. In such cases the initial values will be strings, where each string corresponds to a separate array element. Remember, however, that an array must be declared static if it is initialized within a function.

An advantage to this scheme is that a fixed block of memory need not be reserved in advance, as is done when initializing a conventional array. Thus, if the initial declaration includes many strings and some of them are relatively short, there may be a substantial savings in memory allocation. Moreover, if some of the strings are particularly long, there is no need to worry about the possibility of exceeding some maximum specified string length (i.e., the maximum number of characters per row). Arrays of this type are often referred to as *ragged arrays*.

Example 10.27 The following array declaration appears within a function:

```
static char *names[10] = {
                          "Pacific",
                          "Atlantic",
                          "Indian",
                          "Caribbean",
                          "Bering",
                          "Black",
                          "Red",
                          "North",
                          "Baltic",
                          "Caspian"
                  };
```

In this example, names is a 10-element array of pointers. The first array element (i.e., the first pointer) will point to Pacific, the second array element will point to Atlantic, and so on.

Notice that the array is declared as static so that it can be initialized within the function. If the array declaration were external to all program functions, the static storage class designation would not be necessary.

Since the array declaration includes initial values, it is really not necessary to include an explicit size designation within the declaration. The size of the array will automatically be set equal to the number of strings present. As a result, the above declaration can be written as

```
static char *names[] = {
                        "Pacific",
                        "Atlantic",
                        "Indian",
                        "Caribbean",
                        "Bering",
                        "Black",
                        "Red",
                        "North",
                        "Baltic",
                        "Caspian"
                    };
```

It should be understood that the ragged-array concept refers only to the *initialization* of string arrays, not to the assignment of individual strings that may be read into the computer via the scanf function. Thus, applications that require strings to be read into the computer and then processed, as in Example 10.26, still require the allocation of a specified amount of memory for each array element.

Initialized string values can be accessed by referring to their corresponding pointers (i.e., their corresponding array elements), in the usual manner. These pointers can be reassigned other string constants elsewhere in the program if necessary.

Example 10.28   Displaying the Day of the Year   Let us develop a program that will accept three integer quantities, indicating the month, day and year, and then display the corresponding day of the week, the month, the day of the month and the year more legibly. For example, suppose we were to enter the date 5 24 87; this would produce the output Sunday, May 24, 1987. Programs of this type are often used to display information stored in a computer's internal memory in an encoded format.

Our basic strategy will be to enter a date into the computer, in the form *month, day, year* (mm dd yy), and then convert this date into the number of days relative to some base date. The day of the week corresponding to the specified date can then be determined quite easily, provided we know the day of the week corresponding to the base date. Let us arbitrarily choose Monday, January 1, 1900 as the base date. We will then convert any date between January 1, 1900 and December 31, 1999 into an equivalent day of the week.

The computation can be carried out using the following empirical rules:

1. Determine the approximate day of the current year, as

$$\text{ndays} = (\text{long}) (30.42 * (\text{mm} - 1)) + \text{dd};$$

2. If mm == 2 (February), increase the value of ndays by 1.

3. If mm > 2 and mm < 8 (March, April, May, June or July), decrease the value of ndays by 1.

4. If (yy % 4) == 0 and mm > 2 (leap year), increase the value of ndays by 1.

5. Determine the number of complete four-year cycles beyond the base date as (yy / 4). For each complete four-year cycle, add 1461 to ndays.

6. Determine the number of full years beyond the last complete four-year cycle as (yy % 4). For each full year, add 365 to ndays. Then add 1, because the first year beyond a full four-year cycle will be a leap year.

7. If ndays > 59 (i.e., if the date is any day beyond February 28, 1900), decrease the value of ndays by 1, because 1900 is *not* a leap year. (Note that the first year of each century is *not* a leap year, though every fourth year thereafter *is* a leap year.)

8. Determine the numerical day of the week corresponding to the specified date as day = (ndays % 7).

Note that day == 1 corresponds either to the base date, which is a Monday, or another date that also occurs on a Monday. Hence, day == 2 will refer to a Tuesday, day == 3 will refer to a Wednesday, . . . , day == 6 will refer to a Saturday, and day == Ø will refer to a Sunday.

Here is a complete function, called convert, that carries out these steps. Note that convert accepts the integers mm, dd and yy as input parameters, and returns the integer quantity (ndays % 7). Also, notice that ndays is a long integer variable, whereas all other variables are ordinary integers.

```
convert(int mm, int dd, int yy)    /* convert date to numerical day of week */

{
    long ndays;            /* number of days from start of 1900 */
    int ncycles;           /* number of 4-year cycles beyond 1900 */
    int nyears;            /* number of years beyond last 4-year cycle */
    int day;               /* day of week (Ø, 1,..., 6) */

    /* numerical conversions */
    ndays = (long) (30.42 * (mm - 1)) + dd; /* approximate day of year */
    if (mm == 2) ++ndays;                    /* adjust for February */
    if ((mm > 2) && (mm < 8)) --ndays;       /* adjust for March — July */
    if ((yy % 4 == Ø) && (mm > 2)) ++ndays; /* adjust for leap year */

    ncycles = yy / 4;                        /* 4-year cycles beyond 1900 */
    ndays += 1461 * ncycles;                 /* add days for 4-year cycles */

    nyears = yy % 4;           /* years beyond last 4-year cycle */
    if (nyears > Ø)            /* add days for yrs beyond last 4-year cycle */
        ndays += 365 * nyears + 1;

    if (ndays > 59) --ndays;   /* adjust for 1900 (NOT a leap year) */
    day = ndays % 7;
    return(day);
}
```

The names of the days of the week can be stored as strings in a seven-element array, as follows:

```
static char *weekday[] = {"Sunday", "Monday", "Tuesday", "Wednesday",
                          "Thursday", "Friday", "Saturday"};
```

Each day corresponds to the value assigned to day, where day = (ndays % 7). The days begin with Sunday because Sunday corresponds to day == Ø, as explained above. If the base date were not a Monday, this particular ordering of the days of the week would have to be changed.

Similarly, the names of the months can be stored as strings in a 12-element array, as follows:

```
static char *month[] = {"January", "February", "March", "April",
                        "May", "June", "July", "August", "September",
                        "October", "November", "December"};
```

Each month corresponds to the value of mm - 1.

Here is an entire C program that will carry out the conversion interactively.

```
#include <stdio.h>

/* convert a numerical date (mm dd yy) into "day of week, month, day, year"

                   (e.g., 5 24 87 -> Sunday, May 24, 1987") */
```

```
main()

{
    int mm, dd, yy;
    int day_of_week;      /* day of the week (0 -> Sunday,
                                               1 -> Monday,
                                                  ...
                                               6 -> Saturday) */


    static char *weekday[] = {"Sunday", "Monday", "Tuesday", "Wednesday",
                              "Thursday", "Friday", "Saturday"};

    static char *month[] = {"January", "February", "March", "April",
                            "May", "June", "July", "August", "September",
                            "October", "November", "December"};

    void readinput(int *pm, int *pd, int *py);    /* function declaration */
    int convert(int mm, int dd, int yy);          /* function declaration */


    /* opening message */
    printf("Date Conversion Routine\nTo STOP, enter 0 0 0");
    readinput(&mm, &dd, &yy);

    /* convert date to numerical day of week */
    while (mm > 0)    {
        day_of_week = convert(mm, dd, yy);
        printf("\n%s, %s %d, 19%d", weekday[day_of_week], month[mm-1], dd, yy);
        readinput(&mm, &dd, &yy);
    }
}

void readinput(int *pm, int *pd, int *py)    /* read in the numerical date */
{
    printf("\n\nEnter mm dd yy: ");
    scanf("%d %d %d", pm, pd, py);
    return;
}

convert(int mm, int dd, int yy)    /* convert date to numerical day of week */
{
    long ndays;          /* number of days from start of 1900 */
    int ncycles;         /* number of 4-year cycles beyond 1900 */
    int nyears;          /* number of years beyond last 4-year cycle */
    int day;             /* day of week (0, 1,..., 6) */

    /* numerical conversions */
    ndays = (long) (30.42 * (mm - 1)) + dd; /* approximate day of year */
    if (mm == 2) ++ndays;                   /* adjust for February */
    if ((mm > 2) && (mm < 8)) --ndays;      /* adjust for March - July */
    if ((yy % 4 == 0) && (mm > 2)) ++ndays; /* adjust for leap year */

    ncycles = yy / 4;                       /* 4-year cycles beyond 1900 */
    ndays += 1461 * ncycles;                /* add days for 4-year cycles */

    nyears = yy % 4;              /* years beyond last 4-year cycle */
    if (nyears > 0)              /* add days for yrs beyond last 4-year cycle */
        ndays += 365 * nyears + 1;

    if (ndays > 59) --ndays;     /* adjust for 1900 (NOT a leap year) */
    day = ndays % 7;
    return(day);
}
```

This program includes a loop that repeatedly accepts a date in the form of three integers (i.e., mm dd yy) and returns the corresponding day and date in a more legible form. The program will continue to run until a value of ∅ is entered for mm. Note that the prompt indicates that three zeros must be entered (∅ ∅ ∅) in order to stop the program execution. Actually, however, the program only checks the value of mm.

A typical interactive session is shown below. As usual, the user's responses are underlined.

```
Date Conversion Routine
To STOP, enter ∅ ∅ ∅

Enter mm dd yy: 1 1 80

Tuesday, January 1, 198∅

Enter mm dd yy: 11 27 82

Saturday, November 27, 1982

Enter mm dd yy: 5 24 87

Sunday, May 24, 1987

Enter mm dd yy: 4 12 88

Tuesday, April 12, 1988

Enter mm dd yy: 12 29 89

Friday, December 29, 1989

Enter mm dd yy: 5 13 90

Sunday, May 13, 199∅

Enter mm dd yy: ∅ ∅ ∅
```

10.8 PASSING FUNCTIONS TO OTHER FUNCTIONS

When a function declaration appears within another function, the name of the function being declared becomes a pointer to that function. Thus, if process is declared within main, then process will be interpreted as a pointer variable within main. Such pointers can be passed to other functions as arguments. This has the effect of passing one function to another, as though the first function was a variable. The first function can then be accessed within the second function. Successive calls to the second function can pass different pointers (i.e., different functions) to the second function.

When a function accepts another function's name as an argument, a formal argument declaration must identify that argument as a pointer to another function. In its simplest form, a formal argument that is a pointer to a function can be declared as

```
data-type (*function-name)();
```

where *data-type* refers to the data type of the quantity returned by the function. This function can then be accessed by means of the indirection operator. To do so, the indirection operator must precede the function name (i.e., the formal argument). Both the indirection operator and the function name must be enclosed in parentheses, that is,

```
(*function-name)(argument 1, argument 2, ..., argument n);
```

where *argument 1, argument 2, ..., argument n* refer to the arguments required in the function call.

The following example should clarify much of the confusion.

Example 10.29   The skeletal outline of a C program is shown below. This program consists of four functions: `main`, `process`, `funct1` and `funct2`. Each of the three subordinate functions returns an integer quantity.

```
main()
{
    int i, j;
    int process();         /* function declaration */
    int funct1();          /* function declaration */
    int funct2();          /* function declaration */

    ...

    i = process(funct1);   /* pass funct1 to process; return a value for i */

    ...

    j = process(funct2);   /* pass funct2 to process; return a value for j */

    ...
}


process(pf)    /* function definition */
int (*pf)();   /* formal argument declaration (formal argument is a
                                            pointer to a function) */
{
    int a, b, c;

    ...

    c = (*pf)(a, b);    /* access the function passed to this function;
                                            return a value for c */

    ...

    return(c);
}

funct1(a, b)   /* function definition */
int a, b;
{
    int c;

    c = ···     /* use a and b to evaluate c */

    return(c);
}

funct2(x, y)   /* function definition */
int x, y;
{
    int z;

    z = ···     /* use x and y to evaluate z */

    return(z);
}
```

Notice that main calls process twice. The first call passes funct1 to process, whereas the second call passes funct2 to process. Each call returns an integer value. These values are assigned to the integer variables i and j, respectively.

Now examine the definition of process. This function has one formal argument, pf, which is declared to be a pointer to a function. The function to which pf points will return an integer value.

Within process, we see that the function to which pf points is called once. Two integer quantities (a and b) are passed to this function as arguments. The function then returns an integer quantity, which is assigned to the integer variable c.

The remaining function definitions (for funct1 and funct2) are straightforward. These are the functions passed from main to process. Each of these functions accepts two integer quantities as arguments, and returns an integer quantity to the calling function. Each of the return quantities is assumed to be obtained from the arguments, though the details of the calculations are unspecified. It should be understood, however, that each function presumably processes its input arguments differently (otherwise there would be no need for two separate functions).

Most compilers allow function declarations to include at least the data types of the arguments (see Secs. 7.5 and 7.6). In such cases, a function that accepts a pointer to another function as an argument can be declared as follows:

```
funct-data-type  funct-name(arg-data-type  (*)(type 1, type 2,...),
                            ‾‾‾‾‾‾‾‾‾‾‾‾‾‾‾‾‾‾‾‾‾‾‾‾‾‾‾‾‾‾‾‾‾‾‾‾‾‾‾‾‾‾‾‾‾
                            pointer to function passed as an argument
```

```
                                   data types of other funct args);
```

where *funct-data-type* refers to the data type of the quantity returned by the function being declared; *funct-name* refers to the name of the function being declared; *arg-data-type* refers to the data type of the quantity returned by the embedded argument function, and *type 1, type 2, ...* refer to the data types of this function's arguments. Notice that the indirection operator appears in parentheses, to indicate a pointer to the embedded function. Moreover, the data types of the embedded function's arguments follow in a separate pair of parentheses, to indicate that they are function arguments.

When full function prototyping is used, the declaration is expanded as follows:

```
funct-data-type  funct-name
       (arg-data-type (*pt-var)(type 1 arg 1, type 2 arg 2,...),
        ‾‾‾‾‾‾‾‾‾‾‾‾‾‾‾‾‾‾‾‾‾‾‾‾‾‾‾‾‾‾‾‾‾‾‾‾‾‾‾‾‾‾‾‾‾‾‾‾‾‾‾‾
        pointer to function passed as an argument
```

```
                        data types and names of other funct args);
```

The notation is the same as above, except that *pt-var* refers to the pointer variable pointing to the embedded argument function, and *type 1 arg 1, type 2 arg 2, ...* refer to the data types and the corresponding names of the embedded function's arguments.

Example 10.30 Here is the same skeletal outline shown in the previous example, except that the data types of the arguments are now included in the function declarations.

```
main()
{
    int i, j;
    int process(int (*)(int, int));      /* function declaration */
    int funct1(int, int);                 /* function declaration */
    int funct2(int, int);                 /* function declaration */


    ...

    i = process(funct1);   /* pass funct1 to process; return a value for i */

    ...

    j = process(funct2);   /* pass funct2 to process; return a value for j */

    ...

}
```

```
process(pf)           /* function definition */
int (*pf)(int, int);  /* formal argument declaration
                         (this formal argument is a pointer to a function) */
{
    int a, b, c;

    ...

    c = (*pf)(a, b);   /* access the function passed to this function;
                                                return a value for c */

    ...

    return(c);
}


funct1(a, b)   /* function definition */
int a, b;
{
    int c;

    c = ...    /* use a and b to evaluate c */

    return(c);
}


funct2(x, y)   /* function definition */
int x, y;
{
    int z;

    z = ...    /* use x and y to evaluate z */

    return(z);
}
```

Notice that main contains three function declarations, as before. The declarations for funct1 and funct2 are straightforward. The declaration for process, however, requires some explanation. This declaration states that process returns an integer quantity and has one argument. The argument is a pointer to another function that returns an integer quantity and has two integer arguments. The argument designation is written as

```
int (*)(int, int)
```

Notice the way the argument designation fits into the entire function declaration, i.e.,

```
int process(int (*)(int, int));
```

Now consider the formal argument declaration that appears within process, i.e.,

```
int (*pf)(int, int);
```

This declaration states that pf is a pointer to a function. This function will return an integer quantity and require two integer arguments.

Here is another version of this same outline, utilizing full function prototyping.

```
main()
{
    int i, j;
    int process(int (*pf)(int a, int b));    /* function declaration */
    int funct1(int a, int b);                 /* function declaration */
    int funct2(int a, int b);                 /* function declaration */

    . . .

    i = process(funct1);    /* pass funct1 to process; return a value for i */

    . . .

    j = process(funct2);    /* pass funct2 to process; return a value for j */

    . . .
}


process(int (*pf)(int a, int b))    /* function definition */
{
    int a, b, c;

    . . .

    c = (*pf)(a, b);    /* access the function passed to this function;
                                            return a value for c */

    . . .

    return(c);
}


funct1(int a, int b)    /* function definition */
{
    int c;

    c = . . .               /* use a and b to evaluate c */

    return(c);
}


funct2(int x, int y)    /* function definition */
{
    int z;

    z = . . .               /* use x and y to evaluate z */

    return(z);
}
```

The function declarations within main now include argument names as well as argument data types. Moreover, the declaration for process now includes the name of the variable (pf) that points to the function passed to process.

Within each subordinate function, the formal argument declarations are combined with the first line of the function definition. Notice that the declaration for the formal argument `pf` within `process` is consistent with the declaration for `process` that appears within `main`.

Some programming applications can be formulated quite naturally in terms of one function being passed to another. For example, one function might represent a mathematical equation, and the other might contain a computational strategy to process the equation. In such cases the function representing the equation might be passed to the function that processes the equation. This is particularly useful if the program contains several different mathematical equations, one of which the user selects each time the program is executed.

Example 10.31   Future Value of Monthly Deposits (Compound Interest Calculations)   Suppose that a person decides to save a fixed amount of money at the end of every month for n years. If the money earns interest at i percent per year, then it is natural to ask how much money will accumulate after n years (i.e., after $12n$ monthly deposits). The answer, of course, depends upon how much money is deposited each month, the interest rate, and the frequency with which the interest is compounded. For example, if the interest is compounded annually, semiannually, quarterly or monthly, the future amount of money that will accumulate after n years is given by

$$F = \frac{12A}{m}\left[\frac{(1 + i/m)^{mn} - 1}{i/m}\right] = 12A\left[\frac{(1 + i/m)^{mn} - 1}{i}\right]$$

where F is the future accumulation, A is the amount of money deposited each month, i is the annual interest rate (expressed as a decimal), and m is the number of compounding periods per year (e.g., $m = 1$ for annual compounding, $m = 2$ for semiannual compounding, $m = 4$ for quarterly compounding and $m = 12$ for monthly compounding).

If the compounding periods are shorter than the payment periods, such as in the case of daily compounding, then the future amount of money is determined by

$$F = A\left[\frac{(1 + i/m)^{mn} - 1}{(1 + i/m)^{m/12} - 1}\right]$$

Note that m is customarily assigned a value of 360 when the interest is compounded daily.

Finally, in the case of continuous compounding, the future amount of money is determined as

$$F = A\left[\frac{e^{in} - 1}{e^{i/12} - 1}\right]$$

Suppose that we wish to determine F as a function of the annual interest rate i, for given values of A, m and n. Let us develop a program that will read the required input data into `main`, and then carry out the calculations within a separate function, called `table`. Each of the three formulas for determining the ratio F/A will be placed in one of three independent functions, called `md1`, `md2` and `md3`, respectively. Thus, the program will consist of five different functions, including `main`.

When `table` is called from `main`, one of the arguments passed to `table` will be the name of the function containing the appropriate formula, as indicated by an input parameter (`freq`). The values of A, m and n that are read into `main` will also be passed to `table` as arguments. A loop will then be initiated within `table`, in which values of F are determined for interest rates ranging from 0.01 (i.e., 1 percent per year) to 0.20 (20 percent per year). The calculated values will be written out as they are generated.

Here is a complete program to carry out the calculations.

```c
#include <stdio.h>
#include <stdlib.h>
#include <math.h>

/* personal finance calculations */

main()   /* calculate the future value of a series of monthly deposits */
{
    int m;       /* number of compounding periods per year */
    double n;    /* number of years */
    double a;    /* amount of each monthly payment */
    char freq;   /* frequency of compounding indicator */

    /* function prototypes */
    void table (double (*pf)(double i, int m, double n),
                            double a, int m, double n);
    double md1(double i, int m, double n);
    double md2(double i, int m, double n);
    double md3(double i, int m, double n);

    /* enter input data */
    printf("\nFUTURE VALUE OF A SERIES OF MONTHLY DEPOSITS\n\n");
    printf("Amount of Each Monthly Payment: ");
    scanf("%lf", &a);
    printf("Number of Years: ");
    scanf("%lf", &n);

    /* enter frequency of compounding */
    do  {
            printf("Frequency of Compounding (A, S, Q, M, D, C): ");
            scanf("%1s", &freq);
            freq = toupper(freq);    /* convert to uppercase */
            if (freq == 'A')  {
                m = 1;
                printf("\nAnnual Compounding\n");
            }
            else if (freq == 'S')  {
                m = 2;
                printf("\nSemiannual Compounding\n");
            }
            else if (freq == 'Q')  {
                m = 4;
                printf("\nQuarterly Compounding\n");
            }
            else if (freq == 'M')  {
                m = 12;
                printf("\nMonthly Compounding\n");
            }
            else if (freq == 'D')  {
                m = 360;
                printf("\nDaily Compounding\n");
            }
```

```
                   else if (freq == 'C')    {
                      m = Ø;
                      printf("\nContinuous Compounding\n");
                   }
                   else
                      printf("\nERROR - Please Repeat\n\n");
                }
      while (freq != 'A' && freq != 'S' && freq != 'Q' &&
             freq != 'M' && freq != 'D' && freq != 'C');

      /* carry out calculations */
      if (freq == 'C')
         table(md3, a, m, n);    /* continuous compounding */
      else if (freq == 'D')
         table(md2, a, m, n);    /* daily compounding */
      else
         table(md1, a, m, n);    /* annual, semiannual, quarterly or monthly
                                                        compounding */
   }


void table (double (*pf)(double i, int m, double n),
                         double a, int m, double n)
/* table generator
   (this function accepts a pointer to another function as an argument)

   NOTE: the formal argument

         double (*pf)(double i, int m, double n)

         is a POINTER TO A FUNCTION */

{

   int count;   /* loop counter */
   double i;    /* annual interest rate */
   double f;    /* future value */

   printf("\nInterest Rate    Future Amount\n\n");
   for (count = 1; count <= 2Ø; ++count)    {
      i = Ø.Ø1 * count;
      f = a * (*pf)(i, m, n);  /* ACCESS THE FUNCTION PASSED AS A POINTER */
      printf("      %2d                %.2f\n", count, f);
   }
   return;
}


double md1(double i, int m, double n)
/* monthly deposits, periodic compounding */

{

   double factor, ratio;

   factor = 1 + i/m;
   ratio = 12 * (pow(factor, m*n) - 1) / i;
   return(ratio);
}
```

```
double md2(double i, int m, double n)
/* monthly deposits, daily compounding */

{
    double factor, ratio;

    factor = 1 + i/m;
    ratio = (pow(factor, m*n) - 1) / (pow(factor, m/12) - 1);
    return(ratio);
}


double md3(double i, int dummy, double n)
/* monthly deposits, continuous compounding */

{
    double ratio;

    ratio = (exp(i*n) - 1) / (exp(i/12) - 1);
    return(ratio);
}
```

Notice the function declarations within main, particularly the declaration for table. The first argument passed to table is a pointer to another function that receives two double-precision arguments and an integer argument, and returns a double-precision quantity. This pointer is intended to represent md1, md2 or md3. The declarations for these three functions follow the declaration for table. Each function accepts two double-precision arguments and an integer argument, and returns a double-precision quantity, as required.

An interactive dialog for the input data is generated within main. In particular, the program accepts numerical values for a and n. It also accepts a one-character string for the character variable freq, which indicates the frequency of compounding. The only allowable characters that can be assigned to freq are A, S, Q, M, D or C (for Annual, Semiannual, Quarterly, Monthly, Daily or Continuous compounding, respectively). This character can be entered in either upper- or lowercase, since it is converted to uppercase within the program. Note, however, that the program contains an error trap which prevents characters other than A, S, Q, M, D or C from being entered.

An appropriate numerical value is assigned to m as soon as the frequency of compounding is determined. The program then accesses table, passing either md1, md2 or md3 as an argument, as determined by the character assigned to freq. (See the multiple if - else statement at the end of main.)

Now examine the function table. The last three formal arguments (a, m and n) are declared as ordinary double-precision or integer variables. However, the first formal argument (pf) is declared as a pointer to a function that accepts two double-precision arguments and an integer argument, and returns a double-precision quantity. These formal argument declarations are consistent with the declaration for table appearing in main.

The values for i (i.e., the interest rates) are generated internally within table. These values are determined as 0.01 * count. Since count ranges from 1 to 20, we see that the interest rates range from 0.01 to 0.20, as required. Notice the manner in which the values for f are calculated, that is,

```
f = a * (*pf)(i, m, n);
```

The expression (*pf) refers to the function whose name is passed to table (i.e., md1, md2 or md3). This is accompanied by the required list of arguments, containing the current values for i, m and n. The value returned by the function is then multiplied by a, and the product is assigned to f.

The three remaining functions, md1, md2 and md3, are straightforward. Notice that the second argument in md3 is called dummy, because the value of this argument is not utilized within the function. We could have done this with md2 as well, since the value of m is always 360 in the case of daily compounding.

Execution of the program produces the following representative dialog:

```
FUTURE VALUE OF A SERIES OF MONTHLY DEPOSITS

Amount of Each Monthly Payment: 100
Number of Years: 3
Frequency of Compounding (A, S, Q, M, D, C): p

ERROR - Please Repeat

Frequency of Compounding (A, S, Q, M, D, C): m

Monthly Compounding

Interest Rate     Future Amount

     1            3653.00
     2            3707.01
     3            3762.06
     4            3818.16
     5            3875.33
     6            3933.61
     7            3993.01
     8            4053.56
     9            4115.27
    10            4178.18
    11            4242.31
    12            4307.69
    13            4374.33
    14            4442.28
    15            4511.55
    16            4582.17
    17            4654.18
    18            4727.60
    19            4802.45
    20            4878.78
```

10.9 MORE ABOUT POINTER DECLARATIONS

Before leaving this chapter we mention that pointer declarations can become complicated, and some care is required in their interpretation. This is especially true of declarations that involve functions or arrays.

One difficulty is the dual use of parentheses. In particular, parentheses are used to indicate functions, and they are used for nesting purposes (to establish precedence) within more complicated declarations. Thus, the declaration

```
int *p(int a);
```

indicates a function that accepts an integer argument, and returns a pointer to an integer. On the other hand, the declaration

```
int (*p)(int a);
```

indicates a *pointer to a function* that accepts an integer argument, and returns an integer. In this last declaration, the first pair of parentheses is used for nesting, and the second pair is used to indicate a function.

The interpretation of more complex declarations can be increasingly troublesome. For example, consider the declaration

```
int *(*p)(int (*a)[]);
```

In this declaration, `(*p)(...)` indicates a pointer to a function. Hence, `int *(*p)(...)` indicates a pointer to a function that returns a pointer to an integer. Within the last pair of parentheses (the function's argument specification), `(*a)[]` indicates a pointer to an array. As a result, `int (*a)[]` represents a pointer to an array of integers. Putting the pieces together, `(*p)(int (*a)[])` represents a pointer to a function whose argument is a pointer to an array of integers. And finally, the entire declaration

```
int *(*p)(int (*a)[]);
```

represents a pointer to a function that accepts a pointer to an array of integers as an argument, and returns a pointer to an integer.

Remember that a left parenthesis immediately following an identifier name indicates that the identifier represents a function. Similarly, a left square bracket immediately following an identifier name indicates that the identifier represents an array. Parentheses that identify functions and square brackets that identify arrays have a higher precedence than the unary indirection operator (see Appendix C). Therefore, additional parentheses are required when declaring a pointer to a function or a pointer to an array.

The following example provides a number of illustrations.

Example 10.32 Several declarations involving pointers are shown below. The individual declarations range from simple to complex.

```
int *p;                    /* p is a pointer to an integer quantity */
int *p[10];                /* p is a 10-element array of pointers to integer
                              quantities */
int (*p)[10];              /* p is a pointer to a 10-element integer array */
int *p(void);              /* p is a function that
                              returns a pointer to an integer quantity */
int p(char *a);            /* p is a function that
                              accepts an argument which is a pointer to a character
                              returns an integer quantity */
int *p(char *a);           /* p is a function that
                              accepts an argument which is a pointer to a character
                              returns a pointer to an integer quantity */
int (*p)(char *a);         /* p is a pointer to a function that
                              accepts an argument which is a pointer to a character
                              returns an integer quantity */
int (*p(char *a))[10];     /* p is a function that
                              accepts an argument which is a pointer to a character
                              returns a pointer to a 10-element integer array */
int p(char (*a)[]);        /* p is a function that
                              accepts an argument which is a pointer to a
                                 character array
                              returns an integer quantity */
int p(char *a[]);          /* p is a function that
                              accepts an argument which is an array of pointers to
                                 characters
                              returns an integer quantity */
```

```
int *p(char a[]);       /* p is a function that
                           accepts an argument which is a character array
                           returns a pointer to an integer quantity */

int *p(char (*a)[]);    /* p is a function that
                           accepts an argument which is a pointer to a
                               character array
                           returns a pointer to an integer quantity */

int *p(char *a[]);      /* p is a function that
                           accepts an argument which is an array of pointers
                               to characters
                           returns a pointer to an integer quantity */

int (*p)(char (*a)[]);  /* p is a pointer to a function that
                           accepts an argument which is a pointer to a
                               character array
                           returns an integer quantity */

int *(*p)(char (*a)[]); /* p is pointer to a function that
                           accepts an argument which is a pointer to a
                               character array
                           returns a pointer to an integer quantity */

int *(*p)(char *a[]);   /* p is a pointer to a function that
                           accepts an argument which is an array of pointers
                               to characters
                           returns a pointer to an integer quantity */

int (*p[10])(void);     /* p is a 10-element array of pointers to functions;
                           each function returns an integer quantity */

int (*p[10])(char a);   /* p is a 10-element array of pointers to functions;
                           each function accepts an argument which is a
                           character, and returns an integer quantity */

int *(*p[10])(char a);  /* p is a 10-element array of pointers to functions;
                           each function accepts an argument which is a
                           character, and returns a pointer to an integer
                           quantity */

int *(*p[10])(char *a); /* p is a 10-element array of pointers to functions;
                           each function accepts an argument which is a
                           pointer to a character, and returns a pointer to an
                           integer quantity */
```

Review Questions

10.1 For the version of C available on your particular computer, how many memory cells are required to store a single character? An integer quantity? A long integer? A floating-point quantity? A double-precision quantity?

10.2 What is meant by the address of a memory cell? How are addresses usually numbered?

10.3 How is a variable's address determined?

10.4 What kind of information does a pointer variable represent?

10.5 What is the relationship between the address of a variable v and the corresponding pointer variable pv?

10.6 What is the purpose of the indirection operator? To what type of operand must the indirection operator be applied?

10.7 What is the relationship between the data item represented by a variable v and the corresponding pointer variable pv?

10.8 What precedence is assigned to the unary operators compared with the multiplication, division and modulus operators? In what order are the unary operators evaluated?

10.9 Can the address operator act upon an arithmetic expression, such as 2 * (u + v)? Explain the reasons for your answer.

10.10 Can an expression involving the indirection operator appear on the left side of an assignment statement? Explain.

10.11 What kinds of objects can be associated with pointer variables?

10.12 How is a pointer variable declared? What is the purpose of the data type included in the declaration?

10.13 In what way can the assignment of an initial value be included in the declaration of a pointer variable?

10.14 Are integer values ever assigned to pointer variables? Explain.

10.15 Why is it sometimes desirable to pass a pointer to a function as an argument?

10.16 Suppose a function receives a pointer as an argument. Explain how this function is declared within its calling function. In particular, explain how the data type of the pointer argument is represented.

10.17 Suppose a function receives a pointer as an argument. Explain how the pointer argument is declared within the function definition.

10.18 What is the relationship between an array name and a pointer? How is an array name interpreted when it appears as an argument to a function?

10.19 Suppose a formal argument within a function definition is an array. How can the array be declared within the function?

10.20 How can a portion of an array be passed to a function?

10.21 How can a function return a pointer to its calling routine?

10.22 Describe two different ways to specify the address of an array element.

10.23 Why is the value of an array subscript sometimes referred to as an offset when the subscript is a part of an expression indicating the address of an array element?

10.24 Describe two different ways to access an array element. Compare your answer to that of question 10.22.

10.25 Can an address be assigned to an array name or an array element? Can an address be assigned to a pointer variable whose object is an array?

10.26 How is the library function `malloc` used to associate a block of memory with a pointer variable? How is the size of the memory block specified? What kind of information does the `malloc` function return?

10.27 Suppose a numerical array is defined in terms of a pointer variable. Can the individual array elements be initialized?

10.28 Suppose a character-type array is defined in terms of a pointer variable. Can the individual array elements be initialized? Compare your answer with that of the previous question.

10.29 Suppose an integer quantity is added to or subtracted from a pointer variable. How will the sum or difference be interpreted?

10.30 Under what conditions can one pointer variable be subtracted from another? How will this difference be interpreted?

10.31 Under what conditions can two pointer variables be compared? Under what conditions are such comparisons useful?

10.32 How is a multidimensional array defined in terms of a pointer to a collection of contiguous arrays of lower dimensionality?

10.33 How can the indirection operator be used to access a multidimensional array element?

10.34 How is a multidimensional array defined in terms of an array of pointers? What does each pointer represent? How does this definition differ from a pointer to a collection of contiguous arrays of lower dimensionality?

10.35 How can a one-dimensional array of pointers be used to represent a collection of strings?

10.36 If several strings are stored within a one-dimensional array of pointers, how can an individual string be accessed?

10.37 If several strings are stored within a one-dimensional array of pointers, what happens if the strings are reordered? Are the strings actually moved to different locations within the array?

10.38 Under what conditions can the elements of a multidimensional array be initialized if the array is defined in terms of an array of pointers?

10.39 What is the relationship between a function name and a pointer?

10.40 Suppose a formal argument within a function definition is a pointer to another function. How is the formal argument declared? Within the formal argument declaration, to what does the data type refer?

10.41 Suppose a formal argument within the definition of function p is a pointer to function q. How is the formal argument declared within p? In this declaration, to what does the data type refer? How is function q accessed within function p?

10.42 Suppose that function p is declared within main, and one of p's arguments is a pointer to function q. How would the declaration for p be written if full function prototyping is used?

10.43 For what types of applications is it particularly useful to pass one function to another?

Problems

10.44 Explain the meaning of each of the following declarations:

(a) `int *px;`

(b) `float a, b;`
   `float *pa, *pb;`

(c) `float a = -0.167;`
   `float *pa = &a;`

(d) `char c1, c2, c3;`
   `char *pc1, *pc2, *pc3 = &c1;`

(e) `double funct(double *a, double *b, int *c);`

(f) `double *funct(double *a, double *b, int *c);`

(g) `double (*a)[12];`

(h) `double *a[12];`

(i) `char *a[12];`

(j) `char *d[4] = {"north", "south", "east", "west" };`

(k) `long (*p)[10][20];`

(l) `long *p[10][20];`

(m) `char sample(int (*pf)(char a, char b));`

(n) `int (*pf)(void);`

(o) `int (*pf)(char a, char b);`

(p) `int (*pf)(char *a, char *b);`

10.45 Write an appropriate declaration for each of the following situations:

(a) Declare two pointers whose objects are the integer variables i and j.

(b) Declare a pointer to a floating-point quantity and a pointer to a double-precision quantity.

(c) Declare a function that accepts two integer arguments and returns a pointer to a long integer.

(d) Declare a function that accepts two arguments and returns a long integer. Each argument will be a pointer to an integer quantity.

(e) Declare a one-dimensional, floating-point array using pointer notation.

(f) Declare a two-dimensional floating-point array, with 15 rows and 30 columns, using pointer notation.

(g) Declare an array of strings whose initial values are "red", "green" and "blue".

(h) Declare a function that accepts another function as an argument and returns a pointer to a character. The function passed as an argument will accept an integer argument and return an integer quantity.

(i) Declare a pointer to a function that accepts three integer arguments and returns a floating-point quantity.

(j) Declare a pointer to a function that accepts three pointers to integer quantities as arguments and returns a pointer to a floating-point quantity.

10.46 A C program contains the following statements:

```
char u, v = 'A';
char *pu, *pv = &v;

...

*pv = v + 1;
u = *pv + 1;
pu = &u;
```

Suppose each character occupies 1 byte of memory. If the value assigned to u is stored in (hexadecimal) address F8C and the value assigned to v is stored in address F8D, then

    (a)   What value is represented by &v?
    (b)   What value is assigned to pv?
    (c)   What value is represented by *pv?
    (d)   What value is assigned to u?
    (e)   What value is represented by &u?
    (f)   What value is assigned to pu?
    (g)   What value is represented by *pu?

10.47   A C program contains the following statements:

```
int i, j = 25;
int *pi, *pj = &j;

. . .

*pj = j + 5;
i = *pj + 5;
pi = pj;
*pi = i + j;
```

Suppose each integer quantity occupies 2 bytes of memory. If the value assigned to i begins at (hexadecimal) address F9C and the value assigned to j begins at address F9E, then

    (a)   What value is represented by &i?
    (b)   What value is represented by &j?
    (c)   What value is assigned to pj?
    (d)   What value is assigned to *pj?
    (e)   What value is assigned to i?
    (f)   What value is represented by pi?
    (g)   What final value is assigned to *pi?
    (h)   What value is represented by (pi + 2)?
    (i)   What value is represented by the expression (*pi + 2)?
    (j)   What value is represented by the expression *(pi + 2)?

10.48   A C program contains the following statements:

```
float a = 0.001;
float b = 0.003;
float c, *pa, *pb;

pa = &a;
*pa = 2 * a;
pb = &b;
c = 3 * (*pb - *pa);
```

Suppose each floating-point number occupies 4 bytes of memory. If the value assigned to a begins at (hexadecimal) address 1130 the value assigned to b begins at address 1134, and the value assigned to c begins at 1138, then

    (a)   What value is assigned to &a?
    (b)   What value is assigned to &b?
    (c)   What value is assigned to &c?
    (d)   What value is assigned to pa?
    (e)   What value is represented by *pa?
    (f)   What value is represented by &(*pa)?

(*g*)   What value is assigned to pb?
(*h*)   What value is represented by *pb?
(*i*)   What value is assigned to c?

10.49   The skeletal structure of a C program is shown below.

```
main()
{
    char a = 'X';
    char b = 'Y';
    int i, j;
    int funct1(char a, char b);
    int funct2(char *pa, char *pb);

    . . .

    i = funct1(a, b);
    printf("a=%c    b=%c\n", a, b);

    . . .

    j = funct2(&a, &b);
    printf("a=%c    b=%c", a, b);
}


int funct1(char c1, char c2)
{
    c1 = 'P';
    c2 = 'Q';

    . . .

    return((c1 < c2) ? c1 : c2);
}


int funct2(char *c1, char *c2)
{
    *c1 = 'P';
    *c2 = 'Q';

    . . .

    return((*c1 == *c2) ? *c1 : *c2);
}
```

(*a*)   Within main, what value is assigned to i?
(*b*)   What value is assigned to j?
(*c*)   What values are displayed by the first printf statement?
(*d*)   What values are displayed by the second printf statement?

   Assume ASCII characters.

10.50   The skeletal structure of a C program is shown below.

```
main()
{
    static int a[5] = {10, 20, 30, 40, 50};
    void funct(int *p);


    . . .


    funct(a);


    . . .


}


void funct(int *p)
{
    int i, sum = 0;
    for (i = 0; i < 5; ++i)
        sum += *(p + i);
    printf("sum=%d", sum);
    return;
}
```

(a) What kind of argument is passed to funct?
(b) What kind of information is returned by funct?
(c) What kind of formal argument is defined within funct?
(d) What is the purpose of the for loop that appears within funct?
(e) What value is displayed by the printf statement within funct?

10.51 The skeletal structure of a C program is shown below.

```
main()
{
    static int a[5] = {10, 20, 30, 40, 50};
    void funct(int *p);


    . . .


    funct(a + 3);


    . . .


}


void funct(int *p)
{
    int i, sum = 0;
    for (i = 3; i < 5; ++i)
        sum += *(p + i);
    printf("sum=%d", sum);
    return;
}
```

(a) What kind of argument is passed to funct?
(b) What kind of information is returned by funct?

(c) What information is actually passed to funct?

(d) What is the purpose of the for loop that appears within funct?

(e) What value is displayed by the printf statement within funct?

Compare your answers with those of the previous problem. In what ways do these two skeletal outlines differ?

10.52 The skeletal structure of a C program is shown below.

```
main()
{
    static int a[5] = {10, 20, 30, 40, 50};
    int *ptmax;
    int *funct(int *p);


    . . .


    ptmax = funct(a);
    printf("max=%d", *ptmax);


    . . .


}


int *funct(int *p)
{
    int i, imax, max = 0;
    for (i = 0; i < 5; ++i)
        if (*(p + i) > max)      {
            max = *(p + i);
            imax = i;
        }
    return(p + imax);
}
```

(a) Within main, what is ptmax?

(b) What kind of information is returned by funct?

(c) What is assigned to ptmax when the function is accessed?

(d) What is the purpose of the for loop that appears within funct?

(e) What value is displayed by the printf statement within main?

Compare your answers with those of the previous two problems. In what ways are the skeletal outlines different?

10.53 A C program contains the following declaration:

```
static int x[8] = {10, 20, 30, 40, 50, 60, 70, 80};
```

(a) What is the meaning of x?

(b) What is the meaning of (x + 2)?

(c) What is the value of *x?

(d) What is the value of (*x + 2)?

(e) What is the value of *(x + 2)?

10.54 A C program contains the following declaration:

```
static float table[2][3] = {
                             {1.1, 1.2, 1.3},
                             {2.1, 2.2, 2.3}
                          };
```

(a) What is the meaning of table?

(b) What is the meaning of (table + 1)?

   (c)   What is the meaning of *(table + 1)?
   (d)   What is the meaning of (*(table + 1) + 1)?
   (e)   What is the meaning of (*(table) + 1)?
   (f)   What is the value of *(*(table + 1) + 1)?
   (g)   What is the value of *(*(table) + 1)?
   (h)   What is the value of *(*(table + 1))?
   (i)   What is the value of *(*(table) + 1) + 1?

10.55 A C program contains the following declaration:

```
static char *color[6] = {"red", "green", "blue",
                         "white", "black", "yellow"};
```

   (a)   What is the meaning of color?
   (b)   What is the meaning of (color + 2)?
   (c)   What is the value of *color?
   (d)   What is the value of *(color + 2)?
   (e)   How do color[5] and *(color + 5) differ?

10.56 The skeletal structure of a C program is shown below.

```
main()
{
    float a, b;
    float one(float x, float y);
    float two(float x, float y);
    float three(float (*pt)(float x, float y));

    . . .

    a = three(one);

    . . .

    b = three(two);

    . . .
}


float one(float x, float y)
{
    float z;

    z = . . .

    return(z);
}


float two(float p, float q)
{
    float r;

    r = . . . .

    return(r);
}
```

```
float three(float (*pt)(float x, float y))
{
    float a, b, c;

    . . .

    c = (*pt)(a, b);

    . . .

    return(c);
}
```

(a) Interpret each of the declarations appearing in main.
(b) Interpret the definitions of the functions one and two.
(c) Interpret the definition of the function three. How does three differ from one and two?
(d) What happens within main each time three is accessed?

10.57 The skeletal structure of a C program is shown below.

```
main()
{
    float *pa, *pb;
    float one(float *px, float *py);
    float two(float *px, float *py);
    float *three(float (*pt)(float *px, float *py));

    . . .

    pa = three(one);

    . . .

    pb = three(two);

    . . .
}


float one(float *px, float *py)
{
    float z;

    z = . . .

    return(z);
}


float two(float *pp, float *pq)
{
    float r;

    r = . . .

    return(r);
}
```

```
float *three(float (*pt)(float *px, float *py))
{
    float a, b, c;

    . . .

    c = (*pt)(&a, &b);

    . . .

    return(&c);
}
```

(a) Interpret each of the declarations appearing in main.

(b) Interpret the definitions of the functions one and two.

(c) Interpret the definition of the function three. How does three differ from one and two?

(d) What happens within main each time three is accessed?

(e) How does this program outline differ from the outline shown in the last example?

10.58 Explain the purpose of each of the following declarations:

(a) `float (*x)(int *a);`

(b) `float (*x(int *a))[20];`

(c) `float x(int (*a)[]);`

(d) `float x(int *a[]);`

(e) `float *x(int a[]);`

(f) `float *x(int (*a)[]);`

(g) `float *x(int *a[]);`

(h) `float (*x)(int (*a)[]);`

(i) `float *(*x)(int *a[]);`

(j) `float (*x[20])(int a);`

(k) `float *(*x[20])(int *a);`

10.59 Write an appropriate declaration for each of the following situations involving pointers:

(a) Declare a function that accepts an argument which is a pointer to an integer quantity and returns a pointer to a six-element character array.

(b) Declare a function that accepts an argument which is a pointer to an integer array and returns a character.

(c) Declare a function that accepts an argument which is an array of pointers to integer quantities and returns a character.

(d) Declare a function that accepts an argument which is an integer array and returns a pointer to a character.

(e) Declare a function that accepts an argument which is a pointer to an integer array and returns a pointer to a character.

(f) Declare a function that accepts an argument which is an array of pointers to integer quantities and returns a pointer to a character.

(g) Declare a pointer to a function that accepts an argument which is a pointer to an integer array and returns a character.

(h) Declare a pointer to a function that accepts an argument which is a pointer to an integer array and returns a pointer to a character.

(i) Declare a pointer to a function that accepts an argument which is an array of pointers to integer quantities and returns a pointer to a character.

(j) Declare a 12-element array of pointers to functions. Each function will accept two double-precision quantities as arguments and will return a double-precision quantity.

(k) Declare a 12-element array of pointers to functions. Each function will accept two double-precision quantities as arguments and will return a pointer to a double-precision quantity.

(l) Declare a 12-element array of pointers to functions. Each function will accept two pointers to double-precision quantities as arguments and will return a pointer to a double-precision quantity.

Programming Problems

10.60 Modify the program shown in Example 10.1 as follows:

(a) Use floating-point data rather than integer data. Assign an initial value of 0.3 to u.
(b) Use double-precision data rather than integer data. Assign an initial value of 0.3×10^{45} to u.
(c) Use character data rather than integer data. Assign an initial value of 'C' to u.

Execute each modification and compare the results with those given in Example 10.1. Be sure to modify the printf statements accordingly.

10.61 Modify the program shown in Example 10.3 as follows:

(a) Use floating-point data rather than integer data. Assign an initial value of 0.3 to v.
(b) Use double-precision data rather than integer data. Assign an initial value of 0.3×10^{45} to v.
(c) Use character data rather than integer data. Assign an initial value of 'C' to v.

Execute each modification and compare the results with those given in Example 10.3. Be sure to modify the printf statements accordingly.

10.62 Modify the program shown in Example 10.7 so that a single one-dimensional, character-type array is passed to funct1. Delete funct2 and all references to funct2. Initially, assign the string "red" to the array within main. Then reassign the string "green" to the array within funct1. Execute the program and compare the results with those shown in Example 10.7. Remember to modify the printf statements accordingly.

10.63 Modify the program shown in Example 10.8 (analyzing a line of text) so that it also counts the number of words and the total number of characters in the line of text. (*Note:* A new word can be recognized by the occurrence of a whitespace character followed by a nonwhitespace character.) Test the program using the line of text given in Example 10.8.

10.64 Modify the program shown in Example 10.8 (analyzing a line of text) so that it can process multiple lines of text. First enter and store all lines of text. Then determine the number of vowels, consonants, digits, whitespace characters and "other" characters for each line. Finally, determine the average number of vowels per line, consonants per line, and so on. Write and execute the program two different ways.

(a) Store the multiple lines of text in a two-dimensional array of characters.
(b) Store the multiple lines of text as individual strings whose maximum length is unspecified. Maintain a pointer to each string within a one-dimensional array of pointers.

In each case, identify the last line of text in some predetermined manner (e.g., by entering the string "END"). Test the program using several lines of text of your own choosing.

10.65 Modify the program shown in Example 10.12 so that the elements of x are long integers rather than integers. Execute the program and compare the results with those shown in Example 10.12. Remember to modify the printf statement to accommodate the long integer quantities.

10.66 Modify the program shown in Example 10.15 (reordering a list of numbers) so that any one of the following rearrangements can be carried out:

(a) smallest to largest, by magnitude
(b) smallest to largest, algebraic
(c) largest to smallest, by magnitude
(d) largest to smallest, algebraic

Use pointer notation to represent individual integer quantities, as in Example 10.15. (Recall that an array version of this problem was presented in Example 9.13.) Include a menu that will allow the user to select which rearrangement will be used each time the program is executed. Test the program using the following 10 values:

4.7	−8.0
−2.3	11.4
12.9	5.1
8.8	−0.2
6.0	−14.7

10.67 Modify the program shown in Example 10.22 (adding two tables of numbers) so that each element in the table c is the larger of the corresponding elements in tables a and b (rather than the sum of the corresponding elements in a and b). Represent each table (each array) as a pointer to a group of one-dimensional arrays, as in Example 10.22. Use pointer notation to access the individual table elements. Test the program using the tabular data provided in Example 9.19. (You may wish to experiment with this program, using several different ways to represent the arrays and the individual array elements.)

10.68 Repeat the previous problem, representing each table (each array) as a one-dimensional array of pointers, as discussed in Example 10.24.

10.69 Modify the program shown in Example 10.26 (reordering a list of strings) so that the list of strings can be rearranged into either alphabetical or reverse-alphabetical order. Use pointer notation to represent the beginning of each string. Include a menu that will allow the user to select which rearrangement will be used each time the program is executed. Test the program using the data provided in Example 9.20.

10.70 Modify the program shown in Example 10.28 (displaying the day of the year) so that it can determine the number of days between two dates, assuming that both dates are beyond the base date of January 1, 1900. (*Hint*: Determine the number of days between the first specified date and the base date, then determine the number of days between the second specified date and the base date. Finally, determine the difference between these two calculated values.)

10.71 Modify the program shown in Example 10.31 (compound interest calculations) so that it generates a table of F-values for various interest rates, using different compounding frequencies. Assume that A and n are input values. Display the output in the following manner:

$$A = \ldots$$
$$n = \ldots$$

Interest rate =	5%	6%	7%	8%	9%	10%	11%	12%	13%	14%	15%
Frequency of Compounding											
Annual	—	—	—	—	—	—	—	—	—	—	—
Semiannual	—	—	—	—	—	—	—	—	—	—	—
Quarterly	—	—	—	—	—	—	—	—	—	—	—
Monthly	—	—	—	—	—	—	—	—	—	—	—
Daily	—	—	—	—	—	—	—	—	—	—	—
Continuously	—	—	—	—	—	—	—	—	—	—	—

Notice that the first four rows are generated by one function with different arguments, and each of the last two rows is generated by a different function.

10.72 Modify the program shown in Example 10.31 (compound interest calculations) so that it generates a table of F-values for various time periods, using different compounding frequencies. Assume that A and i are input values. Display the output in the following manner:

$$A = \ldots$$
$$i = \ldots$$

Time period (n) =	1	2	3	4	5	6	7	8	9	10
Frequency of Compounding										
Annual	—	—	—	—	—	—	—	—	—	—
Semiannual	—	—	—	—	—	—	—	—	—	—
Quarterly	—	—	—	—	—	—	—	—	—	—
Monthly	—	—	—	—	—	—	—	—	—	—
Daily	—	—	—	—	—	—	—	—	—	—
Continuously	—	—	—	—	—	—	—	—	—	—

Notice that the first four rows are generated by one function with different arguments, and each of the last two rows is generated by a different function.

10.73 Repeat the previous problem, but transpose the table so that each row represents a different value for n and each column represents a different compounding frequency. Consider integer values of n ranging from 1 to 50. Note that this table will consist of 50 rows and six columns. (*Hint:* Generate the table by columns, storing each column in a two-dimensional array. Display the entire array after all the values have been generated.)

Compare the programming effort required for this problem with the programming effort required for the preceding problem.

10.74 Examples 9.8 and 9.9 present programs to calculate the average of a list of numbers and then calculate the deviations about the average. Both programs make use of one-dimensional, floating-point arrays. Modify both programs so that they utilize pointer notation. (Note that the program shown in Example 9.9 includes the assignment of initial values to individual array elements.) Test both programs using the data given in the examples.

10.75 Modify the program given in Example 9.14 (piglatin generator) so that it uses character-type arrays and pointer notation. Test the program using several lines of text of your own choosing.

10.76 Write a complete C program, using pointer notation in place of arrays, for each of the following problems taken from the end of Chap. 9.

(*a*) Problem 9.39 (read in a line of text, store it within the computer's memory, and then write it out backwards).

(*b*) Problem 9.40 (process a set of student exam scores). Test the program using the data given in Problem 9.40.

(*c*) Problem 9.42 (process a set of weighted student exam scores, and calculate the deviation of each student's average about the overall class average). Test the program using the data given in Problem 9.40.

(*d*) Problem 9.44 (generate a table of compound interest factors).

(*e*) Problem 9.45 (convert from one foreign currency to another).

(*f*) Problem 9.46 (determine the capital of a specified country, or the country whose capital is specified). Test the program using the list of countries and their capitals given in Problem 9.46.

(*g*) Problem 9.47(*a*) (matrix/vector multiplication). Test the program using the data given in Problem 9.47(*a*).

(*h*) Problem 9.47(*b*) (matrix multiplication). Test the program using the data given in Problem 9.47(*b*).

(*i*) Problem 9.47(*d*) (Lagrange interpolation). Test the program using the data given in Problem 9.47(*d*).

(*j*) Problem 9.48(*a*) (blackjack).

(*k*) Problem 9.48(*b*) (roulette).

(*l*) Problem 9.48(*c*) (BINGO).

(*m*) Problem 9.49 (encode or decode a line of text).

10.77 Write a complete C program, using pointer notation, that will generate a table containing the following three columns:

$$t \qquad ae^{bt} \sin ct \qquad ae^{bt} \cos ct$$

Structure the program in the following manner: Write two special functions, f1 and f2, where f1 evaluates the quantity $ae^{bt} \sin ct$ and f2 evaluates $ae^{bt} \cos ct$. Have main read in the values of a, b and c, and then call a function, table_gen which will generate the actual table. Pass f1 and f2 to table_gen as arguments.

Test the program using the values a = 2, b = −0.1, c = 0.5 where the values of t are 1, 2, 3, ..., 60.

Chapter 11

Structures and Unions

In Chap. 9 we studied the array, which is a data structure whose elements are all of the same data type. We now turn our attention to the *structure,* which is a data structure whose individual elements can differ in type. Thus, a single structure might contain integer elements, floating-point elements and character elements. Pointers, arrays and other structures can also be included as elements within a structure. The individual structure elements are referred to as *members.*

This chapter is concerned with the use of structures within a C program. We will see how structures are defined, and how their individual members are accessed and processed within a program. The relationships between structures and pointers, arrays and functions will also be examined.

Closely associated with the structure is the *union,* which also contains multiple members. Unlike a structure, however, the members of a union share the same storage area, even though the individual members may differ in type. Thus, a union permits several different data items to be stored in the same portion of the computer's memory at different times. We will see how unions are defined and utilized within a C program.

11.1 DEFINING A STRUCTURE

Structure declarations are somewhat more complicated than array declarations, since a structure must be defined in terms of its individual members. In general terms, the composition of a structure may be defined as

```
struct  tag {
    member 1;
    member 2;
    . . .
    member m;
};
```

In this declaration, `struct` is a required keyword, *tag* is a name that identifies structures of this type (i.e., structures having this composition), and *member 1, member 2, . . . member m* are individual member declarations. (*Note:* There is no formal distinction between a structure *definition* and a structure *declaration;* the terms are used interchangeably.)

The individual members can be ordinary variables, pointers, arrays, or other structures. The member names within a particular structure must be distinct from one another, though a member name can be the same as the name of a variable defined outside of the structure. A storage class, however, cannot be assigned to an individual member, and individual members cannot be initialized within a structure-type declaration.

Once the composition of the structure has been defined, individual structure-type variables can be declared as follows:

```
storage-class struct tag variable 1, variable 2, ..., variable n;
```

where *storage-class* is an optional storage class specifier, `struct` is a required keyword, *tag* is the name that appeared in the structure type declaration, and *variable 1, variable 2, ..., variable n* are structure variables of type *tag.*

337

Example 11.1 A typical structure declaration is shown below.

```
struct account  {
     int acct_no;
     char acct_type;
     char name[80];
     float balance;
};
```

This structure is named `account` (i.e., the tag is `account`). It contains four members: an integer quantity (`acct_no`), a single character (`acct_type`), an 80-element character array (`name[80]`), and a floating-point quantity (`balance`). Figure 11.1 illustrates the composition of this account schematically.

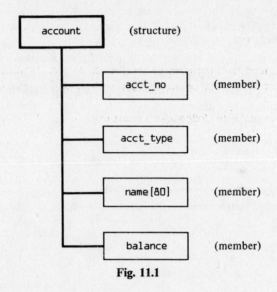

Fig. 11.1

We can now declare the structure variables `oldcustomer` and `newcustomer` as follows:

```
struct account oldcustomer, newcustomer;
```

Thus, `oldcustomer` and `newcustomer` are variables of type `account`. In other words, `oldcustomer` and `newcustomer` are structure-type variables whose composition is identified by the tag `account`.

It is possible to combine the declaration of the structure composition with that of the structure variables, as shown below.

```
storage-class  struct  tag  {
          member 1;
          member 2;
          . . .
          member m;
}  variable 1,  variable 2,  ...,  variable n;
```

The *tag* is optional in this situation.

Example 11.2 The following single declaration is equivalent to the two declarations presented in the previous example.

```
struct account  {
    int acct_no;
    char acct_type;
    char name[80];
    float balance;
} oldcustomer, newcustomer;
```

Thus, oldcustomer and newcustomer are structure variables of type account.

Since the variable declarations are now combined with the declaration of the structure type, the tag (i.e., account) need not be included. As a result, the above declaration can also be written as

```
struct  {
    int acct_no;
    char acct_type;
    char name[80];
    float balance;
} oldcustomer, newcustomer;
```

A structure may be defined as a member of another structure. In such situations, the declaration of the embedded structure must appear before the declaration of the outer structure.

Example 11.3   A C program contains the following structure declarations:

```
struct date  {
    int month;
    int day;
    int year;
};

struct account  {
    int acct_no;
    char acct_type;
    char name[80];
    float balance;
    struct date lastpayment;
} oldcustomer, newcustomer;
```

The structure account now contains another structure, date, as one of its members. Note that the declaration of date precedes the declaration of account. Figure 11.2 shows the composition of account schematically.

The members of a structure variable can be assigned intial values in much the same manner as the elements of an array. The initial values must appear in the order in which they will be assigned to their corresponding structure members, enclosed in braces and separated by commas. The general form is

storage-class struct *tag variable* = {*value 1, value 2, ..., value m* };

where *value 1* refers to the value of the first member, *value 2* refers to the value of the second member, and so on. A structure variable, like an array, can be initialized only if its storage class is either external or static.

Example 11.4   This example illustrates the assignment of initial values to the members of a structure variable.

```
struct date  {
    int month;
    int day;
    int year;
};
```

```
struct account  {
     int acct_no;
     char acct_type;
     char name[80];
     float balance;
     struct date lastpayment;
};

static  struct  account  customer =
                {12345, 'R', "John W. Smith", 586.30, 5, 24, 90};
```

Thus, customer is a static structure variable of type account, whose members are assigned initial values. The first member (acct_no) is assigned the integer value 12345, the second member (acct_type) is assigned the character 'R', the third member (name[80]) is assigned the string "John W. Smith", and the fourth member (balance) is assigned the floating-point value 586.30. The last member is itself a structure that contains three integer members (month, day and year). Therefore, the last member of customer is assigned the integer values 5, 24 and 90.

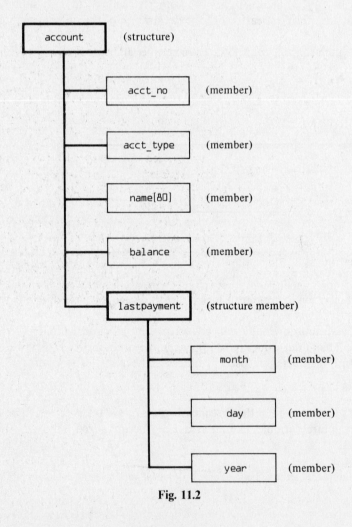

Fig. 11.2

It is also possible to define an array of structures, that is, an array in which each element is a structure. The procedure is illustrated in the following example.

Example 11.5   A C program contains the following structure declarations:

```
struct date  {
     int month;
     int day;
     int year;
};

struct account  {
     int acct_no;
     char acct_type;
     char name[80];
     float balance;
     struct date lastpayment;
}  customer[100];
```

In this declaration customer is a 100-element array of structures. Hence, each element of customer is a separate structure of type account (i.e., each element of customer represents an individual customer record).

Note that each structure of type account includes an array (name[80]) and another structure (date) as members. Thus, we have an array and a structure embedded within another structure, which is itself an element of an array.

It is, of course, also permissible to define customer in a separate declaration, as shown below.

```
struct date  {
     int month;
     int day;
     int year;
};

struct account  {
     int acct_no;
     char acct_type;
     char name[80];
     float balance;
     struct date lastpayment;
};

struct  account  customer[100];
```

Both declarations are equivalent; the choice depends on the individual programmer's preferences.

An array of structures can be assigned initial values just as any other array can. Remember that each array element is a structure that must be assigned a corresponding set of initial values, as illustrated below.

Example 11.6 A C program contains the following declarations:

```
struct date  {
     char name[80];
     int month;
     int day;
     int year;
};

static  struct  date  birthday[] = {"Amy" 12, 30, 73,
                                    "Gail", 5, 13, 66,
                                    "Marc", 7, 15, 72,
                                    "Marla", 11, 29, 70,
                                    "Megan", 2, 4, 77,
                                    "Sharon", 12, 29, 63,
                                    "Susan", 4, 12, 69};
```

In this example `birthday` is an array of structures whose size is unspecified. The initial values will define the size of the array, and the amount of memory required to store the array.

Notice that each row in the variable declaration contains four constants. These constants represent the initial values, i.e., the name, month, day and year, for one array element. Since there are seven rows (seven sets of constants), the array will contain seven elements, numbered 0 to 6.

Some programmers may prefer to embed each set of constants within a separate pair of braces in order to delineate the individual array elements more clearly. This is entirely permissible. Thus, the array declaration can be written

```
static  struct  date  birthday[] = {
                                {"Amy", 12, 30, 73},
                                {"Gail", 5, 13, 66},
                                {"Marc", 7, 15, 72},
                                {"Marla", 11, 29, 70},
                                {"Megan", 2, 4, 77},
                                {"Sharon", 12, 29, 63},
                                {"Susan", 4, 12, 69}
                        };
```

Remember that each structure is a self-contained entity with respect to member definitions. Thus, the same member name can be used in different structures to represent different data. In other words, the scope of a member name is confined to the particular structure within which it is defined.

Example 11.7 Two different structures, called `first` and `second`, are declared below.

```
struct first  {
    float a;
    int b;
    char c;
};

struct second  {
    char a;
    float b, c;
};
```

Notice that the individual member names a, b and c appear in both structure declarations, but the associated data types are different. Thus, a represents a floating-point quantity in `first` and a character in `second`. Similarly, b represents an integer quantity in `first` and a floating-point quantity in `second`, whereas c represents a character in `first` and a floating-point quantity in `second`. This duplication of member names is permissible, since the scope of each set of member definitions is confined to its respective structure. Within each structure the member names are distinct, as required.

11.2 PROCESSING A STRUCTURE

The members of a structure are usually processed individually, as separate entities. Therefore, we must be able to access the individual structure members. A structure member can be accessed by writing

variable.member

where *variable* refers to the name of a structure-type variable, and *member* refers to the name of a member within the structure. Notice the period (.) that separates the variable name from the member name. This period is an operator; it is a member of the highest precedence group, and its associativity is left-to-right (see Appendix C).

Example 11.8 Consider the following structure declarations:

```
struct date  {
    int month;
    int day;
    int year;
};
```

```
struct account  {
    int acct_no;
    char acct_type;
    char name[80];
    float balance;
    struct date lastpayment;
}  customer;
```

In this example `customer` is a structure variable of type `account`. If we wanted to access the customer's account number, we would write

```
customer.acct_no
```

Similarly, the customer's name and the customer's balance can be accessed by writing

```
customer.name
```

and

```
customer.balance
```

Since the period operator is a member of the highest precedence group, this operator will take precedence over the unary operators as well as the various arithmetic, relational, logical and assignment operators. For example, an expression of the form `++variable.member` is equivalent to `++(variable.member)`, i.e., the `++` operator will apply to the structure member, not the entire structure variable. Similarly, the expression `&variable.member` is equivalent to `&(variable.member)`; thus, the expression accesses the address of the structure member, not the starting address of the structure variable.

Example 11.9   Consider the structure declarations given in Example 11.8, i.e.,

```
struct date  {
    int month;
    int day;
    int year;
};

struct account  {
    int acct_no;
    char acct_type;
    char name[80];
    float balance;
    struct date lastpayment;
}  customer;
```

Several expressions involving the structure variable `customer` and its members are given below.

Expression	Interpretation
++customer.balance	increment the value of customer.balance
customer.balance++	increment the value of customer.balance after accessing its value
--customer.acct_no	decrement the value of customer.acct_no
&customer	access the beginning address of customer
&customer.acct_no	access the address of customer.acctno

More complex expressions involving the repeated use of the period operator may also be written. For example, if a structure member is itself a structure, then a member of the embedded structure can be accessed by writing

```
variable.member.submember
```

where *member* refers to the name of the member within the outer structure, and *submember* refers to the name of the member within the embedded structure. Similarly, if a structure member is an array, then an individual array element can be accessed by writing

```
variable.member[expression]
```

where *expression* is a nonnegative value that indicates the array element.

Example 11.10 Consider once again the structure declarations presented in Example 11.8.

```
struct date {
    int month;
    int day;
    int year;
};

struct account {
    int acct_no;
    char acct_type;
    char name[80];
    float balance;
    struct date lastpayment;
} customer;
```

The last member of customer is customer.lastpayment, which is itself a structure of type date. To access the month of the last payment, we would therefore write

```
customer.lastpayment.month
```

Moreover, this value can be incremented by writing

```
++customer.lastpayment.month
```

Similarly, the third member of customer is the character array customer.name. The third character within this array can be accessed by writing

```
customer.name[2]
```

This character's address can be obtained as

```
&customer.name[2]
```

The use of the period operator can be extended to arrays of structures, by writing

```
array[expression].member
```

where *array* refers to the array name, and *array[expression]* is an individual array element (a structure variable). Therefore, *array[expression].member* will refer to a specific member within a particular structure.

Example 11.11   Consider the following structure declarations, which were originally presented in Example 11.5:

```
struct date {
    int month;
    int day;
    int year;
};


struct account {
    int acct_no;
    char acct_type;
    char name[80];
    float balance;
    struct date lastpayment;
} customer[100];
```

In this example customer is an array that may contain as many as 100 elements. Each element is a structure of type account. Thus, if we wanted to access the account number of the 14th customer (i.e., customer[13], since the subscripts begin with 0), we would write customer[13].acct_no. Similarly, this customer's balance can be accessed by writing customer[13].balance.

The 14th customer's name can be accessed by writing customer[13].name. Moreover, we can access an individual character within the name by specifying a subscript. For example, the eighth character within the customer's name can be accessed by writing customer[13].name[7]. Similarly, we can access the month, day and year of the 14th customer's last payment by specifying the individual members of customer[13].lastpayment, that is, customer[13].lastpayment.month, customer[13].lastpayment.day, and customer[13].lastpayment.year. Moreover, the expression ++customer[13].lastpayment.day causes the value of the day to be incremented.

Structure members can be processed in the same manner as ordinary variables of the same data type. Single-valued structure members can appear in expressions, they can be passed to functions, and they can be returned from functions, as though they were ordinary single-valued variables. Complex structure members are processed in the same way as ordinary data items of that same type. For example, a structure member that is an array can be processed in the same manner as an ordinary array, with the same restrictions. Similarly, a structure member that is itself a structure can be processed on a member-by-member basis (the members here refer to the embedded structure), the same as any other structure.

Example 11.12   Several statements or groups of statements that access individual structure members are shown below. All of the structure members conform to the declarations given in Example 11.8.

```
customer.balance = 0;

customer.balance -= payments;

customer.lastpayment.month = 12;

printf("Name: %s\n", customer.name);

if (customer.acct_type == 'P')
    printf("Preferred account no.: %d\n", customer.acct_no);
else
    printf("Regular account no.: %d\n", customer.acct_no);
```

The first statement assigns a value of zero to customer.balance, whereas the second statement causes the value of customer.balance to be decreased by the value of payment. The third statement causes the value 12 to be assigned to `customer.lastpayment.month`. Note that `customer.lastpayment.month` is a member of the embedded structure `customer.lastpayment`.

The fourth statement passes the array `customer.name` to the `printf` function, causing the customer name to be displayed. Finally, the last example illustrates the use of structure members in an `if - else` statement. Also, we see a situation in which the structure member `customer.acct_no` is passed to a function as an argument.

In some of the older versions of C, structures must be processed on a member-by member basis. With this restriction, the only permissible operation on an entire structure is to take its address (more about this later). Most newer versions, however, permit entire structures to be assigned to one another provided the structures have the same composition. This feature is included in the new ANSI standard.

Example 11.13 Suppose that `oldcustomer` and `newcustomer` are structure variables having the same composition, that is,

```
struct date  {
     int month;
     int day;
     int year;
};

struct account  {
     int acct_no;
     char acct_type;
     char name[80];
     float balance;
     struct date lastpayment;
}  oldcustomer, newcustomer;
```

as declared in Example 11.8. Let us assume that all the members of `oldcustomer` have been assigned individual values. In most newer versions of C, it is possible to copy these values to `newcustomer` simply by writing

```
newcustomer = oldcustomer;
```

On the other hand, some older versions of C may require the values to be copied individually, member-by-member; for example,

```
newcustomer.acct_no = oldcustomer.acct_no;
newcustomer.acct_type = oldcustomer.acct_type;
```

. . .

```
newcustomer.lastpayment.year = oldcustomer.lastpayment.year;
```

It is also possible to pass entire structures to and from functions, though the way this is done varies from one version of C to another. Older versions of C allow only pointers to be passed, whereas newer versions allow the structures themselves to be passed. We will discuss this further in Sec. 11.5. Before moving on to the relationship between structures and pointers and the methods for passing structures to functions, however, let us consider a more comprehensive example that involves the processing of structure members.

Example 11.14 Updating Customer Records To illustrate further how the individual members of a structure can be processed, consider a very simple customer billing system. In this system the customer records will be stored within an array of structures. Each record will be stored as an individual structure (i.e., as an array element) containing the customer's name, street address, city and state, account number, account status (current, overdue or delinquent), previous balance, current payment, new balance and payment date.

The overall strategy will be to enter each customer record into the computer, updating it as soon as it is entered, to reflect current payments. All the updated records will then be displayed, along with the current status of each account. The account status will be based upon the size of the current payment relative to the customer's previous balance.

The structure declarations are shown below.

```
struct date {
    int month;
    int day;
    int year;
};

struct account {
    char name[80];
    char street[80];
    char city[80];
    int acct_no;
    char acct_type;
    float oldbalance;
    float newbalance;
    float payment;
    struct date lastpayment;
} customer[100];
```

Notice that `customer` is a 100-element array of structures. Thus, each array element (each structure) will represent one customer record. Each structure includes three members that are character-type arrays (`name`, `street` and `city`), and one member that is another structure (`lastpayment`).

The status of each account will be determined in the following manner:

1. If the current payment is greater than zero but less than 10 percent of the previous outstanding balance, the account will be overdue.

2. If there is an outstanding balance and the current payment is zero, the account will be delinquent.

3. Otherwise, the account will be current.

The overall program strategy will be as follows:

1. Specify the number of customer accounts (i.e., the number of structures) to be processed.

2. For each customer, read in the following items:
   (a) name   (e) previous balance
   (b) street   (f) current payment
   (c) city   (g) payment date
   (d) account number

3. As each customer record is read into the computer, update it in the following manner:
   (a) Compare the current payment with the previous balance and determine the appropriate account status.
   (b) Calculate a new account balance by subtracting the current payment from the previous balance (a negative balance will indicate a credit).

4. After all customer records have been entered and processed, write out the following information for each customer:
   (a) name   (e) old balance
   (b) account number (f) current payment
   (c) street   (g) new balance
   (d) city   (h) account status

Let us write the program in a modular manner, with one function to enter and update each record and another function to display the updated data. Ideally, we would like to pass each customer record (i.e., each array element) to each of these functions. Since each customer record is a structure, however, and we have not yet discussed how to pass a structure to or from a function, we will define the array of structures as an external array. This will allow us to access the array elements, and the individual structure members, directly from all the functions.

The individual program modules are straightforward, though some care is required in reading the individual structure members into the computer. Here is the entire program.

```
#include <stdio.h>

/* update a series of customer accounts (simplified billing system) */
/* maintain the customer accounts as an external array of structures */

struct date {
    int month;
    int day;
    int year;
};

struct account {
    char name[80];
    char street[80];
    char city[80];
    int acct_no;                /* (positive integer) */
    char acct_type;             /* C (current), O (overdue), or D (delinquent) */
    float oldbalance;           /* (nonnegative quantity) */
    float newbalance;           /* (nonnegative quantity) */
    float payment;              /* (nonnegative quantity) */
    struct date lastpayment;
} customer[100];                /* maintain as many as 100 customers */

main()

/* read customer accounts, process each account, and display output */

{
    int i, n;
    void readinput(int i);
    void writeoutput(int i);

    printf("CUSTOMER BILLING SYSTEM\n\n");
    printf("How many customers are there? ");
    scanf("%d", &n);

    for (i = 0; i < n; ++i)   {
        readinput(i);

        /* determine account status */

        if (customer[i].payment > 0)
            customer[i].acct_type =
                (customer[i].payment < 0.1 * customer[i].oldbalance) ? 'O' : 'C';
        else
            customer[i].acct_type =
                (customer[i].oldbalance > 0) ? 'D' : 'C';

        /* adjust account balance */

        customer[i].newbalance = customer[i].oldbalance - customer[i].payment;
    };

    for (i = 0; i < n; ++i)
        writeoutput(i);
}
```

```
void readinput(int i)

/* read input data and update record for each customer */

{
    printf("\nCustomer no. %d\n", i + 1);
    printf("   Name: ");
    scanf(" %[^\n]", customer[i].name);
    printf("   Street: ");
    scanf(" %[^\n]", customer[i].street);
    printf("   City: ");
    scanf(" %[^\n]", customer[i].city);
    printf("   Account number: ");
    scanf("%d", &customer[i].acct_no);
    printf("   Previous balance: ");
    scanf("%f", &customer[i].oldbalance);
    printf("   Current payment: ");
    scanf("%f", &customer[i].payment);
    printf("   Payment date (mm/dd/yyyy): ");
    scanf("%d/%d/%d", &customer[i].lastpayment.month,
                      &customer[i].lastpayment.day,
                      &customer[i].lastpayment.year);

    return;
}


void writeoutput(int i)

/* write out current information for each customer */

{
    printf("\nName:    %s", customer[i].name);
    printf("      Account number: %d\n", customer[i].acct_no);
    printf("Street: %s\n", customer[i].street);
    printf("City:    %s\n\n", customer[i].city);
    printf("Old balance: %7.2f", customer[i].oldbalance);
    printf("   Current payment: %7.2f", customer[i].payment);
    printf("   New balance: %7.2f\n\n", customer[i].newbalance);
    printf("Account status: ");

    switch (customer[i].acct_type)  {
        case 'C':
                printf("CURRENT\n\n");
                break;
        case 'O':
                printf("OVERDUE\n\n");
                break;
        case 'D':
                printf("DELINQUENT\n\n");
                break;
        default:
                printf("ERROR\n\n");
    }
    return;
}
```

Now suppose that the program is used to process four fictitious customer records. The input dialog is shown below, with the user's responses underlined.

CUSTOMER BILLING SYSTEM

How many customers are there? 4

Customer no. 1
     Name: Richard L. Warren
     Street: 123 Vistaview Drive
     City: Denver, CO
     Account number: 4208
     Previous balance: 247.88
     Current payment: 25.00
     Payment date (mm/dd/yyyy): 6/14/1988

Customer no. 2
     Name: Marcia Korenstein
     Street: 4383 Affluent Avenue
     City: Beechview, OH
     Account number: 2219
     Previous balance: 135.00
     Current payment: 135.00
     Payment date (mm/dd/yyyy): 8/10/1989

Customer no. 3
     Name: Mark Singer
     Street: 1787 Larynx Lane
     City: Indianapolis, IN
     Account number: 8452
     Previous balance: 387.42
     Current payment: 35.00
     Payment date (mm/dd/yyyy): 9/22/1988

Customer no. 4
     Name: Phyllis W. Smith
     Street: 1000 Great White Way
     City: New York, NY
     Account number: 711
     Previous balance: 260.00
     Current payment: 0
     Payment date (mm/dd/yyyy): 11/27/1988

The program will then generate the following output data:

Name: Richard L. Warren   Account number: 4208
Street: 123 Vistaview Drive
City: Denver, CO

Old balance: 247.88   Current payment: 25.00   New balance: 222.88

Account status: CURRENT

Name: Marcia Korenstein   Account number: 2219
Street: 4383 Affluent Avenue
City: Beechview, OH

Old balance: 135.00   Current payment: 135.00   New balance: 0.00

Account status: CURRENT

```
Name:   Mark Singer      Account number: 8452
Street: 1787 Larynx Lane
City:   Indianapolis, IN

Old balance:  387.42   Current payment:   35.00   New balance:  352.42

Account status: OVERDUE



Name:   Phyllis W. Smith      Account number: 711
Street: 1000 Great White Way
City:   New York, NY

Old balance:  260.00   Current payment:    0.00   New Balance:  260.00

Account status: DELINQUENT
```

It should be understood that this example is unrealistic from a practical standpoint, for two reasons. First, the array of structures (customer) is defined to be external to all of the functions within the program. It would be preferable to declare customer within main, and then pass it to or from readinput or writeoutput as required. We will learn how this is done in Sec. 11.4.

A more serious problem is that a real customer billing system will store the customer records within a data file on an auxiliary storage device, such as a hard disk or a magnetic tape. To update a record we would access the record from the data file, change the data where necessary, and then write the updated record back to the data file. The use of data files will be discussed in Chap. 12. Since the current example does not make use of data files, we must reenter all of the customer records whenever the program is run. This is rather contrived, though it does provide a simple example illustrating the manner in which structures can be processed on a member-by-member basis.

It is sometimes useful to determine the number of bytes required by an array or a structure. This information can be obtained through the use of the sizeof operator, originally discussed in Sec. 3.2. For example, the size of a structure can be determined by writing either sizeof *variable* or sizeof (struct *tag*).

Example 11.15 An elementary C program is shown below.

```c
#include <stdio.h>

main()   /* determine the size of a structure */
{
    struct date {
         int month;
         int day;
         int year;
    };

    struct account  {
         int acct_no;
         char acct_type;
         char name[80];
         float balance;
         struct date lastpayment;
    } customer;

    printf("%d\n", sizeof customer);
    printf("%d", sizeof (struct account));
}
```

This program makes use of the sizeof operator to determine the number of bytes associated with the structure variable customer (or equivalently, the structure account). The two printf statements illustrate different ways to utilize the sizeof operator. Both printf statements will produce the same output.

Executing the program will result in the following output:

```
93
93
```

Thus, the structure variable customer (or the structure account) will occupy 93 bytes. This value is obtained as follows:

Structure Member	Number of Bytes
acct_no	2
acct_type	1
name	80
balance	4
lastpayment	6
Total	93

Some compilers may assign two bytes to acct_type in order to maintain an even number of bytes. Hence, the total byte count may be 94 rather than 93.

11.3 USER-DEFINED DATA TYPES (typedef)

The typedef feature allows users to define new data types that are equivalent to existing data types. Once a user-defined data type has been established, then new variables, arrays, structures, and so on, can be declared in terms of this new data type.

In general terms, a new data type is defined as

```
typedef  type  new-type;
```

where type refers to an existing data type (either a standard data type, or a previous user-defined data type), and new-type refers to the new user-defined data type. It should be understood, however, that the new data type will be new in name only. In reality, this new data type will not be fundamentally different from one of the standard data types.

Example 11.16   Here is a simple declaration involving the use of typedef.

```
typedef  int  age;
```

In this declaration age is a user-defined data type equivalent to type int. Hence, the variable declaration

```
age  male, female;
```

is equivalent to writing

```
int  male, female;
```

In other words, male and female are regarded as variables of type age, though they are actually integer-type variables.

Similarly, the declarations

```
typedef  float  height[100];
height  men, women;
```

define height as a 100-element, floating-point array type. Hence, men and women are 100-element, floating-point arrays. Another way to express this is

```
typedef float height;
height men[100], women[100];
```

though the former declaration is somewhat simpler.

The `typedef` feature is particularly convenient when defining structures, since it eliminates the need to repeatedly write `struct tag` whenever a structure is referenced. As a result, the structure can be referenced more concisely. In addition, the name given to a user-defined structure type often suggests the purpose of the structure within the program.

In general terms, a user-defined structure type can be written as

```
typedef struct {
    member 1;
    member 2;
    . . .
    member m;
} new-type;
```

where *new-type* is the user-defined structure type. Structure variables can then be defined in terms of the new data type.

Example 11.17 The following declarations are comparable to the structure declarations presented in Examples 11.1 and 11.2. Now, however, we introduce a user-defined data type to describe the structure.

```
typedef struct {
    int acct_no;
    char acct_type;
    char name[80];
    float balance;
} record;

record oldcustomer, newcustomer;
```

The first declaration defines `record` as a user-defined data type. The second declaration defines `oldcustomer` and `newcustomer` as structure variables of type `record`.

The `typedef` feature can be used repeatedly, to define one data type in terms of other user-defined data types.

Example 11.18 Here are some variations of the structure declarations presented in Example 11.5.

```
typedef struct {
    int month;
    int day;
    int year;
} date;

typedef struct {
    int acct_no;
    char acct_type;
    char name[80];
    float balance;
    date lastpayment;
} record;

record customer[100];
```

In this example `date` and `record` are user-defined structure types, and `customer` is a 100-element array whose elements are structures of type `record`. (Recall that `date` was a tag rather than an actual data type in Example 11.5.) The individual members within the ith element of `customer` can be written as `customer[i].acct_no`, `customer[i].name`, `customer[i].lastpayment.month`, and so on, as before.

There are, of course, variations on this theme. Thus, an alternate declaration can be written as

```
typedef struct  {
    int month;
    int day;
    int year;
}  date;

typedef struct  {
    int acct_no;
    char acct_type;
    char name[80];
    float balance;
    date lastpayment;
}  record[100];

record customer;
```

or simply

```
typedef struct  {
    int month;
    int day;
    int year;
}  date;

struct  {
    int acct_no;
    char acct_type;
    char name[80];
    float balance;
    date lastpayment;
}  customer[100];
```

All three sets of declarations are equivalent.

11.4 STRUCTURES AND POINTERS

The beginning address of a structure can be accessed in the same manner as any other address, through the use of the address (&) operator. Thus, if *variable* represents a structure-type variable, then *&variable* represents the starting address of that variable. Moreover, we can declare a pointer variable for a structure by writing

type **ptvar*;

where *type* is a data type that identifies the composition of the structure, and *ptvar* represents the name of the pointer variable. We can then assign the beginning address of a structure variable to this pointer by writing

ptvar = &variable;

Example 11.19 Consider the following structure declaration, which is a variation of the declaration presented in Example 11.1:

```
typedef struct  {
    int acct_no;
    char acct_type;
    char name[80];
    float balance;
}  account;

account  customer, *pc;
```

In this example, `customer` is a structure variable of type `account`, and `pc` is a pointer variable whose object is a structure variable of type `account`. Thus, the beginning address of `customer` can be assigned to `pc` by writing

```
pc = &customer;
```

The variable and pointer declarations can be combined with the structure declaration by writing

```
struct  {
    member 1;
    member 2;
    . . .
    member m;
}  variable,  *ptvar;
```

where *variable* again represents a structure-type variable and *ptvar* represents the name of a pointer variable.

Example 11.20 The following single declaration is equivalent to the two declarations presented in the previous example:

```
struct  {
    int acct_no;
    char acct_type;
    char name[80];
    float balance;
}  customer, *pc;
```

The beginning address of `customer` can be assigned to `pc` by writing

```
pc = &customer;
```

as in the previous example.

An individual structure member can be accessed in terms of its corresponding pointer variable by writing

```
ptvar->member
```

where *ptvar* refers to a structure-type pointer variable and the operator -> is comparable to the period (.) operator discussed in Sec. 11.2. Thus, the expression

```
ptvar->member
```

is equivalent to writing

variable.member

where *variable* is a structure-type variable, as discussed in Sec. 11.2. The operator -> falls into the highest precedence group, like the period operator (.). Its associativity is left-to-right (see Appendix C).

The -> operator can be combined with the period operator to access a submember within a structure (i.e., to access a member of a structure that is itself a member of another structure). Hence, a submember can be accessed by writing

ptvar->member.submember

Similarly, the -> operator can be used to access an element of an array that is a member of a structure. This is accomplished by writing

ptvar->member[expression]

where *expression* is a nonnegative integer that indicates the array element.

Example 11.21 Here is a variation of the declarations shown in Example 11.8.

```
typedef struct {
    int month;
    int day;
    int year;
} date;

struct {
    int acct_no;
    char acct_type;
    char name[80];
    float balance;
    date lastpayment;
} customer, *pc = &customer;
```

Notice that the pointer variable pc is initialized by assigning it the beginning address of the structure variable customer. In other words, pc will point to customer.

If we wanted to access the customer's account number, we could write any of the following:

```
customer.acct_no       pc->acct_no       (*pc).acct_no
```

The parentheses are required in the last expression because the period operator has a higher precedence than the indirection operator (*). Without the parentheses the compiler would generate an error, because pc (a pointer) is not directly compatible with the dot operator.

Similarly, the customer's balance can be accessed by writing any of the following:

```
customer.balance       pc->balance       (*pc).balance
```

and the month of the last payment can be accessed by writing any of the following:

```
customer.lastpayment.month       pc->lastpayment.month
(*pc).lastpayment.month
```

Finally, the customer's name can be accessed by writing any of the following:

```
customer.name       pc->name        (*pc).name
```

Therefore, the third character of the customer's name can be accessed by writing any of the following (see Sec. 10.4):

```
customer.name[2]        pc->name[2]         (*pc).name[2]
*(customer.name + 2)    pc->(name + 2)      *((*pc).name + 2)
```

A structure can also include one or more pointers as members. Thus, if *ptmember* is both a pointer and a member of *variable*, then *variable.ptmember* will access the value to which *ptmember* points. Similarly, if *ptvar* is a pointer variable that points to a structure and *ptmember* is a member of that structure, then *ptvar->ptmember* will access the value to which *ptmember* points.

Example 11.22 Consider the simple C program shown below.

```c
#include <stdio.h>

main()

{
    int n = 3333;
    char t = 'C';
    float b = 99.99;

    typedef struct {
        int month;
        int day;
        int year;
    } date;

    struct {
        int *acct_no;
        char *acct_type;
        char *name;
        float *balance;
        date lastpayment;
    } customer, *pc = &customer;

    customer.acct_no = &n;
    customer.acct_type = &t;
    customer.name = "Smith";
    customer.balance = &b;

    printf("%d %c %s %.2f\n", *customer.acct_no, *customer.acct_type,
                        customer.name, *customer.balance);
    printf("%d %c %s %.2f", *pc->acct_no, *pc->acct_type,
                        pc->name, *pc->balance);

}
```

Within the second structure, the members acct_no, acct_type, name and balance are written as pointers. Thus. the value to which acct_no points can be accessed by writing either *customer.acct_no or *pc->acct_no. The same is true for acct_type and balance. Moreover, recall that a string can be assigned directly to a character-type pointer. Therefore, if name points to the beginning of a string, then the string can be accessed by writing either customer.name or pc->name.

Execution of this simple program results in the following two lines of output:

```
3333 C Smith 99.99
3333 C Smith 99.99
```

The two lines of output are identical, as expected.

Since the -> operator is a member of the highest precedence group, it will be given the same high priority as the period (.) operator, with left-to-right associativity. Moreover, this operator, like the period operator, will take precedence over any unary, arithmetic, relational, logical or assignment operators that may appear in an expression. We have already discussed this point, as it applies to the period operator, in Sec. 11.2. However, some additional consideration should be given to certain unary operators, such as ++, as they apply to structure-type pointer variables.

We already know that expressions such as ++ptvar->member and ++ptvar->member. submember are equivalent to ++(ptvar->member) and ++(ptvar->member. submember), respectively. Thus, such expressions will cause the value of the member or the submember to be incremented, as discussed in Sec. 11.2. On the other hand, the expression ++ptvar will cause the value of ptvar to increase by whatever number of bytes is associated with the structure to which ptvar points. (The number of bytes associated with a particular structure can be determined through the use of the sizeof operator, as illustrated in Example 11.15.) Hence, the address represented by ptvar will change as a result of this expression. Similarly, the expression (++ptvar). member will cause the value of ptvar to increase by this number of bytes before accessing member. There is some danger in attempting operations like these, because ptvar may no longer point to a structure variable once its value has been altered.

Example 11.23 Here is a variation of the simple C program shown in Example 11.15.

```
#include <stdio.h>

main()    /* determine the size of a structure */
{
    typedef struct {
        int month;
        int day;
        int year;
    } date;

    struct {
        int acct_no;
        char acct_type;
        char name[80];
        float balance;
        date lastpayment;
    } customer, *pt = &customer;

    printf("Number of bytes (dec): %d\n", sizeof *pt);
    printf("Number of bytes (hex): %x\n\n", sizeof *pt);
    printf("Starting address (hex): %x\n", pt);
    printf("Incremented address (hex): %x", ++pt);
}
```

Notice that pt is a pointer variable whose object is the structure variable customer.

The first printf statement causes the number of bytes associated with customer to be displayed as a decimal quantity. The second printf statement displays this same value as a hexadecimal quantity. The third printf statement causes the value of pt (i.e., the starting address of customer) to be displayed in hexadecimal, whereas the fourth printf statement shows what happens when pt is incremented.

Execution of the program causes the following output to be generated:

```
Number of bytes (dec): 93
Number of bytes (hex): 5d

Starting address (hex): f72
Incremented address (hex): fcf
```

Thus, we see that customer requires 93 decimal bytes, which is 5d in hexadecimal. The initial value assigned to pt (i.e., the starting address of customer) is f72, in hexadecimal. When pt is incremented, its value increases by 5d hexadecimal bytes, to fcf.

It is interesting to alter this program by replacing the character array member name[80] with the character pointer *name, and then execute the program. What do you think will happen?

11.5 PASSING STRUCTURES TO A FUNCTION

There are several different ways to pass structure-type information to or from a function. Structure members can be transferred individually, or entire structures can be transferred. The mechanics for carrying out the transfers vary, depending on the type of transfer (individual members or complete structures) and the particular version of C.

Individual structure members can be passed to a function as arguments in the function call, and a single structure member can be returned via the return statement. To do so, each structure member is treated the same way as an ordinary, single-valued variable.

Example 11.24 The skeletal outline of a C program is shown below. This outline makes use of the structure declarations presented earlier.

```
main()

{
      typedef struct  {                    /* structure declaration */
            int month;
            int day;
            int year;
      }  date;

      struct  {                            /* structure declaration */
            int acct_no;
            char acct_type;
            char name[80];
            float balance;
            date lastpayment;
      }  customer;

      float adjust(char name[], int acct_no, float balance);    /* funct decl */

      ...

      customer.balance = adjust(customer.name, customer.acct_no, customer.balance);

      ...

}
```

```
float adjust(char name[], int acct_no, float balance)

{
    float newbalance;                    /* local variable declaration */

    ...

    newbalance = ...;                    /* adjust value of balance */

    ...

    return(newbalance);
}
```

This program outline illustrates the manner in which structure members can be passed to a function. In particular, customer.name, customer.acct_no and customer.balance are passed to the function adjust. Within adjust, the value assigned to newbalance presumably makes use of the information passed to the function. This value is then returned to main, where it is assigned to the structure member customer.balance.

Notice the function declaration in main. This declaration could also have been written without the argument names, as follows:

```
float adjust(char [], int, float);
```

Some programmers prefer this form, since it avoids the specification of dummy argument names for data items that are actually structure members. We will continue to utilize full function prototypes, however, to take advantage of the resulting error checking.

A complete structure can be transferred to a function by passing a structure-type pointer as an argument. In principle, this is similar to the procedure used to transfer an array to a function. However, we must use explicit pointer notation to represent a structure that is passed as an argument.

It should be understood that a structure passed in this manner will be passed by reference rather than by value. Hence, if any of the structure members are altered within the function, the alterations will be recognized outside the function. Again, we see a direct analogy with the transfer of arrays to a function.

Example 11.25   Consider the simple C program shown below.

```
#include <stdio.h>

typedef struct {
    char *name;
    int acct_no;
    char acct_type;
    float balance;
} record;

main()  /* transfer a structure-type pointer to a function */

{
    void adjust(record *pt);        /* function declaration */

    static record customer = {"Smith", 3333, 'C', 33.33};

    printf("%s %d %c %.2f\n", customer.name, customer.acct_no,
                            customer.acct_type, customer.balance);
    adjust(&customer);
    printf("%s %d %c %.2f\n", customer.name, customer.acct_no,
                            customer.acct_type, customer.balance);
}
```

```
void adjust(record *pt)                        /* function definition */

{
     pt->name = "Jones";
     pt->acct_no = 9999;
     pt->acct_type = 'R';
     pt->balance = 99.99;
     return;
}
```

This program illustrates the transfer of a structure to a function by passing the structure's address (a pointer) to the function. In particular, customer is a static structure of type record, whose members are assigned an initial set of values. These initial values are displayed when the program begins to execute. The structure's address is then passed to the function adjust, where different values are assigned to the members of the structure.

Within adjust, notice the formal argument declaration that defines pt as a pointer to a structure of type record. Also, notice the empty return statement; nothing is explicitly returned from adjust to main.

Within main, we see that the current values assigned to the members of customer are again displayed after adjust has been accessed. Thus, the program illustrates whether or not the changes made in adjust carry over to the calling portion of the program.

Executing the program results in the following output:

```
Smith 3333 C 33.33
Jones 9999 R 99.99
```

Notice that the values assigned to the members of customer within adjust are recognized within main, as expected.

A pointer to a structure can be returned from a function to the calling portion of the program. This feature may be useful when several structures are passed to a function, but only one structure is returned.

Example 11.26 Locating Customer Records   Here is a simple C program that illustrates how an array of structures is passed to a function, and how a pointer to a particular structure is returned.

Suppose we specify an account number for a particular customer and then locate and display the complete record for that customer. Each customer record will be maintained in a structure, as in the last example. Now, however, the entire set of customer records will be stored in an array called customer. Note that each element of customer will be an independent structure.

The basic strategy will be to enter an account number, and then transfer both the account number and the array of records to a function called search. Within search, the specified account number will be compared with the account number that is stored within each customer record until a match is found, or until the entire list of records has been searched. If a match is found, a pointer to that array element (the structure containing the desired customer record) is returned to main and the contents of the record are displayed.

If a match is not found after searching the entire array, then the function returns a value of NULL (zero) to main. The program then displays an error message requesting that the user re-enter the account number. This overall search will continue until a value of zero is entered for the account number.

The complete program is shown below.

```
#include <stdio.h>

#define N   3
#define NULL 0

typedef struct {
     char *name;
     int acct_no;
     char acct_type;
     float balance;
}  record;
```

```
main()

/* find a customer record that corresponds to a specified account number */

{
    static record customer[N] = {
                                  {"Smith", 3333, 'C', 33.33},
                                  {"Jones", 6666, 'O', 66.66},
                                  {"Brown", 9999, 'D', 99.99}
                            };                        /* array of structures */

    int acctn;                                      /* variable declaration */
    record *pt;                                     /* pointer declaration */
    record *search(record table[], int acctn);     /* function declaration */

    printf("Customer Account Locator\n");
    printf("To END, enter 0 for the account number\n");
    printf("\nAccount no.: ");                      /* enter first account number */
    scanf("%d", &acctn);

    while (acctn != 0)   {
        pt = search(customer, acctn);

        if (pt != NULL)   {                   /* found a match */
            printf("\nName: %s\n", pt->name);
            printf("Account no.: %d\n", pt->acct_no);
            printf("Account type: %c\n", pt->acct_type);
            printf("Balance: %.2f\n", pt->balance);
        }
        else
            printf("\nERROR - Please try again\n");

        printf("\nAccount no.: ");             /* enter next account number */
        scanf("%d", &acctn);
    }
}


record *search(record table[N], int acctn)      /* function definition */

/* accept an array of structures and an account number,
   return a pointer to a particular structure (an array element)
   if the account number matches a member of that structure */

{
    int count;

    for (count = 0; count < N; ++count)
        if (table[count].acct_no == acctn)          /* found a match */
            return(&table[count]);    /* return pointer to array element */

    return(NULL);
}
```

Notice that `customer` is an array of structures of type `record` and `pt` is a pointer to a structure of this same type. Also, `search` is a function that accepts two arguments and returns a pointer to a structure of type `record`. The arguments are an array of structures of type `record` and an integer quantity, respectively. Within `search`, the quantity returned is either the address of an array element or NULL (zero).

The array size is expressed in terms of the symbolic constant N. For this simple example we have selected a value of N = 3. That is, we are storing only three sample records within the array. In a more realistic example, N would have a much greater value.

Finally, it should be mentioned that there are much better ways to search through a set of records than examining each record sequentially. We have selected this simple, though inefficient, procedure in order to concentrate on the mechanics of transferring structures between `main` and its subordinate function `search`.

Shown below is a typical dialog that might result from executing the program. The user's responses are underlined, as usual.

```
Customer Account Locator
To END, enter 0 for the account number

Account no.: 3333

Name: Smith
Account no.: 3333
Account type: C
Balance: 33.33

Account no.: 9999

Name: Brown
Account no.: 9999
Account type: D
Balance: 99.99

Account no.: 666

ERROR - Please try again

Account no.: 6666

Name: Jones
Account no.: 6666
Account type: O
Balance: 66.66

Account no.: 0
```

Most newer versions of C permit an entire structure to be transferred directly to a function as an argument and to be returned directly from a function via the `return` statement. (Notice the contrast with arrays, which *cannot* be returned via the `return` statement.) These features are included in the new ANSI standard.

When a structure is passed directly to a function, the transfer is by value rather than by reference. This is consistent with other direct (nonpointer) transfers in C. Therefore, if any of the structure members are altered within the function, the alterations *will not* be recognized outside of the function. However, if the altered structure is returned to the calling portion of the program, then the changes *will* be recognized within this broader scope.

Example 11.27 In Example 11.25 we saw a program that transferred a structure-type pointer to a function. Two different `printf` statements within `main` illustrated that transfers of this type are by reference, that is, alterations made to the structure within the function are recognized within main. A similar program is shown below. The current program, however, transfers a complete structure, rather than a structure-type pointer, to the function.

```c
#include <stdio.h>

typedef struct {
    char *name;
    int acct_no;
    char acct_type;
    float balance;
} record;

main()   /* transfer a structure to a function */

{
    void adjust(record customer);           /* function declaration */

    static record customer = {"Smith", 3333, 'C', 33.33};

    printf("%s %d %c %.2f\n", customer.name, customer.acct_no,
                              customer.acct_type, customer.balance);
    adjust(customer);
    printf("%s %d %c %.2f\n", customer.name, customer.acct_no,
                              customer.acct_type, customer.balance);
}


void adjust(record cust)           /* function defintion */

{
    cust.name = "Jones";
    cust.acct_no = 9999;
    cust.acct_type = 'R';
    cust.balance = 99.99;
    return;
}
```

Notice that the function adjust now accepts a structure of type record as an argument, rather than a pointer to a structure of type record, as in Example 11.25. Nothing is returned from adjust to main in either program.
When the program is executed, the following output is obtained:

```
Smith 3333 C 33.33
Smith 3333 C 33.33
```

Thus, the new assignments made within adjust are not recognized within main. This is expected, since the transfer of the structure customer from main to adjust is by value rather than by reference. (Compare with the output shown in Example 11.25.)
Now suppose we modify this program so that the altered structure is returned from adjust to main. Here is the modified program.

```c
#include <stdio.h>

typedef struct {
    char *name;
    int acct_no;
    char acct_type;
    float balance;
} record;
```

```
main()   /* transfer a structure to a function and return the structure */

{
    record adjust(record customer);        /* function declaration */

    static record customer = {"Smith", 3333, 'C', 33.33};

    printf("%s %d %c %.2f\n", customer.name, customer.acct_no,
                              customer.acct_type, customer.balance);
    customer = adjust(customer);
    printf("%s %d %c %.2f\n", customer.name, customer.acct_no,
                              customer.acct_type, customer.balance);
}


record adjust(record cust)      /* function defintion */

{
    cust.name = "Jones";
    cust.acct_no = 9999;
    cust.acct_type = 'R';
    cust.balance = 99.99;
    return(cust);
}
```

Notice that adjust now returns a structure of type record to main. The return statement is modified accordingly.

Executing this program results in the following output:

```
Smith 3333 C 33.33
Jones 9999 R 99.99
```

Thus, the alterations made within adjust are now recognized within main. This is expected, since the altered structure is now returned directly to the calling portion of the program. (Compare this with the output shown in Example 11.25 and the output shown earlier in this example.)

Most versions of C allow complicated data structures to be transferred freely between functions. We have already seen examples involving the transfer of individual structure members, entire structures, pointers to structures and arrays of structures. As a practical matter, however, there are some limitations on the complexity of data structures that can easily be transferred to or from a function. In particular, some compilers may have difficulty executing programs that involve complex data structure transfers, because of certain memory restrictions. Beginning programmers should be aware of these limitations, though the details of this topic are beyond the scope of the current text.

Example 11.28   Updating Customer Records   Example 11.14 presented a simple customer billing system illustrating the use of structures to maintain and update customer records. In that example the customer records were stored within a global (external) array of structures. We now consider two variations of that program. In each new program the array of structures is maintained locally, within main. The individual array elements (i.e., individual customer records) are transferred back and forth between functions, as required.

In the first program, complete structures are transferred between the functions. In particular, the function readinput allows information defining each customer record to be entered into the computer. When an entire record has been entered, the corresponding structure is returned to main, where it is stored within the 100-element array called customer and adjusted for the proper account type. After all the records have been entered and adjusted, they are transferred individually to the function writeoutput, where certain information is displayed for each customer.

Here is the entire program.

```
#include <stdio.h>

/* update a series of customer accounts (simplified billing system) */

/* maintain the customer accounts as an array of structures,
   transfer complete structures to and from functions            */

typedef struct  {
    int month;
    int day;
    int year;
}  date;

typedef struct  {
    char name[80];
    char street[80];
    char city[80];
    int acct_no;               /* (positive integer) */
    char acct_type;            /* C (current), O (overdue), or D (delinquent) */
    float oldbalance;          /* (nonnegative quantity) */
    float newbalance;          /* (nonnegative quantity) */
    float payment;             /* (nonnegative quantity) */
    date lastpayment;
}  record;


main()

/* read customer accounts, process each account, and display output */

{
    int i, n;                       /* variable declaration */
    record customer[100];           /* array declaration (array of structures) */
    record readinput(int i);        /* function declaration */
    void writeoutput(record customer);  /* function declaration */

    printf("CUSTOMER BILLING SYSTEM\n\n");
    printf("How many customers are there? ");
    scanf("%d", &n);

    for (i = 0; i < n; ++i)   {
        customer[i] = readinput(i);

        /* determine account status */

        if (customer[i].payment > 0)
            customer[i].acct_type =
                (customer[i].payment < 0.1 * customer[i].oldbalance) ? 'O' : 'C';
        else
            customer[i].acct_type =
                (customer[i].oldbalance > 0) ? 'D' : 'C';

        /* adjust account balance */

        customer[i].newbalance = customer[i].oldbalance - customer[i].payment;
    }

    for (i = 0; i < n; ++i)
        writeoutput(customer[i]);
}
```

```
record readinput(int i)

/* read input data for a customer */

{
    record customer;

        printf("\nCustomer no. %d\n", i + 1);
        printf("   Name: ");
        scanf(" %[^\n]", customer.name);
        printf("   Street: ");
        scanf(" %[^\n]", customer.street);
        printf("   City: ");
        scanf(" %[^\n]", customer.city);
        printf("   Account number: ");
        scanf("%d", &customer.acct_no);
        printf("   Previous balance: ");
        scanf("%f", &customer.oldbalance);
        printf("   Current payment: ");
        scanf("%f", &customer.payment);
        printf("   Payment date (mm/dd/yyyy): ");
        scanf("%d/%d/%d", &customer.lastpayment.month,
                          &customer.lastpayment.day,
                          &customer.lastpayment.year);
        return(customer);
}


void writeoutput(record customer)

/* write out current information for a customer */

{
    printf("\nName:    %s", customer.name);
    printf("     Account number: %d\n", customer.acct_no);
    printf("Street: %s\n", customer.street);
    printf("City:    %s\n\n", customer.city);
    printf("Old balance: %7.2f", customer.oldbalance);
    printf("   Current payment: %7.2f", customer.payment);
    printf("   New balance: %7.2f\n\n", customer.newbalance);
    printf("Account status: ");

    switch (customer.acct_type)   {
       case 'C':
                printf("CURRENT\n\n");
                break;
       case 'O':
                printf("OVERDUE\n\n");
                break;
       case 'D':
                printf("DELINQUENT\n\n");
                break;
       default:
                printf("ERROR\n\n");
    }
    return;
}
```

The next program is very similar to the previous program. Now, however, the transfers involve pointers to structures rather than the structures themselves. Thus, the structures are now transferred by reference, whereas they were transferred by value in the previous program.

For brevity, this program is outlined rather than listed in its entirety. The missing blocks are identical to the corresponding portions of the previous program.

```
#include <stdio.h>

/* update a series of customer accounts (simplified billing system) */

/* maintain the customer accounts as an array of structures,
   transfer pointers to structures to and from functions         */

/* (structure definitions) */

main()

/* read customer accounts, process each account, and display output */

{
    int i, n;                       /* variable declaration */
    record customer[100];           /* array declaration (array of structures) */
    record *readinput(int i);       /* function declaration */
    void writeoutput(record *cust); /* function declaration */

    ...

    for (i = 0; i < n; ++i)   {
        customer[i] = *readinput(i);

        /* determine account status */

        ...

        /* adjust account balance */

        ...
    }

    for (i = 0; i < n; ++i)
        writeoutput(&customer[i]);
}


record *readinput(int i)

/* read input data for a customer */

{
    record customer;

    /* enter input data */

    return(&customer);
}
```

```
void writeoutput(record *pt)

/* write out current information for a customer */

{
    record customer;

    customer = *pt;

    /* display output data */

    return;
}
```

Both of these programs will behave in the same manner as the program given in Example 11.14 when executed. Because of the complexity of the data structure (i.e., the array of structures, where each structure contains embedded arrays and embedded structures), however, the compiled programs may not be executable with certain compilers. In particular, a stack overflow condition (a type of inadequate memory condition) may be experienced with some compilers.

This problem would not exist if the program were more realistic, that is, if the customer records were stored within a file on an auxiliary storage device, rather than in an array that is stored within the computer's memory. We will discuss this problem in Chap. 12, where we consider the use of data files for situations such as this.

11.6 SELF-REFERENTIAL STRUCTURES

It is sometimes desirable to include within a structure one member that is a pointer to the parent structure type. In general terms, this can be expressed as

```
struct   tag  {
    member 1;
    member 2;
    . . .
    struct   tag *name;
};
```

where *name* refers to the name of a pointer variable. Thus, the structure of type *tag* will contain a member that points to another structure of type *tag*. Such structures are known as *self-referential* structures.

Example 11.29 A C program contains the following structure declaration:

```
struct   list_element  {
        char item[40];
        struct   list_element   *next;
};
```

This is a structure of type list_element. The structure contains two members: a 40-element character array, called item, and a pointer to another structure of the same type (i.e., a pointer to another structure of type list_element), called next. Therefore, this is a self-referential structure.

Self-referential structures are very useful in applications that involve linked data structures, such as lists and trees. We will see a comprehensive example illustrating the processing of a linked list in Example 11.32. First, however, we present a brief summary of linked data structures.

The basic idea of a linked data structure is that each component within the structure includes a pointer indicating where the next component can be found. Therefore, the relative order of the components can easily be changed, simply the altering the pointers. In addition, individual components can easily be added or deleted, again by altering the pointers. As a result, a linked data structure is not confined to some maximum number of components. Rather, the data structure can expand or contract in size as required.

Example 11.30 Figure 11.3(*a*) illustrates a linked list containing three components. Each component consists of two data items: a string, and a pointer that references the next component within the list. Thus, the first component contains the string `red`, the second contains `green` and the third contains `blue`. The beginning of the list is indicated by a separate pointer, labeled `start`. Also, the end of the list is indicated by a special pointer, called `NULL`.

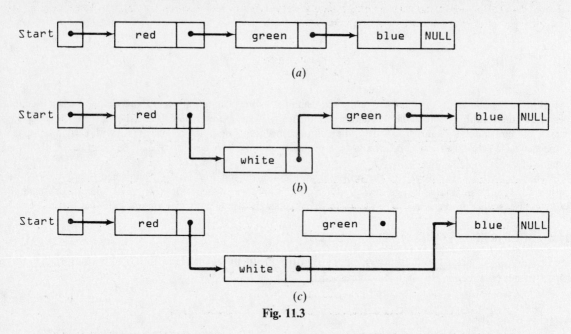

Fig. 11.3

Now let us add another component, whose value is `white`, between `red` and `green`. To do so, we merely change the pointers, as illustrated in Fig. 11.3(*b*). Similarly, if we choose to delete the component whose value is `green`, we simply change the pointer associated with the second component, as shown in Fig. 11.3(*c*).

There are several different kinds of linked data structures, including *linear* linked lists, in which the components are all linked together in some sequential manner; linked lists with multiple pointers, which permit forward and backward traversal within the list; *circular* linked lists, which have no beginning and no end; and *trees*, in which the components are arranged hierarchically. We have already seen an illustration of a linear linked list in Example 11.30. Other kinds of linked lists are illustrated in the next example.

Example 11.31 In Fig. 11.4 we see a linear linked list similar to that shown in Fig. 11.3(*a*). Now, however, we see that there are *two* pointers associated with each component: a forward pointer and a backward pointer. This double set of pointers allows us to traverse the list in either direction, from beginning to end, or from end to beginning.

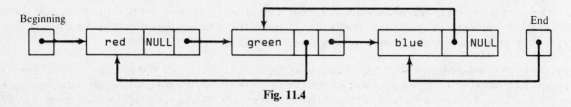

Fig. 11.4

Now consider the list shown in Fig. 11.5. This list is similar to that shown in Fig. 11.3(*a*), except that the last data item (`blue`) points to the first data item (`red`). Hence, this list has no beginning and no end. Such lists are referred to as *circular lists*.

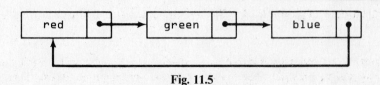

Fig. 11.5

Finally, in Fig. 11.6(*a*) we see an example of a *tree*. Trees consist of nodes and branches, arranged in some hierarchical manner, which indicates a corresponding hierarchical structure within the data. (A *binary tree* is a tree in which every node has no more than two branches.)

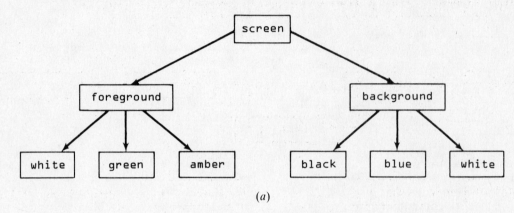

(*a*)

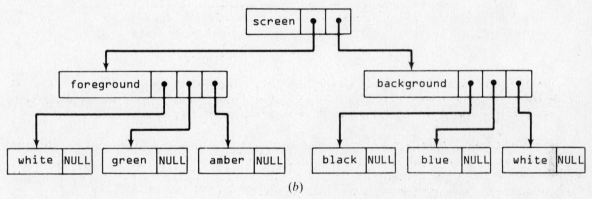

(*b*)

Fig. 11.6

In Fig. 11.6(*a*) the *root node* has the value `screen`, and the associated branches lead to the nodes whose values are `foreground` and `background`, respectively. Similarly, the branches associated with `foreground` lead to the nodes whose values are `white`, `green` and `amber`, and the branches associated with `background` lead to the nodes whose values are `black`, `blue` and `white`.

Figure 11.6(*b*) illustrates the manner in which pointers are used to construct the tree.

Self-referential structures are ideally suited for applications involving linked data structures. Each structure will represent a single component (i.e., one node) within the linked data structure. The self-referential pointer will indicate the next component's location.

Example 11.32 Processing a Linked List We now present an interactive C program that allows us to create a linear linked list, add new components to the linked list, or delete existing components from the linked list. Each component will consist of a string and a pointer to the next component. The program will be menu driven to facilitate its use by nonprogrammers. We will include a provision to display the list after the selection of any menu item (i.e., after any change has been made to the list).

This program is somewhat more complex than the preceding example programs. It utilizes both recursion (see Sec. 7.7) and dynamic memory allocation (see Examples 10.14, 10.22, 10.24 and 10.26).

The program is shown below in its entirety. Following the program, each individual function is discussed in some detail.

```
#include <stdio.h>
#include <stdlib.h>

#define  NULL  0

/* menu-driven program to process a linked list of strings */

struct list_element  {
        char item[40];                  /* data item for this node */
        struct list_element *next;      /* pointer to the next node */
};

typedef struct list_element node;       /* structure type declaration */

main()

{
    node *start;                        /* pointer to beginning of list*/
    int choice;                         /* local variable declaration */

    int menu(void);                     /* function declaration */
    void create(node *pt);              /* function declaration */
    node *insert(node *pt);             /* function declaration */
    node *delete(node *pt);             /* function declaration */
    void display(node *pt);             /* function declaration */

    do  {
        choice = menu();

        switch (choice)  {

        case 1:     /* create the linked list */
            start = (node *) malloc(sizeof(node));  /* allocate space
                                                for first node */
            create(start);
            printf("\n");
            display(start);
            continue;

        case 2:     /* add one component */
            start = insert(start);
            printf("\n");
            display(start);
            continue;

        case 3:     /* delete one component */
            start = delete(start);
            printf("\n");
            display(start);
            continue;

        default:    /* terminate computation */
            printf("End of computation\n");
        }
    }
    while (choice != 4);
}
```

```c
int menu(void)        /* generate the main menu */

{
    int choice;

    do  {
            printf("\nMain menu:\n");
            printf("  1 - CREATE the linked list\n");
            printf("  2 - ADD a component\n");
            printf("  3 - DELETE a component\n");
            printf("  4 - END\n");
            printf("Please enter your choice (1, 2, 3 or 4) -> ");
            scanf("%d", &choice);
            if (choice < 1 || choice > 4)
                printf("\nERROR - Please try again\n");
    }
    while (choice < 1 || choice > 4);
    printf("\n");
    return(choice);
}


void create(node *record)      /* create a linked list */

/* argument points to the current node */

{
    printf("Data item (type \'END\' when finished): ");
    scanf(" %[^\n]", record->item);

    if (strcmpi(record->item, "END") == 0)
            record->next = NULL;

    else {
            /* allocate space for next node */
            record->next = (node *) malloc(sizeof(node));

            /* create the next node */
            create(record->next);
    }
    return;
}


void display(node *record)      /* display the linked list */

/* argument points to the current node*/

{
    if (record->next != NULL)  {
        printf("%s\n", record->item;     /* display this data item */
        display(record->next);           /* get the next data item */
    }
    return;
}
```

```
node *insert(node *first)      /* add one component to the linked list
                                  return pointer to beginning of modified list */

/* argument points to the first node */

{
    node *locate(node *, char[]);    /* function declaration */
    node *newrecord;                 /* pointer to new node */
    node *tag;                       /* pointer to node BEFORE target node */
    char newitem[40];                /* new data item */
    char target[40];                 /* data item following the new entry */

    printf("New data item: ");
    scanf(" %[^\n]", newitem);
    printf("Place before (type \'END\' if last): ");
    scanf(" %[^\n]", target);

    if (strcmpi(first->item, target) == 0)   {
        /* new node is first in list */

        /* allocate space for the new node */
        newrecord = (node *) malloc(sizeof(node));

        /* assign the new data item to newrecord->item */
        strcpy(newrecord->item, newitem);

        /* assign the current pointer to newrecord->next */
        newrecord->next = first;

        /* new pointer becomes the beginning of the list */
        first = newrecord;
    }

    else   {
        /* insert new node after an existing node */

        /* locate the node PRECEDING the target node */
        tag = locate(first, target);

        if (tag == NULL)
            printf("\nMatch not found - Please try again\n");
        else   {
            /* allocate space for the new node */
            newrecord = (node *) malloc(sizeof(node));

            /* assign the new data item to newrecord->item */
            strcpy(newrecord->item, newitem);

            /* assign the next pointer to newrecord->next */
            newrecord->next = tag->next;

            /* assign the new pointer to tag->next */
            tag->next = newrecord;
        }
    }
    return(first);
}
```

```
node *locate(node *record, char target[])       /* locate a node */

/* return a pointer to the node BEFORE the target node
   first argument points to the current node
   second argument is the target string              */

{
    if (strcmpi(record->next->item, target) == 0)      /* found a match */
        return(record);
    else
        if (record->next->next == NULL)                /* end of list */
            return(NULL);
        else
            locate(record->next, target);              /* try next node */
}



node *delete(node *first)     /*delete one component from the linked list
                                return pointer to beginning of modified list */

/* argument points to the first node */

{
    node *locate(node *, char[]);   /* function declaration */
    node *tag;                      /* pointer to node BEFORE target node */
    node *temp;                     /* temporary pointer */
    char target[40];                /* data item to be deleted */

    printf("Data item to be deleted: ");
    scanf(" %[^\n]", target);

    if (strcmpi(first->item, target) == 0)   {
        /* delete the first node */

        /* mark the node following the target node */
        temp = first->next;

        /* free space for the target node */
        free(first);

        /* adjust the pointer to the first node */
        first = temp;
    }
    else
        /* delete a data item other than the first */

        /* locate the node PRECEDING the target node */
        tag = locate(first, target);

        if (tag == NULL)
            printf("\nMatch not found - Please try again\n");
        else   {
            /* mark the node following the target node */
            temp = tag->next->next;

            /* free space for the target node */
            free(tag->next);

            /* adjust the link to the next node */
            tag->next = temp;
        }
    return(first);
}
```

The program begins with the usual #include statements and a definition of the symbolic constant NULL to represent the value Ø. Following these statements is a declaration for the self-referential structure list_element. This structure declaration is the same as that shown in Example 11.29. Thus, list_element identifies a structure consisting of two members: a 40-element character array (item), and a pointer (next) to another structure of the same type. The character array will represent a string, and the pointer will identify the location of the next component in the linked list. Finally, node is defined as a data type, identifying structures having composition list_element.

Note that these declarations are external. They will therefore be recognized by all of the functions that make up the program.

The main function consists of several declarations, followed by a do - while loop that permits repetitious execution of the entire process. Within the declarations, notice that start is a pointer to a structure of type node. This pointer will indicate the beginning of the linked list. The remaining declarations identify the integer variable choice, which represents a menu selection, and several additional functions that are called from main.

The do - while loop calls the function menu, which generates the main menu, and returns a value for choice, indicating the user's menu selection. A switch statement then calls the appropriate functions, in accordance with the user's selection. Notice that the program will stop executing if choice is assigned a value of 4.

If choice is assigned a value of 1, indicating that a new linked list will be created, a block of memory must be allocated for the first data item before calling the function create. This is accomplished using dynamic memory allocation, as follows:

```
start = (node *) malloc(sizeof(node));
```

This statement reserves a block of memory whose size (in bytes) is sufficient for one node. The statement returns a pointer to a structure of type node. This pointer indicates the beginning of the linked list. Thus, it is passed to create as an argument.

Note that the type cast (node *) is required as a part of the memory allocation statement. Without it, the malloc function would return a pointer to a char rather than a pointer to a structure of type node. (See Sec. 10.4, and especially Example 10.14, for more information about dynamic memory allocation.)

Now consider the function menu, which is used to generate the main menu. This function accepts a value for choice after the menu has been generated. The only permissible values for choice are 1, 2, 3 or 4. An error trap, in the form of a do - while statement, causes an error message to be displayed and a new menu to be generated if a value other than 1, 2, 3 or 4 is entered in response to the menu.

The linked list is created by the function create. This is a recursive function that accepts a pointer to the current node (i.e., the node that is being created) as an argument. The pointer variable is called record.

The function begins by prompting for the current data item, i.e., the string that is to reside in the current node. If the user enters the string END (in either upper- or lowercase), then NULL is assigned to the pointer that indicates the location of the next node, and the recursion stops. If the user enters any string other than END, however, then memory is allocated for the next node via the malloc function and the function calls itself recursively. Thus, the recursion will continue until the user has entered END for one of the data items.

Once the linked list has been created, it is displayed via the function display. This function is called from main, after the call to create. Notice that display accepts a pointer to the current node as an argument. The function then executes recursively, until it receives a pointer whose value is NULL. The recursion therefore causes the entire linked list to be displayed.

Now consider the function insert, which is used to add a new component (i.e., a new node) to the linked list. This function asks the user where the insertion is to occur. Note that the function accepts a pointer to the beginning of the list as an argument, and then returns a pointer to the beginning of the list, after the insertion has been made. These two pointers will be the same unless the insertion is made at the beginning of the list.

Notice that insert does not execute recursively. It first prompts for the new data item (newitem), followed by a prompt for the existing data item that will follow the new data item (the existing data item is called target). If the insertion is to be made at the beginning of the list, then memory is allocated for the new node, newitem is assigned to the first member and the pointer originally indicating the beginning of the linked list (first) is assigned to the second member. The pointer returned by malloc, which indicates the beginning of the new node, is then assigned to first. Hence, the beginning of the new node becomes the beginning of the entire list.

If the insertion is to be made after an existing node, then function locate is called to determine the location of the insertion. This function returns a pointer to the node *preceding* the target node. The value returned is assigned to the pointer tag. Hence, tag points to the node which will precede the new node. If locate cannot find a match between the value entered for target and an existing data item, then it will return NULL.

If a match is found by `locate`, then the insertion is made in the following manner: memory is allocated for the new node, `newitem` is assigned to the first member of `newrecord` (i.e., to `newrecord->item`) and the pointer to the target node (i.e., `tag->next`) is assigned to the second member of `newrecord` (i.e., `newrecord->next`). The pointer returned by `malloc`, which indicates the beginning of the new node, is then assigned to `tag->next`. Hence, the pointer in the preceding node will point to the new node, and the pointer in the new node will point to the target node.

Now consider the function `locate`. This is a simple recursive function that accepts a pointer to the current node and the target string as arguments, and returns a pointer to the node that *precedes* the current node. Therefore, if the data item in the node following the current node matches the target string, the function will return the pointer to the current node. Otherwise, one of two possible actions will be taken. If the pointer in the node following the current node is `NULL`, indicating the end of the linked list, a match has not been found. Therefore, the function will return `NULL`. But, if the pointer in the node following the current node is something other than `NULL`, the function will call itself recursively, thus testing the next node for a match.

Finally, consider the function `delete`, which is used to delete an existing component (i.e., an existing node) from the linked list. This function is similar to `insert`, though somewhat simpler. It accepts a pointer to the beginning of the linked list as an argument and returns a pointer to the beginning of the linked list after the deletion has been made.

The `delete` function begins by prompting for the data item to be deleted (`target`). If this is the first data item, then the pointers are adjusted as follows: the pointer indicating the location of the second node is temporarily assigned to the pointer variable `temp`; the memory utilized by the first node is freed, using the library function `free`; and the location of the second node (which is now the first node, because of the deletion) is assigned to `first`. Hence, the beginning of the (former) second node becomes the beginning of the entire list.

If the data item to be deleted is not the first data item in the list, then `locate` is called to determine the location of the deletion. This function will return a pointer to the node *preceding* the target node. The value returned is assigned to the pointer variable `temp`. If this value is `NULL`, a match cannot be found. An error message is then generated, requesting that the user try again.

If `locate` returns a value other than `NULL`, the target node is deleted in the following manner: the pointer to the node following the target node is temporarily assigned to the pointer variable `temp`; the memory utilized by the target node is then freed, using the library function `free`; and the value of `temp` is then assigned to `tag->next`. Hence, the pointer in the preceding node will point to the node following the target node.

Let us now utilize this program to create a linked list containing the following cities: Boston, Chicago, Denver, New York, Pittsburgh and San Francisco. We will then add several cities and delete several cities, thus illustrating all of the program's features. We will maintain the list of cities alphabetically throughout the exercise. (We could, of course, have the computer do the sorting for us, though this would further complicate an already complex program.)

The entire interactive session is shown below. As usual, the user's responses have been underlined.

```
Main menu:
  1 - CREATE the linked list
  2 - ADD a component
  3 - DELETE a component
  4 - END
Please enter your choice (1, 2, 3 or 4) -> 1

Data item (type 'END' when finished): Boston
Data item (type 'END' when finished): Chicago
Data item (type 'END' when finished): Denver
Data item (type 'END' when finished): New York
Data item (type 'END' when finished): Pittsburgh
Data item (type 'END' when finished): San Francisco
Data item (type 'END' when finished): end

Boston
Chicago
Denver
New York
Pittsburgh
San Francisco
```

```
Main menu:
  1 - CREATE the linked list
  2 - ADD a component
  3 - DELETE a component
  4 - END
Please enter your choice (1, 2, 3 or 4) -> 2

New data item: Atlanta
Place before (type 'END' if last): Boston

Atlanta
Boston
Chicago
Denver
New York
Pittsburgh
San Francisco

Main menu:
  1 - CREATE the linked list
  2 - ADD a component
  3 - DELETE a component
  4 - END
Please enter your choice (1, 2, 3 or 4) -> 2

New data item: Seattle
Place before (type 'END' if last): end

Atlanta
Boston
Chicago
Denver
New York
Pittsburgh
San Francisco
Seattle

Main menu:
  1 - CREATE the linked list
  2 - ADD a component
  3 - DELETE a component
  4 - END
Please enter your choice (1, 2, 3 or 4) -> 3

Data item to be deleted: New York

Atlanta
Boston
Chicago
Denver
Pittsburgh
San Francisco
Seattle

Main menu:
  1 - CREATE the linked list
  2 - ADD a component
  3 - DELETE a component
  4 - END
Please enter your choice (1, 2, 3 or 4) -> 2
```

```
New data item: Washington
Place before (type 'END' if last): Williamsburg

Match not found - Please try again

Atlanta
Boston
Chicago
Denver
Pittsburgh
San Francisco
Seattle

Main menu:
    1 - CREATE the linked list
    2 - ADD a component
    3 - DELETE a component
    4 - END
Please enter your choice (1, 2, 3 or 4) -> 2

New data item: Washington
Place before (type 'END' if last): end

Atlanta
Boston
Chicago
Denver
Pittsburgh
San Francisco
Seattle
Washington

Main menu:
    1 - CREATE the linked list
    2 - ADD a component
    3 - DELETE a component
    4 - END
Please enter your choice (1, 2, 3 or 4) -> 3

Data item to be deleted: Atlanta

Boston
Chicago
Denver
Pittsburgh
San Francisco
Seattle
Washington

Main menu:
    1 - CREATE the linked list
    2 - ADD a component
    3 - DELETE a component
    4 - END
Please enter your choice (1, 2, 3 or 4) -> 2

New data item: Dallas
Place before (type 'END' if last): Denver
```

```
Boston
Chicago
Dallas
Denver
Pittsburgh
San Francisco
Seattle
Washington

Main menu:
   1 - CREATE the linked list
   2 - ADD a component
   3 - DELETE a component
   4 - END
Please enter your choice (1, 2, 3 or 4) -> 3

Data item to be deleted: Miami

Match not found - Please try again

Boston
Chicago
Dallas
Denver
Pittsburgh
San Francisco
Seattle
Washington

Main menu:
   1 - CREATE the linked list
   2 - ADD a component
   3 - DELETE a component
   4 - END
Please enter your choice (1, 2, 3 or 4) -> 3

Data item to be deleted: Washington

Boston
Chicago
Dallas
Denver
Pittsburgh
San Francisco
Seattle

Main menu:
   1 - CREATE the linked list
   2 - ADD a component
   3 - DELETE a component
   4 - END
Please enter your choice (1, 2, 3 or 4) -> 5

ERROR - Please try again
```

```
Main menu:
  1 - CREATE the linked list
  2 - ADD a component
  3 - DELETE a component
  4 - END
Please enter your choice (1, 2, 3 or 4) -> 4

End of computation
```

11.7 UNIONS

Unions, like structures, contain members whose individual data types may differ from one another. However, the members that compose a union all share the same storage area within the computer's memory, whereas each member within a structure is assigned its own unique storage area. Thus, unions are used to conserve memory. They are useful for applications involving multiple members, where values need not be assigned to all of the members at any one time.

Within a union, the bookkeeping required to store members whose data types are different (having different memory requirements) is handled automatically by the compiler. However, the user must keep track of what type of information is stored at any given time. An attempt to access the wrong type of information will produce meaningless results.

In general terms, the composition of a union may be defined as

```
union  tag  {
    member 1;
    member 2;
    . . .
    member m;
};
```

where union is a required keyword and the other terms have the same meaning as in a structure definition (see Sec. 11.1). Individual union variables can then be declared as

storage-class union *tag variable 1, variable 2, . . ., variable n;*

where *storage-class* is an optional storage class specifier, union is a required keyword, *tag* is the name that appeared in the union definition, and *variable 1, variable 2, . . ., variable n* are union variables of type *tag*.

The two declarations may be combined, just as we did with structures. Thus, we can write

```
storage-class  union  tag  {
          member 1;
          member 2;
          . . .
          member m;
}  variable 1,  variable 2,  . . .,  variable n;
```

The *tag* is optional in this type of declaration.

Example 11.33 A C program contains the following union declaration:

```
union  id  {
    char color[12];
    int size;
}  shirt, blouse;
```

Here we have two union variables, `shirt` and `blouse`, of type `id`. Each variable can represent either a 12-character string (`color`) or an integer quantity (`size`) at any one time.

The 12-character string will require more storage area within the computer's memory than the integer quantity. Therefore, a block of memory large enough for the 12-character string will be allocated to each union variable. The compiler will automatically distinguish between the 12-character array and the integer quantity within the given block of memory, as required.

A union may be a member of a structure, and a structure may be a member of a union. Moreover, structures and unions may be freely mixed with arrays.

Example 11.34 A C program contains the following declarations:

```
union  id  {
    char color[12];
    int size;
};

struct  clothes  {
    char manufacturer[20];
    float cost;
    union id description;
} shirt, blouse;
```

Now `shirt` and `blouse` are structure variables of type `clothes`. Each variable will contain the following members: a string (`manufacturer`), a floating-point quantity (`cost`), and a union (`description`). The union may represent either a string (`color`), or an integer quantity (`size`).

Another way to declare the structure variables `shirt` and `blouse` is to combine the above two declarations, as follows:

```
struct  clothes  {
    char manufacturer[20];
    float cost;
    union  {
        char color[12];
        int size;
    } description;
} shirt, blouse;
```

This declaration is more concise, though perhaps less straightforward than the original declarations.

An individual union member can be accessed in the same manner as an individual structure member, using the operators . and ->. Thus, if *variable* is a union variable, then *variable.member* refers to a member of the union. Similarly, if *ptvar* is a pointer variable that points to a union, then *ptvar->member* refers to a member of that union.

Example 11.35 Consider the simple C program shown below.

```
#include <stdio.h>

main()

{
    union id  {
        char color;
        int size;
    };
```

```
        struct  {
            char manufacturer[20];
            float cost;
            union id description;
        } shirt, blouse;

        printf("%d\n", sizeof(union id));

        /* assign a value to color */
        shirt.description.color = 'w';
        printf("%c %d\n", shirt.description.color, shirt.description.size);


        /* assign a value to size */
        shirt.description.size = 12;
        printf("%c %d\n", shirt.description.color, shirt.description.size);
}
```

This program contains declarations similar to those shown in Example 11.34. Notice, however, that the first member of the union is now a single character rather than the 12-character array shown in the previous example. This change is made to simplify the assignment of appropriate values to the union members.

Following the declarations and the initial `printf` statement, we see that the character `'w'` is assigned to the union member `shirt.description.color`. Note that the other union member, `shirt.description.size`, will not have a meaningful value. The values of both union members are then displayed.

We then assign the value 12 to `shirt.description.size`, thus overwriting the value of `shirt.description.color`. The values of both union members are then displayed once more.

Executing the program results in the following output:

```
2
w -24713
@ 12
```

The first line indicates that the union is allocated 2 bytes of memory, to accommodate an integer quantity. In line two, the first data item (w) is meaningful, but the second (-24713) is not. In line three, the first data item (@) is meaningless, but the second data item (12) is meaningful. Thus, each line of output contains one meaningful value, in accordance with the assignment statement preceding each `printf` statement.

A union variable can be initialized, provided its storage class is either `external` or `static`. Remember, however, that only one member of a union can be assigned a value at any one time. Most compilers will accept an initial value for only one union member, and they will assign this value to the first member within the union.

Example 11.36 Shown below is a simple C program that includes the assignment of initial values to a structure variable.

```
#include <stdio.h>

main()

{
    union id  {
        char color[12];
        int size;
    };

    struct clothes {
        char manufacturer[20];
        float cost;
        union id description;
    };
```

```
      static struct clothes shirt = {"American", 25.00, "white"};

      printf("%d\n", sizeof(union id));
      printf("%s %5.2f ", shirt.manufacturer, shirt.cost);
      printf("%s %d\n", shirt.description.color, shirt.description.size);

      shirt.description.size = 12;
      printf("%s %5.2f ", shirt.manufacturer, shirt.cost);
      printf("%s %d\n", shirt.description.color, shirt.description.size);
}
```

Notice that `shirt` is a static structure variable of type `clothes`. One of its members is `description`, which is a union of type `id`. This union consists of two members: a 12-character array and an integer quantity.

The structure variable declaration includes the assignment of the following initial values: "American" is assigned to the array member `shirt.manufacturer`, 25.00 is assigned to the integer member `shirt.cost`, and "white" is assigned to the union member `shirt.description.color`. Notice that the second union member within the structure, i.e., `shirt.description.size`, remains unspecified.

The program first displays the size of the memory block allocated to the union, followed by the value of each member of `shirt`. Then 12 is assigned to `shirt.description.size` and the value of each member of `shirt` is again displayed.

When the program is executed, the following output is generated:

```
12
American 25.00 white 26743
American 25.00 ~ 12
```

The first line indicates that 12 bytes of memory are allocated to the union, in order to accommodate the 12-character array. The second line shows the values initially assigned to `shirt.manufacturer`, `shirt.cost` and `shirt.description.color`. The value shown for `shirt.description.size` is meaningless. In the third line we see that `shirt.manufacturer` and `shirt.cost` are unchanged. Now, however, the reassignment of the union members causes `shirt.description.color` to have a meaningless value, but `shirt.description.size` shows the newly assigned value of 12.

In all other respects, unions are processed in the same manner, and with the same restrictions, as structures. Thus, individual union members can be processed as though they were ordinary variables of the same data type, and pointers to unions can be passed to or from functions (by reference). Moreover, most of the newer C compilers permit an entire union to be assigned to another, provided both unions have the same composition. These compilers also permit entire unions to be passed to or from functions (by value), as indicated by the new ANSI standard.

Example 11.37   Raising a Number to a Power   This example is a bit contrived, though it does illustrate how a union can be used to pass information to a function. The problem is to raise a number to a power. Thus, we wish to evaluate the formula $y = x^n$, where x and y are floating-point values and n can be either integer or floating point.

If n is an integer, then y can be evaluated by multiplying x by itself an appropriate number of times. For example, the quantity x^3 could be expressed in terms of the product $(x)(x)(x)$. If n is a floating-point value, then we can write $\log y = n \log x$, or $y = e^{(n \log x)}$. In the latter case, x must be a positive quantity, since we cannot take the log of zero or the log of a negative quantity.

Now let us introduce the following declarations:

```
typedef union  {
    float fexp;            /* floating-point exponent */
    int nexp;              /* integer exponent */
} nvals;

typedef struct  {
    float x;               /* value to be raised to a power */
    char flag;             /* 'f' if exponent is floating-point,
                              'i' if exponent is integer */
    nvals exp;             /* union containing exponent */
} values;

values a;
```

Thus, nvals is a user-defined union type, consisting of the floating-point member fexp and the integer member nexp. These two members represent the two possible types of exponents in the expression $y = x^n$. Similarly, values is a user-defined structure type, consisting of a floating-point member x, a character member flag and a union of type nvals called exp. Note that flag indicates the type of exponent currently represented by the union. If flag represents 'i', then the union will represent an integer exponent (nexp will currently be assigned a value); and if flag represents 'f', then the union will represent a floating-point exponent (fexp will currently be assigned a value). Finally, we see that a is a structure variable of type values.

With these declarations, it is easy to write a function that will evaluate the formula $y = x^n$, as follows:

```
float power(values a)   /* carry out the exponentiation */

{
    int i;
    float y = a.x;

    if (a.flag == 'i') {            /* integer exponent */
        if (a.exp.nexp == 0)
            y = 1.0;                /* zero exponent */
        else {
            for (i = 1; i < abs(a.exp.nexp); ++i)
                y *= a.x;
            if (a.exp.nexp < 0)
                y = 1./y;           /* negative integer exponent */
        }
    }
    else                            /* floating-point exponent */
        y = exp(a.exp.fexp * log(a.x));

    return(y);
}
```

This function accepts a structure variable (a) of type values as an argument. The method used to carry out the calculations depends on the value assigned to a.flag. If a.flag is assigned the character 'i', then the exponentiation is carried out by multiplying a.x by itself an appropriate number of times. Otherwise, the exponentiation is carried out using the formula $y = e^{(n \log x)}$. Notice that the function contains corrections to accommodate a zero exponent ($y = 1.0$), and for a negative integer exponent.

Let us add a main function which prompts for the values of x and n, determines whether or not n is an integer (by comparing n with its truncated value), assigns appropriate values to a.flag and a.exp, calls power, and then writes out the result. We also include a provision for generating an error message if n is a floating-point exponent and the value of x is less than or equal to zero.

Here is the entire program.

```
#include <stdio.h>
#include <math.h>

typedef union {
    float fexp;         /* floating-point exponent */
    int nexp;           /* integer exponent */
} nvals;

typedef struct {
    float x;            /* value to be raised to a power */
    char flag;          /* 'f' if exponent is floating-point,
                           'i' if exponent is integer */

    nvals exp;          /* union containing exponent */
} values;
```

```
main()    /* program to raise a number to a power */

{
    values a;                    /* structure containing x, flag and fexp/nexp */
    float power(values a);    /* function declaration */
    int i;
    float n, y;

    /* enter input data */
    printf("y = x^n\n\n\nEnter a value for x: ");
    scanf("%f", &a.x);
    printf("Enter a value for n: ");
    scanf("%f", &n);

    /* determine type of exponent */
    i = (int) n;
    a.flag = (i == n) ? 'i' : 'f';
    if (a.flag == 'i')
       a.exp.nexp = i;
    else
       a.exp.fexp = n;

    /* raise x to the appropriate power and display the result */
    if (a.flag == 'f' && a.x <= 0.0)    {
       printf("\nERROR - Cannot raise a nonpositive number to a ");
       printf("floating-point power");
    }
    else {
       y = power(a);
       printf("\ny = %.4f", y);
    }
}


float power(values a)   /* carry out the exponentiation */

{
    int i;
    float y = a.x;

    if (a.flag == 'i') {              /* integer exponent */
       if (a.exp.nexp == 0)
          y = 1.0;                     /* zero exponent */
       else  {
          for (i = 1; i < abs(a.exp.nexp); ++i)
             y *= a.x;
          if (a.exp.nexp < 0)
             y = 1./y;                 /* negative integer exponent */
       }
    }
    else                             /* floating-point exponent */
       y = exp(a.exp.fexp * log(a.x));

    return(y);
}
```

Notice that the union and structure declarations are external to the program functions, but the structure variable a is defined locally within each function.

The program does not execute repetitiously. Several typical dialogs, each representing a separate program execution, are shown below. As usual, the user's responses are underlined.

```
Enter a value for x: 2
Enter a value for n: 3

y = 8.0000

Enter a value for x: -2
Enter a value for n: 3

y = -8.0000

Enter a value for x: 2.2
Enter a value for n: 3.3

y = 13.4895

Enter a value for x: -2.2
Enter a value for n: 3.3

ERROR - Cannot raise a nonpositive number to a floating-point power
```

It should be pointed out that most C compilers include the library function pow, which is used to raise a number to a power. We have used pow in several earlier programming examples (see Examples 5.2, 5.4, 6.20, 8.13 and 10.31). The current program is not meant to replace pow; it is presented only to illustrate the use of a union in a representative programming situation.

Review Questions

11.1 What is a structure? How does a structure differ from an array?

11.2 What is a member? What is the relationship between a member and a structure?

11.3 Describe the syntax for defining the composition of a structure. Can individual members be initialized within a structure type declaration?

11.4 How can structure variables be declared? How do structure variable declarations differ from structure type declarations?

11.5 What is a tag? Must a tag be included in a structure type definition? Must a tag be included in a structure variable declaration? Explain fully.

11.6 Can a structure variable be defined as a member of another structure? Can an array be included as a member of a structure? Can an array have structures as elements?

11.7 How are the members of a structure variable assigned initial values? What restrictions apply to the structure's storage class when initial values are assigned?

11.8 How is an array of structures initialized?

11.9 What is the scope of a member name? What does this imply with respect to the naming of members within different structures?

11.10 How is a structure member accessed? How can a structure member be processed?

11.11 What is the precedence of the period operator? What is its associativity?

11.12 Can the period operator (.) be used with an array of structures? Explain.

11.13 What is the only operation that can be applied to an entire structure in some of the older versions of C? How is this rule modified in the newer, ANSI-compatible versions of the language?

11.14 How can the size of a structure be determined? In what units is the size reported?

11.15 What is the purpose of the typedef feature? How is this feature used in conjunction with structures?

11.16 How is a structure type pointer variable declared? To what does this type of variable point?

11.17 How can an individual structure member be accessed in terms of its corresponding pointer variable?

11.18 What is the precedence of the -> operator? What is its associativity? Compare this with your answers to Question 11.11.

11.19 Suppose a pointer variable points to a structure that contains another structure as a member. How can a member of the embedded structure be accessed?

11.20 Suppose a pointer variable points to a structure that contains an array as a member. How can an element of the embedded array be accessed?

11.21 Suppose a member of a structure is a pointer variable. How can the object of the pointer be accessed in terms of the structure variable name and the member name?

11.22 What happens when a pointer to a structure is incremented? What danger is associated with this type of operation?

11.23 How can an entire structure be passed to a function? Describe fully, both for older and newer versions of C.

11.24 How can an entire structure be returned from a function? Describe fully, both for older and newer versions of C.

11.25 What is a self-referential structure? For what kinds of applications are self-referential structures useful?

11.26 What is the basic idea behind a linked data structure? What advantages are there in the use of linked data structures?

11.27 Summarize several types of commonly used linked data structures.

11.28 What is a union? How does a union differ from a structure?

11.29 For what kinds of applications are unions useful?

11.30 In what sense can unions, structures and arrays be intermixed?

11.31 How is a union member accessed? How can a union member be processed? Compare this with your answers to Question 11.10.

11.32 How is a member of a union variable assigned an initial value? In what way does the initialization of a union variable differ from the initialization of a structure variable?

11.33 Summarize the rules that apply to processing unions. Compare with the rules that apply to processing structures.

Problems

11.34 Define a structure consisting of two floating-point members called real and imaginary. Include the tag complex within the definition.

11.35 Declare the variables x1, x2 and x3 to be structure variables of type complex, as described in the preceding problem.

11.36 Combine the structure definition and the variable declarations described in Problems 11.34 and 11.35 into one declaration.

11.37 Declare a variable x to be a structure variable of type complex, as described in Problem 11.34. Assign the initial values 1.3 and −2.2 to the members x.real and x.imaginary, respectively.

11.38 Declare a pointer variable, px, which points to a structure of type complex, as described in Problem 11.34. Write expressions for the structure members in terms of the pointer variable.

11.39 Declare a one-dimensional, 100-element array called cx whose elements are structures of type complex, as described in Problem 11.34.

11.40 Combine the structure definition and the array declaration, described in Problems 11.34 and 11.39, into one declaration.

11.41 Suppose that cx is a one-dimensional, 100-element array of structures, as described in Problem 11.39. Write expressions for the members of the 18th array element (i.e., element number 17).

11.42 Define a structure that contains the following three members:

(a) an integer quantity called won
(b) an integer quantity called lost
(c) a floating-point quantity called percentage

Include the user-defined data type record within the definition.

11.43 Define a structure that contains the following two members:

(*a*) a 40-element character array called `name`
(*b*) a structure called `stats`, of type `record`, as defined in Problem 11.42

Include the user-defined data type `team` within the definition.

11.44 Declare a variable `t` to be a structure variable of type `team`, as described in Problem 11.43. Write an expression for each member and each submember of `t`.

11.45 Declare a variable `t` to be a structure variable of type `team`, as in Problem 11.44. Now, however, initialize `t` as follows:

```
name : Chicago Bears

won :   14

lost :  2

percentage : 87.5
```

11.46 Write a statement that will display the size of the memory block associated with the variable `t` which was described in Problem 11.44.

11.47 Declare a pointer variable `pt`, which points to a structure of type `team`, as described in Problem 11.43. Write an expression for each member and each submember within the structure.

11.48 Declare a one-dimensional, 48-element array called `league` whose elements are structures of type `team`, as described in Problem 11.43. Write expressions for the name and percentage of the fifth team in the league (i.e., team number 4).

11.49 Define a self-referential structure containing the following three members:

(*a*) a 40-element character array called `name`
(*b*) a structure called `stats`, of type `record`, as defined in Problem 11.42
(*c*) a pointer to another structure of this same type, called `next`

Include the tag `team` within the structure definition. Compare your solution with that of Problem 11.43.

11.50 Declare `pt` to be a pointer to a structure whose composition is described in Problem 11.49. Then write a statement that will allocate an appropriate block of memory, with `pt` pointing to the beginning of the memory block.

11.51 Define a structure of type `hms` that contains three integer members, called `hour`, `minute` and `second`, respectively. Then define a union that contains two members, each a structure of type `hms`. Call the union members `local` and `home`, respectively. Declare a pointer variable called `time` that points to this union.

11.52 Define a union of type `ans` that contains the following three members:

(*a*) an integer quantity called `ians`
(*b*) a floating-point quantity called `fans`
(*c*) a double-precision quantity called `dans`

Then define a structure that contains the following four members:

(*a*) a union of type `ans`, called `answer`
(*b*) a single character called `flag`
(*c*) integer quantities called `a` and `b`

Finally, declare two structure variables, called `x` and `y`, whose composition is as described above.

11.53 Declare a structure variable called `v` whose composition is as described in Problem 11.52. Assign the following initial values within the declaration:

```
answer : 14

flag : 'i'

a : -2

b : 5
```

11.54 Modify the structure definition described in Problem 11.52 so that it contains an additional member, called `next`, which is a pointer to another structure of the same type. (Note that the structure will now be self-referential.) Add a declaration of two variables, called x and px, where x is a structure variable and px is a pointer to a structure variable. Assign the starting address of x to px within the declaration.

11.55 Describe the output generated by each of the following programs. Explain any difference between them.

(a)
```c
#include <stdio.h>

typedef struct {
    char *a;
    char *b;
    char *c;
} colors;

main()

{
    void funct(colors sample);
    static colors sample = {"red", "green", "blue"};

    printf("%s %s %s\n", sample.a, sample.b, sample.c);
    funct(sample);
    printf("%s %s %s\n", sample.a, sample.b, sample.c);
}


void funct(colors sample)

{
    sample.a = "cyan";
    sample.b = "magenta";
    sample.c = "yellow";
    printf("%s %s %s\n", sample.a, sample.b, sample.c);
    return;
}
```

(b)
```c
#include <stdio.h>

typedef struct {
    char *a;
    char *b;
    char *c;
} colors;

main()

{
    void funct(colors *pt);
    static colors sample = {"red", "green", "blue"};

    printf("%s %s %s\n", sample.a, sample.b, sample.c);
    funct(&sample);
    printf("%s %s %s\n", sample.a, sample.b, sample.c);
}
```

```
                void funct(colors *pt)

                {
                    pt->a = "cyan";
                    pt->b = "magenta";
                    pt->c = "yellow";
                    printf("%s %s %s\n", pt->a, pt->b, pt->c);
                    return;
                }
```

(c)   `#include <stdio.h>`

```
        typedef struct {
            char *a;
            char *b;
            char *c;
        } colors;

        main()

        {
            colors funct(colors sample);
            static colors sample = {"red", "green", "blue"};

            printf("%s %s %s\n", sample.a, sample.b, sample.c);
            sample = funct(sample);
            printf("%s %s %s\n", sample.a, sample.b, sample.c);
        }


        colors funct(colors sample)

        {
            sample.a = "cyan";
            sample.b = "magenta";
            sample.c = "yellow";
            printf("%s %s %s\n", sample.a, sample.b, sample.c);
            return(sample);
        }
```

11.56 Describe the output generated by the following program. Distinguish between meaningful and meaningless output.

```
        #include <stdio.h>

        main()

        {
            union {
                int i;
                float f;
                double d;
            } u;

            printf("%d\n", sizeof u);
            u.i = 100;
            printf("%d %f %f\n", u.i, u.f, u.d);
            u.f = 0.5;
            printf("%d %f %f\n", u.i, u.f, u.d);
            u.d = 0.0166667;
            printf("%d %f %f\n", u.i, u.f, u.d);
        }
```

11.57 Describe the output generated by the following programs. Explain any differences between the programs.

(a)
```c
#include <stdio.h>

typedef union {
    int i;
    float f;
} udef;

main()

{
    udef u;
    void funct(udef u);

    u.i = 100;
    u.f = 0.5;
    funct(u);
    printf("%d %f\n", u.i, u.f);
}


void funct(udef u)

{
    u.i = 200;
    printf("%d %f\n", u.i, u.f);
    return;
}
```

(b)
```c
#include <stdio.h>

typedef union {
    int i;
    float f;
} udef;

main()

{
    udef u;
    void funct(udef u);

    u.i = 100;
    u.f = 0.5;
    funct(u);
    printf("%d %f\n", u.i, u.f);
}


void funct(udef u)

{
    u.f = -0.3;
    printf("%d %f\n", u.i, u.f);
    return;
}
```

(c) #include <stdio.h>

```
    typedef union {
        int i;
        float f;
    } udef;

    main()

    {
        udef u;
        udef funct(udef u);

        u.i = 100;
        u.f = 0.5;
        u = funct(u);
        printf("%d %f\n", u.i, u.f);
    }


    udef funct(udef u)

    {
        u.f = -0.3;
        printf("%d %f\n", u.i, u.f);
        return(u);
    }
```

Programming Problems

11.58 Answer the following questions as they pertain to your particular C compiler or interpreter:

(a) Can an entire structure variable (or union variable) be assigned to another structure (union) variable, provided both variables have the same composition?

(b) Can an entire structure variable (or union variable) be passed to a function as an argument?

(c) Can an entire structure variable (or union variable) be returned from a function to its calling routine?

(d) Can a pointer to a structure (or a union) be passed to a function as an argument?

(e) Can a pointer to a structure (or a union) be returned from a function to its calling routine?

11.59 Modify the program given in Example 11.26 (locating customer records) so that the function search returns a complete structure rather than a pointer to a structure. (Do not attempt this problem if your version of C does not support the return of entire structures from a function.)

11.60 Modify the customer billing program given in Example 11.28 so that any of the following reports can be written out:

(a) status of all customers (now generated by the program)

(b) status of overdue and delinquent customers only

(c) status of delinquent customers only

Include a provision for displaying a menu when the program is executed, from which the user may choose which report will be generated. Have the program return to the menu after printing each report, thus allowing for the possibility of generating several different reports.

11.61 Modify the customer billing program presented in Example 11.28 so that the structure of type record now includes a union containing the members office_address and home_address. Each union member should itself be a structure consisting of two, 80-character arrays, called street and city, respectively. Add another member to the primary structure (of type record), which is a single character called flag. This member should be assigned a character (e.g., 'o' or 'h') to indicate which type of address is currently stored in the union.

Modify the remainder of the program so that the user is asked which type of address will be supplied for each customer. Then display the appropriate address, with a corresponding label, along with the rest of the output.

11.62 Modify the program given in Example 11.37 so that a number raised to a floating-point power can be executed in either single-precision or double-precision, as specified by the user in response to a prompt. The union type `nvals` should now contain a third member, which should be a double-precision quantity called `dexp`.

11.63 Rewrite each of the following C programs so that it makes use of structure variables:

(a) The depreciation program presented in Example 7.20.

(b) The program given in Example 10.28 for displaying the day of the year.

(c) The program for determining the future value of monthly deposits, given in Example 10.31.

11.64 Modify the piglatin generator presented in Example 9.14 so that it will accept multiple lines of text. Represent each line of text with a separate structure. Include the following three members within each structure:

(a) the original line of text

(b) the number of words within the line

(c) the modified line of text (i.e., the piglatin equivalent of the original text)

Include the enhancements described in Problem 9.36 (i.e., provisions for punctuation marks, uppercase letters and double-letter sounds).

11.65 Write a C program that reads several different names and addresses into the computer, rearranges the names into alphabetical order, and then writes out the alphabetized list. (See Examples 9.20 and 10.26.) Make use of structure variables within the program.

11.66 For each of the following programming problems described in earlier chapters, write a complete C program that makes use of structure variables

(a) The student exam score averaging problem described in Problem 9.40.

(b) The more comprehensive version of the student exam score averaging problem described in Problem 9.42.

(c) The problem that matches the names of countries with their corresponding capitals, described in Problem 9.46.

(d) The text encoding-decoding problem as described in Problem 9.49, but extended to accommodate multiple lines of text.

11.67 Write a complete C program that will accept the following information for each team in either a baseball or a football league:

1. Team name, including the city (e.g., Pittsburgh Steelers)

2. Number of wins

3. Number of losses

For a baseball team, add the following information:

4. Number of hits

5. Number of runs

6. Number of errors

7. Number of extra-inning games

Similarly, add the following information for a football team:

4. Number of ties

5. Number of touchdowns

6. Number of field goals

7. Number of turnovers

8. Total yards gained (season total)

9. Total yards given up to opponents

Enter this information for all of the teams in the league. Then reorder and print the list of teams according to their win-lose records, using the reordering techniques described in Examples 9.13 and 10.15 (see also Examples 9.20 and 10.26). Store the information in an array of structures, where each array element (i.e., each structure) contains the information for a single team. Make use of a union to represent the variable information (either baseball or football) that is included as a part of the structure. This union should itself contain two structures, one for baseball-related statistics and the other for football-related statistics.

Test the program using a current set of league statistics. (Ideally, the program should be tested using both baseball and football statistics.)

11.68 Modify the program given in Example 11.32 so that it makes use of each of the following linked structures:

(a) A linear linked list with two sets of pointers: one set pointing forward, the other pointing backward.

(b) A circular linked list. Be sure to include a pointer to identify the beginning of the circular list.

11.69 Modify the program given in Example 11.32 so that each node contains the following information:

(a) Name
(b) Street address
(c) City/State/ZIP code
(d) Account number
(e) Account status (a single character indicating current, overdue or delinquent status)

11.70 Write a complete C program that will allow you to enter and maintain a computerized version of your family tree. Begin by specifying the number of generations (i.e., the number of levels within the tree). Then enter the names and nationalities hierarchically, beginning with your own name and nationality. Include capabilities for modifying the tree and for adding new names (new nodes) to the tree. Also, include a provision for displaying the entire tree automatically after each update.

Test the program, including at least three generations if possible (you, your parents and your grandparents). Obviously, the tree becomes more interesting as the number of generations increases.

11.71 An RPN calculator utilizes a scheme whereby each new numerical value is followed by the operation that is to be performed between the new value and its predecessor. (RPN stands for "reverse Polish notation.") Thus, adding two numbers, say 3.3 and 4.8, would require the following keystrokes:

```
3.3  ⟨enter⟩

4.8  +
```

The sum, 8.1, would then be displayed in the calculator's single visible register.

RPN calculators make use of a *stack*, typically containing four registers (four components), as illustrated in Fig. 11.7. Each new number is entered into the X register, causing all previously entered values to be pushed up in the stack. If the top register (i.e., the T register) was previously occupied, then the old number will be lost (it will be overwritten by the value that is pushed up from the Z register).

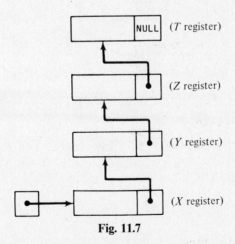

Fig. 11.7

Arithmetic operations are always carried out between the numbers in the X and Y registers. The result of such an operation will always be displayed in the X register, causing everything in the upper registers to drop down one level (thus "popping" the stack). This procedure is illustrated in Figs. 11.8(a) to 11.8(c) for the addition of the values 3.3 and 4.8, as described above.

Write an interactive C program that will simulate an RPN calculator. Display the contents of the stack after each operation, as in Figs. 11.8(a) to 11.8(c). Include a provision for carrying out each of the following operations:

Operation		Keystrokes
enter new data	(value)	⟨enter⟩
addition	(value)	+
subtraction	(value)	–
multiplication	(value)	*
division	(value)	/

Test the program using any numerical data of your choice.

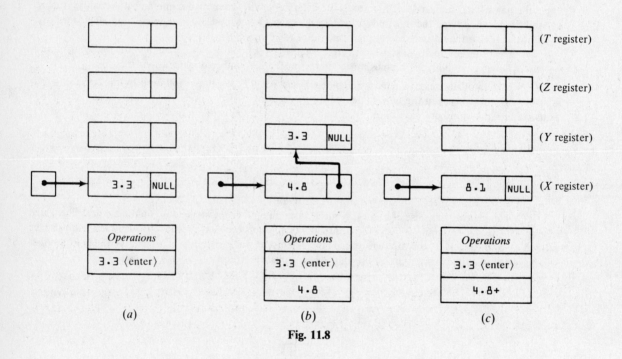

(a)   (b)   (c)

Fig. 11.8

Chapter 12

Data Files

Many applications require that information be written to or read from an auxiliary storage device. Such information is stored on the device in the form of a *data file*. Thus, data files allow us to store information permanently, and to access and alter that information whenever necessary.

In C, an extensive set of library functions is available for creating and processing data files. Unlike other programming languages, C does not distinguish between sequential and direct access (random access) data files. There are, however, two different types of data files, called *stream-oriented* (or *standard*) data files, and *system-oriented* (or *low-level*) data files. Stream-oriented data files are generally easier to work with than system-oriented data files and are therefore more commonly used.

Stream-oriented data files can be divided into two categories. In the first category are data files comprising consecutive characters. These characters can be interpreted as individual data items or as components of strings or numbers. The manner in which these characters are interpreted is determined either by the particular library functions used to transfer the information or by format specifications within the library functions, as in the scanf and printf functions discussed in Chap. 4.

The second category of stream-oriented data files, often referred to as *unformatted* data files, organizes data into blocks containing contiguous bytes of information. These blocks represent more complex data structures, such as arrays and structures. A separate set of library functions is available for processing stream-oriented data files of this type. These library functions provide single instructions that can transfer entire arrays or structures to or from data files.

System-oriented data files are more closely related to the computer's operating system than are stream-oriented data files. They are somewhat more complicated to work with, though their use may be more efficient for certain kinds of applications. A separate set of procedures, with accompanying library functions, is required to process system-oriented data files.

This chapter is concerned only with stream-oriented data files. The overall approach is relatively standardized, though the details may vary from one version of C to another. Thus, the examples presented in this chapter may not apply to all versions of the language in exactly the manner shown. Nevertheless, you should have little difficulty in relating this material to your particular version to C.

12.1 OPENING AND CLOSING A DATA FILE

When working with a stream-oriented data file, the first step is to establish a *buffer area*, where information is temporarily stored while being transferred between the computer's memory and the data file. This buffer area allows information to be read from or written to the data file more rapidly than would otherwise be possible. The buffer area is established by writing

```
FILE *ptvar;
```

where FILE (uppercase letters required) is a special structure type that establishes the buffer area, and *ptvar* is a pointer variable that indicates the beginning of the buffer area. The structure type FILE is defined within a system include file, typically stdio.h. The pointer *ptvar* is often referred to as a *stream pointer*, or simply as a *stream*.

A data file must then be *opened* before it can be created or processed. This associates the file name with the buffer area (i.e., with the stream). It also specifies how the data file will be utilized, that is, as a read-only file, a write-only file, or a read/write file, in which both operations are permitted.

The library function `fopen` is used to open a file. This function is typically written as

ptvar = fopen(*file-name*, *file-type*);

where *file-name* and *file-type* are strings that represent the name of the data file and the manner in which the data file will be utilized, respectively. The name chosen for the *file-name* must be consistent with the rules for naming files, as determined by the computer's operating system. The *file-type* must be one of the strings shown in Table 12-1.

Table 12-1 File-Type Specifications

File-Type	Meaning
"r"	Open an existing file for reading only.
"w"	Open a new file for writing only. If a file with the specified *file-name* currently exists, it will be destroyed and a new file created in its place.
"a"	Open an existing file for appending (i.e., for adding new information at the end of the file). A new file will be created if the file with the specified *file-name* does not exist.
"r+"	Open an existing file for both reading and writing.
"w+"	Open a new file for both reading and writing. If a file with the specified *file-name* currently exists, it will be destroyed and a new file created in its place.
"a+"	Open an existing file for both reading and appending. A new file will be created if the file with the specified *file-name* does not exist.

The `fopen` function returns a pointer to the beginning of the buffer area associated with the file. A NULL value is returned if the file cannot be opened as, for example, when an existing data file cannot be found.

Finally, a data file must be *closed* at the end of the program. This can be accomplished with the library function `fclose`. The syntax is simply

fclose(*ptvar*);

It is good programming practice to close a data file explicitly using the `fclose` function, though most C compilers will automatically close a data file at the end of program execution if a call to `fclose` is not present.

Example 12.1 A C program contains the following statements:

```
#include <stdio.h>

FILE *fpt;

fpt = fopen("sample.dat", "w");

...

fclose(fpt);
```

The first statement causes the header file `stdio.h` to be included in the program. The second statement defines a pointer called `fpt` which will point to a structure of type FILE, indicating the beginning of the data file buffer area. Note that FILE is defined in `stdio.h`.

The third statement opens a new data file called `sample.dat` as a write-only file. Moreover, the `fopen` function returns a pointer to the beginning of the buffer area and assigns it to the pointer variable `fpt`. Thus, `fpt` points to the buffer area associated with the data file `sample.dat`. All subsequent file processing statements (which are not shown explicitly in this example) will access the data file via the pointer variable `fpt` rather than by the file name.

Finally, the last statement closes the data file. Note that the argument is the pointer variable `fpt`, not the file name `sample.dat`.

The value returned by the `fopen` function can be used to generate an error message if a data file cannot be opened, as illustrated in the next example.

Example 12.2 A C program contains the following statements:

```c
#include <stdio.h>
#define  NULL  0

FILE *fpt;

fpt = fopen("sample.dat", "r+");

if (fpt == NULL)
   printf("\nERROR - Cannot open the designated file\n");
else {

   ...

   fclose(fpt);
}
```

This program attempts to open an existing data file called `sample.dat` for both reading and writing. An error message will be generated if this data file cannot be found. Otherwise, the data file will be opened and processed as indicated.

The `fopen` and the `if` statements are often combined, as follows:

```c
if ((fpt = fopen("sample.dat", "r+")) == NULL)
   printf("\nERROR - Cannot open the designated file\n");
```

Either method is acceptable.

12.2 CREATING A DATA FILE

A data file must be created before it can be processed. A stream-oriented data file can be created in two ways. One is to create the file directly, using a text editor or a word processor. The other is to write a program that enters information into the computer and then writes it out to the data file. Unformatted data files can only be created with such specially written programs.

When creating a new data file with a specially written program, the approach generally used is to enter the information from the keyboard and then write it out to the data file. If the data file consists of individual characters, the library functions `getchar` and `putc` can be used to enter the data from the keyboard and to write it out to the data file. (We discussed the use of `getchar` in Sec. 4.2.) The `putc` function is new, though its use is analogous to `putchar`, which we discussed in Sec. 4.3.

Example 12.3 Creating a Data File (Lowercase to Uppercase Text Conversion) Here is a variation of several earlier programs, which read a line of lowercase text into the computer and write it out in uppercase (see Examples 4.4,

6.6, 6.9, 6.13 and 9.2). In this example we will read the text into the computer character-by-character using the getchar function and then write it out to a data file using putc. The toupper library function will carry out the lowercase to uppercase conversion, as before.

```
#include <stdio.h>

/* read in a line of lower-case text and store its
   upper-case equivalent within a data file */

main()

{

    FILE *fpt;    /* define a pointer to pre-defined structure type FILE */

    char c;

    /* open a new data file for writing only */
    fpt = fopen("sample.dat", "w");

    /* read each character and write its upper-case equivalent
                                            to the data file */
    do
        putc(toupper(c = getchar()), fpt);
    while (c != '\n');

    /* close the data file */
    fclose(fpt);
}
```

The program begins by defining the stream pointer fpt, indicating the beginning of the data-file buffer area. A new data file, called sample.dat, is then opened for writing only. Next, a do - while loop reads a series of characters from the keyboard and writes their uppercase equivalents to the data file. The putc function is used to write each character to the data file. Notice that putc requires specification of the stream pointer fpt as an argument.

The loop continues as long as a newline character (\n) is not entered from the keyboard. Once a newline character is detected, the loop ceases and the data file is closed.

After the program has been executed, the data file sample.dat will contain an uppercase equivalent of the line of text entered into the computer from the keyboard. For example, if the original line of text had been

```
We, the people of the United States
```

the data file would contain the text

```
WE, THE PEOPLE OF THE UNITED STATES
```

A data file that has been created in this manner can be viewed in several different ways. For example, the data file can be viewed directly, using an operating system command such as print or type. The data file can also be examined using a text editor or a word processor.

Another approach is to write a program that will read the data file and display its contents. Such a program will, in a sense, be a mirror image of the one described above; i.e., the library function getc will read the individual characters from the data file and putchar will display them on the screen. This is a more complicated way to display a data file, but it offers a great deal of flexibility, since the individual data items can be processed as they are read.

Example 12.4　Reading a Data File　The following program will read a line of text from a data file character-by-character and display the text on the screen. The program makes use of the library functions getc and putchar (see Sec. 4.3) to read and display the data. It complements the program presented in Example 12.3.

```
#include <stdio.h>

#define NULL 0

/* read a line of text from a data file and display it on the screen */

main()

{
    FILE *fpt;    /* define a pointer to pre-defined structure type FILE */

    char c;

    /* open the data file for reading only */
    if ((fpt = fopen("sample.dat", "r")) == NULL)
       printf("\nERROR - Cannot open the designated file\n");

    else    /* read and display each character from the data file */
       do
          putchar(c = getc(fpt));
       while (c != '\n');

    /* close the data file */
    fclose(fpt);
}
```

The logic is directly analogous to that of the program shown in Example 12.3. Note, however, that this program opens the data file sample.dat as a read-only file, whereas the previous program opened sample.dat as a write-only file. An error message is generated if sample.dat cannot be opened. Finally, notice that getc requires that the stream pointer fpt be specified as an argument.

Data files consisting entirely of strings can often be created and read more easily with programs that utilize special string-oriented library functions. Some commonly used functions of this type are gets, puts, fgets and fputs. The functions gets and puts read or write strings to or from the standard output devices, whereas fgets and fputs exchange strings with data files. Since the use of these functions is straightforward, we will not pursue this topic further. You may wish to experiment with these functions, however, by reprogramming some of the character-oriented read/write programs presented earlier.

Many data files contain more complicated data structures, such as records that include various combinations of numeric and character information. Such data files can be processed using the library functions fscanf and fprintf, which are analogous to the functions scanf and printf discussed in Secs. 4.4 and 4.6. Thus, the fscanf function permits formatted data to be read from a data file associated with a particular stream, and fprintf permits formatted data to be written to the data file. The actual format specifications are the same as those used with the scanf and printf functions.

Example 12.5　Creating a File Containing Customer Records　Chapter 11 presented three programs that supposedly were used to create and update customer records (see Examples 11.14 and 11.28). When describing the programs we remarked that the examples were unrealistic, because data files should be used for applications of this type. We now turn our attention to a program that creates such a data file for a series of customer records whose composition is as follows:

```
typedef struct  {
    int month;
    int day;
    int year;
}  date;

typedef struct  {
    char name[80];
    char street[80];
    char city[80];
    int acct_no;
    char acct_type;
    float oldbalance;
    float newbalance;
    float payment;
    struct date lastpayment;
}  record;
```

The overall strategy will be to provide the current date, and then enter a loop that will process a series of customer records. For each customer, the customer's name, street, city, account number (acct_no) and initial balance (oldbalance) will be read into the computer. An initial value of Ø will then be assigned to the structure members newbalance and payment, the character 'C' will be assigned to acct_type (indicating a current status), and the current date assigned to lastpayment. Each customer record will then be written to a write-only data file called records.dat.

The procedure will continue until a customer name is encountered whose first three characters are END (in either upper- or lowercase). When END is encountered, it will be written to the data file, indicating an end-of-file condition.

Here is the complete C program.

```
#include  ⟨stdio.h⟩

#define   TRUE   1

/* create a data file containing customer records */

typedef struct  {
    int month;
    int day;
    int year;
}  date;

typedef struct  {
    char name[80];
    char street[80];
    char city[80];
    int acct_no;              /* (positive integer) */
    char acct_type;           /* C (current), O (overdue), or D (delinquent) */
    float oldbalance;         /* (nonnegative quantity) */
    float newbalance;         /* (nonnegative quantity) */
    float payment;            /* (nonnegative quantity) */
    date lastpayment;
}  record;
```

```
FILE *fpt;                          /* pointer to pre-defined structure FILE */

main()

{
    int flag = TRUE;                    /* variable declaration */
    record customer;                    /* structure variable declaration */
    record readscreen(record customer); /* function declaration */
    void writefile(record customer);    /* function declaration */

    /* open a new data file for writing only */
    fpt = fopen("records.dat", "w");

    /* enter date and assign initial values */
    printf("CUSTOMER BILLING SYSTEM - INITIALIZATION\n\n");
    printf("Please enter today\'s date (mm/dd/yyyy): ");
    scanf("%d/%d/%d", &customer.lastpayment.month,
                      &customer.lastpayment.day,
                      &customer.lastpayment.year);
    customer.newbalance = Ø;
    customer.payment = Ø;
    customer.acct_type = 'C';

    /* main loop */
    while (flag)  {

        /* enter customer's name and write to data file */
        printf("\nName (enter \'END\' when finished): ");
        scanf(" %[^\n]", customer.name);
        fprintf(fpt, "\n%s\n", customer.name);

        /* test for stopping condition */
        if (strcmpi(customer.name, "END") == Ø)
           break;

        customer = readscreen(customer);
        writefile(customer);
    }

    fclose(fpt);
}


record readscreen(record customer)   /* read remaining data */

{
    printf("Street: ");
    scanf(" %[^\n]", customer.street);
    printf("City: ");
    scanf(" %[^\n]", customer.city);
    printf("Account number: ");
    scanf("%d", &customer.acct_no);
    printf("Current balance: ");
    scanf("%f", &customer.oldbalance);
    return(customer);
}
```

```
void writefile(record customer)     /* write remaining data to data file */

{
    fprintf(fpt, "%s\n", customer.street);
    fprintf(fpt, "%s\n", customer.city);
    fprintf(fpt, "%d\n", customer.acct_no);
    fprintf(fpt, "%c\n", customer.acct_type);
    fprintf(fpt, "%.2f\n", customer.oldbalance);
    fprintf(fpt, "%.2f\n", customer.newbalance);
    fprintf(fpt, "%.2f\n", customer.payment);
    fprintf(fpt, "%d/%d/%d\n", customer.lastpayment.month,
                               customer.lastpayment.day,
                               customer.lastpayment.year);
    return;
}
```

The program begins by defining the composition of each customer record and the stream pointer fpt. Within main, a new data file, called records.dat, is then opened for writing only. Next, the program prompts for the current date, and initial values are assigned to the structure members newbalance, payment and acct_type.

The program then enters a while loop, which prompts for a customer name and writes the name to the data file. Next, the program tests to see if the name that has been entered is END (upper- or lowercase). If so, the program breaks out of the loop, the data file is closed, and the computation terminates. Otherwise, the remaining information for the current customer is entered via function readscreen and then written to the data file via function writefile.

Within main and readscreen we see that the various data items are entered interactively, using the familiar formatted printf and scanf functions. On the other hand, within main and writefile the data are written to the data file via the fprintf function. The syntax governing the use of this function is the same as the syntax used with printf, except that a stream pointer must be included as an additional argument. Notice that the control string makes use of the same character groups (i.e., the same formatting features) as the printf function described in Chap. 4.

When the program is executed, the information for each customer record is entered interactively, as shown below. As usual, the user's responses are underlined.

```
CUSTOMER BILLING SYSTEM - INITIALIZATION

Please enter today's date (mm/dd/yyyy): 5/24/1989

Name (enter 'END' when finished): Richard L. Warren
Street: 123 Vistaview Drive
City: Denver, CO
Account number: 4208
Current Balance: 247.88

Name (enter 'END' when finished): Marcia Korenstein
Street: 4383 Affluent Avenue
City: Beechview, OH
Account number: 2219
Current Balance: 135.00

Name (enter 'END' when finished): Mark Singer
Street: 1787 Larynx Lane
City: Indianapolis, IN
Account number: 8452
Current Balance: 387.42

Name (enter 'END' when finished): Phyllis W. Smith
Street: 1000 Great White Way
City: New York, NY
Account number: 711
Current Balance: 260.00

Name (enter 'END' when finished): end
```

After the program has been executed, the data file `records.dat` will have been created, containing the following information:

```
Richard L. Warren
123 Vistaview Drive
Denver, CO
4208
C
247.88
0.00
0.00
5/24/1989

Marcia Korenstein
4383 Affluent Avenue
Beechview, OH
2219
C
135.00
0.00
0.00
5/24/1989

Mark Singer
1787 Larynx Lane
Indianapolis, IN
8452
C
387.42
0.00
0.00
5/24/1989

Phyllis W. Smith
1000 Great White Way
New York, NY
711
C
260.00
0.00
0.00
5/24/1989

end
```

In the next section we will see a program that updates the information contained in this file.

12.3   PROCESSING A DATA FILE

Most data file applications require that a data file be altered as it is being processed. For example, in an application involving customer record processing, it may be desirable to add new records to the file (either at the end of the file or interspersed among the existing records), to delete existing records, to modify the contents of existing records, or to rearrange the records. These requirements in turn suggest several different computational strategies.

Consider, for example, the problem of updating the records within a data file. There are several approaches to this problem. Perhaps the most obvious approach is to read each record from a data file, update the record as required, and then write the updated record to the same data file. There are, however, some problems with this strategy. In particular, it is difficult to read and write formatted data to the same data file without disrupting the arrangement of data items within the file. Moreover, the original set of records may become inaccessible if something goes wrong during the program execution.

Another approach is to work with two different data files—an old file (a source) and a new file. Each record is read from the old file, updated as necessary, and then written to the new file. When all the records have been updated, the old file is deleted or placed into archival storage and the new file renamed. Hence, the new file will become the source for the next round of updates.

Historically, the origin of this method goes back to the early days of computing, when data files were maintained on magnetic tapes. The method is still used, however, because it provides a series of old source files that can be used to generate a customer history. The most recent source file can also be used to recreate the current file if the current file is damaged or destroyed.

Example 12.6   Updating a File Containing Customer Records   Example 12.5 presents a program to create a data file called records.dat that contains customer records. We now present a program to update the records within this data file. The program will make use of the two-file update procedure described above. Hence, we will assume that the previously created data file records.dat has been renamed records.old. This will be the source file.

Our overall strategy will be similar to that described in Example 12.5. We will first provide the current date, and then enter a loop that will read a series of customer records from records.old and write the corresponding updated records to a new data file called records.new. Each pass through the loop will read one record, update it if necessary, and then write the record to records.new. Note that all the records will be written to records.new, whether updated or not.

The procedure will continue until the customer name END has been read from the source file (in either upper- or lowercase). Once this happens, END will be written to the new data file, indicating an end-of-file condition.

The complete program is given below.

```c
#include <stdio.h>

#define  NULL  0
#define  TRUE  1

/* update a data file containing customer records */

typedef struct  {
    int month;
    int day;
    int year;
}  date;


typedef struct  {
    char name[80];
    char street[80];
    char city[80];
    int acct_no;            /* (positive integer) */
    char acct_type;         /* C (current), O (overdue), or D (delinquent) */
    float oldbalance;       /* (nonnegative quantity) */
    float newbalance;       /* (nonnegative quantity) */
    float payment;          /* (nonnegative quantity) */
    date lastpayment;
}  record;

FILE *ptold, *ptnew;        /* pointers to pre-defined structure FILE */
int month, day, year;       /* global variable declarations */
```

```
main()

{
    int flag = TRUE;                    /* local variable declaration */
    record customer;                    /* structure variable declaration */
    record readfile(record customer);   /* function declaration */
    record update(record customer);     /* function declaration */
    void writefile(record customer);    /* function declaration */

    /* open data files */
    if ((ptold = fopen("records.old", "r")) == NULL)   {
       printf("\nERROR - Cannot open the designated read file\n");
       return;
    }
    ptnew = fopen("records.new", "w");

    /* enter current date */
    printf("CUSTOMER BILLING SYSTEM - UPDATE\n\n");
    printf("Please enter today\'s date (mm/dd/yyyy): ");
    scanf("%d/%d/%d", &month, &day, &year);

    /* main loop */
    while (flag)  {

        /* read a name from old data file and write to new data file */
        fscanf(ptold, " %[^\n]", customer.name);
        fprintf(ptnew, "\n%s\n", customer.name);

        /* test for stopping condition */
        if (strcmpi(customer.name, "END") == 0)
           break;

        /* read remaining data from old data file */
        customer = readfile(customer);

        /* prompt for updated information */
        customer = update(customer);

        /* write updated information to new data file */
        writefile(customer);
    }
    fclose(ptold);
    fclose(ptnew);
}


record readfile(record customer)   /* read remaining data from old data file */

{
    fscanf(ptold, " %[^\n]", customer.street);
    fscanf(ptold, " %[^\n]", customer.city);
    fscanf(ptold, " %d", &customer.acct_no);
    fscanf(ptold, " %c", &customer.acct_type);
    fscanf(ptold, " %f", &customer.oldbalance);
    fscanf(ptold, " %f", &customer.newbalance);
    fscanf(ptold, " %f", &customer.payment);
    fscanf(ptold, " %d/%d/%d", &customer.lastpayment.month,
                               &customer.lastpayment.day,
                               &customer.lastpayment.year);

    return(customer);
}
```

```
record update(record customer)    /* prompt for new information,
                                      update records and display summary data */

{
    printf("\n\nName:    %s", customer.name);
    printf("    Account number: %d\n", customer.acct_no);
    printf("\nOld balance: %7.2f", customer.oldbalance);
    printf("    Current payment: ");
    scanf("%f", &customer.payment);

    if (customer.payment > 0)    {
       customer.lastpayment.month = month;
       customer.lastpayment.day = day;
       customer.lastpayment.year = year;
       customer.acct_type =
          (customer.payment < 0.1 * customer.oldbalance) ? 'O' : 'C';
    }
    else
       customer.acct_type = (customer.oldbalance > 0) ? 'D' : 'C';

    customer.newbalance = customer.oldbalance - customer.payment;
    printf("New balance: %7.2f", customer.newbalance);

    printf("    Account status: ");

    switch (customer.acct_type)    {
       case 'C':
                printf("CURRENT\n");
                break;
       case 'O':
                printf("OVERDUE\n");
                break;
       case 'D':
                printf("DELINQUENT\n");
                break;
       default:
                printf("ERROR\n");
    }

    return(customer);
}


void writefile(record customer)    /* write updated information to
                                                    new data file */

{
    fprintf(ptnew, "%s\n", customer.street);
    fprintf(ptnew, "%s\n", customer.city);
    fprintf(ptnew, "%d\n", customer.acct_no);
    fprintf(ptnew, "%c\n", customer.acct_type);
    fprintf(ptnew, "%.2f\n", customer.oldbalance);
    fprintf(ptnew, "%.2f\n", customer.newbalance);
    fprintf(ptnew, "%.2f\n", customer.payment);
    fprintf(ptnew, "%d/%d/%d\n", customer.lastpayment.month,
                                 customer.lastpayment.day,
                                 customer.lastpayment.year);

    return;
}
```

The program begins by defining the composition of each customer record, using the same definitions presented in Example 12.5. These definitions are followed by definitions of the stream pointers `ptold` and `ptnew`.

Within the `main` function, the two data files are both opened; `records.old` is opened as an existing read-only file, and `records.new` is a new write-only file. An error message is generated if `records.old` cannot be opened. Next, the program enters a `while` loop which reads successive customer records from `records.old` (actually, from stream `ptold`), updates each record as required, and writes each record to `records.new` (to stream `ptnew`).

Within `main`, each customer name is read from the source file and then written to the new file. The remaining information for each record is read from the source file, updated, and written to the new file within the functions `readfile`, `update` and `writefile`, respectively. This process continues until a record is encountered containing the customer name END, as discussed above. Both data files are then closed, and the computation terminates.

The function `readfile` reads additional information for each customer record from the source file. The various data items are represented as members of the structure variable `customer`. This structure variable is passed to the function as an argument. The library function `fscanf` is used to read each data item, using a syntax essentially identical to that used with the `scanf` function, as described in Chap. 4. With `fscanf`, however, the stream pointer `ptold` must be included as an additional argument within each function call. Once all the information has been read from the source file, the customer record is returned to `main`.

The function `update` is similar, though it requires that a value for `customer.payment` be entered from the keyboard. Additional information is then assigned to `customer.lastpayment`, `customer.acct_type` and `customer.newbalance`. The values assigned depend on the value provided for `customer.payment`. The updated record is then returned to `main`.

The remaining function, `writefile`, simply accepts each customer record as an argument and writes it to the new data file. Within `writefile`, the library function `fprintf` is used to transfer the information to the new data file, using the same procedures shown in Example 12.5.

When the program is executed, the name, account number and old balance are displayed for each customer. The user is then prompted for a value for the current payment. Once this value has been entered, the customer's new balance and current account status are shown.

A typical interactive session, based upon the data file created in Example 12.5, is shown below. The user's responses are underlined, as usual.

```
CUSTOMER BILLING SYSTEM - UPDATE

Please enter today's date (mm/dd/yyyy): 12/29/1989


Name:   Richard L. Warren     Account number: 4208

Old balance:   247.88    Current payment: 25.00
New balance:   222.88    Account status: CURRENT


Name:   Marcia Korenstein     Account number: 2219

Old balance:   135.00    Current payment: 135.00
New balance:     0.00    Account status: CURRENT


Name:   Mark Singer    Account number: 8452

Old balance:   387.42    Current payment: 35.00
New balance:   352.42    Account status: OVERDUE


Name:   Phyllis W. Smith    Account number: 711

Old balance:   260.00    Current payment: 0
New balance:   260.00    Account status: DELINQUENT
```

After all the customer records have been processed, the new data file `records.new` will have been created, containing the following information:

```
Richard L. Warren
123 Vistaview Drive
Denver, CO
4208
C
247.88
222.88
25.00
12/29/1989

Marcia Korenstein
4383 Affluent Avenue
Beechview, OH
2219
C
135.00
0.00
135.00
12/29/1989

Mark Singer
1787 Larynx Lane
Indianapolis, IN
8452
O
387.42
352.42
35.00
12/29/1989

Phyllis W. Smith
1000 Great White Way
New York, NY
711
D
260.00
260.00
0.00
5/24/1989

end
```

Note that the old data file, `records.old`, is still available in its original form; it can be stored for archival purposes. Before this program can be run again, however, the new data file will have to be renamed `records.old`. (Usually, this is done at the operating system level.)

12.4 UNFORMATTED DATA FILES

Some applications involve the use of data files to store blocks of data, where each block consists of a fixed number of contiguous bytes. Each block will generally represent a complex data structure, such as a structure or an array. For example, a data file may consist of multiple structures having the same composition, or it may contain multiple arrays of the same type and size. For such applications it may be desirable to read the entire block from the data file, or write the entire block to the data file, rather than reading or writing the individual components (i.e., structure members or array elements) within each block separately.

The library functions fread and fwrite are intended to be used in situations of this type. These functions are often referred to as *unformatted* read and write functions. Similarly, data files of this type are often referred to as unformatted data files.

Each of these functions requires four arguments: a pointer to the data block, the size of the data block, the number of data blocks being transferred, and the stream pointer. Thus, a typical fwrite function might be written as

```
fwrite(&customer, sizeof(record), 1, fpt);
```

where customer is a structure variable of type record, and fpt is the stream pointer associated with a data file that has been opened for output.

Example 12.7   Creating an Unformatted Data File Containing Customer Records   Consider a variation of the program presented in Example 12.5, for creating a data file containing customer records. Now, however, we will write each customer record to the data file data.bin as a single, unformatted block of information. This is in contrast to the earlier program, where we wrote the items within each record (i.e., the individual structure members) as separate, formatted data items.

Here is the complete program.

```
#include <stdio.h>
#include <string.h>

#define  TRUE  1

/* create an unformatted data file containing customer records */

typedef struct  {
    int month;
    int day;
    int year;
}  date;

typedef struct  {
    char name[80];
    char street[80];
    char city[80];
    int acct_no;              /* (positive integer) */
    char acct_type;           /* C (current), O (overdue), or D (delinquent) */
    float oldbalance;         /* (nonnegative quantity) */
    float newbalance;         /* (nonnegative quantity) */
    float payment;            /* (nonnegative quantity) */
    date lastpayment;
}  record;

FILE *fpt;                    /* pointer to pre-defined structure FILE */
```

```
main()

{
    int flag = TRUE;                       /* variable declaration */
    record customer;                       /* structure variable declaration */
    record readscreen(record customer);   /* function declaration */

    /* open a new data file for writing only */
    fpt = fopen("data.bin", "w");

    /* enter date and assign initial values */
    printf("CUSTOMER BILLING SYSTEM - INITIALIZATION\n\n");
    printf("Please enter today\'s date (mm/dd/yyyy): ");
    scanf("%d/%d/%d", &customer.lastpayment.month,
                      &customer.lastpayment.day,
                      &customer.lastpayment.year);
    customer.newbalance = 0;
    customer.payment = 0;
    customer.acct_type = 'C';

    /* main loop */
    while (flag) {

        /* enter customer's name */
        printf("\nName (enter \'END\' when finished): ");
        scanf(" %[^\n]", customer.name);

        /* test for stopping condition */
        if (strcmpi(customer.name, "END") == 0)
            break;

        /* enter remaining data and write to data file */
        customer = readscreen(customer);
        fwrite(&customer, sizeof(record), 1, fpt);

        /* erase strings */
        strset(customer.name, ' ');
        strset(customer.street, ' ');
        strset(customer.city, ' ');
    }

    fclose(fpt);
}


record readscreen(record customer)   /* read remaining data */

{
    printf("Street: ");
    scanf(" %[^\n]", customer.street);
    printf("City: ");
    scanf(" %[^\n]", customer.city);
    printf("Account number: ");
    scanf("%d", &customer.acct_no);
    printf("Current balance: ");
    scanf("%f", &customer.oldbalance);
    return(customer);
}
```

Comparing this program with that shown in Example 12.5, we see that the two programs are very similar. Within `main`, the current program reads each customer name and tests for a stopping condition (`END`) but does not write the customer name to the data file, as in the earlier program. Rather, if a stopping condition is not indicated, the current program reads the remainder of the customer record interactively and then writes the entire customer record to the data file with the single `fwrite` statement

```
fwrite(&customer, sizeof(record), 1, fpt);
```

Note that the data file created by this program is called `data.bin`, as indicated by the first argument within the call to the `fopen` function.

The programmer-defined `writefile` function shown in Example 12.5 is not required in this program, since the `fwrite` library function takes its place. On the other hand, both programs make use of the same programmer-defined function `readscreen`, which causes the information for a given customer record to be entered into the computer interactively.

After each record has been written to the data file, the string members `customer.name`, `customer.street` and `customer.city` are cleared (i.e., replaced with blanks), so that none of the previous information will be included in each new record. The library function `strset` is used for this purpose. Thus, the statement

```
strset(customer.name, ' ');
```

causes the contents of `customer.name` to be replaced with repeated blank characters, as indicated by ' '. Note that the header file `string.h` is included in this program, in support of the `strset` function.

Execution of this program produces the same interactive dialog as that shown in Example 12.5. Thus, during program execution the user cannot tell whether the data file being created is formatted or unformatted. Once the new data file `data.bin` has been created, however, its contents will not be legible unless the file is read by a specially written program. Such a program will be presented in the next example.

Once an unformatted data file has been created, the question arises as to how to detect an end-of-file condition. The library function `feof` is available for this purpose. (Actually, `feof` will indicate an end-of-file condition for any stream-oriented data file, not just an unformatted data file.) This function returns a nonzero value (`TRUE`) if an end-of-file condition has been detected and a value of zero (`FALSE`) if an end-of-file is *not* detected. Hence, a program that reads an unformatted data file can utilize a loop that continues to read successive records, as long as the value returned by `feof` is not `TRUE`.

Example 12.8   Updating an Unformatted Data File Containing Customer Records   We now consider another program for reading and updating the unformatted data file created in Example 12.7. We will again make use of a two-file update procedure, as in Example 12.6. Now, however, the files will be called `data.old` and `data.new`. Therefore, the file created in the previous example, called `data.bin`, will have to be renamed `data.old` before the current program can be run.

This program will make use of the library functions `fread` and `fwrite` to read unformatted customer records from `data.old` and to write the updated records to `data.new`. Therefore, the current program will not make use of programmer-defined functions `readfile` and `writefile`, as in Example 12.6.

The entire C program is shown below.

```
#include <stdio.h>

#define  NULL  0

/* update an unformatted data file containing customer records */

typedef struct {
    int month;
    int day;
    int year;
} date;
```

```
typedef struct  {
    char name[80];
    char street[80];
    char city[80];
    int acct_no;                /* (positive integer) */
    char acct_type;             /* C (current), O (overdue), or D (delinquent) */
    float oldbalance;           /* (nonnegative quantity) */
    float newbalance;           /* (nonnegative quantity) */
    float payment;              /* (nonnegative quantity) */
    date lastpayment;
}  record;

FILE *ptold, *ptnew;            /* pointers to pre-defined structure FILE */
int month, day, year;           /* global variable declarations */

main()

{
    record customer;                        /* structure variable declaration */
    record update(record customer);     /* function declaration */

    /* open data files */
    if ((ptold = fopen("data.old", "r")) == NULL)    {
        printf("\nERROR - Cannot open the designated read file\n");
        return;
    }
    ptnew = fopen("data.new", "w");

    /* enter current date */
    printf("CUSTOMER BILLING SYSTEM - UPDATE\n\n");
    printf("Please enter today\'s date (mm/dd/yyyy): ");
    scanf("%d/%d/%d", &month, &day, &year);

    /* read the first record from old data file */
    fread(&customer, sizeof(record), 1, ptold);

    /* main loop (continue until end-of-file is detected) */
    while (!feof(ptold))  {

        /* prompt for updated information */
        customer = update(customer);

        /* write updated information to new data file */
        fwrite(&customer, sizeof(record), 1, ptnew);

        /* read next record from old data file */
        fread(&customer, sizeof(record), 1, ptold);
    }

    fclose(ptold);
    fclose(ptnew);
}
```

```
record update(record customer)    /* prompt for new information,
                                      update records and display summary data */

{
      printf("\n\nName:    %s", customer.name);
      printf("     Account number: %d\n", customer.acct_no);
      printf("\nOld balance: %7.2f", customer.oldbalance);
      printf("     Current payment: ");
      scanf("%f", &customer.payment);

      if (customer.payment > 0)   {
         customer.lastpayment.month = month;
         customer.lastpayment.day = day;
         customer.lastpayment.year = year;
         customer.acct_type =
            (customer.payment < 0.1 * customer.oldbalance) ? 'O' : 'C';
      }
      else
         customer.acct_type = (customer.oldbalance > 0) ? 'D' : 'C';

      customer.newbalance = customer.oldbalance - customer.payment;
      printf("New balance: %7.2f", customer.newbalance);

      printf("     Account status: ");

      switch (customer.acct_type)   {
         case 'C':
                   printf("CURRENT\n");
                   break;
         case 'O':
                   printf("OVERDUE\n");
                   break;
         case 'D':
                   printf("DELINQUENT\n");
                   break;
         default:
                   printf("ERROR\n");
      }

      return(customer);
}
```

The overall program logic is similar to that presented in Example 12.6. That is, a record is read from data.old, updated interactively, and then written to data.new. This procedure continues until an end-of-file condition has been detected during the most recent fread operation. Note the manner in which the end-of-file test is built into the specification of the while loop, i.e., while (!feof(ptold)).

Each record is updated interactively, via the user-defined function update. This function is identical to that shown in Example 12.6.

Execution of the program results in the same interactive dialog as that shown in Example 12.6.

We will not pursue the use of data files further within this book. Remember, however, that most versions of C contain many different library functions for carrying out various file-oriented operations. Some of these functions are intended to be used with standard input/output devices (i.e., reading from the keyboard and writing to the screen), some are intended for stream-oriented data files and others are available for use with system-oriented data files. Thus, we have only scratched the surface of this important topic within the current chapter. Readers are encouraged to find out what file-related functions are available for their particular versions of the language.

Review Questions

12.1 What is the primary advantage to using a data file?

12.2 Describe the different ways in which data files can be categorized in C.

12.3 What is the purpose of a buffer area when working with a stream-oriented data file? How is a buffer area defined?

12.4 When defining a buffer area for use with a stream-oriented data file, what does the symbol FILE represent? Where is FILE defined?

12.5 What is a stream pointer? What is the relationship between a stream pointer and a buffer area?

12.6 What is meant by opening a data file? How is this accomplished?

12.7 Summarize the rules governing the use of the fopen function. Describe the information that is returned by this function.

12.8 Summarize the different file types that can be specified by the fopen function.

12.9 What is the purpose of the fclose function? Must a call to this function appear within a program that utilizes a data file?

12.10 Describe a commonly used programming construct in which a provision for an error message accompanies a call to the fopen function.

12.11 Describe two different methods for creating a stream-oriented data file. Can both methods be used with unformatted data files?

12.12 Describe the general procedure for creating a stream-oriented data file using a specially written C program. What file-oriented library functions might be used within the program?

12.13 How can a stream-oriented data file be viewed once it has been created? Does your answer apply to unformatted data files?

12.14 Describe the general procedure for reading a stream-oriented data file using a specially written C program. What file-oriented library functions might be used within the program? Compare your answer with the answer to Problem 12.12.

12.15 Describe two different approaches to updating a data file. Which approach is better, and why?

12.16 Contrast the use of the fscanf and fprintf functions with the use of the scanf and printf functions described in Chap. 4. How do the grammatical rules differ?

12.17 For what kinds of applications are unformatted data files well suited?

12.18 Contrast the use of the fread and fwrite functions with the use of the fscanf and fprintf functions. How do the grammatical rules differ? For what kinds of applications is each group of functions well suited?

12.19 What is the purpose of the library function strset? Why might strset be included in a program that creates an unformatted data file?

12.20 What is the purpose of the library function feof? How might the feof function be utilized within a program that updates an unformatted data file?

Problems

12.21 Associate the stream pointer pointr with a new stream-oriented data file called students.dat. Open the data file for writing only.

12.22 Associate the stream pointer pointr with an existing stream-oriented data file called students.dat. Open the data file so that new information can be appended to the end of the file.

12.23 Associate the stream pointer pointr with a new stream-oriented data file called sample.dat. Open the data file so that information can either be read from or written to the file. Show how the data file can be closed at the end of the program.

12.24 Associate the stream pointer pointr with an existing stream-oriented data file called sample.dat. Open the data file so that information can either be read from or written to the file. Show how the data file can be closed at the end of the program.

12.25 Repeat Problem 12.24, adding a provision for generating an error message in the event that the data file cannot be opened (if, for example, the data file is not present).

12.26 The skeletal outline of a C program is shown below.

```
#include <stdio.h>

main()

{
    FILE *fpt;

    int a;
    float b;
    char c;

    fpt = fopen("sample.dat", "w");

    . . .

    fclose(fpt);
}
```

Enter values for a, b and c from the keyboard, in response to prompts generated by the program. Then write the values to the data file. Format the floating-point value so that not more than two decimals are written to the data file.

12.27 The skeletal outline of a C program is shown below.

```
include <stdio.h>

main()

{
    FILE *fpt;

    int a;
    float b;
    char c;

    fpt = fopen("sample.dat", "r");

    . . .

    fclose(fpt);
}
```

Read the values of a, b and c from the data file and display them on the screen.

12.28 The skeletal outline of a C program is shown below.

```
#include <stdio.h>

main()

{
    FILE *pt1, *pt2;

    int a;
    float b;
    char c;

    pt1 = fopen("sample.old", "r");
    pt2 = fopen("sample.new", "w");

    . . .

    fclose(pt1);
    fclose(pt2);
}
```

(a) Read the values of a, b and c from the data file sample.old.

(b) Display each value on the screen and enter an updated value.

(c) Write the new values to the data file sample.new. Format the floating-point value so that not more than two decimals are written to sample.new.

12.29 The skeletal outline of a C program is shown below.

```
#include <stdio.h>

main()

{
    FILE *pt1, *pt2;

    char name[20];

    pt1 = fopen("sample.old", "r");
    pt2 = fopen("sample.new", "w");


    ...


    fclose(pt1);
    fclose(pt2);
}
```

(a) Read the string represented by name from the data file sample.old.

(b) Display it on the screen.

(c) Enter an updated string.

(d) Write the new string to the data file sample.new.

12.30 The skeletal outline of a C program is shown below.

```
#include <stdio.h>

main()

{
    struct {
        int a;
        float b;
        char c;
        char name[20];
    } values;

    pt1 = fopen("data.old", "r+");
    pt2 = fopen("data.new", "w+");


    ...


    fclose(pt1);
    fclose(pt2);
}
```

(a) Read the value of values.name from the formatted data file data.old and display it on the screen.

(b) Enter values for values.a, values.b and values.c from the keyboard, in response to programmed prompts.

(c) Write the values of values.name, values.a, values.b and values.c to the formatted data file data.new.

12.31　Repeat Problem 12.30, treating the two data files as unformatted data files. (Read an entire record from `data.old`, and write the entire updated record to `data.new`.)

Programming Problems

12.32　Modify the program given in Example 12.3 (read in a line of lowercase text and write the uppercase equivalent to a data file) so that each character entered from the keyboard is tested to determine its case and is then written to the data file in the opposite case. (Hence, lowercase is converted to uppercase and uppercase is converted to lowercase.) Use the library function `isupper` or `islower` to test the case of each incoming character, and use the functions `toupper` and `tolower` to carry out the conversions.

12.33　Modify the programs given in Examples 12.3 and 12.4 so that multiple lines of text can be processed. As a stopping condition, check for END (either upper- or lowercase) in the first three characters within each line.

12.34　Modify the program given in Example 12.6 (updating a file containing customer records) so that it uses only one file, i.e., each updated customer record replaces the original record. Use the library function `ftell` to determine the current file position, and the function `fseek` to change the file position, as needed. Be sure to open a data file of the proper type.

12.35　Expand the program given in Example 12.6 so that new customer records can be added, old records can be deleted or existing records can be modified. Be sure to maintain the records in alphabetical order. Allow the user to choose which option will be executed before each record is processed.

12.36　Modify the program given in Example 12.8 (updating an unformatted data file containing customer records) so that it uses only one file, i.e., each updated customer record replaces the original record. Use the library function `ftell` to determine the current file position and the function `fseek` to change the file position, as needed. Be sure to open a data file of the proper type.

12.37　Write a program that will read successive records from the new data file created in Example 12.8 and display each record on the screen in an appropriately formatted form.

12.38　Expand the program described in Problem 12.36 so that new customer records can be added, old records can be deleted or existing records can be modified. Be sure to maintain the records in alphabetical order. Allow the user to choose which option will be executed before each record is processed.

12.39　Write an interactive C program that will encode or decode multiple lines of text, using the encoding/decoding procedure described in Problem 9.49. Store the encoded text within a data file, so that it can be retrieved and decoded at any time. The program should include the following features:

(a)　Enter text from the keyboard, encode the text and store the encoded text in a data file.
(b)　Retrieve the encoded text and display it in its encoded form.
(c)　Retrieve the encoded text, decode it and then display the decoded text.
(d)　End the computation.

Test the program using several lines of text of your choice.

12.40　Extend the program described in Problem 12.39 so that multiple random integers can be generated, where each successive integer is used to encode each consecutive line. Thus, the first random integer will be used to encode the first line of text, the second random integer will be used to encode the second line of text, and so on. Include a provision for reproducing the sequence of random integers, so that the same random integers can be used to decode the text. Test the program using several lines of text of your choice.

12.41　Modify the craps game simulator given in Examples 7.12 and 7.16 so that it simulates a specified number of games and saves the outcome of each game in a data file. At the end of the simulation, read the data file to determine the percentage of wins and losses that the player has experienced.

　　　Test the program by simulating 500 consecutive games. Based upon these results, estimate the odds of winning when playing craps.

12.42　Modify the piglatin generator presented in Example 9.14 so that multiple lines of text can be entered from the keyboard. Save the entire English text in a data file, and save the corresponding piglatin in another data file.

　　　Include within the program a provision for generating a menu which will allow the user to select any one of the following features:

(a)　Enter new text, convert to piglatin and save. (Save both the original text and the piglatin, as described above.)

     (b)   Read previously entered text from a data file and display.

     (c)   Read the piglatin equivalent of previously entered text and display.

     (d)   End the computation.

     Test the program using several arbitrary lines of text.

12.43 Write a complete C program that will generate a data file containing the student exam data presented in Problem 6.69 (k). Let each file component be a structure containing the name and exam scores for a single student. Run the program, creating a data file for use in the next problem.

12.44 Write a file-oriented C program that will process the student exam scores given in Problem 6.69 (k). Read the data from the data file created in the previous problem. Then create a report containing the name, exam scores and average grade for each student.

12.45 Extend the program written for Problem 12.44 so that an overall class average is determined, followed by the deviation of each student's average about the class average. Write the output onto a new data file. Then display the output in the form of a well-labeled report.

12.46 Write an interactive, file-oriented C program that will maintain a list of names, addresses and telephone numbers in alphabetical order (by last names). Consider the information associated with each name to be a separate record. Represent each record as a structure.

     Include a menu that will allow the user to select any of the following features:

     (a)   Add a new record.

     (b)   Delete a record.

     (c)   Modify an existing record.

     (d)   Retrieve and display an entire record for a given name.

     (e)   Generate a complete list of all names, addresses and telephone numbers.

     (f)   End the computation.

     Be sure to rearrange the records whenever a new record is added or a record is deleted, so that the records are always maintained in alphabetical order. Utilize a linear linked list, as described in Example 11.32.

12.47 Write a program that will generate a data file containing the list of countries and their corresponding capitals given in Problem 9.46. Place the name of each country and its corresponding capital in a separate structure. Treat each structure as a separate record. Run the program, creating a data file for use in the next problem.

12.48 Write an interactive, menu-driven C program that will access the data file generated in the preceding problem and then allow one of the following operations to be executed:

     (a)   Determine the capital of a specified country.

     (b)   Determine the country whose capital is specified.

     (c)   Terminate the computation.

12.49 Extend the program written for Problem 12.48 to include the following additional features:

     (a)   Add a new record (i.e., a new country and its corresponding capital).

     (b)   Delete a record.

     (c)   Generate a listing of all of the countries and their corresponding capitals.

12.50 Write a complete C program that can be used as a simple line-oriented text editor. This program must have the following capabilities:

     (a)   Enter several lines of text and store in a data file.

     (b)   List the data file.

     (c)   Retrieve and display a particular line, determined by line number.

     (d)   Insert n lines.

     (e)   Delete n lines.

     (f)   Save the newly edited text and end the computation.

     Carry out each of these tasks in response to a one-letter command, preceded by a dollar sign ($). The find (retrieve) command should be followed by an unsigned integer to indicate which line should be retrieved. Also, the insert and delete commands can be followed by an optional unsigned integer if several consecutive lines are to be inserted or deleted.

     Each command should appear on a line by itself, thus providing a means of distinguishing commands from lines of text. (A command line will always begin with a dollar sign, followed by a single-letter command, an optional unsigned integer, and a newline designation.)

The following commands are recommended:

$E —enter new text

$L —list the entire block of text

Fk$—find (retrieve) line number k

In$—insert n lines after line number k

Dn$—delete n lines after line number k

$S —save the edited block of text and end the computation

12.51 Extend the program described in Problem 11.67 so that the team information is maintained in a data file rather than an array. Each file component should be a structure containing the data for one team. Include provisions for each of the following operations:

(*a*) Entering new records (adding new teams).
(*b*) Updating existing records.
(*c*) Deleting records (removing teams).
(*d*) Generating a summary report for all the teams in the league.

Chapter 13

Low-Level Programming

From the material presented in the first twelve chapters of this book, it should be clear that C is a full-fledged, high-level programming language. However, C also possesses certain "low-level" features that allow the programmer to carry out operations normally available only in assembly language or machine language. For example, it is possible to store the values of certain variables within the central processing unit's registers. This will usually speed up any computation associated with these values.

Moreover, C permits the manipulation of individual bits within a word. Thus, bits can be shifted to the left or the right, inverted (1s and 0s reversed), or masked (extracted selectively). Applications requiring such operations are familiar to assembly language programmers. C also allows the bits within a word of memory to be organized into individual groups. This permits multiple data items to be packed within a single word.

This chapter shows how to carry out low-level operations in C. Readers who lack background in this area may wish to skip some of this material, particularly Sec. 13.2.

13.1 REGISTER VARIABLES

In Chap. 8 we mentioned that there are four different storage class specifications in C, and we examined three of them—automatic, external and static—in detail. We now turn our attention to the last of these, which is the *register* storage class.

Registers are special storage areas within a computer's central processing unit. The actual arithmetic and logical operations that comprise a program are carried out within these registers. Normally, these operations are carried out by transferring information from the computer's memory to these registers, carrying out the indicated operations, and then transferring the results back to the computer's memory. This general procedure is repeated many times during the course of a program's execution.

For some programs, the execution time can be reduced considerably if certain values can be stored within these registers rather than in the computer's memory. Such programs may also be somewhat smaller in size (i.e., they may require fewer instructions), since fewer data transfers will be required. Usually, however, the size reduction will not be dramatic and will be less significant than the savings in execution time.

In C, the values of *register variables* are stored within the central processing unit's registers. A variable can be assigned this storage class simply by preceding the type declaration with the keyword register. There can, however, be only a few register variables (typically, two or three) within any one function. The exact number depends on the particular computer, and the specific C compiler. Usually, only integer variables are assigned the register storage class (more about this later in this section).

The register and automatic storage classes are closely related. In particular, their visibility (i.e., their scope) is the same. Thus, register variables, like automatic variables, are local to the function in which they are declared. Furthermore, the rules governing the use of register variables are the same as those for automatic variables (see Sec. 8.2), except that the address operator (&) cannot be applied to register variables.

The similarities between register and automatic variables is not coincidental, because the register storage class can be assigned only to variables that would otherwise have the storage class automatic. Moreover, declaring certain variables to be register variables does not guarantee that they will actually be treated as register variables. The declaration will be valid only if the requested register space is available. If a register declaration cannot be honored, the variables will be treated as having the storage class automatic.

Example 13.1   A C program contains the variable declaration

```
register int a, b, c;
```

This declaration specifies that the variables a, b and c will be integer variables with storage class `register`. Hence, the values of a, b and c will be stored within the registers of the computer's central processing unit rather than in memory, provided the register space is available.

If the register space is not available, then the variables will be treated as integer variables with storage class `automatic`. This is equivalent to the declaration

```
auto int a, b, c;
```

or simply

```
int a, b, c;
```

as explained in Sec. 8.2.

Unfortunately, there is no way to determine whether a `register` declaration will be honored, other than to run a program with and without the declaration and compare the results. A program that makes use of register variables should run faster than the corresponding program without register variables. It may also be somewhat smaller in size.

Example 13.2   Generating Fibonacci Numbers   The program presented below is a variation of that shown in Example 8.7, for generating a series of Fibonacci numbers.

```
#include <stdio.h>
#include <time.h>

/* calculate the first 23 Fibonacci numbers 30,000 times,
   to illustrate the use of register variables */

main()

{
    time_t start, finish;               /* start and finish times */
    register int f, f1, f2;
    int count, loop, n = 23;

    /* tag the starting time */
    time(&start);

    /* do 30,000 loops */
    for (loop = 1; loop <= 30000; ++loop) {
        f1 = 1;
        f2 = 1;

        /* generate the first n Fibonacci numbers */
        for (count = 1; count <= n; ++count) {
            f = (count < 3) ? 1 : f1 + f2;
            f2 = f1;
            f1 = f;
        }
    }
```

```
        /* adjust the counter and tag the completion time */
        --count;
        time(&finish);

        /* display the output */
        printf("i = %2d   F = %d\n", count, f);
        printf("elapsed time: %.0lf seconds", difftime(finish, start));
}
```

This program includes three integer variables that have the register storage class. Only 23 Fibonacci numbers will be calculated, since the value of an integer quantity on some personal computers cannot exceed $2^{15} - 1 = 32,767$. (Note that the values of the 23rd and 24th Fibonacci numbers are 28,657 and 46,368, respectively.)

The calculation of the Fibonacci numbers is repeated 30,000 times, in order to obtain a reasonably accurate assessment of the time required to execute the program. The only output generated is the value of the 23rd Fibonacci number, calculated at the end of the last loop. Thus, the program is computationally intensive (minimal input/output), in order to emphasize the advantage in using the register storage class.

Notice that the program includes its own timing mechanism. In particular, the program makes use of the library function time, which assigns the current time (in seconds) to the variables start and finish. These variables are of type time_t, as defined in the header file time.h. The program also makes use of the library function difftime, which returns the time difference defined by the variables finish and start.

Executing the program (on an IBM Personal Computer model AT, running at 8 MHz) results in the following output:

```
i = 23   F = 28657
elapsed time: 7 seconds
```

If the program is rerun without the register declaration (i.e., if the variables f, f1 and f2 are declared as ordinary integer variables), the output is

```
i = 23   F = 28657
elapsed time: 11 seconds
```

Thus, a 36 percent savings in computation time is experienced by using register type variables.

On the other hand, the sizes of the compiled object programs (using Microsoft's Quick C Compiler) are not significantly different. Specifically, the size of the first program (with the register variables) is 22,774 bytes, whereas the size of the second program (without register variables) is 22,790 bytes.

Though the register storage class is usually associated with integer variables, some compilers allow the register storage class to be associated with other types of variables having the same word size (e.g., short or unsigned integers). Moreover, *pointers* to such variables may also be permitted.

The register storage class specification can be included as a part of a formal argument declaration within a function, or as a part of an argument type specification within a function prototype. (*Note*: register is the *only* storage class specifier that can be used in this manner.)

Example 13.3 The skeletal outline of a C program is shown below.

```
main()

{
    register unsigned u;                  /* variable declaration */
    register int *pt;                     /* pointer declaration */

    void funct(register unsigned u, register int *pt);   /* function prototype */

    u = 5;                                /* assign an integer quantity */
    *pt = 12;                             /* assign an integer quantity */

    funct(u, pt);
}
```

```
void funct(register unsigned u, register int *pt)     /* function definition */

{

    ...

    return;

}
```

Within main, we see that u is an unsigned integer, and pt is a pointer to an integer. Both of these variables are assigned the register storage class. Thus, u will represent an unsigned integer that is stored within one register of the computer's central processing unit, and pt will point to the contents of another such register. In both cases, the use of the computer's registers will be contingent upon their availability.

The function prototype indicates that the first argument transferred to funct is an unsigned integer having the register storage class and the second argument is a pointer to an integer having this same storage class. Notice that the corresponding formal argument declarations within funct are consistent with the argument specifications shown in the function prototype.

Following the function prototype, a value of 5 is assigned to u, and a value of 12 is assigned to the location to which pt points. These values will be stored in the computer's registers, provided the registers are available. The variables u and pt are then passed to funct, where they are processed in some unspecified manner.

13.2 BITWISE OPERATIONS

Some applications require the manipulation of individual bits within a word of memory. Assembly language or machine language is normally required for operations of this type. However, C contains several special operators that allow such bitwise operations to be carried out easily and efficiently. These bitwise operators can be divided into three general categories: the one's complement operator, the logical bitwise operators, and the shift operators. C also contains several operators that combine bitwise operations with ordinary assignment. Each category is discussed separately below.

The One's Complement Operator

The *one's complement operator* (~) is a unary operator that causes the bits of its operand to be inverted (i.e., reversed) so that 1s become 0s and 0s become 1s. This operator always precedes its operand. The operand must be an integer-type quantity (including integer, long, short, unsigned, or char). Generally, the operand will be an unsigned octal or an unsigned hexadecimal quantity, though this is not a firm requirement.

Example 13.4 Consider the hexadecimal constant 0x7ff. The corresponding bit pattern, expressed in terms of a 16-bit word, is 0000 0111 1111 1111 (see Appendix A). The one's complement of this bit pattern is 1111 1000 0000 0000, which corresponds to the hexadecimal constant 0xf800. Thus, we see that the value of the expression ~0x7ff is 0xf800. (Note that the bit patterns in this example have been arranged into groups of four for convenience only.)

Several other expressions that make use of the one's complement operator, and their corresponding values, are shown below. All results are expressed in terms of a 16-bit word.

Expression	Value	
~0xc5	0xff3a	(hexadecimal constants)
~0x1111	0xeeee	(hexadecimal constants)
~0xffff	0	(hexadecimal constants)
~052	0177725	(octal constants)
~0177777	0	(octal constants)

In the octal constants 0177725 and 0177777, the leftmost octal digit is equivalent to only one bit (otherwise, the total bit pattern would exceed 16 bits).

You are encouraged to show the validity of these expressions by writing out the equivalent bit patterns, as shown above.

The one's complement operator is sometimes referred to as the *complementation operator*. It is a member of the same precedence group as the other unary operators; thus, its associativity is right-to-left.

Example 13.5 Consider the simple C program shown below.

```
#include <stdio.h>

main()

{
    unsigned i = 0x5b3c;

    printf("hexadecimal values:  i = %x   ~i = %x\n", i, ~i);
    printf("decimal equivalents: i = %u   ~i = %u", i, ~i);
}
```

Executing this program on a computer with a 16-bit word size results in the following output:

```
hexadecimal values:  i = 5b3c   ~i = a4c3
decimal equivalents: i = 23356   ~i = 42179
```

To understand these results, first consider the bit patterns corresponding to the values for i and ~i.

```
 i = 0101 1011 0011 1100
~i = 1010 0100 1100 0011
```

The decimal equivalent of the first bit pattern can be determined by writing

$$i= 0 \times 2^{15} + 1 \times 2^{14} + 0 \times 2^{13} + 1 \times 2^{12} + 1 \times 2^{11} + 0 \times 2^{10} + 1 \times 2^9 + 1 \times 2^8 +$$
$$0 \times 2^7 + 0 \times 2^6 + 1 \times 2^5 + 1 \times 2^4 + 1 \times 2^3 + 1 \times 2^2 + 0 \times 2^1 + 0 \times 2^0 =$$
$$16384 + 4096 + 2048 + 512 + 256 + 32 + 16 + 8 + 4 = 23356$$

Thus, the decimal equivalent of 0x5b3c is 23356.

Similarly, the decimal equivalent of the second bit pattern can be determined by writing

$$~i= 1 \times 2^{15} + 0 \times 2^{14} + 1 \times 2^{13} + 0 \times 2^{12} + 0 \times 2^{11} + 1 \times 2^{10} + 0 \times 2^9 + 0 \times 2^8 +$$
$$1 \times 2^7 + 1 \times 2^6 + 0 \times 2^5 + 0 \times 2^4 + 0 \times 2^3 + 0 \times 2^2 + 1 \times 2^1 + 1 \times 2^0 =$$
$$32768 + 8192 + 1024 + 128 + 64 + 2 + 1 = 42179$$

Thus, we see that the decimal equivalent of 0xa4c3 is 42179.

The Logical Bitwise Operators

There are three logical bitwise operators: *bitwise and* (&), *bitwise exclusive or* (^), and *bitwise or* (¦). Each of these operators requires two integer-type operands. The operations are carried out independently on each pair of corresponding bits within the operands. Thus, the least significant bits (i.e., the rightmost bits) within the two operands will be compared, then the next least significant bits, and so on, until all of the bits have been compared. The results of these comparisons are:

- A *bitwise and* expression will return a 1 if both bits have a value of 1 (i.e., if both bits are true). Otherwise, it will return a value of 0.

- A *bitwise exclusive or* expression will return a 1 if one of the bits has a value of 1 and the other has a value of 0 (one bit is true, the other false). Otherwise, it will return a value of 0.

- A *bitwise or* expression will return a 1 if one or more of the bits have a value of 1 (one or both bits are true). Otherwise, it will return a value of 0.

These results are summarized in Table 13-1. In this table, b1 and b2 represent the corresponding bits within the first and second operands, respectively.

Table 13-1   Logical Bitwise Operations

b1	b2	b1 & b2	b1 ^ b2	b1 ¦ b2
1	1	1	0	1
1	0	0	1	1
0	1	0	1	1
0	0	0	0	0

Example 13.6   Suppose a and b are unsigned integer variables whose values are 0x6db7 and 0xa726, respectively. The results of several bitwise operations on these variables are shown below.

```
~a = 0x9248;

~b = 0x58d9;

a & b = 0x2526;

a ^ b = 0xca91;

a ¦ b = 0xefb7;
```

The validity of these expressions can be verified by expanding each of the bit patterns. Thus,

```
     a = 0110 1101 1011 0111
         ─────────────────────
    ~a = 1001 0010 0100 1000
       = 0x9248


     b = 1010 0111 0010 0110
         ─────────────────────
    ~b = 0101 1000 1101 1001
       = 0x58d9


     a = 0110 1101 1011 0111
     b = 1010 0111 0010 0110
         ─────────────────────
 a & b = 0010 0101 0010 0110
       = 0x2526


     a = 0110 1101 1011 0111
     b = 1010 0111 0010 0110
         ─────────────────────
 a ^ b = 1100 1010 1001 0001
       = 0xca91


     a = 0110 1101 1011 0111
     b = 1010 0111 0010 0110
         ─────────────────────
 a ¦ b = 1110 1111 1011 0111
       = 0xefb7
```

Each of the logical bitwise operators has its own precedence. The *bitwise and* (&) operator has the highest precedence, followed by *bitwise exclusive or* (^), then *bitwise or* (¦). *Bitwise and* follows the equality operators (== and !=). *Bitwise or* is followed by logical *and* (&&). The associativity for each bitwise operator is left-to-right. (See Appendix C for a summary of all C operators, showing their precedences and associativities.)

Masking

Masking is a process in which a given bit pattern is transformed into another bit pattern by means of a logical bitwise operation. The original bit pattern is one of the operands in the bitwise operation. The second operand, called the *mask*, is a specially selected bit pattern that brings about the desired transformation.

There are several different kinds of masking operations. For example, a portion of a given bit pattern can be copied to a new word, while the remainder of the new word is filled with 0s. Thus, part of the original bit pattern will be "masked off" from the final result. The *bitwise and* operator (&) is used for this type of masking operation, as illustrated below.

Example 13.7 Suppose a is an unsigned integer variable whose value is 0x6db7. Extract the rightmost 6 bits of this value and assign them to the unsigned integer variable b. Assign 0s to the 10 leftmost bits of b.

To carry out this operation, we write the bitwise expression

```
b = a & 0x3f;
```

The second operand, i.e., the hexadecimal constant 0x3f, will serve as a mask. Thus, the resulting value of b will be 0x37.

The validity of this result can be established by examining the corresponding bit patterns.

```
   a = 0110 1101 1011 0111
mask = 0000 0000 0011 1111
       _____
   b = 0000 0000 0011 0111
     = 0x37.
```

Notice that the mask prevents the leftmost 10 bits from being copied from a to b.

The mask in the last example contained 1s in the rightmost bit positions (i.e., the least significant bit positions) and 0s in the leftmost bit positions (the most significant bit positions). Such masks are independent of the word length, since 0s are used to fill the remainder of the word after the required 1s have been placed in the low-order bit positions. If 1s were required in the leftmost bit positions, the mask would be related to the length of the word. (Remember that the rightmost bit position always represents 2^0, whereas the leftmost bit position represents 2^{n-1}, where n is the number of bits in the word.) Such dependence can often be removed, however, by writing the mask in terms of its one's complement.

Example 13.8 Suppose once again that a is an unsigned integer variable whose value is 0x6db7. Now extract the *leftmost* 6 bits of this value and assign them to the unsigned integer variable b. Assign 0s to the 10 rightmost bits of b.

To carry out this operation, we can write the bitwise expression

```
b = a & 0xfc00;
```

Thus, the hexadecimal constant 0xfc00 will serve as a mask. The resulting value of b will be 0x6c00.

The validity of this result can be established by again examining the corresponding bit patterns.

```
   a = 0110 1101 1011 0111
mask = 1111 1100 0000 0000
       _____
   b = 0110 1100 0000 0000
     = 0x6c00.
```

The mask now blocks the rightmost 10 bits in a.

The mask is dependent on the 16-bit word size in this situation, since the 1s appear in the leftmost bit positions. If the mask is written in terms of its one's complement, however, the 1s appear in the rightmost bit positions and the remaining bit positions are filled with 0s. The mask therefore becomes independent of the word size.

The one's complement of the original mask is the hexadecimal constant 0x3ff. We can therefore express this masking operation as

```
b = a & ~0x3ff;
```

The resulting value of b will be 0x6c00, as before.

The validity of this result can be seen by examining the corresponding bit patterns shown below.

```
 0x3ff = 0000 0011 1111 1111
         _____

~0x3ff = 1111 1100 0000 0000 = 0xfc00      (the original mask)


     a = 0110 1101 1011 0111
~0x3ff = 1111 1100 0000 0000
         _____

     b = 0110 1100 0000 0000
       = 0x6c00.
```

Another type of masking operation allows a portion of a given bit pattern to be copied to a new word, while the remainder of the new word is filled with 1s. The *bitwise or* operator is used for this purpose. (Note the distinction between this and the previous masking operation, which allowed a portion of a bit pattern to be copied to a new word, while the remainder of the new word was filled with 0s.)

Example 13.9 Suppose that a is an unsigned integer variable whose value is 0x6db7, as before. Transform the corresponding bit pattern into another bit pattern in which the rightmost 8 bits are all 1s, and the leftmost 8 bits retain their original value. Assign this new bit pattern to the unsigned integer variable b.

This operation is carried out with the bitwise expression

```
b = a | 0xff;
```

The hexadecimal constant 0xff is the mask. The resulting value of b will be 0x6dff.

Now let us examine the corresponding bit patterns, in order to verify the accuracy of this result.

```
   a = 0110 1101 1011 0111
mask = 0000 0000 1111 1111
       _____

   b = 0110 1101 1111 1111
     = 0x6dff
```

Remember that the bitwise operation is now *bitwise or*, not *bitwise and*, as in the previous examples. Thus, when each of the rightmost 8 bits in a is compared with the corresponding 1 in the mask, the result is always 1. When each of the leftmost 8 bits in a is compared with the corresponding 0 in the mask, however, the result will be the same as the original bit in a.

Now suppose we wish to transform the bit pattern of a into another bit pattern in which the *leftmost* 8 bits are all 1s, and the *rightmost* 8 bits retain their original value. This can be accomplished by either of the following two expressions:

```
b = a | 0xff00;
```

or

```
b = a | ~0xff;
```

In either case, the resulting value of b will be 0xffb7. The second expression is preferable because it is independent of the word size.

You should verify the accuracy of these results by expanding the corresponding bit patterns and carrying out the indicated bitwise operations.

A portion of a given bit pattern can be copied to a new word, while the remainder of the original bit pattern is inverted within the new word. This type of masking operation makes use of *bitwise exclusive or*. The details are illustrated in the following example.

Example 13.10   Suppose that a is an unsigned integer variable whose value is 0x6db7, as in the last several examples. Now let us reverse the rightmost 8 bits, and preserve the leftmost 8 bits. This new bit pattern will be assigned to the unsigned integer variable b.

To do this, we make use of the *bitwise exclusive or* operation.

```
b = a ^ 0xff;
```

The hexadecimal constant 0xff is the mask. This expression will result in the value 0x6d48 being assigned to b.
Here are the corresponding bit patterns.

```
   a = 0110 1101 1011 0111
mask = 0000 0000 1111 1111
       ─────────────────────
   b = 0110 1101 0100 1000
     = 0x6d48
```

Remember that the bitwise operation is now *bitwise exclusive or* rather than *bitwise and* or *bitwise or*. Therefore, when each of the rightmost 8 bits in a is compared with the corresponding 1 in the mask, the resulting bit will be the opposite of the bit originally in a. On the other hand, when each of the leftmost 8 bits in a is compared with the corresponding 0 in the mask, the resulting bit will be the same as the bit originally in a.

If we wanted to invert the leftmost 8 bits in a while preserving the original rightmost 8 bits, we could write either

```
b = a ^ 0xff00;
```

or the more desirable expression (because it is independent of the word size)

```
b = a ^ ~0xff;
```

The resulting value of each expression is 0x92b7.

The *exclusive or* operation can be used repeatedly as a *toggle*, to change the value of a particular bit within a word. In other words, if a particular bit has a value of 1, the *exclusive or* operation will change its value to 0, and vice versa. Such operations are particularly common in programs that interact closely with the computer's hardware.

Example 13.11   Suppose that a is an unsigned integer variable whose value is 0x6db7, as in the previous examples. The expression

```
a ^ 0x4
```

will invert the value of bit number 2 (the third bit from the right) within a. If this operation is carried out repeatedly, the value of a will alternate between 0x6db7 and 0x6db3. Thus, using this operation repeatedly will toggle the third bit from the right on and off.

The corresponding bit patterns are shown below.

```
0x6db7 = 0110 1101 1011 0111
  mask = 0000 0000 0000 0100
         ─────────────────────
0x6db3 = 0110 1101 1011 0011
  mask = 0000 0000 0000 0100
         ─────────────────────
0x6db7 = 0110 1101 1011 0111
```

The Shift Operators

The two bitwise shift operators are *shift left* (<<) and *shift right* (>>). Each operator requires two operands. The first is an integer-type operand that represents the bit pattern to be shifted. The second is an unsigned integer that indicates the number of displacements (i.e., whether the bits in the first operand will be shifted by 1 bit position, 2 bit positions, 3 bit positions, and so on). This value cannot exceed the number of bits associated with the word size of the first operand.

The left-shift operator causes all the bits in the first operand to be shifted to the left by the number of positions indicated by the second operand. The leftmost bits (i.e., the overflow bits) in the original bit pattern will be lost. The rightmost bit positions that become vacant will be filled with 0s.

Example 13.12   Suppose a is an unsigned integer variable whose value is 0x6db7. The expression

```
b = a << 6;
```

will shift all bits of a six places to the left and assign the resulting bit pattern to the unsigned integer variable b. The resulting value of b will be 0x6dc0.

To see how the final result was obtained, let us write out the corresponding bit patterns.

```
                  lost bits
             ┌─────────┴─────────┐
    a  =   0110  1101  1011  0111


                    shift left


    a << 6 =  0110  1101  1100  0000  =  0x6dc0
              └────────┘
              filled with 0s
```

All the bits originally assigned to a are shifted to the left six places, as the arrows indicate. The leftmost 6 bits (originally 0110 11) are lost. The rightmost 6 bit positions are filled with 00 0000.

The right-shift operator causes all the bits in the first operand to be shifted to the right by the number of positions indicated by the second operand. The rightmost bits (i.e., the underflow bits) in the original bit pattern will be lost. If the bit pattern being shifted represents an *unsigned* integer, then the leftmost bit positions that become vacant will be filled with 0s. Hence, the behavior of the right-shift operator is similar to that of the left-shift operator when the first operand is an unsigned integer.

Example 13.13   Suppose a is an unsigned integer variable whose value is 0x6db7. The expression

```
b = a >> 6;
```

will shift all bits of a six places to the right and assign the resulting bit pattern to the unsigned integer variable b. The resulting value of b will be 0x1b6.

To see how the final result was obtained, let us once again write out the corresponding bit patterns.

```
                         lost bits
                    ┌────────┴────────┐
    a  =   0110  1101  1011  0111


                    shift right


    a >> 6 =  0000  0001  1011  0110  =  0x1b6
              └────────┘
              filled with 0s
```

We see that all the bits originally assigned to a are shifted to the right six places, as the arrows indicate. The rightmost 6 bits (originally 11 0111) are lost. The leftmost 6 bit positions are filled with 00 0000.

If the bit pattern representing a *signed* integer is shifted to the right, the outcome of the shift operation may depend on the value of the leftmost bit (the sign bit). Most compilers will fill the vacant bit positions with the contents of this bit. (Negative integers have a 1 in this position, whereas positive integers have a 0 here.) Some compilers, however, will fill the vacant bit positions with 0s, regardless of the sign of the original integer quantity. You should determine how your particular compiler will handle this situation.

Example 13.14 Here is a simple C program that illustrates the use of the right-shift operator.

```
#include <stdio.h>

main()

{
    unsigned a = 0xf05a;
    int b = a;

    printf("%u %d\n", a, b);
    printf("%x\n", a >> 6);
    printf("%x\n", b >> 6);
}
```

Notice that a represents an unsigned integer quantity, whereas b represents an ordinary (signed) integer. Both variables are initially assigned the (hexadecimal) value 0xf05a. Since the leftmost bit position will contain a 1, the signed integer (b) will interpret this value as a negative number.

The program displays the decimal values represented by the bit patterns assigned to a and b. We therefore see the result of a 6-bit right-shift operation for each quantity. Thus, if the program is run with a compiler that copies the contents of the sign bit into the vacated bit positions, the following output will be obtained:

```
61530 -4006
3c1
ffc1
```

The first line shows that the hexadecimal quantity 0xf05a is equivalent to the unsigned decimal quantity 61530, and the signed decimal quantity −4006. When the unsigned integer is shifted six places to the right, the vacated bit positions are filled with 0s. Hence, the hexadecimal equivalent of the resulting bit pattern is 0x3c1. When the *signed* integer is shifted six places to the right, however, the vacated bit positions are filled with 1s (the value of the sign bit). Therefore, the hexadecimal equivalent of the resulting bit pattern in this case is ffc1.

The actual bit patterns, before and after the right-shift operations, are shown below.

```
    a = 1111 0000 0101 1010

a >> 6 = 0000 0011 1100 0001 = 0x3c1


    b = 1111 0000 0101 1010

b >> 6 = 1111 1111 1100 0001 = 0xffc1
```

The Bitwise Assignment Operators

C also contains the following *bitwise assignment* operators.

$$\&= \qquad \hat{}= \qquad |= \qquad <<= \qquad >>=$$

These operators combine the preceding bitwise operations with ordinary assignment. The left operand must be an assignable, integer-type identifier (e.g., an integer variable), and the right operand must be a bitwise expression. The left operand is interpreted as the first operand in the bitwise expression. The

value of the bitwise expression is then assigned to the left operand. For example, the expression
a &= 0x7f is equivalent to a = a & 0x7f.

The bitwise assignment operators are members of the same precedence group as the other assignment operators in C. Their associativity is right-to-left (see Appendix C).

Example 13.15 Several bitwise assignment expressions are shown below. In each expression, assume that a is an unsigned integer variable whose initial value is 0x6db7.

Expression	Equivalent Expression	Final Value
a &= 0x7f	a = a & 0x7f	0x37
a ^= 0x7f	a = a ^ 0x7f	0x6dc8
a |= 0x7f	a = a | 0x7f	0x6dff
a <<= 5	a = a << 5	0xb6e0
a >>= 5	a = a >> 5	0x36d

Many applications involve the use of multiple bitwise operations. In fact, two or more bitwise operations often appear in the same expression.

Example 13.16   Displaying Bit Patterns   Most versions of C do not include a library function to convert a decimal integer into a binary bit pattern. A complete C program to carry out this conversion is shown below. The program will display the bit pattern corresponding to either a positive or a negative integer quantity.

```
#include <stdio.h>

/* display the bit pattern corresponding to a signed decimal integer */

main()

{

    int a, b, m, count, nbits;
    unsigned mask;

    /* determine the word size in bits and set the initial mask */
    nbits = 8 * sizeof(int);
    m = 0x1 << (nbits - 1);            /* place 1 in leftmost position */

    /* main loop */
    do  {

        /* read a signed integer */
        printf("\n\nEnter an integer value (0 to stop): ", a);
        scanf("%d", &a);

        /* output the bit pattern */
        mask = m;
        for (count = 1; count <= nbits; count++)  {
            b = (a & mask) ? 1 : 0;   /* set display bit on or off */
            printf("%x", b);          /* print display bit */
            if (count % 4 == 0)
                printf(" ");          /* blank space after every 4th digit */
            mask >>= 1;               /* shift mask 1 position to the right */
        }

    } while (a != 0);
}
```

The program is written so that it is independent of the integer word size. Therefore it can be used on any computer. It begins by determining the word size in bits. It then assigns an appropriate initial value to the integer variable m. This value will be used as a mask in a *bitwise and* operation. Notice that m contains a 1 in the leftmost bit position and 0s in all the other bit positions.

The main part of the program is a do - while loop that allows multiple integer quantities to be converted into equivalent bit patterns. Each pass through the loop causes one integer quantity to be entered into the computer and converted into an equivalent bit pattern, which is then displayed. The computation continues until a value of 0 is entered into the computer and converted into a succession of 0 bits.

Once an integer quantity has been entered into the computer, the mask is assigned the initial value defined at the beginning of the program. A for loop is then used to examine the integer quantity bit-by-bit, beginning with the most significant bit (i.e., the leftmost bit). A masking operation, based upon the use of *bitwise and*, is used to examine each bit position. The content of the bit position is then displayed. Finally, the 1 within the mask is shifted one bit position to the right, in anticipation of examining the next bit.

Note that all the bits are displayed on the same line. A blank space is displayed after every group of 4 bits, to enhance the legibility of the display.

The interactive dialog resulting from a typical program execution is shown below. The user's responses are underlined.

```
Enter an integer value (Ø to stop): 1
0000 0000 0000 0001

Enter an integer value (Ø to stop): -1
1111 1111 1111 1111

Enter an integer value (Ø to stop): 129
0000 0000 1000 0001

Enter an integer value (Ø to stop): -129
1111 1111 0111 1111

Enter an integer value (Ø to stop): 1024
0000 0100 0000 0000

Enter an integer value (Ø to stop): -1024
1111 1100 0000 0000

Enter an integer value (Ø to stop): 7033
0001 1011 0111 1001

Enter an integer value (Ø to stop): -7033
1110 0100 1000 0111

Enter an integer value (Ø to stop): 32767
0111 1111 1111 1111

Enter an integer value (Ø to stop): -32768
1000 0000 0000 0000

Enter an integer value (Ø to stop): Ø
0000 0000 0000 0000
```

Notice that each positive number has a 0 in the leftmost bit position, and each negative number has a 1 in this position. (Actually, the bit pattern for a negative number is the *two's complement* of the bit pattern for a positive number. To obtain the two's complement, form the one's complement and then add 1 to the rightmost bit position.)

13.3 BIT FIELDS

In some applications it may be desirable to work with data items that consist of only a few bits (e.g., a single-bit flag to indicate a true/false condition, a 3-bit integer whose values can range from 0 through 7, or a 7-bit ASCII character.) Several such data items can be packed into an individual word of memory.

To do so, the word is subdivided into individual *bit fields*. These bit fields are defined as members of a structure. Each bit field can then be accessed individually, like any other member of a structure.

In general terms, the decomposition of a word into distinct bit fields can be written as

```
struct   tag  {
     member 1;
     member 2;
     . . .
     member m;
};
```

where the individual elements have the same meaning as in a structure declaration. Each member declaration must now include a specification indicating the size of the corresponding bit field. To do so, the member name must be followed by a colon and an unsigned integer indicating the field size.

The interpretation of these bit fields may vary from one C compiler to another. For example, some C compilers may order the bit fields from right-to-left, whereas other C compilers will order them from left-to-right. We will assume right-to-left ordering in the examples shown below.

Example 13.17 A C program contains the following declarations:

```
struct   sample   {
     unsigned a :  1;
     unsigned b :  3;
     unsigned c :  2;
     unsigned d :  1;
};

struct   sample   v;
```

The first declaration defines a structure which is subdivided into four bit fields, called a, b, c and d. These bit fields have widths of 1 bit, 3 bits, 2 bits and 1 bit, respectively. Hence, the bit fields occupy a total of 7 bits within a word of memory. Any additional bits within the word will remain uncommitted.

Figure 13.1 illustrates the layout of the bit fields within the word, assuming a 16-bit word with the fields ordered from right-to-left.

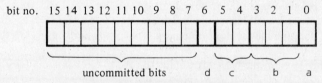

Fig. 13.1   Bit fields within a 16-bit word

The second declaration states that v is a structure variable of type sample. Thus, v. a is a field within v whose width is 1 bit. Similarly, v. b is a field whose width is 3 bits, and so on.

A bit field can only be defined as a portion of an integer or an unsigned word. (Some compilers also permit a bit field to be a portion of a char or a long word.) In all other respects, however, the rules for defining bit fields are the same as the rules that govern other kinds of structures.

Example 13.18 The declarations in Example 13.17 can be combined to read

```
struct   sample   {
     unsigned a :  1;
     unsigned b :  3;
     unsigned c :  2;
     unsigned d :  1;
} v;
```

The interpretation of the variable v is the same as that given in Example 13.17. Moreover, the tag can be omitted, so that the above declaration can be further shortened to

```
struct  {
    unsigned a :  1;
    unsigned b :  3;
    unsigned c :  2;
    unsigned d :  1;
} v;
```

if desired.

A field within a structure cannot overlap a word within the computer's memory. This issue does not arise if the sum of the field widths does not exceed the size of an unsigned integer quantity. If the sum of the field widths does exceed this word size, however, then any overlapping field will automatically be forced to the beginning of the next word.

Example 13.19   Consider the simple C program shown below.

```
#include ⟨stdio.h⟩

main()

{
    static struct  {
        unsigned a : 5;         /* begin first word */
        unsigned b : 5;
        unsigned c : 5;
        unsigned d : 5;         /* forced to second word */
    } v = {1, 2, 3, 4};

    printf("v.a = %d   v.b = %d   v.c = %d   v.d = %d\n", v.a, v.b, v.c, v.d);
    printf("v requires %d bytes\n", sizeof(v));
}
```

The four fields within v require a total of 20 bits. If the computer only allows 16 bits for an unsigned integer quantity, this structure declaration will require 2 words of memory. The first three fields will be stored in the first word. Since the last field will straddle the word boundary, it is automatically forced to the beginning of the second word.

Figure 13.2 shows the layout of the bit fields within the two, 16-bit words.

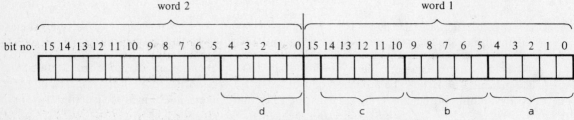

Fig. 13.2   Four bit fields within two 16-bit words

Executing this program will produce the following output:

```
v.a = 1   v.b = 2   v.c = 3   v.d = 4
v requires 4 bytes
```

The second line verifies the need for 2 words, since each word is equivalent to 2 bytes.

Unnamed fields can be used to control the alignment of bit fields within a word of memory. Such fields provide padding within the word. The size of the unnamed field determines the extent of the padding.

Example 13.20 Consider the simple C program shown below.

```
#include <stdio.h>

main()

{
    static struct  {
        unsigned a : 5;
        unsigned b : 5;
        unsigned c : 5;
    } v = {1, 2, 3};

    printf("v.a = %d   v.b = %d   v.c = %d\n", v.a, v.b, v.c);
    printf("v requires %d bytes\n", sizeof(v));
}
```

This program is similar to that shown in the previous example. Now, however, only three fields (15 bits) are defined within v. Hence, only 1 word of memory is required to store this structure.

Executing this program results in the following output:

```
v.a = 1   v.b = 2   v.c = 3
v requires 2 bytes
```

The second line of output verifies that all three fields can be stored within a single, unsigned word (2 bytes).

Let us alter this program by adding an unnamed field whose field width is 6 bits, i.e.,

```
#include <stdio.h>

main()

{
    static struct  {
        unsigned a : 5;     /* begin first word */
        unsigned b : 5;
        unsigned   : 6;     /* fill out first word */
        unsigned c : 5;     /* begin second word */
    } v = {1, 2, 3};

    printf("v.a = %d   v.b = %d   v.c = %d\n", v.a, v.b, v.c);
    printf("v requires %d bytes\n", sizeof(v));
}
```

Now 2 words of memory will be required. The first two fields will be stored within the first word, followed by 6 vacant bits (for a total of 16 bits, thus filling the first word). The last field will therefore be aligned with the beginning of the second word, as illustrated in, Fig. 13.3.

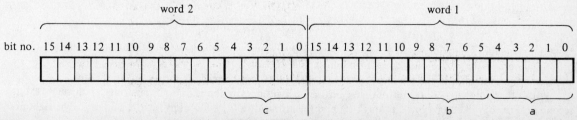

Fig. 13.3   Three bit fields within two 16-bit words

When this program is executed, the following output is produced:

```
v.a = 1    v.b = 2    v.c = 3
v requires 4 bytes
```

From the last line of output, we see that 2 words (4 bytes) are now required to store the three fields because of the additional padding.

Another way to control the alignment of bit fields is to include an unnamed field whose width is zero. This will automatically force the next field to be aligned with the beginning of a new word.

Example 13.21   Consider the simple C program shown below.

```
#include <stdio.h>

main()

{
    static struct  {
        unsigned a : 5;          /* begin first word */
        unsigned b : 5;
        unsigned   : 0;          /* force alignment with second word */
        unsigned c : 5;          /* begin second word */
    } v = {1, 2, 3};

    printf("v.a = %d    v.b = %d    v.c = %d\n", v.a, v.b, v.c);
    printf("v requires %d bytes\n", sizeof(v));
}
```

This program is similar to the second program shown in the last example. Now, however, the structure declaration includes an unnamed bit field whose field width is zero. This will automatically force the last field to the beginning of a new word, as illustrated previously in Fig. 13.3.

When this program is executed, the following output is generated:

```
v.a = 1    v.b = 2    v.c = 3
v requires 4 bytes
```

The last line verifies that 2 words (4 bytes) are required to store the three fields, as defined above.

The reader is again reminded that some compilers order bit fields from right-to-left (i.e., from low-order bits to high-order bits) within a word, whereas other compilers order the fields from left-to-right (high-order to low-order bits). Check your programmer's reference manual to determine how this is done on your particular computer.

Example 13.22   Consider the first structure declaration presented in Example 13.20, that is,

```
static struct  {
    unsigned a : 5;
    unsigned b : 5;
    unsigned c : 5;
} v = {1, 2, 3};
```

With some computers, the first field (v.a) will occupy the rightmost 5 bits (i.e., bits 0 through 4), the second field (v.b) will occupy the next 5 bits (bits 5 through 9), and the last field (v.c) will occupy bits 10 through 14. The leftmost bit (i.e, bit 15, which is the most significant bit) will be unoccupied, as shown in Fig. 13.4(a).

With other computers, however, the first field (v.a) will occupy the leftmost 5 bits (bits 11 through 15), the second field (v.b) will occupy bits 6 through 10, and the last field (v.c) will occupy bits 1 through 5. The rightmost

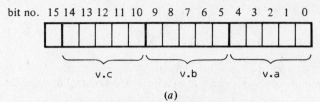

Fig. 13.4a　Bit fields with right-to-left ordering

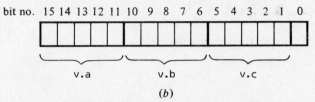

Fig. 13.4b　Bit fields with left-to-right ordering

bit (i.e., bit 0, which is the least significant bit) will be unoccupied, as shown in Fig. 13.4(*b*). Thus, a program written for one type of computer may produce incorrect results when run on the other type of computer.

Bit fields are accessed in the same manner as other structure members, and they may appear within arithmetic expressions as unsigned integer quantities. There are, however, several restrictions on their use. In particular, arrays of bit fields are not permitted, the address operator (&) cannot be applied to a bit field, a pointer cannot access a bit field, and a function cannot return a bit field.

Example 13.23　Data Compression (Storing Names and Birthdates)　This example presents a program that stores the names and birthdates of several students within an array. The overall strategy will be to first enter each student's name and birthdate. The program will then display the name, birthday (i.e., day of the week on which the student was born) and date of birth for each student. The birthdays will be determined using the method described in Example 10.28.

Each birthdate will consist of three integer quantities: the month, day and year of birth. (The year will be entered and stored as a two-digit integer, representing the number of years since 1900, as described in Example 10.28. Thus, the year 1989 will be entered and stored simply as 89.) To conserve memory, these three integer quantities will be stored in bit fields within a single 16-bit word as follows:

```
typedef struct   {
    unsigned month : 4;
    unsigned day   : 5;
    unsigned year  : 7;
} date;
```

Notice that the month will be stored as a 4-bit unsigned integer, whose values can range from 0 to 15 (note that $2^4 - 1 = 15$). Of course, we will be concerned only with the values 1 through 12. Similarly, the day will be stored as a 5-bit unsigned integer. Its values can range from 0 to 31 (note that $2^5 - 1 = 31$). And the year will be stored as a 7-bit integer, whose values can range from 0 to 127 (note that $2^7 - 1 = 127$), though we will be concerned only with the values 0 through 99. Therefore, we will be able to compress these three integer quantities into the space that would normally be allocated to a single integer quantity.

Here is the entire program.

```
#include <stdio.h>

/* Store students' names and birthdates within an array, using bit fields
   for the birthdates.

   When finished, display each student's name and birthdate.
   Display each birthdate as follows: day_of_week, month, day, year   */
```

```
main()

{
    int mm, dd, yy, count = Ø;
    int day_of_week;     /* day of the week (Ø -> Sunday,
                                              1 -> Monday,
                                                ...
                                              6 -> Saturday) */

    typedef struct   {
        unsigned month : 4;
        unsigned day   : 5;
        unsigned year  : 7;
    } date;

    struct   {
        char name[3Ø];
        date birthdate;
    } student[4Ø];

    static char *weekday[] = {"Sunday", "Monday", "Tuesday", "Wednesday",
                              "Thursday", "Friday", "Saturday"};

    static char *month[] = {"January", "February", "March", "April",
                            "May", "June", "July", "August", "September",
                            "October", "November", "December"};

    int convert(int mm, int dd, int yy);        /* function declaration */

    */ opening message */
    printf("Data Entry Routine\nType \'END\' when finished\n");
    printf("\nName: ");
    scanf(" %[^\n]", student[count].name);

    /* enter data for all students */
    while (strcmpi(student[count].name, "END") != Ø)   {
        printf("Birthdate (mm dd yy): ");
        scanf("%d %d %d", &mm, &dd, &yy);

        /* assign integer input data to bit fields */
        student[count].birthdate.month = mm;
        student[count].birthdate.day = dd;
        student[count].birthdate.year = yy;

        printf("\nName: ");
        scanf(" %[^\n]", student[++count].name);
    }

    /* convert birthdates and display output for all students */
    count = Ø;
    while (strcmpi(student[count].name, "END") != Ø)   {
        day_of_week = convert(student[count].birthdate.month,
                              student[count].birthdate.day,
                              student[count].birthdate.year);
        printf("\n%s      ", student[count].name);
        printf("%s %s %d, 19%d\n", weekday[day_of_week],
                              month[student[count].birthdate.month-1],
                              student[count].birthdate.day,
                              student[count].birthdate.year);

        ++count;
    }
}
```

```
convert(int mm, int dd, int yy)    /* convert date to numerical day of week */

{
    long ndays;           /* number of days from start of 1900 */
    int ncycles;          /* number of 4-year cycles beyond 1900 */
    int nyears;           /* number of years beyond last 4-year cycle */
    int day;              /* day of week (0, 1, ..., 6) */

    /* numerical conversions */
    ndays = (long) (30.42 * (mm - 1)) + dd;   /* approximate day of year */
    if (mm == 2) ++ndays;                     /* adjust for February */
    if ((mm > 2) && (mm < 8)) --ndays;        /* adjust for March - July */
    if ((yy % 4 == 0) && (mm > 2)) ++ndays;   /* adjust for leap year */

    ncycles = yy / 4;                     /* 4-year cycles beyond 1900 */
    ndays += 1461 * ncycles;              /* add days for 4-year cycles */

    nyears = yy % 4;            /* years beyond last 4-year cycle */
    if (nyears > 0)            /* add days for years beyond last 4-yr cycle */
        ndays += 365 * nyears + 1;

    if (ndays > 59) --ndays;   /* adjust for 1900 (NOT a leap year) */
    day = ndays % 7;
    return(day);
}
```

Within this program, we see that student is a 40-element array of structures. Each array element (i.e., each structure) consists of a 30-element character array (name) that represents the student's name, and another structure (birthdate) that contains the student's date of birth. This last structure contains the three bit fields birthdate.month, birthdate.day and birthdate.year as members.

The program also contains two arrays of pointers, whose elements represent the days of the week and the months of the year, respectively. These arrays are discussed in Example 10.28. In addition, the program includes the function convert, which is used to convert any date between January 1, 1900 and December 31, 1999 into an equivalent (integer-valued) day of the week. This function is identical to the function described in Example 10.28.

The main function consists essentially of two while loops. The first loop is used to enter and store input data for all the students. Each pass through the loop will enter and store data for a different student. This process will continue until the word "END" has been detected for a student name (in either upper- or lowercase). Notice the manner in which values are assigned to the bit fields in this loop.

The second loop causes each student's birthdate to be converted into a day of the week and then displayed, along with the student's name and date of birth. The details governing the birthdate conversion and the display of information are given in Example 10.28, and need not be repeated here. Notice the manner in which the bit fields are accessed within the function calls.

The input dialog and the corresponding output resulting from a typical program execution are shown below. As usual, the user's responses are underlined.

```
Data Entry Routine
Type 'END' when finished

Name: Rob Smith
Birthdate (mm dd yy): 7 20 66

Name: Judy Thompson
Birthdate (mm dd yy): 11 27 72

Name: Jim Williams
Birthdate (mm dd yy): 12 29 83

Name: Mort Davis
Birthdate (mm dd yy): 6 10 58
```

```
Name: end
```

Rob Smith   Wednesday July 2Ø, 1966

Judy Thompson   Monday November 27, 1972

Jim Williams   Thursday December 29, 1983

Mort Davis   Tuesday June 1Ø, 1958

Before leaving this example, a few additional observations are in order. First, it should be pointed out that the memory savings resulting from the use of bit fields has not been dramatic. The benefit of this data compression technique would be greater, however, if the dimensionality of the student array were to increase.

Second, some additional data compression could be realized by storing eight 7-bit ASCII characters in 7 bytes of memory, using the bitwise shift operators. Each byte would then contain one complete character, plus 1 bit from the eighth character. This would result in a 12.5 percent reduction in the memory requirements. The details of this technique are beyond the scope of our present discussion, though interested readers may wish to experiment with this technique on their own. (See Problem 13.55 at the end of this chapter.)

Review Questions

13.1   What is meant by low-level programming?

13.2   What are registers? In general terms, for what are registers used?

13.3   What is the purpose of the `register` storage class? What benefits are obtained from the use of this storage class? What types of variables can be assigned this storage class?

13.4   What is the scope of register variables?

13.5   Summarize the rules for using register variables.

13.6   Why might a `register` declaration not be honored? If a `register` declaration is not honored, how are the register variables treated?

13.7   How can a programmer tell if a `register` declaration is honored within a program?

13.8   What is meant by bitwise operations?

13.9   What is the purpose of the one's complement operator? To what types of operands does it apply? To what percedence group does it belong? What is its associativity?

13.10 Describe the three logical bitwise operators. What is the purpose of each?

13.11 What types of operands do each of the logical bitwise operators require?

13.12 Summarize the values returned by each of the logical bitwise operations. Consider all possible operand values in your answer.

13.13 Describe the precedence and the associativity for each of the logical bitwise operators.

13.14 What is a masking operation? What is the purpose of each operand? Which operand is the mask, and how is it chosen?

13.15 Describe a masking operation in which a portion of a given bit pattern is copied while the remaining bits are all set to 0. Which logical bitwise operation is used for this operation? How is the mask selected?

13.16 Describe a masking operation in which a portion of a given bit pattern is copied while the remaining bits are all set to 1. Which logical bitwise operation is used for this operation? How is the mask defined? Compare your answer with the answer to Question 13.15.

13.17 Describe a masking operation in which a portion of a given bit pattern is copied while the remaining bits are inverted. Which logical bitwise operation is used for this operation? How is the mask defined? Compare your answer with the answers to the previous two questions.

13.18 Why is the one's complement operator sometimes used in a masking operation? Under what conditions is its use desirable?

13.19 How can a particular bit be toggled on and off repeatedly? Which logical bitwise operation is used for this purpose?

13.20 Describe the two bitwise shift operators. What requirement must the operands satisfy? What is the purpose of each operand?

13.21 Describe the precedence and the associativity for the bitwise shift operators.

13.22 When shifting bits either to the left or to the right, what happens to the bits shifted out of the original word position?

13.23 When shifting bits to the left, what value fills the rightmost bit positions vacated by the shifting bits?

13.24 When shifting bits to the right, what value fills the leftmost bit positions vacated by the shifting bits? Does the type of operand being shifted affect this value? Explain fully. Compare your answer with the answer to Question 13.23.

13.25 Do all C compilers handle right-shift operations in the same manner? Explain fully.

13.26 List the bitwise assignment operators and describe their purpose.

13.27 Describe each of the operands in a bitwise assignment operation.

13.28 Describe the precedence and the associativity for the bitwise assignment operators.

13.29 What are bit fields? To what type of data structure do bit fields belong? How are individual bit fields accessed?

13.30 Summarize the rules for defining bit fields.

13.31 What data type must be associated with each bit field?

13.32 What happens if a bit field overlaps a word within the computer's memory?

13.33 Within a bit field declaration, what interpretation is given to an unnamed bit field? What interpretation is given to a zero-width bit field?

13.34 In what order are the bit fields arranged within a word? Is this convention uniform among all compilers?

13.35 What restrictions apply to the use of bit fields within a program, after they have been properly declared?

Problems

13.36 Declare the variables u and v to be unsigned integer variables with the `register` storage class.

13.37 Declare the variables u, v, x and y to be integer variables whose initial values are 1, 2, 3 and 4, respectively. Assume that u and v will be automatic variables. Assign the `register` storage class to x and y.

13.38 Suppose that `funct` is a function that accepts a pointer to an unsigned integer register variable as an argument, and returns a pointer to an unsigned integer. Write a skeletal outline of the `main` calling routine and `funct`, illustrating how these features are defined.

13.39 Suppose that a is an unsigned integer whose value is (hexadecimal) 0xa2c3. Write the corresponding bit pattern for this value. Then evaluate each of the following bitwise expressions, first showing the resulting bit pattern and then the equivalent hexadecimal value. Utilize the original value of a in each expression. Assume that a is stored in a 16-bit word.

(a) ~a	(h) a >> 3	(o) a & ~(0x3f06 << 8)
(b) a & 0x3f06	(i) a << 5	(p) a ^ ~0x3f06 << 8
(c) a ^ 0x3f06	(j) a & ~a	(q) (a ^ ~0x3f06) << 8
(d) a ¦ 0x3f06	(k) a ^ ~a	(r) a ^ ~(0x3f06 << 8)
(e) a & ~0x3f06	(l) a ¦ ~a	(s) a ¦ ~0x3f06 << 8
(f) a ^ ~0x3f06	(m) a & ~0x3f06 << 8	(t) (a ¦ ~0x3f06) << 8
(g) a ¦ ~0x3f06	(n) (a & ~0x3f06) << 8	(u) a ¦ ~(0x3f06 << 8)

13.40 Rewrite each of the following bitwise expressions in the form of a bitwise assignment statement, where the value of each expression is assigned to the variable a.

(a) Problem 13.39 (b)	(d) Problem 13.39 (h)	(g) Problem 13.39 (o)
(b) Problem 13.39 (c)	(e) Problem 13.39 (i)	
(c) Problem 13.39 (g)	(f) Problem 13.39 (k)	

13.41 Define a mask and write the appropriate masking operation for each of the situations described below.

(a) Copy the odd bits (bits 1, 3, 5, ..., 15) and place 0s in the even bit locations (bits 0, 2, 4, ..., 14) of a 16-bit, unsigned integer quantity represented by the variable v. Assume that bit 0 is the rightmost bit.

(b) Strip the most significant bit (the leftmost bit) from an 8-bit character represented by the variable c. (Certain word processors use this bit to control text formatting within a document. Stripping this bit, i.e., setting it to 0, can transform the word processor document into a text file consisting of ordinary ASCII characters.)

(c) Copy the odd bits (bits 1, 3, 5, . . . , 15) and place 1s in the even bit locations (bits 0, 2, 4, . . . , 14) of a 16-bit, unsigned integer quantity represented by the variable v. Assume that bit 0 is the rightmost bit.

(d) Toggle (invert) the values of bits 1 and 6 of a 16-bit, unsigned integer quantity represented by the variable v, while preserving all remaining bits. Assign the new bit pattern to v. Assume that bit 0 is the rightmost bit.

13.42 (a) Suppose that v is a signed, 16-bit integer quantity whose hexadecimal value is 0x369c. Evaluate each of the following shift expressions. (Utilize the original value of v in each expression.)

(i) v << 4
(ii) v >> 4

(b) Now suppose the value of v is changed to 0xc369. Evaluate each of the following shift expressions and compare the results with those obtained in part (a). Explain any differences.

(i) v << 4
(ii) v >> 4

13.43 Describe the composition of each of the following structures. Assume a 16-bit integer word.

(a)
```
struct {
       unsigned u : 3;
       unsigned v : 1;
       unsigned w : 7;
       unsigned x : 5;
};
```

(d)
```
struct {
       unsigned u : 7;
       unsigned   : 9;
       unsigned v : 7;
       unsigned   : 2;
       unsigned w : 7;
};
```

(b)
```
static struct {
       unsigned u : 3;
       unsigned v : 1;
       unsigned w : 7;
       unsigned x : 5;
} a = {2, 1, 16, 8};
```

(e)
```
struct {
       unsigned u : 7;
       unsigned   : 0;
       unsigned v : 7;
       unsigned   : 0;
       unsigned w : 7;
};
```

(c)
```
struct {
       unsigned u : 7;
       unsigned v : 7;
       unsigned w : 7;
} a;
```

13.44 Write a structure declaration for each of the following situations. Assume a 16-bit integer word.

(a) Define three bit fields, called a, b and c, whose widths are 6 bits, 4 bits and 6 bits, respectively.

(b) Declare a structure-type variable v having the composition defined in part (a) above. Assign the initial values 3, 5 and 7, respectively, to the three bit fields. Are the bit fields large enough to accommodate these values?

(c) What are the largest values that can be assigned to each of the bit fields defined in part (a) above?

(d) Define three bit fields, called a, b and c, whose widths are 8 bits, 6 bits and 5 bits, respectively. How will these fields be stored within the computer's memory?

(e) Define three bit fields called a, b and c, whose widths are 8 bits, 6 bits and 5 bits, respectively. Separate a and b with two vacant bits.

(f) Define three bit fields, called a, b and c, whose widths are 8 bits, 6 bits and 5 bits, respectively. Force b to the beginning of a second word of storage. Separate b and c with two vacant bits.

Programming Problems

13.45 Modify the program presented in Example 13.2 (repeated calculation of a sequence of Fibonacci numbers) so that f, f1 and f2 are pointers to integer quantities stored within registers.

13.46   Problem 6.69(f) describes a method for calculating prime numbers, and suggests writing a program to calculate the first n prime numbers, where n is a specified quantity (e.g., $n = 100$). Modify this problem statement so that the list of n prime numbers is generated 30,000 times. Display the list only once, after the last pass through the loop.

Solve the problem with and without the `register` storage class specification. Compare the execution times and the sizes of the compiled object programs.

13.47   Another way to generate a list of prime numbers is to use the famous *sieve of Eratosthenes*. This method proceeds as follows:

(*a*)   Generate an ordered list of integers ranging from 2 to n.
(*b*)   For some particular integer i within the list, carry out the following operations:

  (*i*)   Tag the integer as a prime (you may wish to place it in an array or write it out to a data file).
  (*ii*)   Then remove all succeeding integers that are multiples of i.

(*c*)   Repeat part (*b*) for each successive value of i within the list, beginning with $i = 2$ and ending with the last remaining integer.

Write a C program that uses this method to determine the primes within a list of numbers ranging from 1 to n, where n is an input quantity. Repeat the calculation 30,000 times, displaying the list of prime numbers at the end of the last pass through the loop.

Solve the problem with and without the `register` storage class specification. Compare the execution times and the sizes of the compiled object programs.

13.48   Write a C program that will accept a hexadecimal number as input and then display a menu that will permit any of the following operations to be carried out:

(*a*)   Display the hexadecimal equivalent of the one's complement.
(*b*)   Carry out a masking operation and then display the hexadecimal equivalent of the result.
(*c*)   Carry out a bit shifting operation and then display the hexadecimal equivalent of the result.
(*d*)   Exit.

If the masking operation is selected, prompt the user for the type of operation (*bitwise and*, *bitwise exclusive or*, or *bitwise or*) and then a (hexadecimal) value for the mask. If the bit shifting operation is selected, prompt the user for the type of shift (left or right), and then the number of bits.

Test the program with several different (hexadecimal) input values of your own choice.

13.49   Modify the program written for Problem 13.48 above so that binary bit patterns are displayed in addition to hexadecimal values. Use a separate function, patterned after the program shown in Example 13.16, to display the binary bit patterns.

13.50   Modify the program written for Problem 13.49 so that the input quantity can be a decimal, hexadecimal or octal constant. Begin by displaying a menu that allows the user to specify the type of number (i.e., the desired number system) before entering the actual value. Then display the input value in the other two number systems and in terms of its equivalent binary bit pattern.

After the input quantity has been entered and displayed, generate the main menu prompting for the type of operation, as described in Problem 13.48. If a masking operation is selected, enter the mask as either a hexadecimal or an octal constant. Display the result of each operation in decimal, hexadecimal, octal and binary.

13.51   Write a C program that will illustrate the equivalence between

(*a*)   Shifting a binary number to the left n bits and multiplying the binary number by 2^n.
(*b*)   Shifting a binary number to the right n bits and dividing the binary number by 2^n (or equivalently, multiplying the binary number by 2^{-n}).

Choose the initial binary number carefully, so that bits will not be lost as a result of the shifting operation. (For the shift left, choose a relatively small number so that there will be several leading zeros in the leftmost bit positions. For the shift right, choose a relatively large number, with zeros in the rightmost bit positions.)

13.52   Write a complete C program that will encode and decode the contents of a text file (i.e., a character-oriented data file) by replacing each character with its one's complement. Note that the one's complement of a one's complement is the original character. Hence, the process of obtaining the one's complement can be used either to encode the original text or to decode the encoded text.

Include the following features in your program:

(*a*)   Enter the contents of an ordinary text file from the keyboard.
(*b*)   Save the current text file in its present state (either encoded or decoded).

(c) Retrieve a text file that has been saved (either encoded or decoded).

(d) Encode or decode the current text file (i.e., reverse its current state by obtaining the one's complement of each of the characters).

(e) Display the current text file in its present state (either encoded or decoded).

Generate a menu that will allow the user to select any of these features, as desired.

13.53 Alter the program written for Problem 13.52 so that the encoding and decoding is carried out using a *bitwise exclusive or* masking operation rather than the one's complement operation. Include a provision that will allow the user to specify a *key* (i.e., a mask, which will be the second operand in the *exclusive or* operation). Since *exclusive or* provides a toggling operation, it can be used either to encode the original text or to decode the encoded text. The same key must be used for both the encoding and the decoding.

13.54 Modify the data compression program shown in Example 13.23 so that it displays each student's age (in years), in addition to the output that is currently generated. Then add the following capabilities as separate features:

(a) Display the age of a student whose name and birthdate are specified as input items.

(b) Display the names of all students whose age is specified by the user.

(c) Display the names of all students who are the same age or younger than a certain value specified by the user.

(d) Display the names of all students who are the same age or older than a certain value specified by the user.

Generate a menu that will allow the user to select any of these features, as desired.

13.55 Modify the program presented in Example 10.8 (analyzing a line of text) so that the 80 characters within each line of text are stored within a 70-byte character array. (Assume 7-bit ASCII characters.) To do so, use the bitwise shift operators in such a manner that a group of eight characters is stored in seven consecutive array elements (i.e., 7 bytes). Each array element will contain one complete character, plus 1 bit from the eighth character.

Include a provision to display the contents of the 70-byte array (using hexadecimal constants) in compressed form and in the equivalent uncompressed form.

Use the program to analyze the following line of text:

```
Personal computers with memories in excess of 1024 KB have become very common.
```

(Note that this line of text, including punctuation and blank spaces between the words, contains a total of 78 characters.) Examine the hexadecimal output as well as the results of the analysis to verify that the program executes correctly.

Chapter 14

Some Additional Features of C

In this last chapter we consider several new, unrelated features of C, and we present some additional information about certain other features that have already been discussed. We begin with a discussion of enumerations—a data type which defines a set of integer-type identifiers that can be assigned to corresponding enumeration variables. Enumeration variables are useful in programs that require flags to identify various internal logical conditions.

We then consider command line arguments, which allow parameters to be transferred to a program when the compiled object program is executed from the operating system. File names, for example, can easily be transferred to a program in this manner.

A discussion of the C library functions is then presented, in which the library functions provided by most commercial C compilers are viewed from a broader perspective. This is followed by a discussion of macros, which provide an alternative to the use of library functions. The use of macros may be more desirable than the use of library functions in certain situations. The chapter concludes with a discussion of the C preprocessor, which is a set of special commands carried out at the beginning of the compilation process.

14.1 ENUMERATIONS

An *enumeration* is a data type, similar to a structure or a union. Its members are constants that are written as identifiers, though they have signed integer values. These constants represent values that can be assigned to corresponding enumeration variables.

In general terms, an enumeration may be defined as

```
enum   tag   {member 1,   member 2,   ...,   member m};
```

where enum is a required keyword, *tag* is a name that identifies enumerations having this composition, and *member 1, member 2, ... member m* represent the individual identifiers that may be assigned to variables of this type (see below). The member names must differ from one another, and they must be distinct from other identifiers whose scope is the same as that of the enumeration.

Once the enumeration has been defined, corresponding enumeration variables can be declared as

```
storage-class   enum   tag  variable 1,   variable 2,   ...,   variable n;
```

where *storage-class* is an optional storage class specifier, enum is a required keyword, *tag* is the name that appeared in the enumeration definition, and *variable 1, variable 2, ..., variable n* are enumeration variables of type *tag*.

The enumeration definition can be combined with the variable declarations, as indicated below.

```
storage-class   enum   tag   {member 1,   member 2,   ...,   member m}
                               variable 1,   variable 2,   ...   variable n;
```

The *tag* is optional in this situation.

447

Example 14.1   A C program contains the following declarations:

```
enum  colors  {black, blue, cyan, green, magenta, red, white, yellow};

colors  foreground, background;
```

The first line defines an enumeration named `colors` (i.e., the tag is `colors`). The enumeration consists of eight constants whose names are `black, blue, cyan, green, magenta, red, white` and `yellow`.

The second line declares the variables `foreground` and `background` to be enumeration variables of type `colors`. Thus, each variable can be assigned any one of the constants `black, blue, cyan, ..., yellow`.

The two declarations can be combined if desired, resulting in

```
enum  colors  {black, blue, cyan, green, magenta, red, white, yellow}
                                            foreground, background;
```

or, without the tag, simply

```
enum  {black, blue, cyan, green, magenta, red, white, yellow}
                                            foreground, background;
```

Enumeration constants are automatically assigned equivalent integer values, beginning with 0 for the first constant, with each successive constant increasing by 1. Thus, *member 1* will automatically be assigned the value 0, *member 2* will be assigned 1, and so on.

Example 14.2   Consider the enumeration defined in Example 14.1, i.e.,

```
enum  colors  {black, blue, cyan, green, magenta, red, white, yellow};
```

The enumeration constants will represent the following integer values:

```
black      0
blue       1
cyan       2
green      3
magenta    4
red        5
white      6
yellow     7
```

These automatic assignments can be overridden within the definition of the enumeration. That is, some constants can be assigned explicit integer values which differ from the default values. To do so, each constant (i.e., each member) which is assigned an explicit value is expressed as an ordinary assignment expression, i.e., *member = int*, where *int* represents a signed integer quantity. Those constants that are not assigned explicit values will automatically be assigned values which increase successively by 1 from the last explicit assignment. This may cause two or more enumeration constants to have the same integer value.

Example 14.3   Here is a variation of the enumeration defined in Examples 14.1 and 14.2.

```
enum  colors  {black = -1, blue, cyan, green, magenta, red = 2, white, yellow};
```

The enumeration constants will now represent the following integer values:

```
black      -1
blue        0
cyan        1
green       2
magenta     3
red         2
white       3
yellow      4
```

The constants `black` and `red` are now assigned the explicit values −1 and 2, respectively. The remaining enumeration constants are automatically assigned values that increase successively by 1 from the last explicit assignment. Thus, `blue`, `cyan`, `green` and `magenta` are assigned the values 0, 1, 2 and 3, respectively. Similarly, `white` and `yellow` are assigned the values 3 and 4. Notice that there are now duplicate assignments, i.e., `green` and `red` both represent 2, whereas `magenta` and `white` both represent 3.

Enumeration variables can be processed in the same manner as other integer variables; that is, they can be assigned new values, compared and so on. It should be understood, however, that enumeration variables are used internally, to indicate various conditions that can arise within a program. Hence, there are certain restrictions associated with their use. In particular, an enumeration constant cannot be read into the computer and assigned to an enumeration variable. (It is possible to enter an *integer* and assign it to an enumeration variable, though this is generally not done.) Moreover, only the integer value of an enumeration variable can be written out of the computer.

Example 14.4   Consider once again the declarations presented in Example 14.1, i.e.,

```
enum  colors  {black, blue, cyan, green, magenta, red, white, yellow};

colors  foreground, background;
```

Several typical statements involving the use of the enumeration variables `foreground` and `background` are shown below.

```
foreground = white;
```

```
background = blue;
```

```
if (background == blue)
   foreground = yellow;
else
   foreground = white;
```

```
if (foreground == background)
   foreground = (enum colors)  (++background % 8);
```

```
switch (background)  {

case black:
        foreground = white;
        break;

case blue:
     cyan:
     green:
     magenta:
     red:
        foreground = yellow;
        break;

case white:
        foreground = black;
        break;

case yellow:
        foreground = blue;
        break;

case default:
        printf("ERROR IN SELECTION OF BACKGROUND COLOR\n");
}
```

Using enumeration variables within a program can often increase the logical clarity of that program. Enumeration variables are particularly useful as flags, to indicate various options for carrying out a calculation, or to identify various conditions that may have arisen as a result of previous internal calculations. From this perspective, the use of enumeration variables within a complex program is encouraged. It should be understood, however, that ordinary integer variables can always be used in place of enumeration variables. Thus, enumeration variables do not provide any fundamentally new capabilities.

Example 14.5 Raising a Number to a Power In Example 11.37 we saw a C program to evaluate the formula $y = x^n$, where x and y are floating-point values and n is either an integer or a floating-point exponent. That program made use of the following data structures:

```
typedef  union  {
    float fexp;              /* floating-point exponent */
    int nexp;               /* integer exponent */
} nvals;

typedef  struct  {
    float x;                 /* value to be raised to a power */
    char flag;               /* 'f' if exponent is floating-point,
                                'i' if exponent is integer */
    nvals exp;               /* union containing exponent */
} values;
```

Note that the union contains the value of the exponent, which may be either an integer or a floating-point quantity. The structure includes the value of x, a flag (a single character, which indicates the nature of the exponent) and the union, which contains the exponent.

We now present another version of this program, in which the single-character flag is replaced with an enumeration variable. The data structures are therefore modified as follows:

```
typedef  enum  {floating_exp, integer_exp}  exp_type;

typedef  union  {
    float fexp;              /* floating-point exponent */
    int nexp;                /* integer exponent */
} nvals;

typedef  struct  {
    float x;                 /* value to be raised to a power */
    exp_type flag;           /* flag indicating type of exponent */
    nvals exp;               /* union containing exponent */
} values;
```

Notice that flag, which is a member of the structure of type values, is now an enumeration variable of type exp_type. This variable can take on the value floating_exp or integer_exp, indicating either a floating-point exponent or an integer exponent, respectively.

The calculations will be carried out differently, depending on the nature of the exponent. In particular, the exponentiation will be carried out by repeated multiplication in the case of an integer exponent, and by utilizing logarithms in the case of a floating-point exponent.

Here is the modified version of the program.

```
#include <stdio.h>
#include <math.h>

typedef  enum  {floating_exp, integer_exp}  exp_type;

typedef  union  {
    float fexp;              /* floating-point exponent */
    int nexp;                /* integer exponent */
} nvals;

typedef  struct  {
    float x;                 /* value to be raised to a power */
    exp_type flag;           /* flag indicating type of exponent */
    nvals exp;               /* union containing exponent */
} values;

main()    /* program to raise a number to a power */

{
    values a;                   /* structure containing x, flag and fexp/nexp */
    float power(values a);   /* function declaration */
    int i;
    float n, y;

    /* enter input data */
    printf("y = x^n\n\nEnter a value for x: ");
    scanf("%f", &a.x);
    printf("Enter a value for n: ");
    scanf("%f", &n);

    /* determine type of exponent */
    i = (int) n;
    a.flag = (i == n) ? integer_exp : floating_exp;
    if (a.flag == integer_exp)
        a.exp.nexp = i;
    else
        a.exp.fexp = n;
```

```
      /* raise x to the appropriate power and display the result */
      if (a.flag == floating_exp && a.x <= 0.0)   {
         printf("\nERROR - Cannot raise a non-positive number to a ");
         printf("floating-point power");
      }
      else  {
         y = power(a);
         printf("\ny = %.4f", y);
      }
}

float power(values a)   /* carry out the exponentiation */

{
      int i;
      float y = a.x;

      if (a.flag == integer_exp)  {   /* integer exponent */
         if (a.exp.nexp == 0)
            y = 1.0;                       /* zero exponent */
         else  {
            for (i = 1; i < abs(a.exp.nexp); ++i)
               y *= a.x;
            if (a.exp.nexp < 0)
               y = 1./y;                   /* negative integer exponent */
         }
      }
      else                               /* floating-point exponent */
         y = exp(a.exp.fexp * log(a.x));

      return(y);
}
```

When executed, this program behaves in exactly the same manner as the earlier version. You may wish to verify this by executing the program using the input values shown in Example 11.37.

This version of the program does not represent a dramatic improvement over the earlier version. The advantage in using enumeration variables becomes greater, however, in programs that include more complicated options.

An enumeration variable can be initialized, in much the same manner as other variables in C. The initialization can be accomplished by assigning either an enumeration constant or an integer value to the variable. Usually, however, the variable will be assigned an enumeration constant, as illustrated below (also, see Example 14.13).

Example 14.6   A C program contains the following declarations:

```
enum  colors  {black, blue, cyan, green, magenta, red, white, yellow};

colors  foreground = yellow, background = red;
```

Thus, the enumeration variables foreground and background are assigned the initial values yellow and red, respectively. These initialization assignments are equivalent to writing

```
foreground = 7;

background = 5;
```

However, enumeration variables are typically assigned enumeration constants rather than their equivalent integer values.

14.2 COMMAND LINE PARAMETERS

Have you been wondering about the empty parentheses in the first line of the main function, i.e., main()? These parentheses may contain special arguments that allow parameters to be passed to main from the operating system. Most versions of C permit two such arguments, which are traditionally called argc and argv, respectively. The first of these, argc, must be an integer variable, while the second, argv, is an array of pointers to characters, i.e., an array of strings. Each string in this array will represent a parameter that is passed to main. The value of argc will indicate the number of parameters passed.

Example 14.7 The following outline indicates how the arguments argc and argv are defined within main:

```
main(argc, argv)
int argc;
char *argv[];

{

    ...

}
```

In most newer versions of C, this outline can be written more concisely as

```
main(int argc, char *argv[])

{

    ...

}
```

Execution of a program is normally initiated by specifying the name of the program (actually, the name of the file containing the compiled object program) at the operating system level, as explained in Sec. 5.4. The program name is interpreted as an operating system command. Hence, the line in which it appears is generally referred to as the *command line*.

In order to pass one or more parameters to the program when the program execution is initiated, the parameters must follow the program name on the command line, for example,

program-name parameter 1 parameter 2 ... parameter n

The individual items must be separated from one another either by blank spaces or by tabs. Some operating systems permit blank spaces to be included within a parameter, as long as the entire parameter is enclosed in quotation marks.

The program name will be stored as the first item in argv, followed by each of the parameters. Hence, if the program name is followed by n parameters, there will be $(n + 1)$ entries in argv, ranging from argv[0] to argv[n]. Moreover, argc will automatically be assigned the value $(n + 1)$. Note that the value for argc is *not* supplied explicitly from the command line.

Example 14.8 Consider the following simple C program:

```
#include <stdio.h>

main(int argc, char *argv[])

{
    int count;

    printf("argc = %d\n", argc);

    for (count = 0; count < argc; ++count)
        printf("argv[%d] = %s\n", count, argv[count]);
}
```

This program will allow an unspecified number of parameters to be entered from the command line. When the program is executed, the current value for argc and the elements of argv will be displayed as separate lines of output.

Suppose, for example, that the program name is sample and the command line initiating the program execution is

```
sample  red  white  blue
```

Then the program will be executed, resulting in the following output:

```
argc = 4
argv[0] = sample.exe
argv[1] = red
argv[2] = white
argv[3] = blue
```

The output tells us that four separate items have been entered from the command line. The first is the program name, sample.exe, followed by the three parameters, red, white and blue. Each item is an element in the array argv. (Note that sample.exe is the name of the object file resulting from the compilation of the source code sample.c.)

Similarly, if the command line is

```
sample  red  "white  blue"
```

the resulting output will be

```
argc = 3
argv[0] = sample.exe
argv[1] = red
argv[2] = white  blue
```

In this case the string "white blue" will be interpreted as a single parameter, because of the quotation marks.

Once the parameters have been entered, they can be utilized within the program in any desired manner. One particularly common application is to specify the names of data files as command line parameters. This technique is illustrated below.

Example 14.9 Reading a Data File Here is a variation of the program shown in Example 12.4, which reads a line of text from a data file character-by-character and displays the text on the screen. In its original form, the program read the text from a data file called sample.dat, i.e., the name of the data file was built into the program. Now, however, the file name is entered as a command line parameter. Thus, the program is applicable to *any* data file; it is no longer confined to sample.dat.

Here is the entire program.

```
#include <stdio.h>

#define  NULL  0

/* read a line of text from a data file and display it on the screen */

main(int argc, char *argv[])

{
    FILE *fpt;    /* define a pointer to pre-defined structure type FILE */

    charc c;

    /* open the data file for reading only */
    if ((fpt = fopen(argv[1], "r")) == NULL)
        printf("\nERROR - Cannot open the designated file\n");

    else    /* read and display each character from the data file */
        do
            putchar(c = getc(fpt));
        while (c != '\n');

    /* close the data file */
    fclose(fpt);
}
```

Notice that the main function now includes the formal arguments argc and argv, defined in the manner described earlier. Also, the fopen function is now written as fopen(argv[1], "r") rather than fopen("sample.dat", "r") as in the earlier version of the program.

Now suppose that the program name is readfile. To execute this program and read the data file sample.dat, the command line would be written

```
readfile  sample.dat
```

The program will then behave in exactly the same manner as the earlier version shown in Example 12.4.

14.3 MORE ABOUT LIBRARY FUNCTIONS

By now we have learned that the C library functions are extensive, both in number and in purpose. We have seen evidence of this in the programming examples presented earlier in this book, and in the list of commonly used library functions given in Appendix H. Throughout this book we have used these library functions freely, wherever they were needed.

It should be understood, however, that all the library functions presented in this book fall into a few basic categories. In particular, they facilitate various input/output operations, mathematical function evaluations, data conversions, character classifications and conversions, string manipulations, dynamic memory allocation, and certain miscellaneous operations associated with clock time.

Most commercial C compilers include many additional library functions. Some of these functions fall into the categories described above, while others fall into new categories that have not been described elsewhere in this book. For example, most compilers include library functions that can manipulate buffer areas (i.e., blocks of memory in which arrays of characters are stored temporarily), facilitate file handling and file management, and provide capabilities for carrying out searching and sorting. In addition, there may be library functions that provide access to certain operating system commands and to the computer's internal hardware (especially instructions embedded in the computer's read-only memory). And finally, some compilers include categories of library functions for more specialized applications, such as process control and computer graphics.

These library functions simplify the writing of comprehensive C programs in a number of important areas. For example, C is used to write operating systems, as well as office automation applications such as word processors, spreadsheets and data base management programs. The well-known UNIX® operating system is written primarily in C. So are many commercial office automation programs.

The process control functions permit applications in which programs are executed simultaneously, in a hierarchical manner. Similarly, the graphics functions facilitate the writing of various graphics applications, such as "paint" programs and computer-aided design (CAD) applications. The use of C for other types of commercial applications appears to be increasing rapidly.

Detailed discussions of such comprehensive programming applications are well beyond the scope of the present text. However, readers should be aware that it is practical to write such applications in C, largely because of the availability of the extensive C library. Readers who wish to pursue these topics further should familiarize themselves with the library functions that accompany their particular C compilers.

14.4   MACROS

We have already seen that the #define statement can be used to define symbolic constants within a C program. At the beginning of the compilation process, all symbolic constants are replaced by their equivalent text (see Sec. 2.9). Thus, symbolic constants provide a form of shorthand notation that can simplify a program's organization.

The #define statement can be used for more, however, than simply defining symbolic constants. In particular, it can be used to define *macros*, i.e., single identifiers that are equivalent to expressions, complete statements or groups of statements. Macros resemble functions in this sense. They are defined in an altogether different manner than functions, however, and they are treated differently during the compilation process.

Example 14.10   Consider the simple C program shown below.

```
#include <stdio.h>

#define  area  length * width

main()

{
    int length, width;

    printf("length = ");
    scanf("%d", &length);
    printf("width = ");
    scanf("%d", &width);

    printf("area = %d", area);
}
```

This program contains the macro area, which represents the expression length * width. When the program is compiled, the expression length * width will replace the identifier area within the printf statement, so that the printf statement will become

```
printf("area = %d", length * width);
```

Note that the *string* "area = %d" is unaffected by the #define statement (see Sec. 2.9).

When the program is executed, the values for length and width are entered interactively from the keyboard and the corresponding value for area is displayed. A typical interactive session is shown below. The user's responses are underlined, as usual.

```
length = 3
width = 4
area = 12
```

Macro definitions are customarily placed at the beginning of a file, ahead of the first function definition. The scope of a macro definition extends from its point of definition to the end of the file. A macro defined in one file is not recognized within another file.

Multiline macros can be defined by placing a backward slash (\) at the end of each line except the last. This feature permits a single macro (i.e., a single identifier) to represent a compound statement.

Example 14.11   Here is another simple C program that contains a macro.

```
#include <stdio.h>

#define  loop  for (lines = 1; lines <= n; lines++)  {            \
                  for (count = 1; count <= n - lines; count++)     \
                    putchar(' ');                                  \
                  for (count = 1; count <= 2 * lines - 1; count++) \
                    putchar('*');                                  \
                  printf("\n");                                    \
                }

main()

{
    int count, lines, n;

    printf("number of lines = ");
    scanf("%d", &n);
    printf("\n");

    loop
}
```

This program contains a multiline macro, which represents a compound statement. The compound statement consists of several embedded `for` loops. Notice the backward slash (\) at the end of each line, except the last.

When this program is compiled, the reference to the macro is actually replaced by the statements contained within the macro definition. Thus, the above program becomes

```
#include <stdio.h>

main()

{
    int count, lines, n;

    printf("number of lines = ");
    scanf("%d", &n);
    printf("\n");

    for (lines = 1; lines <= n; lines++)  {
        for (count = 1; count <= n - lines; count++)
            putchar(' ');
        for (count = 1; count <= 2 * lines - 1; count++)
            putchar('*');
        printf("\n");

    }
}
```

When the program is executed it displays a triangle of asterisks, whose size, in terms of the number of lines, is determined by a user-supplied value (i.e., the value for n). The result of a typical execution is shown below. Again, the user's response is underlined.

```
number of lines = 6

     *
    ***
   *****
  *******
 *********
***********
```

A macro definition may include arguments, which are enclosed in parentheses. The left parenthesis must appear immediately after the macro name, i.e., there can be no space separating the macro name from the left parenthesis. When a macro is defined in this manner, its appearance within a program resembles a function call.

Example 14.12 Here is another variation of the program shown in Example 14.11.

```
#include <stdio.h>

#define  loop(n)  for (lines = 1; lines <= n; lines++)  {           \
                    for (count = 1; count <= n - lines; count++)     \
                        putchar(' ');                                \
                    for (count = 1; count <= 2 * lines - 1; count++) \
                        putchar('*');                                \
                    printf("\n");                                    \
                  }

main()

{
    int count, lines, n;

    printf("number of lines = ");
    scanf("%d", &n);
    printf("\n");

    loop(n)
}
```

The program now passes the value of n to the macro, as though it were an actual argument in a function call. This program behaves in exactly the same manner as the program shown in Example 14.11 when it is executed.

Macros are sometimes used in place of functions within a program. The use of a macro in place of a function eliminates the time delays associated with the function calls. If a program contains many repeated function calls, the time savings resulting from the use of macros can become significant.

On the other hand, macro substitution will take place wherever a reference to a macro appears within a program. Thus, a program that contains several references to the same macro may become unreasonably long. We are therefore faced with a tradeoff between execution speed and size of the compiled object program. The use of a macro is most advantageous in applications where there are relatively few function calls but the function is called repeatedly (e.g., a single function call within a loop).

Example 14.13 Future Value of Monthly Deposits (Compound Interest Calculations) In Example 10.31 we saw a C program that generates the future value of a given sum of money over a specified time period for various interest rates. The program was originally structured in a manner that illustrates how one function can be passed as an argument to another function. In particular, main passed another function, either md1, md2 or md3, to table, which generated a table of future value vs. interest rate.

We now present two variations of that program. The first version utilizes function calls directly from main, whereas the second version makes use of macro substitution. Here is the first version.

```c
/* personal finance calculations, using function calls */

#include <stdio.h>
#include <stdlib.h>
#include <math.h>

main()    /* calculate the future value of a series of monthly deposits */
{
    enum {A = 1, S = 2, Q = 4, M = 12, D = 360, C} m;
                /* number of compounding periods per year */
    int count;   /* loop counter */
    double n;    /* number of years */
    double a;    /* amount of each monthly payment */
    double i;    /* annual interest rate */
    double f;    /* future value */
    char freq;   /* frequency of compounding indicator */

    /* function prototypes */
    double md1(double i, int m, double n);
    double md2(double i, int m, double n);
    double md3(double i, double n);

    /* enter input data */
    printf("\nFUTURE VALUE OF A SERIES OF MONTHLY DEPOSITS\n\n");
    printf("Amount of Each Monthly Payment: ");
    scanf("%lf", &a);
    printf("Number of Years: ");
    scanf("%lf", &n);

    /* enter frequency of compounding */
    do  {
            printf("Frequency of Compounding (A, S, Q, M, D, C): ");
            scanf("%1s", &freq);
            freq = toupper(freq);    /* convert to upper-case */
            if (freq == 'A')   {
                m = A;
                printf("\nAnnual Compounding\n");
            }
            else if (freq == 'S')   {
                m = S;
                printf("\nSemiannual Compounding\n");
            }
            else if (freq == 'Q')   {
                m = Q;
                printf("\nQuarterly Compounding\n");
            }
            else if (freq == 'M')   {
                m = M;
                printf("\nMonthly Compounding\n");
            }
            else if (freq == 'D')   {
                m = D;
                printf("\nDaily Compounding\n");
            }
```

```
            else if (freq == 'C')    {
                m = C;
                printf("\nContinuous Compounding\n");
            }
            else
                printf("\nERROR - Please Repeat\n\n");
        }
    while (freq != 'A' && freq != 'S' && freq != 'Q' &&
           freq != 'M' && freq != 'D' && freq != 'C');

    /* carry out the calculations */
    printf("\nInterest Rate    Future Amount\n\n");
    for (count = 1; count <= 20; ++count)    {
        i = 0.01 * count;
        if (m == C)
            f = a * md3(i, n);         /* continuous compounding */
        else if (m == D)
            f = a * md2(i, m, n);    /* daily compounding */
        else
            f = a * md1(i, m, n);    /* annual, semiannual, quarterly or
                                                monthly compounding */
        printf("      %2d               %.2f\n", count, f);
    }
}


double md1(double i, int m, double n)
/* monthly deposits, periodic compounding */

{
    double factor, ratio;

    factor = 1 + i/m;
    ratio = 12 * (pow(factor, m*n) - 1) / i;
    return(ratio);
}


double md2(double i, int m, double n)
/* monthly deposits, daily compounding */

{
    double factor, ratio;

    factor = 1 + i/m;
    ratio = (pow(factor, m*n) - 1) / (pow(factor, m/12) - 1);
    return(ratio);
}


double md3(double i, double n)
/* monthly deposits, continuous compounding */

{
    double ratio;

    ratio = (exp(i*n) - 1) / (exp(i/12) - 1);
    return(ratio);
}
```

Notice that the function `table`, which was included in the original program, is now combined with `main`, thus avoiding the need to pass one function to another. The current program utilizes an enumeration to simplify the internal bookkeeping somewhat.

Here is the second version, which utilizes macro substitution in place of the functions.

```c
/* personal finance calculations, using macro substitutions */

#include <stdio.h>
#include <stdlib.h>
#include <math.h>

#define  md1(i, m, n)  {    /* monthly deposits, periodic compounding */    \
             factor = 1 + i/m;                                              \
             ratio = (12/m) * (pow(factor, m*n) - 1) / (i/m);              \
        }

#define  md2(i, m, n)  {    /* monthly deposits, daily compounding */       \
             factor = 1 + i/m;                                              \
             ratio = (pow(factor, m*n) - 1) / (pow(factor, m/12) - 1);     \
        }

#define  md3(i, n)     {    /* monthly deposits, continuous compounding */ \
             ratio = (exp(i*n) - 1) / (exp(i/12) - 1);                     \
        }


main()    /* calculate the future value of a series of monthly deposits */
{
    enum {A = 1, S = 2, Q = 4, M = 12, D = 360, C} m;
                              /* number of compounding periods per year */
    int count;                /* loop counter */
    double n;                 /* number of years */
    double a;                 /* amount of each monthly payment */
    double i;                 /* annual interest rate */
    double f;                 /* future value */
    double factor, ratio;     /* internal parameters */
    char freq;                /* frequency of compounding indicator */

    /* enter input data */
    printf("\nFUTURE VALUE OF A SERIES OF MONTHLY DEPOSITS\n\n");
    printf("Amount of Each Monthly Payment: ");
    scanf("%lf", &a);
    printf("Number of Years: ");
    scanf("%lf", &n);

    /* enter frequency of compounding */
    do  {
            printf("Frequency of Compounding (A, S, Q, M, D, C): ");
            scanf("%1s", &freq);
            freq = toupper(freq);   /* convert to upper-case */
            if (freq == 'A')  {
                m = A;
                printf("\nAnnual Compounding\n");
            }
            else if (freq == 'S')  {
                m = S;
                printf("\nSemiannual Compounding\n");
            }
```

```
        else if (freq == 'Q')   {
            m = Q;
            printf("\nQuarterly Compounding\n");
        }
        else if (freq == 'M')   {
            m = M;
            printf("\nMonthly Compounding\n");
        }
        else if (freq == 'D')   {
            m = D;
            printf("\nDaily Compounding\n");
        }
        else if (freq == 'C')   {
            m = C;
            printf("\nContinuous Compounding\n");
        }
        else
            printf("\nERROR - Please Repeat\n\n");
    }
    while (freq != 'A' && freq != 'S' && freq != 'Q' &&
           freq != 'M' && freq != 'D' && freq != 'C');

    /* carry out the calculations */
    printf("\nInterest Rate    Future Amount\n\n");
    for (count = 1; count <= 20; ++count)   {
        i = 0.01 * count;
        if (m == C)
            md3(i, n)                       /* continuous compounding */
        else if (m == D)
            md2(i, m, n)                    /* daily compounding */
        else
            md1(i, m, n)                    /* annual, semiannual, quarterly or
                                               monthly compounding */
        f = a * ratio;
        printf("      %2d            %.2f\n", count, f);
    }
}
```

Examine these two programs carefully, comparing the use of macro substitution in place of the functions. In particular, notice the manner in which the functions are accessed in the first program, compared with the references to the macros in the second program (refer to the nested if - else statements at the end of main).

When executed, both of these programs behave in exactly the same manner as the original program given in Example 10.31.

Many commercial C compilers offer certain library functions both as macros and as true functions. The macros are defined in the various header files. The programmer may then choose which form is most appropriate for each particular application. You should understand, however, that there are certain disadvantages associated with the use of macros in place of functions, aside from the potentially significant increase in program length. In particular:

1. When passing arguments to a macro, the number of arguments will be checked, but their data types will not. Thus, there is less error checking than with a function call.

2. A macro identifier is not associated with an address, so that a macro cannot be utilized as a pointer. Thus, a macro identifier cannot be passed to a function as an argument in the same sense that a function can be passed to another function as an argument (see Sec. 10.8). Moreover, a macro cannot call itself recursively.

3.   There are possible undesirable side effects associated with the use of macros, particularly when calling arguments are involved.

Example 14.14   Consider the macro definition

```
#define root(a, b)  sqrt(a*a + b*b)
```

Now suppose that this macro is utilized within a program in the following manner:

```
root(a+1, b+2)
```

The intent, of course, is to evaluate the formula

```
sqrt((a+1)*(a+1) + (b+2)*(b+2))
```

However, each appearance of a is replaced by a + 1 (without parentheses), and each appearance of b is replaced by b + 2. Therefore, the result of the macro substitution will be

```
sqrt(a+1*a+1 + b+2*b+2)
```

This expression is equivalent to

```
sqrt(2*a+1 + 3*b+2) = sqrt(2*a + 3*b + 3)
```

which is clearly incorrect. The source of error can be corrected, however, by placing additional parentheses within the macro definition, that is,

```
#define  root(a, b)  sqrt((a)*(a) + (b)*(b))
```

   A more subtle error occurs if we write

```
root(a++, b++)
```

The macro substitution results in the expression

```
sqrt(a*(a+1) + b*(b+1))
```

rather than

```
sqrt(a*a + b*b)
```

as intended. This is an example of an undesired side effect. Placing additional parentheses within the macro definition will not correct this problem.

14.5   THE C PREPROCESSOR

The C preprocessor is a collection of special statements, called *directives*, that are executed at the beginning of the compilation process. The #include and #define statements considered earlier in this book are preprocessor directives. Additional preprocessor directives are #if, #elif, #else, #endif, #ifdef, #ifndef, #line and #undef. The preprocessor also includes three special operators: defined, #, and ##.

   Preprocessor directives usually appear at the beginning of a program, though this is not a firm requirement. Thus, a preprocessor directive may appear anywhere within a program. However, the directive will apply only to the portion of the program following its appearance.

   For the beginning programmer, some of the preprocessor directives are relatively unimportant. Hence, we will not describe each preprocessor feature in detail. The more important features are discussed below.

The #if, #elif, #else and #endif directives are used most frequently. They permit conditional compilation of the source program, depending on the value of one or more true/false conditions. They are sometimes used in conjunction with the defined operator, which is used to determine whether or not a symbolic constant or a macro identifier has been defined within a program.

Example 14.15 The following preprocessor directives illustrate the conditional compilation of a C program. The conditional compilation depends on the status of the symbolic constant FOREGROUND.

```
#if defined(FOREGROUND)
    #define  BACKGROUND  0
#else
    #define  FOREGROUND  0
    #define  BACKGROUND  7
#endif
```

Thus, if FOREGROUND has already been defined, the symbolic constant BACKGROUND will represent the value 0. Otherwise, FOREGROUND and BACKGROUND will represent the values 0 and 7, respectively.

Here is another way to accomplish the same thing.

```
#ifdef  FOREGROUND
    #define  BACKGROUND  0
#else
    #define  FOREGROUND  0
    #define  BACKGROUND  7
#endif
```

The directive #ifdef is equivalent to #if defined(). Similarly, the directive #ifndef is equivalent to #if !defined(), i.e., "if not defined." The original approach, in which the defined operator appears explicitly, is the preferred form.

In each of these examples, the last directive is #endif. The preprocessor requires that any set of directives beginning with #if, #ifdef or #ifndef must end with #endif.

The directive #elif is analogous to an else – if clause using ordinary C control statements. An #if directive can be followed by any number of #elif directives, though there can be only one #else directive. The appearance of the #else directive is optional, as determined by the required program logic.

Example 14.16 Here is another illustration of conditional compilation. In this situation the conditional compilation will depend on the value that is represented by the symbolic constant BACKGROUND.

```
#if BACKGROUND == 7
    #define  FOREGROUND  0
#elif BACKGROUND == 6
    #define  FOREGROUND  1
#else
    #define  FOREGROUND  6
#endif
```

In this example we see that FOREGROUND will represent 0 if BACKGROUND represents 7, and FOREGROUND will represent 1 if BACKGROUND represents 6. Otherwise, FOREGROUND will represent 6.

The #undef directive "undefines" a symbolic constant or a macro identifier, i.e., it negates the effect of a #define directive that may have appeared earlier in the program.

Example 14.17   The following example illustrates the use of the #undef directive within a C program:

```
#define  FOREGROUND  7
#define  BACKGROUND  Ø

main()

{

    ...

    #undef  FOREGROUND

    ...

    #undef  BACKGROUND

    ...

}
```

The symbolic constants FOREGROUND and BACKGROUND are defined by the first two directives. These definitions are then negated by the #undef directives, when they appear later in the program. Before the #undef directives, any references to FOREGROUND or BACKGROUND will be associated with the values 7 and Ø, respectively. After the #undef directives, any references to FOREGROUND or BACKGROUND will be ignored.

The "stringizing" operator # allows a formal argument within a macro definition to be converted to a string. If a formal argument in a macro definition is preceded by this operator, the corresponding actual argument will automatically be enclosed in double quotes. Consecutive whitespace characters inside the actual argument will be replaced by a single blank space, and any special characters, such as ', " and \, will be replaced by their corresponding escape sequences, e.g., \', \" and \\. In addition, the resulting string will automatically be concatenated (combined) with any adjacent strings.

Example 14.18   Here is an illustration of the use of the "stringizing" operator, #.

```
#define  display(text)  printf(#text "\n")

main()

{
    ...

    display (Please do not sleep in class. );

    ...

    display(Please - don't snore during the professor's lecture!);
}
```

Within main, the macros are equivalent to

```
printf("Please do not sleep in class. \n");
```

and

```
printf("Please   -   don\'t snore during the professor\'s lecture!\n");
```

Notice that each actual argument is converted to a string within the `printf` function. Each argument is concatenated with a newline character (\n), which is written as a separate string within the macro definition. Also, notice that the consecutive blank spaces appearing in the second argument are replaced by single blank spaces, and each apostrophe (') is replaced by its corresponding escape sequence (\').

Executing this program will result in the following output:

```
Please do not sleep in class.


Please - don't snore during the professor's lecture!
```

The "token-pasting" operator `##` causes individual items within a macro definition to be concatenated, thus forming a single item. The various rules governing the use of this operator are somewhat complicated. However, the general purpose of the token-pasting operator is illustrated in the following example.

Example 14.19 A C program contains the following macro definition:

```
#define  display(i)  printf("x" #i " = %f\n", x##i)
```

Suppose this macro is accessed by writing

```
display(3);
```

The result will be

```
printf("x3 = %f\n", x3);
```

Thus, the expression `x##i` becomes the variable `x3`, since 3 is the current value of the argument `i`.

Notice that this example illustrates the use of both the stringizing operator (`#`) and the token-pasting operator (`##`).

Refer to the programmer's reference manual for your particular C compiler for more information on the use of the C preprocessor.

Review Questions

14.1 What is an enumeration? How is an enumeration defined?

14.2 What are enumeration constants? In what form are they written?

14.3 Summarize the rules for assigning names to enumeration constants.

14.4 Summarize the rules for assigning numerical values to enumeration constants. What default values are assigned to enumeration constants?

14.5 Can two or more enumeration constants have the same numerical value? Explain.

14.6 What are enumeration variables? How are they declared?

14.7 In what ways can enumeration variables be processed? What restrictions apply to the processing of enumeration variables?

14.8 What advantage is there in using enumeration variables within a program?

14.9 Summarize the rules for assigning initial values to enumeration variables. Compare your answer with that for Question 14.4.

14.10 Most C programs recognize two formal arguments in the definition of function `main`. What are they traditionally called? What are their respective data types?

14.11 Describe the information represented by each formal argument in function `main`. Is information passed explicitly to each argument?

14.12 When parameters are passed to a program from the command line, how is the program execution initiated? Where do the parameters appear?

14.13 What useful purpose can be served by command line parameters when executing a program involving the use of data files?

14.14 The library functions discussed in earlier chapters of this book are all members of a few broad categories of library functions. Describe each category, in general terms.

14.15 Describe, in general terms, some additional categories of library functions that are provided with most commercial C compilers. What is the purpose of each category?

14.16 What is a macro? Summarize the similarities and differences between macros and functions.

14.17 How is a multiline macro defined?

14.18 Describe the use of arguments within a macro.

14.19 What is the principal advantage in the use of a macro rather than a function? What is the principal disadvantage? What other disadvantages are there?

14.20 Summarize the various preprocessor directives, other than `#include` and `#define`. Indicate the purpose of the more commonly used directives.

14.21 What is the scope of a preprocessor directive within a program file?

14.22 Summarize the special preprocessor operators `#` and `##`. What is the purpose of each?

14.23 What is meant by conditional compilation? In general terms, how is conditional compilation carried out? What preprocessor directives are available for this purpose?

Problems

14.24 Define an enumeration type called `flags`, having the following members: `first`, `second`, `third`, `fourth` and `fifth`.

14.25 Define an enumeration variable called `event`, of type `flags` (see the preceding problem).

14.26 Define two enumeration variables, called `soprano` and `bass`, whose members are as follows: `do`, `re`, `mi`, `fa`, `sol`, `la` and `ti`. Assign the following integer values to these members:

```
do    1
re    2
mi    3
fa    4
sol   5
la    6
ti    7
```

14.27 Define an enumeration type called `money`, having the following members: `penny`, `nickel`, `dime`, `quarter`, `half` and `dollar`. Assign the following integer values to these members:

```
penny      1
nickel     5
dime       1Ø
quarter    25
half       5Ø
dollar     1ØØ
```

14.28 Define an enumeration variable called `coins`, of type `money` (see the preceding problem). Assign the initial value `dime` to `coins`.

14.29 In the following enumeration declaration, determine the value of each member:

```
enum  compass  {north = 2, south, east = 1, west};
```

14.30 Determine the value associated with each of the following enumeration variables (see the preceding problem):

```
enum  compass  move_1 = south, move_2 = north;
```

14.31 Explain the purpose of the following program outline (refer to Problem 14.29 for the meaning of compass):

```
int score = 0;
enum compass move;

. . .

switch (move)  {

case north:
    score += 10:
    break;

case south:
    score += 20:
    break;

case east:
    score += 30:
    break;

case west:
    score += 40:
    break;

default:
    printf("ERROR - Please try again\n");
}
```

14.32 The outline of a C program is shown below.

```
main(int argc, char *argv[])

{

    . . .

}
```

(a) Suppose the compiled object program is stored in a file called demo.exe, and the following commands are issued to initiate the execution of the program:

```
demo  debug  fast
```

Determine the value of argc and the nonempty elements of argv.

(b) Suppose the command line is written as

```
demo  "debug  fast"
```

How will this change affect the values of argc and argv?

14.33 Describe the purpose of the C program shown below.

```
#include <stdio.h>

main(int argc, char *argv[])

{
    char letter[80];
    int count, tag;

    for (count = 0; (letter[count] = getchar()) != '\n'; ++count)
        ;
    tag = count;
    for (count = 0; count < tag; ++count)
        if (strcmpi(argv[1], "upper") == 0)
            putchar(toupper(letter[count]));
        else if (strcmpi(argv[1], "lower") == 0)
                putchar(tolower(letter[count]));
            else {
                puts("ERROR IN COMMAND LINE - PLEASE TRY AGAIN");
                break;
            }
}
```

14.34   Consider the program shown below, which reads a line of text from an existing data file, displays it on the screen and writes it out to a new data file.

```
#include <stdio.h>

#define  NULL   0

/* read a line of text from a data file, display it on the screen
                                and write it to a new data file */

main(int argc, char *argv[])

{
    FILE *fpt1, *fpt2;

    char c;

    /* open the old data file for reading only */
    if ((fpt1 = fopen(argv[1], "r")) == NULL)
        printf("\nERROR - Cannot open the designated file\n");

    /* read, display and write each character from the old data file */
    else
        fpt2 = fopen(argv[2], "w");
        do {
                putchar(c = getc(fpt1));
                putc(c, fpt2);
        } while (c != '\n');

    /* close the data files */
    fclose(fpt1);
    fclose(fpt2);
}
```

Suppose the program is stored in a file called transfer.exe, the old data file is called data.old and the new data file is called data.new. How should the command line be written in order to execute this program?

14.35 Write a symbolic constant or a macro definition for each of the following situations. Do not include arguments unless the problem asks you to do so.

(a) Define the symbolic constant PI to represent the value 3.1415927.

(b) Define a macro called AREA, which will calculate the area of a circle in terms of its radius. Use the constant PI, defined in Problem 14.35(a), in the calculation.

(c) Rewrite the macro described in the preceding problem so that the radius is expressed as an argument.

(d) Define a macro called CIRCUMFERENCE, which will calculate the circumference of a circle in terms of its radius. Use the constant PI, defined in Problem 14.35(a), in the calculation.

(e) Rewrite the macro described in the preceding problem so that the radius is expressed as an argument.

(f) Write a multiline macro called interest, which will evaluate the compound interest formula

$$F = P(1 + i)^n$$

where F is the future amount of money that will accumulate after n years, P is the principal (i.e., the original amount of money), $i = 0.01r$ and r is the annual interest rate expressed as a percentage.

        Evaluate i on one line of the macro, and evaluate F on a separate line. Assume that all of the symbols represent floating-point quantities.

(g) Rewrite the macro described in the preceding problem so that P, r and n are expressed as arguments.

(h) Write a macro called max that utilizes the conditional operator (? :) to determine the maximum of a and b, where a and b are integer quantities.

(i) Rewrite the macro described in the preceding problem so that a and b are expressed as arguments.

14.36 Explain the purpose of each of the following groups of preprocessor directives:

(a)
```
#if !defined(FLAG)
    #define  FLAG  1
#endif
```

(b)
```
#if defined(PASCAL)
    #define  BEGIN  {
    #define  END    }
#endif
```

(c)
```
#ifdef  CELSIUS
    #define  temperature(t)  0.5555555 * (t - 32)
#else
    #define  temperature(t)  1.8 * t + 32
#endif
```

(d)
```
#ifndef  DEBUG
    #define  out  printf("x = %f\n", x)
#elif  LEVEL == 1
    #define  out  printf("i = %d   y = %f\n", i, y[i])
#else
    #define  out  for (count = 1; count <= n; ++count)
                      printf("i = %d   y = %f\n", i, y[i])
#endif
```

(e)
```
#if defined(DEBUG)
    #undef  DEBUG
#endif
```

(f)
```
#ifdef  ERROR_CHECKS
    #define  message(line)  printf(#line)
#endif
```

(g)
```
#if defined(ERROR_CHECKS)
    #define  message(n)  printf("%s\n", message##n)
#endif
```

14.37 Write one or more preprocessor directives for each of the following situations:

  (a) If the symbolic constant BOOLEAN has been defined, define the symbolic constants TRUE and FALSE so that their values are 1 and Ø, respectively, and negate the definitions of the symbolic constants YES and NO.

  (b) If flag has a value of Ø, define the symbolic constant COLOR to have a value of 1. Otherwise, if the value of flag is less than 3, define COLOR to have a value of 2; and if the value of flag equals or exceeds 3, define COLOR to have a value of 3.

  (c) If the symbolic constant SIZE has the same value as the symbolic constant WIDE, define the symbolic constant WIDTH to have a value of 132; otherwise, define WIDTH to have a value of 8Ø.

  (d) Use the "stringizing" operator to define a macro called error(text) that will display text as a string.

  (e) Use the "token-pasting" operator to define a macro called error(i) that will print the value of the string variable errori (e.g., error1).

14.38 Familiarize yourself with the library functions and the header files that accompany your particular C compiler. Are some functions available both as macros and as true functions?

14.39 Does the library accompanying your particular C compiler include graphics or process control routines? Are other special routines included? If so, what are they?

Programming Problems

14.40 Modify the programs given in Example 14.13 (future value of monthly deposits) so that they accept a command line parameter, which indicates the frequency of compounding. The command line parameter should be a single character, selected from A, S, Q, M, D or C (either upper- or lowercase), as explained in the example.

14.41 Modify the program given in Example 6.21 (solution of an algebraic equation) so that flag is an enumeration variable whose value is either true or false.

14.42 Modify the program given in Example 6.32 (searching for palindromes) so that flag is an enumeration variable whose value is either true or false.

14.43 Modify the program given in Example 7.9 (largest of three integer quantities) so that the function maximum is written as a multiline macro.

14.44 Modify the program given in Example 7.16 (shooting craps) so that the function throw is written as a multiline macro. Can an enumeration variable be used effectively in this particular problem?

14.45 Modify the program given in Example 7.10 (calculating factorials) so that the function factorial is written as a multiline macro.

14.46 Write a complete C program to solve the problem described in Problem 7.42 (roots of a quadratic equation). Include an enumeration variable within the program.

14.47 Write a complete C program to solve the problem described in Problem 9.46 (names of countries and their capitals). Use an enumeration variable to distinguish between the two program options (i.e., find the name of a capital for a specified country, or find the country whose capital is specified).

14.48 Modify the program given in Example 10.28 (displaying the day of the year) so that it makes use of an enumeration variable to represent the months of the year.

14.49 Write a complete C program to solve the problem described in Problem 11.67 (maintaining baseball/football team statistics). Include an enumeration variable to distinguish between baseball and football.

14.50 Write a complete C program to solve the problem described in Problem 11.71 (an RPN calculator). Include an enumeration variable to identify the types of arithmetic operations that will be carried out by the calculator.

14.51 Repeat Problem 14.50, utilizing macros in place of functions.

14.52 Modify the program given in each of the following examples so that the required file name is entered as a command line parameter:

  (a) Example 12.3 (creating a data file)
  (b) Example 12.4 (reading a data file)

14.53 Modify the program given in each of the following examples so that the required file names are entered as command line parameters. Utilize an enumeration variable to represent internal true/false conditions within each program.

(a) Example 12.5 (creating a file containing customer records)
(b) Example 12.6 (updating a file containing customer records)
(c) Example 12.7 (creating an unformatted data file containing customer records)
(d) Example 12.8 (updating an unformatted data file containing customer records)

14.54 Write a complete C program to solve each of the following problems:

(a) Problem 12.50 (line-oriented text editor)
(b) Problem 12.51 (maintaining baseball/football team statistics in a data file)

For each program, enter the required file names as command line parameters.

14.55 Each of the following problems requires that one or more numerical values be specified as command line parameters. Use the library functions atoi and atof to convert the command line parameters into integers and floating-point values, respectively.

(a) Write a complete C program to solve the problem described in Problem 7.49(a) (recursive generation of Legendre polynomials). Enter the values of n and x as command line parameters.
(b) Write a complete C program to solve the problem described in Problem 7.49(b) (calculate the sum of n floating-point numbers recursively). Enter the value of n as a command line parameter (but enter the individual floating-point numbers interactively, as before).
(c) Write a complete C program to solve the problem described in Problem 7.49(c) (calculate the first n terms of a series recursively). Enter the value of n as a command line parameter.
(d) Write a complete C program to solve the problem described in Problem 7.49(d) (calculate the product of n floating-point numbers recursively). Enter the value of n as a command line parameter. (Enter the individual floating-point numbers interactively, however, as before.)
(e) Modify the program given in Example 8.4 (search for a maximum) in the following ways:

 (i) Enter values for CNST, a and b as command line parameters.
 (ii) Write the function curve as a macro.

(f) Modify the program given in Example 8.7 (generating Fibonacci numbers) so that the value for n is entered as a command line parameter.
(g) Modify the program given in Example 9.13 (reordering a list of numbers) so that the value for n is entered as a command line parameter.
(h) Modify the program given in Example 9.19 (adding two tables of numbers) so that the values of nrows and ncols are entered as command line parameters.

14.56 Write a complete C program to generate the table described in Problem 9.43. Use a macro to evaluate the formula

$$y = 2e^{-0.1t} \sin 0.5t$$

14.57 Write a complete C program to generate the table described in Problem 9.44. Use a macro to evaluate the formula

$$F/P = (1 + i/100)^n$$

14.58 Write a complete C program to solve the problem described in Problem 7.44 (evaluating the formula $y = x^n$). Use a multiline macro in place of the function to carry out the exponentiation.

Appendix A

Number Systems

Decimal	Binary	Octal	Hexadecimal
0	0000	0	0
1	0001	1	1
2	0010	2	2
3	0011	3	3
4	0100	4	4
5	0101	5	5
6	0110	6	6
7	0111	7	7
8	1000	10	8
9	1001	11	9
10	1010	12	A
11	1011	13	B
12	1100	14	C
13	1101	15	D
14	1110	16	E
15	1111	17	F

Notice that there are eight octal digits and 16 hexadecimal digits. The octal digits range from 0 to 7; the hexadecimal digits range from 0 to 9, and then from A to F.

Each octal digit is equivalent to three binary digits (3 bits), and each hexadecimal digit is equivalent to four binary digits (4 bits). Thus, octal or hexadecimal numbers offer a convenient and concise way to represent binary bit patterns. For example, the bit pattern 1Ø11Ø111 can be represented in hexadecimal as B7. To see this relationship more clearly, rearrange the bits into groups of four and represent each group by a single hexadecimal digit, i.e., 1Ø11 Ø111 -> B 7.

Similarly, this same bit pattern (1Ø11Ø111) can be represented in octal as 267. To see this relationship more clearly, add a leading zero (so that the number of bits in the bit pattern will be some multiple of 3), rearrange the bits into groups of three, and represent each group by a single octal digit, i.e., Ø1Ø 11Ø 111 -> 2 6 7.

Most computers use hexadecimal numbers to represent bit patterns, though some computers use octal numbers for this purpose.

Appendix B

Escape Sequences

Character	Escape Sequence	ASCII Value
bell (alert)	\a	007
backspace	\b	008
horizontal tab	\t	009
newline (line feed)	\n	010
vertical tab	\v	011
form feed	\f	012
carriage return	\r	013
quotation mark ('')	\''	034
apostrophe (')	\'	039
question mark (?)	\?	063
backslash (\)	\\	092
null	\0	000
octal number	\ooo	(o represents an octal digit)

Usually, not more than three octal digits are permitted.
Examples: \5,   \005,   \123,   \177

hexadecimal number	\xhh	(h represents a hexadecimal digit)

Usually, any number of hexadecimal digits are permitted.
Examples: \x5,   \x05,   \x53,   \x7f

Most compilers permit the apostrophe (') and the question mark (?) to appear within a string constant as either an ordinary character or an escape sequence.

Operator Summary

Precedence Group	Operators	Associativity
function, array, structure member, pointer to structure member	() [] . ->	L → R
unary operators	- ++ -- ! ~ * & sizeof (*type*)	R → L
arithmetic multiply, divide and remainder	* / %	L → R
arithmetic add and subtract	+ -	L → R
bitwise shift operators	<< >>	L → R
relational operators	< <= > >=	L → R
equality operators	== !=	L → R
bitwise *and*	&	L → R
bitwise *exclusive or*	^	L → R
bitwise *or*	|	L → R
logical *and*	&&	L → R
logical *or*	||	L → R
conditional operator	? :	R → L
assignment operators	= += -= *= /= %= &= ^= |= <<= >>=	R → L
comma operator	,	L → R

Note: The precedence groups are listed from highest to lowest. Some newer C compilers also include a unary plus (+) operator, to complement the unary minus (-) operator. However, a unary plus expression is equivalent to the value of its operand, i.e., +v has the same value as v.

Appendix D

Data Types and Data Conversion Rules

Data Type	Description	Typical Memory Requirements
int	integer quantity	2 bytes or 1 word (varies from one computer to another)
short	short integer quantity (may contain fewer digits than int)	2 bytes or 1 word (varies from one computer to another)
long	long integer quantity (may contain more digits than int)	1 or 2 words (varies from one computer to another)
unsigned	unsigned (nonnegative) integer quantity (maximum permissible quantity is approximately twice as large as int)	2 bytes or 1 word (varies from one computer to another)
char	single character	1 byte
signed char	single character, with numerical values ranging from −128 to +127	1 byte
unsigned char	single character, with numerical values ranging from 0 to 255	1 byte
float	floating-point number (i.e., a number containing a decimal point and/or an exponent)	1 word
double	double-precision floating-point number (i.e., more significant figures and an exponent that may be larger in magnitude)	2 words
long double	double-precision floating-point number (may be higher precision than double)	2 or more words (varies from one computer to another)
void	special data type for functions that do not return any value	(not applicable)
enum	enumeration constant (special type of int)	2 bytes or 1 word (varies from one computer to another)

Note: The qualifier unsigned may appear with short int or long int, i.e., unsigned short int (or unsigned short), or unsigned long int (or unsigned long).

CONVERSION RULES

These rules apply to arithmetic operations between two operators with dissimilar data types. There may be some variation from one version of C to another.

1. If one of the operands is long double, the other will be converted to long double and the result will be long double.
2. Otherwise, if one of the operands is double, the other will be converted to double and the result will be double.
3. Otherwise, if one of the operands is float, the other will be converted to float and the result will be float.
4. Otherwise, if one of the operands is unsigned long int, the other will be converted to unsigned long int and the result will be unsigned long int.

5. Otherwise, if one of the operands is `long int` and the other is `unsigned int`, then:
    (*a*) If `unsigned int` can be converted to `long int`, the `unsigned int` operand will be converted as such and the result will be `long int`.
    (*b*) Otherwise, both operands will be converted to `unsigned long int` and the result will be `unsigned long int`.

6. Otherwise, if one of the operands is `long int`, the other will be converted to `long int` and the result will be `long int`.

7. Otherwise, if one of the operands is `unsigned int`, the other will be converted to `unsigned int` and the result will be `unsigned int`.

8. If none of the above conditions applies, then both operands will be converted to `int` (if necessary), and the result will be `int`.

Note that some versions of C automatically convert all floating-point operands to double-precision.

ASSIGNMENT RULES

If the two operands in an assignment expression are of different data types, then the value of the righthand operand will automatically be converted to the type of the operand on the left. The entire assignment expression will then be of this same data type. Moreover,

1. A floating-point value may be truncated if assigned to an integer identifier.

2. A double-precision value may be rounded if assigned to a floating-point (single-precision) identifier.

3. An integer quantity may be altered if assigned to a shorter integer identifier or to a character identifier (some high-order bits may be lost).

Appendix E

The ASCII Character Set

ASCII Value	Character	ASCII Value	Character	ASCII Value	Character	ASCII Value	Character
000	NUL	032	blank	064	@	096	`
001	SOH	033	!	065	A	097	a
002	STX	034	"	066	B	098	b
003	ETX	035	#	067	C	099	c
004	EOT	036	$	068	D	100	d
005	ENQ	037	%	069	E	101	e
006	ACK	038	&	070	F	102	f
007	BEL	039	'	071	G	103	g
008	BS	040	(	072	H	104	h
009	HT	041	)	073	I	105	i
010	LF	042	*	074	J	106	j
011	VT	043	+	075	K	107	k
012	FF	044	,	076	L	108	l
013	CR	045	-	077	M	109	m
014	SO	046	.	078	N	110	n
015	SI	047	/	079	O	111	o
016	DLE	048	0	080	P	112	p
017	DC1	049	1	081	Q	113	q
018	DC2	050	2	082	R	114	r
019	DC3	051	3	083	S	115	s
020	DC4	052	4	084	T	116	t
021	NAK	053	5	085	U	117	u
022	SYN	054	6	086	V	118	v
023	ETB	055	7	087	W	119	w
024	CAN	056	8	088	X	120	x
025	EM	057	9	089	Y	121	y
026	SUB	058	:	090	Z	122	z
027	ESC	059	;	091	[	123	{
028	FS	060	<	092	\	124	|
029	GS	061	=	093	]	125	}
030	RS	062	>	094	↑	126	~
031	US	063	?	095	—	127	DEL

Note: The first 32 characters and the last character are control characters; they cannot be printed.

Control Statement Summary

Statement	General Form	Example
break	break;	```for (n = 1; n <= 100; ++n) {` ` scanf("%f", &x);` ` if (x < 0) {` ` printf("ERROR - NEGATIVE VALUE FOR X");` ` break;` ` }` ` ...` `}```
continue	continue;	```for (n = 1; n <= 100; ++n) {` ` scanf("%f", &x);` ` if (x < 0) {` ` printf("ERROR - NEGATIVE VALUE FOR X");` ` continue;` ` }` ` ...` `}```
do - while	do *statement* while (*expression*);	```do` ` printf("%d\n", digit++);` `while (digit <= 9);```
for	for (*exp 1*; *exp 2*; *exp 3*) *statement*	```for (digit = 0; digit <= 9; ++digit)` ` printf("%d\n", digit);```
goto	goto *label*; ... *label*: *statement*	```if (x < 0)` ` goto flag;` `...` `flag: printf("ERROR");```
if	if (*expression*) *statement*	```if (x < 0)` ` printf("%f", x);```

Statement	General Form	Example

if – else	if (*expression*)
	    statement 1
	else
	    statement 2
		if (status == 'S')
		    tax = 0.20 * pay;
		else
		    tax = 0.14 * pay;

return	return *expression*;	return (n1 + n2);

switch	switch (*expression*) {
	
	case *expression 1*:
	    statement 1
	    statement 2
	    ...
	    statement m
	    break;
	
	case *expression 2*:
	    statement 1
	    statement 2
	    ...
	    statement n
	    break;
	
	...
	
	default:
	    statement 1
	    statement 2
	    ...
	    statement k
	}
		switch (choice = getchar()) {
		
		case 'R':
		    printf("RED");
		    break;
		
		case 'W':
		    printf("WHITE");
		    break;
		
		case 'B';
		    printf("BLUE");
		    break;
		
		default:
		    printf("ERROR");
		}

while	while (*expression*) *statement*	while (digit <= 9) printf(%d\n", digit++);

Appendix G

Commonly Used *scanf* and *printf* Conversion Characters

scanf Conversion Characters

Conversion Character	Meaning
c	data item is a single character
d	data item is a decimal integer
e	data item is a floating-point value
f	data item is a floating-point value
g	data item is a floating-point value
h	data item is a short integer
i	data item is a decimal, hexadecimal, or octal integer
o	data item is an octal integer
s	data item is a string followed by a whitespace character (the null character \0 will automatically be added at the end)
u	data item is an unsigned decimal integer
x	data item is a hexadecimal integer
[. . .]	data item is a string which may include whitespace characters

A *prefix* may precede certain conversion characters.

Prefix	Meaning
h	short data item (short integer or short unsigned integer)
l	long data item (long integer, long unsigned integer or double)
L	long data item (long double)

Example:

```
int a;
short b;
long c;
unsigned d;
double x;
char str[80];

scanf("%5d %3hd %12ld %12lu %15lf", &a, &b, &c, &d, &x);

scanf("%[^\n]", str);
```

481

printf Conversion Characters

Conversion Character	Meaning
c	data item is displayed as a single character
d	data item is displayed as a signed decimal integer
e	data item is displayed as a floating-point value with an exponent
f	data item is displayed as a floating-point value without an exponent
g	data item is displayed as a floating-point value using either e-type or f-type conversion, depending on value; trailing zeros, trailing decimal point will not be displayed.
i	data item is displayed as a signed decimal integer
o	data item is displayed as an octal integer, without a leading zero
s	data item is displayed as a string
u	data item is displayed as an unsigned decimal integer
x	data item is displayed as a hexadecimal integer, without the leading Øx

Note that some of these characters are interpreted differently than with the scanf function.

A *prefix* may precede certain conversion characters.

Prefix	Meaning
h	short data item (short integer or short unsigned integer)
l	long data item (long integer, long unsigned integer or double)
L	long data item (long double)

Example:

```
int a;
short b;
long c;
unsigned d;
double x;
char str[8Ø];

printf("%5d  %3hd  %12ld  %12lu  %15.7le\n", a, b, c, d, x);

printf("%4Øs\n", str);
```

Flags

Flag	Meaning
−	Data item is left-justified within the field (blank spaces required to fill the minimum field-width will be added *after* the data item rather than *before* the data item.)
+	A sign (either + or −) will precede each signed numerical data item. Without this flag, only negative data items are preceded by a sign.
∅	Causes leading zeros to appear instead of leading blanks. Applies only to data items that are right-justified within a field whose minimum size is larger than the data item. (*Note:* Some compilers consider the zero flag to be a part of the field-width specification rather than an actual flag. This assures that the ∅ is processed last, if multiple flags are present.)
` ` (blank space)	A blank space will precede each positive signed numerical data item. This flag is overridden by the + flag if both are present.
# (with o- and x-type conversion)	Causes octal and hexadecimal data items to be preceded by ∅ and ∅x, respectively.
# (with e-, f- and g-type conversion)	Causes a decimal point to be present in all floating-point numbers, even if the data item is a whole number. Also prevents the truncation of trailing zeros in g-type conversion.

Example:

```
int a;
short b;
long c;
unsigned d;
double x;

printf("%+5d  %+5hd  %+12ld  %-12lu  %#15.7le\n", a, b, c, d, x);
```

Appendix H

Library Functions

Function	Type	Purpose	include *File*
abs(i)	int	Return the absolute value of i.	stdlib.h
acos(d)	double	Return the arc cosine of d.	math.h
asin(d)	double	Return the arc sine of d.	math.h
atan(d)	double	Return the arc tangent of d.	math.h
atan2(d1,d2)	double	Return the arc tangent of d1/d2.	math.h
atof(s)	double	Convert string s to a double-precision quantity.	stdlib.h
atoi(s)	int	Convert string s to an integer.	stdlib.h
atol(s)	long	Convert string s to a long integer.	stdlib.h
calloc(u1,u2)	void*	Allocate memory for an array having u1 elements, each of length u2 bytes. Return a pointer to the beginning of the allocated space.	malloc.h, or stdlib.h
ceil(d)	double	Return a value rounded up to the next higher integer.	math.h
cos(d)	double	Return the cosine of d.	math.h
cosh(d)	double	Return the hyperbolic cosine of d.	math.h
difftime(l1,l2)	double	Return the time difference l1 - l2, where l1 and l2 represent elapsed times beyond a designated base time (see the time function).	time.h
exit(u)	void	Close all files and buffers, and terminate the program. (Value of u is assigned by the function, to indicate termination status.)	stdlib.h
exp(d)	double	Raise e to the power d (e = 2.7182818... is the base of the natural [Naperian] system of logarithms).	math.h
fabs(d)	double	Return the absolute value of d.	math.h
fclose(f)	int	Close file f. Return 0 if file is successfully closed.	stdio.h
feof(f)	int	Determine if an end-of-file condition has been reached. If so, return a nonzero value; otherwise, return 0.	stdio.h
fgetc(f)	int	Enter a single character from file f.	stdio.h
fgets(s,i,f)	char*	Enter string s, containing i characters, from file f.	stdio.h
floor(d)	double	Return a value rounded down to the next lower integer.	math.h
fmod(d1,d2)	double	Return the remainder of d1/d2 (with same sign as d1).	math.h
fopen(s1,s2)	file*	Open a file named s1 of type s2. Return a pointer to the file.	stdio.h
fprintf(f,...)	int	Send data items to file f (remaining arguments are complicated—see Appendix G).	stdio.h
fputc(c,f)	int	Send a single character to file f.	stdio.h
fputs(s,f)	int	Send string s to file f.	stdio.h

Function	Type	Purpose	include *File*
fread(s,i1,i2,f)	int	Enter i2 data items, each of size i1 bytes, from file f to string s.	stdio.h
free(p)	void	Free a block of allocated memory whose beginning is indicated by p.	malloc.h, or stdlib.h
fscanf(f,...)	int	Enter data items from file f (remaining arguments are complicated—see Appendix G)	stdio.h
fseek(f,l,i)	int	Move the pointer for file f a distance l bytes from location i (i may represent the beginning of the file, the current pointer position, or the end of the file).	stdio.h
ftell(f)	long int	Return the current pointer position within file f.	stdio.h
fwrite(s,i1,i2,f)	int	Send i2 data items, each of size i1 bytes, from string s to file f.	stdio.h
getc(f)	int	Enter a single character from file f.	stdio.h
getchar(void)	int	Enter a single character from the standard input device.	stdio.h
gets(s)	char*	Enter string s from the standard input device.	stdio.h
isalnum(c)	int	Determine if argument is alphanumeric. Return nonzero value if true; $\emptyset$ otherwise.	ctype.h
isalpha(c)	int	Determine if argument is alphabetic. Return nonzero value if true; $\emptyset$ otherwise.	ctype.h
isascii(c)	int	Determine if argument is an ASCII character. Return nonzero value if true; $\emptyset$ otherwise.	ctype.h
iscntrl(c)	int	Determine if argument is an ASCII control character. Return nonzero value if true; $\emptyset$ otherwise.	ctype.h
isdigit(c)	int	Determine if argument is a decimal digit. Return nonzero value if true; $\emptyset$ otherwise.	ctype.h
isgraph(c)	int	Determine if argument is a graphic printing ASCII character (hex $\emptyset$x21-$\emptyset$x7e; octal $\emptyset$41-176). Return nonzero value if true; $\emptyset$ otherwise.	ctype.h
islower(c)	int	Determine if argument is lowercase. Return nonzero value if true; $\emptyset$ otherwise.	ctype.h
isodigit(c)	int	Determine if argument is an octal digit. Return nonzero value if true; $\emptyset$ otherwise.	ctype.h
isprint(c)	int	Determine if argument is a printing ASCII character (hex $\emptyset$x20-$\emptyset$x7e; octal $\emptyset$40-176). Return nonzero value if true; $\emptyset$ otherwise.	ctype.h
ispunct(c)	int	Determine if argument is a punctuation character. Return nonzero value if true; $\emptyset$ otherwise.	ctype.h
isspace(c)	int	Determine if argument is a whitespace character. Return nonzero value if true; $\emptyset$ otherwise.	ctype.h
isupper(c)	int	Determine if argument is uppercase. Return nonzero value if true; $\emptyset$ otherwise.	ctype.h
isxdigit(c)	int	Determine if argument is a hexadecimal digit. Return nonzero value if true; $\emptyset$ otherwise.	ctype.h
labs(l)	long int	Return the absolute value of l.	math.h
log(d)	double	Return the natural logarithm of d.	math.h
log1$\emptyset$(d)	double	Return the logarithm (base 10) of d.	math.h
malloc(u)	void*	Allocate u bytes of memory. Return a pointer to the beginning of the allocated space.	malloc.h, or stdlib.h

Function	Type	Purpose	include File
pow(d1,d2)	double	Return d1 raised to the d2 power.	math.h
printf(...)	int	Send data items to the standard output device (arguments are complicated—see Appendix G).	stdio.h
putc(c,f)	int	Send a single character to file f.	stdio.h
putchar(c)	int	Send a single character to the standard output device.	stdio.h
puts(s)	int	Send string s to the standard output device.	stdio.h
rand(void)	int	Return a random positive integer.	stdlib.h
rewind(f)	void	Move the pointer to the beginning of file f.	stdio.h
scanf(...)	int	Enter data items from the standard input device (arguments are complicated—see Appendix G).	stdio.h
sin(d)	double	Return the sine of d.	math.h
sinh(d)	double	Return the hyperbolic sine of d.	math.h
sqrt(d)	double	Return the square root of d.	math.h
srand(u)	void	Initialize the random number generator.	stdlib.h
strcmp(s1,s2)	int	Compare two strings lexicographically. Return a negative value if s1 < s2; $\emptyset$ if s1 and s2 are identical; and a positive value if s1 > s2.	string.h
strcmpi(s1,s2)	int	Compare two strings lexicographically, without regard to case. Return a negative value if s1 < s2; $\emptyset$ if s1 and s2 are identical; and a positive value if s1 > s2.	string.h
strcpy(s1,s2)	char*	Copy string s2 to string s1.	string.h
strlen(s)	int	Return the number of characters in string s.	string.h
strset(s,c)	char*	Set all characters within s to c (excluding the terminating null character \$\emptyset$).	string.h
system(s)	int	Pass command string s to the operating system. Return $\emptyset$ if the command is successfully executed; otherwise, return a nonzero value, typically -1.	stdlib.h
tan(d)	double	Return the tangent of d.	math.h
tanh(d)	double	Return the hyperbolic tangent of d.	math.h
time(p)	long int	Return the number of seconds elapsed beyond a designated base time.	time.h
toascii(c)	int	Convert value of argument to ASCII.	ctype.h
tolower(c)	int	Convert letter to lowercase.	ctype.h, or stdlib.h
toupper(c)	int	Convert letter to uppercase.	ctype.h, or stdlib.h

Notes: *Type* refers to the data type of the quantity returned by the function. An asterisk (*) denotes a pointer.

    c denotes a character-type argument

    d denotes a double-precision argument

    f denotes a file argument

    i denotes an integer argument

    l denotes a long integer argument

    p denotes a pointer argument

    s denotes a string argument

    u denotes an unsigned integer argument

    Most commercial C compilers are accompanied by many more library functions. Consult the C reference manual for your particular compiler for more detailed information on each of the above functions, and for a list of additional functions.

Answers to Selected Problems

CHAPTER 1

1.31 (*a*) This program prints the message Welcome to the Wonderful World of Computing!. The program does not contain any variables. The line containing printf is an output statement. There are no assignment or input statements.

(*b*) This program also prints the message Welcome to the Wonderful World of Computing!. The program does not contain any variables. (MESSAGE is a symbolic constant, not a variable.) The line containing printf is an output statement. There are no assignment or input statements.

(*c*) This program calculates the area of a triangle from its base and height. The variables are base, height and area. The alternating printf - scanf statements provide interactive input. The final printf statement is an output statement. The statement that begins with area = is an assignment statement.

(*d*) This program calculates net (after tax) salary, given the gross salary and the tax rate (which is expressed as a constant 14%). The variables are gross, tax and net. The initial printf - scanf statements provide interactive input. The final two printf statements are output statements. The statements containing tax = and net = are assignment statements.

(*e*) This program uses a function to determine the smaller of two integer quantities. The variables are a, b and min. The alternating pairs of printf - scanf statements provide interactive input. The final printf statement is an output statement. The statement min = smaller(a, b) references the function, which is called smaller. This function contains an if - else statement that returns the smaller of the two quantities to the main portion of the program.

(*f*) This program processes n pairs of integer quantities, and determines the smaller of each pair. A for loop is used to process the multiple pairs of integer quantities. In all other respects, this program is similar to that shown in Problem 1.31(*e*).

(*g*) This program processes an unspecified number of pairs of integer quantities, and determines the smaller of each pair. The computation continues until a pair of zeros is entered into the computer. A while loop is used to process the multiple pairs of integer quantities. In all other respects, this program is similar to that shown in Problem 1.31(*f*).

(*h*) This program processes an unspecified number of pairs of integer quantities, and determines the smaller of each pair. The original values and the corresponding minimum values are stored in the arrays a, b and min. Each array can store as many as 100 integer values.

  After all the data have been entered and all the minimum values have been determined, the number of data sets is "tagged" with the assignment statement n = --i; a for loop is then used to display the data. In all other respects, this program is similar to that shown in Problem 1.31(*g*).

CHAPTER 2

2.39 (*a*) Valid
(*b*) An identifier must begin with a letter or an underscore.
(*c*) Valid
(*d*) return is a reserved word.
(*e*) An identifier must begin with a letter or an underscore.
(*f*) Valid
(*g*) Blank spaces are not allowed.
(*h*) Valid
(*i*) Dash (minus sign) is not allowed.
(*j*) An identifier must begin with a letter or an underscore.

2.40 (*a*) Distinct   (*c*) Identical   (*e*) Distinct
(*b*) Distinct   (*d*) Distinct   (*f*) Distinct

2.41 (*a*) Valid (real)
(*b*) Illegal character (,)
(*c*) Valid (real)
(*d*) Valid (real)
(*e*) Valid (decimal integer)

(f) Valid (long integer)

(g) Valid (real)

(h) Illegal character (blank space)

(i) Valid (octal constant)

(j) Illegal characters (C, D, F), if intended as an octal constant. If intended as a hexadecimal constant, an X or an x must be included (i.e., ∅X18CDF).

(k) Valid (hexadecimal long integer)

(l) Illegal character (h)

2.42 (a) Valid

(b) Valid

(c) Valid

(d) Escape sequences must be written with a backward slash.

(e) Valid

(f) Valid

(g) Valid

(h) Valid (null-character escape sequence).

(i) A character constant cannot consist of multiple characters.

(j) Valid (octal escape sequence). Note that octal 52 is equivalent to decimal 42. In the ASCII character set, this value represents an asterisk (*).

2.43 (a) A string constant must be enclosed in double quotation marks.

(b) Valid

(c) Trailing quotation mark is missing.

(d) Valid

(e) Valid

(f) Valid

(g) Quotation marks and (optionally) the apostrophe within the string must be expressed as escape sequences, i.e., "The professor said, \"Please don\'t sleep in class\""

2.44
(a)
```
int p, q;
float x, y, z;
char a, b, c;
```
(b)
```
float root1, root2;
long counter;
short flag;
```
(c)
```
int index;
unsigned cust_no;
double gross, tax, net;
```
(d)
```
char current, last;
unsigned count;
float error;
```
(e)
```
char first, last;
char message[80];
```

2.45
(a)
```
float a = -8.2, b = ∅.∅∅5;
int x = 129, y = 87, z = -22;
char c1 = 'w', c2 = '&';
```
(b)
```
double d1 = 2.88e-8, d2 = -8.4e5;
int u = ∅711, v = ∅xffff;
```
(c)
```
long big = 123456789L;
double const = ∅.3333333333;
char eol = '\n';
```
(d)
```
char message[]= "ERROR";
```

2.46 (a) Subtract the value of b from the value of a.

(b) Add the values of b and c, then multiply the sum by the value of a.

(c) Add the values of b and c and multiply the sum by the value of a. Then assign the result to d.

(d) Determine whether or not the value of a is greater than or equal to the value of b. The result will be either true or false, represented by the value 1 (true) or 0 (false).

(e) Divide the value of a by 5, and determine whether or not the remainder is equal to zero. The result will be either true or false.

(f) Divide the value of b by the value of c, and determine whether or not the value of a is less than the quotient. The result will be either true or false.

(g) Decrement the value of a, i.e., decrease the value of a by 1.

2.47 (a) Expression statement

(b) Control statement containing a compound statement. (The compound statement is enclosed in braces.)

(c) Control statement

(d) Compound statement containing expression statements and a control statement.

(e) Compound statement containing an expression statement and a control statement. The control statement itself contains two compound statements.

2.48 (a) #define FACTOR -18   (d) #define NAME "Sharon"
          (b) #define ERROR 0.0001   (e) #define EOLN '\n'
          (c) #define BEGIN {   (f) #define COST "$19.95"
              #define END   }

CHAPTER 3

3.36 (a) 6   (e) −1   (i) −1
          (b) 45   (f) 3   (j) −16
          (c) 2   (g) −4
          (d) 2   (h) 0 (because b / c is zero)

3.37 (a) 7.1
          (b) 49
          (c) 2.51429
          (d) The remainder operation is not defined for floating-point operands.
          (e) −5.17647
          (f) −2.68571
          (g) 20.53333
          (h) 1.67619

3.38 (a) 69   (c) 51   (e) 98   (g) 100   (i) 159
          (b) 79   (d) 3   (f) 6   (h) 63   (j) 2703

3.39 (a) integer
          (b) float (some versions of C will convert to double-precision)
          (c) double-precision
          (d) long integer
          (e) float (or double-precision)
          (f) integer
          (g) long integer
          (h) integer
          (i) long integer

3.40 (a) 14   (h) 1.005   (o) 1   (v) 0
          (b) 18   (i) −1.01   (p) 0   (w) 0
          (c) −466.6667   (j) 0   (q) 1   (x) 1
          (d) −13   (k) 0   (r) 0.01   (y) 1
          (e) 9   (l) 1   (s) 1   (z) 0
          (f) 9   (m) 0   (t) 1
          (g) 4   (n) 1   (u) 0

3.41 (a) k = 13
          (b) z = −0.005
          (c) i = 5
          (d) k = 0
          (e) k = 99
          (f) z = 1.0
          (g) b = 100, a = 100 (*Note:* 100 is the encoded value for 'd' in the ASCII character set.)
          (h) j = 1, i = 1
          (i) k = 0, z = 0.0
          (j) z = 0.005, k = 0 (compare with (i) above)
          (k) i = 10
          (l) y = −0.015
          (m) x = 0.010
          (n) i = 1
          (o) i = 3
          (p) i = 11
          (q) k = 8

   (r) k = 5

   (s) z = 0.005

   (t) z = 0.0

   (u) a = 'c'

   (v) i = 3

3.42 (a) Return the absolute value of the integer expression $(i - 2 * j)$.

  (b) Return the absolute value of the floating-point expression $(x + y)$.

  (c) Determine if the character represented by c is a printing ASCII character.

  (d) Determine if the character represented by c is a decimal digit.

  (e) Convert the character represented by c to uppercase.

  (f) Round the value of x up to the next higher integer.

  (g) Round the value of $(x + y)$ down to the next lower integer.

  (h) Determine if the character represented by c is lowercase.

  (i) Determine if the character represented by j is uppercase.

  (j) Return the value e^x.

  (k) Return the natural logarithm of x.

  (l) Return the square root of the expression $(x*x + y*y)$.

  (m) Determine if the value of the expression $(10 * j)$ can be interpreted as an alphanumeric character.

  (n) Determine if the value of the expression $(10 * j)$ can be interpreted as an alphabetic character.

  (o) Determine if the value of the expression $(10 * j)$ can be interpreted as an ASCII character.

  (p) Convert the value of the expression $(10 * j)$ to an ASCII character.

  (q) Divide the value of x by the value of y, and return the remainder with the same sign as x.

  (r) Convert the ASCII character whose numerical code is 65 to lowercase.

  (s) Determine the difference between the value of x and the value of y, then raise this difference to the 3.0 power.

  (t) Evaluate the expression $(x - y)$ and return its sine.

  (u) Return the number of characters in the string "hello".

  (v) Return the position of the first occurrence of the letter e in the string "hello".

3.43

(a)	2	(h)	0.0	(o)	0.011180	(v)	$3.375e - 6$
(b)	0.005	(i)	-1.0	(p)	1	(w)	0.014999
(c)	1	(j)	1	(q)	0	(x)	5
(d)	0	(k)	0	(r)	1	(y)	1 (0 indicates first position)
(e)	'D'	(l)	1.005013	(s)	'2'	(z)	1.002472
(f)	1.0	(m)	-5.298317	(t)	0.005		
(g)	0.0	(n)	0.005	(u)	'a'		

CHAPTER 4

4.50 (a) ```a = getchar();``` (b) ```putchar(a);```

    ```b = getchar();```   ```putchar(b);```

    ```c = getchar();```   ```putchar(c);```

4.51 (a) ```scanf("%c%c%c", &a, &b, &c);```   (b) ```printf("%c%c%c", a, b, c);```

   or ```scanf("%c %c %c", &a, &b, &c);```   or ```printf("%c %c %c", a, b, c);```

4.52 (a) ```for (count = 0; count < 60; ++count)```

     ```text[count] = getchar();```

  (b) ```for (count = 0; count < 60; ++count)```

     ```putchar(text[count]);```

   (*Note:* count is assumed to be an integer variable.)

4.53 ```for (count = 0; (text[count] = getchar()) != '\n'; ++count)```

   ```;```

4.54 ```scanf("%[^\n]", text);```

  The method used in Problem 4.53 indicates the number of characters that have been read.

4.55 (a) ```scanf("%d %d %d", &i, &j, &k);```   (c) ```scanf("%x %x %o", &i, &j, &k);```

  (b) ```scanf("%d %o %x", &i, &j, &k);```

4.56 (a) ```scanf("%6d %6d %6d", &i, &j, &k);``` (c) ```scanf("%7x %7x %7o", &i, &j, &k);```

  (b) ```scanf("%8d %8o %8x", &i, &j, &k);```
   ```

4.57 (a) a will be assigned a long decimal integer with a maximum field width of 12; b will be assigned a short decimal integer with a maximum field width of 5; c and d will be assigned double-precision quantities with maximum field widths of 15.

(b) a will be assigned a long hexadecimal integer with a maximum field width of 10; b will be assigned a short octal integer with a maximum field width of 6; c will be assigned a short unsigned integer with a maximum field width of 6; and d will be assigned a long unsigned integer with a maximum field width of 14.

(c) a will be assigned a long decimal integer with a maximum field width of 12; b will be assigned a short decimal integer whose maximum field width is unspecified; c and d will be assigned floating-point quantities with maximum field widths of 15.

(d) a will be assigned a decimal integer with a maximum field width of 8; another decimal integer will then be read into the computer but not assigned; c and d will then be assigned double-precision quantities with maximum field widths of 12.

4.58 (a) `scanf("%d %d %e %le", &i, &j, &x, &dx);`
or `scanf("%d %d %f %lf", &i, &j, &x, &dx);`

(b) `scanf("%d %ld %d %f %u", &i, &ix, &j, &x, &u);`

(c) `scanf("%d %u %c", &i, &u, &c);`

(d) `scanf("%c %f %lf %hd", &c, &x, &dx, &s);`
or `scanf("%c %e %le %hd", &c, &x, &dx, &s);`

4.59 (a) `scanf("%4d %4d %8e %15le", &i, &j, &x, &dx);`
or `scanf("%4d %4d %8f %15lf", &i, &j, &x, &dx);`

(b) `scanf("%5d %12ld %5d %10f %5u", &i, &ix, &j, &x, &u);`

(c) `scanf("%6d %6u %c", &i, &u, &c);`

(d) `scanf("%c %9f %16lf %6hd", &c, &x, &dx, &s);`
or `scanf("%c %9e %16le %6hd", &c, &x, &dx, &s);`

4.60 `scanf("%s", text);`

4.61 `scanf("%[ abcdefghijklmnopqrstuvwxyz\n]", text);`

4.62 `scanf("%[ ABCDEFGHIJKLMNOPQRSTUVWXYZ1234567890$ ]", text);`

4.63 `scanf("%[^*]", text);`

4.64 (a) $*@   (no spaces separating the characters)

(b) $ * @   (one or more blank spaces between the characters)

(c) $ * @   (one or more whitespace characters between the characters)

(d) $ * @   (one or more blank spaces between the characters. Other whitespace characters may also appear with the blank spaces.)

(e) $*@   (no spaces separating the characters)

4.65 (a) 12 -8 0.011 -2.2e6

(b) 12 -8 0.011 -2.2e6

(c) 12 -8 0.011 -2.2e6

(d) 12 -8 0.011 -2.2e6

Note: The specified field widths cannot be exceeded; one or more blank spaces must separate the successive numerical quantities. The most convenient representation of the floating-point values is as shown, irrespective of the particular conversion characters in each scanf function.

4.66 (a) `printf("%d %d %d", i, j, k);`

(b) `printf("%d %d", (i + j), (i - k));`

(c) `printf("%f %d", sqrt(i + j), abs(i - k));`

4.67 (a) `printf("%3d %3d %3d", i, j, k);`

(b) `printf("%5d %5d", (i + j), (i - k));`

(c) `printf("%9f %7d", sqrt(i + j), abs(i - k));`

4.68 (a) `printf("%f %f %f", x, y, z);`

(b) `printf("%f %f", (x + y), (x - z));`

(c) `printf("%f %f", sqrt(x + y), fabs(x - z));`

Note: e- or g-type conversion could also be used, e.g.,
`printf("%e %e %e", x, y, z);`

4.69 (a) `printf("%6f %6f %6f", x, y, z);`
(b) `printf("%8f %8f", (x + y), (x - z));`
(c) `printf("%12f %9f", sqrt(x + y), fabs(x - z));`

4.70 (a) `printf("%6e %6e %6e", x, y, z);`
(b) `printf("%8e %8e", (x + y), (x - z));`
(c) `printf("%12e %9e", sqrt(x + y), fabs(x - z));`

In each case, the numerical values will include exponents.

4.71 (a) `printf("%8.4f %8.4f %8.4f", x, y, z);`
(b) `printf("%9.3f %9.3f", (x + y), (x - z));`
(c) `printf("%12.4f %10.4f", sqrt(x + y), fabs(x - z));`

4.72 (a) `printf("%12.4e %12.4e %12.4e", x, y, z);`
(b) `printf("%14.5e %14.5e", (x + y), (x - z));`
(c) `printf("%12.7e %15.7e", sqrt(x + y), fabs(x - z));`

4.73 (a) `printf("%o %o %x %x", a, b, c, d);`
(b) `printf("%o %x", (a + b), (c - d));`

4.74 (a) `printf("%d %d %g %g", i, j, x, dx);`
(b) `printf("%d %ld %d %g %u", i, ix, j, x, u);`
(c) `printf("%d %u %c", i, u, c);`
(d) `printf("%c %g %g %ld", c, x, dx, ix);`

Note: e- or f-type conversion may be used in place of the g-type conversion.

4.75 (a) `printf("%4d %4d %14.8e %14.8e", i, j, x, dx);`
(b) `printf("%4d\n %4d\n %14.8e\n %14.8e", i, j, x, dx);`
(c) `printf("%5d %12ld %5d %10.5f %5u", i, ix, j, x, u);`
(d) `printf("%5d %12ld %5d\n\n %10.5f %5u", i, ix, j, x, u);`
(e) `printf("%6d   %6u   %c", i, u, c);`
(f) `printf("%5d %5u %11.4f", j, u, x);`
(g) `printf("%-5d %-5u %-11.4f", j, u, x);`
(h) `printf("%+5d %5u %+11.4f", j, u, x);`
(i) `printf("%05d %05u %11.4f", j, u, x);`
(j) `printf("%5d %5u %#11.4f", j, u, x);`

4.76 (a) `printf("%8o %8d %8x", i, j, k);`
(b) `printf("%-8o %-8d %-8x", i, j, k);`
(c) `printf("%#8o %08d %#8x", i, j, k);`

4.77 (a) `12345 -13579 -24680 123456789 -2222 5555`
(b) `12345 -13579 -24680`
`123456789 -2222 5555`
(c) `    12345    -13579    -24680`
`        123456789    -2222        5555`
(d) `12345    -13579`
`-24680    123456789`
`-2222    5555`
(e) `  +12345    -13579`
`   -24680        +123456789`
`    -2222     5555`
(f) `00012345 -0013579`
`-0024680 000000123456789`
`-0002222 00005555`

4.78 (a) `12345 abcd9 77777`
(b) `12345 abcd9 77777`
(c) `    12345    abcd9    77777`
(d) `12345    abcd9    77777`
(e) `  +12345    abcd9    77777`
(f) `00012345 0xabcd9 077777`

4.79 (*a*) 2.500000 0.000500 3000.000000
  (*b*) 2.500000 0.000500 3000.000000
  (*c*) 2.500000 0.000500 3000.000000
  (*d*)   2.5000   0.0005 3000.0000
  (*e*)   2.500   0.001 3000.000
  (*f*) 2.500000e+000 5.000000e-004 3.000000e+003
  (*g*) 2.500000e+000 5.000000e-004 3.000000e+003
  (*h*) 2.500000e+000 5.000000e-004 3.000000e+003
  (*i*)   2.5000e+000   5.0000e-004   3.0000e+003
  (*j*) 2.50e+000 5.00e-004 3.00e+003
  (*k*) 2.500000 0.000500 3000.000000
  (*l*) +2.500000 +0.000500 +3000.000000
  (*m*) 2.500000 0.000500 3000.000000
  (*n*) 2.500000 0.000500 3000.000000
  (*o*) 2.5 0.0005 3000
  (*p*) 2.500000 0.000500 3000.000000

4.80 (*a*) A B C
  (*b*) ABC
  (*c*)   A   B   C
  (*d*)   A   B   C
  (*e*) c1=A c2=B c3=C

4.81 (*a*) printf("%s", text);
  (*b*) printf("%.8s", text);
  (*c*) printf("%13.8s", text);
  (*d*) printf("%-13.8s", text);

4.82 (*a*) Programming with C can be a challenging creative activity.
  (*b*) Programming with C can be a challenging creative activity.
  (*c*) Programming with C
  (*d*)   Program
  (*e*) Program

4.83 (*a*) printf("Please enter your name: ");
         scanf("%[^\n]", name);
  (*b*) printf("x1 = %4.1f   x2 = %4.1f", x1, x2);
  (*c*) printf("Please enter a value for a: ");
         scanf("%d", &a);
         printf("Please enter a value for b: ");
         scanf("%d", &b);
         printf("\nThe sum is %d", (a + b));

The last statement can also be written as

         printf("\n%s %d", "The sum is", (a + b));

CHAPTER 5
5.31 (*a*) #include <stdio.h>

```
         /* "HELLO!" program */

         main()

         {
             printf("%s", "HELLO!");
         }
```

(b) #include ⟨stdio.h⟩

```
/* "WELCOME - LET'S BE FRIENDS" program */

main()

{
    char name[2Ø];

    printf("%s", "HI, WHAT\'S YOUR NAME? ");
    scanf("%[^\n]", name);
    printf("\n\n%s%s\n%s", "WELCOME ", name, "LET\'S BE FRIENDS!");
}
```

(c) #include ⟨stdio.h⟩

```
/* temperature conversion - fahrenheit to celsius */

main()

{
    float c, f;

    printf("%s", "Please enter a value for the temperature in degrees F: ");
    scanf("%f", &f);


    c = (5. / 9.) * (f - 32.);

    printf("\n%s%5.1f", "The corresponding value for C is: ", c);
}
```

(d) #include ⟨stdio.h⟩

```
/* piggy-bank problem */

main()

{
    int halfs, quarters, dimes, nickels, pennies;
    float dollars;

    printf("%s", "How many half-dollars? ");
    scanf("%d", &halfs);
    printf("%s", "How many quarters? ");
    scanf("%d", &quarters);
    printf("%s", "How many dimes? ");
    scanf("%d", &dimes);
    printf("%s", "How many nickels? ");
    scanf("%d", &nickels);
    printf("%s", "How many pennies? ");
    scanf("%d", &pennies);

    dollars = Ø.5 * halfs + Ø.25 * quarters + Ø.1 * dimes +
                            Ø.Ø5 * nickels + Ø.Ø1 * pennies;

    printf("\n%s%6.2f%s", "The total is ", dollars, " dollars");
}
```

(e)
```
#include <stdio.h>

#define PI 3.1415927

/* volume and area of a sphere */

main()

{
    float radius, volume, area;

    printf("%s", "Please enter a value for the radius: ");
    scanf("%f", &radius);

    volume = (4. / 3.) * PI * radius * radius * radius;
    area  = 4. * PI * radius * radius;

    printf("\n%s%.3e\n%s%.3e", "The volume is ", volume,
                                "The area is ", area);
}
```

(f)
```
#include <stdio.h>

/* mass of air in an automobile tire */

main()

{
    float p, v, m, t;

    printf("%s", "Please enter a value for the volume, in cubic feet: ");
    scanf("%f", &v);
    printf("%s", "Please enter a value for the pressure, in psi: ");
    scanf("%f", &p);
    printf("%s", "Please enter a value for the temperature, in degrees F: ");
    scanf("%f", &t);

    m = (p * v) / (0.37 * (t + 460.));
    printf("\nMass of air: %g pounds", m);
}
```

(g)
```
#include <stdio.h>

/* encoding of a 5-letter word */

main()

{
    char c1, c2, c3, c4, c5;

    printf("%s", "Please enter a 5-letter word: ");
    scanf("%c%c%c%c%c", &c1, &c2, &c3, &c4, &c5);
    printf("%c%c%c%c%c", (c1-30), (c2-30), (c3-30), (c4-30), (c5-30));
}
```

(*h*)   #include ⟨stdio.h⟩

```
/* decoding of a 5-letter word */

main()

{
    char c1, c2, c3, c4, c5;

    printf("%s", "Please enter the encoded 5-letter word: ");
    scanf("%c%c%c%c%c", &c1, &c2, &c3, &c4, &c5);
    printf("%c%c%c%c%c", (c1+30), (c2+30), (c3+30), (c4+30), (c5+30));
}
```

(*i*)   #include ⟨stdio.h⟩

```
/* encoding and decoding a line of text */

main()

{
    int count, tag;
    char text[80];

    /* read and encode the line of text */

    printf("%s", "Please enter a line of text below: \n");
    for (count = 0; (text[count] = getchar() - 30) != ('\n' - 30); ++count)
        ;
    tag = count;

    /* write out the encoded text */

    printf("\nEncoded text:\n");
    for (count = 0; count < tag; ++count)
        putchar(text[count]);

    /* decode and write out, returning the original text */

    printf("\n\nDecoded (original) text:\n");
    for (count = 0; count < tag; ++count)
        putchar(text[count] + 30);
}
```

(*j*)   #include ⟨stdio.h⟩
        #include ⟨ctype.h⟩

```
/* reversing upper-case and lower-case letters in a line of text */

main()

{
    int count, tag;
    char c, text[80];
```

```
        /* read a line of input */

        printf("%s", "Please enter a line of text below: \n");
        for (count = 0; (text[count] = getchar()) != '\n'; ++count)
            ;
        tag = count;

        /* write the reversed line of output */

        for (count = 0; count < tag; ++count)   {
            c = islower(text[count]) ? toupper(text[count])
                                     : tolower(text[count]);
            putchar(c);
        }
    }
```

CHAPTER 6

6.43 If the value of x is smaller in magnitude than the value of xmin, then the value of xmin is assigned to x if x has a positive value, and the value of -xmin is assigned to x if x has a negative value or if x equals zero. This is not a compound statement, and there are no embedded compound statements.

6.44 (*1*) The program segment itself is a compound statement.
(*2*) The do - while statement, which is embedded in the program segment, contains a compound statement.
(*3*) The if statement, which is embedded in the do - while statement, contains a compound statement.

6.45 (*a*)
```
sum = 0;
i = 2;
while (i < 100)   {
    sum += i;
    i += 3;
}
```
(*c*)
```
sum = 0;
for (i = 2; i < 100; i += 3)
    sum += i;
```

(*b*)
```
sum = 0;
i = 2;
do {
    sum += i;
    i += 3;
} while (i < 100);
```

6.46 (*a*)
```
sum = 0;
i = nstart;
while (i <= nstop)   {
    sum += i;
    i += n;
}
```
(*c*)
```
sum = 0;
for (i = nstart; i <= nstop; i += n)
    sum += i;
```

(*b*)
```
sum = 0;
i = nstart;
do {
    sum += i;
    i += n;
} while (i <= nstop);
```

6.47 (*a*)
```
count = 0;                              or    count = 0;
while (count < n)   {                         while (count < n)
    printf("%d ", text[count]);                   printf("%d ", text[count++]);
    ++count;
}
```

```
(b)  count = 0;                            or   count = 0;
     do {                                       do
          printf("%d ", text[count]);               printf("%d ", text[count++]);
          ++count;                              while (count < n);
     } while (count < n);

(c)  for (count = 0; count < n; ++count)
          printf("%d ", text[count]);
```

6.48
```
(a)  count = 0;                            or   count = 0;
     while (text[count] != '*')   {            while (text[count] != '*')
          printf("%d ", text[count]);               printf("%d ", text[count++]);
          ++count;
     }

(b)  count = 0;                            or   count = 0;
     do {                                       do
          printf("%d ", text[count]);               printf("%d ", text[count++]);
          ++count;                              while (text[count]) != '*');
     } while (text[count] != '*');

(c)  for (count = 0; text[count] != '*'; ++count)
          printf("%d ", text[count]);
```

6.49
```
(a)  for (j = 2; j <= 13; ++j)   {        (c)  for (j = 2; j <= 13; ++j)   {
          sum = 0;                                   sum = 0;
          i = 2;                                     for (i = 2; i < 100; i += j)
          while (i < 100)   {                            sum += i;
               sum += i;                             printf("%d", sum);
               i += j;                          }
          }
          printf("%d", sum);
     }

(b)  for (j = 2; j <= 13; ++j)   {
          sum = 0;
          i = 2;
          do {
               sum += i;
               i += j;
          } while (i < 100);
          printf("%d", sum);
     }
```

6.50
```
(a)  sum = 0;                              (b)  sum = 0;
     for (i = 2; i < 100; i += 3)               for (i = 2; i < 100; i += 3)
          sum = (i % 5 == 0) ? += i : += 0;         if (i % 5 == 0) sum += i;
```

6.51
```
(a)  sum = 0;
     for (i = nstart; i <= nstop; i += n)
          sum = (i % k == 0) ? += i : += 0;
(b)  sum = 0;
     for (i = nstart; i <= nstop; i += n)
          if (i % k == 0) sum += i;
```

6.52
```
letters = digits = whitesp = other = 0;
for (count = 0; count < 80; ++count)   {
     if ((text[count] >= 'a' && text[count] <= 'z') ||
         (text[count] >= 'A' && text[count] <= 'Z'))
              ++letters;
     else if (text[count] >= '0' && text[count] <= '9')
              ++digits;
          else if (text[count] == ' ' || text[count] == '\n'
                                       || text[count] == '\t')
                       ++whitesp;
                  else ++other;
}
```

```
6.53   vowels = consonants = 0;
       for (count = 0; count < 80; ++count)     {
           if (isalpha(text[count])
               if (text[count] == 'a' || text[count] == 'A' ||
                   text[count] == 'e' || text[count] == 'E' ||
                   text[count] == 'i' || text[count] == 'I' ||
                   text[count] == 'o' || text[count] == 'O' ||
                   text[count] == 'u' || text[count] == 'U')
                       ++vowels;
               else ++consonants;
       }
```

The loop can also be written as

```
       vowels = consonants = 0;
       for (count = 0; count < 80; ++count)     {
           if (isalpha(text[count])
               if (tolower(text[count]) == 'a' ||
                   tolower(text[count]) == 'e' ||
                   tolower(text[count]) == 'i' ||
                   tolower(text[count]) == 'o' ||
                   tolower(text[count]) == 'u')
                       ++vowels;
               else ++consonants;
       }
```

```
6.54   switch (flag)    {

       case 1:   printf("HOT");
                 break;

       case 2:   printf("LUKE WARM");
                 break;

       case 3:   printf("COLD");
                 break;

       default: printf("OUT OF RANGE");
       }
```

```
6.55   switch (color)    {

       case 'r':
       case 'R':
             printf("RED");
             break:

       case 'g':
       case 'G':
             printf("GREEN");
             break;

       case 'b':
       case 'B':
             printf("BLUE");
             break;

       default:
             printf("BLACK");
             break;
       }
```

6.56
```
if (temp < 0.)
    printf("ICE");
else if (temp <= 100.)
        printf("WATER");
    else
        printf("STEAM");
```

A `switch` statement cannot be used because:

(a) The tests involve floating-point quantities rather than integer quantities.

(b) The tests involve ranges of values rather than exact values.

6.57
```
for (i = 0, j = 79; i < 80; ++i, --j)
    backtext[j] = text[i];
```

6.58 (a) 0 5 15 30   (g) 0 1 3 5 8 12 15 19 24 30
               x = 30   x = 30

         (b) 1 2 3 4   (h) 0 1 3 6
               x = 4   x = 6

         (c) 1 2 3 4   (i) 0
               x = 4   x = 0

         (d) 1 0 3 2 7 6 13 12 21   (j) 0 0 2 4 5 9 10 14 14 20
               x = 21   x = 20

         (e) 1 0 3 2 7 6 13 12 21   (k) 1 3 5 7 9 12 14 17 20 23
               x = 21   x = 23

         (f) 1   (l) 1 6 11 16 21 24 29 32 35 38
               x = 1   x = 38

CHAPTER 7

7.32 (a) f accepts an integer argument and returns an integer quantity.

         (b) f accepts two arguments and returns a double-precision quantity. The first argument is a double-precision quantity, and the second is an integer.

         (c) f accepts three arguments and returns nothing. The first argument is a long integer, the second is a short integer and the third is an unsigned integer.

         (d) f does not accept any argument but returns a single character.

         (e) f accepts two unsigned integer arguments and returns an unsigned integer.

7.33 (a) f accepts two floating-point arguments and returns a floating-point value.

         (b) f accepts a long integer and returns a long integer.

         (c) f accepts an integer and returns nothing.

         (d) f accepts nothing but returns a character.

7.34 (a) `float funct(float a, float b)`   (c) `long funct(int x, long y)`
```
    {                                      {
        . . .                                  . . .
    }                                      }
```

         (b) `char funct(char c1, char c2)`
```
    {
        . . .
    }
```

7.35 (a) `sample(void)`   Could also be written as   `int sample(void)`

         (b) `float root(a,b)`
```
    int a, b;
```
              or
```
    float root(int a, int b)
```

(c) ```
char convert(c)
char c;
```

    or

    ```
char convert(char c)
```

(d) ```
char transfer(i)
long int i;
```

    or

    ```
char transfer(long i)
```

(e) ```
long int inverse(i)
char c;
```

    or

    ```
long inverse(char c)
```

(f) ```
double process(i, a, b)
int i;
float a, b;
```

    or

    ```
double process(int i, float a, float b)
```

(g) ```
void value(x, y, i)
double x, y;
short int i;
```

    or

    ```
void value(double x, double y, short i)
```

7.36 (a)
```
main()
{
    int a, b, c;
    funct1(int a, int b);   /* add this declaration */

    ...

    c = funct1(a, b);

    ...
}

funct1(int x, int y)
{

    ...

}
```

(b)
```
main()
{
    double a, b, c;
    double funct1(double a, double b);   /* add this decl */

    ...

    c = funct1(a, b);

    ...
}
```
```

```
    double funct1(double x, double y)
    {

        . . .

    }

(c) main()
    {
        int a;
        float b;
        long int c;
        long int funct1(int a, float b);   /* add this decl */

        . . .

        c = funct1(a, b);

        . . .
    }

    long int funct1(int x, float y)
    {

        . . .

    }

(d) main()
    {
        double a, b, c, d;
        double funct1(double a, double b);   /* add this decl */
        double funct2(double a, double b);   /* add this decl */

        . . .

        c = funct1(a, b);

        . . .

        d = funct2(a + b, a + c);
    }

    double funct1(double x, double y)
    {
        double z;
        double funct2(double x, double y);   /* add this decl */

        . . .

        z = funct2(x, y);

        . . .

    }

    double funct2(double x, double y)
    {

        . . .

    }
```

7.37 (a) 1   4   9   16   25

(b) ```
#include <stdio.h>

main()
{
    int count;
    int funct1(int count);

    for (count = 1; count <= 5; ++count)
        printf("%d ", funct1(count));
}

int funct1(int x)
{
    return(x * x);
}
```

(c)  55

(d)  30

**7.38** (a)  $y = x_n + \sum_{i=1}^{n-1} x_i$   or:

$y_1 = x_1$   and   $y_n = x_n + y_{n-1}$   for   $n > 1$

(b)  $y = (-1)^n x^n/n! + \sum_{i=0}^{n-1} (-1)^i x^i/i!$   or:

$y_0 = 1$   and   $y_n = (-1)^n x^n/n! + y_{n-1}$   for   $n > 0$

(c)  $p = f_t * \prod_{j=1}^{t-1} f_j$   or:

$p_1 = f_1$   and   $p_t = f_t * p_{t-1}$   for   $t > 1$

## CHAPTER 8

**8.25** (a)  1   2   3   4   5      (b)  1   3   6   10   15      (c)  6   15   28   45   66

**8.26** (a)  `extern float solver(float a, float b)`
*Note:*  extern can be omitted, i.e., the first line can be written as
`float solver(float a, float b)`

(b)  `static float solver(float a, float b)`

**8.27** (a)  *First file:*

```
extern double funct1(double a, double b);  /* added */

main()
{
    double x, y, z;

    . . .

    z = funct1(x, y);

    . . .
}
```

Second file:

```
double funct1(double a, double b)
{
    . . .
}
```
```

(b)   *First file:*

```
extern double funct1(double x, double y);   /* added */

main()
{
    double x, y, z;

    . . .

    z = funct1(x, y);

    . . .

}
```

Second file:

```
double funct1(double a, double b)
{
    double c;
    double funct2(double x, double y);   /* added */

    c = funct2(a, b);

    . . .

}

static double funct2(double a, double b)
{

    . . .

}
```

8.28 (a)   4   6   9   13   18
       (b)   100   196   80   184   60   164   40   136   20   100
       (c)   104   116   136   136   100
       (d)   101   102   106   124   200
       (e)   6   11   16   21   26
       (f)   6   11   16   21   26
       (g)   9   25   57   121   249
       (h)   This program will return the number of characters within a line of text entered from the keyboard. The terminating newline character will not be included in the sum.

CHAPTER 9

9.27 (a)   name is a one-dimensional, 30-element character array
       (b)   c is a one-dimensional, six-element floating-point array
       (c)   a is a one-dimensional, 50-element integer array
       (d)   params is a two-dimensional, 25-element integer array (five rows, five columns)
       (e)   memo is a two-dimensional, 8712-element character array (66 rows, 132 columns)
       (f)   accounts is a three-dimensional, 80,000-element double-precision array (50 pages, 20 rows, 80 columns)

9.28 (a)   c is a one-dimensional eight-element floating-point array

           c[0] = 2.   c[1] = 5.   c[2] = 3.   c[3] = -4.
           c[4] = 12.   c[5] = 12.   c[6] = 0.   c[7] = 8.

       (b)   c is a one-dimensional eight-element floating-point array

           c[0] = 2.   c[1] = 5.   c[2] = 3.   c[3] = -4.
           c[4] = 0.   c[5] = 0.   c[6] = 0.   c[7] = 0.

(c) z is a one-dimensional, 12-element integer array

z[2] = 8   z[5] = 6   All other elements are assigned zeros

(d) flag is a one-dimensional, four-element character array

flag[0] = 'T'   flag[1] = 'R'   flag[2] = 'U'   flag[3] = 'E'

(e) flag is a one-dimensional, five-element character array

flag[0] = 'T'   flag[1] = 'R'   flag[2] = 'U'   flag[3] = 'E'
flag[4] is assigned zero

(f) flag is a one-dimensional, five-element character array

flag[0] = 'T'   flag[1] = 'R'   flag[2] = 'U'   flag[3] = 'E'
flag[4] = '\0'

(g) flag is a one-dimensional, six-element character array

flag[0] = 'F'   flag[1] = 'A'   flag[2] = 'L'   flag[3] = 'S'
flag[4] = 'E'   flag[5] = '\0'

(h) p is a two-dimensional, 2 × 4 integer array

p[0][0] = 1   p[0][1] = 3   p[0][2] = 5   p[0][3] = 7
p[1][0] = 0   p[1][1] = 0   p[1][2] = 0   p[1][3] = 0

(i) p is a two-dimensional 2 × 4 integer array

p[0][0] = 1   p[0][1] = 1   p[0][2] = 3   p[0][3] = 3
p[1][0] = 5   p[1][1] = 5   p[1][2] = 7   p[1][3] = 7

(j) p is a two-dimensional, 2 × 4 integer array

p[0][0] = 1   p[0][1] = 3   p[0][2] = 5   p[0][3] = 7
p[1][0] = 2   p[1][1] = 4   p[1][2] = 6   p[1][3] = 8

(k) p is a two-dimensional, 2 × 4 integer array

p[0][0] = 1   p[0][1] = 3   p[0][2] = 0   p[0][3] = 0
p[1][0] = 5   p[1][1] = 7   p[1][2] = 0   p[1][3] = 0

(l) c is a three-dimensional, 2 × 3 × 4 integer array

c[0][0][0] = 1   c[0][0][1] = 2   c[0][0][2] = 3   c[0][0][3] = 0
c[0][1][0] = 4   c[0][1][1] = 5   c[0][1][2] = 0   c[0][1][3] = 0
c[0][2][0] = 6   c[0][2][1] = 7   c[0][2][2] = 8   c[0][2][3] = 9
c[1][0][0] = 10   c[1][0][1] = 11   c[1][0][2] = 0   c[1][0][3] = 0
c[1][1][0] = 0   c[1][1][1] = 0   c[1][1][2] = 0   c[1][1][3] = 0
c[1][2][0] = 12   c[1][2][1] = 13   c[1][2][2] = 14   c[1][2][3] = 0

(m) colors is a two-dimensional, 3 × 6 character array

```
colors[0][0] = 'R'     colors[0][1] = 'E'     colors[0][2] = 'D'
colors[0][3] = 0       colors[0][4] = 0       colors[0][5] = 0
colors[1][0] = 'G'     colors[1][1] = 'R'     colors[1][2] = 'E'
colors[1][3] = 'E'     colors[1][4] = 'N'     colors[1][5] = 0
colors[2][0] = 'B'     colors[2][1] = 'L'     colors[2][2] = 'U'
colors[2][3] = 'E'     colors[2][4] = 0       colors[2][5] = 0
```

9.29 (a) `int c[12] = {1, 4, 7, 10, 13, 16, 19, 22, 25, 28, 31, 34};`
(b) `char point[] = "NORTH";`
(c) `char letters[4] = {'N', 'S', 'E', 'W'};`
(d) `float consts[6] = {0.005, -0.032, 1e-6, 0.167, -0.3e8, 0.015};`
(e) `int n[3][4] = {10, 12, 14, 16, 20, 22, 24, 26, 30, 32, 34, 36};`

Another way to assign the initial values is as follows:

```
int n[3][4] = {
                  {10, 12, 14, 16},
                  {20, 22, 24, 26},
                  {30, 32, 34, 36}
              };
```

(f) `int n[3][4] = {10, 12, 14, 0, 0, 20, 22, 0, 0, 30, 32, 0};`

or

```
int n[3][4] = {
                  {10, 12, 14},
                  {0, 20, 22},
                  {0, 30, 32}
              };
```

(g) `int n[3][4] = {10, 12, 14, 16, 20, 22};`

9.30 (a)
```
main()
{
    float a, b, x;
    int jstar[20];
    float sample(float a, float b, int jstar[]);

    . . .

    x = sample(a, b, jstar);

    . . .
}

float sample(float a, float b, int jstar[])
{

    . . .

}
```

```
(b)  main()
     {
          int n;
          char c;
          float x;
          double values[50];
          float sample(int n, char c, double values[]);


          ...


          x = sample(n, c, values);


          ...

     }

     float sample(int n, char c, double values[])
     {

          ...

     }

(c)  main()
     {
          float x;
          char text[12][80];
          float sample(char text[][80]);


          ...


          x = sample(text);


          ...

     }

     float sample(char text[][80])
     {

          ...

     }

(d)  main()
     {
          float x;
          char message[40];
          float accounts[50][100];
          float sample(char message[], float accounts[][100]);


          ...


          x = sample(message, accounts);


          ...

     }

     float sample(char message[], float accounts[][100])
     {

          ...

     }
```

9.31 (a)   2∅ (sum of the array elements whose values are even)

     (b)   25 (sum of the even array elements)

     (c)   Will not run (automatic arrays cannot be initialized)

     (d)   25 (sum of the external array elements whose values are odd)

     (e)   1 (smallest value)

     (f)   1   5   9   (smallest value within each row)

     (g)   9 1∅ 11 12 (largest value within each column)

     (h)   ∅   2   2   4

              4   6   6   8

              8 1∅ 1∅ 12   (if the value of an element is odd, reduce its value by 1; then display the entire array)

     (i)   PPoorrmmiiggwwtt   aa eeggeettffnn (skip the even numbered array elements; print each odd numbered array element twice)

CHAPTER 10

10.44 (a)   px is a pointer to an integer quantity.

     (b)   a and b are floating-point variables; pa and pb are pointers to floating-point quantities (though not necessarily to a or b).

     (c)   a is a floating-point variable whose initial value is −0.167; pa is a pointer to a floating-point quantity; the address of a is assigned to pa as an initial value.

     (d)   c1, c2 and c3 are char-type variables; pc1, pc2 and pc3 are pointers to characters; the address of c1 is assigned to pc3.

     (e)   funct is a function that accepts three arguments and returns a double-precision quantity. The first two arguments are pointers to double-precision quantities; the third argument is a pointer to an integer quantity.

     (f)   funct is a function that accepts three arguments and returns a pointer to a double-precision quantity. The first two arguments are pointers to double-precision quantities; the third argument is a pointer to an integer quantity.

     (g)   a is a pointer to a group of contiguous, one-dimensional, double-precision arrays; equivalent to double a[][12];

     (h)   a is a one-dimensional array of pointers to double-precision quantities (equivalent to a two-dimensional array of double-precision quantities).

     (i)   a is a one-dimensional array of pointers to single characters or strings (equivalent to a two-dimensional array of characters).

     (j)   d is a one-dimensional array of pointers to the strings "north", "south", "east" and "west".

     (k)   p is a pointer to a group of contiguous, two-dimensional, long-integer arrays; equivalent to p[][1∅][2∅];

     (l)   p is a two-dimensional array of pointers to long-integer quantities (equivalent to a three-dimensional array of long integers).

     (m)   sample is a function that accepts an argument which is a function and returns a character. The function passed as an argument accepts two character arguments and returns an integer quantity.

     (n)   pf is a pointer to a function that accepts no arguments but returns an integer quantity.

     (o)   pf is a pointer to a function that accepts two character arguments and returns an integer quantity.

     (p)   pf is a pointer to a function that accepts two pointers to characters as arguments and returns an integer quantity.

10.45 (a)
```
int i, j;
int *pi = &i;
int *pj = &j;
```

     (b)
```
float *pf;
double *pd;
```

     (c)   `long *funct(int a, int b);`

     (d)   `long funct(int *a, int *b);`

     (e)   `float *x;`

     (f)   `float (*x)[3∅]; or float *x[15];`

     (g)   `char *color[3] = {"red", "green", "blue"};`

     (h)   `char *funct(int (*pf)(int a));`

     (i)   `float (*pf)(int a, int b, int c);`

     (j)   `float *(*pf)(int *a, int *b, int *c);`

10.46 (a) F8D (c) 'B' (e) F8C (g) 'C'
     (b) F8D (d) 'C' (f) F8C

10.47 (a) F9C
     (b) F9E
     (c) F9E
     (d) 30 (note that this changes the value of j)
     (e) 35
     (f) F9E
     (g) (i + j) = 35 + 30 = 65
     (h) FA2
     (i) 67
     (j) unspecified

10.48 (a) 1130 (d) 1130 (g) 1134
     (b) 1134 (e) 0.002 (h) 0.003
     (c) 1138 (f) &(*pa) = pa = 1130 (i) 0.003

10.49 (a) 80
     (b) 81
     (c) a=88   b=89
     (d) a=80   b=81

10.50 (a) A pointer to an integer.
     (b) Nothing is returned.
     (c) A pointer to an integer quantity.
     (d) Calculate the sum of the elements of p (p is a five-element integer array).
     (e) sum=150

10.51 (a) A pointer to an integer.
     (b) Nothing is returned.
     (c) The last two elements of a five-element integer array.
     (d) Calculate the sum of the last two elements of the five-element integer array.
     (e) sum=90

10.52 (a) A pointer to an integer quantity.
     (b) A pointer to an integer quantity.
     (c) The address of the element of p whose value is the largest (p is actually a five-element integer array).
     (d) Determine the largest value of the elements of p.
     (e) max=50

10.53 (a) Address of x[0] (d) 12 (i.e., 10 + 2)
     (b) Address of x[2] (e) 30 (this is the value of x[2])
     (c) 10

10.54 (a) Address of table[0][0]
     (b) Address of row 1 (the second row) of table
     (c) Address of table[1][0]
     (d) Address of table[1][1]
     (e) Address of table[0][1]
     (f) 2.2 (i.e., 1.2 + 1)
     (g) 1.2
     (h) 2.1
     (i) 2.2

10.55 (a) Address of color[0] (the beginning of the first string)
     (b) Address of color[2] (the beginning of the third string)
     (c) "red"
     (d) "blue"
     (e) They both refer to the same array element (pointer to "yellow")

10.56 (a) a and b are ordinary floating-point variables. one, two and three are functions, each of which returns a floating-point quantity. one and two each accept two floating-point quantities as arguments. three accepts a function as an argument; the argument function will accept two floating-point quantities as its own arguments and will return a floating-point quantity. (*Note:* Either one or two can appear as an argument to three.)

(b) one and two are conventional function definitions. Each accepts two floating-point quantities and returns a floating-point quantity that is calculated within the function.

(c) three accepts a pointer to a function as an argument. The argument function accepts two floating-point quantities and returns a floating-point quantity. Within three, the argument function is accessed and the calculated result is assigned to c. The value of c is then returned to main.

(d) A different function is passed to three each time it is accessed. Therefore, the value returned by three will be calculated differently each time three is accessed.

10.57 (a) a and b are pointers to floating-point quantities. one, two and three are functions; one and two each return a floating-point quantity, and three returns a pointer to a floating-point quantity. one and two each accept two pointers to floating-point quantities as arguments. three accepts a function as an argument; the argument function will accept two pointers to floating-point quantities as its own arguments, and it will return a floating-point quantity. (*Note:* Either one or two can appear as an argument to three.)

(b) one and two are conventional function definitions. Each accepts two pointers to floating-point quantities and returns a floating-point quantity that is calculated within the function.

(c) three accepts a pointer to a function as an argument. The argument function accepts two pointers to floating-point quantities and returns a floating-point quantity. Within three, the argument function is accessed and the calculated result is assigned to c. The address of c is then returned to main.

(d) A different function is passed to three each time it is accessed. Therefore, the value whose address is returned by three will be calculated differently each time three is accessed.

(e) In this outline one and two accept pointers as arguments, whereas one and two accept ordinary floating-point variables as arguments in the previous outline. Also, in this outline three returns a pointer whereas three returns an ordinary floating-point quantity in the previous outline.

10.58 (a) x is a pointer to a function that accepts an argument which is a pointer to an integer quantity and returns a floating-point quantity.

(b) x is a function that accepts an argument which is a pointer to an integer quantity and returns a pointer to a 20-element floating-point array.

(c) x is a function that accepts an argument which is a pointer to an integer array and returns a floating-point quantity.

(d) x is a function that accepts an argument which is an array of pointers to integer quantities and returns a floating-point quantity.

(e) x is a function that accepts an argument which is an integer array and returns a pointer to a floating-point quantity.

(f) x is a function that accepts an argument which is a pointer to an integer array and returns a pointer to a floating-point quantity.

(g) x is a function that accepts an argument which is an array of pointers to integer quantities and returns a pointer to a floating-point quantity.

(h) x is a pointer to a function that accepts an argument which is a pointer to an integer array and returns a floating-point quantity.

(i) x is a pointer to a function that accepts an argument which is an array of pointers to integer quantities and returns a pointer to a floating-point quantity.

(j) x is a 20-element array of pointers to functions; each function accepts an argument which is an integer quantity and returns a floating-point quantity.

(k) x is a 20-element array of pointers to functions; each function accepts an argument which is a pointer to an integer quantity and returns a floating-point quantity.

10.59

(a) `char (*p(int *a))[6]);`   (g) `char (*p)(int (*a)[]);`

(b) `char p(int (*a)[]);`   (h) `char *(*p)(int (*a)[]);`

(c) `char p(int *a[]);`   (i) `char *(*p)(int *a[]);`

(d) `char *p(int a[]);`   (j) `double (*f[12])(double a, double b);`

(e) `char *p(int (*a)[]);`   (k) `double *(*f[12])(double a, double b);`

(f) `char *p(int *a[]);`   (l) `double *(*f[12])(double *a, double *b);`

CHAPTER 11

11.34
```
struct  complex  {
     float real;
     float imaginary;
};
```

11.35 `struct complex x1, x2, x3;`

11.36
```
struct complex {
      float real;
      float imaginary;
} x1, x2, x3;
```
Including the tag (`complex`) is optional in this situation.

11.37 `struct complex x = {1.3, -2.2};`

Remember that `x` must be either `static` or `external`.

11.38 `struct complex *px;`

The structure members are `px->real` and `px->imaginary`.

11.39 `struct complex cx[100];`

11.40
```
struct complex {
      float real;
      float imaginary;
} cx[100];
```
Including the tag (`complex`) is optional in this situation.

11.41 The structure members are `cx[17].real` and `cx[17].imaginary`.

11.42
```
typedef struct {
      int won;
      int lost;
      float percentage;
} record;
```

11.43
```
typedef struct {
      char name[40];
      record stats;
} team;
```
where the structure type `record` is defined in Problem 11.42.

11.44 `team t;`

The structure members are `t.name`, `t.stats.won`, `t.stats.lost`, and `t.stats.percentage`. The characters that make up `t.name` can also be accessed individually, e.g., `t.name[0]`, `t.name[1]`, `t.name[2]`,..., and so on.

11.45 `team t = {"Chicago Bears", 14, 2, 87.5};`

11.46 `printf("%d\n", sizeof t);`

or

`printf("%d\n", sizeof (team));`

11.47 `team *pt;`

The structure members are `pt->name`, `pt->stats.won`, `pt->stats.lost`, and `pt->stats.percentage`. The characters that make up `t->name` can also be accessed individually, e.g., `pt->name[0]`.

11.48 `team league[48];`

The individual items are `league[4].name` and `league[4].stats.percentage`.

11.49
```
struct team {
      char name[40];
      record stats;
      struct team *next;
};
```

11.50 Two solutions are given, either of which is correct.

(*a*) `struct team *pt;`

`pt = (struct team *) malloc(sizeof(struct team));`

(b)
```
typedef struct team city;
city *pt;

pt = (city *) malloc(sizeof(city));
```

11.51 Two solutions are given, either of which is correct.

(a)
```
struct hms {
    int hour;
    int minute;
    int second;
}

union {
    struct hms local;
    struct hms home;
} *time;
```

(b)
```
typedef struct {
            int hour;
            int minute;
            int second;
} hms;

union {
    hms local;
    hms home;
} *time;
```

11.52 Two solutions are given, either of which is correct.

(a)
```
union ans {
    int ians;
    float fans;
    double dans;
};

struct {
    union ans answer;
    char flag;
    int a;
    int b;
} x, y;
```

(b)
```
typedef union {
            int ians;
            float fans;
            double dans;
} ans;

struct {
    ans answer;
    char flag;
    int a;
    int b;
} x, y;
```

11.53
```
union ans {
    int ians;
    float fans;
    double dans;
};

struct sample {
    union ans answer;
    char flag;
    int a;
    int b;
};

struct sample v = {14, 'i', -2, 5};
```

11.54
```
union ans {
    int ians;
    float fans;
    double dans;
};

struct sample {
    union ans answer;
    char flag;
    int a;
    int b;
    struct sample *next;
};

typedef struct sample struct_type;
struct_type x, *px = &x;
```

11.55 (a)
```
red green blue
cyan magenta yellow
red green blue
```

The structure variable sample is passed to funct by value. Hence, the reassignments within funct are not recognized within main.

(b)
```
red green blue
cyan magenta yellow
cyan magenta yellow
```

The structure variable sample is passed to funct by reference. (Actually, a pointer to the beginning of sample is passed to funct.) Therefore, the reassignments within funct are recognized within main.

(c)
```
red green blue
cyan magenta yellow
cyan magenta yellow
```

The structure variable sample is passed to funct by value, as in (a). Now, however, the altered structure variable is returned to main.

11.56
```
8
100 0.000000 -0.000000
0 0.500000 -0.000000
-25098 391364288.000000 0.016667
```

The first line represents the size of the union (8 bytes, to accommodate a double-precision number). In the second line, only the first value (100) is meaningful. In the third line, only the second value (0.500000) is meaningful. And in the last line, only the last value (0.016667) is meaningful.

11.57 (a) 200 0.500012
                0 0.500000

The union variable u is passed to funct by value. Hence, the reassignment within funct is not recognized within main. *Note:* Only the first value is meaningful in the first line of output, and only the second value is meaningful in the last line.

(b) -26214 -0.300000
      0 0.500000

The union variable u is again passed to funct by value. Hence, the reassignment within funct is not recognized within main. The first value in each line is meaningless.

(c) -26214 -0.300000
     -26214 -0.300000

The union variable u is passed to funct by value, but the altered union variable is then returned to main. Hence, the reassignment within funct will be recognized within main. The first value in each line is meaningless.

CHAPTER 12

12.21
```
#include <stdio.h>

FILE *pointr;

pointr = fopen("students.dat", "w");
```

12.22
```
#include <stdio.h>

FILE *pointr;

pointr = fopen("students.dat", "a");
```

12.23
```
#include <stdio.h>

FILE *pointr;

pointr = fopen("sample.dat", "w+");

fclose(pointr);
```

12.24
```
#include <stdio.h>

FILE *pointr;

pointr = fopen("sample.dat", "r+");

fclose(pointr);
```

12.25
```
#include <stdio.h>
#define  NULL  0

FILE *pointr;

pointr = fopen("sample.dat", "r+");
if (pointr == NULL)
    printf("\nERROR - Cannot open the designated file\n");

fclose(pointr);
```

The fopen and if statements are often combined, e.g.,

```
if ((pointr = fopen("sample.dat", "r+")) == NULL)
    printf("\nERROR - Cannot open the designated file\n");
```

12.26
```
printf("Enter values for a, b and c: ");
scanf("%d %f %c", &a, &b, &c);
fprintf(fpt, "%d %.2f %c", a, b, c);
```
Newline characters (\n) may be included within the fprintf control string, as desired.

12.27
```
fscanf(fpt, "%d %f %c", &a, &b, &c);
printf("a = %d   b = %f   c = %c", a, b, c);
```

12.28 (a) `fscanf(pt1, "%d %f %c", &a, &b, &c);`
    (b)
```
printf("a = %d   New value: ", a);
scanf("%d", &a);
printf("b = %f   New value: ", b);
scanf("%f", &b);
printf("c = %c   New value: ", c);
scanf("%c", &c);
```
    (c) `fprintf(pt2, "%d %.2f %c", a, b, c);`
Newline characters (\n) may be included within the fprintf control string, as desired.

12.29 (a) `fscanf(pt1, "%s", name);`
    (b) `printf("Name: %s\n", name);`
    (c)
```
printf("New name: ");
scanf(" %[^\n]", name);
```
    (d) `fprintf(pt2, "%s", name);`
Here is another solution.

    (a) `fgets(name, 20, pt1);`
    (b) `printf("Name: %s\n", name);`
    (c)
```
puts("New name: ");
gets(name);
```
    (d) `fputs(name, pt2);`

12.30 (a)
```
fscanf(pt1, "%s", values.name);
printf("%s", values.name);
```
    (b)
```
printf("a = ");
scanf("%d", &values.a);
printf("b = ");
scanf("%f", &values.b);
printf("c = ");
scanf("%c", &values.c);
```
    (c) `fprintf(pt2, "%s %d %f %c", values.name, values.a, values.b, values.c);`
    or
    `fprintf(pt2, "%s\n%d\n%f\n%c\n", values.name, values.a, values.b, values.c);`
    or
```
fprintf(pt2, "%s\n", values.name);
fprintf(pt2, "%d\n", values.a);
fprintf(pt2, "%f\n", values.b);
fprintf(pt2, "%c\n", values.c);
```

12.31 (a)
```
fread(&values, sizeof values, 1, pt1);
printf("%s", values.name);
```

```
(b)  printf("a = ");
     scanf("%d", &values.a);
     printf("b = ");
     scanf("%f", &values.b);
     printf("c = ");
     scanf("%c", &values.c);
(c)  fwrite(&values, sizeof values, 1, pt2);
```

CHAPTER 13

13.36 `register unsigned u, v;`

13.37 `int u = 1, v = 2;`
`register int x = 3, y = 4;`

13.38
```
main()

{
    register unsigned *pt1;                          /* pointer declaration */
    unsigned *pt2;                                   /* pointer declaration */
    unsigned *funct(register unsigned *pt1);         /* function declaration */

    . . .

    pt2 = funct(pt1);

    . . .

}


unsigned *funct(register unsigned *pt1)             /* function definition */

{
    unsigned *pt2;

    . . .

    pt2 = ...;

    . . .

    return(pt2);
}
```

13.39 Bit pattern corresponding to a: `1010 0010 1100 0011`

(a)	5d3c	`0101 1101 0011 1100`	
(b)	2202	`0010 0010 0000 0010`	
(c)	9dc5	`1001 1101 1100 0101`	
(d)	bfc7	`1011 1111 1100 0111`	
(e)	80c1	`1000 0000 1100 0001`	
(f)	623a	`0110 0010 0011 1010`	
(g)	e2fb	`1110 0010 1111 1011`	
(h)	1458	`0001 0100 0101 1000`	
(i)	5860	`0101 1000 0110 0000`	
(j)	0	`0000 0000 0000 0000`	(valid for any value of a)
(k)	ffff	`1111 1111 1111 1111`	(valid for any value of a)
(l)	ffff	`1111 1111 1111 1111`	(valid for any value of a)
(m)	a000	`1010 0000 0000 0000`	
(n)	c100	`1100 0001 0000 0000`	

(o)	a0c3	1010 0000 1100 0011
(p)	5bc3	0101 1011 1100 0011
(q)	3a00	0011 1010 0000 0000
(r)	5b3c	0101 1011 0011 1100
(s)	fbc3	1111 1011 1100 0011
(t)	fb00	1111 1011 0000 0000
(u)	fbff	1111 1011 1111 1111

13.40 (a) `a &= 0x3f06`   (d) `a >>= 3`   (g) `a &= ~(0x3f06 << 8)`

      (b) `a ^= 0x3f06`   (e) `a <<= 5`

      (c) `a |= ~0x3f06`   (f) `a ^= ~a`

13.41 (a) `v & 0xaaaa` or `v & ~0x5555`   (c) `v | 0x5555`

      (b) `c & 0x7f`   (d) `v ^= 0x42`

13.42 (a) Note that v represents a positive number, since the leftmost bit is 0 (the equivalent decimal value is 13980). Hence, the vacated bits resulting from both shift operations will be filled with 0s. The resulting values are

      (i) `0x69c0`   (ii) `0x369`

     (b) Now v represents a negative number, since the leftmost bit is 1 (the equivalent decimal value is -15511). Hence, the vacated bits in the left-shift operation will be filled with 0s, but the vacated bits in the right-shift operation will be filled with 1s. The resulting values are

      (i) `0x3690`   (ii) `0xfc36`

13.43 Each structure defines several bit fields.

     (a) u consists of 3 bits, v consists of 1 bit, w consists of 7 bits, and x consists of 5 bits. The total bit count is 16. Hence, all the bit fields will fit into 1 word.

     (b) The individual bit fields are the same as in part (a). Now, however, each bit field is assigned an initial value. Note that each value is small enough to fit within its corresponding bit field (i.e., 2 requires 2 bits, 1 requires 1 bit, 16 requires 5 bits, and 8 requires 4 bits).

     (c) u, v and w are each 7 bits wide. 2 words of memory will be required. u and v will fit into 1 word, but w will be forced to the beginning of the next word.

     (d) u, v and w are each 7 bits wide. 2 words will be required. u will be placed within the first word, followed by 9 empty bits. v and w will fit into the second word, separated by two empty bits.

     (e) u, v and w are each 7 bits wide. 3 words will be utilized to store these bit fields. u will be placed within the first word, v will be forced to the beginning of the second word, and w will be forced to the beginning of the third word. Each bit field will be followed by nine empty bits.

13.44 (a)
```
struct fields {
    unsigned a : 6;
    unsigned b : 4;
    unsigned c : 6;
};
```

     (b)
```
static struct fields v = {3, 5, 7};
```
or
```
static struct {
    unsigned a : 6;
    unsigned b : 4;
    unsigned c : 6;
} v = {3, 5, 7};
```
Each value can fit into a 3-bit field.

     (c) The 6-bit fields can accommodate a value as large as 63, since $63 = 2^6 - 1 = 1 \times 2^5 + 1 \times 2^4 + 1 \times 2^3 + 1 \times 2^2 + 1 \times 2^1 + 1 \times 2^0$. The 4-bit field can accommodate a value as large as 15, since $15 = 2^4 - 1 = 1 \times 2^3 + 1 \times 2^2 + 1 \times 2^1 + 1 \times 2^0$.

     (d)
```
static struct {
    unsigned a : 8;
    unsigned b : 6;
    unsigned c : 5;
};
```
a and b will be stored within one 16-bit word, and c will be stored within a second 16-bit word.

```
(e)  static  struct  {
          unsigned a : 8;
          unsigned   : 2;
          unsigned b : 6;
          unsigned c : 5;
     };
(f)  static  struct  {
          unsigned a : 8;
          unsigned   : 0;
          unsigned b : 6;
          unsigned   : 2;
          unsigned c : 5;
     };
```

CHAPTER 14

14.24   `enum  flags  {first, second, third, fourth, fifth};`

14.25   `enum  flags  event;`

     or

     `enum  {first,  second,  third,  fourth,  fifth}  event;`

14.26   `enum  {do = 1, re, mi, fa, sol, la, ti}  soprano, bass;`

14.27   `enum  money  {penny = 1, nickel = 5, dime = 10,`
                      `quarter = 25, half = 50, dollar = 100};`

14.28   `enum  money  coins = dime;`

     or

     `enum  {penny = 1, nickel = 5, dime = 10, quarter = 25,`
        `half = 50, dollar = 100}  coins = dime;`

14.29   `north = 2`
       `south = 3`
       `east = 1`
       `west = 2`

14.30   `move_1 = 3`
       `move_2 = 2`

14.31   This `switch` statement calculates a cumulative score, using rules that depend on the values assigned to the enumeration variable `move`. The rules are as follows: If `move` = `north` add 10 points to `score`; if `move` = `south` add 20 points to `score`; if `move` = `east` add 30 points to `score`; and if `move` = `west` add 40 points to `score`. An error message is displayed if `move` is assigned anything other than `north`, `south`, `east` or `west`.

14.32   (a) `argc = 3, argv[0] = demo, argv[1] = debug, and argv[2] = fast`
       (b) `argc = 2, argv[0] = demo, and argv[1] = debug  fast`

14.33   This program will read in a line of text and display it in either upper- or lowercase, depending on the second command line parameter. This parameter must be either `upper` or `lower`. If it is neither `upper` nor `lower`, an error message is generated and the text is not displayed.

14.34   `transfer.exe  data.old  data.new`

     or, with some compilers,

     `transfer  data.old  data.new`

14.35   (a) `#define  PI  3.1415927`
       (b) `#define  AREA  PI * radius * radius`
       (c) `#define  AREA(radius)  PI * radius * radius`
       (d) `#define  CIRCUMFERENCE  2 * PI * radius`
       (e) `#define  CIRCUMFERENCE(radius)  2 * PI * radius`
       (f) `#define  interest  {                    \`
                     `i = 0.01 * r;            \`
                     `f = p * pow((1 + i), n); \`
             `}`

This assumes that the variables i, r, f, p and n have all been declared to be double-precision variables.

(g)
```
#define  interest(p, r, n)  {           \
                i = 0.01 * r;           \
                f = p * pow((1 + i), n);  \
             }
```

(h)
```
#define  max  (a >= b) ? a : b
```
or
```
#define  max  (((a) >= (b)) ? (a) : (b))
```
The second version will minimize the likelihood of undesirable side effects.

(i)
```
#define  max(a, b)  (a >= b) ? a : b
```
or
```
#define  max(a, b)  (((a) >= (b)) ? (a) : (b))
```

14.36 (a) If the symbolic constant FLAG has not been defined previously, define FLAG to represent the value 1.

(b) If the symbolic constant PASCAL has been defined previously, define the symbolic constants BEGIN and END to represent the symbols { and }, respectively.

(c) If the symbolic constant CELSIUS has been defined previously, define the macro temperature(t) to represent the expression 0.5555555 * (t - 32); otherwise, define temperature so that it represents the expression 1.8 * t + 32.

(d) If the symbolic constant DEBUG has not been defined previously, define the macro out as
```
printf("x = %f\n", x)
```
Otherwise, if the symbolic constant LEVEL has a value of 1, define out as
```
printf("i = %d   y = %f\n", i, y[i])
```
and if LEVEL does not have a value of 1, define out as the multiline macro
```
for (count = 1; count <= n; ++count)         \
    printf("i = %d   y = %f\n", i, y[i])
```
(Assume that the variables x, i, y, count and n have been properly declared.)

(e) "Undefine" the symbolic constant DEBUG if it has been defined previously.

(f) This problem illustrates the use of the "stringizing" operator (#). If the symbolic constant ERROR_CHECKS has been defined previously, then the macro message(line) is defined in such a manner that the argument line is converted into a string and then displayed.

(g) This problem illustrates the use of the "token-pasting" operator (##). If the symbolic constant ERROR_CHECKS has been defined previously, then the macro message(n) is defined in such a manner that the value of messagen (e.g., message3) is displayed.

14.37 (a)
```
#if defined(BOOLEAN)        or      #ifdef  BOOLEAN
    #define  TRUE   1                   #define  TRUE   1
    #define  FALSE  0                   #define  FALSE  0
    #undef   YES                        #undef   YES
    #undef   NO                         #undef   NO
#endif                              #endif
```

(b)
```
#if flag == 0
    #define  COLOR  1
#elif flag < 3
    #define  COLOR  2
#else
    #define  COLOR  3
#endif
```

(c)
```
#if SIZE == WIDE
    #define  WIDTH  132
#else
    #define  WIDTH  80
#endif
```

(d)
```
#define  error(text)  printf(#text)
```

(e)
```
#define  error(i)  printf("%s\n", error##i)
```

Index

Index